Professor Phillip H Kenny,
LLB, Dip Crim, LLM, Solicitor
Professor of Law and Head of Department of Law
Northumbria University

Russell Hewitson,
LLB, Solicitor
Senior Lecturer in Law
Northumbria University

Butterworths
London, Dublin, Edinburgh
1994

United Kingdom	Butterworths a Division of Reed Elsevier (UK) Ltd, Halsbury House, 35 Chancery Lane, LONDON WC2A 1EL and 4 Hill Street, EDINBURGH EH2 3JZ
Australia	Butterworths, SYDNEY, MELBOURNE, BRISBANE, ADELAIDE, PERTH, CANBERRA and HOBART
Canada	Butterworths Canada Ltd, TORONTO and VANCOUVER
Ireland	Butterworth (Ireland) Ltd, DUBLIN
Malaysia	Malayan Law Journal Sdn Bhd, KUALA LUMPUR
New Zealand	Butterworths of New Zealand Ltd, WELLINGTON and AUCKLAND
Puerto Rico	Butterworth of Puerto Rico, Inc, SAN JUAN
Singapore	Reed Elsevier (Singapore) Pte Ltd, SINGAPORE
South Africa	Butterworths Publishers Pty Ltd, DURBAN
USA	Michie, CHARLOTTESVILLE, Virginia

Reprinted 1995

Crown copyright material is reproduced with the permission of the Controller of Her Majesty's Stationery Office.

A CIP catalogue record for this book is available from the British Library.

ISBN 0 406 03145 2

Printed and bound in Great Britain by Clays Ltd, St Ives plc

Preface

Land Law, Trusts, Succession and Conveyancing—these are names to strike terror into the hearts of students. The authors firmly believe that the subjects become clearer and more interesting not by mastering a superficial guide but by coming to grips with the intricate and enthralling detail of each subject of property law. Very much of this detail is contained in the statute law. The good property lawyer is thoroughly familiar with and able to make a confident reference to the statutory framework. This familiarity and confidence can come only from frequent reading and use of the statutes. It would be hard to claim that any one of these statutes is, taken as a whole, well or coherently drafted and their study presents difficulty, *but* not studying them leaves property law opaque. When the statutory framework is monitored the case law becomes more accessible. The complex picture of English property law begins to move into focus. Soon its study and practise will be enjoyed. It is the authors' hope that this set of materials will encourage students along the path to the enjoyment of property law in all its aspects.

P H Kenny, R Hewitson
February 1994

Contents

Contents

PRESCRIPTION ACT 1832

(C 71)

An Act for shortening the Time of Prescription in certain cases

[1 August 1832]

[1]   Claims to right of common and other profits a prendre (except tithes, etc), not to be defeated after thirty years enjoyment by merely showing the commencement of the right; after sixty years enjoyment the right to be absolute, unless shown to be had by consent or agreement

. . . No claim which may be lawfully made at the common law, by custom, prescription, or grant, to any right of common or other profit or benefit to be taken and enjoyed from or upon any land of our sovereign lord the King, . . . or any land being parcel of the duchy of Lancaster or the duchy of Cornwall, or of any ecclesiastical or lay person, or body corporate, except such matters and things as are herein specially provided for, and except tithes, rent, and services, shall, where such right, profit, or benefit shall have been actually taken and enjoyed by any person claiming right thereto without interruption for the full period of thirty years, be defeated or destroyed by showing only that such right, profit, or benefit was first taken or enjoyed at any time prior to such period of thirty years, but nevertheless such claim may be defeated in any other way by which the same is now liable to be defeated; and when such right, profit, or benefit shall have been so taken and enjoyed as aforesaid for the full period of sixty years, the right thereto shall be deemed absolute and indefeasible, unless it shall appear that the same was taken and enjoyed by some consent or agreement expressly made or given for that purpose by deed or writing.

[1]

NOTES

Words omitted repealed by the Statute Law Revision Act 1890.

2   In claims of rights of way or other easements the periods to be twenty years and forty years

. . . No claim which may be lawfully made at the common law, by custom, prescription, or grant, to any way or other easement, or to any watercourse, or the use of any water, to be enjoyed or derived upon, over, or from any land or water of our said lord the King . . . or being parcel of the duchy of Lancaster or of the duchy of Cornwall, or being the property of any ecclesiastical or lay person, or body corporate, when such way or other matter as herein last before mentioned shall have been actually enjoyed by any person claiming right thereto without interruption for the full period of twenty years, shall be defeated or destroyed by showing only that such way or other matter was first enjoyed at any time prior to such period of twenty years, but nevertheless such claim may be defeated in any other way by which the same is now liable to be defeated; and where such way or other matter as herein last before mentioned shall have been so enjoyed as aforesaid for the full period of forty years, the right thereto shall be deemed absolute and indefeasible, unless it shall appear that the same was enjoyed by some consent or agreement expressly given or made for that purpose by deed or writing.

[2]

NOTES

Words omitted repealed by the Statute Law Revision (No 2) Act 1888 and the Statute Law Revision Act 1890.

3 Right to the use of light enjoyed for twenty years, indefeasible, unless shown to have been by consent

. . . When the access and use of light to and for any dwelling house, workshop, or other building shall have been actually enjoyed therewith for the full period of twenty years without interruption, the right thereto shall be deemed absolute and indefeasible, any local usage or custom to the contrary notwithstanding, unless it shall appear that the same was enjoyed by some consent or agreement expressly made or given for that purpose by deed or writing.

[3]

NOTES
Words omitted repealed by the Statute Law Revision (No 2) Act 1888.

4 The before-mentioned periods to be deemed those next before a suit or action in which the claim is brought in question—What shall constitute an interruption

. . . Each of the respective periods of years herein-before mentioned shall be deemed and taken to be the period next before some suit or action wherein the claim or matter to which such period may relate shall have been or shall be brought into question; and . . . no act or other matter shall be deemed to be an interruption, within the meaning of this statute, unless the same shall have been or shall be submitted to or acquiesced in for one year after the party interrupted shall have had or shall have notice thereof, and of the person making or authorizing the same to be made.

[4]

NOTES
Words omitted repealed by the Statute Law Revision (No 2) Act 1888.

5 In actions on the case, etc, the claimant may allege his right generally, as at present—In pleas to trespass and other pleadings, where party used to allege his claim from time immemorial, enjoyment during the period mentioned in this Act may be alleged; and exceptions or other matters must be replied specially

. . . In all actions upon the case and other pleadings, wherein the party claiming may now by law allege his right generally, without averring the existence of such right from time immemorial, such general allegation shall still be deemed sufficient, and if the same shall be denied, all and every the matters in this Act mentioned and provided, which shall be applicable to the case, shall be admissible in evidence to sustain or rebut such allegation; and . . . in all pleadings to actions of trespass, and in all other pleadings wherein before the passing of this Act it would have been necessary to allege the right to have existed from time immemorial, it shall be sufficient to allege the enjoyment thereof as of right by the occupiers of the tenement in respect whereof the same is claimed for and during such of the periods mentioned in this Act as may be applicable to the case, and without claiming in the name or right of the owner of the fee, as is now usually done; and if the other party shall intend to rely on any proviso, exception, incapacity, disability, contract, agreement, or other matter herein-before mentioned, or on any cause or matter of fact or of law not inconsistent with the simple fact of enjoyment, the same shall be specially alleged and set forth in answer to the allegation of the party claiming, and shall not be received in evidence on any general traverse or denial of such allegation.

[5]

NOTES

Words omitted repealed by the Statute Law Revision (No 2) Act 1888.

6   No presumption to be allowed in support of a claim on proof of enjoyment for less than the requisite number of years

. . . In the several cases mentioned in and provided for by this Act, no presumption shall be allowed or made in favour or support of any claim, upon proof of the exercise or enjoyment of the right or matter claimed for any less period of time or number of years than for such period or number mentioned in this Act as may be applicable to the case and to the nature of the claim.

[6]

NOTES

Words omitted repealed by the Statute Law Revision (No 2) Act 1888.

7   Proviso where any person capable of resisting a claim is an infant, etc

Provided also, that the time during which any person otherwise capable of resisting any claim to any of the matters before mentioned shall have been or shall be an infant, idiot, non compos mentis, feme covert, or tenant for life, or during which any action or suit shall have been pending, and which shall have been diligently prosecuted, until abated by the death of any party or parties thereto, shall be excluded in the computation of the periods herein-before mentioned, except only in cases where the right or claim is hereby declared to be absolute and indefeasible.

[7]

8   Time to be excluded in certain cases in computing the term of forty years appointed by this Act

Provided always, . . . that when any land or water upon, over, or from which any such way or other convenient watercourse or use of water shall have been or shall be enjoyed or derived hath been or shall be held under or by virtue of any term of life, or any term of years exceeding three years from the granting thereof, the time of the enjoyment of any such way or other matter as herein last before mentioned, during the continuance of such term, shall be excluded in the computation of the said period of forty years, in case the claim shall within three years next after the end or sooner determination of such term be resisted by any person entitled to any reversion expectant on the determination thereof.

[8]

NOTES

Words omitted repealed by the Statute Law Revision (No 2) Act 1888.

9   Extent of Act

This Act shall not extend to Scotland . . .

[9]

NOTES

Words omitted repealed by the Statute Law Revision Act 1874.

WILLS ACT 1837

(C 26)

An Act for the amendment of the Laws with respect to Wills

[3 July 1837]

[1] Meaning of certain words in this Act

. . . the words and expressions herein-after mentioned, which in their ordinary signification have a more confined or a different meaning, shall in this Act, except where the nature of the provisions or the context of the Act shall exclude such construction, be interpreted as follows; (that is to say,) the word "will" shall extend to a testament, and to a codicil, and to an appointment by will or by writing in the nature of a will in exercise of a power, [and also to an appointment by will of a guardian of a child], . . . and to any other testamentary disposition; and the words "real estate" shall extend to manors, advowsons, messuages, lands, tithes, rents, and hereditaments, . . . whether corporeal, incorporeal, or personal, and to any undivided share thereof, and to any estate, right, or interest (other than a chattel interest) therein; and the words "personal estate" shall extend to leasehold estates and other chattels real, and also to monies, shares of government and other funds, securities for money (not being real estates), debts, choses in action, rights, credits, goods, and all other property whatsoever which by law devolves upon the executor or administrator, and to any share or interest therein; and every word importing the singular number only shall extend and be applied to several persons or things as well as one person or thing; and every word importing the masculine gender only shall extend and be applied to a female as well as a male.

[10]

NOTES
First words omitted repealed by the Statute Law Revision Act 1893; second and third words omitted repealed by the Statute Law (Repeals) Act 1969; words in square brackets substituted by the Children Act 1989, s 108(5), Sch 13, para 1.

3 All property may be disposed of by will

. . . it shall be lawful for every person to devise, bequeath, or dispose of, by his will executed in manner herein-after required, all real estate and all personal estate which he shall be entitled to, either at law or in equity, at the time of his death, and which, if not so devised, bequeathed, and disposed of, would devolve . . . upon his executor or administrator; and . . . the power hereby given shall extend . . . to all contingent, executory or other future interests in any real or personal estate, whether the testator may or may not be ascertained as the person or one of the persons in whom the same respectively may become vested, and whether he may be entitled thereto under the instrument by which the same respectively were created, or under any disposition thereof by deed or will; and also to all rights of entry for conditions broken, and other rights of entry; and also to such of the same estates, interests, and rights respectively, and other real and personal estate, as the testator may be entitled to at the time of his death, notwithstanding that he may become entitled to the same subsequently to the execution of his will.

[11]

NOTES
First and third words omitted repealed by the Statute Law Revision (No 2) Act 1888; second and fourth words omitted repealed by the Statute Law (Repeals) Act 1969.

7   No will of a person under age valid

. . . no will made by any person under the age of [eighteen years] shall be valid.

[12]

NOTES

Words omitted repealed by the Statute Law Revision (No 2) Act 1888; words in square brackets substituted by the Family Law Reform Act 1969, s 3(1)(a).

[9   Signing and attestation of wills

No will shall be valid unless—
- (a)   it is in writing, and signed by the testator, or by some other person in his presence and by his direction; and
- (b)   it appears that the testator intended by his signature to give effect to the will; and
- (c)   the signature is made or acknowledged by the testator in the presence of two or more witnesses present at the same time; and
- (d)   each witness either—
  - (i)   attests and signs the will; or
  - (ii)   acknowledges his signature,

  in the presence of the testator (but not necessarily in the presence of any other witness),

but no form of attestation shall be necessary.]

[13]

NOTES

Substituted by the Administration of Justice Act 1982, s 17.

10   Appointments by will to be executed like other wills, and to be valid, although other required solemnities are not observed

. . . no appointment made by will, in exercise of any power, shall be valid, unless the same be executed in manner herein-before required; and every will executed in manner herein-before required shall, so far as respects the execution and attestation thereof, be a valid execution of a power of appointment by will, notwithstanding it shall have been expressly required that a will made in exercise of such power should be executed with some additional or other form of execution or solemnity.

[14]

NOTES

Words omitted repealed by the Statute Law Revision (No 2) Act 1888.

11   Saving as to wills of soldiers and mariners

Provided always, . . . that any soldier being in actual military service, or any mariner or seaman being at sea, may dispose of his personal estate as he might have done before the making of this Act.

[15]

NOTES

Words omitted repealed by the Statute Law Revision (No 2) Act 1888.

13   Publication of will not requisite

. . . every will executed in manner herein-before required shall be valid without any other publication thereof.

[16]

NOTES

Words omitted repealed by the Statute Law Revision (No 2) Act 1888.

14   Will not to be void on account of incompetency of attesting witness

. . . if any person who shall attest the execution of a will shall at the time of the execution thereof or at any time afterwards be incompetent to be admitted a witness to prove the execution thereof, such will shall not on that account be invalid.

[17]

NOTES

Words omitted repealed by the Statute Law Revision (No 2) Act 1888.

15   Gifts to an attesting witness, or his or her wife or husband, to be void

. . . if any person shall attest the execution of any will to whom or to whose wife or husband any beneficial devise, legacy, estate, interest, gift, or appointment, of or affecting any real or personal estate (other than and except charges and directions for the payment of any debt or debts), shall be thereby given or made, such devise, legacy, estate, interest, gift, or appointment shall, so far only as concerns such person attesting the execution of such will, or the wife or husband of such person, or any person claiming under such person or wife or husband, be utterly null and void, and such person so attesting shall be admitted as a witness to prove the execution of such will, or to prove the validity or invalidity thereof, notwithstanding such devise, legacy, estate, interest, gift, or appointment mentioned in such will.

[18]

NOTES

Words omitted repealed by the Statute Law Revision (No 2) Act 1888.

16   Creditor attesting a will charging estate with debts shall be admitted a witness

. . . in case by any will any real or personal estate shall be charged with any debt or debts, and any creditor, or the wife or husband of any creditor, whose debt is so charged, shall attest the execution of such will, such creditor notwithstanding such charge shall be admitted a witness to prove the execution of such will, or to prove the validity or invalidity thereof.

[19]

NOTES

Words omitted repealed by the Statute Law Revision (No 2) Act 1888.

17   Executor shall be admitted a witness

. . . no person shall, on account of his being an executor of a will, be incompetent to be admitted a witness to prove the execution of such will, or a witness to prove the validity or invalidity thereof.

[20]

NOTES

Words omitted repealed by the Statute Law Revision (No 2) Act 1888.

[18   Wills to be revoked by marriage, except in certain cases

(1)   Subject to subsections (2) to (4) below, a will shall be revoked by the testator's marriage.

(2)   A disposition in a will in exercise of a power of appointment shall take effect notwithstanding the testator's subsequent marriage unless the property so appointed would in default of appointment pass to his personal representatives.

(3)   Where it appears from a will that at the time it was made the testator was expecting to be married to a particular person and that he intended that the will should not be revoked by the marriage, the will shall not be revoked by his marriage to that person.

(4)   Where it appears from a will that at the time it was made the testator was expecting to be married to a particular person and that he intended that a disposition in the will should not be revoked by his marriage to that person,—

   (a)   that disposition shall take effect notwithstanding the marriage; and
   (b)   any other disposition in the will shall take effect also, unless it appears from the will that the testator intended the disposition to be revoked by the marriage.]

[21]

NOTES

Substituted by the Administration of Justice Act 1982, s 18(1).

[18A   Effect of dissolution or annulment of marriage on wills

(1)   Where, after a testator has made a will, a decree of a court [of civil jurisdiction in England and Wales] dissolves or annuls his marriages [or his marriage is dissolved or annulled and the divorce or annulment is entitled to recognition in England and Wales by virtue of Part II of the Family Law Act 1986],—

   (a)   the will shall take effect as if any appointment of the former spouse as an executor or as the executor and trustee of the will were omitted; and
   (b)   any devise or bequest to the former spouse shall lapse,

except in so far as a contrary intention appears by the will.

(2)   Subsection (1)(b) above is without prejudice to any right of the former spouse to apply for financial provision under the Inheritance (Provision for Family and Dependants) Act 1975.

(3)   Where—

   (a)   by the terms of a will an interest in remainder is subject to a life interest; and
   (b)   the life interest lapses by virtue of subsection (1)(b) above,

the interest in remainder shall be treated as if it had not been subject to the life interest and, if it was contingent upon the termination of the life interest, as if it had not been so contingent.]

[22]

NOTES

Inserted by the Administration of Justice Act 1982, s 18(2).

Sub-s (1): words in first pair of square brackets inserted and words in second pair of square brackets substituted by the Family Law Act 1986, s 53.

19   No will to be revoked by presumption from altered circumstances

. . . no will shall be revoked by any presumption of an intention on the ground of an alteration in circumstances.

[23]

NOTES

Words omitted repealed by the Statute Law Revision (No 2) Act 1888.

20   No will to be revoked otherwise than as aforesaid or by another will or codicil, or by destruction thereof

. . . no will or codicil, or any part thereof, shall be revoked otherwise than as aforesaid, or by another will or codicil executed in manner herein-before required, or by some writing declaring an intention to revoke the same and executed in the manner in which a will is herein-before required to be executed, or by the burning, tearing, or otherwise destroying the same by the testator, or by some person in his presence and by his direction, with the intention of revoking the same.

[24]

NOTES

Words omitted repealed by the Statute Law Revision (No 2) Act 1888.

21   No alteration in a will after execution except in certain cases, shall have any effect, unless executed as a will

. . . no obliteration, interlineation, or other alteration made in any will after the execution thereof shall be valid or have any effect, except so far as the words or effect of the will before such alteration shall not be apparent, unless such alteration shall be executed in like manner as herein-before is required for the execution of the will; but the will, with such alteration as part thereof, shall be deemed to be duly executed if the signature of the testator and the subscription of the witnesses be made in the margin or on some other part of the will opposite or near to such alteration, or at the foot or end of or opposite to a memorandum referring to such alteration, and written at the end of some other part of the will.

[25]

NOTES

Words omitted repealed by the Statute Law Revision (No 2) Act 1888.

22   No revoked will shall be revived otherwise than by re-execution or a codicil, etc

. . . no will or codicil, or any part thereof, which shall be in any manner revoked, shall be revived otherwise than by the re-execution thereof or by a codicil executed in manner herein-before required and showing an intention to revive the same; and when any will or codicil which shall be partly revoked, and afterwards wholly revoked, shall be revived, such revival shall not extend to so much thereof as shall have been revoked before the revocation of the whole thereof, unless an intention to the contrary shall be shown.

[26]

NOTES

Words omitted repealed by the Statute Law Revision (No 2) Act 1888.

23 Subsequent conveyance or other act not to prevent operation of will

. . . no conveyance or other act made or done subsequently to the execution of a will of or relating to any real or personal estate therein comprised, except an act by which such will shall be revoked as aforesaid, shall prevent the operation of the will with respect to such estate or interest in such real or personal estate as the testator shall have power to dispose of by will at the time of his death.

[27]

NOTES

Words omitted repealed by the Statute Law Revision (No 2) Act 1888.

24 Wills shall be construed, as to the estate comprised, to speak from the death of the testator

. . . every will shall be construed, with reference to the real estate and personal estate comprised in it, to speak and take effect as if it had been executed immediately before the death of the testator, unless a contrary intention shall appear by the will.

[28]

NOTES

Words omitted repealed by the Statute Law Revision (No 2) Act 1888.

25 Residuary devises shall include estates comprised in lapsed and void devises

. . . unless a contrary intention shall appear by the will, such real estate or interest therein as shall be comprised or intended to be comprised in any devise in such will contained, which shall fail or be void by reason of the death of the devisee in the lifetime of the testator, or by reason of such devise being contrary to law or otherwise incapable of taking effect shall be included in the residuary devise (if any) contained in such will.

[29]

NOTES

Words omitted repealed by the Statute Law Revision (No 2) Act 1888.

26 A general devise of the testator's lands shall include copyhold and leasehold as well as freehold lands, in the absence of a contrary intention

. . . a devise of the land of the testator, or of the land of the testator in any place or in the occupation of any person mentioned in his will, or otherwise described in a general manner, and any other general devise which would describe a . . . leasehold estate if the testator had no freehold estate which could be described by it, shall be construed to include the . . . leasehold estates of the testator, or his . . . leasehold estates, or any of them, to which such description shall extend, as the case may be, as well as freehold estates, unless a contrary intention shall appear by the will.

[30]

NOTES

First words omitted repealed by the Statute Law Revision (No 2) Act 1888; other words omitted repealed by the Statute Law (Repeals) Act 1969.

27   A general gift of realty or personalty shall include property over which the testator has a general power of appointment

. . . a general devise of the real estate of the testator, or of the real estate of the testator in any place or in the occupation of any person mentioned in his will, or otherwise described in a general manner, shall be construed to include any real estate, or any real estate to which such description shall extend (as the case may be), which he may have power to appoint in any manner he may think proper, and shall operate as an execution of such power, unless a contrary intention shall appear by the will; and in like manner a bequest of the personal estate of the testator, or any bequest of personal property described in a general manner, shall be construed to include any personal estate, or any personal estate to which such description shall extend (as the case may be), which he may have power to appoint in any manner he may think proper, and shall operate as an execution of such power, unless a contrary intention shall appear by the will.

[31]

NOTES

Words omitted repealed by the Statute Law Revision (No 2) Act 1888.

28   A devise of real estate without any words of limitations shall pass the fee, etc

. . . where any real estate shall be devised to any person without any words of limitation, such devise shall be construed to pass the fee simple, or other the whole estate or interest which the testator had power to dispose of by will in such real estate, unless a contrary intention shall appear by the will.

[32]

NOTES

Words omitted repealed by the Statute Law Revision (No 2) Act 1888.

29   The words "die without issue," or "die without leaving issue," etc, shall mean a want or failure of issue in the lifetime or at the death of the person, except in certain cases

. . . in any devise or bequest of real or personal estate the words "die without issue" or "die without leaving issue," or "have no issue," or any other words which may import either a want or failure of issue of any person in his lifetime or at the time of his death, or an indefinite failure of his issue, shall be construed to mean a want or failure of issue in the lifetime or at the time of the death of such person, and not an indefinite failure of his issue, unless a contrary intention shall appear by the will, by reason of such person having a prior estate tail, or of a preceding gift, being, without any implication arising from such words, a limitation of an estate tail to such person or issue, or otherwise: Provided, that this Act shall not extend to cases where such words as aforesaid import if no issue described in a preceding gift shall be born, or if there shall be no issue who shall live to attain the age or otherwise answer the description required for obtaining a vested estate by a preceding gift to such issue.

[33]

NOTES

Words omitted repealed by the Statute Law Revision (No 2) Act 1888.

30   Devise of realty to trustees or executors shall pass the fee, etc, except in certain cases

. . . where any real estate (other than or not being a presentation to a church) shall be devised to any trustee or executor, such devise shall be construed to pass the fee simple or other the whole estate or interest which the testator had power to dispose of by will in such real estate, unless a definite term of years, absolute or determinable, or an estate of freehold, shall thereby be given to him expressly or by implication.

[34]

NOTES

Words omitted repealed by the Statute Law Revision (No 2) Act 1888.

31   Trustees under an unlimited devise, where the trust may endure beyond the life of a person beneficially entitled for life, shall take the fee, etc

. . . where any real estate shall be devised to a trustee, without any express limitation of the estate to be taken by such trustee, and the beneficial interest in such real estate, or in the surplus rents and profits thereof, shall not be given to any person for life, or such beneficial interest shall be given to any person for life, but the purposes of the trust may continue beyond the life of such person, such devise shall be construed to vest in such trustee the fee simple, or other the whole legal estate which the testator had power to dispose of by will in such real estate, and not an estate determinable when the purposes of the trust shall be satisfied.

[35]

NOTES

Words omitted repealed by the Statute Law Revision (No 2) Act 1888.

32   Devises of estates tail shall not lapse where inheritable issue survives, etc

. . . where any person to whom any real estate shall be devised for an estate tail or an estate in quasi entail shall die in the lifetime of the testator leaving issue who would be heritable under such entail, and any such issue shall be living at the time of the death of the testator, such devise shall not lapse, but shall take effect as if the death of such person had happened immediately after the death of the testator, unless a contrary intention shall appear by the will.

[36]

NOTES

Words omitted repealed by the Statute Law Revision (No 2) Act 1888.

[33   Gifts to children or other issue who leave issue living at the testator's death shall not lapse

(1)   Where—
   (a)   a will contains a devise or bequest to a child or remoter descendant of the testator; and
   (b)   the intended beneficiary dies before the testator, leaving issue; and
   (c)   issue of the intended beneficiary are living at the testator's death,

then, unless a contrary intention appears by the will, the devise or bequest shall take effect as a devise or bequest to the issue living at the testator's death.

(2)   Where—
   (a)   a will contains a devise or bequest to a class of persons consisting of children or remoter descendants of the testator; and
   (b)   a member of the class dies before the testator, leaving issue, and
   (c)   issue of that member are living at the testator's death,

then, unless a contrary intention appears by the will, the devise or bequest shall take effect as if the class included the issue of its deceased member living at the testator's death.

(3)   Issue shall take under this section through all degrees, according to their stock, in equal shares if more than one, any gift or share which their parent would have taken and so that no issue shall take whose parent is living at the testator's death and so capable of taking.

(4)   For the purposes of this section—
   (a)   the illegitimacy of any person is to be disregarded; and
   (b)   a person conceived before the testator's death and born living thereafter is to be taken to have been living at the testator's death.]

[37]

NOTES

Substituted by the Administration of Justice Act 1982, s 19.

34   Act not to extend to wills made before 1838, or to estates pur autre vie of persons who die before 1838

. . . this Act shall not extend to any will made before the first day of January one thousand eight hundred and thirty-eight; and every will re-executed or republished, or revived by any codicil, shall for the purposes of this Act be deemed to have been made at the time at which the same shall be so re-executed, republished or revived; and this Act shall not extend to any estate pur autre vie of any person who shall die before the first day of January one thousand eight hundred and thirty-eight.

[38]

NOTES

Words omitted repealed by the Statute Law Revision (No 2) Act 1888.

35   Act not to extend to Scotland

. . . this Act shall not extend to Scotland.

[39]

NOTES

Words omitted repealed by the Statute Law Repeals (No 2) Act 1888.

COMMON LAW PROCEDURE ACT 1852

(C 76)

An Act to amend the Process, Practice, and Mode of Pleading in the Superior Courts of Common Law at Westminster, and in the Superior Courts of the Counties Palatine of Lancaster and Durham

[30 June 1852]

Ejectment

210   Proceedings in ejectment by landlord for non-payment of rent

In all cases between landlord and tenant, as often as it shall happen that one half year's rent shall be in arrear, and the landlord or lessor, to whom the same is due, hath right by law to re-enter for the non-payment thereof, such landlord or lessor shall and may, without any formal demand, or re-entry, serve a writ in ejectment for the recovery of the demised premises; . . . which service . . . shall stand in the place and stead of a demand and re-entry; and in case of judgment against the defendant for nonappearance, if it shall be made appear to the court where the said action is depending, by affidavit, or be proved upon the trial in case the defendant appears, that half a year's rent was due before the said writ was served, and that no sufficient distress was to be found on the demised premises, countervailing the arrears then due, and that the lessor had power to re-enter, then and in every such case the lessor shall recover judgment and execution, in the same manner as if the rent in arrear had been legally demanded, and a re-entry made; and in case the lessee or his assignee, or other person claiming or deriving under the said lease, shall permit and suffer judgment to be had and recovered on such trial in ejectment, and execution to be executed thereon, without paying the rent and arrears, together with full costs, and without proceeding for relief in equity within six months after such execution executed, then and in such case the said lessee, his assignee, and all other persons claiming and deriving under the said lease, shall be barred and foreclosed from all relief or remedy in law or equity, other than by bringing error for reversal of such judgment, in case the same shall be erroneous; and the said landlord or lessor shall from thenceforth hold the said demised premises discharged from such lease; . . . provided that nothing herein contained shall extend to bar the right of any mortgagee of such lease, or any part thereof, who shall not be in possession, so as such mortgagee shall and do, within six months after such judgment obtained and execution executed pay all rent in arrear, and all costs and damages sustained by such lessor or person entitled to the remainder or reversion as aforesaid, and perform all the covenants and agreements which, on the part and behalf of the first lessee, are and ought to be performed.

[40]

NOTES

Words omitted repealed by the Statute Law Revision Act 1892.

211   Lessee proceeding in equity not to have injunction or relief without payment of rent and costs

In case the said lessee, his assignee, or other person claiming any right, title, or interest, in law or equity, of, in, or to the said lease, shall, within the time aforesaid, proceed for relief in any court of equity, such person shall not have or continue any injunction against the proceedings at law on such ejectment, unless he does or shall, within forty days next after a full and perfect answer shall be made by the claimant in such ejectment, bring into court, and lodge with the proper officer such sum and sums of money as the lessor or landlord shall in his answer swear to be due and in arrear over and above all just allowances, and also the costs taxed in the said suit, there to remain till the hearing of the cause, or to be paid out to the lessor or landlord on good security, subject to the decree of the court; and in case such proceedings for relief in equity shall be taken within the time aforesaid, and after execution is executed, the lessor or landlord shall be accountable only for so much and no more as he shall really and bona fide, without fraud, deceit, or wilful neglect, make of the demised premises from the time of his entering into the actual possession thereof; and if what shall be so made by the lessor or landlord happen to be less than the rent reserved on the said lease, then the said lessee or his assignee, before he shall be restored to his possession, shall pay such lessor or landlord what the money so by him made fell short of the reserved rent for the time such lessor or landlord held the said lands.

[41]

212 Tenant paying all rent, with costs, proceedings to cease

If the tenant or his assignee do or shall, at any time before the trial in such ejectment, pay or tender to the lessor or landlord, his executors or administrators, or his or their attorney in that cause, or pay into the court where the same cause is depending, all the rent and arrears, together with the costs, then and in such case all further proceedings on the said ejectment shall cease and be discontinued; and if such lessee, his executors, administrators, or assigns, shall, upon such proceedings as aforesaid, be relieved in equity, he and they shall have, hold, and enjoy the demised lands, according to the lease thereof made, without any new lease.

[42]

235 Short title

In citing this Act in any instrument, document, or proceeding, it shall be sufficient to use the expression "The Common Law Procedure Act 1852."

[43]

236 Extent of Act

Nothing in this Act shall extend to Ireland or Scotland . . .

[44]

NOTES
Words omitted repealed by the Statute Law Revision Act 1892.

MARRIED WOMEN'S PROPERTY ACT 1882

(C 75)

An Act to consolidate and amend the Acts relating to the Property of Married Women
[18 August 1882]

17 Questions between husband and wife as to property to be decided in a summary way

In any question between husband and wife as to the title to or possession of property, either party, . . . may apply by summons or otherwise in a summary way [to the High Court or such county court as may be prescribed and the court may, on such an application (which may be heard in private), make such order with respect to the property as it thinks fit.

In this section "prescribed" means prescribed by rules of court and rules made for the purposes of this section may confer jurisdiction on county courts whatever the situation or value of the property in dispute.]

[45]

NOTES
Words omitted repealed by the Statute Law (Repeals) Act 1969; words in square brackets substituted by the Matrimonial and Family Proceedings Act 1984, s 43.

---

26 Extent of Act

This Act shall not extend to Scotland.

[46]

27 Short title

This Act may be cited as the Married Women's Property Act 1882.

[47]

WILLS (SOLDIERS AND SAILORS) ACT 1918

(C 58)

An Act to amend the Law with respect to Testamentary Dispositions by Soldiers and Sailors
[6 February 1918]

1 Explanation of s 11 of Wills Act 1837

In order to remove doubts as to the construction of the Wills Act 1837, it is hereby declared and enacted that section eleven of that Act authorises and always has authorised any soldier being in actual military service, or any mariner or seaman being at sea, to dispose of his personal estate as he might have done before the passing of that Act, though under the age of [eighteen years].

[48]

NOTES

Words in square brackets substituted by the Family Law Reform Act 1969, s 3(1)(b).

2 Extension of s 11 of Wills Act 1837

Section eleven of the Wills Act 1837, shall extend to any member of His Majesty's naval or marine forces not only when he is at sea but also when he is so circumstanced that if he were a soldier he would be in actual military service within the meaning of that section.

[49]

3 Validity of testamentary dispositions of real property made by soldiers and sailors

(1) A testamentary disposition of any real estate in England or Ireland made by a person to whom section eleven of the Wills Act 1837, applies, and who dies after the passing of this Act, shall, notwithstanding that the person making the disposition was at the time of making it under [eighteen years] of age or that the disposition has not been made in such manner or form as was at the passing of this Act required by law, be valid in any case where the person making the disposition was of such age and the disposition has been made in such manner and form that if the disposition had been a disposition of personal estate made by such a person domiciled in England or Ireland it would have been valid.

(2) A testamentary disposition of any heritable property in Scotland made after the passing of this Act by a person to whom section eleven of the Wills Act 1837, applies or to whom it would apply if he were domiciled in England, shall not be invalid by reason only of the fact that such person is under twenty-one years of age, provided always that he is of such age that he could, if domiciled in Scotland, have made a valid testamentary disposition of moveable property.

[50]

NOTES

Sub-s (1): words in square brackets substituted by the Family Law Reform Act 1969, s 3(1)(b).

4 Power to appoint testamentary guardians

Where any person dies after the passing of this Act having made a will which is, or which, if it had been a disposition of property, would have been rendered valid by section eleven of the Wills Act 1837, any appointment contained in that will of any person as guardian of the infant children of the testator shall be of full force and effect.

[51]

5 Short title and interpretation

(1)   This Act may be cited as the Wills (Soldiers and Sailors) Act 1918.

(2)   For the purposes of section eleven of the Wills Act 1837, and this Act the expression "soldier" includes a member of the Air Force, and references in this Act to the said section eleven include a reference to that section as explained and extended by this Act.

[52]

LAW OF PROPERTY ACT 1922

(C 16)

An Act to assimilate and amend the law of Real and Personal Estate, to abolish copyhold and other special tenures, to amend the law relating to commonable lands and of intestacy, and to amend the Wills Act 1837, the Settled Land Acts 1882 to 1890, the Conveyancing Acts 1881 to 1911, the Trustee Act 1893, and the Land Transfer Acts 1875 and 1897

[29 June 1922]

PART VII
PROVISIONS RESPECTING LEASEHOLDS

Conversion of Perpetually Renewable Leaseholds into Long Terms

145 Conversion of perpetually renewable leaseholds

For the purpose of converting perpetually renewable leases and underleases (not being an interest in perpetually renewable copyhold land enfranchised by Part V of this Act, but including a perpetually renewable underlease derived out of an interest in perpetually renewable copyhold land) into long terms, for preventing the creation of perpetually renewable leasehold interests and for providing for the interests of the persons affected, the provisions contained in the Fifteenth Schedule to this Act shall have effect.

[53]

PART XI
GENERAL PROVISIONS

191 Short title, commencement and extent

(1)   This Act may be cited as the Law of Property Act 1922.

(2)   . . .

(3)   This Act (including the repeals therein) shall not extend to Scotland or Ireland.

[54]

NOTES

Sub-s (2): repealed by the Statute Law Revision Act 1950.

FIFTEENTH SCHEDULE
PROVISIONS RELATING TO PERPETUALLY RENEWABLE LEASES AND UNDERLEASES

Section 145

1   Conversion of perpetually renewable leases into long terms

(1) Land comprised in a perpetually renewable lease which was subsisting at the commencement of this Act shall, by virtue of this Act, vest in the person who at such commencement was entitled to such lease, for a term of two thousand years, to be calculated from the date at which the existing term or interest commenced, at the rent and subject to the lessees' covenants and conditions (if any) which under the lease would have been payable or enforceable during the subsistence of such term or interest.

(2) The rent, covenants and conditions (if any) shall (subject to the express provisions of this Act to the contrary) be payable and enforceable during the subsistence of the term created by this Act; and that term shall take effect in substitution for the term or interest created by the lease, and be subject to the like power of re-entry (if any) and other provisions which affected the term or interest created by the lease, but without any right of renewal.

2   Conversion of perpetually renewable underleases into long terms

(1) Land comprised in any underlease, which at the commencement of this Act was perpetually renewable and was derived out of a head term affected by this Act, shall, by virtue of this Act, vest in the person who at such commencement was entitled to the subterm or interest for a term of two thousand years less one day, to be calculated from the date at which the head term created by this Act commenced, at the rent and subject to the underlessee's covenants and conditions (if any) which under the underlease would have been payable or enforceable during the subsistence of such subterm or interest.

(2) The rent, covenants and conditions (if any) shall (subject to the express provisions of this Act to the contrary) be payable and enforceable during the subsistence of the subterm created by this Act; and that subterm shall take effect in substitution for the subterm or interest created by the underlease, and be subject to the like power of re-entry (if any) and other provisions which affected the subterm or interest created by the underlease, but without any right of renewal.

(3) The foregoing provisions of this section shall also apply to any perpetually renewable subterm or interest which, at the commencement of this Act, was derived out of any other subterm or interest, but so that in every case the subterm created by this Act shall be one day less in duration than the derivative term created by this Act, out of which it takes effect.

5   Dispositions purporting to create perpetually renewable leaseholds

A grant, after the commencement of this Act, of a term, subterm, or other leasehold interest with a covenant or obligation for perpetual renewal, which would have been valid if this Part of this Act had not been passed, shall (subject to the express provisions of this Act) take effect as a demise for a term of two thousand years or in the case of a subdemise for a term less in duration by one day than the term out of which it is derived, to commence from the date fixed for the commencement of the term, subterm, or other interest, and in every case free from any obligation for renewal or for payment of any fines, fees, costs, or other money in respect of renewal.

[54A]

SETTLED LAND ACT 1925

(C 18)

An Act to consolidate the enactments relating to Settled Land in England and Wales

[9 April 1925]

PART I
GENERAL PRELIMINARY PROVISIONS

Settlements and Settled Land

1 What constitutes a settlement

(1) Any deed, will, agreement for a settlement or other agreement, Act of Parliament, or other instrument, or any number of instruments, whether made or passed before or after, or partly before and partly after, the commencement of this Act, under or by virtue of which instrument or instruments any land, after the commencement of this Act, stands for the time being—

    (i)   limited in trust for any persons by way of succession; or

    (ii) limited in trust for any person in possession—

        (a) for an entailed interest whether or not capable of being barred or defeated;

        (b) for an estate in fee simple or for a term of years absolute subject to an executory limitation, gift, or disposition over on failure of his issue or in any other event;

        (c) for a base or determinable fee or any corresponding interest in leasehold land;

        (d) being an infant, for an estate in fee simple or for a term of years absolute; or

    (iii) limited in trust for any person for an estate in fee simple or for a term of years absolute contingently on the happening of any event; or

    (iv) . . .

    (v) charged, whether voluntarily or in consideration of marriage or by way of family arrangement, and whether immediately or after an interval, with the payment of any rentcharge for the life of any person, or any less period, or of any capital, annual, or periodical sums for the portions, advancement, maintenance, or otherwise for the benefit of any persons, with or without any term of years for securing or raising the same;

creates or is for the purposes of this Act a settlement and is in this Act referred to as a settlement, or as the settlement, as the case requires;

Provided that, where land is the subject of a compound settlement, references in this Act to the settlement shall be construed as meaning such compound settlement, unless the context otherwise requires.

(2) Where an infant is beneficially entitled to land for an estate in fee simple or for a term of years absolute and by reason of an intestacy or otherwise there is no instrument under which the interest of the infant arises or is acquired, a settlement shall be deemed to have been made by the intestate, or by the person whose interest the infant has acquired.

(3) An infant shall be deemed to be entitled in possession notwithstanding any subsisting right of dower (not assigned by metes and bounds) affecting the land, and such a right of dower shall be deemed to be an interest comprised in the subject of the settlement and coming to the dowress under or by virtue of the settlement.

Where dower has been assigned by metes and bounds, the letters of administration or probate granted in respect of the estate of the husband of the dowress shall be deemed a settlement made by the husband.

(4)   An estate or interest not disposed of by a settlement and remaining in or reverting to the settlor, or any person deriving title under him, is for the purposes of this Act an estate or interest comprised in the subject of the settlement and coming to the settlor or such person under or by virtue of the settlement.

(5)   Where—

(a)   a settlement creates an entailed interest which is incapable of being barred or defeated, or a base or determinable fee, whether or not the reversion or right of reverter is in the Crown, or any corresponding interest in leasehold land; or

(b)   the subject of a settlement is an entailed interest, or a base or determinable fee, whether or not the reversion or right of reverter is in the Crown, or any corresponding interest in leasehold land;

the reversion or right of reverter upon the cesser of the interest so created or settled shall be deemed to be an interest comprised in the subject of the settlement, and limited by the settlement.

(6)   Subsection (4) and (5) of this section bind the Crown.

[(7)   This section does not apply to land held upon trust for sale.]

[55]

NOTES

Sub-s (1): para (iv) repealed by the Married Women (Restraint upon Anticipation) Act 1949, s 1(4), Sch 2.
Sub-s (7): inserted by the Law of Property (Amendment) Act 1926, s 7, Schedule.

2   What is settled land

Land which is or is deemed to be the subject of a settlement is for the purposes of this Act settled land, and is in relation to the settlement referred to in this Act as the settled land.

[56]

3   Duration of settlements

Land [not held upon trust for sale] which has been subject to a settlement shall be deemed for the purposes of this Act to remain and be settled land, and the settlement shall be deemed to be a subsisting settlement for the purposes of this Act so long as—

(a)   any limitation, charge, or power of charging under the settlement subsists, or is capable of being exercised; or

(b)   the person who, if of full age, would be entitled as beneficial owner to have that land vested in him for a legal estate is an infant.

[57]

NOTES

Words in square brackets inserted by the Law of Property (Amendment) Act 1926, s 7, Schedule.

4   Authorised method of settling land inter vivos

(1)   Every settlement of a legal estate in land inter vivos shall, save as in this Act otherwise provided, be effected by two deeds, namely, a vesting deed and a trust instrument and if effected in any other way shall not operate to transfer or create a legal estate.

(2)   By the vesting deed the land shall be conveyed to the tenant for life or statutory owner (and if more than one as joint tenants) for the legal estate the subject of the intended settlement:

Provided that, where such legal estate is already vested in the tenant for life or statutory owner, it shall be sufficient, without any other conveyance, if the vesting deed declares that the land is vested in him for that estate.

(3)   The trust instrument shall—
   (a)   declare the trusts affecting the settled land;
   (b)   appoint or constitute trustees of the settlement:
   (c)   contain the power, if any, to appoint new trustees of the settlement;
   (d)   set out, either expressly or by reference, any powers intended to be conferred by the settlement in extension of those conferred by this Act;
   (e)   bear any ad valorem stamp duty which may be payable (whether by virtue of the vesting deed or otherwise) in respect of the settlement.

[58]

5   Contents of vesting deeds

(1)   Every vesting deed for giving effect to a settlement or for conveying settled land to a tenant for life or statutory owner during the subsistence of the settlement (in this Act referred to as a "principal vesting deed") shall contain the following statements and particulars, namely:—
   (a)   A description, either specific or general, of the settled land;
   (b)   A statement that the settled land is vested in the person or persons to whom it is conveyed or in whom it is declared to be vested upon the trusts from time to time affecting the settled land;
   (c)   The names of the persons who are the trustees of the settlement;
   (d)   Any additional or larger powers conferred by the trust instrument relating to the settled land which by virtue of this Act operate and are exercisable as if conferred by this Act on a tenant for life;
   (e)   The name of any person for the time being entitled under the trust instrument to appoint new trustees of the settlement.

(2)   The statements or particulars required by this section may be incorporated by reference to an existing vesting instrument, and, where there is a settlement subsisting at the commencement of this Act, by reference to that settlement and to any instrument whereby land has been conveyed to the uses or upon the trusts of that settlement, but not (save as last aforesaid) by reference to a trust instrument nor by reference to a disentailing deed.

(3)   A principal vesting deed shall not be invalidated by reason only of any error in any of the statements or particulars by this Act required to be contained therein.

[59]

6   Procedure in the case of settlements by will

Where a settlement is created by the will of an estate owner who dies after the commencement of this Act—
   (a)   the will is for the purposes of this Act a trust instrument; and
   (b)   the personal representatives of the testator shall hold the settled land on trust, if and when required so to do, to convey it to the person who, under the will, or by virtue of this Act, is the tenant for life or statutory owner, and, if more than one, as joint tenants.

[60]

7   Procedure on change of ownership

(1)   If, on the death of a tenant for life or statutory owner, or of the survivor of two or more tenants for life or statutory owners, in whom the settled land was vested, the land remains settled land, his personal representatives shall hold the settled land on trust, if and when required so to do, to convey it to the person who under the trust instrument or by virtue of this Act becomes the tenant for life or statutory owner and, if more than one, as joint tenants.

(2)   If a person by reason of attaining full age becomes a tenant for life for the purposes of this Act of settled land, he shall be entitled to require the trustees of the settlement, personal representatives, or other persons in whom the settled land is vested, to convey the land to him.

(3)   If a person who, when of full age, will together with another person or other persons constitute the tenant for life for the purposes of this Act of settled land attains that age, he shall be entitled to require the tenant for life, trustees of the settlement, personal representatives or other persons in whom the settled land is vested to convey the land to him and the other person or persons who together with him constitute the tenant for life as joint tenants.

(4)   If by reason of forfeiture, surrender, or otherwise the estate owner of any settled land ceases to have the statutory powers of a tenant for life and the land remains settled land, he shall be bound forthwith to convey the settled land to the person who under the trust instrument, or by virtue of this Act, becomes the tenant for life or statutory owner and, if more than one, as joint tenants.

(5)   If any person of full age becomes absolutely entitled to the settled land (whether beneficially, or as personal representative, or as trustee for sale, or otherwise) free from all limitations, powers, and charges taking effect under the settlement, he shall be entitled to require the trustees of the settlement, personal representatives, or other persons in whom the settled land is vested, to convey the land to him, and if more persons than one being of full age become so entitled to the settled land they shall be entitled to require such persons as aforesaid to convey the land to them as joint tenants.

[61]

8   Mode and costs of conveyance, and saving of rights of personal representatives and equitable chargees

(1)   A conveyance by personal representatives under either of the last two preceding sections may be made by an assent in writing signed by them which shall operate as a conveyance.

(2)   Every conveyance under either of the last two preceding sections shall be made at the cost of the trust estate.

(3)   The obligations to convey settled land imposed by the last two preceding sections are subject and without prejudice—
   (a)   where the settlement is created by a will, to the rights and powers of the personal representatives for purposes of administration; and
   (b)   in any case, to the person on whom the obligation is imposed being satisfied that provision has been or will be made for the payment of any unpaid death duties in respect of the land or any interest therein for which he is accountable, and any interest and costs in respect of such duties, or that he is otherwise effectually indemnified against such duties, interest and costs.

(4) Where the land is or remains settled land a conveyance under either of the last two preceding sections shall—

    (a) if by deed, be a principal vesting deed; and

    (b) if by an assent, be a vesting assent, which shall contain the like statements and particulars as are required by this Act in the case of a principal vesting deed.

(5) Nothing contained in either of the last two preceding sections affects the right of personal representatives to transfer or create such legal estates to take effect in priority to a conveyance under either of those sections as may be required for giving effect to the obligations imposed on them by statute.

(6) A conveyance under either of the last two preceding sections, if made by deed, may contain a reservation to the person conveying of a term of years absolute in the land conveyed, upon trusts for indemnifying him against any unpaid death duties in respect of the land conveyed or any interest therein, and any interest and costs in respect of such duties.

(7) Nothing contained in either of the last two preceding sections affects any right which a person entitled to an equitable charge for securing money actually raised, and affecting the whole estate the subject of the settlement, may have to require effect to be given thereto by a legal mortgage, before the execution of a conveyance under either of those sections.

[62]

9 Procedure in the case of settlement and of instruments deemed to be trust instruments

(1) Each of the following settlements or instruments shall for the purposes of this Act be deemed to be a trust instrument, and any reference to a trust instrument contained in this Act shall apply thereto, namely:—

    (i) An instrument executed, or, in case of a will, coming into operation, after the commencement of this Act which by virtue of this Act is deemed to be a settlement;

    (ii) A settlement which by virtue of this Act is deemed to have been made by any person after the commencement of this Act;

    (iii) An instrument inter vivos intended to create a settlement of a legal estate in land which is executed after the commencement of this Act, and does not comply with the requirements of this Act with respect to the method of effecting such a settlement; and

    (iv) A settlement made after the commencement of this Act (including a settlement by the will of a person who dies after such commencement) of any of the following interests—

        (a) an equitable interest in land which is capable, when in possession, of subsisting at law; or

        (b) an entailed interest; or

        (c) a base or determinable fee or any corresponding interest in leasehold land,

    but only if and when the interest settled takes effect free from all equitable interests and powers under every prior settlement (if any).

(2) As soon as practicable after a settlement, or an instrument which for the purposes of this Act is deemed to be a trust instrument, takes effect as such, the trustees of the settlement may, and on the request of the tenant for life or statutory

owner shall, execute a principal vesting deed, containing the proper statements and particulars, declaring that the legal estate in the settled land shall vest or is vested in the person or persons therein named, being the tenant for life or statutory owner, and including themselves if they are the statutory owners, and such deed shall, unless the legal estate is already so vested, operate to convey or vest the legal estate in the settled land to or in the person or persons aforesaid and, if more than one, as joint tenants.

(3)   If there are no trustees of the settlement, then (in default of a person able and willing to appoint such trustees) an application under this Act shall be made to the court for the appointment of such trustees.

(4)   The provisions of the last preceding section with reference to a conveyance shall apply, so far as they are applicable, to a principal vesting deed under this section.

[63]

13   Dispositions not to take effect until vesting instrument is made

Where a tenant for life or statutory owner has become entitled to have a principal vesting deed or a vesting assent executed in his favour, then until a vesting instrument is executed or made pursuant to this Act in respect of the settled land, any purported disposition thereof inter vivos by any person, other than a personal representative (not being a disposition which he has power to make in right of his equitable interests or powers under a trust instrument), shall not take effect except in favour of a purchaser of a legal estate [without notice of such tenant for life or statutory owner having become so entitled as aforesaid] but, save as aforesaid, shall operate only as a contract for valuable consideration to carry out the transaction after the requisite vesting instrument has been executed or made, and a purchaser of a legal estate shall not be concerned with such disposition unless the contract is registered as a land charge.

[Nothing in this section affects the creation or transfer of a legal estate by virtue of an order of the court or the Minister or other competent authority.]

[64]

NOTES
Words in first pair of square brackets substituted and words in second pair of square brackets inserted by the Law of Property (Amendment) Act 1926, ss 6, 7, Schedule.

Enforcement of Equitable Interests and powers against Estate Owner and discharge on termination of Settlement

16   Enforcement of equitable interests and powers against estate owner

(1)   All equitable interests and powers in or over settled land (whether created before or after the date of any vesting instrument affecting the legal estate) shall be enforceable against the estate owner in whom the settled land is vested (but in the case of personal representatives without prejudice to their rights and powers for purposes of administration) in manner following (that is to say):—

  (i)   The estate owner shall stand possessed of the settled land and the income thereof upon such trusts and subject to such powers and provisions as may be requisite for giving effect to the equitable interests and powers affecting the settled land or income thereof of which he has notice according to their respective priorities;

  (ii) Where any person of full age becomes entitled to require a legal estate in the settled land to be vested in him in priority to the settlement, by reason of a right of reverter, statutory or otherwise, or an equitable right of entry taking effect, or on the ground that his interest ought no longer to be capable of being overreached under the powers of this Act, the estate owner shall be bound, if so requested in writing, to transfer or create such legal estate as may be required for giving legal effect to the rights of the person so entitled;

(iii) Where—

(a) any principal sum is required to be raised on the security of the settled land, by virtue of any trust, or by reason of the exercise of an equitable power affecting the settled land, or by any person or persons who under the settlement is or are entitled or together entitled to or has or have a general power of appointment over the settled land, whether subject to any equitable charges or powers of charging subsisting under the settlement or not; or

(b) the settled land is subject to any equitable charge for securing money actually raised and affecting the whole estate the subject of the settlement;

the estate owner shall be bound, if so requested in writing, to create such legal estate or charge by way of legal mortgage as may be required for raising the money or giving legal effect to the equitable charge:

Provided that, so long as the settlement remains subsisting, any legal estate or charge by way of legal mortgage so created shall take effect and shall be expressed to take effect subject to any equitable charges or powers of charging subsisting under the settlement which have priority to the interests or powers of the person or persons by or on behalf of whom the money is required to be raised or legal effect is required to be given to the equitable charge, unless the persons entitled to the prior charges or entitled to exercise the powers consent in writing to the same being postponed, but it shall not be necessary for such consent to be expressed in the instrument creating such legal estate or charge by way of legal mortgage.

(2) Where a mortgage or charge is expressed to be made by an estate owner pursuant to this section, then, in favour of the mortgagee or chargee and persons deriving title under him, the same shall take effect in priority to all the trusts of the settlement and all equitable interests and powers subsisting or to arise under the settlement except those to which it is expressly made subject, and shall so take effect, whether the mortgagee or chargee has notice of any such trusts, interests, or powers, or not, and the mortgagee or chargee shall not be concerned to see that a case had arisen to authorise the mortgage or charge, or that no more money than was wanted was raised.

(3) Nothing contained in paragraph (iii) of subsection (1) of this section affects the power conferred by this Act on a tenant for life of raising money by mortgage or of directing money to be applied in discharge of incumbrances.

(4) Effect may be given by means of a legal mortgage to an agreement for a mortgage, or a charge or lien, whether or not arising by operation of law, if the agreement charge or lien ought to have priority over the settlement.

(5) Save as hereinbefore expressly provided, no legal estate shall, so long as the settlement is subsisting, be transferred or created by the estate owner for giving effect to any equitable interest or power under the settlement.

(6) If a question arises or a doubt is entertained whether any and what legal estate ought to be transferred or created pursuant to this section, an application may be made to the court for directions as hereinafter provided.

(7)   If an estate owner refuses or neglects for one month after demand in writing to transfer or create any such legal estate, or if by reason of his being outside the United Kingdom, or being unable to be found, or by reason of the dissolution of a corporation, or for any other reason, the court is satisfied that the transaction cannot otherwise be effected, or cannot be effected without undue delay or expense, the court may, on the application of any person interested, make a vesting order transferring or creating the requisite legal estate.

(8)   This section does not affect a purchaser of a legal estate taking free from any equitable interest or power.

[65]

17   Deed of discharge on termination of settlement

(1)   Where the estate owner of any settled land holds the land free from all equitable interests and powers under a trust instrument, the persons who in the last or only principal vesting instrument or the last or only endorsement on or annex thereto are declared to be the trustees of the settlement or the survivors of them shall, save as hereinafter mentioned, be bound to execute, at the cost of the trust estate, a deed declaring that they are discharged from the trust so far as regards that land:

Provided that, if the trustees have notice of any derivative settlement, trust for sale or equitable charge affecting such land, they shall not execute a deed of discharge until—

(a)   in the case of a derivative settlement, or trust for sale, a vesting instrument or a conveyance has been executed or made for giving effect thereto; and

(b)   in the case of an equitable charge, they are satisfied that the charge is or will be secured by a legal mortgage, or is protected by registration as a land charge, or by deposit of the documents of title, or that the owner thereof consents to the execution of the deed of discharge.

Where the land is affected by a derivative settlement or trust for sale, the deed of discharge shall contain a statement that the land is settled land by virtue of such vesting instrument as aforesaid and the trust instrument therein referred to, or is held on trust for sale by virtue of such conveyance as aforesaid, as the case may require.

(2)   If, in the circumstances mentioned in subsection (1) of this section and when the conditions therein mentioned have been complied with, the trustees of a settlement on being requested to execute a deed of discharge—

(a)   by the estate owner; or

(b)   by a person interested under, or by the trustees of, a derivative settlement; or

(c)   by the trustees of a conveyance on trust for sale;

refuse to do so, or if for any reason the discharge cannot be effected without undue delay or expense, the estate owner, person interested, or trustees may apply to the court for an order discharging the first mentioned trustees as respects the whole or any part of the settled land, and the court may make such order as it may think fit.

(3)   Where a deed or order of discharge contains no statement to the contrary, a purchaser of a legal estate in the land to which the deed or order relates shall be entitled to assume that the land has ceased to be settled land, and is not subject to any trust for sale.

[66]

Restrictions on dispositions of Settled Land where Trustees have not been Discharged

18 Restrictions on dispositions of settled land where trustees have not been discharged

(1)   Where land is the subject of a vesting instrument and the trustees of the settlement have not been discharged under this Act, then—

    (a)   any disposition by the tenant for life or statutory owner of the land, other than a disposition authorised by this Act or any other statute, or made in pursuance of any additional or larger powers mentioned in the vesting instrument, shall be void, except for the purpose of conveying or creating such equitable interests as he has power, in right of his equitable interests and powers under the trust instrument, to convey or create; and

    (b)   if any capital money is payable in respect of a transaction, a conveyance to a purchaser of the land shall only take effect under this Act if the capital money is paid to or by the direction of the trustees of the settlement or into court; and

    (c)   notwithstanding anything to the contrary in the vesting instrument, or the trust instrument, capital money shall not, except where the trustee is a trust corporation, be paid to or by the direction of fewer persons than two as trustees of the settlement.

(2)   The restrictions imposed by this section do not affect—

    (a)   the right of a personal representative in whom the settled land may be vested to convey or deal with the land for the purposes of administration;

    (b)   the right of a person of full age who has become absolutely entitled (whether beneficially or as trustee for sale or personal representative or otherwise) to the settled land, free from all limitations, powers, and charges taking effect under the trust instrument, to require the land to be conveyed to him;

    (c)   the power of the tenant for life, statutory owner, or personal representative in whom the settled land is vested to transfer or create such legal estates, to take effect in priority to the settlement, as may be required for giving effect to any obligations imposed on him by statute, but where any capital money is raised or received in respect of the transaction the money shall be paid to or by the direction of the trustees of the settlement or in accordance with an order of the court.

[67]

Tenants for Life and Persons with Powers of Tenant for Life

19 Who is tenant for life

(1)   The person of full age who is for the time being beneficially entitled under a settlement to possession of settled land for his life is for the purposes of this Act the tenant for life of that land and the tenant for life under that settlement.

(2)   If in any case there are two or more persons of full age so entitled as joint tenants, they together constitute the tenant for life for the purposes of this Act.

(3)   If in any case there are two or more persons so entitled as joint tenants and they are not all of full age, such one or more of them as is or are for the time being of full age is or (if more than one) together constitute the tenant for life for the purposes of this Act, but this subsection does not affect the beneficial interests of such of them as are not for the time being of full age.

(4)   A person being tenant for life within the foregoing definitions shall be deemed to be such notwithstanding that, under the settlement or otherwise, the settled land, or his estate or interest therein, is incumbered or charged in any manner or to any extent, and notwithstanding any assignment by operation of law or otherwise of his estate or interest under the settlement, whether before or after it came into possession, other than an assurance which extinguishes that estate or interest.

[68]

20   Other limited owners having powers of tenant for life

(1)   Each of the following persons being of full age shall, when his estate or interest is in possession, have the powers of a tenant for life under this Act, (namely):—

   (i)   A tenant in tail, including a tenant in tail after possibility of issue extinct, and a tenant in tail who is by Act of Parliament restrained from barring or defeating his estate tail, and although the reversion is in the Crown, but not including such a tenant in tail where the land in respect whereof he is so restrained was purchased with money provided by Parliament in consideration of public services;

   (ii)   A person entitled to land for an estate in fee simple or for a term of years absolute with or subject to, in any of such cases, an executory limitation, gift, or disposition over on failure of his issue or in any other event;

  (iii)   A person entitled to a base or determinable fee, although the reversion or right of reverter is in the Crown, or to any corresponding interest in leasehold land;

  (iv)   A tenant for years determinable on life, not holding merely under a lease at a rent;

  (v)   A tenant for the life of another, not holding merely under a lease at a rent;

  (vi)   A tenant for his own or any other life, or for years determinable on life, whose estate is liable to cease in any event during that life, whether by expiration of the estate, or by conditional limitation, or otherwise, or to be defeated by an executory limitation, gift, or disposition over, or is subject to a trust for accumulation of income for any purpose;

  (vii)   A tenant by the curtesy;

 (viii)   A person entitled to the income of land under a trust or direction for payment thereof to him during his own or any other life, whether or not subject to expenses of management or to a trust for accumulation of income for any purpose, or until sale of the land, or until forfeiture, cesser or determination by any means of his interest therein, unless the land is subject to an immediate binding trust for sale;

  (ix)   A person beneficially entitled to land for an estate in fee simple or for a term of years absolute subject to any estates, interests, charges, or powers of charging, subsisting or capable of being exercised under a settlement;

  (x)   . . .

(2)   In every such case as is mentioned in subsection (1) of this section, the provisions of this Act referring to a tenant for life, either as conferring powers on him or otherwise, shall extend to each of the persons aforesaid, and any reference in this Act to death as regards a tenant for life shall, where necessary, be deemed to refer to the determination by death or otherwise of the estate or interest of the person on whom the powers of a tenant for life are conferred by this section.

(3)   For the purposes of this Act the estate or interest of a tenant by the curtesy shall be deemed to be an estate or interest arising under a settlement made by his wife.

(4)　Where the reversion of right or reverter or other reversionary right is in the Crown, the exercise by a person on whom the powers of a tenant for life are conferred by this section of his powers under this Act, binds the Crown.

[69]

NOTES

　　Sub-s (1): para (x) repealed by the Married Women (Restraint upon Anticipation) Act 1949, s 1(4), Sch 2.

21　Absolute owners subject to certain interests to have the powers of tenant for life

(1)　Where a person of full age is beneficially entitled in possession to a legal estate subject to any equitable interests or powers, then, for the purpose of overreaching such interests or powers, he may, notwithstanding any stipulation to the contrary, by deed (which shall have effect as a principal vesting deed within the meaning of this Act) declare that the legal estate is vested in him on trust to give effect to all equitable interests and powers affecting the legal estate, and that deed shall be executed by two or more individuals approved or appointed by the court or a trust corporation, who shall be stated to be the trustees of the settlement for the purposes of this Act.

　　Thereupon so long as any of the equitable interests and powers are subsisting the following provisions shall have effect:—

> (a)　The person so entitled as aforesaid and each of his successors in title being an estate owner shall have the powers of a tenant for life and the land shall be deemed to be settled land;
>
> (b)　The instrument (if any) under which his estate arises or is acquired, and the instrument (if any) under which the equitable interests or powers are subsisting or capable of taking effect shall be deemed to be the trust instrument:
>
> 　　Provided that where there is no such instrument as last aforesaid then a deed (which shall take effect as a trust instrument) shall be executed contemporaneously with the vesting deed, and shall declare the trusts affecting the land;
>
> (c)　The persons stated in the principal vesting deed to be the trustees of the settlement for the purposes of this Act shall also be the trustees of the trust instrument for those purposes; and
>
> (d)　Capital money arising on any disposition of the land shall be paid to or by the direction of the trustees of the settlement or into court, and shall be applicable towards discharging or providing for payment in due order of any principal money payable in respect of such interests or charges as are overreached by such disposition, and until so applied shall be invested or applied as capital money under the trust instrument, and the income thereof shall be applied as the income of such capital money, and be liable for keeping down in due order any annual or periodical sum which may be overreached by the disposition.

(2)　The following equitable interests and powers are excepted from the operation of subsection (1) of this section namely—

> (i)　an equitable interest protected by a deposit of documents relating to the legal estate affected;
>
> (ii)　the benefit of a covenant or agreement restrictive of the user of land;
>
> (iii)　an easement, liberty or privilege over or affecting land and being merely an equitable interest;

(iv) the benefit of a contract to convey or create a legal estate, including a contract conferring either expressly or by statutory implication a valid option of purchase, a right of pre-emption, or any other like right;

(v) any equitable interest protected by registration under the Land Charges Act 1925, other than—

(a) an annuity within the meaning of Part II of that Act;

(b) a limited owner's charge or a general equitable charge within the meaning of that Act.

(3)   Subject to the powers conferred by this Act on a tenant for life, nothing contained in this section shall deprive an equitable chargee of any of his rights or of his remedies for enforcing those rights.

[70]

23   Powers of trustees, etc, when there is no tenant for life

(1)   Where under a settlement there is no tenant for life nor, independently of this section, a person having by virtue of this Act the powers of a tenant for life then—

(a) any person of full age on whom such powers are by the settlement expressed to be conferred; and

(b) in any other case the trustees of the settlement;

shall have the powers of a tenant for life under this Act.

(2)   This section applies to trustees of settlements of land purchased with money provided by Parliament in consideration of public services where the tenant in tail is restrained from barring or defeating his estate tail, except that, if the tenant in tail is of full age and capacity, the powers shall not be exercised without his consent, but a purchaser shall not be concerned to see or inquire whether such consent has been given.

[71]

24   As to a tenant for life who has parted with his interest

(1)   If it is shown to the satisfaction of the court that a tenant for life, who has by reason of bankruptcy, assignment, incumbrance, or otherwise ceased in the opinion of the court to have a substantial interest in his estate or interest in the settled land or any part thereof, has unreasonably refused to exercise any of the powers conferred on him by this Act, or consents to an order under this section, the court may, on the application of any person interested in the settled land or the part thereof affected, make an order authorising the trustees of the settlement, to exercise in the name and on behalf of the tenant for life, any of the powers of a tenant for life under this Act, in relation to the settled land or the part thereof affected, either generally and in such manner and for such period as the court may think fit, or in a particular instance, and the court may by the order direct that any documents of title in the possession of the tenant for life relating to the settled land be delivered to the trustees of the settlement.

(2)   While any such order is in force, the tenant for life shall not, in relation to the settled land or the part thereof affected, exercise any of the powers thereby authorised to be exercised in his name and on his behalf, but no person dealing with the tenant for life shall be affected by any such order, unless the order is for the time being registered as an order affecting land.

(3)   An order may be made under this section at any time after the estate or interest of the tenant for life under the settlement has taken effect in possession, and notwithstanding that he disposed thereof when it was an estate or interest in remainder or reversion.

[72]

26   Infants, how to be affected

(1)   Where an infant is beneficially entitled in possession to land for an estate in fee simple or for a term of years absolute or would if of full age be a tenant for life of or have the powers of a tenant for life over settled land, then, during the minority of the infant—

(a)   if the settled land is vested in a personal representative, the personal representative, until a principal vesting instrument has been executed pursuant to the provisions of this Act; and

(b)   in every other case, the trustees of the settlement;

shall have, in reference to the settled land and capital money, all the powers conferred by this Act and the settlement on a tenant for life, and on the trustees of the settlement.

(2)   If the settled land is vested in a personal representative, then, if and when during the minority the infant, if of full age, would have been entitled to have the legal estate in the settled land conveyed to or otherwise vested in him pursuant to the provisions of this Act, a principal vesting instrument shall, if the trustees of the settlement so require, be executed, at the cost of the trust estate, for vesting the legal estate in themselves, and in the meantime the personal representative shall, during the minority, give effect to the directions of the trustees of the settlement, and shall not be concerned with the propriety of any conveyance directed to be made by those trustees if the conveyance appears to be a proper conveyance under the powers conferred by this Act or by the settlement, and the capital money, if any, arising under the conveyance is paid to or by the direction of the trustees of the settlement or into court, but a purchaser dealing with the personal representative and paying the capital money, if any, to him shall not be concerned to see that the money is paid to trustees of the settlement or into court, or to inquire whether the personal representative is liable to give effect to any such directions, or whether any such directions have been given.

(3)   Subsection (2) of this section applies whether the infant becomes entitled before or after the commencement of this Act, and has effect during successive minorities until a person of full age becomes entitled to require the settled land to be vested in him.

(4)   This section does not apply where an infant is beneficially entitled in possession to land for an estate in fee simple or for a term of years absolute jointly with a person of full age (for which case provision is made in the Law of Property Act 1925), but it applies to two or more infants entitled as aforesaid jointly, until one of them attains full age.

(5)   This section does not apply where an infant would, if of full age, constitute the tenant for life or have the powers of a tenant for life together with another person of full age, but it applies to two or more infants who would, if all of them were of full age, together constitute the tenant for life or have the powers of a tenant for life, until one of them attains full age.

(6)   Nothing in this section affects prejudicially any beneficial interest of an infant.

[73]

27   Effect of conveying legal estate to infant

(1)   A conveyance of a legal estate in land to an infant alone, or to two or more persons jointly, both or all of whom are infants, for his or their own benefit shall operate only as an agreement for valuable consideration to execute a settlement by

means of a principal vesting deed and a trust instrument in favour of the infant or infants, and in the meantime to hold the land in trust for the infant or infants.

(2)   Nothing in this Act prevents an equitable interest in settled land being vested in or transferred to an infant.

(3)   . . .

[74]

NOTES
   Sub-s (3): repealed by the Family Law Reform Act 1969, s 11(a).

29   Charitable and public trusts

(1)   For the purposes of this section, all land vested or to be vested in trustees on or for charitable, ecclesiastical, or public trusts or purposes shall be deemed to be settled land, and the trustees shall, without constituting them statutory owners, have in reference to the land, all the powers which are by this Act conferred on a tenant for life and on the trustees of a settlement.

In connexion only with the exercise of those powers, and not so as to impose any obligation in respect of or to affect—
   (a)   the mode of creation or the administration of such trusts; or
   (b)   the appointment or number of trustees of such trusts;

the statute or other instrument creating the trust or under which it is administered shall be deemed the settlement, and the trustees shall be deemed the trustees of the settlement, and, save where the trust is created by a will coming into operation after the commencement of this Act, a separate instrument shall not be necessary for giving effect to the settlement.

Any conveyance of land held on charitable, ecclesiastical or public trusts shall state that the land is held on such trusts, and, where a purchaser has notice that the land is held on charitable, ecclesiastical, or public trusts, he shall be bound to see that any consents or orders requisite for authorising the transaction have been obtained.

(2)   The said powers shall be exercisable subject to such consents or orders, if any, being obtained as would, if this Act had not been passed, have been requisite if the transaction were being effected under an express power conferred by the instrument creating the trust, and where the land is vested in . . . persons having no powers of management, the said powers shall be exercisable by the managing trustees or committee of management, and the . . . persons aforesaid shall not be liable for giving effect to directions given by the managing trustees or committee of management:

Provided that where—
   (a)   a disposition or dealing is to be effected for a nominal price or rent, or for less than the best price or rent that can be reasonably obtained or gratuitously; or
   (b)   any interest in land is to be acquired;

the like consent or order (if any) shall be required in reference to the disposition, dealing or acquisition, as would have been requisite if the intended transaction were a sale.

(3)   Nothing in this section affects the jurisdiction of the court, Charity Commissioners, Board of Education, or other competent authority, in regard to the administration of charitable, ecclesiastical, or public trusts.

(4)   . . .

(5)   Where any trustees or the majority of any set of trustees have power to transfer or create any legal estate, that estate shall be transferred or created by them in the names and on behalf of the persons . . . in whom the legal estate is vested.

(6)   This section applies (save as otherwise provided) whether the trust was created before or after the commencement of this Act, but does not apply to land to which the Universities and College Estates Act 1925, applies.

[75]

NOTES

Sub-ss (2), (5): words omitted repealed by the Charities Act 1960, s 48(2), Sch 7, Pt I.

Sub-s (4): repealed by the Charities Act 1960, s 48 (2), Sch 7, Pt II.

See further, in relation to charities: the Charities Act 1993, ss 37(6), 39(5).

Trustees of Settlement

30 Who are trustees for purposes of Act

(1)   Subject to the provisions of this Act, the following persons are trustees of a settlement for the purposes of this Act, and are in this Act referred to as the "trustees of the settlement" or "trustees of a settlement", namely—

    (i)   the persons, if any, who are for the time being under the settlement trustees with power of sale of the settled land (subject or not to the consent of any person), or with power of consent to or approval of the exercise of such a power of sale, or if there are no such persons; then

    (ii)   the persons, if any, for the time being, who are by the settlement declared to be trustees thereof for the purposes of the Settled Land Acts 1882 to 1890, or any of them, or this Act, or if there are no such persons; then

    (iii)   the persons, if any, who are for the time being under the settlement trustees with power of or upon trust for sale of any other land comprised in the settlement and subject to the same limitations as the land to be sold or otherwise dealt with, or with power of consent to or approval of the exercise of such a power of sale, or, if there are no such persons; then

    (iv)   the persons, if any, who are for the time being under the settlement trustees with future power of sale, or under a future trust for sale of the settled land, or with power of consent to or approval of the exercise of such a future power of sale, and whether the power or trust takes effect in all events or not, or, if there are no such persons; then

    (v)   the persons, if any, appointed by deed to be trustees of the settlement by all the persons who at the date of the deed were together able, by virtue of their beneficial interests or by the exercise of an equitable power, to dispose of the settled land in equity for the whole estate the subject of the settlement.

(2)   Paragraphs (i), (iii) and (iv) of the last preceding subsection take effect in like manner as if the powers therein referred to had not by this Act been made exercisable by the tenant for life or statutory owner.

(3)   Where a settlement is created by will, or a settlement has arisen by the effect of an intestacy, and apart from this subsection there would be no trustees for the purposes of this Act of such settlement, then the personal representatives of the deceased shall, until other trustees are appointed, be by virtue of this Act the trustees of the settlement, but where there is a sole personal representative, not being a trust corporation, it shall be obligatory on him to appoint an additional trustee to act with him for the purposes of this Act, and the provisions of the Trustee Act 1925, relating to the appointment of new trustees and the vesting of trust property shall apply accordingly.

[76]

34   Appointment of trustees by court

(1)   If at any time there are no trustees of a settlement, or where in any other case it is expedient, for the purposes of this Act, that new trustees of a settlement be appointed, the court may, if it thinks fit, on the application of the tenant for life, statutory owner, or of any other person having, under the settlement, an estate or interest in the settled land, in possession, remainder or otherwise, or, in the case of an infant, of his testamentary or other guardian or next friend, appoint fit persons to be trustees of the settlement.

(2)   The persons so appointed, and the survivors and survivor of them, while continuing to be trustees or trustee, and, until the appointment of new trustees, the personal representatives or representative for the time being of the last surviving or continuing trustee, shall become and be the trustees or trustee of the settlement.

[77]

35   Procedure on appointment of new trustees

(1)   Whenever a new trustee for the purposes of this Act is appointed of a trust instrument or a trustee thereof for the purposes aforesaid is discharged from the trust without a new trustee being appointed, a deed shall be executed supplemental to the last or only principal vesting instrument containing a declaration that the persons therein named, being the persons who after such appointment or discharge, as the case may be, are the trustees of the trust instrument for the purposes aforesaid, are the trustees of the settlement for those purposes; and a memorandum shall be endorsed on or annexed to the last or only principal vesting instrument in accordance with the Trustee Act 1925.

(2)   Every such deed as aforesaid shall, if the trustee was appointed or discharged by the court be executed by such person as the court may direct, and, in any other case, shall be executed by—

    (i)   the person, if any, named in the principal vesting instrument as the person for the time being entitled to appoint new trustees of the settlement, or if no person is so named, or the person is dead or unable or unwilling to act, the persons who if the principal vesting instrument had been the only instrument constituting the settlement would have had power to appoint new trustees thereof;

    (ii)   the persons named in the deed of declaration as the trustees of the settlement; and

    (iii)   any trustee who is discharged as aforesaid or retires.

(3)   A statement contained in any such deed of declaration as is mentioned in this section to the effect that the person named in the principal vesting instrument as the person for the time being entitled to appoint new trustees of the settlement is unable or unwilling to act, or that a trustee has remained outside the United Kingdom for more than twelve months, or refuses or is unfit to act, or is incapable of acting, shall in favour of a purchaser of a legal estate be conclusive evidence of the matter stated.

[78]

Provisions as to Undivided Shares

36   Undivided shares to take effect behind a trust for sale of the land

(1)   If and when, after the commencement of this Act, settled land is held in trust for persons entitled in possession under a trust instrument in undivided shares, the trustees of the settlement (if the settled land is not already vested in them) may require the estate

owner in whom the settled land is vested (but in the case of a personal representative subject to his rights and powers for purposes of administration), at the cost of the trust estate, to convey the land to them, or assent to the land vesting in them as joint tenants, and in the meantime the land shall be held on the same trusts as would have been applicable thereto if it had been so conveyed to or vested in the trustees.

(2)   If and when the settled land so held in trust in undivided shares is or becomes vested in the trustees of the settlement, the land shall be held by them (subject to any incumbrances affecting the settled land which are secured by a legal mortgage, but freed from any incumbrances affecting the undivided shares or not secured as aforesaid, and from any interests, powers and charges subsisting under the trust instrument which have priority to the trust for the persons entitled to the undivided shares) upon the statutory trusts.

(3)   If the estate owner refuses or neglects for one month after demand in writing to convey the settled land so held in trust in undivided shares in manner aforesaid, or if by reason of his being outside the United Kingdom or being unable to be found, or by reason of the dissolution of a corporation, or for any other reason, the court is satisfied that the conveyance cannot otherwise be made, or cannot be made without undue delay or expense, the court may, on the application of the trustees of the settlement, make an order vesting the settled land in them on the statutory trusts.

(4)   An undivided share in land shall not be capable of being created except under a trust instrument or under the Law of Property Act 1925, and shall then only take effect behind a trust for sale.

(5)   Nothing in this section affects the priority inter se of any incumbrances whether affecting the entirety of the land or an undivided share.

(6)   For the purposes of this section land held upon the statutory trusts shall be held upon the trusts and subject to the provisions following, namely, upon trust to sell the same, with power to postpone the sale of the whole or any part thereof, and to stand possessed of the net proceeds of sale, after payment of costs, and of the net rents and profits until sale, after payment of rates, taxes, costs of insurance, repairs, and other outgoings, upon such trusts and subject to such powers and provisions as may be requisite for giving effect to the rights of the persons interested in the settled land, [and the right of a person who, if the land had not been made subject to a trust for sale by virtue of this Act, would have been entitled to an entailed interest in an undivided share in the land, shall be deemed to be a right to a corresponding entailed interest in the net proceeds of sale attributable to that share].

(7)   The provisions of this section bind the Crown.

[79]

NOTES

Sub-s (6): words in square brackets added by the Law of Property (Entailed Interests) Act 1932, s 1(1).

PART II
POWERS OF A TENANT FOR LIFE

Sale and Exchange

38   Powers of sale and exchange

A tenant for life—

      (i)   May sell the settled land, or any part thereof, or any easement, right or privilege of any kind over or in relation to the land; and

(ii) . . .
(iii) May make an exchange of the settled land, or any part thereof, or of any easement, right, or privilege of any kind, whether or not newly created, over or in relation to the settled land, or any part thereof, for other land, or for any easement, right or privilege of any kind, whether or not newly created, over or in relation to other land, including an exchange in consideration of money paid for equality of exchange.

[80]

NOTES

Para (ii) repealed by the Statute Law (Repeals) Act 1969.

39 Regulations respecting sales

(1) Save as hereinafter provided every sale shall be made for the best consideration in money that can reasonably be obtained.

(2) A sale may be made in consideration wholly or partially of a perpetual rent, or a terminable rent consisting of principal and interest combined, payable yearly or half yearly to be secured upon the land sold, or the land to which the easement, right or privilege sold is to be annexed in enjoyment or an adequate part thereof.

In the case of a terminable rent, the conveyance shall distinguish the part attributable to principal and that attributable to interest, and the part attributable to principal shall be capital money arising under this Act:

Provided that, unless the part of the terminable rent attributable to interest varies according to the amount of the principal repaid, the trustees of the settlement shall, during the subsistence of the rent, accumulate the income of the said capital money in the way of compound interest by investing it and the resulting income thereof in securities authorised for the investment of capital money and shall add the accumulations to capital.

(3) The rent to be reserved on any such sale shall be the best rent that can reasonably be obtained, regard being had to any money paid as part of the consideration, or laid out, or to be laid out, for the benefit of the settled land, and generally to the circumstances of the case, but a peppercorn rent, or a nominal or other rent less than the rent ultimately payable, may be made payable during any period not exceeding five years from the date of the conveyance.

(4) Where a sale is made in consideration of a rent, the following provisions shall have effect:—

(i) The conveyance shall contain a covenant by the purchaser for payment of the rent, and [the statutory powers and remedies for the recovery of the rent shall apply];
(ii) A duplicate of the conveyance shall be executed by the purchaser and delivered to the tenant for life or statutory owner, of which execution and delivery the execution of the conveyance by the tenant for life or statutory owner shall be sufficient evidence;
(iii) A statement, contained in the conveyance or in an indorsement thereon, signed by the tenant for life of statutory owner, respecting any matter of fact or of calculation under this Act in relation to the sale, shall, in favour of the purchaser and of those claiming under him, be sufficient evidence of the matter stated.

(5) The consideration on a sale to any company incorporated by special Act of Parliament or by provisional order confirmed by Parliament or by any other order,

scheme or certificate having the force of an Act of Parliament, may, with the consent of the tenant for life, consist, wholly or in part, of fully-paid securities of any description of the company, and such securities shall be vested in the trustees of the settlement and shall be subject to the provisions of this Act relating to securities representing capital money arising under this Act, and may be retained and held by the trustees in like manner as if they had been authorised by this Act for the investment of capital money.

(6)   A sale may be made in one lot or in several lots, and either by auction or by private contract, and may be made subject to any stipulations respecting title, or evidence of title, or other things.

(7)   On a sale the tenant for life may fix reserve biddings and may buy in at an auction.

[81]

NOTES

Sub-s (4): words in square brackets substituted by the Law of Property (Amendment) Act 1926, s 7, Schedule.

---

40   Regulations respecting exchanges

(1)   Save as in this Part of this Act provided, every exchange shall be made for the best consideration in land or in land and money that can reasonably be obtained.

(2)   An exchange may be made subject to any stipulations respecting title, or evidence of title, or other things.

(3)   Settled land in England or Wales shall not be given in exchange for land out of England or Wales.

[82]

Leasing Powers

41   Power to lease for ordinary or building or mining or forestry purposes

A tenant for life may lease the settled land, or any part thereof, or any easement, right, or privilege of any kind over or in relation to the land, for any purpose whatever, whether involving waste or not, for any term not exceeding—
  (i)   In case of a building lease, nine hundred and ninety-nine years;
  (ii)   In case of a mining lease, one hundred years;
  (iii)   In case of a forestry lease, nine hundred and ninety-nine years;
  (iv)   In case of any other lease, fifty years.

[83]

42   Regulations respecting leases generally

(1)   Save as hereinafter provided, every lease—
  (i)   shall be by deed, and be made to take effect in possession not later than twelve months after its date, or in reversion after an existing lease having not more than seven years to run at the date of the new lease;
  (ii)   shall reserve the best rent that can reasonably be obtained, regard being had to any fine taken, and to any money laid out or to be laid out for the benefit of the settled land, and generally to the circumstances of the case;
  (iii)   shall contain a covenant by the lessee for payment of the rent, and a condition of re-entry on the rent not being paid within a time therein specified not exceeding thirty days.

(2)   A counterpart of every lease shall be executed by the lessee and delivered to the tenant for life or statutory owner, of which execution and delivery the execution of the lease by the tenant for life or statutory owner shall be sufficient evidence.

(3)   A statement, contained in a lease or in an indorsement thereon, signed by the tenant for life or statutory owner, respecting any matter of fact or of calculation under this Act in relation to the lease, shall, in favour of the lessee and of those claiming under him, be sufficient evidence of the matter stated.

(4)   A fine received on the grant of a lease under any power conferred by this Act shall be deemed to be capital money arising under this Act.

(5)   A lease at the best rent that can be reasonably obtained without fine, and whereby the lessee is not exempted from punishment for waste, may be made—
> (i)   Where the term does not exceed twenty-one years—
>> (a) without any notice of an intention to make the lease having been given under this Act; and
>> (b) notwithstanding that there are no trustees of the settlement; and
> (ii) Where the term does not extend beyond three years from the date of the writing, by any writing under hand only containing an agreement instead of a covenant by the lessee for payment of rent.

[84]

43   Leasing powers for special objects

The leasing power of a tenant for life extends to the making of—
> (i)   a lease for giving effect (in such manner and so far as the law permits) to a covenant of renewal, performance whereof could be enforced against the owner for the time being of the settled land; and
> (ii) a lease for confirming, as far as may be, a previous lease being void or voidable, but so that every lease, as and when confirmed, shall be such a lease as might at the date of the original lease have been lawfully granted under this Act or otherwise, as the case may require.

[85]

Provisions as to building, mining and forestry leases

44   Regulations respecting building leases

(1)   Every building lease shall be made partly in consideration of the lessee, or some person by whose direction the lease is granted, or some other person, having erected or agreeing to erect buildings, new or additional, or having improved or repaired or agreeing to improve or repair buildings, or having executed or agreeing to execute on the land leased, an improvement authorised by this Act for or in connexion with building purposes.

(2)   A peppercorn rent or a nominal or other rent less than the rent ultimately payable, may be made payable for the first five years or any less part of the term.

(3)   Where the land is contracted to be leased in lots, the entire amount of rent to be ultimately payable may be apportioned among the lots in any manner:

Provided that—
> (i)   the annual rent reserved by any lease shall not be less than [50p]; and
> (ii) the total amount of the rents reserved on all leases for the time being granted shall not be less than the total amount of the rents which, in order that the leases may be in conformity with this Act, ought to be reserved in respect of the whole land for the time being leased; and

(iii) the rent reserved by any lease shall not exceed one-fifth part of the full annual value of the land comprised in that lease with the buildings thereon when completed.

[86]

NOTES

Sub-s (3): sum in square brackets substituted by virtue of the Decimal Currency Act 1969, s 10(1).

45 Regulations respecting mining leases

(1) In a mining lease—
  (i) the rent may be made to be ascertainable by or to vary according to the acreage worked, or by or according to the quantities of any mineral or substance gotten, made merchantable, converted, carried away, or disposed of, in or from the settled land, or any other land, or by or according to any facilities given in that behalf; and
  (ii) the rent may also be made to vary according to the price of the minerals or substances gotten, or any of them, and such price may be the saleable value, or the price or value appearing in any trade or market or other price list or return from time to time, or may be the marketable value as ascertained in any manner prescribed by the lease (including a reference to arbitration), or may be an average of any such prices or values taken during a specified period; and
  (iii) a fixed or minimum rent may be made payable, with or without power for the lessees, in case the rent, according to acreage or quantity or otherwise, in any specified period does not produce an amount equal to the fixed or minimum rent, to make up the deficiency in any subsequent specified period, free of rent other than the fixed or minimum rent.

(2) A lease may be made partly in consideration of the lessee having executed, or agreeing to execute, on the land leased an improvement authorised by this Act, for or in connexion with mining purposes.

[87]

46 Variation of building or mining lease according to circumstances of district

(1) Where it is shown to the court with respect to the district in which any settled land is situate, either—
  (i) that it is the custom for land therein to be leased for building or mining purposes for a longer term or on other conditions than the term or conditions specified in that behalf in this Act; or
  (ii) that it is difficult to make leases for building or mining purposes of land therein, except for a longer term or on other conditions than the term and conditions specified in that behalf in this Act;

the court may, if it thinks fit, authorise generally the tenant for life or statutory owner to make from time to time leases of or affecting the settled land in that district, or parts thereof for any term or on any conditions as in the order of the court expressed, or may, if it thinks fit, authorise the tenant for life or statutory owner to make any such lease in any particular case.

(2) Thereupon the tenant for life or statutory owner, and, subject to any direction in the order of the court to the contrary, each of his successors in title being a tenant for life or statutory owner, may make in any case, or in the particular case, a lease of the settled land, or part thereof, in conformity with the order.

[88]

47 Capitalisation of part of mining rent

Under a mining lease, whether the mines or minerals leased are already opened or in work or not, unless a contrary intention is expressed in the settlement, there shall be from time to time set aside, as capital money arising under this Act, part of the rent as follows, namely—where the tenant for life or statutory owner is impeachable for waste in respect of minerals, three fourth parts of the rent, and otherwise one fourth part thereof, and in every such case the residue of the rent shall go as rents and profits.

[89]

48 Regulations respecting forestry leases

(1) In the case of a forestry lease—

   (i) a peppercorn rent or a nominal or other rent less than the rent ultimately payable, may be made payable for the first ten years or any less part of the term;

   (ii) the rent may be made to be ascertainable by, or to vary according to the value of the timber on the land comprised in the lease, or the produce thereof, which may during any year be cut, converted, carried away, or otherwise disposed of;

   (iii) a fixed or minimum rent may be made payable, with or without power for the lessee, in case the rent according to value in any specified period does not produce an amount equal to the fixed or minimum rent, to make up the deficiency in any subsequent specified period, free of rent other than the fixed or minimum rent; and

   (iv) any other provisions may be made for the sharing of the proceeds or profits of the user of the land between the reversioner and the Forestry Commissioners.

(2) In this section the expression "timber" includes all forest products.

[90]

Miscellaneous Powers

64 General power for the tenant for life to effect any transaction under an order of the court

(1) Any transaction affecting or concerning the settled land, or any part thereof, or any other land (not being a transaction otherwise authorised by this Act, or by the settlement) which in the opinion of the court would be for the benefit of the settled land, or any part thereof, or the persons interested under the settlement, may, under an order of the court, be effected by a tenant for life, if it is one which could have been validly effected by an absolute owner.

(2) In this section "transaction" includes any sale, . . . exchange, assurance, grant, lease, surrender, reconveyance, release, reservation, or other disposition, and any purchase or other acquisition, and any covenant, contract, or option, and any application of capital money, . . . and any compromise or other dealing, or arrangement; . . . and "effected" has the meaning appropriate to the particular transaction; and the references to land include references to restrictions and burdens affecting land.

[91]

NOTES

   Sub-s (2): first words omitted repealed by the Statute Law (Repeals) Act 1969; second and third words omitted repealed by the Settled Land and Trustee Acts (Court's General Powers) Act 1943, s 2.

Provisions as to special classes of property

65   Power to dispose of mansion

(1)   The powers of disposing of settled land conferred by this Act on a tenant for life may be exercised as respects the principal mansion house, if any, on any settled land, and the pleasure grounds and park and lands, if any, usually occupied therewith:

Provided that those powers shall not be exercised without the consent of the trustees of the settlement or an order of the court—
   (a)   if the settlement is a settlement made or coming into operation before the commencement of this Act and the settlement does not expressly provide to the contrary; or
   (b)   if the settlement is a settlement made or coming into operation after the commencement of this Act and the settlement expressly provides that these powers or any of them shall not be exercised without such consent or order.

(2)   Where a house is usually occupied as a farmhouse, or where the site of any house and the pleasure grounds and park and lands, if any, usually occupied therewith do not together exceed twenty-five acres in extent, the house is not to be deemed a principal mansion house within the meaning of this section, and may accordingly be disposed of in like manner as any other part of the settled land.

[92]

Raising of Money

71   Power to raise money by mortgage

(1)   Where money is required for any of the following purposes namely:—
   (i)   Discharging an incumbrance on the settled land or part thereof;
   (ii)   Paying for any improvement authorised by this Act or by the settlement;
   (iii)   Equality of exchange;
(iv), (v)   . . . ;
   (vi)   Redeeming a compensation rentcharge in respect of the extinguishment of manorial incidents and affecting the settled land;
   (vii)   Commuting any additional rent made payable on the conversion of a perpetually renewable leasehold interest into a long term;
   (viii)   Satisfying any claims for compensation on the conversion of a perpetually renewable leasehold interest into a long term by any officer, solicitor, or other agent of the lessor in respect of fees or remuneration which would have been payable by the lessee or under-lessee on any renewal;
   (ix)   Payment of the costs of any transaction authorised by this section or either of the two last preceding sections;

the tenant for life may raise the money so required, on the security of the settled land, or of any part thereof, by a legal mortgage, and the money so raised shall be capital money for that purpose, and may be paid or applied accordingly.

(2)   "Incumbrance" in this section does not include any annual sum payable only during a life or lives or during a term of years absolute or determinable.

(3)   The restrictions imposed by this Part of this Act on the leasing powers of a tenant for life do not apply in relation to a mortgage term created under this Act.

[93]

NOTES

Sub-s (1): paras (iv), (v) repealed by the Statute Law (Repeals) Act 1969.

Modification: any reference to solicitor(s) etc modified to include references to bodies recognised under the Administration of Justice Act 1985, s 9, by the Solicitors' Incorporated Practices Order 1991, SI 1991/2684, arts 4, 5, Sch 1.

PART V
MISCELLANEOUS PROVISIONS

93   Reference of questions to court

If a question arises or a doubt is entertained—

    (a) respecting the exercise or intended exercise of any of the powers conferred by this Act, or any enactment replaced by this Act, or the settlement, or any matter relating thereto; or

    (b) as to the person in whose favour a vesting deed or assent ought to be executed, or as to the contents thereof; or

    (c) otherwise in relation to property subject to a settlement;

the tenant for life or statutory owner, or the trustees of the settlement, or any other person interested under the settlement, may apply to the court for its decision or directions thereon, or for the sanction of the court to any conditional contract, and the court may make such order or give such directions respecting the matter as the court thinks fit.

[94]

PART VI
GENERAL PROVISIONS AS TO TRUSTEES

94   Number of trustees to act

(1)   Notwithstanding anything in this Act, capital money arising under this Act shall not be paid to fewer than two persons as trustees of a settlement, unless the trustee is a trust corporation.

(2)   Subject as aforesaid the provisions of this Act referring to the trustees of a settlement apply to the surviving or continuing trustees or trustee of the settlement for the time being.

[95]

95   Trustees' receipts

The receipt or direction in writing of or by the trustees of the settlement, or where a sole trustee is a trust corporation, of or by that trustee, or of or by the personal representatives of the last surviving or continuing trustee, for or relating to any money or securities, paid or transferred to or by the direction of the trustees, trustee, or representatives, as the case may be, effectually discharges the payer or transferor therefrom, and from being bound to see to the application or being answerable for any loss or misapplication thereof, and, in case of a mortgagee or other person advancing money, from being concerned to see that any money advanced by him is wanted for any purpose of this Act, or that no more than is wanted is raised.

[96]

96 Protection of each trustee individually

Each person who is for the time being a trustee of a settlement is answerable for what he actually receives only, notwithstanding his signing any receipt for conformity, and in respect of his own acts, receipts, and defaults only, and is not answerable in respect of those of any other trustee, or of any banker, broker, or other person, or for the insufficiency or deficiency of any securities, or for any loss not happening through his own wilful default.

[97]

97 Protection of trustees generally

The trustees of a settlement, or any of them—

(a) are not liable for giving any consent, or for not making, bringing, taking, or doing any such application, action, proceeding, or thing, as they might make, bring, take, or do; and

(b) in case of a purchase of land with capital money arising under this Act, or of an exchange, lease, or other disposition, are not liable for adopting any contract made by the tenant for life or statutory owner, or bound to inquire as to the propriety of the purchase, exchange, lease, or other disposition, or answerable as regards any price, consideration, or fine; and

(c) are not liable to see to or answerable for the investigation of the title, or answerable for a conveyance of land, if the conveyance purports to convey the land in the proper mode; and

(d) are not liable in respect of purchase-money paid by them by the direction of the tenant for life or statutory owner to any person joining in the conveyance as a conveying party, or as giving a receipt for the purchase-money, or in any other character, or in respect of any other money paid by them by the direction of the tenant for life or statutory owner on the purchase, exchange, lease, or other disposition.

[98]

98 Protection of trustees in particular cases

(1) Where the tenant for life or statutory owner directs capital money to be invested on any authorised security or investment, the trustees of the settlement shall not be liable for the acts of any agent employed by the tenant for life or statutory owner in connexion with the transaction, or for not employing a separate agent in or about the valuation of the subject of the security or the investigation of the title thereto, or for the form of the security or of any deed conveying the subject thereof to the trustees.

(2) The trustees of the settlement shall not be liable for paying or applying any capital money by the direction of the tenant for life or statutory owner for any authorised purpose.

(3) The trustees of the settlement shall not be liable in any way on account of any vesting instrument or other documents of title relating to the settled land, other than securities for capital money, being placed in the possession of the tenant for life or statutory owner:

Provided that where, if the settlement were not disclosed, it would appear that the tenant for life had a general power of appointment over, or was absolutely and beneficially entitled to the settled land, the trustees of the settlement shall, before they deliver the documents to him, require that notice of the last or only principal vesting instrument be written on one of the documents under which the tenant for life acquired his title, and may, if the documents are not in their possession, require such notice to be written as aforesaid, but, in the latter case, they shall not be liable in any way for not requiring the notice to be written.

(4)   This section applies to dealings and matters effected before as well as after the commencement of this Act.

[99]

101   Notice to trustees

(1)   Save as otherwise expressly provided by this Act, a tenant for life or statutory owner, when intending to make a sale, exchange, lease, mortgage, or charge or to grant an option—

(a)   shall give notice of his intention in that behalf to each of the trustees of the settlement, by posting registered letters, containing the notice, addressed to the trustees severally, each at his usual or last known place of abode in the United Kingdom; and

(b)   shall give a like notice to the solicitor for the trustees, if any such solicitor is known to the tenant for life or statutory owner, by posting a registered letter, containing the notice, addressed to the solicitor at his place of business in the United Kingdom;

every letter under this section being posted not less than one month before the making or granting by the tenant for life or statutory owner of the sale, exchange, lease, mortgage, charge, or option, or of a contract for the same:

Provided that a notice under this section shall not be valid unless at the date thereof the trustee is a trust corporation, or the number of trustees is not less than two.

(2)   The notice required by this section of intention to make a sale, exchange, or lease, or to grant an option, may be notice of a general intention in that behalf.

(3)   The tenant for life or statutory owner is, upon request by a trustee of the settlement, to furnish to him such particulars and information as may reasonably be required by him from time to time with reference to sales, exchanges, or leases effected, or in progress, or immediately intended.

(4)   Any trustee, by writing under his hand, may waive notice either in any particular case, or generally, and may accept less than one month's notice.

(5)   A person dealing in good faith with the tenant for life is not concerned to inquire respecting the giving of any such notice as is required by this section.

[100]

NOTES

Modification: any reference to solicitor(s) etc modified to include references to bodies recognised under the Administration of Justice Act 1985, s 9, by the Solicitors' Incorporated Practices Order 1991, SI 1991/2684, arts 4, 5, Sch 1.

102   Management of land during minority or pending contingency

(1)   If and as long as any person who is entitled to a beneficial interest in possession affecting land is an infant, the trustees appointed for this purpose by the settlement, or if there are none so appointed, then the trustees of the settlement, unless the settlement or the order of the court whereby they or their predecessors in office were appointed to be such trustees expressly provides to the contrary, or if there are none, then any persons appointed as trustees for this purpose by the court on the application of a guardian or next friend of the infant, may enter into and continue in possession of the land on behalf of the infant, and in every such case the subsequent provisions of this section shall apply.

(2)   The trustees shall manage or superintend the management of the land, with full power—

   (a)   to fell timber or cut underwood from time to time in the usual course for sale, or for repairs or otherwise; and

   (b)   to erect, pull down, rebuild, and repair houses, and other buildings and erections; and

   (c)   to continue the working of mines, minerals, and quarries which have usually been worked; and

   (d)   to drain or otherwise improve the land or any part thereof; and

   (e)   to insure against loss by fire; and

   (f)   to make allowances to and arrangements with tenants and others; and

   (g)   to determine tenancies, and to accept surrenders of leases and tenancies; and

   (h)   generally to deal with the land in a proper and due course of management;

but so that, where the infant is impeachable for waste, the trustees shall not commit waste, and shall cut timber on the same terms only, and subject to the same restrictions, on and subject to which the infant could, if of full age, cut the same.

(3)   The trustees may from time to time, out of the income of the land, including the produce of the sale of timber and underwood, pay the expenses incurred in the management, or in the exercise of any power conferred by this section, or otherwise in relation to the land, and all outgoings not payable by any tenant or other person, and shall keep down any annual sum, and the interest of any principal sum, charged on the land.

(4)   This section has effect subject to an express appointment by the settlement, or the court, of trustees for the purposes of this section or of any enactment replaced by this section.

(5)   Where any person is contingently entitled to land, this section shall, subject to any prior interests or charges affecting that land, apply until his interest vests, or, if his interest vests during his minority, until he attains [the age of eighteen years].

This subsection applies only where a person becomes contingently entitled under an instrument coming into operation after the commencement of this Act.

(6)   This section applies only if and as far as a contrary intention is not expressed in the instrument, if any, under which the interest of the infant or person contingently entitled as aforesaid arises, and has effect subject to the terms of that instrument and to the provisions therein contained.

[101]

NOTES

Sub-s (5): words in square brackets substituted by the Family Law Reform Act 1969, s 1(3), Sch 1.

PART VII
RESTRICTIONS, SAVINGS, AND PROTECTION OF PURCHASERS

104   Powers not assignable, and contract not to exercise powers void

(1)   The powers under this Act of a tenant for life are not capable of assignment or release, and do not pass to a person as being, by operation of law or otherwise, an assignee of a tenant for life, and remain exercisable by the tenant for life after and notwithstanding any assignment, by operation of law or otherwise, of his estate or interest under the settlement.

This subsection applies notwithstanding that the estate or interest of the tenant for life under the settlement was not in possession when the assignment was made or took effect by operation of law.

(2)   A contract by a tenant for life not to exercise his powers under this Act or any of them shall be void.

(3)   Where an assignment for value of the estate or interest of the tenant for life was made before the commencement of this Act, this section shall operate without prejudice to the rights of the assignee, and in that case the assignee's rights shall not be affected without his consent, except that—

(a)   unless the assignee is actually in possession of the settled land or the part thereof affected, his consent shall not be requisite for the making of leases thereof by the tenant for life or statutory owner, provided the leases are made at the best rent that can reasonably be obtained, without fine, and in other respects are in conformity with this Act; and

(b)   the consent of the assignee shall not be required to an investment of capital money for the time being affected by the assignment in securities authorised by statute for the investment of trust money.

(4)   Where such an assignment for value is made or comes into operation after the commencement of this Act, the consent of the assignee shall not be requisite for the exercise by the tenant for life of any of the powers conferred by this Act:

Provided that—

(a)   the assignee shall be entitled to the same or the like estate or interest in or charge on the land, money, or securities for the time being representing the land, money, or securities comprised in the assignment, as he had by virtue of the assignment in the last-mentioned land, money, or securities; and

(b)   if the assignment so provides, or if it takes effect by operation of the law of bankruptcy, and after notice thereof to the trustees of the settlement, no investment or application of capital money for the time being affected by the assignment shall be made without the consent of the assignee, except an investment in securities authorised by statute for the investment of trust money; and

(c)   notice of the intended transaction shall, unless the assignment otherwise provides, be given to the assignee, but a purchaser shall not be concerned to see or inquire whether such notice has been given.

(5)   Where such an assignment for value was made before the commencement of this Act, then on the exercise by the tenant for life after such commencement of any of the powers conferred by this Act—

(a)   a purchaser shall not be concerned to see or inquire whether the consent of the assignee has been obtained; and

(b)   the provisions of paragraph (a) of the last subsection shall apply for the benefit of the assignee.

(6)   A trustee or personal representative who is an assignee for value shall have power to consent to the exercise by the tenant for life of his powers under this Act, or to any such investment or application of capital money as aforesaid, and to bind by such consent all persons interested in the trust estate, or the estate of the testator or intestate.

(7)   If by the original assignment, or by any subsequent disposition, the estate or interest assigned or created by the original assignment, or any part thereof, or any derivative interest is settled on persons in succession, whether subject to any prior

charge or not, and there is no trustee or personal representative in whom the entirety of the estate or interest so settled is vested, then the person for the time being entitled in possession under the limitations of that settlement, whether as trustee or beneficiary, or who would, if of full age, be so entitled, and notwithstanding any charge or incumbrance subsisting or to arise under such settlement, shall have power to consent to the exercise by the tenant for life of his powers under this Act, or to any such investment or application of capital money as aforesaid, and to bind by such consent all persons interested or to become interested under such settlement.

(8)   Where an assignee for value, or any person who has power to consent as aforesaid under this section, is an infant, the consent may be given on his behalf by his parents or parent or testamentary or other guardian in the order named.

(9)   The court shall have power to authorise any person interested under any assignment to consent to the exercise by the tenant for life of his powers under this Act, or to any such investment or application of capital money as aforesaid on behalf of himself and all other persons interested, or who may become interested under such assignment.

(10) An assignment by operation of the law of bankruptcy, where the assignment comes into operation after the commencement of this Act, shall be deemed to be an assignment for value for the purposes of this section.

(11) An instrument whereby a tenant for life, in consideration of marriage or as part or by way of any family arrangement, not being a security for payment of money advanced, makes an assignment of or creates a charge upon his estate or interest under the settlement is to be deemed one of the instruments creating the settlement, and not an assignment for value for the purposes of this section:

Provided that this subsection shall not have effect with respect to any disposition made before the eighteenth day of August, eighteen hundred and ninety, if inconsistent with the nature or terms of the disposition.

(12) This section extends to assignments made or coming into operation before or after the commencement of this Act, and in this section "assignment" includes assignment by way of mortgage, and any partial or qualified assignment, and any charge or incumbrance, "assignee" has a corresponding meaning, and "assignee for value" includes persons deriving title under the original assignee.

[102]

105   Effect of surrender of life estate to the next remainderman

(1)   Where the estate or interest of a tenant for life under the settlement has been or is absolutely assured with intent to extinguish the same, either before or after the commencement of this Act, to the person next entitled in remainder or reversion under the settlement, then, . . . the statutory powers of the tenant for life under this Act shall, in reference to the property affected by the assurance, and notwithstanding the provisions of the last preceding section, cease to be exercisable by him, and the statutory powers shall thenceforth become exercisable as if he were dead, but without prejudice to any incumbrance affecting the estate or interest assured, and to the rights to which any incumbrancer would have been entitled if those powers had remained exercisable by the tenant for life.

This subsection applies whether or not any term of years or charge intervenes, or the estate of the remainderman or reversioner is liable to be defeated, and whether or not the estate or interest of the tenant for life under the settlement was in possession at the date of the assurance.

This subsection does not prejudice anything done by the tenant for life before the commencement of this Act, in exercise of any power operating under the Settled Land Acts 1882 to 1890, or, unless the assurance provides to the contrary, operate to accelerate any such intervening term of years or charge as aforesaid.

(2)   In this section "assurance" means any surrender, conveyance, assignment or appointment under a power (whether vested in any person solely, or jointly in two or more persons) which operates in equity to extinguish the estate or interest of the tenant for life, and "assured" has a corresponding meaning.

[103]

NOTES

Sub-s (1): words omitted repealed by the Law of Property (Amendment) Act 1926, s 7, Schedule.

106   Prohibition or limitation against exercise of powers void, and provision against forfeiture

(1)   If in a settlement, will, assurance, or other instrument executed or made before or after, or partly before and partly after, the commencement of this Act a provision is inserted—

   (a)   purporting or attempting, by way of direction, declaration, or otherwise, to forbid a tenant for life or statutory owner to exercise any power under this Act, or his right to require the settled land to be vested in him; or

   (b)   attempting, or tending, or intended, by a limitation, gift, or disposition over of settled land, or by a limitation, gift, or disposition of other real or any personal property, or by the imposition of any condition, or by forfeiture, or in any other manner whatever, to prohibit or prevent him from exercising, or to induce him to abstain from exercising, or to put him into a position inconsistent with his exercising any power under this Act, or his right to require the settled land to be vested in him;

that provision, as far as it purports, or attempts, or tends, or is intended to have, or would or might have, the operation aforesaid, shall be deemed to be void.

(2)   For the purposes of this section an estate or interest limited to continue so long only as a person abstains from exercising any such power or right as aforesaid shall be and take effect as an estate or interest to continue for the period for which it would continue if that person were to abstain from exercising the power or right, discharged from liability to determination or cesser by or on his exercising the same.

(3)   Notwithstanding anything in a settlement, the exercise by the tenant for life or statutory owner of any power under this Act shall not occasion a forfeiture.

[104]

107   Tenant for life trustee for all parties interested

(1)   A tenant for life or statutory owner shall, in exercising any power under this Act, have regard to the interests of all parties entitled under the settlement, and shall, in relation to the exercise thereof by him, be deemed to be in the position and to have the duties and liabilities of a trustee for those parties.

(2)   The provision by a tenant for life or statutory owner, at his own expense, of dwellings available for the working classes on any settled land shall not be deemed to be an injury to any interest in reversion or remainder in that land, but such provision shall not be made by a tenant for life or statutory owner without the previous approval in writing of the trustees of the settlement.

[105]

108 Saving for and exercise of other powers

(1)   Nothing in this Act shall take away, abridge, or prejudicially affect any power for the time being subsisting under a settlement, or by statute or otherwise, exercisable by a tenant for life, or (save as hereinafter provided) by trustees with his consent, or on his request, or by his direction, or otherwise, and the powers given by this Act are cumulative.

(2)   In case of conflict between the provisions of a settlement and the provisions of this Act, relative to any matter in respect whereof the tenant for life or statutory owner exercises or contracts or intends to exercise any power under this Act, the provisions of this Act shall prevail; and, notwithstanding anything in the settlement, any power (not being merely a power of revocation or appointment) relating to the settled land thereby conferred on the trustees of the settlement or other persons exercisable for any purpose, whether or not provided for in this Act, shall, after the commencement of this Act, be exercisable by the tenant for life or statutory owner as if it were an additional power conferred on the tenant for life within the next following section of this Act and not otherwise.

(3)   If a question arises or a doubt is entertained respecting any matter within this section, the tenant for life or statutory owner, or the trustees of the settlement, or any other person interested, under the settlement may apply to the court for its decision thereon, and the court may make such order respecting the matter as the court thinks fit.

[106]

109 Saving for additional or larger powers under settlement

(1)   Nothing in this Act precludes a settlor from conferring on the tenant for life, or (save as provided by the last preceding section) on the trustees of the settlement, any powers additional to or larger than those conferred by this Act.

(2)   Any additional or larger powers so conferred shall, as far as may be, notwithstanding anything in this Act, operate and be exercisable in the like manner, and with all the like incidents, effects, and consequences, as if they were conferred by this Act, and, if relating to the settled land, as if they were conferred by this Act on a tenant for life.

[107]

110 Protection of purchasers, etc

(1)   On a sale, exchange, lease, mortgage, charge, or other disposition, a purchaser dealing in good faith with a tenant for life or statutory owner shall, as against all parties entitled under the settlement, be conclusively taken to have given the best price, consideration, or rent as the case may require, that could reasonably be obtained by the tenant for life or statutory owner, and to have complied with all the requisitions of this Act.

(2)   A purchaser of a legal estate in settled land shall not, except as hereby expressly provided, be bound or entitled to call for the production of the trust instrument or any information concerning that instrument or any ad valorem stamp duty thereon, and whether or not he has notice of its contents he shall, save as hereinafter provided, be bound and entitled if the last or only principal vesting instrument contains the statements and particulars required by this Act to assume that—

    (a)   the person in whom the land is by the said instrument vested or declared to be vested is the tenant for life or statutory owner and has all the powers of a tenant for life under this Act, including such additional or larger powers, if any, as are therein mentioned;

(b) the persons by the said instrument stated to be the trustees of the settlement, or their successors appearing to be duly appointed, are the properly constituted trustees of the settlement;

(c) the statements and particulars required by this Act and contained (expressly or by reference) in the said instrument were correct at the date thereof;

(d) the statements contained in any deed executed in accordance with this Act declaring who are the trustees of the settlement for the purposes of this Act are correct;

(e) the statements contained in any deed of discharge, executed in accordance with this Act, are correct:

Provided that, as regards the first vesting instrument executed for the purpose of giving effect to—

(a) a settlement subsisting at the commencement of this Act; or

(b) an instrument which by virtue of this Act is deemed to be a settlement; or

(c) a settlement which by virtue of this Act is deemed to have been made by any person after the commencement of this Act; or

(d) an instrument inter vivos intended to create a settlement of a legal estate in land which is executed after the commencement of this Act and does not comply with the requirements of this Act with respect to the method of effecting such a settlement;

a purchaser shall be concerned to see—

(i) that the land disposed of to him is comprised in such settlement or instrument;

(ii) that the person in whom the settled land is by such vesting instrument vested, or declared to be vested, is the person in whom it ought to be vested as tenant for life or statutory owner;

(iii) that the persons thereby stated to be the trustees of the settlement are the properly constituted trustees of the settlement.

(3) A purchaser of a legal estate in settled land from a personal representative shall be entitled to act on the following assumptions:—

(i) If the capital money, if any, payable in respect of the transaction is paid to the personal representative, that such representative is acting under his statutory or other powers and requires the money for purposes of administration;

(ii) If such capital money is, by the direction of the personal representative, paid to persons who are stated to be the trustees of a settlement, that such persons are the duly constituted trustees of the settlement for the purposes of this Act, and that the personal representative is acting under his statutory powers during a minority;

(iii) In any other case, that the personal representative is acting under his statutory or other powers.

(4) Where no capital money arises under a transaction, a disposition by a tenant for life or statutory owner shall, in favour of a purchaser of a legal estate, have effect under this Act notwithstanding that at the date of the transaction there are no trustees of the settlement.

(5) If a conveyance of or an assent relating to land formerly subject to a vesting instrument does not state who are the trustees of the settlement for the purposes of this Act, a purchaser of a legal estate shall be bound and entitled to act on the assumption that the person in whom the land was thereby vested was entitled to the land free from all limitations, powers, and charges taking effect under that settlement, absolutely and beneficially, or, if so expressed in the conveyance or assent, as personal

representative, or trustee for sale or otherwise, and that every statement of fact in such conveyance or assent is correct.

PART IX
SUPPLEMENTARY PROVISIONS

117 Definitions

(1)   In this Act, unless the context otherwise requires, the following expressions have the meanings hereby assigned to them respectively, that is to say:—

(i)   "Building purposes" include the erecting and the improving of, and the adding to, and the repairing of buildings; and a "building lease" is a lease for any building purposes or purposes connected therewith;

(ii)   "Capital money arising under this Act" means capital money arising under the powers and provisions of this Act or the Acts replaced by this Act, and receivable for the trusts and purposes of the settlement and includes securities representing capital money;

(iii)   "Death Duty" means estate duty . . . and every other duty leviable or payable on death;

(iv)   "Determinable fee" means a fee determinable whether by limitation or condition;

(v)   "Disposition" and "conveyance" include a mortgage, charge by way of legal mortgage, lease, assent, vesting declaration, vesting instrument, disclaimer, release and every other assurance of property or of an interest therein by any instrument, except a will, and "dispose of" and "convey" have corresponding meanings;

(vi)   "Dower" includes "freebench";

(vii)   "Hereditaments" mean real property which on an intestacy might before the commencement of this Act have devolved on an heir;

(viii)   "Instrument" does not include a statute unless the statute creates a settlement;

(ix)   "Land" includes land of any tenure, and mines and minerals whether or not held apart from the surface, buildings or parts of buildings (whether the division is horizontal, vertical or made in any other way) and other corporeal hereditaments; also a manor, an advowson, and a rent and other incorporeal hereditaments, and an easement, right, privilege, or benefit in, over, or derived from land, and any estate or interest in land not being an undivided share in land;

(x)   "Lease" includes an agreement for a lease, and "forestry lease" means a lease to the Forestry Commissioners for any purpose for which they are authorised to acquire land by the Forestry Act 1919;

(xi)   "Legal mortgage" means a mortgage by demise or sub-demise or a charge by way of legal mortgage, and "legal mortgagee" has a corresponding meaning; "legal estate" means an estate interest or charge in or over land (subsisting or created at law) which is by statute authorised to subsist or to be created at law; and "equitable interests" mean all other interests and charges in or over land or in the proceeds of sale thereof; an equitable interest "capable of subsisting at law" means such an equitable interest as could validly subsist at law, if clothed with the legal estate; and "estate owner" means the owner of a legal estate;

(xii)   "Limitation" includes a trust, and "trust" includes an implied or constructive trust;

(xiii)   . . .

(xiv)   "Manor" includes lordship, and reputed manor or lordship; and "manorial incident" has the same meaning as in the Law of Property Act 1922;

(xv)   "Mines and minerals" mean mines and minerals whether already opened or in work or not, and include all minerals and substances in, on, or under the land, obtainable by underground or by surface working; and "mining purposes" include the sinking and searching for, winning, working, getting, making merchantable, smelting or otherwise converting or working for the purposes of any manufacture, carrying away, and disposing of mines and minerals, in or under the settled land, or any other land, and the erection of buildings, and the execution of engineering and other works suitable for those purposes; and a "mining lease" is a lease for any mining purposes or purposes connected therewith, and includes a grant or licence for any mining purposes;

(xvi)   "Minister" means [the Minister of Agriculture, Fisheries and Food];

(xvii)   "Notice" includes constructive notice;

(xviii)   "Personal representative" means the executor, original or by representation, or administrator, for the time being of a deceased person, and where there are special personal representatives for the purposes of settled land means those personal representatives;

(xix)   "Possession" includes receipt of rents and profits, or the right to receive the same, if any; and "income" includes rents and profits;

(xx)   "Property" includes any thing in action, and any interest in real or personal property;

(xxi)   "Purchaser" means a purchaser in good faith for value, and includes a lessee, mortgagee or other person who in good faith acquires an interest in settled land for value; and in reference to a legal estate includes a chargee by way of legal mortgage;

(xxii)   "Rent" includes yearly or other rent, and toll, duty, royalty, or other reservation, by the acre, or the ton, or otherwise; and in relation to rent, "payment" includes delivery; and "fine" includes premium or fore-gift, and any payment, consideration, or benefit in the nature of a fine, premium, or fore-gift;

(xxiii)   "Securities" include stocks, funds, and shares;

(xxiv)   "Settled land" includes land which is deemed to be settled land; "settlement" includes an instrument or instruments which under this Act or the Acts which it replaces is or are deemed to be or which together constitute a settlement, and a settlement which is deemed to have been made by any person or to be subsisting for the purposes of this Act; "a settlement subsisting at the commencement of this Act" includes a settlement created by virtue of this Act immediately on the commencement thereof; and "trustees of the settlement" mean the trustees thereof for the purposes of this Act howsoever appointed or constituted;

(xxv)   "Small dwellings" mean dwelling-houses of a rateable value not exceeding one hundred pounds per annum;

(xxvi)   "Statutory owner" means the trustees of the settlement or other persons who, during a minority, or at any other time when there is no tenant for life, have the powers of a tenant for life under this Act, but does not include the trustees of the settlement, where by virtue of an order of the court or otherwise the trustees have power to convey the settled land in the name of the tenant for life;

(xxvii)   "Steward" includes deputy steward, or other proper officer, of a manor;

(xxviii) "Tenant for life" includes a person (not being a statutory owner) who has the powers of a tenant for life under this Act, and also (where the context requires) one of two or more persons who together constitute the tenant for life, or have the powers of a tenant for life; and "tenant in tail" includes a person entitled to an entailed interest in any property; and "entailed interest" has the same meaning as in the Law of Property Act 1925;

(xxix) A "term of years absolute" means a term of years, taking effect either in possession or in reversion, with or without impeachment for waste, whether at a rent or not and whether subject or not to another legal estate, and whether certain or liable to determination by notice, re-entry, operation of law, or by a provision for cesser on redemption, or in any other event (other than the dropping of a life, or the determination of a determinable life interest), but does not include any term of years determinable with life or lives or with the cesser of a determinable life interest, nor, if created after the commencement of this Act, a term of years which is not expressed to take effect in possession within twenty-one years after the creation thereof where required by statute to take effect within that period; and in this definition the expression "term of years" includes a term for less than a year, or for a year or years and a fraction of a year or from year to year;

(xxx) "Trust corporation" means the Public Trustee or a corporation either appointed by the court in any particular case to be a trustee or entitled by rules made under subsection (3) of section four of the Public Trustee Act 1906, to act as custodian trustee, and "trust for sale" "trustees for sale" and "power to postpone a sale" have the same meanings as in the Law of Property Act 1925;

(xxxi) In relation to settled land "vesting deed" or "vesting order" means the instrument whereby settled land is conveyed to or vested or declared to be vested in a tenant for life or statutory owner; "vesting assent" means the instrument whereby a personal representative, after the death of a tenant for life or statutory owner, or the survivor of two or more tenants for life or statutory owners, vests settled land in a person entitled as tenant for life or statutory owner; "vesting instrument" means a vesting deed, a vesting assent or, where the land affected remains settled land, a vesting order; "principal vesting instrument" includes any vesting instrument other than a subsidiary vesting deed; and "trust instrument" means the instrument whereby the trusts of the settled land are declared, and includes any two or more such instruments and a settlement or instrument which is deemed to be a trust instrument;

(xxxii) "United Kingdom" means Great Britain and Northern Ireland;

(xxxiii) "Will" includes codicil.

[(1A) Any reference in this Act to money, securities or proceeds of sale being paid or transferred into court shall be construed as referring to the money, securities or proceeds being paid or transferred into the Supreme Court or any other court that has jurisdiction, and any reference in this Act to the court, in a context referring to the investment or application of money, securities or proceeds of sale paid or transferred into court, shall be construed, in the case of money, securities or proceeds paid or transferred into the Supreme Court, as referring to the High Court, and, in the case of money, securities or proceeds paid or transferred into another court, as referring to that other court.]

(2) Where an equitable interest in or power over property arises by statute or operation of law, references to the "creation" of an interest or power include any interest or power so arising.

(3) References to registration under the Land Charges Act 1925, apply to any registration made under any statute which is by the Land Charges Act 1925, to have effect as if the registration had been made under that Act.

[109]

NOTES

Sub-s (1): words omitted from para (iii) repealed by the Finance Act 1949, s 52, Sch 11, Pt IV; para (xiii) repealed by the Mental Health Act 1959, s 149(2), Sch 8, Pt I; words in square brackets in para (xvi) substituted by virtue of the Transfer of Functions (Ministry of Food) Order 1955, SI 1955/554.

Sub-s (1A): inserted by the Administration of Justice Act 1965, s 17(1), Sch 1.

Modification: definition "Trust corporation" modified in relation to charities, by the Charities Act 1993, s 35.

120   Short title, commencement and extent

(1) This Act may be cited as the Settled Land Act 1925.

(2) . . .

(3) This Act extends to England and Wales only.

[110]

NOTES

Sub-s (2): repealed by the Statute Law Revision Act 1950.

FIRST SCHEDULE
Forms of Instruments

Section 15

Form No 1
Vesting Deed for Giving Effect to a Settlement Subsisting at the Commencement of this Act

This Vesting Deed is made [etc] between *X* of [etc] and *Y* of [etc] (hereinafter called the trustees) of the one part and *TL* of [etc] of the other part.

[*Recite the Settlement under which TL is a tenant for life of full age in possession of the freeholds and leaseholds respectively described in the First and Second Schedules and has power to appoint new trustees, and the trustees are trustees for the purposes of the Settled Land Act 1925, also the request by TL that the trustees should execute the requisite vesting deed.*]

Now for giving effect to the requirements of the Settled Land Act 1925, this deed witnesseth as follows:—

1. The trustees as Trustees hereby declare that—

All and singular the hereditaments and premises respectively mentioned in the First and Second Schedules hereto and all other (if any) the premises capable of being vested by this declaration which are now by any means subject to the limitations of the recited settlement are vested in the said *TL* as to the freehold hereditaments mentioned in the First Schedule hereto in fee simple, and as to the leasehold hereditaments mentioned in the Second Schedule hereto, for all the residue of the terms of years for which the same are respectively held.

2. The said *TL* shall stand possessed of the premises upon the trusts and subject to the powers and provisions upon and subject to which under the recited settlement or otherwise the same ought to be held from time to time.

3. The trustees are the trustees of the settlement for the purposes of the Settled Land Act 1925.

4. The following additional or larger powers are conferred by the said settlement in relation to the settled land, and by virtue of the Settled Land Act 1925, operate and are exercisable as if conferred by that Act on a tenant for life [*Here insert the additional powers*].

5. [*Add the usual covenant by TL with the trustees to pay the rent in respect of leasehold hereditaments, observe the lessee's covenants and keep the trustees indemnified.*]

6. The power to appoint a new trustee or new trustees of the settlement is vested in the said *TL* during his life.

In witness [etc].

[NOTE.—Add the schedules. In the first part of the First Schedule give particulars of the manors, advowsons and other incorporeal hereditaments. In the second part give particulars of the freehold land referring, if practicable, to annexed plans, so that the vesting deed may ultimately become a convenient root of title. Unless this is done the deeds referred to will for purposes of the parcels remain part of the title. In the Second Schedule give particulars of the dates of and parties to the leases of the leasehold hereditaments, and short particulars of the properties demised, the terms and the rents. If there are any mortgages having priority to the settlement these should be mentioned in another schedule and referred to in the recitals.]

Form No 2
Vesting Deed on the Settlement of Land

This Vesting Deed made [etc] between John H of [etc] of the first part, Jane W of [etc] of the second part, and X of [etc], Y of [etc], and Z of [etc] (hereinafter called the trustees) of the third part.

Witnesseth and it is hereby declared as follows:—

1. In consideration of the intended marriage between *John H* and *Jane W* the said *John H* as Settlor hereby declares that

All that (*setting out the parcels by reference to a schedule or otherwise*) are vested in *John H* in fee simple (*or in the case of leaseholds refer to the terms*).

Upon the trusts declared concerning the same by a Trust Instrument bearing even date with but intended to be executed contemporaneously with these presents and made between the same parties and in the same order as these presents or upon such other trusts as the same ought to be held from time to time.

2. The trustees are the trustees of the settlement for the purposes of the Settled Land Act 1925.

3. The following additional or larger powers are conferred by the said trust instrument in relation to the settled land and by virtue of the Settled Land Act 1925, operate and are exercisable as if conferred by that Act on a tenant for life. [*Here insert the additional powers.*]

4. The power of appointing a new trustee or new trustees of the settlement is vested in the said [*John H*] during his life.

In witness [etc].

Form No 3
Trust Instrument of the Settlement of Land

This Trust Instrument is made [etc] between *John H* of [etc] (hereinafter called the Settlor) of the first part, *Jane W* of [etc] of the second part, and *X* of [etc], *Y* of [etc], and *Z* of [etc] (hereinafter called the trustees) of the third part.

Whereas by a deed (hereinafter called the Vesting Deed) bearing even date with but executed contemporaneously with these presents, and made between the same parties and in the same order as these presents, certain hereditaments situated at   in the county of   were vested in the Settlor Upon the trusts declared concerning the same by a trust instrument of even date therein referred to (meaning these presents).

Now in consideration of the intended marriage between the Settlor and *Jane W*, this Deed Witnesseth as follows:—

1.   The Settlor hereby agrees that he will hold the hereditaments and property comprised in the Vesting Deed In trust for himself until the solemnisation of the said marriage and thereafter Upon the trusts following, that is to say:—

2.   Upon trust for the Settlor during his life without impeachment of waste with remainder Upon trust if *Jane W* survives him that she shall receive out of the premises during the residue of her life a yearly jointure rentcharge of [etc] and subject thereto Upon trust for the trustees for a term of 800 years from the date of the death of the Settlor without impeachment of waste   Upon the trusts hereinafter declared concerning the same. And subject to the said term and the trusts thereof Upon trust for the first and other sons of the said intended marriage successively according to seniority in tail male with remainder [etc] *with an ultimate remainder in trust for the Settlor in fee simple.*

[*Here add the requisite trusts of the portions term, and any other proper provisions including the appointment of the trustees to be trustees of the settlement for the purposes of the Settled Land Act 1925, extension of Settled Land Act powers, and a power for the tenant for life for the time being of full age to appoint new trustees of the settlement.*]

In witness [etc].

[NOTE.—The Vesting Deed and the Trust Instrument can be executed as escrows till the marriage.]

Form No 4
Subsidiary Vesting Deed on Sale when the Land is Purchased with Capital Money

This Subsidiary Vesting Deed is made [etc] between *Henry V* of [etc] (hereinafter called the Vendor) of the first part, *X* of [etc], *Y* of [etc], and *Z* of [etc] (hereinafter called the trustees) of the second part, and *John H* [etc] (hereinafter called the Purchaser) of the third part.

Whereas the Vendor is entitled for an estate in fee simple in possession free from incumbrances to the hereditaments hereinafter conveyed and has agreed to sell the same to the Purchaser at the price of   pounds.

And whereas by a principal vesting deed (hereinafter called the principal deed) dated [etc], and made [etc] [*Form No 2*], certain hereditaments were vested in the Purchaser Upon the trusts of a trust instrument of even date therewith, and by [endorsements on] the principal deed the trustees were stated to be the trustees of the settlement for the purposes of the Settled Land Act 1925.

Now this Deed witnesseth as follows:—

1. In consideration of the sum of   pounds now paid to the Vendor by the trustees by the direction of the Purchaser (the receipt of which sum the Vendor hereby acknowledges) the Vendor as Beneficial Owner hereby conveys unto the Purchaser All those [etc].

To hold unto the Purchaser [in fee simple] upon and subject to the same trusts and powers as are declared by the principal deed by reference as aforesaid with respect to the hereditaments therein comprised.

2. and 3. [*Same as 2 and 4 in Form No 2*].

In witness [etc].

NOTE.—On a purchase of a term of years absolute out of capital money, the term must be conveyed to the tenant for life, if any, of full age, instead of to the trustees of the settlement. If there is a minority the land will be conveyed to the personal representatives or to the Settled Land Act trustees.

Form No 5
Vesting Assent by Personal Representatives

1. *EF* of [etc] and *GH* of [etc] as the personal representatives of *XY*, late of [etc] deceased, do this   day of   19   hereby, As Personal Representatives, assent to the vesting in *CD* of [etc] of [All that farm, etc] *or* [All the property described in the Schedule hereto] for all the estate or interest of the said *XY* at the time of his death [*or*, for an estate in fee simple].

2. The premises are vested in the said *CD* upon the trusts declared concerning the same by [etc].

3. The said *EF* and *GH* are the trustees of the settlement for the purposes of the Settled Land Act 1925.

4. and 5. [*Same as 3 and 4 in Form No 2*].

As witness, etc.

NOTE.—The expression "conveyance" includes an assent, but an assent will relate back to the death unless a contrary intention appears.

An assent will not be properly postponed merely because death duty remains to be paid. The representatives have only to be satisfied (*eg*, where the tenant for life has directed payment out of capital money or has executed a mortgage for raising the money as and when an instalment becomes due) that the duty will be paid.

TRUSTEE ACT 1925

(C 19)

An Act to consolidate certain enactments relating to trustees in England and Wales

[9 April 1925]

PART I
INVESTMENTS

10   Powers supplementary to powers of investment

(1)   Trustees lending money on the security of any property on which they can lawfully lend may contract that such money shall not be called in during any period not exceeding seven years from the time when the loan was made, provided interest be paid within a specified time not exceeding thirty days after every half-yearly or other day on which it becomes due, and provided there be no breach of any covenant by the mortgagor contained in the instrument of mortgage or charge for the maintenance and protection of the property.

(2)   On a sale of land for an estate in fee simple or for a term having at least five hundred years to run by trustees or by a tenant for life or statutory owner, the trustees, or the tenant for life or statutory owner on behalf of the trustees of the settlement, may, where the proceeds are liable to be invested, contract that the payment of any part, not exceeding two-thirds, of the purchase money shall be secured by a charge by way of legal mortgage or a mortgage by demise or sub-demise for a term of at least five hundred years (less a nominal reversion when by sub-demise), of the land sold, with or without the security of any other property, such charge or mortgage, if any buildings are comprised in the mortgage, to contain a covenant by the mortgagor to keep them insured against loss or damage by fire to the full value thereof.

The trustees shall not be bound to obtain any report as to the value of the land or other property to be comprised in such charge or mortgage, or any advice as to the making of the loan, and shall not be liable for any loss which may be incurred by reason only of the security being insufficient at the date of the charge or mortgage; and the trustees of the settlement shall be bound to give effect to such contract made by the tenant for life or statutory owner.

(3)   Where any securities of a company are subject to a trust, the trustees may concur in any scheme or arrangement—

    (a)   for the reconstruction of the company;

    (b)   for the sale of all or any part of the property and undertaking of the company to another company;

  [(bb)   for the acquisition of the securities of the company, or of control thereof by another company];

    (c)   for the amalgamation of the company with another company;

    (d)   for the release, modification, or variation of any rights, privileges or liabilities attached to the securities or any of them;

in like manner as if they were entitled to such securities beneficially, with power to accept any securities of any denomination or description of the reconstructed or purchasing or new company in lieu of or in exchange for all or any of the first-mentioned securities; and the trustees shall not be responsible for any loss occasioned by any act or thing so done in good faith, and may retain any securities so accepted as aforesaid for any period for which they could have properly retained the original securities.

(4) If any conditional or preferential right to subscribe for any securities in any company is offered to trustees in respect of any holding in such company, they may as to all or any of such securities, either exercise such right and apply capital money subject to the trust in payment of the consideration, or renounce such right, or assign for the best consideration that can be reasonably obtained the benefit of such right or the title thereto to any person, including any beneficiary under the trust, without being responsible for any loss occasioned by any act or thing so done by them in good faith:

Provided that the consideration for any such assignment shall be held as capital money of the trust.

(5) The powers conferred by this section shall be exercisable subject to the consent of any person whose consent to a change of investment is required by law or by the instrument, if any, creating the trust.

(6) Where the loan referred to in subsection (1), or the sale referred to in subsection (2), of this section is made under the order of the court, the powers conferred by those subsections respectively shall apply only if and as far as the court may by order direct.

[112]

NOTES
Sub-s (3): para (bb) inserted by the Trustee Investments Act 1961, s 9(1).

PART II
GENERAL POWERS OF TRUSTEES AND PERSONAL REPRESENTATIVES

General Powers

17 Protection to purchasers and mortgagees dealing with trustees

No purchaser or mortgagee, paying or advancing money on a sale or mortgage purporting to be made under any trust or power vested in trustees, shall be concerned to see that such money is wanted, or that no more than is wanted is raised, or otherwise as to the application thereof.

[113]

25 Power to delegate trusts during absence abroad

[(1) Notwithstanding any rule of law or equity to the contrary, a trustee may, by power of attorney, delegate for a period not exceeding twelve months the execution or exercise of all or any of the trusts, powers and discretions vested in him as trustee either alone or jointly with any other person or persons.

(2) The persons who may be donees of a power of attorney under this section include a trust corporation but not (unless a trust corporation) the only other co-trustee of the donor of the power.

(3) An instrument creating a power of attorney under this section shall be attested by at least one witness.

(4) Before or within seven days after giving a power of attorney under this section the donor shall give written notice thereof (specifying the date on which the power comes into operation and its duration, the donee of the power, the reason why the power is given and, where some only are delegated, the trusts, powers and discretions delegated) to—

(a) each person (other than himself), if any, who under any instrument creating the trust has power (whether alone or jointly) to appoint a new trustee; and

(b) each of the other trustees, if any;

but failure to comply with this subsection shall not, in favour of a person dealing with the donee of the power, invalidate any act done or instrument executed by the donee.

(5)   The donor of a power of attorney given under this section shall be liable for the acts or defaults of the donee in the same manner as if they were the acts or defaults of the donor].

[(6)] For the purpose of executing or exercising the trusts or powers delegated to him, the donee may exercise any of the powers conferred on the donor as trustee by statute or by the instrument creating the trust, including power, for the purpose of the transfer of any inscribed stock, himself to delegate to an attorney power to transfer but not including the power of delegation conferred by this section.

[(7)] The fact that it appears from any power of attorney given under this section, or from any evidence required for the purposes of any such power of attorney or otherwise, that in dealing with any stock the donee of the power is acting in the execution of a trust shall not be deemed for any purpose to affect any person in whose books the stock is inscribed or registered with any notice of the trust.

[(8)   This section applies to a personal representative, tenant for life and statutory owner as it applies to a trustee except that subsection (4) shall apply as if it required the notice there mentioned to be given—

(a) in the case of a personal representative, to each of the other personal representatives, if any, except any executor who has renounced probate;

(b) in the case of a tenant for life, to the trustees of the settlement and to each person, if any, who together with the person giving the notice constitutes the tenant for life;

(c) in the case of a statutory owner, to each of the persons, if any, who together with the person giving the notice constitute the statutory owner and, in the case of a statutory owner by virtue of section 23(1)(a) of the Settled Land Act 1925; to the trustees of the settlement.

[114]

NOTES

Sub-ss (1)–(5): substituted for original sub-ss (1)–(8) by the Powers of Attorney Act 1971, s 9(1), (2).
Sub-ss (6), (7): renumbered as such by the Powers of Attorney Act 1971, s 9(1), (3).
Sub-s (8): substituted for original sub-s (11) by the Powers of Attorney Act 1971, s 9(1), (3).

Maintenance, Advancement and Protective Trusts

31 Power to apply income for maintenance and to accumulate surplus income during a minority

(1)   Where any property is held by trustees in trust for any person for any interest whatsoever, whether vested or contingent, then, subject to any prior interests or charges affecting that property—

(i) during the infancy of any such person, if his interest so long continues, the trustees may, at their sole discretion, pay to his parent or guardian, if any, or otherwise apply for or towards his maintenance, education, or benefit, the whole or such part, if any, of the income of that property as may, in all the circumstances, be reasonable, whether or not there is—

 (a) any other fund applicable to the same purpose; or

 (b) any person bound by law to provide for his maintenance or education; and

 (ii) if such person on attaining the age of [eighteen years] has not a vested interest in such income, the trustees shall thenceforth pay the income of that property and of any accretion thereto under subsection (2) of this section to him, until he either attains a vested interest therein or dies, or until failure of his interest:

Provided that, in deciding whether the whole or any part of the income of the property is during a minority to be paid or applied for the purposes aforesaid, the trustees shall have regard to the age of the infant and his requirements and generally to the circumstances of the case, and in particular to what other income, if any, is applicable for the same purposes; and where trustees have notice that the income of more than one fund is applicable for those purposes, then, so far as practicable, unless the entire income of the funds is paid or applied as aforesaid or the court otherwise directs, a proportionate part only of the income of each fund shall be so paid or applied.

(2) During the infancy of any such person, if his interest so long continues, the trustees shall accumulate all the residue of that income in the way of compound interest by investing the same and the resulting income thereof from time to time in authorised investments, and shall hold those accumulations as follows:—

 (i) If any such person—

  (a) attains the age of [eighteen years], or marries under that age, and his interest in such income during his infancy or until his marriage is a vested interest; or

  (b) on attaining the age of [eighteen years] or on marriage under that age becomes entitled to the property from which such income arose in fee simple, absolute or determinable, or absolutely, or for an entailed interest;

 the trustees shall hold the accumulations in trust for such person absolutely, but without prejudice to any provision with respect thereto contained in any settlement by him made under any statutory powers during his infancy, and so that the receipt of such person after marriage, and though still an infant, shall be a good discharge; and

 (ii) In any other case the trustees shall, notwithstanding that such person had a vested interest in such income, hold the accumulations as an accretion to the capital of the property from which such accumulations arose, and as one fund with such capital for all purposes, and so that, if such property is settled land, such accumulations shall be held upon the same trusts as if the same were capital money arising therefrom;

but the trustees may, at any time during the infancy of such person if his interest so long continues, apply those accumulations, or any part thereof, as if they were income arising in the then current year.

(3) This section applies in the case of a contingent interest only if the limitation or trust carries the intermediate income of the property, but it applies to a future or contingent legacy by the parent of, or a person standing in loco parentis to, the legatee, if and for such period as, under the general law, the legacy carries interest for the maintenance of the legatee, and in any such case as last aforesaid the rate of interest shall (if the income available is sufficient, and subject to any rules of court to the contrary) be five pounds per centum per annum.

(4)   This section applies to a vested annuity in like manner as if the annuity were the income of property held by trustees in trust to pay the income thereof to the annuitant for the same period for which the annuity is payable, save that in any case accumulations made during the infancy of the annuitant shall be held in trust for the annuitant or his personal representatives absolutely.

(5)   This section does not apply where the instrument, if any, under which the interest arises came into operation before the commencement of this Act.

[115]

NOTES

Sub-ss (1), (2): words in square brackets substituted by the Family Law Reform Act 1969, s 1(3), Sch 1, Pt I.

Part III
Appointment and Discharge of Trustees

34   Limitation of the number of trustees

(1)   Where, at the commencement of this Act, there are more than four trustees of a settlement of land, or more than four trustees holding land on trust for sale, no new trustees shall (except where as a result of the appointment the number is reduced to four or less) be capable of being appointed until the number is reduced to less than four, and thereafter the number shall not be increased beyond four.

(2)   In the case of settlements and dispositions on trust for sale of land made or coming into operation after the commencement of this Act—
   (a)   the number of trustees thereof shall not in any case exceed four, and where more than four persons are named as such trustees, the four first named (who are able and willing to act) shall alone be the trustees, and the other persons named shall not be trustees unless appointed on the occurrence of a vacancy;
   (b)   the number of the trustees shall not be increased beyond four.

(3)   This section only applies to settlements and dispositions of land, and the restrictions imposed on the number of trustees do not apply—
   (a)   in the case of land vested in trustees for charitable, ecclesiastical, or public purposes; or
   (b)   where the net proceeds of the sale of the land are held for like purposes; or
   (c)   to the trustees of a term of years absolute limited by a settlement on trusts for raising money, or of a like term created under the statutory remedies relating to annual sums charged on land.

[116]

35   Appointments of trustees of settlements and dispositions on trust for sale of land

(1)   Appointments of new trustees of conveyances on trust for sale on the one hand and of the settlement of the proceeds of sale on the other hand, shall, subject to any order of the court, be effected by separate instruments, but in such manner as to secure that the same persons shall become the trustees of the conveyance on trust for sale as become the trustees of the settlement of the proceeds of sale.

(2)   Where new trustees of a settlement are appointed, a memorandum of the names and addresses of the persons who are for the time being the trustees thereof for

the purposes of the Settled Land Act 1925, shall be endorsed on or annexed to the last or only principal vesting instrument by or on behalf of the trustees of the settlement, and such vesting instrument shall, for that purpose, be produced by the person having the possession thereof of the trustees of the settlement when so required.

(3)   Where new trustees of a conveyance on trust for sale relating to a legal estate are appointed, a memorandum of the persons who are for the time being the trustees for sale shall be endorsed on or annexed thereto by or on behalf of the trustees of the settlement of the proceeds of sale, and the conveyance shall, for that purpose, be produced by the person having the possession thereof to the last-mentioned trustees when so required.

(4)   This section applies only to settlements and dispositions of land.

[117]

36   Power of appointing new or additional trustees

(1)   Where a trustee, either original or substituted, and whether appointed by a court or otherwise, is dead, or remains out of the United Kingdom for more than twelve months, or desires to be discharged from all or any of the trusts or powers reposed in or conferred on him, or refuses or is unfit to act therein, or is incapable of acting therein, or is an infant, then, subject to the restrictions imposed by this Act on the number of trustees,—

   (a)   the person or persons nominated for the purpose of appointing new trustees by the instrument, if any, creating the trust; or
   (b)   if there is no such person, or no such person able and willing to act, then the surviving or continuing trustees or trustee for the time being, or the personal representatives of the last surviving or continuing trustee;

may, by writing, appoint one or more other persons (whether or not being the persons exercising the power) to be a trustee or trustees in the place of the trustee so deceased remaining out of the United Kingdom, desiring to be discharged, refusing, or being unfit or being incapable, or being an infant, as aforesaid.

(2)   Where a trustee has been removed under a power contained in the instrument creating the trust, a new trustee or new trustees may be appointed in the place of the trustee who is removed, as if he were dead, or, in the case of a corporation, as if the corporation desired to be discharged from the trust, and the provisions of this section shall apply accordingly, but subject to the restrictions imposed by this Act on the number of trustees.

(3)   Where a corporation being a trustee is or has been dissolved, either before or after the commencement of this Act, then, for the purposes of this section and of any enactment replaced thereby, the corporation shall be deemed to be and to have been from the date of the dissolution incapable of acting in the trusts or powers reposed in or conferred on the corporation.

(4)   The power of appointment given by subsection (1) of this section or any similar previous enactment to the personal representatives of last surviving or continuing trustee shall be and shall be deemed always to have been exercisable by the executors for the time being (whether original or by representation) of such surviving or continuing trustee who have proved the will of their testator or by the administrators for the time being of such trustee without the concurrence of any executor who has renounced or has not proved.

(5) But a sole or last surviving executor intending to renounce, or all the executors where they all intend to renounce, shall have and shall be deemed always to have had power, at any time before renouncing probate, to exercise the power of appointment given by this section, or by any similar previous enactment, if willing to act for that purpose and without thereby accepting the office of executor.

(6) Where a sole trustee, other than a trust corporation, is or has been originally appointed to act in a trust, or where, in the case of any trust, there are not more than three trustees (none of them being a trust corporation) either original or substituted and whether appointed by the court or otherwise, then and in any such case—

(a) the person or persons nominated for the purpose of appointing new trustees by the instrument, if any, creating the trust; or

(b) if there is no such person, or no such person able and willing to act, then the trustee or trustees for the time being;

may, by writing appoint another person or other persons to be an additional trustee or additional trustees, but it shall not be obligatory to appoint any additional trustee, unless the instrument, if any, creating the trust, or any statutory enactment provides to the contrary, nor shall the number of trustees be increased beyond four by virtue of any such appointment.

(7) Every new trustee appointed under this section as well before as after all the trust property becomes by law, or by assurance, or otherwise, vested in him, shall have the same powers, authorities, and discretions, and may in all respects act as if he had been originally appointed a trustee by the instrument, if any, creating the trust.

(8) The provisions of this section relating to a trustee who is dead include the case of a person nominated trustee in a will but dying before the testator, and those relative to a continuing trustee include a refusing or retiring trustee, if willing to act in the execution of the provisions of this section.

[(9) Where a trustee is incapable, by reason of mental disorder within the meaning of [the Mental Health Act 1983], of exercising his functions as trustee and is also entitled in possession to some beneficial interest in the trust property, no appointment of a new trustee in his place shall be made by virtue of paragraph (b) of subsection (1) of this section unless leave to make the appointment has been given by the authority having jurisdiction under [Part VII of the Mental Health Act 1983].]

[118]

NOTES

Sub-s (9): substituted by the Mental Health Act 1959, s 149(1), Sch 7, Pt I; words in square brackets substituted by the Mental Health Act 1983, s 148, Sch 4, para 4(a).

37 Supplemental provisions as to appointment of trustees

(1) On the appointment of a trustee for the whole or any part of trust property—

(a) the number of trustees may, subject to the restrictions imposed by this Act on the number of trustees, be increased; and

(b) a separate set of trustees, not exceeding four, may be appointed for any part of the trust property held on trusts distinct from those relating to any other part or parts of the trust property, notwithstanding that no new trustees or trustee are or is to be appointed for other parts of the trust property, and any existing trustee may be appointed or remain one of such separate set of trustees, or, if only one trustee was originally appointed, then, save as hereinafter provided, one separate trustee may be so appointed; and

(c) it shall not be obligatory, save as hereinafter provided, to appoint more than one new trustee where only one trustee was originally appointed, or to fill up the original number of trustees where more than two trustees were originally appointed, but, except where only one trustee was originally appointed, and a sole trustee when appointed will be able to give valid receipts for all capital money, a trustee shall not be discharged from his trust unless there will be either a trust corporation or at least two individuals to act as trustees to perform the trust; and

(d) any assurance or thing requisite for vesting the trust property, or any part thereof, in a sole trustee, or jointly in the persons who are the trustees, shall be executed or done.

(2)   Nothing in this Act shall authorise the appointment of a sole trustee, not being a trust corporation, where the trustee, when appointed, would not be able to give valid receipts for all capital money arising under the trust.

[119]

38   Evidence as to a vacancy in a trust

(1)   A statement, contained in any instrument coming into operation after the commencement of this Act by which a new trustee is appointed for any purpose connected with land, to the effect that a trustee has remained out of the United Kingdom for more than twelve months or refuses or is unfit to act, or is incapable of acting, or that he is not entitled to a beneficial interest in the trust property in possession, shall, in favour of a purchaser of a legal estate, be conclusive evidence of the matter stated.

(2)   In favour of such purchaser any appointment of a new trustee depending on that statement, and any vesting declaration, express or implied, consequent on the appointment, shall be valid.

[120]

39   Retirement of trustee without a new appointment

(1)   Where a trustee is desirous of being discharged from the trust, and after his discharge there will be either a trust corporation or at least two individuals to act as trustees to perform the trust, then, if such trustee as aforesaid by deed declares that he is desirous of being discharged from the trust, and if his co-trustees and such other person, if any, as is empowered to appoint trustees, by deed consent to the discharge of the trustee, and to the vesting in the co-trustees alone of the trust property, the trustee desirous of being discharged shall be deemed to have retired from the trust, and shall, by the deed, be discharged therefrom under this Act, without any new trustee being appointed in his place.

(2)   Any assurance or thing requisite for vesting the trust property in the continuing trustees alone shall be executed or done.

[121]

40   Vesting of trust property in new or continuing trustees

(1)   Where by a deed a new trustee is appointed to perform any trust, then—

(a) if the deed contains a declaration by the appointor to the effect that any estate or interest in any land subject to the trust, or in any chattel so subject, or the right to recover or receive any debt or other thing in action so subject, shall vest in the persons who by virtue of the deed become or are the trustees for performing the trust, the deed shall operate, without any conveyance or assignment, to vest in those persons as joint tenants and for the purposes of the trust the estate interest or right to which the declaration relates; and

(b) if the deed is made after the commencement of this Act and does not contain such a declaration, the deed shall, subject to any express provision to the contrary therein contained, operate as if it had contained such a declaration by the appointor extending to all the estates interests and rights with respect to which a declaration could have been made.

(2) Where by a deed a retiring trustee is discharged under the statutory power without a new trustee being appointed, then—

(a) if the deed contains such a declaration as aforesaid by the retiring and continuing trustees, and by the other person, if any, empowered to appoint trustees, the deed shall, without any conveyance or assignment, operate to vest in the continuing trustees alone, as joint tenants, and for the purposes of the trust, the estate, interest, or right to which the declaration relates; and

(b) if the deed is made after the commencement of this Act and does not contain such a declaration, the deed shall, subject to any express provision to the contrary therein contained, operate as if it had contained such a declaration by such persons as aforesaid extending to all the estates, interests and rights with respect to which a declaration could have been made.

(3) An express vesting declaration, whether made before or after the commencement of this Act, shall, notwithstanding that the estate, interest or right to be vested is not expressly referred to, and provided that the other statutory requirements were or are complied with, operate and be deemed always to have operated (but without prejudice to any express provision to the contrary contained in the deed of appointment or discharge) to vest in the persons respectively referred to in subsections (1) and (2) of this section, as the case may require, such estates, interests and rights as are capable of being and ought to be vested in those persons.

(4) This section does not extend—

(a) to land conveyed by way of mortgage for securing money subject to the trust, except land conveyed on trust for securing debentures or debenture stock;

(b) to land held under a lease which contains any covenant, condition or agreement against assignment or disposing of the land without licence or consent, unless, prior to the execution of the deed containing expressly or impliedly the vesting declaration, the requisite licence or consent has been obtained, or unless, by virtue of any statute or rule of law, the vesting declaration, express or implied, would not operate as a breach of covenant or give rise to a forfeiture;

(c) to any share, stock, annuity or property which is only transferable in books kept by a company or other body, or in manner directed by or under an Act of Parliament.

In this subsection lease includes an underlease and an agreement for a lease or underlease.

(5) For purposes of registration of the deed in any registry, the person or persons making the declaration expressly or impliedly, shall be deemed the conveying party or parties, and the conveyance shall be deemed to be made by him or them under a power conferred by this Act.

(6) This section applies to deeds of appointment or discharge executed on or after the first day of January, eighteen hundred and eighty-two.

PART IV
POWERS OF THE COURT

Appointment of new Trustees

41 Power of court to appoint new trustees

(1)   The court may, whenever it is expedient to appoint a new trustee or new trustees, and it is found inexpedient difficult or impracticable so to do without the assistance of the court, make an order appointing a new trustee or new trustees either in substitution for or in addition to any existing trustee or trustees, or although there is no existing trustee.

In particular and without prejudice to the generality of the foregoing provision, the court may make an order appointing a new trustee in substitution for a trustee who . . . is [incapable, by reason of mental disorder within the meaning of [the Mental Health Act 1983], of exercising his functions as trustee], or is a bankrupt, or is a corporation which is in liquidation or has been dissolved.

(2)   The power conferred by this section may, in the case of a deed of arrangement within the meaning of the Deeds of Arrangement Act 1914, be exercised either by the High Court or by the court having jurisdiction in bankruptcy in the district in which the debtor resided or carried on business at the date of the execution of the deed.

(3)   An order under this section, and any consequential vesting order or conveyance, shall not operate further or otherwise as a discharge to any former or continuing trustee than an appointment of new trustees under any power for that purpose contained in any instrument would have operated.

(4)   Nothing in this section gives power to appoint an executor or administrator.

[123]

NOTES

   Sub-s (1): words omitted repealed by the Criminal Law Act 1967, s 10, Sch 3, Pt III; words in first (outer) pair of square brackets substituted by the Mental Health Act 1959, s 149(1), Sch 7, Pt I, words in square brackets therein substituted by the Mental Health Act 1983, s 148, Sch 4, para 4(b).

---

42 Power to authorise remuneration

Where the court appoints a corporation, other than the Public Trustee, to be a trustee either solely or jointly with another person, the court may authorise the corporation to charge such remuneration for its services as trustee as the court may think fit.

[124]

43 Powers of new trustee appointed by the court

Every trustee appointed by a court of competent jurisdiction shall, as well before as after the trust property becomes by law, or by assurance, or otherwise, vested in him, have the same powers, authorities, and discretions, and may in all respects act as if he had been originally appointed a trustee by the instrument, if any, creating the trust.

[125]

Vesting Orders

44   Vesting orders of land

In any of the following cases, namely:—

(i) Where the court appoints or has appointed a trustee, or where a trustee has been appointed out of court under any statutory or express power;

(ii) Where a trustee entitled to or possessed of any land or interest therein, whether by way of mortgage or otherwise, or entitled to a contingent right therein, either solely or jointly with any other person

    (a) is under disability; or

    (b) is out of the jurisdiction of the High Court; or

    (c) cannot be found, or, being a corporation, has been dissolved;

(iii) Where it is uncertain who was the survivor of two or more trustees jointly entitled to or possessed of any interest in land;

(iv) Where it is uncertain whether the last trustee known to have been entitled to or possessed of any interest in land is living or dead;

(v) Where there is no personal representative of a deceased trustee who was entitled to or possessed of any interest in land, or where it is uncertain who is the personal representative of a deceased trustee who was entitled to or possessed of any interest in land;

(vi) Where a trustee jointly or solely entitled to or possessed of any interest in land, or entitled to a contingent right therein, has been required, by or on behalf of a person entitled to require a conveyance of the land or interest or a release of the right, to convey the land or interest or to release the right, and has wilfully refused or neglected to convey the land or interest or release the right for twenty-eight days after the date of the requirement;

(vii) Where land or any interest therein is vested in a trustee whether by way of mortgage or otherwise, and it appears to the court to be expedient;

the court may make an order (in this Act called a vesting order) vesting the land or interest therein in any such person in any such manner and for any such estate or interest as the court may direct, or releasing or disposing of the contingent right to such person as the court may direct:

Provided that—

(a) Where the order is consequential on the appointment of a trustee the land or interest therein shall be vested for such estate as the court may direct in the persons who on the appointment are the trustees; and

(b) Where the order relates to a trustee entitled or formerly entitled jointly with another person, and such trustee is under disability or out of the jurisdiction of the High Court or cannot be found, or being a corporation has been dissolved, the land interest or right shall be vested in such other person who remains entitled, either alone or with any other person the court may appoint.

[126]

45   Orders as to contingent rights of unborn persons

Where any interest in land is subject to a contingent right in an unborn person or class of unborn persons who, on coming into existence would, in respect, thereof, become entitled to or possessed of that interest on any trust, the court may make an order releasing the land or interest therein from the contingent right, or may make an order vesting in any person the estate or interest to or of which the unborn person or class of unborn persons would, on coming into existence, be entitled or possessed in the land.

[127]

PART V
GENERAL PROVISIONS

64 Application of Act to Settled Land Act Trustees

(1) All the powers and provisions contained in this Act with reference to the appointment of new trustees, and the discharge and retirement of trustees, apply to and include trustees for the purposes of the Settled Land Act 1925, and trustees for the purpose of the management of land during a minority, whether such trustees are appointed by the court or by the settlement, or under provisions contained in any instrument.

(2) Where, either before or after the commencement of this Act, trustees of a settlement have been appointed by the court for the purposes of the Settled Land Acts 1882 to 1890, or of the Settled Land Act 1925, then, after the commencement of this Act—

    (a) the person or persons nominated for the purpose of appointing new trustees by the instrument, if any, creating the settlement, though no trustees for the purposes of the said Acts were thereby appointed; or

    (b) if there is no such person, or no such person able and willing to act, the surviving or continuing trustees or trustee for the time being for the purposes of the said Acts or the personal representatives of the last surviving or continuing trustee for those purposes,

shall have the powers conferred by this Act to appoint new or additional trustees of the settlement for the purposes of the said Acts.

(3) Appointments of new trustees for the purposes of the said Acts made or expressed to be made before the commencement of this Act by the trustees or trustee or personal representatives referred to in paragraph (b) of the last preceding subsection or by the persons referred to in paragraph (a) of that subsection are, without prejudice to any order of the court made before such commencement, hereby confirmed.

[128]

71 Short title, commencement, extent

(1) This Act may be cited as the Trustee Act, 1925.

(2) . . .

(3) This Act, except where otherwise expressly provided, extends to England and Wales only.

(4) The provisions of this Act bind the Crown.

[129]

NOTES
Sub-s (2): repealed by the Statute Law Revision Act 1950.

LAW OF PROPERTY ACT 1925

(C 20)

An Act to consolidate the enactments relating to Conveyancing and the Law of Property in England and Wales

[9 April 1925]

PART I
GENERAL PRINCIPLES AS TO LEGAL ESTATES, EQUITABLE INTERESTS AND POWERS

1 Legal estates and equitable interests

(1) The only estates in land which are capable of subsisting or of being conveyed or created at law are—

    (a) An estate in fee simple absolute in possession;

    (b) A term of years absolute.

(2) The only interests or charges in or over land which are capable of subsisting or of being conveyed or created at law are—

    (a) An easement, right, or privilege in or over land for an interest equivalent to an estate in fee simple absolute in possession or a term of years absolute;

    (b) A rentcharge in possession issuing out of or charged on land being either perpetual or for a term of years absolute;

    (c) A charge by way of legal mortgage;

    (d) . . . and any other similar charge on land which is not created by an instrument;

    (e) Rights of entry exercisable over or in respect of a legal term of years absolute, or annexed, for any purpose, to a legal rentcharge.

(3) All other estates, interests, and charges in or over land take effect as equitable interests.

(4) The estates, interests, and charges which under this section are authorised to subsist or to be conveyed or created at law are (when subsisting or conveyed or created at law) in this Act referred to as "legal estates", and have the same incidents as legal estates subsisting at the commencement of this Act; and the owner of a legal estate is referred to as "an estate owner" and his legal estate is referred to as his estate.

(5) A legal estate may subsist concurrently with or subject to any other legal estate in the same land in like manner as it could have done before the commencement of this Act.

(6) A legal estate is not capable of subsisting or of being created in an undivided share in land or of being held by an infant.

(7) Every power of appointment over, or power to convey or charge land or any interest therein, whether created by a statute or other instrument or implied by law, and whether created before or after the commencement of this Act (not being a power vested in a legal mortgagee or an estate owner in right of his estate and exercisable by him or by another person in his name and on his behalf), operates only in equity.

(8) Estates, interests, and charges in or over land which are not legal estates are in this Act referred to as "equitable interests", and powers which by this Act are to operate in equity only are in this Act referred to as "equitable powers".

(9)   The provisions in any statute or other instrument requiring land to be conveyed to uses shall take effect as directions that the land shall (subject to creating or reserving thereout any legal estate authorised by this Act which may be required) be conveyed to a person of full age upon the requisite trusts.

(10)   The repeal of the Statute of Uses (as amended) does not affect the operation thereof in regard to dealings taking effect before the commencement of this Act.

[130]

NOTES
   Sub-s (2): words omitted repealed by the Finance Act 1963, s 73(8)(b), Sch 14, Pt IV and by the Tithe Act 1936, s 48(3), Sch 9.

2   Conveyances overreaching certain equitable interests and powers

(1)   A conveyance to a purchaser of a legal estate in land shall overreach any equitable interest or power affecting that estate, whether or not he has notice thereof, if—

   (i)   the conveyance is made under the powers conferred by the Settled Land Act 1925 or any additional powers conferred by a settlement, and the equitable interest or power is capable of being overreached thereby, and the statutory requirements respecting the payment of capital money arising under the settlement are complied with;

   (ii)   the conveyance is made by trustees for sale and the equitable interest or power is at the date of the conveyance capable of being overreached by such trustees under the provisions of subsection (2) of this section or independently of that subsection, and the statutory requirements respecting the payment of capital money arising under a disposition upon trust for sale are complied with;

   (iii) the conveyance is made by a mortgagee or personal representative in the exercise of his paramount powers, and the equitable interest or power is capable of being overreached by such conveyance, and any capital money arising from the transaction is paid to the mortgagee or personal representative;

   (iv)   the conveyance is made under an order of the court and the equitable interest or power is bound by such order, and any capital money arising from the transaction is paid into, or in accordance with the order of, the court.

(2)   [Where the legal estate affected is subject to a trust for sale, then if at the date of a conveyance made after the commencement of this Act under the trust for sale or the powers conferred on the trustees for sale, the trustees (whether original or substituted) are either—]

   (a)   two or more individuals approved or appointed by the court or the successors in office of the individuals so approved or appointed; or

   (b)   a trust corporation,

[any equitable interest or power having priority to the trust for sale] shall, notwithstanding any stipulation to the contrary, be overreached by the conveyance, and shall, according to its priority, take effect as if created or arising by means of a primary trust affecting the proceeds of sale and the income of the land until sale.

(3)   The following equitable interests and powers are excepted from the operation of subsection (2) of this section, namely—

   (i)   Any equitable interest protected by a deposit of documents relating to the legal estate affected;

   (ii)   The benefit of any covenant or agreement restrictive of the user of land;

   (iii) Any easement, liberty, or privilege over or affecting land and being merely an equitable interest (in this Act referred to as an "equitable easement");

    (iv) The benefit of any contract (in this Act referred to as an "estate contract") to convey or create a legal estate, including a contract conferring either expressly or by statutory implication a valid option to purchase, a right of pre-emption, or any other like right;

    (v) Any equitable interest protected by registration under the Land Charges Act 1925 other than—

        (a) an annuity within the meaning of Part II of that Act;

        (b) a limited owner's charge or a general equitable charge within the meaning of that Act.

(4)   Subject to the protection afforded by this section to the purchaser of a legal estate, nothing contained in this section shall deprive a person entitled to an equitable charge of any of his rights or remedies for enforcing the same.

(5)   So far as regards the following interests, created before the commencement of this Act (which accordingly are not within the provisions of the Land Charges Act 1925), namely—

    (a) the benefit of any covenant or agreement restrictive of the user of the land;

    (b) any equitable easement;

    (c) the interest under a puisne mortgage within the meaning of the Land Charges Act 1925 unless and until acquired under a transfer made after the commencement of this Act;

    (d) the benefit of an estate contract, unless and until the same is acquired under a conveyance made after the commencement of this Act;

a purchaser of a legal estate shall only take subject thereto if he has notice thereof, and the same are not overreached under the provisions contained or in the manner referred to in this section.

[131]

NOTES

Sub-s (2): words in square brackets substituted by the Law of Property (Amendment) Act 1926, s 7, Schedule.

Land Charges Act 1925: see now the Land Charges Act 1972.

3 Manner of giving effect to equitable interests and powers

(1)   All equitable interests and powers in or over land shall be enforceable against the estate owner of the legal estate affected in manner following (that is to say):—

    (a) Where the legal estate affected is settled land, the tenant for life or statutory owner shall be bound to give effect to the equitable interests and powers in manner provided by the Settled Land Act 1925;

    (b) Where the legal estate affected is vested in trustees for sale—

        (i) The trustees shall stand possessed of the net proceeds of sale after payment of costs and of the net rents and profits of the land until sale after payment of rates, taxes, costs of insurance, repairs, and other outgoings, upon such trusts and subject to such powers and provisions as may be requisite for giving effect to the equitable interests and powers affecting the same respectively, of which they have notice, and whether created before or after the disposition upon trust for sale, according to their respective priorities:

        (ii) Where, by reason of the exercise of any equitable power or under any trust affecting the proceeds of sale, any principal sum is required to be raised, or any person of full age becomes entitled to require a legal estate in the land to be vested in him in priority to the trust for sale, then, unless the claim is satisfied out of the net proceeds of sale, the trustees for sale shall (if so requested in writing) be bound to transfer or create such legal estates, to take effect in priority to the trust for sale, as may be required for raising the money by way of legal mortgage or for giving legal effect to the rights of the person so entitled:

Provided that, if the proceeds of sale are held in trust for persons of full age in undivided shares absolutely free from incumbrances affecting undivided shares, those persons cannot require the land to be conveyed to them in undivided shares, but may (subject to effect being given by way of legal mortgage to incumbrances affecting the entirety) require the same to be vested in any of them (not exceeding four) as joint tenants on trust for sale; and if the conveyance purports to transfer the land to any of them in undivided shares or to more than four such persons, it shall operate only as a transfer to them or (if more than four) to the four first named therein as joint tenants on trust for sale:

(c) Where the legal estate affected is neither settled land nor vested in trustees for sale, the estate owner shall be bound to give effect to the equitable interests and powers affecting his estate of which he has notice according to their respective priorities. This provision does not affect the priority or powers of a legal mortgagee, or the powers of personal representatives for purposes of administration.

(2)   Effect may be given by means of a legal mortgage to an agreement for a mortgage, charge or lien (whether or not arising by operation of law) if the agreement, charge or lien ought to have priority over the trust for sale.

(3)   Where, by reason . . . of an equitable right of entry taking effect, or for any other reason, a person becomes entitled to require a legal estate to be vested in him, then and in any such case the estate owner whose estate is affected shall be bound to convey or create such legal estate as the case may require.

(4)   If any question arises whether any and what legal estate ought to be transferred or created as aforesaid, any person interested may apply to the court for directions in the manner provided by this Act.

(5)   If the trustees for sale or other estate owners refuse or neglect for one month after demand to transfer or create any such legal estate, or if by reason of their being out of the United Kingdom or being unable to be found, or by reason of the dissolution of a corporation, or for any other reason, the court is satisfied that the transaction cannot otherwise be effected, or cannot be effected without undue delay or expense, the court may, on the application of any person interested, make a vesting order transferring or creating a legal estate in the manner provided by this Act.

(6)   This section does not affect a purchaser of a legal estate taking free from an equitable interest or power.

[(7)   The county court has jurisdiction under this section where the land which is to be dealt with in the court does not exceed [£30,000] in capital value . . .]

[132]

NOTES

Sub-s (3): words omitted repealed by the Reverter of Sites Act 1987, s 8(2), (3), Schedule.

Sub-s (7): added by the County Courts Act 1984, s 148(1), Sch 2, Pt II, para 2(1), (3); sum in square brackets substituted and words omitted repealed by the High Court and County Courts Jurisdiction Order 1991, SI 1991/724, art 2(3)(a), (8), Schedule, Pt I.

4 Creation and disposition of equitable interests

(1) Interests in land validly created or arising after the commencement of this Act, which are not capable of subsisting as legal estates, shall take effect as equitable interests, and, save as otherwise expressly provided by statute, interests in land which under the Statute of Uses or otherwise could before the commencement of this Act have been created as legal interests, shall be capable of being created as equitable interests:

Provided that, after the commencement of this Act (and save as hereinafter expressly enacted), an equitable interest in land shall only be capable of being validly created in any case in which an equivalent equitable interest in property real or personal could have been validly created before such commencement.

(2) All rights and interests in land may be disposed of, including—
   (a) a contingent, executory or future equitable interest in any land, or a possibility coupled with an interest in any land, whether or not the object of the gift or limitation of such interest or possibility be ascertained;
   (b) a right of entry, into or upon land whether immediate or future, and whether vested or contingent.

(3) All rights of entry affecting a legal estate which are exercisable on condition broken or for any other reason may after the commencement of this Act, be made exercisable by any person and the persons deriving title under him, but, in regard to an estate in fee simple (not being a rentcharge held for a legal estate) only within the period authorised by the rule relating to perpetuities.

[133]

7 Saving of certain legal estates and statutory powers

(1) A fee simple which, by virtue of the Lands Clauses Acts, . . . or any similar statute, is liable to be divested, is for the purposes of this Act a fee simple absolute, and remains liable to be divested as if this Act had not been passed, [and a fee simple subject to a legal or equitable right of entry or re-entry is for the purposes of this Act a fee simple absolute].

(2) A fee simple vested in a corporation which is liable to determine by reason of the dissolution of the corporation is, for the purposes of this Act, a fee simple absolute.

(3) The provisions of—
   (a) . . . ;
   (b) the Friendly Societies Act 1896, in regard to land to which that Act applies;
   (c) any other statutes conferring special facilities or prescribing special modes (whether by way of registered memorial or otherwise) for disposing of or acquiring land, or providing for the vesting (by conveyance or otherwise) of the land in trustees or any person, or the holder for the time being of an office or any corporation sole or aggregate (including the Crown);

shall remain in full force.

This subsection does not authorise an entailed interest to take effect otherwise than as an equitable interest.

(4) Where any such power for disposing of or creating a legal estate is exercisable by a person who is not the estate owner, the power shall, when practicable, be exercised in the name and on behalf of the estate owner.

NOTES
Sub-s (1): words omitted repealed by the Reverter of Sites Act 1987, s 8(3), Schedule; words in square brackets inserted by the Law of Property (Amendment) Act 1926, s 7, Schedule.
Sub-s (3): para (a) repealed by the Criminal Justice Act 1948, s 83, Sch 10.
Friendly Societies Act 1896: see now the Friendly Societies Act 1974.

10   Title to be shown to legal estates

(1)   Where title is shown to a legal estate in land, it shall be deemed not necessary or proper to include in the abstract of title an instrument relating only to interests or powers which will be over-reached by the conveyance of the estate to which title is being shown; but nothing in this Part of this Act affects the liability of any person to disclose an equitable interest or power which will not be so over-reached, or to furnish an abstract of any instrument creating or affecting the same.

(2)   A solicitor delivering an abstract framed in accordance with this Part of this Act shall not incur any liability on account of an omission to include therein an instrument which, under this section, is to be deemed not necessary or proper to be included, nor shall any liability be implied by reason of the inclusion of any such instrument.

[135]

NOTES
Modification: any reference to solicitor(s) etc modified to include references to bodies recognised under the Administration of Justice Act 1985, s 9, by the Solicitors' Incorporated Practices Order 1991, SI 1991/2684, arts 4, 5, Sch 1.

14   Interests of persons in possession

This Part of this Act shall not prejudicially affect the interest of any person in possession or in actual occupation of land to which he may be entitled in right of such possession or occupation.

[136]

Infants and Lunatics

19   Effect of conveyances of legal estates to infants

(1)   A conveyance of a legal estate in land to an infant alone or to two or more persons jointly both or all of whom are infants, shall have such operation as is provided for in the Settled Land Act 1925.

(2)   A conveyance of a legal estate in land to an infant, jointly with one or more other persons of full age, shall operate to vest the legal estate in the other person or persons on the statutory trusts, but not so as to sever any joint tenancy in the net proceeds of sale or in the rents and profits until sale, or affect the right of a tenant for life or statutory owner to have settled land vested in him.

(3)   The foregoing provisions of this section do not apply to conveyances on trust or by way of mortgage.

(4)   A conveyance of a legal estate to an infant alone or to two or more persons jointly, both or all of whom are infants, on any trusts, shall operate as a declaration of trust and shall not be effectual to pass any legal estate.

(5)   A conveyance of a legal estate in land to an infant jointly with one or more other persons of full age on any trusts shall operate as if the infant had not been

named therein, but without prejudice to any beneficial interest in the land intended to be thereby provided for the infant.

(6)   A grant or transfer of a legal mortgage of land to an infant shall operate only as an agreement for valuable consideration to execute a proper conveyance when the infant attains full age, and in the meantime to hold any beneficial interest in the mortgage debt in trust for the persons for whose benefit the conveyance was intended to be made:

Provided that, if the conveyance is made to the infant and another person or other persons of full age, it shall operate as if the infant had not been named therein, but without prejudice to any beneficial interest in the mortgage debt intended to be thereby provided for the infant.

[137]

20   Infants not to be appointed trustees

The appointment of an infant to be a trustee in relation to any settlement or trust shall be void, but without prejudice to the power to appoint a new trustee to fill the vacancy.

[138]

21   Receipts by married infants

A married infant shall have power to give valid receipts for all income (including statutory accumulations of income made during the minority) to which the infant may be entitled in like manner as if the infant were of full age.

[138A]

[22   Conveyances on behalf of persons suffering from mental disorder and as to land held by them on trust for sale

(1)   Where a legal estate in land (whether settled or not) is vested in a person suffering from mental disorder, either solely or jointly with any other person or persons, his receiver or (if no receiver is acting for him) any person authorised in that behalf shall, under an order of the authority having jurisdiction under [Part VII of the Mental Health Act 1983], or of the court, or under any statutory power, make or concur in making all requisite dispositions for conveying or creating a legal estate in his name and on his behalf.

(2)   If land held on trust for sale is vested, either solely or jointly with any other person or persons, in a person who is incapable, by reason of mental disorder, of exercising his functions as trustee, a new trustee shall be appointed in the place of that person, or he shall be otherwise discharged from the trust, before the legal estate is dealt with under the trust for sale or under the powers vested in the trustees for sale.]

[138B]

NOTES
Substituted by the Mental Health Act 1959, s 149(1), Sch 7, Pt I.
Sub-s (1): words in square brackets substituted by the Mental Health Act 1983, s 148, Sch 4, para 5(a).

Dispositions on Trust for Sale

23   Duration of trusts for sale

Where land has, either before or after the commencement of this Act, become subject to an express or implied trust for sale, such trust shall, so far as regards the safety and protection of any purchaser thereunder, be deemed to be subsisting until the land has been conveyed to or under the direction of the persons interested in the proceeds of sale.

This section applies to sales whether made before or after the commencement of this Act, but operates without prejudice to an order of any court restraining a sale.

[138C]

24 Appointment of trustees of dispositions on trust for sale

(1) The persons having power to appoint new trustees of a conveyance of land on trust for sale shall be bound to appoint the same persons (if any) who are for the time being trustees of the settlement of the proceeds of sale, but a purchaser shall not be concerned to see whether the proper persons are appointed to be trustees of the conveyance of the land.

(2) This section applies whether the settlement of the proceeds of sale or the conveyance on trust for sale comes into operation before or after the commencement of this Act.

[138D]

25 Power to postpone sale

(1) A power to postpone sale shall, in the case of every trust for sale of land, be implied unless a contrary intention appears.

(2) Where there is a power to postpone the sale, then (subject to any express direction to the contrary in the instrument, if any, creating the trust for sale) the trustees for sale shall not be liable in any way for postponing the sale, in the exercise of their discretion for any indefinite period; nor shall a purchaser of a legal estate be concerned in any case with any directions respecting the postponement of a sale.

(3) The foregoing provisions of this section apply whether the trust for sale is created before or after the commencement or by virtue of this Act.

(4) Where a disposition or settlement coming into operation after the commencement of this Act contains a trust either to retain or sell land the same shall be construed as a trust to sell the land with power to postpone the sale.

[138E]

26 Consents to the execution of a trust for sale

(1) If the consent of more than two persons is by the disposition made requisite to the execution of a trust for sale of land, then, in favour of a purchaser, the consent of any two of such persons to the execution of the trust or to the exercise of any statutory or other powers vested in the trustees for sale shall be deemed sufficient.

(2) Where the person whose consent to the execution of any such trust or power is expressed to be required in a disposition is not sui juris or becomes subject to disability, his consent shall not, in favour of a purchaser, be deemed to be requisite to the execution of the trust or the exercise of the power; but the trustees shall, in any such case, obtain the separate consent of the parent or testamentary or other guardian of an infant or of the . . . receiver (if any) of a [person suffering from mental disorder].

[(3) Trustees for sale shall so far as practicable consult the persons of full age for the time being beneficially interested in possession in the rents and profits of the land until sale, and shall, so far as consistent with the general interest of the trust, give effect to the wishes of such persons, or, in the case of dispute, of the majority (according to the value of their combined interests) of such persons, but a purchaser shall not be concerned to see that the provisions of this subsection have been complied with.

In the case of a trust for sale, not being a trust for sale created by or in pursuance of the powers conferred by this or any other Act, this subsection shall not apply unless the contrary intention appears in the disposition creating the trust.]

(4)   This section applies whether the trust for sale is created before or after the commencement or by virtue of this Act.

[138F]

NOTES
Sub-s (2): words omitted repealed and words in square brackets substituted by the Mental Health Act 1959, s 149(1), Sch 7, Pt I.

Sub-s (3): substituted by the Law of Property (Amendment) Act 1926, s 7, Schedule.

27   Purchaser not to be concerned with the trusts of the proceeds of sale which are to be paid to two or more trustees or to a trust corporation

(1)   A purchaser of a legal estate from trustees for sale shall not be concerned with the trusts affecting the proceeds of sale of land subject to a trust for sale (whether made to attach to such proceeds by virtue of this Act or otherwise), or affecting the rents and profits of the land until sale, whether or not those trusts are declared by the same instrument by which the trust for sale is created.

[(2)   Notwithstanding anything to the contrary in the instrument (if any) creating a trust for sale of land or in the settlement of the net proceeds, the proceeds of sale or other capital money shall not be paid to or applied by the direction of fewer than two persons as trustees for sale, except where the trustee is a trust corporation, but this subsection does not affect the right of a sole personal representative as such to give valid receipts for, or direct the application of, proceeds of sale or other capital money, nor, except where capital money arises on the transaction, render it necessary to have more than one trustee.]

[138G]

NOTES
Sub-s (2): substituted by the Law of Property (Amendment) Act 1926, s 7, Schedule.

28   Powers of management, etc, conferred on trustees for sale

(1)   Trustees for sale shall, in relation to land or to manorial incidents and to the proceeds of sale, have all the powers of a tenant for life and the trustees of a settlement under the Settled Land Act 1925, including in relation to the land the powers of management conferred by that Act during a minority: [and where by statute settled land is or becomes vested in the trustees of the settlement upon the statutory trusts, such trustees and their successors in office shall also have all the additional or larger powers (if any) conferred by the settlement on the tenant for life, statutory owner, or trustees of the settlement] and (subject to any express trust to the contrary) all capital money arising under the said powers shall, unless paid or applied for any purpose authorised by the Settled Land Act 1925, be applicable in the same manner as if the money represented proceeds of sale arising under the trust for sale.

All land acquired under this subsection shall be conveyed to the trustees on trust for sale.

The powers conferred by this subsection shall be exercised with such consents (if any) as would have been required on a sale under the trust for sale, and when exercised shall operate to overreach any equitable interests or powers which are by virtue of this Act or otherwise made to attach to the net proceeds of sale as if created by a trust affecting those proceeds.

(2) Subject to any direction to the contrary in the disposition on trust for sale or in the settlement of the proceeds of sale, the net rents and profits of the land until sale, after keeping down costs of repairs and insurance and other outgoings shall be paid or applied, except so far as any part thereof may be liable to be set aside as capital money under the Settled Land Act 1925, in like manner as the income of investments representing the purchase money would be payable or applicable if a sale had been made and the proceeds had been duly invested.

(3) Where the net proceeds of sale have under the trusts affecting the same become absolutely vested in persons of full age in undivided shares (whether or not such shares may be subject to a derivative trust) the trustees for sale may, with the consent of the persons, if any, of full age, not being annuitants, interested in possession in the net rents and profits of the land until sale:—

(a) partition the land remaining unsold or any part thereof; and

(b) provide (by way of mortgage or otherwise) for the payment of any equality money;

and, upon such partition being arranged, the trustees for sale shall give effect thereto by conveying the land so partitioned in severalty (subject or not to any legal mortgage created for raising equality money) to persons of full age and either absolutely or on trust for sale or, where any part of the land becomes settled land, by a vesting deed, or partly in one way and partly in another in accordance with the rights of the persons interested under the partition, but a purchaser shall not be concerned to see or inquire whether any such consent as aforesaid has been given:

Provided that—

(i) If a share in the net proceeds belongs to a [person suffering from mental disorder] the consent of his . . . receiver shall be sufficient to protect the trustees for sale:

(ii) If a share in the net proceeds is affected by an incumbrance the trustees for sale may either give effect thereto or provide for the discharge thereof by means of the property allotted in respect of such share, as they may consider expedient.

(4) If a share in the net proceeds is absolutely vested in an infant, the trustees for sale may act on his behalf and retain land (to be held on trust for sale) or other property to represent his share, but in other respects the foregoing power shall apply as if the infant had been of full age.

(5) This section applies to dispositions on trust for sale coming into operation either before or after the commencement or by virtue of this Act.

[138H]

NOTES

Sub-s (1): words in square brackets inserted by the Law of Property (Amendment) Act 1926, s 7, Schedule.

Sub-s (3): words in square brackets substituted and words omitted repealed by the Mental Health Act 1959, s 149(1), Sch 7, Pt I.

See further, in relation to the application of capital money, the Agricultural Tenancies Act 1995, s 33(1), (2).

29 Delegation of powers of management by trustees for sale

(1)   The powers of and incidental to leasing, accepting surrenders of leases and management, conferred on trustees for sale whether by this Act or otherwise, may, until sale of the land, be revocably delegated from time to time, by writing, signed by them, to any person of full age (not being merely an annuitant) for the time being beneficially entitled in possession to the net rents and profits of the land during his life or for any less period: and in favour of a lessee such writing shall, unless the contrary appears, be sufficient evidence that the person named therein is a person to whom the powers may be delegated, and the production of such writing shall, unless the contrary appears, be sufficient evidence that the delegation has not been revoked.

(2)   Any power so delegated shall be exercised only in the names and on behalf of the trustees delegating the power.

(3)   The persons delegating any power under this section shall not, in relation to the exercise or purported exercise of the power, be liable for the acts or defaults of the person to whom the power is delegated, but that person shall, in relation to the exercise of the power by him, be deemed to be in the position and to have the duties and liabilities of a trustee.

(4)   Where, at the commencement of this Act, an order made under section seven of the Settled Land Act 1884 is in force, the person on whom any power is thereby conferred shall, while the order remains in force, exercise such power in the names and on behalf of the trustees for sale in like manner as if the power had been delegated to him under this section.

[138I]

30 Powers of court where trustees for sale refuse to exercise powers

[(1)] If the trustees for sale refuse to sell or to exercise any of the powers conferred by either of the last two sections, or any requisite consent cannot be obtained, any person interested may apply to the court for a vesting or other order for giving effect to the proposed transaction or for an order directing the trustees for sale to give effect thereto, and the court may make such order as it thinks fit.

[(2)   The county court has jurisdiction under this section . . .]

[138J]

NOTES

Sub-s (1): numbered as such by the County Courts Act 1984, s 148(1), Sch 2, Pt II, para 2.

Sub-s (2): added by the County Courts Act 1984, s 148(1), Sch 2, Pt II, para 2; words omitted repealed by the High Court and County Courts Jurisdiction Order 1991, SI 1991/724, art 2(1)(a), (8), Schedule, Pt I.

---

31 Trust for sale of mortgaged property where right of redemption is barred

(1)   Where any property, vested in trustees by way of security, becomes, by virtue of the statutes of limitation, or of an order for foreclosure or otherwise, discharged from the right of redemption, it shall be held by them on trust for sale.

(2)   The net proceeds of sale, after payment of costs and expenses, shall be applied in like manner as the mortgage debt, if received, would have been applicable, and the income of the property until sale shall be applied in like manner as the interest, if received, would have been applicable; but this subsection operates without prejudice to any rule of law relating to the apportionment of capital and income between tenant for life and remainderman.

(3)   This section does not affect the right of any person to require that, instead of a sale, the property shall be conveyed to him or in accordance with his directions.

(4)   Where the mortgage money is capital money for the purposes of the Settled Land Act 1925 the trustees shall, if the tenant for life or statutory owner so requires, instead of selling any land, forming the whole or part of such property, execute such subsidiary vesting deed with respect thereto as would have been required if the land had been acquired on a purchase with capital money.

(5)   This section applies whether the right of redemption was discharged before or after the first day of January, nineteen hundred and twelve, but has effect without prejudice to any dealings or arrangements made before that date.

                                                                              [138K]

32   Implied trust for sale in personalty settlements

(1)   Where a settlement of personal property or of land held upon trust for sale contains a power to invest money in the purchase of land, such land shall, unless the settlement otherwise provides, be held by the trustees on trust for sale; and the net rents and profits until sale, after keeping down costs of repairs and insurance and other outgoings, shall be paid or applied in like manner as the income of investments representing the purchase-money would be payable or applicable if a sale had been made and the proceeds had been duly invested in personal estate.

(2)   This section applies to settlements (including wills) coming into operation after the thirty-first day of December, nineteen hundred and eleven, and does not apply to capital money arising under the Settled Land Act 1925 or money liable to be treated as such.

                                                                              [138L]

33   Application of Part I to personal representatives

The provisions of this Part of this Act relating to trustees for sale apply to personal representatives holding on trust for sale, but without prejudice to their rights and powers for purposes of administration.

                                                                              [139]

Undivided Shares and Joint Ownership

34   Effect of future dispositions to tenants in common

(1)   An undivided share in land shall not be capable of being created except as provided by the Settled Land Act 1925 or as hereinafter mentioned.

(2)   Where, after the commencement of this Act, land is expressed to be conveyed to any persons in undivided shares and those persons are of full age, the conveyance shall (notwithstanding anything to the contrary in this Act) operate as if the land had been expressed to be conveyed to the grantees, or, if there are more than four grantees, to the four first named in the conveyance, as joint tenants upon the statutory trusts hereinafter mentioned and so as to give effect to the rights of the persons who would have been entitled to the shares had the conveyance operated to create those shares:

Provided that, where the conveyance is made by way of mortgage the land shall vest in the grantees or such four of them as aforesaid for a term of years absolute (as provided by this Act) as joint tenants subject to cesser on redemption in like manner as if the mortgage money had belonged to them on a joint account, but without prejudice to the beneficial interests in the mortgage money and interest.

(3)   A devise bequest or testamentary appointment, coming into operation after the commencement of this Act, of land to two or more persons in undivided shares shall operate as a devise bequest or appointment of the land to the trustees (if any) of the will for the purposes of the Settled Land Act 1925 or, if there are no such trustees, then to the personal representatives of the testator, and in each case (but without prejudice to the rights and powers of the personal representatives for purposes of administration) upon the statutory trusts hereinafter mentioned.

(4)   Any disposition purporting to make a settlement of an undivided share in land shall only operate as a settlement of a corresponding share of the net proceeds of sale and of the rents and profits until sale of the entirety of the land.

[140]

35   Meaning of the statutory trusts

For the purposes of this Act land held upon the "statutory trusts" shall be held upon the trusts and subject to the provisions following, namely, upon trust to sell the same and to stand possessed of the net proceeds of sale, after payment of costs, and of the net rents and profits until sale after payment of rates, taxes, costs of insurance, repairs, and other outgoings, upon such trusts, and subject to such powers and provisions, as may be requisite for giving effect to the rights of the persons (including an incumbrancer of a former undivided share or whose incumbrance is not secured by a legal mortgage) interested in the land [and the right of a person who, if the land had not been made subject to a trust for sale by virtue of this Act, would have been entitled to an entailed interest in an undivided share in the land, shall be deemed to be a right to a corresponding entailed interest in the net proceeds of sale attributable to that share].

[Where—
(a)   an undivided share was subject to a settlement, and
(b)   the settlement remains subsisting in respect of other property, and
(c)   the trustees thereof are not the same persons as the trustees for sale,

then the statutory trusts include a trust for the trustees for sale to pay the proper proportion of the net proceeds of sale or other capital money attributable to the share to the trustees of the settlement to be held by them as capital money arising under the Settled Land Act 1925.]

[141]

NOTES

Words in first pair of square brackets inserted by the Law of Property (Entailed Interests) Act 1932, s 1; words in second pair of square brackets inserted by the Law of Property (Amendment) Act 1926, s 7, Schedule.

36   Joint tenancies

(1)   Where a legal estate (not being settled land) is beneficially limited to or held in trust for any persons as joint tenants, the same shall be held on trust for sale, in like manner as if the persons beneficially entitled were tenants in common, but not so as to sever their joint tenancy in equity.

(2)   No severance of a joint tenancy of a legal estate, so as to create a tenancy in common in land, shall be permissible, whether by operation of law or otherwise, but this subsection does not affect the right of a joint tenant to release his interest to the other joint tenants, or the right to sever a joint tenancy in an equitable interest whether or not the legal estate is vested in the joint tenants:

Provided that, where a legal estate (not being settled land) is vested in joint tenants beneficially, and any tenant desires to sever the joint tenancy in equity, he shall give to the other joint tenants a notice in writing of such desire or do such other acts or things as would, in the case of personal estate, have been effectual to sever the tenancy in equity, and thereupon under the trust for sale affecting the land the net proceeds of sale, and the net rents and profits until sale, shall be held upon the trusts which would have been requisite for giving effect to the beneficial interests if there had been an actual severance.

[Nothing in this Act affects the right of a survivor of joint tenants, who is solely and beneficially interested, to deal with his legal estate as if it were not held on trust for sale.]

(3)   Without prejudice to the right of a joint tenant to release his interest to the other joint tenants no severance of a mortgage term or trust estate, so as to create a tenancy in common, shall be permissible.

[142]

NOTES

Sub-s (2): words in square brackets inserted by the Law of Property (Amendment) Act 1926, s 7, Schedule.

37 Rights of husband and wife

A husband and wife shall, for all purposes of acquisition of any interest in property, under a disposition made or coming into operation after the commencement of this Act, be treated as two persons.

[143]

PART II
CONTRACTS, CONVEYANCES AND OTHER INSTRUMENTS

Contracts

40 Contracts for sale, etc, of land to be in writing

(1)   No action may be brought upon any contract for the sale or other disposition of land or any interest in land, unless the agreement upon which such action is brought, or some memorandum or note thereof, is in writing, and signed by the party to be charged or by some other person thereunto by him lawfully authorised.

(2)   This section applies to contracts whether made before or after the commencement of this Act and does not affect the law relating to part performance, or sales by the court.

[144]

NOTES

Repealed by the Law of Property (Miscellaneous Provisions) Act 1989, ss 2(8), 4, Sch 2.

42 Provisions as to contracts

(1)   A stipulation that a purchaser of a legal estate in land shall accept a title made with the concurrence of any person entitled to an equitable interest shall be void, if a title can be made discharged from the equitable interest without such concurrence—

(a) under a trust for sale; or

(b) under this Act, or the Settled Land Act 1925, or any other statute.

(2)   A stipulation that a purchaser of a legal estate in land shall pay or contribute towards the costs of or incidental to—

(a)   obtaining a vesting order, or the appointment of trustees of a settlement, or the appointment of trustees of a conveyance on trust for sale; or

(b)   the preparation stamping or execution of a conveyance on trust for sale, or of a vesting instrument for bringing into force the provisions of the Settled Land Act 1925;

shall be void.

(3)   A stipulation contained in any contract for the sale or exchange of land made after the commencement of this Act, to the effect that an outstanding legal estate is to be traced or got in by or at the expense of a purchaser or that no objection is to be taken on account of an outstanding legal estate, shall be void.

(4)   If the subject matter of any contract for the sale or exchange of land—

(i)   is a mortgage term and the vendor has power to convey the fee simple in the land, or, in the case of a mortgage of a term of years absolute, the leasehold reversion affected by the mortgage, the contract shall be deemed to extend to the fee simple in the land or such leasehold reversion;

(ii)   is an equitable interest capable of subsisting as a legal estate, and the vendor has power to vest such legal estate in himself or in the purchaser or to require the same to be so vested, the contract shall be deemed to extend to such legal estate;

(iii)   is an entailed interest in possession and the vendor has power to vest in himself or in the purchaser the fee simple in the land, (or, if the entailed interest is an interest in a term of years absolute, such term,) or to require the same to be so vested, the contract shall be deemed to extend to the fee simple in the land or the term of years absolute.

(5)   This section does not affect the right of a mortgagee of leasehold land to sell his mortgage term only if he is unable to convey or vest the leasehold reversion expectant thereon.

(6)   Any contract to convey an undivided share in land made before or after the commencement of this Act, shall be deemed to be sufficiently complied with by the conveyance of a corresponding share in the proceeds of sale of the land in like manner as if the contract had been to convey that corresponding share.

(7)   Where a purchaser has power to acquire land compulsorily, and a contract, whether by virtue of a notice to treat or otherwise, is subsisting under which title can be made without payment of the compensation money into court, title shall be made in that way unless the purchaser, to avoid expense or delay or for any special reason, considers it expedient that the money should be paid into court.

(8)   A vendor shall not have any power to rescind a contract by reason only of the enforcement of any right under this section.

(9)   This section only applies in favour of a purchaser for money or money's worth.

[145]

44   Statutory commencements of title

(1)   After the commencement of this Act [fifteen years] shall be substituted for forty years as the period of commencement of title which a purchaser of land may require; nevertheless earlier title than [fifteen years] may be required in cases similar to those

in which earlier title than forty years might immediately before the commencement of this Act be required.

(2) Under a contract to grant or assign a term of years, whether derived or to be derived out of freehold or leasehold land, the intended lessee or assign shall not be entitled to call for the title to the freehold.

(3) Under a contract to sell and assign a term of years derived out of a leasehold interest in land, the intended assign shall not have the right to call for the title to the leasehold reversion.

(4) On a contract to grant a lease for a term of years to be derived out of a leasehold interest, with a leasehold reversion, the intended lessee shall not have the right to call for the title to that reversion.

(5) Where by reason of any of the three last preceding subsections, an intending lessee or assign is not entitled to call for the title to the freehold or to a leasehold reversion, as the case may be, he shall not, where the contract is made after the commencement of this Act, be deemed to be affected with notice of any matter or thing of which, if he had contracted that such title should be furnished, he might have had notice.

(6) Where land of copyhold or customary tenure has been converted into freehold by enfranchisement, then, under a contract to sell and convey the freehold, the purchaser shall not have the right to call for the title to make the enfranchisement.

(7) Where the manorial incidents formerly affecting any land have been extinguished, then, under a contract to sell and convey the freehold, the purchaser shall not have the right to call for the title of the person entering into any compensation agreement or giving a receipt for the compensation money to enter into such agreement or to give such receipt, and shall not be deemed to be affected with notice of any matter or thing of which, if he had contracted that such title should be furnished, he might have had notice.

(8) A purchaser shall not be deemed to be or ever to have been affected with notice of any matter or thing of which, if he had investigated the title or made enquiries in regard to matters prior to the period of commencement of title fixed by this Act, or by any other statute, or by any rule of law, he might have had notice, unless he actually makes such investigation or enquiries.

(9) Where a lease whether made before or after the commencement of this Act, is made under a power contained in a settlement, will, Act of Parliament, or other instrument, any preliminary contract for or relating to the lease shall not, for the purpose of the deduction of title to an intended assign, form part of the title, or evidence of the title, to the lease.

(10) This section, save where otherwise expressly provided, applies to contracts for sale whether made before or after the commencement of this Act, and applies to contracts for exchange in like manner as to contracts for sale, save that it applies only to contracts for exchange made after such commencement.

(11) This section applies only if and so far as a contrary intention is not expressed in the contract.

[146]

NOTES
Sub-s (1): words in square brackets substituted by the Law of Property Act 1969, s 23.

45 Other statutory conditions of sale

(1) A purchaser of any property shall not—

    (a) require the production, or any abstract or copy, of any deed, will, or other document, dated or made before the time prescribed by law, or stipulated, for the commencement of the title, even though the same creates a power subsequently exercised by an instrument abstracted in the abstract furnished to the purchaser; or

    (b) require any information, or make any requisition, objection, or inquiry, with respect to any such deed, will, or document, or the title prior to that time, notwithstanding that any such deed, will, or other document, or that prior title, is recited, agreed to be produced, or noticed;

and he shall assume, unless the contrary appears, that the recitals, contained in the abstracted instruments, of any deed, will, or other document, forming part of that prior title, are correct, and give all the material contents of the deed, will, or other document so recited, and that every document so recited was duly executed by all necessary parties, and perfected, if and as required, by fine, recovery, acknowledgment, inrolment, or otherwise:

Provided that this subsection shall not deprive a purchaser of the right to require the production, or an abstract or copy of—

    (i) any power of attorney under which any abstracted document is executed; or

    (ii) any document creating or disposing of an interest, power or obligation which is not shown to have ceased or expired, and subject to which any part of the property is disposed of by an abstracted document; or

    (iii) any document creating any limitation or trust by reference to which any part of the property is disposed of by an abstracted document.

(2) Where land sold is held by lease (other than an under-lease), the purchaser shall assume, unless the contrary appears, that the lease was duly granted; and, on production of the receipt for the last payment due for rent under the lease before the date of actual completion of the purchase, he shall assume, unless the contrary appears, that all the covenants and provisions of the lease have been duly performed and observed up to the date of actual completion of the purchase.

(3) Where land sold is held by under-lease, the purchaser shall assume, unless the contrary appears, that the under-lease and every superior lease were duly granted; and, on production of the receipt for the last payment due for rent under the under-lease before the date of actual completion of the purchase, he shall assume, unless the contrary appears, that all the covenants and provisions of the under-lease have been duly performed and observed up to the date of actual completion of the purchase, and further that all rent due under every superior lease, and all the covenants and provisions of every superior lease, have been paid and duly performed and observed up to that date.

(4) On a sale of any property, the following expenses shall be borne by the purchaser where he requires them to be incurred for the purpose of verifying the abstract or any other purpose, that is to say—

    (a) the expenses of the production and inspection of all Acts of Parliament, inclosure awards, records, proceedings of courts, court rolls, deeds, wills, probates, letters of administration, and other documents, not in the possession of the vendor or his mortgagee or trustee, and the expenses of all journeys incidental to such production or inspection; and

    (b)   the expenses of searching for, procuring, making, verifying, and producing all certificates, declarations, evidences, and information not in the possession of the vendor or his mortgagee or trustee, and all attested, stamped, office or other copies or abstracts of, or extracts from, any Acts of Parliament or other documents aforesaid, not in the possession of the vendor or his mortgagee or trustee;

and where the vendor or his mortgagee or trustee retains possession of any document, the expenses of making any copy thereof, attested or unattested, which a purchaser requires to be delivered to him, shall be borne by that purchaser.

(5) On a sale of any property in lots, a purchaser of two or more lots, held wholly or partly under the same title, shall not have a right to more than one abstract of the common title, except at his own expense.

(6) Recitals, statements, and descriptions of facts, matters, and parties contained in deeds, instruments, Acts of Parliament, or statutory declarations, twenty years old at the date of the contract, shall, unless and except so far as they may be proved to be inaccurate, be taken to be sufficient evidence of the truth of such facts, matters, and descriptions.

(7) The inability of a vendor to furnish a purchaser with an acknowledgment of his right to production and delivery of copies of documents of title or with a legal covenant to produce and furnish copies of documents of title shall not be an objection to title in case the purchaser will, on the completion of the contract, have an equitable right to the production of such documents.

(8) Such acknowledgments of the right of production or covenants for production and such undertakings or covenants for safe custody of documents as the purchaser can and does require shall be furnished or made at his expense, and the vendor shall bear the expense of perusal and execution on behalf of and by himself, and on behalf of and by necessary parties other than the purchaser.

(9) A vendor shall be entitled to retain documents of title where—
    (a)   he retains any part of the land to which the documents relate; or
    (b)   the document consists of a trust instrument or other instrument creating a trust which is still subsisting, or an instrument relating to the appointment or discharge of a trustee of a subsisting trust.

(10) This section applies to contracts for sale made before or after the commencement of this Act, and applies to contracts for exchange in like manner as to contracts for sale, except that it applies only to contracts for exchange made after such commencement:

    Provided that this section shall apply subject to any stipulation or contrary intention expressed in the contract.

(11) Nothing in this section shall be construed as binding a purchaser to complete his purchase in any case where, on a contract made independently of this section, and containing stipulations similar to the provisions of this section, or any of them, specific performance of the contract would not be enforced against him by the court.

[146A]

46 Forms of contracts and conditions of sale

The Lord Chancellor may from time to time prescribe and publish forms of contracts and conditions of sale of land, and the forms so prescribed shall, subject to any modification, or any stipulation or intention to the contrary, expressed in the correspondence, apply to contracts by correspondence, and may, but only by express reference thereto, be made to apply to any other cases for which the forms are made available.

[146B]

47   Application of insurance money on completion of a sale or exchange

(1)   Where after the date of any contract for sale or exchange of property, money becomes payable under any policy of insurance maintained by the vendor in respect of any damage to or destruction of property included in the contract, the money shall, on completion of the contract, be held or receivable by the vendor on behalf of the purchaser and paid by the vendor to the purchaser on completion of the sale or exchange, or so soon thereafter as the same shall be received by the vendor.

(2)   This section applies only to contracts made after the commencement of this Act, and has effect subject to—
   (a)   any stipulation to the contrary contained in the contract,
   (b)   any requisite consents of the insurers,
   (c)   the payment by the purchaser of the proportionate part of the premium from the date of the contract.

(3)   This section applies to a sale or exchange by an order of the court, as if—
   (a)   for references to the "vendor" there were substituted references to the "person bound by the order";
   (b)   for the reference to the completion of the contract there were substituted a reference to the payment of the purchase or equality money (if any) into court;
   (c)   for the reference to the date of the contract there were substituted a reference to the time when the contract becomes binding.

[146C]

48   Stipulations preventing a purchaser, lessee, or underlessee from employing his own solicitor to be void

(1)   Any stipulation made on the sale of any interest in land after the commencement of this Act to the effect that the conveyance to, or the registration of the title of, the purchaser shall be prepared or carried out at the expense of the purchaser by a solicitor appointed by or acting for the vendor, and any stipulation which might restrict a purchaser in the selection of a solicitor to act on his behalf in relation to any interest in land agreed to be purchased, shall be void; and, if a sale is effected by demise or subdemise, then, for the purposes of this subsection, the instrument required for giving effect to the transaction shall be deemed to be a conveyance:

   Provided that nothing in this subsection shall affect any right reserved to a vendor to furnish a form of conveyance to a purchaser from which the draft can be prepared, or to charge a reasonable fee therefor, or, where a perpetual rentcharge is to be reserved as the only consideration in money or money's worth, the right of a vendor to stipulate that the draft conveyance is to be prepared by his solicitor at the expense of the purchaser.

(2)   Any covenant or stipulation contained in, or entered into with reference to any lease or underlease made before or after the commencement of this Act—
   (a)   whereby the right of preparing, at the expense of a purchaser, any conveyance of the estate or interest of the lessee or underlessee in the demised premises or in any part thereof, or of otherwise carrying out, at the expense of the purchaser, any dealing with such estate or interest, is expressed to be reserved to or vested in the lessor or underlessor or his solicitor; or

(b) which in any way restricts the right of the purchaser to have such conveyance carried out on his behalf by a solicitor appointed by him;

shall be void:

Provided that, where any covenant or stipulation is rendered void by this subsection, there shall be implied in lieu thereof a covenant or stipulation that the lessee or underlessee shall register with the lessor or his solicitor within six months from the date thereof, or as soon after the expiration of that period as may be practicable, all conveyances and devolutions (including probates or letters of administration) affecting the lease or underlease and pay a fee of one guinea in respect of each registration, and the power of entry (if any) on breach of any covenant contained in the lease or underlease shall apply and extend to the breach of any covenant so to be implied.

(3) Save where a sale is effected by demise or subdemise, this section does not affect the law relating to the preparation of a lease or underlease or the draft thereof.

(4) In this section "lease" and "underlease" include any agreement therefor or other tenancy, and "lessee" and "underlessee" and "lessor" and "underlessor" have corresponding meanings.

[146D]

NOTES

Modification: any reference to solicitor(s) etc modified to include references to bodies recognised under the Administration of Justice Act 1985, s 9, by the Solicitors' Incorporated Practices Order 1991, SI 1991/2684, arts 4, 5, Sch 1.

Modified by the Administration of Justice Act 1985, ss 9, 34(2), Sch 2, para 37 and by the Building Societies Act 1986, s 124, Sch 21, paras 9, 12.

49 Applications to the court by vendor and purchaser

(1) A vendor or purchaser of any interest in land, or their representatives respectively, may apply in a summary way to the court, in respect of any requisitions or objections, or any claim for compensation, or any other question arising out of or connected with the contract (not being a question affecting the existence or validity of the contract), and the court may make such order upon the application as to the court may appear just, and may order how and by whom all or any of the costs of and incident to the application are to be borne and paid.

(2) Where the court refuses to grant specific performance of a contract, or in any action for the return of a deposit, the court may, if it thinks fit, order the repayment of any deposit.

(3) This section applies to a contract for the sale or exchange of any interest in land.

[(4) The county court has jurisdiction under this section where the land which is to be dealt with in the court does not exceed [£30,000] in capital value . . .]

[146E]

NOTES

Sub-s (4): added by the County Courts Act 1984, s 148(1), Sch 2, Pt II, para 2(1), (3); sum in square brackets substituted and words omitted repealed by the High Court and County Courts Jurisdiction Order 1991, SI 1991/724, art 2(3)(a), (8), Schedule, Pt I.

50 Discharge of incumbrances by the court on sales or exchanges

(1) Where land subject to any incumbrance, whether immediately realisable or payable or not, is sold or exchanged by the court, or out of court, the court may, if it

thinks fit, on the application of any party to the sale or exchange, direct or allow payment into court of such sum as is hereinafter mentioned, that is to say—

(a) in the case of an annual sum charged on the land, or of a capital sum charged on a determinable interest in the land, the sum to be paid into court shall be of such amount as, when invested in Government securities, the court considers will be sufficient, by means of the dividends thereof, to keep down or otherwise provide for that charge; and

(b) in any other case of capital money charged on the land, the sum to be paid into court shall be of an amount sufficient to meet the incumbrance and any interest due thereon;

but in either case there shall also be paid into court such additional amount as the court considers will be sufficient to meet the contingency of further costs, expenses and interests, and any other contingency, except depreciation of investments, not exceeding one-tenth part of the original amount to be paid in, unless the court for special reason thinks fit to require a larger additional amount.

(2)   Thereupon, the court may, if it thinks fit, and either after or without any notice to the incumbrancer, as the court thinks fit, declare the land to be freed from the incumbrance, and make any order for conveyance, or vesting order, proper for giving effect to the sale or exchange, and give directions for the retention and investment of the money in court and for the payment or application of the income thereof.

(3)   The court may declare all other land, if any, affected by the incumbrance (besides the land sold or exchanged) to be freed from the incumbrance, and this power may be exercised either after or without notice to the incumbrancer, and notwithstanding that on a previous occasion an order, relating to the same incumbrance, has been made by the court which was confined to the land then sold or exchanged.

(4)   On any application under this section the court may, if it thinks fit, as respects any vendor or purchaser, dispense with the service of any notice which would otherwise be required to be served on the vendor or purchaser.

(5)   After notice served on the persons interested in or entitled to the money or fund in court, the court may direct payment or transfer thereof to the persons entitled to receive or give a discharge for the same, and generally may give directions respecting the application or distribution of the capital or income thereof.

(6)   This section applies to sales or exchanges whether made before or after the commencement of this Act, and to incumbrances whether created by statute or otherwise.

[147]

Conveyances and other Instruments

51 Lands lie in grant only

(1)   All lands and all interests therein lie in grant and are incapable of being conveyed by livery or livery and seisin, or by feoffment, or by bargain and sale; and a conveyance of an interest in land may operate to pass the possession or right to possession thereof, without actual entry, but subject to all prior rights thereto.

(2)   The use of the word grant is not necessary to convey land or to create any interest therein.

[148]

52   Conveyances to be by deed

(1)   All conveyances of land or of any interest therein are void for the purpose of conveying or creating a legal estate unless made by deed.

(2)   This section does not apply to—

    (a)   assents by a personal representative;

    (b)   disclaimers made in accordance with [sections 178 to 180 or sections 315 to 319 of the Insolvency Act 1986], or not required to be evidenced in writing;

    (c)   surrenders by operation of law, including surrenders which may, by law, be effected without writing;

    (d)   leases or tenancies or other assurances not required by law to be made in writing;

    (e)   receipts [other than those falling within section 115 below];

    (f)   vesting orders of the court or other competent authority;

    (g)   conveyances taking effect by operation of law.

[149]

NOTES

Sub-s (2): words in square brackets in para (b) substituted by the Insolvency Act 1986, s 439(2), Sch 14; words in square brackets in para (e) substituted by the Law of Property (Miscellaneous Provisions) Act 1989, s 1(8), Sch 1, para 2.

53   Instruments required to be in writing

(1)   Subject to the provisions hereinafter contained with respect to the creation of interests in land by parol—

    (a)   no interest in land can be created or disposed of except by writing signed by the person creating or conveying the same, or by his agent thereunto lawfully authorised in writing, or by will, or by operation of law;

    (b)   a declaration of trust respecting any land or any interest therein must be manifested and proved by some writing signed by some person who is able to declare such trust or by his will;

    (c)   a disposition of an equitable interest or trust subsisting at the time of the disposition, must be in writing signed by the person disposing of the same, or by his agent thereunto lawfully authorised in writing or by will.

(2)   This section does not affect the creation or operation of resulting, implied or constructive trusts.

[150]

54   Creation of interests in land by parol

(1)   All interests in land created by parol and not put in writing and signed by the persons so creating the same, or by their agents thereunto lawfully authorised in writing, have, notwithstanding any consideration having been given for the same, the force and effect of interests at will only.

(2)   Nothing in the foregoing provisions of this Part of this Act shall affect the creation by parol of leases taking effect in possession for a term not exceeding three years (whether or not the lessee is given power to extend the term) at the best rent which can be reasonably obtained without taking a fine.

[151]

55   Savings in regard to last two sections

Nothing in the last two foregoing sections shall—

(a) invalidate dispositions by will; or
(b) affect any interest validly created before the commencement of this Act; or
(c) affect the right to acquire an interest in land by virtue of taking possession; or
(d) affect the operation of the law relating to part performance.

[152]

56   Persons taking who are not parties and as to indentures

(1)   A person may take an immediate or other interest in land or other property, or the benefit of any condition, right of entry, covenant or agreement over or respecting land or other property, although he may not be named as a party to the conveyance or other instrument.

(2)   A deed between parties, to effect its objects, has the effect of an indenture though not indented or expressed to be an indenture.

[153]

60   Abolition of technicalities in regard to conveyances and deeds

(1)   A conveyance of freehold land to any person without words of limitation, or any equivalent expression, shall pass to the grantee the fee simple or other the whole interest which the grantor had power to convey in such land, unless a contrary intention appears in the conveyance.

(2)   A conveyance of freehold land to a corporation sole by his corporate designation without the word "successors" shall pass to the corporation the fee simple or other the whole interest which the grantor had power to convey in such land, unless a contrary intention appears in the conveyance.

(3)   In a voluntary conveyance a resulting trust for the grantor shall not be implied merely by reason that the property is not expressed to be conveyed for the use or benefit of the grantee.

(4)   The foregoing provisions of this section apply only to conveyances and deeds executed after the commencement of this Act:

Provided that in a deed executed after the thirty-first day of December, eighteen hundred and eighty-one, it is sufficient—
(a) In the limitation of an estate in fee simple, to use the words "in fee simple," without the word "heirs";
(b) In the limitation of an estate tail, to use the words "in tail" without the words "heirs of the body"; and
(c) In the limitation of an estate in tail male or in tail female, to use the words "in tail male" or "in tail female," as the case requires, without the words "heirs male of the body," or "heirs female of the body".

[154]

61   Construction of expressions used in deeds and other instruments

In all deeds, contracts, wills, orders and other instruments executed, made or coming into operation after the commencement of this Act, unless the context otherwise requires—
(a) "Month" means calendar month;
(b) "Person" includes a corporation;
(c) The singular includes the plural and vice versa;
(d) The masculine includes the feminine and vice versa.

[155]

62   General words implied in conveyances

(1)   A conveyance of land shall be deemed to include and shall by virtue of this Act operate to convey, with the land, all buildings, erections, fixtures, commons, hedges, ditches, fences, ways, waters, watercourses, liberties, privileges, easements, rights, and advantages whatsoever, appertaining or reputed to appertain to the land, or any part thereof, or, at the time of conveyance, demised, occupied, or enjoyed with or reputed or known as part or parcel of or appurtenant to the land or any part thereof.

(2)   A conveyance of land, having houses or other buildings thereon, shall be deemed to include and shall by virtue of this Act operate to convey, with the land, houses, or other buildings, all outhouses, erections, fixtures, cellars, areas, courts, courtyards, cisterns, sewers, gutters, drains, ways, passages, lights, watercourses, liberties, privileges, easements, rights, and advantages whatsoever, appertaining or reputed to appertain to the land, houses, or other buildings conveyed, or any of them, or any part thereof, or, at the time of conveyance, demised, occupied, or enjoyed with, or reputed or known as part or parcel of or appurtenant to, the land, houses, other buildings conveyed, or any of them, or any part thereof.

(3)   A conveyance of a manor shall be deemed to include and shall by virtue of this Act operate to convey, with the manor, all pastures, feedings, wastes, warrens, commons, mines, minerals, quarries, furzes, trees, woods, underwoods, coppices, and the ground and soil thereof, fishings, fisheries, fowlings, courts leet, courts baron, and other courts, view of frankpledge and all that to view of frankpledge doth belong, mills, mulctures, customs, tolls, duties, reliefs, heriots, fines, sums of money, amerciaments, waifs, estrays, chief-rents, quitrents, rentscharge, rents seck, rents of assize, fee farm rents, services, royalties, jurisdictions, franchises, liberties, privileges, easements, profits, advantages, rights, emoluments, and hereditaments whatsoever, to the manor appertaining or reputed to appertain, or, at the time of conveyance, demised, occupied, or enjoyed with the same, or reputed or known as part, parcel, or member thereof.

For the purposes of this subsection the right to compensation for manorial incidents on the extinguishment thereof shall be deemed to be a right appertaining to the manor.

(4)   This section applies only if and as far as a contrary intention is not expressed in the conveyance, and has effect subject to the terms of the conveyance and to the provisions therein contained.

(5)   This section shall not be construed as giving to any person a better title to any property, right, or thing in this section mentioned than the title which the conveyance gives to him to the land or manor expressed to be conveyed, or as conveying to him any property, right, or thing in this section mentioned, further or otherwise than as the same could have been conveyed to him by the conveying parties.

(6)   This section applies to conveyances made after the thirty-first day of December, eighteen hundred and eighty-one.

[156]

63   All estate clause implied

(1)   Every conveyance is effectual to pass all the estate, right, title, interest, claim, and demand which the conveying parties respectively have, in, to, or on the property conveyed, or expressed or intended so to be, or which they respectively have power to convey in, to, or on the same.

(2)   This section applies only if and as far as a contrary intention is not expressed in the conveyance, and has effect subject to the terms of the conveyance and to the provisions therein contained.

(3)   This section applies to conveyances made after the thirty-first day of December, eighteen hundred and eighty-one.

[157]

64   Production and safe custody of documents

(1)   Where a person retains possession of documents, and gives to another an acknowledgment in writing of the right of that other to production of those documents, and to delivery of copies thereof (in this section called an acknowledgment), that acknowledgment shall have effect as in this section provided.

(2)   An acknowledgment shall bind the documents to which it relates in the possession or under the control of the person who retains them, and in the possession or under the control of every other person having possession or control thereof from time to time, but shall bind each individual possessor or person as long only as he has possession or control thereof; and every person so having possession or control from time to time shall be bound specifically to perform the obligations imposed under this section by an acknowledgment, unless prevented from so doing by fire or other inevitable accident.

(3)   The obligations imposed under this section by an acknowledgment are to be performed from time to time at the request in writing of the person to whom an acknowledgment is given, or of any person, not being a lessee at a rent, having or claiming any estate, interest, or right through or under that person, or otherwise becoming through or under that person interested in or affected by the terms of any document to which the acknowledgment relates.

(4)   The obligations imposed under this section by an acknowledgment are—
    (i)   An obligation to produce the documents or any of them at all reasonable times for the purpose of inspection, and of comparison with abstracts or copies thereof, by the person entitled to request production or by any person by him authorised in writing; and
    (ii)   An obligation to produce the documents or any of them at any trial, hearing, or examination in any court, or in the execution of any commission, or elsewhere in the United Kingdom, on any occasion on which production may properly be required, for proving or supporting the title or claim of the person entitled to request production, or for any other purpose relative to that title or claim; and
    (iii) An obligation to deliver to the person entitled to request the same true copies or extracts, attested or unattested, of or from the documents or any of them.

(5)   All costs and expenses of or incidental to the specific performance of any obligation imposed under this section by an acknowledgment shall be paid by the person requesting performance.

(6)   An acknowledgment shall not confer any right to damages for loss or destruction of, or injury to, the documents to which it relates, from whatever cause arising.

(7)   Any person claiming to be entitled to the benefit of an acknowledgment may apply to the court for an order directing the production of the documents to which it relates, or any of them, or the delivery of copies of or extracts from those documents

or any of them to him, or some person on his behalf; and the court may, if it thinks fit, order production, or production and delivery, accordingly, and may give directions respecting the time, place, terms, and mode of production or delivery, and may make such order as it thinks fit respecting the costs of the application, or any other matter connected with the application.

(8)   An acknowledgment shall by virtue of this Act satisfy any liability to give a covenant for production and delivery of copies of or extracts from documents.

(9)   Where a person retains possession of documents and gives to another an undertaking in writing for safe custody thereof, that undertaking shall impose on the person giving it, and on every person having possession or control of the documents from time to time, but on each individual possessor or person as long only as he has possession or control thereof, an obligation to keep the document safe, whole, uncancelled, and undefaced, unless prevented from so doing by fire or other inevitable accident.

(10)   Any person claiming to be entitled to the benefit of such an undertaking may apply to the court to assess damages for any loss or destruction of, or injury to, the documents or any of them, and the court may, if it thinks fit, direct an inquiry respecting the amount of damages, and order payment thereof by the person liable, and may make such order as it thinks fit respecting the costs of the application, or any other matter connected with the application.

(11)   An undertaking for safe custody of documents shall by virtue of this Act satisfy any liability to give a covenant for safe custody of documents.

(12)   The rights conferred by an acknowledgment or an undertaking under this section shall be in addition to all such other rights relative to the production, or inspection, or the obtaining of copies of documents, as are not, by virtue of this Act, satisfied by the giving of the acknowledgment or undertaking, and shall have effect subject to the terms of the acknowledgment or undertaking, and to any provisions therein contained.

(13)   This section applies only if and as far as a contrary intention is not expressed in the acknowledgment or undertaking.

(14)   This section applies to an acknowledgment or undertaking given, or a liability respecting documents incurred, after the thirty-first day of December, eighteen hundred and eighty-one.

[158]

65   Reservation of legal estates

(1)   A reservation of a legal estate shall operate at law without any execution of the conveyance by the grantee of the legal estate out of which the reservation is made, or any regrant by him, so as to create the legal estate reserved, and so as to vest the same in possession in the person (whether being the grantor or not) for whose benefit the reservation is made.

(2)   A conveyance of a legal estate expressed to be made subject to another legal estate not in existence immediately before the date of the conveyance, shall operate as a reservation, unless a contrary intention appears.

(3)   This section applies only to reservations made after the commencement of this Act.

[159]

68 Receipt in deed or indorsed evidence

(1) A receipt for consideration money or other consideration in the body of a deed or indorsed thereon shall, in favour of a subsequent purchaser, not having notice that the money or other consideration thereby acknowledged to be received was not in fact paid or given, wholly or in part, be sufficient evidence of the payment or giving of the whole amount thereof.

(2) This section applies to deeds executed after the thirty-first day of December, eighteen hundred and eighty-one.

[160]

69 Receipt in deed or indorsed authority for payment to solicitor

(1) Where a solicitor produces a deed, having in the body thereof or indorsed thereon a receipt for consideration money or other consideration, the deed being executed, or the indorsed receipt being signed, by the person entitled to give a receipt for that consideration, the deed shall be a sufficient authority to the person liable to pay or give the same for his paying or giving the same to the solicitor, without the solicitor producing any separate or other direction or authority in that behalf from the person who executed or signed the deed or receipt.

(2) This section applies whether the consideration was paid or given before or after the commencement of this Act.

[161]

NOTES

Modification: any reference to solicitor(s) etc modified to include references to bodies recognised under the Administration of Justice Act 1985, s 9, by the Solicitors' Incorporated Practices Order 1991, SI 1991/2684, arts 4, 5, Sch 1.

70 Partial release of security from rentcharge

(1) A release from a rentcharge of part of the land charged therewith does not extinguish the whole rentcharge, but operates only to bar the right to recover any part of the rentcharge out of the land released, without prejudice to the rights of any persons interested in the land remaining unreleased, and not concurring in or confirming the release.

(2) This section applies to releases made after the twelfth day of August, eighteen hundred and fifty-nine.

[162]

Covenants

78 Benefit of covenants relating to land

(1) A covenant relating to any land of the covenantee shall be deemed to be made with the covenantee and his successors in title and the persons deriving title under him or them, and shall have effect as if such successors and other persons were expressed.

For the purposes of this subsection in connexion with covenants restrictive of the user of land "successors in title" shall be deemed to include the owners and occupiers for the time being of the land of the covenantee intended to be benefited.

(2) This section applies to covenants made after the commencement of this Act, but the repeal of section fifty-eight of the Conveyancing Act 1881 does not affect the operation of covenants to which that section applied.

[163]

79   Burden of covenants relating to land

(1)   A covenant relating to any land of a covenantor or capable of being bound by him, shall, unless a contrary intention is expressed be deemed to be made by the covenantor on behalf of himself his successors in title and the persons deriving title under him or them, and, subject as aforesaid, shall have effect as if such successors and other persons were expressed.

This subsection extends to a covenant to do some act relating to the land, notwithstanding that the subject-matter may not be in existence when the covenant is made.

(2)   For the purposes of this section in connexion with covenants restrictive of the user of land "successors in title" shall be deemed to include the owners and occupiers for the time being of such land.

(3)   This section applies only to covenants made after the commencement of this Act.

[164]

[84   Power to discharge or modify restrictive covenants affecting land

(1)   The Lands Tribunal shall (without prejudice to any concurrent jurisdiction of the court) have power from time to time, on the application of any person interested in any freehold land affected by any restriction arising under covenant or otherwise as to the user thereof or the building thereon, by order wholly or partially to discharge or modify any such restriction on being satisfied—

   (a) that by reason of changes in the character of the property or the neighbourhood or other circumstances of the case which the Lands Tribunal may deem material, the restriction ought to be deemed obsolete; or
   (aa) that (in a case falling within subsection (1A) below) the continued existence thereof would impede some reasonable user of the land for public or private purposes or, as the case may be, would unless modified so impede such user; or
   (b) that the persons of full age and capacity for the time being or from time to time entitled to the benefit of the restriction, whether in respect of estates in fee simple or any lesser estates or interests in the property to which the benefit of the restriction is annexed, have agreed, either expressly or by implication, by their acts or omissions, to the same being discharged or modified; or
   (c) that the proposed discharge or modification will not injure the persons entitled to the benefit of the restriction;

and an order discharging or modifying a restriction under this subsection may direct the applicant to pay to any person entitled to the benefit of the restriction such sum by way of consideration as the Tribunal may think it just to award under one, but not both, of the following heads, that is to say, either—

   (i) a sum to make up for any loss or disadvantage suffered by that person in consequence of the discharge or modification; or
   (ii) a sum to make up for any effect which the restriction had, at the time when it was imposed, in reducing the consideration then received for the land affected by it.

(1A)   Subsection (1)(aa) above authorises the discharge or modification of a restriction by reference to its impeding some reasonable user of land in any case in which the Lands Tribunal is satisfied that the restriction, in impeding that user, either—

(a)   does not secure to persons entitled to the benefit of it any practical benefits of substantial value or advantage to them; or

(b)   is contrary to the public interest;

and that money will be an adequate compensation for the loss or disadvantage (if any) which any such person will suffer from the discharge or modification.

(1B) In determining whether a case is one falling within subsection (1A) above, and in determining whether (in any such case or otherwise) a restriction ought to be discharged or modified, the Lands Tribunal shall take into account the development plan and any declared or ascertainable pattern for the grant or refusal of planning permissions in the relevant areas, as well as the period at which and context in which the restriction was created or imposed and any other material circumstances.

(1C) It is hereby declared that the power conferred by this section to modify a restriction includes power to add such further provisions restricting the user of or the building on the land affected as appear to the Lands Tribunal to be reasonable in view of the relaxation of the existing provisions, and as may be accepted by the applicant; and the Lands Tribunal may accordingly refuse to modify a restriction without some such addition.

(2)   The court shall have power on the application of any person interested—

(a)   to declare whether or not in any particular case any freehold land is, or would in any given event be, affected by a restriction imposed by any instrument; or

(b)   to declare what, upon the true construction of any instrument purporting to impose a restriction, is the nature and extent of the restriction thereby imposed and whether the same is, or would in any given event be, enforceable and if so by whom.

Neither subsections (7) and (11) of this section nor, unless the contrary is expressed, any later enactment providing for this section not to apply to any restrictions shall affect the operation of this subsection or the operation for purposes of this subsection of any other provisions of this section.

(3)   The Lands Tribunal shall, before making any order under this section, direct such enquiries, if any, to be made of any government department or local authority, and such notices, if any, whether by way of advertisement or otherwise, to be given to such of the persons who appear to be entitled to the benefit of the restriction intended to be discharged, modified, or dealt with as, having regard to any enquiries, notices or other proceedings previously made, given or taken, the Lands Tribunal may think fit.

(3A) On an application to the Lands Tribunal under this section the Lands Tribunal shall give any necessary directions as to the persons who are or are not to be admitted (as appearing to be entitled to the benefit of the restriction) to oppose the application, and no appeal shall lie against any such direction; but rules under the Lands Tribunal Act 1949 shall make provision whereby, in cases in which there arises on such an application (whether or not in connection with the admission of persons to oppose) any such question as is referred to in subsection (2)(a) or (b) of this section, the proceedings on the application can and, if the rules so provide, shall be suspended to enable the decision of the court to be obtained on that question by an application under that subsection, or by means of a case stated by the Lands Tribunal, or otherwise, as may be provided by those rules or by rules of court.

(5)   Any order made under this section shall be binding on all persons, whether ascertained or of full age or capacity or not, then entitled or thereafter capable of becoming entitled to the benefit of any restriction, which is thereby discharged,

modified or dealt with, and whether such persons are parties to the proceedings or have been served with notice or not.

(6)   An order may be made under this section notwithstanding that any instrument which is alleged to impose the restriction intended to be discharged, modified, or dealt with, may not have been produced to the court or the Lands Tribunal, and the court or the Lands Tribunal may act on such evidence of that instrument as it may think sufficient.

(7)   This section applies to restrictions whether subsisting at the commencement of this Act or imposed thereafter, but this section does not apply where the restriction was imposed on the occasion of a disposition made gratuitously or for a nominal consideration for public purposes.

(8)   This section applies whether the land affected by the restrictions is registered or not, but, in the case of registered land, the Land Registrar shall give effect on the register to any order under this section in accordance with the Land Registration Act 1925.

(9)   Where any proceedings by action or otherwise are taken to enforce a restrictive covenant, any person against whom the proceedings are taken, may in such proceedings apply to the court for an order giving leave to apply to the Lands Tribunal under this section, and staying the proceedings in the meantime.

(11) This section does not apply to restrictions imposed by the Commissioners of Works under any statutory power for the protection of any Royal Park or Garden or to restrictions of a like character imposed upon the occasion of any enfranchisement effected before the commencement of this Act in any manor vested in His Majesty in right of the Crown or the Duchy of Lancaster, nor (subject to subsection (11A) below) to restrictions created or imposed—

    (a)   for naval, military or air force purposes,

   [(b)   for civil aviation purposes under the powers of the Air Navigation Act 1920, of section 19 or 23 of the Civil Aviation Act 1949 or of section 30 or 41 of the Civil Aviation Act 1982.]

(11A)   Subsection (11) of this section—

    (a)   shall exclude the application of this section to a restriction falling within subsection (11)(a), and not created or imposed in connection with the use of any land as an aerodrome, only so long as the restriction is enforceable by or on behalf of the Crown; and

    (b)   shall exclude the application of this section to a restriction falling within subsection (11)(b), or created or imposed in connection with the use of any land as an aerodrome, only so long as the restriction is enforceable by or on behalf of the Crown or any public or international authority.

(12) Where a term of more than forty years is created in land (whether before or after the commencement of this Act) this section shall, after the expiration of twenty-five years of the term, apply to restrictions, affecting such leasehold land in like manner as it would have applied had the land been freehold:

Provided that this subsection shall not apply to mining leases.]

NOTES

By virtue of the Law of Property Act 1969, s 28(1), this section has effect as set out in Sch 3 to that Act, incorporating amendments made by the Landlord and Tenant Act 1954, s 52(1) and by s 28(1)–(9) of the 1989 Act.

Sub-s (11): para (b) substituted by the Civil Aviation Act 1982, s 109, Sch 15, para 1.

PART III
MORTGAGES, RENTCHARGES, AND POWERS OF ATTORNEY

Mortgages

85   Mode of mortgaging freeholds

(1)   A mortgage of an estate in fee simple shall only be capable of being effected at law either by a demise for a term of years absolute, subject to a provision for cesser on redemption, or by a charge by deed expressed to be by way of legal mortgage:

Provided that a first mortgagee shall have the same right to the possession of documents as if his security included the fee simple.

(2)   Any purported conveyance of an estate in fee simple by way of mortgage made after the commencement of this Act shall (to the extent of the estate of the mortgagor) operate as a demise of the land to the mortgagee for a term of years absolute, without impeachment for waste, but subject to cesser on redemption, in manner following, namely:—

    (a)   A first or only mortgagee shall take a term of three thousand years from the date of the mortgage:

    (b)   A second or subsequent mortgagee shall take a term (commencing from the date of the mortgage) one day longer than the term vested in the first or other mortgagee whose security ranks immediately before that of such second or subsequent mortgagee:

and, in this subsection, any such purported conveyance as aforesaid includes an absolute conveyance with a deed of defeasance and any other assurance which, but for this subsection, would operate in effect to vest the fee simple in a mortgagee subject to redemption.

(3)   This section applies whether or not the land is registered under the Land Registration Act 1925, or the mortgage is expressed to be made by way of trust for sale or otherwise.

(4)   Without prejudice to the provisions of this Act respecting legal and equitable powers, every power to mortgage or to lend money on mortgage of an estate in fee simple shall be construed as a power to mortgage the estate for a term of years absolute, without impeachment for waste, or by a charge by way of legal mortgage or to lend on such security.

[166]

86   Mode of mortgaging leaseholds

(1)   A mortgage of a term of years absolute shall only be capable of being effected at law either by a subdemise for a term of years absolute, less by one day at least than the term vested in the mortgagor, and subject to a provision for cesser on redemption, or by a charge by deed expressed to be by way of legal mortgage; and where a licence to subdemise by way of mortgage is required, such licence shall not be unreasonably refused:

Provided that a first mortgagee shall have the same right to the possession of documents as if his security had been effected by assignment.

(2)   Any purported assignment of a term of years absolute by way of mortgage made after the commencement of this Act shall (to the extent of the estate of the mortgagor) operate as a subdemise of the leasehold land to the mortgagee for a term of years absolute, but subject to cesser on redemption, in manner following, namely:—

(a) The term to be taken by a first or only mortgagee shall be ten days less than the term expressed to be assigned:

(b) The term to be taken by a second or subsequent mortgagee shall be one day longer than the term vested in the first or other mortgagee whose security ranks immediately before that of the second or subsequent mortgagee, if the length of the last mentioned term permits, and in any case for a term less by one day at least than the term expressed to be assigned:

and, in this subsection, any such purported assignment as aforesaid includes an absolute assignment with a deed of defeasance and any other assurance which, but for this subsection, would operate in effect to vest the term of the mortgagor in a mortgagee subject to redemption.

(3)   This section applies whether or not the land is registered under the Land Registration Act 1925, or the mortgage is made by way of sub-mortgage of a term of years absolute, or is expressed to be by way of trust for sale or otherwise.

(4)   Without prejudice to the provisions of this Act respecting legal and equitable powers, every power to mortgage for or to lend money on mortgage of a term of years absolute by way of assignment shall be construed as a power to mortgage the term by subdemise for a term of years absolute or by a charge by way of legal mortgage, or to lend on such security.

[167]

87   Charges by way of legal mortgage

(1)   Where a legal mortgage of land is created by a charge by deed expressed to be by way of legal mortgage, the mortgagee shall have the same protection, powers and remedies (including the right to take proceedings to obtain possession from the occupiers and the persons in receipt of rents and profits, or any of them) as if—

(a) where the mortgage is a mortgage of an estate in fee simple, a mortgage term for three thousand years without impeachment of waste had been thereby created in favour of the mortgagee; and

(b) where the mortgage is a mortgage of a term of years absolute, a sub-term less by one day than the term vested in the mortgagor had been thereby created in favour of the mortgagee.

(2)   Where an estate vested in a mortgagee immediately before the commencement of this Act has by virtue of this Act been converted into a term of years absolute or sub-term, the mortgagee may, by a declaration in writing to that effect signed by him, convert the mortgage into a charge by way of legal mortgage, and in that case the mortgage term shall be extinguished in the inheritance or in the head term as the case may be, and the mortgagee shall have the same protection, powers and remedies (including the right to take proceedings to obtain possession from the occupiers and the persons in receipt of rents and profits or any of them) as if the mortgage term or sub-term had remained subsisting.

The power conferred by this subsection may be exercised by a mortgagee notwithstanding that he is a trustee or personal representative.

(3)   Such declaration shall not affect the priority of the mortgagee or his right to retain possession of documents, nor affect his title to or right over any fixtures or chattels personal comprised in the mortgage.

[168]

88   Realisation of freehold mortgages

(1)   Where an estate in fee simple has been mortgaged by the creation of a term of years absolute limited thereout or by a charge by way of legal mortgage and the mortgagee sells under his statutory or express power of sale—

  (a)   the conveyance by him shall operate to vest in the purchaser the fee simple in the land conveyed subject to any legal mortgage having priority to the mortgage in right of which the sale is made and to any money thereby secured, and thereupon;

  (b)   the mortgage term or the charge by way of legal mortgage and any subsequent mortgage term or charges shall merge or be extinguished as respects the land conveyed;

and such conveyance may, as respects the fee simple, be made in the name of the estate owner in whom it is vested.

(2)   Where any such mortgagee obtains an order for foreclosure absolute, the order shall operate to vest the fee simple in him (subject to any legal mortgage having priority to the mortgage in right of which the foreclosure is obtained and to any money thereby secured), and thereupon the mortgage term, if any, shall thereby be merged in the fee simple, and any subsequent mortgage term or charge by way of legal mortgage bound by the order shall thereupon be extinguished.

(3)   Where any such mortgagee acquires a title under the Limitation Acts, he, or the persons deriving title under him, may enlarge the mortgage term into a fee simple under the statutory power for that purpose discharged from any legal mortgage affected by the title so acquired, or in the case of a chargee by way of legal mortgage may by deed declare that the fee simple is vested in him discharged as aforesaid, and the same shall vest accordingly.

(4)   Where the mortgage includes fixtures or chattels personal any statutory power of sale and any right to foreclose or take possession shall extend to the absolute or other interest therein affected by the charge.

(5)   In the case of a sub-mortgage by subdemise of a long term (less a nominal period) itself limited out of an estate in fee simple, the foregoing provisions of this section shall operate as if the derivative term, if any, created by the sub-mortgage had been limited out of the fee simple, and so as to enlarge the principal term and extinguish the derivative term created by the sub-mortgage as aforesaid, and to enable the sub-mortgagee to convey the fee simple or acquire it by foreclosure, enlargement, or otherwise as aforesaid.

(6)   This section applies to a mortgage whether created before or after the commencement of this Act, and to a mortgage term created by this Act, but does not operate to confer a better title to the fee simple than would have been acquired if the same had been conveyed by the mortgage (being a valid mortgage) and the restrictions imposed by this Act in regard to the effect and creation of mortgages were not in force, and all prior mortgages (if any) not being merely equitable charges had been created by demise or by charge by way of legal mortgage.

[169]

89   Realisation of leasehold mortgages

(1)   Where a term of years absolute has been mortgaged by the creation of another term of years absolute limited thereout or by a charge by way of legal mortgage and the mortgagee sells under his statutory or express power of sale,—

(a) the conveyance by him shall operate to convey to the purchaser not only the mortgage term, if any, but also (unless expressly excepted with the leave of the court) the leasehold reversion affected by the mortgage, subject to any legal mortgage having priority to the mortgage in right of which the sale is made and to any money thereby secured, and thereupon

(b) the mortgage term, or the charge by way of legal mortgage and any subsequent mortgage term or charge, shall merge in such leasehold reversion or be extinguished unless excepted as aforesaid;

and such conveyance may, as respects the leasehold reversion, be made in the name of the estate owner in whom it is vested.

Where a licence to assign is required on a sale by a mortgagee, such licence shall not be unreasonably refused.

(2) Where any such mortgagee obtains an order for foreclosure absolute, the order shall, unless it otherwise provides, operate (without giving rise to a forfeiture for want of a licence to assign) to vest the leasehold reversion affected by the mortgage and any subsequent mortgage term in him, subject to any legal mortgage having priority to the mortgage in right of which the foreclosure is obtained and to any money thereby secured, and thereupon the mortgage term and any subsequent mortgage term or charge by way of legal mortgage bound by the order shall, subject to any express provision to the contrary contained in the order, merge in such leasehold reversion or be extinguished.

(3) Where any such mortgagee acquires a title under the Limitation Acts, he, or the persons deriving title under him, may by deed declare that the leasehold reversion affected by the mortgage and any mortgage term affected by the title so acquired shall vest in him, free from any right of redemption which is barred, and the same shall (without giving rise to a forfeiture for want of a licence to assign) vest accordingly, and thereupon the mortgage term, if any, and any other mortgage term or charge by way of legal mortgage affected by the title so acquired shall, subject to any express provision to the contrary contained in the deed, merge in such leasehold reversion or be extinguished.

(4) Where the mortgage includes fixtures or chattels personal, any statutory power of sale and any right to foreclose or take possession shall extend to the absolute or other interest therein affected by the charge.

(5) In the case of a sub-mortgage by subdemise of a term (less a nominal period) itself limited out of a leasehold reversion, the foregoing provisions of this section shall operate as if the derivative term created by the sub-mortgage had been limited out of the leasehold reversion, and so as (subject as aforesaid) to merge the principal mortgage term therein as well as the derivative term created by the sub-mortgage and to enable the sub-mortgagee to convey the leasehold reversion or acquire it by foreclosure, vesting, or otherwise as aforesaid.

(6) This section takes effect without prejudice to any incumbrance or trust affecting the leasehold reversion which has priority over the mortgage in right of which the sale, foreclosure, or title is made or acquired, and applies to a mortgage whether executed before or after the commencement of this Act, and to a mortgage term created by this Act, but does not apply where the mortgage term does not comprise the whole of the land included in the leasehold reversion unless the rent (if any) payable in respect of that reversion has been apportioned as respects the land affected, or the rent is of no money value or no rent is reserved, and unless the lessee's covenants and conditions (if any) have been apportioned, either expressly or by implication, as respects the land affected.

[In this subsection references to an apportionment include an equitable apportionment made without the consent of the lessor.]

[(7)   The county court has jurisdiction under this section where the amount owing in respect of the mortgage or charge at the commencement of the proceedings does not exceed [£30,000].]

NOTES

Sub-s (6): words in square brackets inserted by the Law of Property (Amendment) Act 1926, s 7, Schedule.

Sub-s (7): added by the County Courts Act 1984, s 148(1), Sch 2, Pt II, para 3(1), (3); sum in square brackets substituted by the High Court and County Courts Jurisdiction Order 1991, SI 1991/724, art 2(4), (8), Schedule, Pt I.

91   Sale of mortgaged property in action for redemption or foreclosure

(1)   Any person entitled to redeem mortgaged property may have a judgment or order for sale instead of for redemption in an action brought by him either for redemption alone, or for sale alone, or for sale or redemption in the alternative.

(2)   In any action, whether for foreclosure, or for redemption, or for sale, or for the raising and payment in any manner of mortgage money, the court, on the request of the mortgagee, or of any person interested either in the mortgage money or in the right of redemption, and, notwithstanding that—

  (a)   any other person dissents; or

  (b)   the mortgagee or any person so interested does not appear in the action;

and without allowing any time for redemption or for payment of any mortgage money, may direct a sale of the mortgaged property, on such terms as it thinks fit, including the deposit in court of a reasonable sum fixed by the court to meet the expenses of sale and to secure performance of the terms.

(3)   But, in an action brought by a person interested in the right of redemption and seeking a sale, the court may, in the application of any defendant, direct the plaintiff to give such security for costs as the court thinks fit, and may give the conduct of the sale to any defendant, and may give such directions as it thinks fit respecting the costs of the defendants or any of them.

(4)   In any case within this section the court may, if it thinks fit, direct a sale without previously determining the priorities of incumbrancers.

(5)   This section applies to actions brought either before or after the commencement of this Act.

(6)   In this section "mortgaged property" includes the estate or interest which a mortgagee would have had power to convey if the statutory power of sale were applicable.

(7)   For the purposes of this section the court may, in favour of a purchaser, make a vesting order conveying the mortgaged property, or appoint a person to do so, subject or not to any incumbrance, as the court may think fit; or, in the case of an equitable mortgage, may create and vest a mortgage term in the mortgagee to enable him to carry out the sale as if the mortgage had been made by deed by way of legal mortgage.

[(8)   The county court has jurisdiction under this section where the amount owing in respect of the mortgage or charge at the commencement of the proceedings does not exceed [£30,000].]

NOTES

Sub-s (8): added by the County Courts Act 1984, s 148(1), Sch 2, Pt II, para 3(1), (3); sum in square brackets substituted by the High Court and County Courts Jurisdiction Order 1991, SI 1991/724, art 2(4), (8), Schedule, Pt I.

93 Restriction on consolidation of mortgages

(1) A mortgagor seeking to redeem any one mortgage is entitled to do so without paying any money due under any separate mortgage made by him, or by any person through whom he claims, solely on property other than that comprised in the mortgage which he seeks to redeem.

This subsection applies only if and as far as a contrary intention is not expressed in the mortgage deeds or one of them.

(2) This section does not apply where all the mortgages were made before the first day of January, eighteen hundred and eighty-two.

(3) Save as aforesaid, nothing in this Act, in reference to mortgages, affects any right of consolidation or renders inoperative a stipulation in relation to any mortgage made before or after the commencement of this Act reserving a right to consolidate.

[172]

94 Tacking and further advances

(1) After the commencement of this Act, a prior mortgagee shall have a right to make further advances to rank in priority to subsequent mortgages (whether legal or equitable)—

    (a) if an arrangement has been made to that effect with the subsequent mortgagees; or

    (b) if he had no notice of such subsequent mortgages at the time when the further advance was made by him; or

    (c) whether or not he had such notice as aforesaid, where the mortgage imposes an obligation on him to make such further advances.

This subsection applies whether or not the prior mortgage was made expressly for securing further advances.

(2) In relation to the making of further advances after the commencement of this Act a mortgagee shall not be deemed to have notice of a mortgage merely by reason that it was registered as a land charge . . . if it was not so registered at the [time when the original mortgage was created] or when the last search (if any) by or on behalf of the mortgagee was made, whichever last happened.

This subsection only applies where the prior mortgage was made expressly for securing a current account or other further advances.

(3) Save in regard to the making of further advances as aforesaid, the right to tack is hereby abolished:

Provided that nothing in this Act shall affect any priority acquired before the commencement of this Act by tacking, or in respect of further advances made without notice of a subsequent incumbrance or by arrangement with the subsequent incumbrancer.

(4) This section applies to mortgages of land made before or after the commencement of this Act, but not to charges registered under the Land Registration Act 1925, or any enactment replaced by that Act.

[173]

NOTES

Sub-s (2): words omitted spent for certain purposes, repealed for remaining purposes by the Law of Property Act 1969, s 16, Sch 2, Pt I; words in square brackets substituted by the Law of Property (Amendment) Act 1926, s 7, Schedule.

95 Obligation to transfer instead of reconveying, and as to right to take possession

(1) Where a mortgagor is entitled to redeem, then subject to compliance with the terms on compliance with which he would be entitled to require a reconveyance or surrender, he shall be entitled to require the mortgagee, instead of re-conveying or surrendering, to assign the mortgage debt and convey the mortgaged property to any third person, as the mortgagor directs; and the mortgagee shall be bound to assign and convey accordingly.

(2) The rights conferred by this section belong to and are capable of being enforced by each incumbrancer, or by the mortgagor, notwithstanding any intermediate incumbrance; but a requisition of an incumbrancer prevails over a requisition of the mortgagor, and, as between incumbrancers, a requisition of a prior incumbrancer prevails over a requisition of a subsequent incumbrancer.

(3) The foregoing provisions of this section do not apply in the case of a mortgagee being or having been in possession.

(4) Nothing in this Act affects prejudicially the right of a mortgagee of land whether or not his charge is secured by a legal term of years absolute to take possession of the land, but the taking of possession by the mortgagee does not convert any legal estate of the mortgagor into an equitable interest.

(5) This section applies to mortgages made either before or after the commencement of this Act, and takes effect notwithstanding any stipulation to the contrary.

[174]

97 Priorities as between puisne mortgages

Every mortgage affecting a legal estate in land made after the commencement of this Act, whether legal or equitable (not being a mortgage protected by the deposit of documents relating to the legal estate affected) shall rank according to its date of registration as a land charge pursuant to the Land Charges Act 1925.

This section does not apply [to mortgages or charges to which the Land Charges Act 1972 does not apply by virtue of section 14(3) of that Act (which excludes certain land charges created by instruments necessitating registration under the Land Registration Act 1925), or] to mortgages or charges of registered land . . .

[175]

NOTES
Words in square brackets substituted by the Land Charges Act 1972, s 18(1), Sch 3, para 1; words omitted spent for certain purposes, repealed for remaining purposes by the Law of Property Act 1969, s 17, Sch 2, Pt II.

Land Charges Act 1925: see now the Land Charges Act 1972.

98 Actions for possession by mortgagors

(1) A mortgagor for the time being entitled to the possession or receipt of the rents and profits of any land, as to which the mortgagee has not given notice of his intention to take possession or to enter into the receipt of the rents and profits thereof, may sue for such possession, or for the recovery of such rents or profits, or to prevent or recover damages in respect of any trespass or other wrong relative thereto, in his own name only, unless the cause of action arises upon a lease or other contract made by him jointly with any other person.

(2) This section does not prejudice the power of a mortgagor independently of this section to take proceedings in his own name only, either in right of any legal estate vested in him or otherwise.

(3) This section applies whether the mortgage was made before or after the commencement of this Act.

99 Leasing powers of mortgagor and mortgagee in possession

(1) A mortgagor of land while in possession shall, as against every incumbrancer, have power to make from time to time any such lease of the mortgaged land, or any part thereof, as is by this section authorised.

(2) A mortgagee of land while in possession shall, as against all prior incumbrancers, if any, and as against the mortgagor, have power to make from time to time any such lease as aforesaid.

(3) The leases which this section authorises are—
   (i) agricultural or occupation leases for any term not exceeding twenty-one years, or, in the case of a mortgage made after the commencement of this Act, fifty years; and
   (ii) building leases for any term not exceeding ninety-nine years, or, in the case of a mortgage made after the commencement of this Act, nine hundred and ninety-nine years.

(4) Every person making a lease under this section may execute and do all assurances and things necessary or proper in that behalf.

(5) Every lease shall be made to take effect in possession not later than twelve months after its date.

(6) Every such lease shall reserve the best rent that can reasonably be obtained, regard being had to the circumstances of the case, but without any fine being taken.

(7) Every such lease shall contain a covenant by the lessee for payment of the rent, and a condition of re-entry on the rent not being paid within a time therein specified not exceeding thirty days.

(8) A counterpart of every such lease shall be executed by the lessee and delivered to the lessor, of which execution and delivery the execution of the lease by the lessor shall, in favour of the lessee and all persons deriving title under him, be sufficient evidence.

(9) Every such building lease shall be made in consideration of the lessee, or some person by whose direction the lease is granted, having erected, or agreeing to erect within not more than five years from the date of the lease, buildings, new or additional, or having improved or repaired buildings, or agreeing to improve or repair buildings within that time, or having executed, or agreeing to execute within that time, on the land leased, an improvement for or in connexion with building purposes.

(10) In any such building lease a peppercorn rent, or a nominal or other rent less than the rent ultimately payable, may be made payable for the first five years, or any less part of the term.

(11) In case of a lease by the mortgagor, he shall, within one month after making the lease, deliver to the mortgagee, or, where there are more than one, to the mortgagee first in priority, a counterpart of the lease duly executed by the lessee, but the lessee shall not be concerned to see that this provision is complied with.

(12) A contract to make or accept a lease under this section may be enforced by or against every person on whom the lease if granted would be binding.

(13) [Subject to subsection (13A) below,] this section applies only if and as far as a contrary intention is not expressed by the mortgagor and mortgagee in the mortgage deed, or otherwise in writing, and has effect subject to the terms of the mortgage deed or of any such writing and to the provisions therein contained.

[(13A)   Subsection (13) of this section—
   (a)   shall not enable the application of any provision of this section to be excluded or restricted in relation to any mortgage of agricultural land made after 1st March 1948 but before 1st September 1995, and
   (b)   shall not enable the power to grant a lease of an agricultural holding to which, by virtue of section 4 of the Agricultural Tenancies Act 1995, the Agricultural Holdings Act 1986 will apply, to be excluded or restricted in relation to any mortgage of agricultural land made on or after 1st September 1995.

(13B)   In subsection (13A) of this section—
   "agricultural holding" has the same meaning as in the Agricultural Holdings Act 1986; and
   "agricultural land" has the same meaning as in the Agriculture Act 1947.]

(14) The mortgagor and mortgagee may, by agreement in writing, whether or not contained in the mortgage deed, reserve to or confer on the mortgagor or the mortgagee, or both, any further or other powers of leasing or having reference to leasing; and any further or other powers so reserved or conferred shall be exercisable, as far as may be, as if they were conferred by this Act, and with all the like incidents, effects, and consequences:

   Provided that the powers so reserved or conferred shall not prejudicially affect the rights of any mortgagee interested under any other mortgage subsisting at the date of the agreement, unless that mortgagee joins in or adopts the agreement.

(15)   Nothing in this Act shall be construed to enable a mortgagor or mortgagee to make a lease for any longer term or on any other conditions than such as could have been granted or imposed by the mortgagor, with the concurrence of all the incumbrancers, if this Act and the enactments replaced by this section had not been passed:

   Provided that, in the case of a mortgage of leasehold land, a lease granted under this section shall reserve a reversion of not less than one day.

(16) Subject as aforesaid, this section applies to any mortgage made after the thirty-first day of December, eighteen hundred and eighty-one, but the provisions thereof, or any of them, may, by agreement in writing made after that date between mortgagor and mortgagee, be applied to a mortgage made before that date, so nevertheless that any such agreement shall not prejudicially affect any right or interest of any mortgagee not joining in or adopting the agreement.

(17) The provisions of this section referring to a lease shall be construed to extend and apply, as far as circumstances admit, to any letting, and to an agreement, whether in writing or not, for leasing or letting.

(18) For the purposes of this section "mortgagor" does not include an incumbrancer deriving title under the original mortgagor.

(19) The powers of leasing conferred by this section shall, after a receiver of the income of the mortgaged property or any part thereof has been appointed by a

mortgagee under his statutory power, and so long as the receiver acts, be exercisable by such mortgagee instead of by the mortgagor, as respects any land affected by the receivership, in like manner as if such mortgagee were in possession of the land, and the mortgagee may, by writing, delegate any of such powers to the receiver.

[177]

NOTES

Commencement: 1 January 1926 (sub-ss (1)–(13), (14)–(19)); 1 September 1995 (sub-ss (13A), (13B)).

Sub-s (13): words in square brackets inserted by the Agricultural Tenancies Act 1995, s 31(1), (2).

Sub-ss (13A), (13B): inserted by the Agricultural Tenancies Act 1995, s 31(1), (3).

100   Powers of mortgagor and mortgagee in possession to accept surrenders of leases

(1)   For the purpose only of enabling a lease authorised under the last preceding section, or under any agreement made pursuant to that section, or by the mortgage deed (in this section referred to as an authorised lease) to be granted, a mortgagor of land while in possession shall, as against every incumbrancer, have, by virtue of this Act, power to accept from time to time a surrender of any lease of the mortgaged land or any part thereof comprised in the lease, with or without an exception of or in respect of all or any of the mines and minerals therein, and, on a surrender of the lease so far as it comprises part only of the land or mines and minerals leased, the rent may be apportioned.

(2)   For the same purpose, a mortgagee of land while in possession shall, as against all prior or other incumbrancers, if any, and as against the mortgagor, have, by virtue of this Act, power to accept from time to time any such surrender as aforesaid.

(3)   On a surrender of part only of the land or mines and minerals leased, the original lease may be varied, provided that the lease when varied would have been valid as an authorised lease if granted by the person accepting the surrender; and, on a surrender and the making of a new or other lease, whether for the same or for any extended or other term, and whether subject or not to the same or to any other covenants, provisions, or conditions, the value of the lessee's interest in the lease surrendered may, subject to the provisions of this section, be taken into account in the determination of the amount of the rent to be reserved, and of the nature of the covenants, provisions, and conditions to be inserted in the new or other lease.

(4)   Where any consideration for the surrender, other than an agreement to accept an authorised lease, is given by or on behalf of the lessee to or on behalf of the person accepting the surrender, nothing in this section authorises a surrender to a mortgagor without the consent of the incumbrancers, or authorises a surrender to a second or subsequent incumbrancer without the consent of every prior incumbrancer.

(5)   No surrender shall, by virtue of this section, be rendered valid unless:—

    (a) An authorised lease is granted of the whole of the land or mines and minerals comprised in the surrender to take effect in possession immediately or within one month after the date of the surrender; and

    (b) The term certain or other interest granted by the new lease is not less in duration than the unexpired term or interest which would have been subsisting under the original lease if that lease had not been surrendered; and

    (c) Where the whole of the land mines and minerals originally leased has been surrendered, the rent reserved by the new lease is not less than the rent which would have been payable under the original lease if it had not been surrendered; or where part only of the land or mines and minerals has been surrendered, the aggregate rents respectively remaining payable or reserved under the original lease and new lease are not less than the rent which would have been payable under the original lease if no partial surrender had been accepted.

(6) A contract to make or accept a surrender under this section may be enforced by or against every person on whom the surrender, if completed, would be binding.

(7) This section applies only if and as far as a contrary intention is not expressed by the mortgagor and mortgagee in the mortgage deed, or otherwise in writing, and shall have effect subject to the terms of the mortgage deed or of any such writing and to the provisions therein contained.

(8) This section applies to a mortgage made after the thirty-first day of December, nineteen hundred and eleven, but the provisions of this section, or any of them, may, by agreement in writing made after that date, between mortgagor and mortgagee, be applied to a mortgage made before that date, so nevertheless that any such agreement shall not prejudicially affect any right or interest of any mortgagee not joining in or adopting the agreement.

(9) The provisions of this section referring to a lease shall be construed to extend and apply, as far as circumstances admit, to any letting, and to an agreement, whether in writing or not, for leasing or letting.

(10) The mortgagor and mortgagee may, by agreement in writing, whether or not contained in the mortgage deed, reserve or confer on the mortgagor or mortgagee, or both, any further or other powers relating to the surrender of leases; and any further or other powers so conferred or reserved shall be exercisable, as far as may be, as if they were conferred by this Act, and with all the like incidents, effects and consequences:

Provided that the powers so reserved or conferred shall not prejudicially affect the rights of any mortgagee interested under any other mortgage subsisting at the date of the agreement, unless that mortgagee joins in or adopts the agreement.

(11) Nothing in this section operates to enable a mortgagor or mortgagee to accept a surrender which could not have been accepted by the mortgagor with the concurrence of all the incumbrancers if this Act and the enactments replaced by this section had not been passed.

(12) For the purposes of this section "mortgagor" does not include an incumbrancer deriving title under the original mortgagor.

(13) The powers of accepting surrenders conferred by this section shall, after a receiver of the income of the mortgaged property or any part thereof has been appointed by the mortgagee, under the statutory power, and so long as the receiver acts, be exercisable by such mortgagee instead of by the mortgagor, as respects any land affected by the receivership, in like manner as if such mortgagee were in possession of the land; and the mortgagee may, by writing, delegate any of such powers to the receiver.

[178]

101 Powers incident to estate or interest of mortgage

(1) A mortgagee, where the mortgage is made by deed, shall, by virtue of this Act, have the following powers, to the like extent as if they had been in terms conferred by the mortgage deed, but not further (namely):—

    (i) A power, when the mortgage money has become due, to sell, or to concur with any other person in selling, the mortgaged property, or any part thereof, either subject to prior charges or not, and either together or in lots, by public auction or by private contract, subject to such conditions respecting title, or evidence of title, or other matter, as the mortgagee thinks fit, with power to vary any contract for sale, and to buy in at an auction, or to rescind any contract for sale, and to re-sell, without being answerable for any loss occasioned thereby; and

(ii) A power, at any time after the date of the mortgage deed, to insure and keep insured against loss or damage by fire any building, or any effects or property of an insurable nature, whether affixed to the freehold or not, being or forming part of the property which or an estate or interest wherein is mortgaged, and the premiums paid for any such insurance shall be a charge on the mortgaged property or estate or interest, in addition to the mortgage money, and with the same priority, and with interest at the same rate, as the mortgage money; and

(iii) A power, when the mortgage money has become due, to appoint a receiver of the income of the mortgaged property, or any part thereof; or, if the mortgaged property consists of an interest in income, or of a rentcharge or an annual or other periodical sum, a receiver of that property or any part thereof; and

(iv) A power, while the mortgagee is in possession, to cut and sell timber and other trees ripe for cutting, and not planted or left standing for shelter or ornament, or to contract for any such cutting and sale, to be completed within any time not exceeding twelve months from the making of the contract.

(2)   Where the mortgage deed is executed after the thirty-first day of December, nineteen hundred and eleven, the power of sale aforesaid includes the following powers as incident thereto (namely):—

(i) A power to impose or reserve or make binding, as far as the law permits, by covenant, condition, or otherwise, on the unsold part of the mortgaged property or any part thereof, or on the purchaser and any property sold, any restriction or reservation with respect to building on or other user of land, or with respect to mines and minerals, or for the purpose of the more beneficial working thereof, or with respect to any other thing:

(ii) A power to sell the mortgaged property, or any part thereof, or all or any mines and minerals apart from the surface:—

(a) With or without a grant or reservation of rights of way, rights of water, easements, rights, and privileges for or connected with building or other purposes in relation to the property remaining in mortgage or any part thereof, or to any property sold: and

(b) With or without an exception or reservation of all or any of the mines and minerals in or under the mortgaged property, and with or without a grant or reservation of powers of working, wayleaves, or rights of way, rights of water and drainage and other powers, easements, rights, and privileges for or connected with mining purposes in relation to the property remaining unsold or any part thereof, or to any property sold: and

(c) With or without covenants by the purchaser to expend money on the land sold.

(3)   The provisions of this Act relating to the foregoing powers, comprised either in this section, or in any other section regulating the exercise of those powers, may be varied or extended by the mortgage deed, and, as so varied or extended, shall, as far as may be, operate in the like manner and with all the like incidents, effects, and consequences, as if such variations or extensions were contained in this Act.

(4)   This section applies only if and as far as a contrary intention is not expressed in the mortgage deed, and has effect subject to the terms of the mortgage deed and to the provisions therein contained.

(5)   Save as otherwise provided, this section applies where the mortgage deed is executed after the thirty-first day of December, eighteen hundred and eighty-one.

(6)   The power of sale conferred by this section includes such power of selling the estate in fee simple or any leasehold reversion as is conferred by the provisions of this Act relating to the realisation of mortgages.

[179]

102   Provision as to mortgages of undivided shares in land

(1)   A person who was before the commencement of this Act a mortgagee of an undivided share in land shall have the same power to sell his share in the proceeds of sale of the land and in the rents and profits thereof until sale, as, independently of this Act, he would have had in regard to the share in the land; and shall also have a right to require the trustees for sale in whom the land is vested to account to him for the income attributable to that share or to appoint a receiver to receive the same from such trustees corresponding to the right which, independently of this Act, he would have had to take possession or to appoint a receiver of the rents and profits attributable to the same share.

(2)   The powers conferred by this section are exercisable by the persons deriving title under such mortgagee.

[180]

103   Regulation of exercise of power of sale

A mortgagee shall not exercise the power of sale conferred by this Act unless and until—

   (i)   Notice requiring payment of the mortgage money has been served on the mortgagor or one of two or more mortgagors, and default has been made in payment of the mortgage money, or of part thereof, for three months after such service; or

 (ii)   Some interest under the mortgage is in arrear and unpaid for two months after becoming due; or

(iii)   There has been a breach of some provision contained in the mortgage deed or in this Act, or in an enactment replaced by this Act, and on the part of the mortgagor, or of some person concurring in making the mortgage, to be observed or performed, other than and besides a covenant for payment of the mortgage money or interest thereon.

[181]

104   Conveyance on sale

(1)   A mortgagee exercising the power of sale conferred by this Act shall have power, by deed, to convey the property sold, for such estate and interest therein as he is by this Act authorised to sell or convey or may be the subject of the mortgage, freed from all estates, interest, and rights to which the mortgage has priority, but subject to all estates, interests, and rights which have priority to the mortgage.

(2)   Where a conveyance is made in exercise of the power of sale conferred by this Act, or any enactment replaced by this Act, the title of the purchaser shall not be impeachable on the ground—

(a)   that no case had arisen to authorise the sale; or
(b)   that due notice was not given; or
(c)   where the mortgage is made after the commencement of this Act, that leave of the court, when so required, was not obtained; or
(d)   whether the mortgage was made before or after such commencement, that the power was otherwise improperly or irregularly exercised;

and a purchaser is not, either before or on conveyance, concerned to see or inquire whether a case has arisen to authorise the sale, or due notice has been given, or the power is otherwise properly and regularly exercised; but any person damnified by an unauthorised, or improper, or irregular exercise of the power shall have his remedy in damages against the person exercising the power.

(3)   A conveyance on sale by a mortgagee, made after the commencement of this Act, shall be deemed to have been made in exercise of the power of sale conferred by this Act unless a contrary intention appears.

[182]

105   Application of proceeds of sale

The money which is received by the mortgagee, arising from the sale, after discharge of prior incumbrances to which the sale is not made subject, if any, or after payment into court under this Act of a sum to meet any prior incumbrance, shall be held by him in trust to be applied by him, first, in payment of all costs, charges, and expenses properly incurred by him as incident to the sale or any attempted sale, or otherwise; and secondly, in discharge of the mortgage money, interest, and costs, and other money, if any, due under the mortgage; and the residue of the money so received shall be paid to the person entitled to the mortgaged property, or authorised to give receipts for the proceeds of the sale thereof.

[183]

106   Provisions as to exercise of power of sale

(1)   The power of sale conferred by this Act may be exercised by any person for the time being entitled to receive and give a discharge for the mortgage money.

(2)   The power of sale conferred by this Act does not affect the right of foreclosure.

(3)   The mortgagee shall not be answerable for any involuntary loss happening in or about the exercise or execution of the power of sale conferred by this Act, or of any trust connected therewith, or, where the mortgage is executed after the thirty-first day of December, nineteen hundred and eleven, of any power or provision contained in the mortgage deed.

(4)   At any time after the power of sale conferred by this Act has become exercisable, the person entitled to exercise the power may demand and recover from any person, other than a person having in the mortgaged property an estate, interest, or right in priority to the mortgage, all the deeds and documents relating to the property, or to the title thereto, which a purchaser under the power of sale would be entitled to demand and recover from him.

[184]

108   Amount and application of insurance money

(1)   The amount of an insurance effected by a mortgagee against loss or damage by fire under the power in that behalf conferred by this Act shall not exceed the amount specified in the mortgage deed, or, if no amount is therein specified, two third parts of the amount that would be required, in case of total destruction, to restore the property insured.

(2)   An insurance shall not, under the power conferred by this Act, be effected by a mortgagee in any of the following cases (namely):—

(i)   Where there is a declaration in the mortgage deed that no insurance is required:

(ii)   Where an insurance is kept up by or on behalf of the mortgagor in accordance with the mortgage deed:

(iii)   Where the mortgage deed contains no stipulation respecting insurance, and an insurance is kept up by or on behalf of the mortgagor with the consent of the mortgagee to the amount to which the mortgagee is by this Act authorised to insure.

(3)   All money received on an insurance of mortgaged property against loss or damage by fire or otherwise effected under this Act, or any enactment replaced by this Act, or on an insurance for the maintenance of which the mortgagor is liable under the mortgage deed, shall, if the mortgagee so requires, be applied by the mortgagor in making good the loss or damage in respect of which the money is received.

(4)   Without prejudice to any obligation to the contrary imposed by law, or by special contract, a mortgagee may require that all money received on an insurance of mortgaged property against loss or damage by fire or otherwise effected under this Act, or any enactment replaced by this Act, or on an insurance for the maintenance of which the mortgagor is liable under the mortgage deed, be applied in or towards the discharge of the mortgage money.

[185]

109   Appointment, powers, remuneration and duties of receiver

(1)   A mortgagee entitled to appoint a receiver under the power in that behalf conferred by this Act shall not appoint a receiver until he has become entitled to exercise the power of sale conferred by this Act, but may then, by writing under his hand, appoint such person as he thinks fit to be receiver.

(2)   A receiver appointed under the powers conferred by this Act, or any enactment replaced by this Act, shall be deemed to be the agent of the mortgagor; and the mortgagor shall be solely responsible for the receiver's acts or defaults unless the mortgage deed otherwise provides.

(3)   The receiver shall have power to demand and recover all the income of which he is appointed receiver, by action, distress, or otherwise, in the name either of the mortgagor or of the mortgagee, to the full extent of the estate or interest which the mortgagor could dispose of, and to give effectual receipts accordingly for the same, and to exercise any powers which may have been delegated to him by the mortgagee pursuant to this Act.

(4)   A person paying money to the receiver shall not be concerned to inquire whether any case has happened to authorise the receiver to act.

(5)   The receiver may be removed, and a new receiver may be appointed, from time to time by the mortgagee by writing under his hand.

(6)   The receiver shall be entitled to retain out of any money received by him, for his remuneration, and in satisfaction of all costs, charges, and expenses incurred by him as receiver, a commission at such rate, not exceeding five per centum on the gross amount of all money received, as is specified in his appointment, and if no rate is so specified, then at the rate of five per centum on that gross amount, or at such other rate as the court thinks fit to allow, on application made by him for that purpose.

(7)   The receiver shall, if so directed in writing by the mortgagee, insure to the extent, if any, to which the mortgagee might have insured and keep insured against loss or damage by fire, out of the money received by him, any building, effects, or property comprised in the mortgage, whether affixed to the freehold or not, being of an insurable nature.

(8)   Subject to the provisions of this Act as to the application of insurance money, the receiver shall apply all money received by him as follows, namely:—

    (i)   In discharge of all rents, taxes, rates, and outgoings whatever affecting the mortgaged property; and

    (ii) In keeping down all annual sums or other payments, and the interest on all principal sums, having priority to the mortgage in right whereof he is receiver; and

    (iii) In payment of his commission, and of the premiums on fire, life, or other insurances, if any, properly payable under the mortgage deed or under this Act, and the cost of executing necessary or proper repairs directed in writing by the mortgagee; and

    (iv) In payment of the interest accruing due in respect of any principal money due under the mortgage; and

    (v) In or towards discharge of the principal money if so directed in writing by the mortgagee;

and shall pay the residue, if any, of the money received by him to the person who, but for the possession of the receiver, would have been entitled to receive the income of which he is appointed receiver, or who is otherwise entitled to the mortgaged property.

[186]

115   Reconveyances of mortgages by endorsed receipts

(1)   A receipt endorsed on, written at the foot of, or annexed to, a mortgage for all money thereby secured, which states the name of the person who pays the money and is executed by the chargee by way of legal mortgage or the person in whom the mortgaged property is vested and who is legally entitled to give a receipt for the mortgage money shall operate, without any reconveyance, surrender, or release—

    (a) Where a mortgage takes effect by demise or subdemise, as a surrender of the term, so as to determine the term or merge the same in the reversion immediately expectant thereon;

    (b) Where the mortgage does not take effect by demise or subdemise, as a reconveyance thereof to the extent of the interest which is the subject matter of the mortgage, to the person who immediately before the execution of the receipt was entitled to the equity of redemption;

and in either case, as a discharge of the mortgaged property from all principal money and interest secured by, and from all claims under the mortgage, but without prejudice to any term or other interest which is paramount to the estate or interest of the mortgagee or other person in whom the mortgaged property was vested.

(2)   Provided that, whereby the receipt the money appears to have been paid by a person who is not entitled to the immediate equity of redemption, the receipt shall operate as if the benefit of the mortgage had by deed been transferred to him; unless—

    (a) it is otherwise expressly provided; or

    (b) the mortgage is paid off out of capital money, or other money in the hands of a personal representative or trustee properly applicable for the discharge of the mortgage, and it is not expressly provided that the receipt is to operate as a transfer.

(3)   Nothing in this section confers on a mortgagor a right to keep alive a mortgage paid off by him, so as to affect prejudicially any subsequent incumbrancer; and where there is no right to keep the mortgage alive, the receipt does not operate as a transfer.

(4)   This section does not affect the right of any person to require a reassignment, surrender, release, or transfer to be executed in lieu of a receipt.

(5)   A receipt may be given in the form contained in the Third Schedule to this Act, with such variations and additions, if any, as may be deemed expedient . . .

(6)   In a receipt given under this section the same covenants shall be implied as if the person who executes the receipt had by deed been expressed to convey the property as mortgagee, subject to any interest which is paramount to the mortgage.

(7)   Where the mortgage consists of a mortgage and a further charge or of more than one deed, it shall be sufficient for the purposes of this section, if the receipt refers either to all the deeds whereby the mortgage money is secured or to the aggregate amount of the mortgage money thereby secured and for the time being owing, and is endorsed on, written at the foot of, or annexed to, one of the mortgage deeds.

(8)   This section applies to the discharge of a charge by way of legal mortgage, and to the discharge of a mortgage, whether made by way of statutory mortgage or not, executed before or after the commencement of this Act, but only as respects discharges effected after such commencement.

(9)   The provisions of this section relating to the operation of a receipt shall (in substitution for the like statutory provisions relating to receipts given by or on behalf of a building . . . society) apply to the discharge of a mortgage made to any such society, provided that the receipt is executed in the manner required by the statute relating to the society . . .

(10) This section does not apply to the discharge of a charge or incumbrance registered under the Land Registration Act 1925.

(11) In this section "mortgaged property" means the property remaining subject to the mortgage at the date of the receipt.

[187]

NOTES

    Sub-s (5): words omitted repealed by the Finance Act 1971, s 69(7), Sch 14, Pt VI.
    Sub-s (9): first words omitted repealed by the Friendly Societies Act 1971, s 14(2), Sch 3 and by the Industrial and Provident Societies Act 1965, s 77(1), Sch 5; second words omitted repealed by the Finance Act 1971, s 69(7), Sch 14, Pt VI.

---

116   Cesser of mortgage terms

Without prejudice to the right of a tenant for life or other person having only a limited interest in the equity of redemption to require a mortgage to be kept alive by transfer or otherwise, a mortgage term shall, when the money secured by the mortgage has been discharged, become a satisfied term and shall cease.

[188]

PART IV
EQUITABLE INTERESTS AND THINGS IN ACTION

130   Creation of entailed interests in real and personal property

(1)   An interest in tail or in tail male or in tail female or in tail special (in this Act referred to as "an entailed interest") may be created by way of trust in any property,

real or personal, but only by the like expressions as those by which before the commencement of this Act a similar estate tail could have been created by deed (not being an executory instrument) in freehold land, and with the like results, including the right to bar the entail either absolutely or so as to create an interest equivalent to a base fee, and accordingly all statutory provisions relating to estates tail in real property shall apply to entailed interests in personal property.

Personal estate so entailed (not being chattels settled as heirlooms) may be invested, applied, and otherwise dealt with as if the same were capital money or securities representing capital money arising under the Settled Land Act 1925, from land settled on the like trusts.

(2)   Expressions contained in an instrument coming into operation after the commencement of this Act, which, in a will, or executory instrument coming into operation before such commencement, would have created an entailed interest in freehold land, but would not have been effectual for that purpose in a deed not being an executory instrument, shall (save as provided by the next succeeding section) operate in equity, in regard to property real or personal, to create absolute, fee simple or other interests corresponding to those which, if the property affected had been personal estate, would have been created therein by similar expressions before the commencement of this Act.

(3)   Where personal estate (including the proceeds of sale of land directed to be sold and chattels directed to be held as heirlooms) is, after the commencement of this Act, directed to be enjoyed or held with, or upon trusts corresponding to trusts affecting, land in which, either before or after the commencement of this Act an entailed interest has been created, and is subsisting, such direction shall be deemed sufficient to create a corresponding entailed interest in such personal estate.

(4)   In default of and subject to the execution of a disentailing assurance or the exercise of the testamentary power conferred by this Act, an entailed interest (to the extent of the property affected) shall devolve as an equitable interest, from time to time, upon the persons who would have been successively entitled thereto as the heirs of the body (either generally or of a particular class) of the tenant in tail or other person, or as tenant by the curtesy, if the entailed interest had, before the commencement of this Act, been limited in respect of freehold land governed by the general law in force immediately before such commencement, and such law had remained unaffected.

(5)   Where personal chattels are settled without reference to settled land on trusts creating entailed interests therein, the trustees, with the consent of the usufructuary for the time being if of full age, may sell the chattels or any of them, and the net proceeds of any such sale shall be held in trust for and shall go to the same persons successively, in the same manner and for the same interests, as the chattels sold would have been held and gone if they had not been sold, and the income of investments representing such proceeds of sale shall be applied accordingly.

(6)   An entailed interest shall only be capable of being created by a settlement of real or personal property or the proceeds of sale thereof (including the will of a person dying after the commencement of this Act), or by an agreement for a settlement in which the trusts to affect property are sufficiently declared.

(7)   In this Act where the context so admits "entailed interest" includes an estate tail (now made to take effect as an equitable interest) created before the commencement of this Act.

136   Legal assignments of things in action

(1)   Any absolute assignment by writing under the hand of the assignor (not purporting to be by way of charge only) of any debt or other legal thing in action, of which express notice in writing has been given to the debtor, trustee or other person from whom the assignor would have been entitled to claim such debt or thing in action, is effectual in law (subject to equities having priority over the right of the assignee) to pass and transfer from the date of such notice—

(a)   the legal right to such debt or thing in action;

(b)   all legal and other remedies for the same; and

(c)   the power to give a good discharge for the same without the concurrence of the assignor:

Provided that, if the debtor, trustee or other person liable in respect of such debt or thing in action has notice—

(a)   that the assignment is disputed by the assignor or any person claiming under him; or

(b)   of any other opposing or conflicting claims to such debt or thing in action;

he may, if he thinks fit, either call upon the persons making claim thereto to interplead concerning the same, or pay the debt or other thing in action into court under the provisions of the Trustee Act 1925.

(2)   This section does not affect the provisions of the Policies of Assurance Act 1867.

[(3)   The county court has jurisdiction (including power to receive payment of money or securities into court) under the proviso to subsection (1) of this section where the amount or value of the debt or thing in action does not exceed [£30,000].]

[190]

NOTES

   Sub-s (3): added by the County Courts Act 1984, s 148(1), Sch 2, Pt II, para 4; sum in square brackets substituted by the High Court and County Courts Jurisdiction Order 1991, SI 1991/724, art 2(5), (8), Schedule, Pt I.

PART V
LEASES AND TENANCIES

140   Apportionment of conditions on severance

(1)   Notwithstanding the severance by conveyance, surrender, or otherwise of the reversionary estate in any land comprised in a lease, and notwithstanding the avoidance or cesser in any other manner of the term granted by a lease as to part only of the land comprised therein, every condition or right of re-entry, and every other condition contained in the lease, shall be apportioned, and shall remain annexed to the severed parts of the reversionary estate as severed, and shall be in force with respect to the term whereon each severed part is reversionary, or the term in the part of the land as to which the term has not been surrendered, or has not been avoided or has not otherwise ceased, in like manner as if the land comprised in each severed part, or the land as to which the term remains subsisting, as the case may be, had alone originally been comprised in the lease.

(2)   In this section "right of re-entry" includes a right to determine the lease by notice to quit or otherwise; but where the notice is served by a person entitled to a severed part of the reversion so that it extends to part only of the land demised, the

lessee may within one month determine the lease in regard to the rest of the land by giving to the owner of the reversionary estate therein a counter notice expiring at the same time as the original notice

$$[. \quad . \quad . \quad . \quad .]$$

(3)   This section applies to leases made before or after the commencement of this Act and whether the severance of the reversionary estate or the partial avoidance or cesser of the term was effected before or after such commencement:

Provided that, where the lease was made before the first day of January eighteen hundred and eighty-two nothing in this section shall affect the operation of a severance of the reversionary estate or partial avoidance or cesser of the term which was effected before the commencement of this Act.

[191]

NOTES

Sub-s (2): proviso omitted added by the Law of Property (Amendment) Act 1926, s 2, repealed by the Agricultural Holdings Act 1948, ss 98, 100(1), Sch 8.

141   Rent and benefit of lessee's covenants to run with the reversion

(1)   Rent reserved by a lease, and the benefit of every covenant or provision therein contained, having reference to the subject-matter thereof, and on the lessee's part to be observed or performed, and every condition of re-entry and other condition therein contained, shall be annexed and incident to and shall go with the reversionary estate in the land, or in any part thereof, immediately expectant on the term granted by the lease, notwithstanding severance of that reversionary estate, and without prejudice to any liability affecting a covenantor or his estate.

(2)   Any such rent, covenant or provision shall be capable of being recovered, received, enforced, and taken advantage of, by the person from time to time entitled, subject to the term, to the income of the whole or any part, as the case may require, of the land leased.

(3)   Where that person becomes entitled by conveyance or otherwise, such rent, covenant or provision may be recovered, received, enforced or taken advantage of by him notwithstanding that he becomes so entitled after the condition of re-entry or forfeiture has become enforceable, but this subsection does not render enforceable any condition of re-entry or other condition waived or released before such person becomes entitled as aforesaid.

(4)   This section applies to leases made before or after the commencement of this Act, but does not affect the operation of—

    (a)   any severance of the reversionary estate; or

    (b)   any acquisition by conveyance or otherwise of the right to receive or enforce any rent covenant or provision;

effected before the commencement of this Act.

[192]

142   Obligation of lessor's covenants to run with reversion

(1)   The obligation under a condition or of a covenant entered into by a lessor with reference to the subject-matter of the lease shall, if and as far as the lessor has power to bind the reversionary estate immediately expectant on the term granted by the lease, be

annexed and incident to and shall go with that reversionary estate, or the several parts thereof, notwithstanding severance of that reversionary estate, and may be taken advantage of and enforced by the person in whom the term is from time to time vested by conveyance, devolution in law, or otherwise; and, if and as far as the lessor has power to bind the person from time to time entitled to that reversionary estate, the obligation aforesaid may be taken advantage of and enforced against any person so entitled.

(2) This section applies to leases made before or after the commencement of this Act, whether the severance of the reversionary estate was effected before or after such commencement:

Provided that, where the lease was made before the first day of January eighteen hundred and eighty-two, nothing in this section shall affect the operation of any severance of the reversionary estate effected before such commencement.

This section takes effect without prejudice to any liability affecting a covenantor or his estate.

[193]

143 Effect of licences granted to lessees

(1) Where a licence is granted to a lessee to do any act, the licence, unless otherwise expressed, extends only—
    (a) to the permission actually given; or
    (b) to the specific breach of any provision or covenant referred to; or
    (c) to any other matter thereby specifically authorised to be done;

and the licence does not prevent any proceeding for any subsequent breach unless otherwise specified in the licence.

(2) Notwithstanding any such licence—
    (a) All rights under covenants and powers of re-entry contained in the lease remain in full force and are available as against any subsequent breach of covenant, condition or other matter not specifically authorised or waived, in the same manner as if no licence had been granted; and
    (b) The condition or right of entry remains in force in all respects as if the licence had not been granted, save in respect of the particular matter authorised to be done.

(3) Where in any lease there is a power or condition of re-entry on the lessee assigning, subletting or doing any other specified act without a licence, and a licence is granted—
    (a) to any one of two or more lessees to do any act, or to deal with his equitable share or interest; or
    (b) to any lessee, or to any one of two or more lessees to assign or underlet part only of the property, or to do any act in respect of part only of the property;

the licence does not operate to extinguish the right of entry in case of any breach of covenant or condition by the co-lessees of the other shares or interests in the property, or by the lessee or lessees of the rest of the property (as the case may be) in respect of such shares or interests or remaining property, but the right of entry remains in force in respect of the shares, interests or property not the subject of the licence.

This subsection does not authorise the grant after the commencement of this Act of a licence to create an undivided share in a legal estate.

(4)   This section applies to licences granted after the thirteenth day of August, eighteen hundred and fifty-nine.

[194]

144   No fine to be exacted for licence to assign

In all leases containing a covenant, condition, or agreement against assigning, underletting, or parting with the possession, or disposing of the land or property leased without licence or consent, such covenant, condition, or agreement shall, unless the lease contains an express provision to the contrary, be deemed to be subject to a proviso to the effect that no fine or sum of money in the nature of a fine shall be payable for or in respect of such licence or consent; but this proviso does not preclude the right to require the payment of a reasonable sum in respect of any legal or other expense incurred in relation to such licence or consent.

[195]

145   Lessee to give notice of ejectment to lessor

Every lessee to whom there is delivered any writ for the recovery of premises demised to or held by him, or to whose knowledge any such writ comes, shall forthwith give notice thereof to his lessor or his bailiff or receiver, and, if he fails so to do, he shall be liable to forfeit to the person of whom he holds the premises an amount equal to the value of three years' improved or rack rent of the premises, to be recovered by action in any court having jurisdiction in respect of claims for such an amount.

[196]

146   Restrictions on and relief against forfeiture of leases and underleases

(1)   A right of re-entry or forfeiture under any proviso or stipulation in a lease for a breach of any covenant or condition in the lease shall not be enforceable, by action or otherwise, unless and until the lessor serves on the lessee a notice—
   (a)   specifying the particular breach complained of; and
   (b)   if the breach is capable of remedy, requiring the lessee to remedy the breach; and
   (c)   in any case, requiring the lessee to make compensation in money for the breach;

and the lessee fails, within a reasonable time thereafter, to remedy the breach, if it is capable of remedy, and to make reasonable compensation in money, to the satisfaction of the lessor, for the breach.

(2)   Where a lessor is proceeding, by action or otherwise, to enforce such a right of re-entry or forfeiture, the lessee may, in the lessor's action, if any, or in any action brought by himself, apply to the court for relief; and the court may grant or refuse relief, as the court, having regard to the proceedings and conduct of the parties under the foregoing provisions of this section, and to all the other circumstances, thinks fit; and in case of relief may grant it on such terms, if any, as to costs, expenses, damages, compensation, penalty, or otherwise, including the granting of an injunction to restrain any like breach in the future, as the court, in the circumstances of each case, thinks fit.

(3)   A lessor shall be entitled to recover as a debt due to him from a lessee, and in addition to damages (if any), all reasonable costs and expenses properly incurred by the lessor in the employment of a solicitor and surveyor or valuer, or otherwise, in reference to any breach giving rise to a right of re-entry in forfeiture which, at the request of the lessee, is waived by the lessor, or from which the lessee is relieved, under the provisions of this Act.

(4)   Where a lessor is proceeding by action or otherwise to enforce a right of re-entry or forfeiture under any covenant, proviso, or stipulation in a lease, or for non-payment of rent, the court may, on application by any person claiming as under-lessee any estate or interest in the property comprised in the lease or any part thereof, either in the lessor's action (if any) or in any action brought by such person for that purpose, make an order vesting, for the whole term of the lease or any less term, the property comprised in the lease or any part thereof in any person entitled as under-lessee to any estate or interest in such property upon such conditions as to execution of any deed or other document, payment of rent, costs, expenses, damages, compensation, giving security, or otherwise, as the court in the circumstances of each case may think fit, but in no case shall any such under-lessee be entitled to require a lease to be granted to him for any longer term than he had under his original sub-lease.

(5)   For the purposes of this section—
  (a) "Lease" includes an original or derivative under-lease; also an agreement for a lease where the lessee has become entitled to have his lease granted; also a grant at a fee farm rent, or securing a rent by condition;
  (b) "Lessee" includes an original or derivative under-lessee, and the persons deriving title under a lessee; also a grantee under any such grant as aforesaid and the persons deriving title under him;
  (c) "Lessor" includes an original or derivative under-lessor, and the persons deriving title under a lessor; also a person making such grant as aforesaid and the persons deriving title under him;
  (d) "Under-lease" includes an agreement for an underlease where the under-lessee has become entitled to have his underlease granted;
  (e) "Under-lessee" includes any person deriving title under an under-lessee.

(6)   This section applies although the proviso or stipulation under which the right of re-entry or forfeiture accrues is inserted in the lease in pursuance of the directions of any Act of Parliament.

(7)   For the purposes of this section a lease limited to continue as long only as the lessee abstains from committing a breach of covenant shall be and take effect as a lease to continue for any longer term for which it could subsist, but determinable by a proviso for re-entry on such a breach.

(8)   This section does not extend—
  (i)   To a covenant or condition against assigning, underletting, parting with the possession, or disposing of the land leased where the breach occurred before the commencement of this Act; or
  (ii) In the case of a mining lease, to a covenant or condition for allowing the lessor to have access to or inspect books, accounts, records, weighing machines or other things, or to enter or inspect the mine or the workings thereof.

(9)   This section does not apply to a condition for forfeiture on the bankruptcy of the lessee or on taking in execution of the lessee's interest if contained in a lease of—
  (a) Agricultural or pastoral land;
  (b) Mines or minerals;
  (c) A house used or intended to be used as a public-house or beershop;
  (d) A house let as a dwelling-house, with the use of any furniture, books, works of art, or other chattels not being in the nature of fixtures;
  (e) Any property with respect to which the personal qualifications of the tenant are of importance for the preservation of the value or character of the property, or on the ground of neighbourhood to the lessor, or to any person holding under him.

(10)   Where a condition of forfeiture on the bankruptcy of the lessee or on taking in execution of the lessee's interest is contained in any lease, other than a lease of any of the classes mentioned in the last subsection, then—

(a)   if the lessee's interest is sold within one year from the bankruptcy or taking in execution, this section applies to the forfeiture condition aforesaid;

(b)   if the lessee's interest is not sold before the expiration of that year, this section only applies to the forfeiture condition aforesaid during the first year from the date of the bankruptcy or taking in execution.

(11)   This section does not, save as otherwise mentioned, affect the law relating to re-entry or forfeiture or relief in case of non-payment of rent.

(12)   This section has effect notwithstanding any stipulation to the contrary.

[(13)   The county court has jurisdiction under this section . . .]

[197]

NOTES

   Sub-s (13): added by the County Courts Act 1984, s 148(1), Sch 2, Pt II, para 5; words omitted repealed by the High Court and County Courts Jurisdiction Order 1991, SI 1991/724, art 2(1)(a), (8), Schedule, Pt I.

   Modification: any reference to solicitor(s) etc modified to include references to bodies recognised under the Administration of Justice Act 1985, s 9, by the Solicitors' Incorporated Practices Order 1991, SI 1991/2684, arts 4, 5, Sch 1.

147   Relief against notice to effect decorative repairs

(1)   After a notice is served on a lessee relating to the internal decorative repairs to a house or other building, he may apply to the court for relief, and if, having regard to all the circumstances of the case (including in particular the length of the lessee's term or interest remaining unexpired), the court is satisfied that the notice is unreasonable, it may, by order, wholly or partially relieve the lessee from liability for such repairs.

(2)   This section does not apply:—

(i)   where the liability arises under an express covenant or agreement to put the property in a decorative state of repair and the covenant or agreement has never been performed;

(ii)   to any matter necessary or proper—

(a)   for putting or keeping the property in a sanitary condition, or

(b)   for the maintenance or preservation of the structure;

(iii)   to any statutory liability to keep a house in all respects reasonably fit for human habitation;

(iv)   to any covenant or stipulation to yield up the house or other building in a specified state of repair at the end of the term.

(3)   In this section "lease" includes an underlease and an agreement for a lease, and "lessee" has a corresponding meaning and includes any person liable to effect the repairs.

(4)   This section applies whether the notice is served before or after the commencement of this Act, and has effect notwithstanding any stipulation to the contrary.

[(5)   The county court has jurisdiction under this section . . .]

[198]

NOTES

   Sub-s (5): added by the County Courts Act 1984, s 148(1), Sch 2, Pt II, para 6; words omitted repealed by the High Court and County Courts Jurisdiction Order 1991, SI 1991/724, art 2(1)(a), (8), Schedule, Pt I.

148   Waiver of a covenant in a lease

(1)   Where any actual waiver by a lessor or the persons deriving title under him of the benefit of any covenant or condition in any lease is proved to have taken place in any particular instance, such waiver shall not be deemed to extend to any instance, or to any breach of covenant or condition save that to which such waiver specially relates, nor operate as a general waiver of the benefit of any such covenant or condition.

(2)   This section applies unless a contrary intention appears and extends to waivers effected after the twenty-third day of July, eighteen hundred and sixty.

[199]

149   Abolition of interesse termini, and as to reversionary leases and leases for lives

(1)   The doctrine of interesse termini is hereby abolished.

(2)   As from the commencement of this Act all terms of years absolute shall, whether the interest is created before or after such commencement, be capable of taking effect at law or in equity, according to the estate interest or powers of the grantor, from the date fixed for commencement of the term, without actual entry.

(3)   A term, at a rent or granted in consideration of a fine, limited after the commencement of this Act to take effect more than twenty-one years from the date of the instrument purporting to create it, shall be void, and any contract made after such commencement to create such a term shall likewise be void; but this subsection does not apply to any term taking effect in equity under a settlement, or created out of an equitable interest under a settlement, or under an equitable power for mortgage, indemnity or other like purposes.

(4)   Nothing in subsections (1) and (2) of this section prejudicially affects the right of any person to recover any rent or to enforce or take advantage of any covenants or conditions, or, as respects terms or interests created before the commencement of this Act, operates to vary any statutory or other obligations imposed in respect of such terms or interests.

(5)   Nothing in this Act affects the rule of law that a legal term, whether or not being a mortgage term, may be created to take effect in reversion expectant on a longer term, which rule is hereby confirmed.

(6)   Any lease or underlease, at a rent, or in consideration of a fine, for life or lives or for any term of years determinable with life or lives, or on the marriage of the lessee, or any contract therefor, made before or after the commencement of this Act, or created by virtue of Part V of the Law of Property Act 1922, shall take effect as a lease, underlease or contract therefor, for a term of ninety years determinable after the death or marriage (as the case may be) of the original lessee, or of the survivor of the original lessees, by at least one month's notice in writing given to determine the same on one of the quarter days applicable to the tenancy, either by the lessor or the persons deriving title under him, to the person entitled to the leasehold interest, or if no such person is in existence by affixing the same to the premises, or by the lessee or other persons in whom the leasehold interest is vested to the lessor or the persons deriving title under him:

Provided that—
    (a)   this subsection shall not apply to any term taking effect in equity under a settlement or created out of an equitable interest under a settlement for mortgage, indemnity, or other like purposes;

(b) the person in whom the leasehold interest is vested by virtue of Part V of the Law of Property Act 1922 shall, for the purposes of this subsection, be deemed an original lessee;

(c) if the lease, underlease, or contract therefor is made determinable on the dropping of the lives of persons other than or besides the lessees, then the notice shall be capable of being served after the death of any person or of the survivor of any persons (whether or not including the lessees) on the cesser of whose life or lives the lease, underlease, or contract is made determinable, instead of after the death of the original lessee or of the survivor of the original lessees;

(d) if there are no quarter days specially applicable to the tenancy, notice may be given to determine the tenancy on one of the usual quarter days.

[200]

150 Surrender of a lease, without prejudice to underleases with a view to the grant of a new lease

(1) A lease may be surrendered with a view to the acceptance of a new lease in place thereof, without a surrender of any under-lease derived thereout.

(2) A new lease may be granted and accepted, in place of any lease so surrendered, without any such surrender of an under-lease as aforesaid, and the new lease operates as if all under-leases derived out of the surrendered lease had been surrendered before the surrender of that lease was effected.

(3) The lessee under the new lease and any person deriving title under him is entitled to the same rights and remedies in respect of the rent reserved by and the covenants, agreements and conditions contained in any under-lease as if the original lease had not been surrendered but was or remained vested in him.

(4) Each under-lessee and any person deriving title under him is entitled to hold and enjoy the land comprised in his under-lease (subject to the payment of any rent reserved by and to the observance of the covenants agreements and conditions contained in the under-lease) as if the lease out of which the under-lease was derived had not been surrendered.

(5) The lessor granting the new lease and any person deriving title under him is entitled to the same remedies, by distress or entry in and upon the land comprised in any such under-lease for rent reserved by or for breach of any covenant, agreement or condition contained in the new lease (so far only as the rents reserved by or the covenants, agreements or conditions contained in the new lease do not exceed or impose greater burdens than those reserved by or contained in the original lease out of which the under-lease is derived) as he would have had—

(a) If the original lease had remained on foot; or

(b) If a new under-lease derived out of the new lease had been granted to the under-lessee or a person deriving title under him;

as the case may require.

(6) This section does not affect the powers of the court to give relief against forfeiture.

[201]

153 Enlargement of residue of long terms into fee simple estates

(1) Where a residue unexpired of not less than two hundred years of a term, which,

as originally created, was for not less than three hundred years, is subsisting in land, whether being the whole land originally comprised in the term, or part only thereof,—

(a) without any trust or right of redemption affecting the term in favour of the freeholder, or other person entitled in reversion expectant on the term; and

(b) without any rent, or with merely a peppercorn rent or other rent having no money value, incident to the reversion, or having had a rent, not being merely a peppercorn rent or other rent having no money value, originally so incident, which subsequently has been released or has become barred by lapse of time, or has in any other way ceased to be payable;

the term may be enlarged into a fee simple in the manner, and subject to the restrictions in this section provided.

(2) This section applies to and includes every such term as aforesaid whenever created, whether or not having the freehold as the immediate reversion thereon; but does not apply to—

(i) Any term liable to be determined by re-entry for condition broken; or

(ii) Any term created by subdemise out of a superior term, itself incapable of being enlarged into fee simple.

(3) This section extends to mortgage terms, where the right of redemption is barred.

(4) A rent not exceeding the yearly sum of one pound which has not been collected or paid for a continuous period of twenty years or upwards shall, for the purposes of this section, be deemed to have ceased to be payable:

Provided that, of the said period, at least five years must have elapsed after the commencement of this Act.

(5) Where a rent incident to a reversion expectant on a term to which this section applies is deemed to have ceased to be payable for the purposes aforesaid, no claim for such rent or for any arrears thereof shall be capable of being enforced.

(6) Each of the following persons, namely—

(i) Any person beneficially entitled in right of the term, whether subject to any incumbrance or not, to possession of any land comprised in the term, and, in the case of a married woman without the concurrence of her husband, whether or not she is entitled for her separate use or as her separate property, . . . ;

(ii) Any person being in receipt of income as trustee, in right of the term, or having the term vested in him in trust for sale, whether subject to any incumbrance or not;

(iii) Any person in whom, as personal representative of any deceased person, the term is vested, whether subject to any incumbrance or not;

shall, so far as regards the land to which he is entitled, or in which he is interested in right of the term, in any such character as aforesaid, have power by deed to declare to the effect that, from and after the execution of the deed, the term shall be enlarged into a fee simple.

(7) Thereupon, by virtue of the deed and of this Act, the term shall become and be enlarged accordingly, and the person in whom the term was previously vested shall acquire and have in the land a fee simple instead of the term.

(8) The estate in fee simple so acquired by enlargement shall be subject to all the same trusts, powers, executory limitations over, rights, and equities, and to all the same

covenants and provisions relating to user and enjoyment, and to all the same obligations of every kind, as the term would have been subject to if it had not been so enlarged.

(9) But where—

  (a) any land so held for the residue of a term has been settled in trust by reference to other land, being freehold land, so as to go along with that other land, or, in the case of settlements coming into operation before the commencement of this Act, so as to go along with that other land as far as the law permits; and

  (b) at the time of enlargement, the ultimate beneficial interest in the term, whether subject to any subsisting particular estate or not, has not become absolutely and indefeasibly vested in any person, free from charges or powers of charging created by a settlement;

the estate in fee simple acquired as aforesaid shall, without prejudice to any conveyance for value previously made by a person having a contingent or defeasible interest in the term, be liable to be, and shall be, conveyed by means of a subsidiary vesting instrument and settled in like manner as the other land, being freehold land, aforesaid, and until so conveyed and settled shall devolve beneficially as if it had been so conveyed and settled.

(10) The estate in fee simple so acquired shall, whether the term was originally created without impeachment of waste or not, include the fee simple in all mines and minerals which at the time of enlargement have not been severed in right or in fact, or have not been severed or reserved by an inclosure Act or award.

[202]

NOTES

Sub-s (6): words omitted from para (i) repealed by the Married Women (Restraint upon Anticipation) Act 1949, s 1, Sch 2.

Part VII
Perpetuities and Accumulations

Perpetuities

161 Abolition of the double possibility rule

(1) The rule of law prohibiting the limitation, after a life interest to an unborn person, of an interest in land to the unborn child or other issue of an unborn person is hereby abolished, but without prejudice to any other rule relating to perpetuities.

(2) This section only applies to limitations or trusts created by an instrument coming into operation after the commencement of this Act.

[203]

162 Restrictions on the perpetuity rule

(1) For removing doubts, it is hereby declared that the rule of law relating to perpetuities does not apply and shall be deemed never to have applied—

  (a) To any power to distrain on or to take possession of land or the income thereof given by way of indemnity against a rent, whether charged upon or payable in respect of any part of that land or not; or

  (b) To any rentcharge created only as an indemnity against another rentcharge, although the indemnity rentcharge may only arise or become payable on breach of a condition or stipulation; or

(c) To any power, whether exercisable on breach of a condition or stipulation or not, to retain or withhold payment of any instalment of a rentcharge as an indemnity against another rentcharge; or

(d) To any grant, exception, or reservation of any right of entry on, or user of, the surface of land or of any easements, rights, or privileges over or under land for the purpose of—

    (i) winning, working, inspecting, measuring, converting, manufacturing, carrying away, and disposing of mines and minerals;

    (ii) inspecting, grubbing up, felling and carrying away timber and other trees, and the tops and lops thereof;

    (iii) executing repairs, alterations, or additions to any adjoining land, or the buildings and erections thereon;

    (iv) constructing, laying down, altering, repairing, renewing, cleansing, and maintaining sewers, water-courses, cesspools, gutters, drains, water-pipes, gas-pipes, electric wires or cables or other like works.

(2) This section applies to instruments coming into operation before or after the commencement of this Act.

[204]

Accumulations

164   General restrictions on accumulation of income

(1) No person may by any instrument or otherwise settle or dispose of any property in such manner that the income thereof shall, save as hereinafter mentioned, be wholly or partially accumulated for any longer period than one of the following, namely:—

    (a) the life of the grantor or settlor; or

    (b) a term of twenty-one years from the death of the grantor, settlor or testator; or

    (c) the duration of the minority or respective minorities of any person or persons living or en ventre sa mere at the death of the grantor, settlor or testator; or

    (d) the duration of the minority or respective minorities only of any person or persons who under the limitations of the instrument directing the accumulations would, for the time being, if of full age, be entitled to the income directed to be accumulated.

In every case where any accumulation is directed otherwise than as aforesaid, the direction shall (save as hereinafter mentioned) be void; and the income of the property directed to be accumulated shall, so long as the same is directed to be accumulated contrary to this section, go to and be received by the person or persons who would have been entitled thereto if such accumulation had not been directed.

(2) This section does not extend to any provision—

    (i) for payment of the debts of any grantor, settlor, testator or other person;

    (ii) for raising portions for—

        (a) any child, children or remoter issue of any grantor, settlor or testator; or

        (b) any child, children or remoter issue of a person taking any interest under any settlement or other disposition directing the accumulations or to whom any interest is thereby limited;

    (iii) respecting the accumulation of the produce of timber or wood;

and accordingly such provisions may be made as if no statutory restrictions on accumulation of income had been imposed.

(3)   The restrictions imposed by this section apply to instruments made on or after the twenty-eighth day of July, eighteen hundred, but in the case of wills only where the testator was living and of testamentary capacity after the end of one year from that date.

[205]

165   Qualification of restrictions on accumulation

Where accumulations of surplus income are made during a minority under any statutory power or under the general law, the period for which such accumulations are made is not (whether the trust was created or the accumulations were made before or after the commencement of this Act) to be taken into account in determining the periods for which accumulations are permitted to be made by the last preceding section, and accordingly an express trust for accumulation for any other permitted period shall not be deemed to have been invalidated or become invalid, by reason of accumulations also having been made as aforesaid during such minority.

[206]

166   Restriction on accumulation for the purchase of land

(1)   No person may settle or dispose of any property in such manner that the income thereof shall be wholly or partially accumulated for the purchase of land only, for any longer period than the duration of the minority or respective minorities of any person or persons who, under the limitations of the instrument directing the accumulation, would for the time being, if of full age, be entitled to the income so directed to be accumulated.

(2)   This section does not, nor do the enactments which it replaces, apply to accumulations to be held as capital money for the purposes of the Settled Land Act 1925 or the enactments replaced by that Act, whether or not the accumulations are primarily liable to be laid out in the purchase of land.

(3)   This section applies to settlements and dispositions made after the twenty-seventh day of June eighteen hundred and ninety-two.

[207]

PART XI
MISCELLANEOUS

Notices

198   Registration under the Land Charges Act 1925 to be notice

(1)   The registration of any instrument or matter [in any register kept under the Land Charges Act 1972 or any local land charges register] shall be deemed to constitute actual notice of such instrument or matter, and of the fact of such registration, to all persons and for all purposes connected with the land affected, as from the date of registration or other prescribed date and so long as the registration continues in force.

(2)   This section operates without prejudice to the provisions of this Act respecting the making of further advances by a mortgagee, and applies only to instruments and matters required or authorised to be registered [in any such register].

[208]

NOTES

Words in square brackets substituted by the Local Land Charges Act 1975, s 17(2), Sch 1.
Land Charges Act 1925: see now the Land Charges Act 1972.

199   Restrictions on constructive notice

(1)   A purchaser shall not be prejudicially affected by notice of—
  (i)   any instrument or matter capable of registration under the provisions of the Land Charges Act 1925, or any enactment which it replaces, which is void or not enforceable as against him under that Act or enactment, by reason of the non-registration thereof;
  (ii) any other instrument or matter or any fact or thing unless—
    (a)   it is within his own knowledge, or would have come to his knowledge if such inquiries and inspections had been made as ought reasonably to have been made by him; or
    (b)   in the same transaction with respect to which a question of notice to the purchaser arises, it has come to the knowledge of his counsel, as such, or of his solicitor or other agent, as such, or would have come to the knowledge of his solicitor or other agent, as such, if such inquiries and inspections had been made as ought reasonably to have been made by the solicitor or other agent.

(2)   Paragraph (ii) of the last subsection shall not exempt a purchaser from any liability under, or any obligation to perform or observe, any covenant, condition, provision, or restriction contained in any instrument under which his title is derived, mediately or immediately; and such liability or obligation may be enforced in the same manner and to the same extent as if that paragraph had not been enacted.

(3)   A purchaser shall not by reason of anything in this section be affected by notice in any case where he would not have been so affected if this section had not been enacted.

(4)   This section applies to purchases made either before or after the commencement of this Act.

                                                                              [209]

NOTES
  Modification: any reference to solicitor(s) etc modified to include references to bodies recognised under the Administration of Justice Act 1985, s 9, by the Solicitors' Incorporated Practices Order 1991, SI 1991/2684, arts 4, 5, Sch 1.
  Land Charges Act 1925: see now the Land Charges Act 1972.

PART XII
CONSTRUCTION, JURISDICTION, AND GENERAL PROVISIONS

205   General definitions

(1)   In this Act unless the context otherwise requires, the following expressions have the meanings hereby assigned to them respectively, that is to say:—
  (i)   "Bankruptcy" includes liquidation by arrangement; also in relation to a corporation means the winding up thereof;
  (ii) "Conveyance" includes a mortgage, charge, lease, assent, vesting declaration, vesting instrument, disclaimer, release and every other assurance of property or of an interest therein by any instrument, except a will; "convey" has a corresponding meaning; and "disposition" includes a conveyance and also a devise, bequest, or an appointment of property contained in a will; and "dispose of" has a corresponding meaning;
  (iii) "Building purposes" include the erecting and improving of, and the adding to, and the repairing of buildings; and a "building lease" is a lease for building purposes or purposes connected therewith;
  [(iiiA) . . .]

(iv)   "Death duty" means estate duty, . . . and every other duty leviable or
       payable on a death;

(v)   "Estate owner" means the owner of a legal estate, but an infant is not
       capable of being an estate owner;

(vi)   "Gazette" means the London Gazette;

(vii) "Incumbrance" includes a legal or equitable mortgage and a trust for
       securing money, and a lien, and a charge of a portion, annuity, or other
       capital or annual sum; and "incumbrancer" has a meaning corresponding
       with that of incumbrance, and includes every person entitled to the benefit
       of an incumbrance, or to require payment or discharge thereof;

(viii) "Instrument" does not include a statute, unless the statute creates a
       settlement;

(ix)   "Land" includes land of any tenure, and mines and minerals, whether or not
       held apart from the surface, buildings or parts of buildings (whether the
       division is horizontal, vertical or made in any other way) and other corporeal
       hereditaments; also a manor, an advowson, and a rent and other incorporeal
       hereditaments, and an easement, right, privilege, or benefit in, over, or
       derived from land; but not an undivided share in land; and "mines and
       minerals" include any strata or seam of minerals or substances in or under any
       land, and powers of working and getting the same but not an undivided share
       thereof; and "manor" includes a lordship, and reputed manor or lordship; and
       "hereditament" means any real property which on an intestacy occurring
       before the commencement of this Act might have devolved upon an heir;

(x)   "Legal estates" mean the estates, interests and charges, in or over land
       (subsisting or created at law) which are by this Act authorised to subsist or
       to be created as legal estates; "equitable interests" mean all the other
       interests and charges in or over land or in the proceeds of sale thereof; an
       equitable interest "capable of subsisting as a legal estate" means such as
       could validly subsist or be created as a legal estate under this Act;

(xi)   "Legal powers" include the powers vested in a chargee by way of legal
       mortgage or in an estate owner under which a legal estate can be transferred
       or created; and "equitable powers" mean all the powers in or over land
       under which equitable interests or powers only can be transferred or created;

(xii) "Limitation Acts" means the Real Property Limitation Acts 1833, 1837
       and 1874, and "limitation" includes a trust;

[(xiii) "Mental disorder" has the meaning assigned to it by [section 1 of the Mental
       Health Act 1983] and "receiver" in relation to a person suffering from
       mental disorder, means a receiver appointed for that person under [Part VIII
       of the Mental Health Act 1959 or Part VII of the said Act of 1983];]

(xiv) a "mining lease" means a lease for mining purposes, that is, the searching
       for, winning, working, getting, making merchantable, carrying away, or
       disposing of mines and minerals, or purposes connected therewith, and
       includes a grant or licence for mining purposes;

(xv)   "Minister" means [the Minister of Agriculture, Fisheries and Food];

(xvi) "Mortgage" includes any charge or lien on any property for securing money
       or money's worth; "legal mortgage" means a mortgage by demise or
       subdemise or a charge by way of legal mortgage and "legal mortgagee" has a
       corresponding meaning; "mortgage money" means money or money's
       worth secured by a mortgage; "mortgagor" includes any person from time
       to time deriving title under the original mortgagor or entitled to redeem a
       mortgage according to his estate interest or right in the mortgaged property;
       "mortgagee" includes a chargee by way of legal mortgage and any person

from time to time deriving title under the original mortgagee; and "mortgagee in possession" is, for the purposes of this Act, a mortgagee who, in right of the mortgage, has entered into and is in possession of the mortgaged property; and "right of redemption" includes an option to repurchase only if the option in effect creates a right of redemption;

(xvii) "Notice" includes constructive notice;

(xviii) "Personal representative" means the executor, original or by representation, or administrator for the time being of a deceased person, and as regards any liability for the payment of death duties includes any person who takes possession of or intermeddles with the property of a deceased person without the authority of the personal representatives or the court;

(xix) "Possession" includes receipt of rents and profits or the right to receive the same, if any; and "income" includes rents and profits;

(xx) "Property" includes any thing in action, and any interest in real or personal property;

(xxi) "Purchaser" means a purchaser in good faith for valuable consideration and includes a lessee, mortgagee or other person who for valuable consideration acquires an interest in property except that in Part I of this Act and elsewhere where so expressly provided "purchaser" only means a person who acquires an interest in or charge on property for money or money's worth; and in reference to a legal estate includes a chargee by way of legal mortgage and where the context so requires "purchaser" includes an intending purchaser; "purchase" has a meaning corresponding with that of "purchaser"; and "valuable consideration" includes marriage but does not include a nominal consideration in money;

(xxii) "Registered land" has the same meaning as in the Land Registration Act 1925, and "Land Registrar" means the Chief Land Registrar under that Act;

(xxiii) "Rent" includes a rent service or a rentcharge, or other rent, toll, duty, royalty, or annual or periodical payment in money or money's worth, reserved or issuing out of or charged upon land, but does not include mortgage interest; "rentcharge" includes a fee farm rent; "fine" includes a premium or foregift and any payment, consideration, or benefit in the nature of a fine, premium or foregift; "lessor" includes an underlessor and a person deriving title under a lessor or underlessor; and "lessee" includes an underlessee and a person deriving title under a lessee or underlessee, and "lease" includes an underlease or other tenancy;

(xxiv) "Sale" includes an extinguishment of manorial incidents, but in other respects means a sale properly so called;

(xxv) "Securities" include stocks, funds and shares;

(xxvi) "Tenant for life", "statutory owner", "settled land", "settlement", "vesting deed", "subsidiary vesting deed", "vesting order", "vesting instrument", "trust instrument", "capital money" and "trustees of the settlement" have the same meanings as in the Settled Land Act 1925;

(xxvii) "Term of years absolute" means a term of years (taking effect either in possession or in reversion whether or not at a rent) with or without impeachment for waste, subject or not to another legal estate, and either certain or liable to determination by notice, re-entry, operation of law, or by a provision for cesser on redemption, or in any other event (other than the dropping of a life, or the determination of a determinable life interest); but does not include any term of years determinable with life or lives or with the cesser of a determinable life interest, nor, if created after the commencement of this Act, a term of years which is not expressed to take effect in possession within twenty-one years after the creation thereof where required by this Act to take effect within that period; and in this definition the expression "term of years" includes a term for less than a year, or for a year or years and a fraction of a year or from year to year;

(xxviii) "Trust Corporation" means the Public Trustee or a corporation either appointed by the court in any particular case to be a trustee or entitled by rules made under subsection (3) of section four of the Public Trustee Act 1906, to act as custodian trustee;

(xxix) "Trust for sale", in relation to land, means an immediate binding trust for sale, whether or not exercisable at the request or with the consent of any person, and with or without a power at discretion to postpone the sale; "trustees for sale" mean the persons (including a personal representative) holding land on trust for sale; and "power to postpone a sale" means power to postpone in the exercise of a discretion;

(xxx) "United Kingdom" means Great Britain and Northern Ireland;

(xxxi) "Will" includes codicil.

[(1A)   Any reference in this Act to money being paid into court shall be construed as referring to the money being paid into the Supreme Court or any other court that has jurisdiction, and any reference in this Act to the court, in a context referring to the investment or application of money paid into court, shall be construed, in the case of money paid into the Supreme Court, as referring to the High Court, and in the case of money paid into another court, as referring to that other court.]

(2)   Where an equitable interest in or power over property arises by statute or operation of law, references to the creation of an interest or power include references to any interest or power so arising.

(3)   References to registration under the Land Charges Act 1925 apply to any registration made under any other statute which is by the Land Charges Act 1925 to have effect as if the registration had been made under that Act.

[210]

NOTES

Sub-s (1): para (iiiA) added by the County Courts Act 1984, s 148(1), Sch 2, Pt II, para 9, repealed by the High Court and County Courts Jurisdiction Order 1991, SI 1991/724, art 2(8), Schedule, Pt I; words omitted from para (iv) repealed by the Finance Act 1949, s 52(9), (10), Sch 11, Pt IV; para (xiii) substituted by the Mental Health Act 1959, s 149(1), Sch 7, Pt I, words in square brackets substituted by the Mental Health Act 1983, s 148, Sch 4, para 5(b); words in square brackets in para (xv) substituted by the Transfer of Functions (Ministry of Food) Order 1955, SI 1955/554.

Sub-s (1A): added by the Administration of Justice Act 1965, ss 17, 18, Sch 1.

Modification: definition "Trust corporation" modified in relation to charities, by the Charities Act 1993, s 35.

Real Property Limitation Acts 1833, 1837, 1874: see now the Limitation Act 1980.

Land Charges Act 1925: see now the Land Charges Act 1972, and the Local Land Charges Act 1975.

---

209   Short title, commencement, extent

(1)   This Act may be cited as the Law of Property Act 1925.

(2)   . . .

(3)   This Act extends to England and Wales only.

[211]

NOTES

Sub-s (2): repealed by the Statute Law Revision Act 1950.

LAND REGISTRATION ACT 1925

(C 21)

An Act to consolidate the Land Transfer Acts and the statute law relating to registered land

[9 April 1925]

PART I
PRELIMINARY

[1 Registers to be continued

(1) The Chief Land Registrar shall continue to keep a register of title to freehold land and leasehold land.

(2) The register need not be kept in documentary form.]

[212]

NOTES

Substituted by the Administration of Justice Act 1982, s 66(1).

---

2 What estates may be registered

(1) After the commencement of this Act, estates capable of subsisting as legal estates shall be the only interests in land in respect of which a proprietor can be registered and all other interests in registered land (except overriding interests and interests entered on the register at or before such commencement) shall take effect in equity, as minor interests, but all interests (except undivided shares in land) entered on the register at such commencement which are not legal estates shall be capable of being dealt with under this Act:

Provided that, on the occasion of the first dealing with any such interest, the register shall be rectified in such manner as may be provided by rules made to secure that the entries therein shall be similar to those which would have been made if the title to the land had been registered after the commencement of this Act.

(2) Subject as aforesaid, and save as otherwise expressly provided by this Act, this Act applies to land registered under any enactment replaced by this Act in like manner as it applies to land registered under this Act.

[213]

3 Interpretation

In this Act unless the context otherwise requires, the following expressions have the meanings hereby assigned to them respectively, that is to say:—

    (i)   "Charge by way of legal mortgage" means a mortgage created by charge under which, by virtue of the Law of Property Act 1925, the mortgagee is to be treated as an estate owner in like manner as if a mortgage term by demise or subdemise were vested in him, and "legal mortgage" has the same meaning as in that Act;

    [(ii) "the court" means the High Court or, where county courts have jurisdiction by virtue of rules made under section 138(1) of this Act, the county court;]

    (iii) . . .

    (iv) "Estate owner" means the owner of a legal estate, but an infant is not capable of being an estate owner;

    (v) "Gazette" means the London Gazette;

    (vi) "Income" includes rents and profits;

(vii) "Instrument" does not include a statute, unless the statute creates a settlement;

(viii) "Land" includes land of any tenure (including land, subject or not to manorial incidents, enfranchised under Part V of the Law of Property Act 1922), and mines and minerals, whether or not held with the surface, buildings or parts of buildings (whether the division is horizontal, vertical or made in any other way) and other corporeal hereditaments; also a manor, . . . and a rent and other incorporeal hereditaments, and an easement, right, privilege, or benefit in, over, or derived from land; but not an undivided share in land; and "hereditaments" mean real property which on an intestacy might, before the commencement of this Act, have devolved on an heir;

[(ix) "Land Charge" means a land charge of any class described in section 2 of the Land Charges Act 1972 or a local land charge;]

(x) "Lease" includes an under-lease and any tenancy or agreement for a lease, under-lease or tenancy;

(xi) "Legal estates" mean the estates interests and charges in or over land subsisting or created at law which are by the Law of Property Act 1925 authorised to subsist or to be created at law; and "Equitable interests" mean all the other interests and charges in or over land or in the proceeds of sale thereof; an equitable interest "capable of subsisting at law" means such as could validly subsist at law if clothed with the legal estate;

(xii) "Limitation Acts" mean the Real Property Limitation Acts 1833, 1837 and 1874, and any Acts amending those Acts;

(xiii) "Manorial incidents" have the same meaning as in Part V of the Law of Property Act 1922;

(xiv) "Mines and minerals" include any strata or seam of minerals or substances in or under any land, and powers of working and getting the same, but not an undivided share thereof;

(xv) "Minor interests" mean the interests not capable of being disposed of or created by registered dispositions and capable of being overridden (whether or not a purchaser has notice thereof) by the proprietors unless protected as provided by this Act, and all rights and interests which are not registered or protected on the register and are not overriding interests, and include—

    (a) in the case of land held on trust for sale, all interests and powers which are under the Law of Property Act 1925 capable of being overridden by the trustees for sale, whether or not such interests and powers are so protected; and

    (b) in the case of settled land, all interests and powers which are under the Settled Land Act 1925, and the Law of Property Act 1925, or either of them, capable of being overridden by the tenant for life or statutory owner, whether or not such interests and powers are so protected as aforesaid;

(xvi) "Overriding interests" mean all the incumbrances, interests, rights, and powers not entered on the register but subject to which registered dispositions are by this Act to take effect, and in regard to land registered at the commencement of this Act include the matters which are by any enactment repealed by this Act declared not to be incumbrances;

(xvii) "Personal representative" means the executor, original or by representation, or administrator for the time being of a deceased person, and as regards any liability for the payment of death duties includes any person who takes possession of or intermeddles with the property of a deceased person without the authority of the personal representatives or the court; and where there are special personal representatives for the purposes of any settled land, it means, in relation to that land, those representatives;

(xviii) "Possession" includes receipt of rents and profits or the right to receive the same, if any;

(xix) "Prescribed" means prescribed by general rules made in pursuance of this Act;

(xx) "Proprietor" means the registered proprietor for the time being of an estate in land or of a charge;

(xxi) "Purchaser" means a purchaser in good faith for valuable consideration and includes a lessee, mortgagee, or other person who for valuable consideration acquires any interest in land or in any charge on land;

(xxii) "Registered dispositions" mean dispositions which take effect under the powers conferred on the proprietor by way of transfer, charge, lease or otherwise and to which (when required to be registered) special effect or priority is given by this Act on registration;

(xxiii) "Registered estate", in reference to land, means the legal estate, or other registered interest, if any, as respects which a person is for the time being registered as proprietor, but does not include a registered charge and a "registered charge" includes a mortgage or incumbrance registered as a charge under this Act;

(xxiv) "Registered land" means land or any estate or interest in land the title to which is registered under this Act or any enactment replaced by this Act, and includes any easement, right, privilege, or benefit which is appurtenant or appendant thereto, and any mines and minerals within or under the same and held therewith;

(xxv) "Rent" includes a rent service or a rentcharge, or other rent, toll, duty, royalty, or annual or periodical payment, in money or money's worth, issuing out of or charged upon land, but does not include mortgage interest;

(xxvi) "Settled land" "settlement" "tenant for life" "statutory owner" "trustees of the settlement" "capital money" . . . "trust corporation" "trust instrument" "vesting deed" "vesting order" "vesting assent" and "vesting instrument" have the same meanings as in the Settled Land Act 1925;

(xxvii) A "term of years absolute" means a term of years, whether at a rent or not, taking effect either in possession or in reversion, with or without impeachment for waste, subject or not to another legal estate and either certain or liable to determination by notice, re-entry, operation of law, or by a provision for cesser on redemption, or in any other event (other than the dropping of a life, or the determination of a determinable life interest), but does not include any term of years determinable with life or lives or with the cesser of a determinable life interest, nor, if created after the commencement of this Act, a term of years which is not expressed to take effect in possession within twenty-one years after the creation thereof where required by the Law of Property Act 1925 to take effect within that period; and in this definition the expression "term of years" includes a term for less than a year, or for a year or years and a fraction of a year or from year to year;

(xxviii) "Trust for sale", in relation to land, means an immediate binding trust for sale, whether or not exercisable at the request or with the consent of any person, and with or without a power at discretion to postpone the sale;

(xxix) "Trustees for sale" mean the persons (including a personal representative) holding land on trust for sale;

(xxx) "United Kingdom" means Great Britain and Northern Ireland;

(xxxi) "Valuable consideration" includes marriage, but does not include a nominal consideration in money;

(xxxii) "Will" includes codicil.

NOTES

Para (ii) substituted by the Administration of Justice Act 1982, s 67, Sch 5, para (a); para (iii) repealed by the Finance Act 1975, ss 52(2), 59(5), Sch 13, Pt I; words omitted from para (viii) repealed by the Patronage (Benefices) Measure 1986 (2), s 6; para (ix) substituted by the Local Land Charges Act 1975, s 17(2), Sch 1; words omitted from para (xxvi) repealed by the Mental Health Act 1959, s 149(2), Sch 8, Pt I.

Real Property Limitation Acts 1833, 1837, 1874: see now the Limitation Act 1980.

PART II
REGISTRATION OF LAND

Freehold Land

4 Application for registration of freehold land

Where the title to be registered is a title to a freehold estate in land—

    (a) any estate owner holding an estate in fee simple (including a tenant for life, statutory owner, personal representative, or trustee for sale) whether subject or not to incumbrances; or

    (b) any other person (not being a mortgagee where there is a subsisting right of redemption or a person who has merely contracted to buy land) who is entitled to require a legal estate in fee simple whether subject or not to incumbrances, to be vested in him;

may apply to the registrar to be registered in respect of such estate, or, in the case of a person not in a fiduciary position, to have registered in his stead any nominee, as proprietor with an absolute title or with a possessory title:

Provided that—

    (i) Where an absolute title is required the applicant or his nominee shall not be registered as proprietor until and unless the title is approved by the registrar;

    (ii) Where a possessory title is required the applicant or his nominee may be registered as proprietor on giving such evidence of title and serving such notices, if any, as may for the time being be prescribed;

    (iii) If, on an application for registration with possessory title, the registrar is satisfied as to the title to the freehold estate, he may register it as absolute, whether the applicant consents to such registration or not, but in that case no higher fee shall be charged than would have been charged for registration with possessory title.

[215]

5 Effect of first registration with absolute title

Where the registered land is a freehold estate, the registration of any person as first proprietor thereof with an absolute title shall vest in the person so registered an estate in fee simple in possession in the land, together with all rights, privileges, and appurtenances belonging or appurtenant thereto, subject to the following rights and interests, that is to say,—

    (a) Subject to the incumbrances, and other entries, if any, appearing on the register; and

    (b) Unless the contrary is expressed on the register, subject to such overriding interests, if any, as affect the registered land; and

    (c) Where the first proprietor is not entitled for his own benefit to the registered land subject, as between himself and the persons entitled to minor interests, to any minor interests of such persons of which he has notice, but free from all other estates and interests whatsoever, including estates and interests of His Majesty.

[216]

6   Effect of first registration with possessory title

Where the registered land is a freehold estate, the registration of any person as first proprietor thereof with a possessory title only shall not affect or prejudice the enforcement of any estate, right or interest adverse to or in derogation of the title of the first proprietor, and subsisting or capable of arising at the time of registration of that proprietor; but save as aforesaid, shall have the same effect as registration of a person with an absolute title.

[217]

7   Qualified title

(1)   Where an absolute title is required, and on the examination of the title it appears to the registrar that the title can be established only for a limited period, or only subject to certain reservations, the registrar may, on the application of the party applying to be registered, by an entry made in the register, except from the effect of registration any estate, right, or interest—

  (a)   arising before a specified date; or

  (b)   arising under a specified instrument or otherwise particularly described in the register,

and a title registered subject to such excepted estate, right, or interest shall be called a qualified title.

(2)   Where the registered land is a freehold estate, the registration of a person as first proprietor thereof with a qualified title shall have the same effect as the registration of such person with an absolute title, save that registration with a qualified title shall not affect or prejudice the enforcement of any estate, right or interest appearing by the register to be excepted.

[218]

Leasehold Land

8   Application for registration of leasehold land

(1)   Where the title to be registered is a title to a leasehold interest in land—

  (a)   any estate owner (including a tenant for life, statutory owner, personal representative, or trustee for sale, but not including a mortgagee where there is a subsisting right of redemption), holding under a lease for a term of years absolute of which more than twenty-one are unexpired, whether subject or not to incumbrances; or

  (b)   any other person (not being a mortgagee as aforesaid and not being a person who has merely contracted to buy the leasehold interest) who is entitled to require a legal leasehold estate held under such a lease as aforesaid (whether subject or not to incumbrances) to be vested in him,

may apply to the registrar to be registered in respect of such estate, or in the case of a person not being in a fiduciary position to have registered in his stead any nominee, as proprietor with an absolute title, with a good leasehold title or with a possessory title:

Provided that—
- (i) Where an absolute title is required, the applicant or his nominee shall not be registered as proprietor until and unless the title both to the leasehold and to the freehold, and to any intermediate leasehold that may exist, is approved by the registrar;
- (ii) Where a good leasehold title is required, the applicant or his nominee shall not be registered as proprietor until and unless the title to the leasehold interest is approved by the registrar;
- (iii) Where a possessory title is required, the applicant or his nominee may be registered as proprietor on giving such evidence of title and serving such notices, if any, as may for the time being be prescribed;
- (iv) If on an application for registration with a possessory title the registrar is satisfied as to the title to the leasehold interest, he may register it as good leasehold, whether the applicant consents to such registration or not, but in that case no higher fee shall be charged than would have been charged for registration with possessory title.

[(1A) An application for registration in respect of leasehold land held under a lease in relation to the grant or assignment of which section 123(1) of this Act applies (whether by virtue of this Act or any later enactment) may be made within the period allowed by section 123(1), or any authorised extension of that period, notwithstanding that the lease was granted for a term of not more than twenty-one years or that the unexpired term of the lease is not more than twenty-one years.]

[(2) Leasehold land held under a lease containing a prohibition or restriction on dealings therewith inter vivos shall not be registered under this Act unless and until provision is made in the prescribed manner for preventing any dealing therewith in contravention of the prohibition or restriction by an entry on the register to that effect, or otherwise.]

(3) Where on an application to register a mortgage term, wherein no right of redemption is subsisting, it appears that the applicant is entitled in equity to the superior term, if any, out of which it was created, the registrar shall register him as proprietor of the superior term without any entry to the effect that the legal interest in that term is outstanding, and on such registration the superior term shall vest in the proprietor and the mortgage term shall merge therein:

Provided that this subsection shall not apply where the mortgage term does not comprise the whole of the land included in the superior term, unless in that case the rent, if any, payable in respect of the superior term has been apportioned, or the rent is of no money value or no rent is reserved, and unless the covenants, if any, entered into for the benefit of the reversion have been apportioned (either expressly or by implication) as respects the land comprised in the mortgage term.

[219]

NOTES

Sub-s (1A): inserted by the Land Registration Act 1986, s 2(2), (5), in relation to the grant or assignment of a lease after 1 January 1987.

Sub-s (2): substituted by the Land Registration Act 1986, s 3, in relation to a lease granted before 1 January 1987 subject to an absolute prohibition on any dealings therewith inter vivos.

---

9 Effect of first registration with absolute title

Where the registered land is a leasehold interest, the registration under this Act of any person as first proprietor thereof with an absolute title shall be deemed to vest in such person the possession of the leasehold interest described, with all implied or expressed rights, privileges, and appurtenances attached to such interest, subject to the following obligations, rights, and interests, that is to say,—

(a) Subject to all implied and express covenants, obligations, and liabilities incident to the registered land; and

(b) Subject to the incumbrances and other entries (if any) appearing on the register; and

(c) Unless the contrary is expressed on the register, subject to such overriding interests, if any, as affect the registered land; and

(d) Where such first proprietor is not entitled for his own benefit to the registered land subject, as between himself and the persons entitled to minor interests, to any minor interests of such persons of which he has notice;

but free from all other estates and interests whatsoever, including estates and interests of His Majesty.

[220]

10 Effect of first registration with good leasehold title

Where the registered land is a leasehold interest, the registration of a person as first proprietor thereof with a good leasehold title shall not affect or prejudice the enforcement of any estate, right or interest affecting or in derogation of the title of the lessor to grant the lease, but, save as aforesaid, shall have the same effect as registration with an absolute title.

[221]

11 Effect of first registration with possessory title

Where the registered land is a leasehold interest, the registration of a person as first proprietor thereof with a possessory title shall not affect or prejudice the enforcement of any estate, right, or interest (whether in respect of the lessor's title or otherwise) adverse to or in derogation of the title of such first registered proprietor, and subsisting or capable of arising at the time of the registration of such proprietor; but, save as aforesaid, shall have the same effect as registration with an absolute title.

[222]

12 Qualified title

(1) Where on examination it appears to the registrar that the title, either of the lessor to the reversion or of the lessee to the leasehold interest, can be established only for a limited period, or subject to certain reservations, the registrar may, upon the request in writing of the person applying to be registered, by an entry made in the register, except from the effect of registration any estate, right or interest—

(a) arising before a specified date, or

(b) arising under a specified instrument, or otherwise particularly described in the register,

and a title registered subject to any such exception shall be called a qualified title.

(2) Where the registered land is a leasehold interest, the registration of a person as first proprietor thereof with a qualified title shall not affect or prejudice the enforcement of any estate, right, or interest appearing by the register to be excepted, but, save as aforesaid, shall have the same effect as registration with a good leasehold title or an absolute title, as the case may be.

[223]

Preliminaries to Registration

13   Regulations as to examination of title by registrar

The examination by the registrar of any title under this Act shall be conducted in the prescribed manner:

Provided that—

    (a) Due notice shall be given, where the giving of such notice is prescribed, and sufficient opportunity shall be afforded to any persons desirous of objecting to come in and state their objections to the registrar; and

    (b) The registrar shall have jurisdiction to hear and determine any such objections, subject to an appeal to the court in the prescribed manner and on the prescribed conditions; and

    (c) If the registrar, upon the examination of any title, is of opinion that the title is open to objection, but is nevertheless a title the holding under which will not be disturbed, he may approve of such title, or may require the applicant to apply to the court, upon a statement signed by the registrar, for its sanction to the registration.

[224]

14   Evidence required before registration

(1)   Before the completion of the registration of any estate in land in respect of which an examination of title is required, the applicant for registration and his solicitor, shall each, if required by the registrar, make an affidavit or declaration that to the best of his knowledge and belief all deeds, wills, and instruments of title, and all charges and incumbrances affecting the title which is the subject of the application, and all facts material to such title, have been disclosed in the course of the investigation of title made by the registrar.

(2)   The registrar may require any person making an affidavit or declaration in pursuance of this section to state in his affidavit or declaration what means he has had of becoming acquainted with the several matters referred to in this section; and if the registrar is of opinion that any further or other evidence is necessary or desirable, he may refuse to complete the registration until such further or other evidence is produced.

(3)   Before the registration of any person who has not previously acquired the estate intended to be registered, the registrar shall be satisfied that all ad valorem stamp duty, if any, which, if the estate had been acquired by him, would have been payable in respect of the instrument vesting that estate in him, has been discharged.

[225]

NOTES

Modification: any reference to a solicitor modified to include a reference to a licensed conveyancer and any reference to a person's solicitor modified to include a reference to a licensed conveyancer acting for that person, by the Administration of Justice Act 1985, s 34(1).

15   Production of deeds

(1)   When an application has been made to the registrar for the registration of any title to land, then if any person has in his possession or custody any deeds, instruments, or evidences of title relating to or affecting such title, to the production of which the applicant or any trustee for him is entitled, the registrar may require such person to show cause, within a time limited, why he should not produce such deeds, instruments, or evidences of title to the registrar, or otherwise, as the registrar

may deem fit; and, unless cause is shown to the satisfaction of the registrar within the time limited, such deeds, instruments, and evidences of title may be ordered by the registrar to be produced at the expense of the applicant, at such time and place, and in such manner, and on such terms, as the registrar thinks fit.

(2)   Any person aggrieved by an order of the registrar under this section may appeal in the prescribed manner to the court, which may annul or confirm the order of the registrar with or without modification.

(3)   If any person disobeys any order of the registrar made in pursuance of this section, the registrar may certify such disobedience to the court, and thereupon such person, subject to such right of appeal as aforesaid, may be punished by the court in the same manner in all respects as if the order made by the registrar were the order of the court.

[226]

16   Deeds to be marked with notice of registration

A person shall not be registered as proprietor until, if required by the registrar, he has produced to him such documents of title, if any, as will, in the opinion of the registrar, when stamped or otherwise marked, give notice to any purchaser or other person dealing with the land of the fact of the registration, and the registrar shall stamp or otherwise mark the same accordingly, unless the registrar is satisfied that without such stamping or marking the fact of such registration cannot be concealed from a purchaser or other person dealing with the land:

   Provided that, in the case of registration with a possessory title, the registrar may act on such reasonable evidence as may be prescribed as to the sufficiency of the documents produced, and as to dispensing with their production in special circumstances.

[227]

PART III
REGISTERED DEALINGS WITH REGISTERED LAND

Dispositions of Freehold Land

18   Powers of disposition of registered freeholds

(1)   Where the registered land is a freehold estate the proprietor may, in the prescribed manner, transfer the registered estate in the land or any part thereof, and, subject to any entry in the register to the contrary, may in the prescribed manner—

   (a)   transfer the fee simple in possession of all or any mines or minerals apart from the surface; or of the surface without all or any of the mines and minerals;

   (b)   grant an annuity or a rentcharge in possession (either perpetual or for a term of years absolute) in any form which sufficiently refers in the prescribed manner to the registered land charged;

   (c)   grant in fee simple in possession any easement, right, or privilege in, over, or derived from the registered land or any part thereof, in any form which sufficiently refers, in the prescribed manner, to the registered servient tenement and to the dominant tenement, whether being registered land or not;

   (d)   transfer the fee simple in possession of the registered land or any part thereof, subject to the creation thereout, by way of reservation, in favour of any person of an annuity or a rentcharge in possession (either perpetual or for a term of years absolute), or of any easement, right, or privilege in possession (either in fee simple or for a term of years absolute);

(e) grant (subject or not to the reservation of an easement, right, or privilege) a lease of the registered land or any part thereof, or of all or any mines and minerals apart from the surface, or of the surface without all or any of the mines and minerals, or of an easement, right or privilege in or over the land, or any part thereof, for any term of years absolute for any purpose (but where by way of mortgage subject to the provisions of this Act and the Law of Property Act 1925 relating thereto), and in any form which sufficiently refers, in the prescribed manner, to the registered land.

(2) A perpetual annuity or rentcharge in possession may be granted or reserved to any person with or without a power of re-entry, exercisable at any time, on default of payment thereof, or on breach of covenant, and shall have incidental thereto all the powers and remedies (as varied if at all by the disposition creating the rentcharge) for recovery thereof conferred by the Law of Property Act 1925; and where an easement, right, or privilege is reserved in a registered disposition for a legal estate, the reservation shall operate to create the same for the benefit of the land for the benefit of which the right is reserved.

(3) A lease for a term, not exceeding twenty-one years, to take effect in possession or within one year from the date thereof . . . may be granted and shall take effect under this section notwithstanding that a caution, notice of deposit of a certificate, restriction, or inhibition (other than a bankruptcy inhibition) may be subsisting, but subject to the interests intended to be protected by any such caution, notice, restriction, or inhibition.

(4) The foregoing powers of disposition shall (subject to the express provisions of this Act and of the Law of Property Act 1925 relating to mortgages) apply to dispositions by the registered proprietor by way of charge or mortgage; but no estate, other than a legal estate, shall be capable of being disposed of, or created under, this section.

(5) In this Act "transfer" or "disposition" when referring to registered freehold land includes any disposition authorised as aforesaid; and "transferee" has a corresponding meaning.

[228]

NOTES

Sub-s (3): words omitted repealed by the Land Registration Act 1986, s 4(2), (5), in relation to dispositions after 1 January 1987.

---

19 Registration of disposition of freeholds

(1) The transfer of the registered estate in the land or part thereof shall be completed by the registrar entering on the register the transferee as the proprietor of the estate transferred, but until such entry is made the transferor shall be deemed to remain proprietor of the registered estate; and, where part only of the land is transferred, notice thereof shall also be noted on the register.

(2) All interests transferred or created by dispositions by the proprietor, other than a transfer of the registered estate in the land, or part thereof, shall, subject to the provisions relating to mortgages, be completed by registration in the same manner and with the same effect as provided by this Act with respect to transfers of registered estates and notice thereof shall also be noted on the register:

Provided that nothing in this subsection—

(a) shall authorise the registration of a lease granted for a term not exceeding twenty-one years, or require the entry of a notice of such a lease . . . ; or

(b) shall authorise the registration of a mortgage term where there is a subsisting right of redemption; or

(c) shall render necessary the registration of any easement, right, or privilege except as appurtenant to registered land, or the entry of notice thereof except as against the registered title of the servient land.

Every such disposition shall, when registered, take effect as a registered disposition, and a lease made by the registered proprietor under the last foregoing section which is not required to be registered or noted on the register shall nevertheless take effect as if it were a registered disposition immediately on being granted.

(3) The general words implied in conveyances under the Law of Property Act 1925 shall apply, so far as applicable thereto, to dispositions of a registered estate.

[229]

NOTES

Sub-s (2): words omitted from para (a) repealed by the Land Registration Act 1986, s 4(3), (5), in relation to dispositions after 1 January 1987.

20 Effect of registration and dispositions of freeholds

(1) In the case of a freehold estate registered with an absolute title, a disposition of the registered land or of a legal estate therein, including a lease thereof, for valuable consideration shall, when registered, confer on the transferee or grantee an estate in fee simple or the term of years absolute or other legal estate expressed to be created in the land dealt with, together with all rights, privileges, and appurtenances belonging or appurtenant thereto, including (subject to any entry to the contrary in the register) the appropriate rights and interests which would, under the Law of Property Act 1925, have been transferred if the land had not been registered, subject—

(a) to the incumbrances and other entries, if any, appearing on the register [and any charge for inheritance tax subject to which the disposition takes effect under section 73 of this Act]; and

(b) unless the contrary is expressed on the register, to the overriding interests, if any, affecting the estate transferred or created,

but free from all other estates and interests whatsoever, including estates and interests of His Majesty, and the disposition shall operate in like manner as if the registered transferor or grantor were (subject to any entry to the contrary in the register) entitled to the registered land in fee simple in possession for his own benefit.

(2) In the case of a freehold estate registered with a qualified title a disposition of the registered land or of a legal estate therein, including a lease thereof, for valuable consideration shall, when registered, have the same effect as it would have had if the land had been registered with an absolute title, save that such disposition shall not affect or prejudice the enforcement of any right or interest appearing by the register to be excepted.

(3) In the case of a freehold estate registered with a possessory title, a disposition of the registered land or of a legal estate therein, including a lease thereof, for valuable consideration shall not affect or prejudice the enforcement of any right or interest adverse to or in derogation of the title of the first registered proprietor, and subsisting or capable of arising at the time of the registration of such proprietor; but, save as aforesaid, shall when registered have the same effect as it would have had if the land had been registered with an absolute title.

(4) Where any such disposition is made without valuable consideration, it shall, so far as the transferee or grantee is concerned, be subject to any minor interests subject to which the transferor or grantor held the same, but, save as aforesaid, shall, when

registered, in all respects, and in particular as respects any registered dealings on the part of the transferee or grantee, have the same effect as if the disposition had been made for valuable consideration.

[230]

NOTES

Sub-s (1): words in square brackets in para (a) inserted by the Finance Act 1975, s 52(1), Sch 12, paras 2, 5(1), (2).

Inheritance tax: except in relation to a liability to tax arising before 25 July 1986 capital transfer tax is to be known as inheritance tax and the Capital Transfer Tax Act 1984 may be cited as the Inheritance Tax Act 1984, by virtue of the Finance Act 1986, s 100. Accordingly references to capital transfer tax have been changed to references to inheritance tax throughout this Act.

Dispositions of Leasehold Land

21 Powers of disposition of registered leaseholds

(1) Where the registered land is a leasehold interest the proprietor may, in the prescribed manner, transfer the registered estate in the land or any part thereof, and, subject to any entry in the register to the contrary may in the prescribed manner—

  (a) transfer all or any of the leasehold mines and minerals apart from the surface; or the surface without all or any of the leasehold mines and minerals;

  (b) grant (to the extent of the registered estate) any annuity or rentcharge in possession, easement, right or privilege in, over, or derived from the registered land or any part thereof, in any form which sufficiently refers, in the prescribed manner, to the registered lease, and to the dominant tenement, whether being registered land or not;

  (c) transfer the registered land or any part thereof subject to a reservation to any person of any such annuity, rentcharge, easement, right, or privilege;

  (d) grant (subject or not to the reservation of an easement, right or privilege) an underlease of the registered land, or any part thereof, or of all or any mines and minerals apart from the surface, or of the surface without all or any of the mines and minerals, or of an easement, right or privilege, in or over the registered land or any part thereof, for any term of years absolute of less duration than the registered estate and for any purpose (but where by way of mortgage, subject to the provisions of this Act and of the Law of Property Act 1925 relating thereto), and in any form which sufficiently refers in the prescribed manner to the registered land, and in the case of an easement, right, or privilege, to the dominant tenement, whether being registered land or not.

(2) A disposition of registered leasehold land may be made subject to a rent legally apportioned in the prescribed manner, or to a rent not so apportioned.

(3) An underlease for a term, not exceeding twenty-one years, to take effect in possession or within one year from the date thereof, . . . , may be granted and shall take effect under this section, notwithstanding that a caution, notice of deposit of a certificate, restriction, or inhibition (other than a bankruptcy inhibition) may be subsisting, but subject to the interests intended to be protected by any such caution, notice, restriction or inhibition.

(4) The foregoing powers of disposition shall (subject to the express provisions of this Act and of the Law of Property Act 1925 relating to mortgages) apply to dispositions by the registered proprietor by way of charge or mortgage, but no estate, other than a legal estate, shall be capable of being disposed of or created under this section.

(5)   In this Act "transfer" or "disposition" when referring to registered leasehold land includes any disposition authorised as aforesaid and "transferee" has a corresponding meaning.

[231]

NOTES

Sub-s (3): words omitted repealed by the Land Registration Act 1986, s 4(2), (5), in relation to dispositions after 1 January 1987.

22   Registration of dispositions of leaseholds

(1)   A transfer of the registered estate in the land or part thereof shall be completed by the registrar entering on the register the transferee as proprietor of the estate transferred, but until such entry is made the transferor shall be deemed to remain the proprietor of the registered estate; and where part only of the land is transferred, notice thereof shall also be noted on the register.

(2)   All interests transferred or created by dispositions by the registered proprietor other than the transfer of his registered estate in the land or in part thereof shall (subject to the provisions relating to mortgages) be completed by registration in the same manner and with the same effect as provided by this Act with respect to transfers of the registered estate, and notice thereof shall also be noted on the register in accordance with this Act:

Provided that nothing in this subsection—
  (a)   shall authorise the registration of an underlease originally granted for a term not exceeding twenty-one years, or require the entry of a notice of such an underlease . . . ; or
  (b)   shall authorise the registration of a mortgage term where there is a subsisting right of redemption, or
  (c)   shall render necessary the registration of any easement, right, or privilege except as appurtenant to registered land, or the entry of notice thereof except as against the registered title of the servient land.

Every such disposition shall, when registered, take effect as a registered disposition, and an underlease made by the registered proprietor which is not required to be registered or noted on the register shall nevertheless take effect as if it were a registered disposition immediately on being granted.

(3)   The general words implied in conveyances under the Law of Property Act 1925 shall apply, so far as applicable thereto, to transfers of a registered leasehold estate.

[232]

NOTES

Sub-s (2): words omitted from para (a) repealed by the Land Registration Act 1986, s 4(3), (5), in relation to dispositions after 1 January 1987.

23   Effect of registration of dispositions of leaseholds

(1)   In the case of a leasehold estate registered with an absolute title, a disposition (including a subdemise thereof) for valuable consideration shall, when registered, be deemed to vest in the transferee or under-lessee the estate transferred or created to the extent of the registered estate, or for the term created by the subdemise, as the case may require, with all implied or expressed rights, privileges, and appurtenances attached to the estate transferred or created, including (subject to any entry to the contrary on the register) the appropriate rights and interests which would under the

Law of Property Act 1925 have been transferred if the land had not been registered, but subject as follows:—

    (a)   To all implied and express covenants, obligations, and liabilities incident to the estate transferred or created; and

    (b)   To the incumbrances and other entries (if any) appearing on the register [and any charge for inheritance tax subject to which the disposition takes effect under section 73 of this Act]; and

    (c)   Unless the contrary is expressed on the register, to the overriding interests, if any, affecting the estate transferred or created,

but free from all other estates and interests whatsoever, including estates and interests of His Majesty; and the transfer or subdemise shall operate in like manner as if the registered transferor or sublessor were (subject to any entry to the contrary on the register) absolutely entitled to the registered lease for his own benefit.

(2)   In the case of a leasehold estate registered with a good leasehold title, a disposition (including a subdemise thereof) for valuable consideration shall, when registered, have the same effect as it would have had if the land had been registered with an absolute title, save that it shall not affect or prejudice the enforcement of any right or interest affecting or in derogation of the lessor to grant the lease.

(3)   In the case of a leasehold estate registered with a qualified title, a disposition (including a subdemise thereof) for valuable consideration shall, when registered, have the same effect as it would have had if the land had been registered with an absolute title, save that such disposition shall not affect or prejudice the enforcement of any right or interest (whether in respect of the lessor's title or otherwise) appearing by the register to be excepted.

(4)   In the case of a leasehold estate registered with a possessory title, a disposition (including a subdemise thereof) for valuable consideration shall not affect or prejudice the enforcement of any right or interest (whether in respect of the lessor's title or otherwise) adverse to or in derogation of the title of the first registered proprietor, and subsisting or capable of arising at the time of the registration of such proprietor, but save as aforesaid shall, when registered, have the same effect as it would have had if the land had been registered with an absolute title.

(5)   Where any such disposition is made without valuable consideration it shall, so far as the transferee or underlessee is concerned, be subject to any minor interests subject to which the transferor or sublessor held the same; but, save as aforesaid, shall, when registered, in all respects, and in particular as respects any registered dealings on the part of the transferee or underlessee, have the same effect as if the disposition had been made for valuable consideration.

                                                                     [233]

NOTES

Sub-s (1): words in square brackets in para (b) inserted by the Finance Act 1975, s 52(1), Sch 12, paras 2, 5(1), (3).

Inheritance tax: except in relation to a liability to tax arising before 25 July 1986 capital transfer tax is to be known as inheritance tax and the Capital Transfer Tax Act 1984 may be cited as the Inheritance Tax Act 1984, by virtue of the Finance Act 1986, s 100. Accordingly references to capital transfer tax have been changed to references to inheritance tax throughout this Act.

24 Implied covenants on transfers of leaseholds

(1)   On the transfer, otherwise than by way of underlease, of any leasehold interest in land under this Act, unless there be an entry on the register negativing such implication, there shall be implied—

(a)   . . .

(b) on the part of the transferee, a covenant with the transferor, that during the residue of the term the transferee and the persons deriving title under him will pay, perform, and observe the rent, covenants, and conditions by and in the registered lease reserved and contained, and on the part of the lessee to be paid, performed, and observed, and will keep the transferor and the persons deriving title under him indemnified against all actions, expenses, and claims on account of the non-payment of the said rent or any part thereof, or the breach of the said covenants or conditions, or any of them.

(2)   On a transfer of part of the land held under a lease, the covenant implied on the part of the transferee by this section shall be limited to the payment of the apportioned rent, if any, and the performance and observance of the covenants by the lessee and conditions in the registered lease so far only as they affect the part transferred. Where the transferor remains owner of part of the land comprised in the lease, there shall also be implied on his part, as respects the part retained, a covenant with the transferee similar to that implied on the part of the transferee under this subsection.

[234]

NOTES

Sub-s (1): para (a) repealed by the Law of Property (Miscellaneous Provisions) Act 1994, s 21(2), Sch 2.

Charges on Freehold and Leasehold Land

25   Proprietor's power to create charges

(1)   The proprietor of any registered land may by deed—

(a) charge the registered land with the payment at an appointed time of any principal sum of money either with or without interest;

(b) charge the registered land in favour of a building society [(within the meaning of the Building Societies Act 1986), in accordance with] the rules of that society.

(2)   A charge may be in any form provided that—

(a) the registered land comprised in the charge is described by reference to the register or in any other manner sufficient to enable the registrar to identify the same without reference to any other document;

(b) the charge does not refer to any other interest or charge affecting the land which—

    (i) would have priority over the same and is not registered or protected on the register.

    (ii) is not an overriding interest.

(3)   Any provision contained in a charge which purports to—

    (i) take away from the proprietor thereof the power of transferring it by registered disposition or of requiring the cessation thereof to be noted on the register; or

    (ii) affect any registered land or charge other than that in respect of which the charge is to be expressly registered,

shall be void.

[235]

NOTES

Sub-s (1): words in square brackets in para (a) substituted by the Building Societies Act 1986, s 120(1), Sch 18, Pt I, para 2.

26   Registration of charges

(1)   The charge shall be completed by the registrar entering on the register the person in whose favour the charge is made as the proprietor of such charge, and the particulars of the charge.

(2)   A charge may be registered notwithstanding that it contains any trust, power to appoint new trustees, or other provisions for giving effect to the security.

(3)   Where the land, in respect of which a charge is registered, is registered with a good leasehold, qualified or possessory title, the charge shall take effect subject to the provisions of this Act with respect to land registered with such a title.

[236]

27   Terms of years implied in or granted by charges

(1)   A registered charge shall, unless made or taking effect by demise or subdemise, and subject to any provision to the contrary contained in the charge, take effect as a charge by way of legal mortgage.

(2)   Subject to the provisions of the Law of Property Act 1925, a registered charge may contain in the case of freehold land, an express demise, and in the case of leasehold land an express subdemise of the land to the creditor for a term of years absolute, subject to a proviso for cesser on redemption.

(3)   Any such demise or subdemise or charge by way of legal mortgage shall take effect from the date of the delivery of the deed containing the same, but subject to the estate or interest of any person (other than the proprietor of the land) whose estate or interest (whenever created) is registered or noted on the register before the date of registration of the charge.

(4)   Any charge registered before the commencement of this Act shall take effect as a demise or subdemise of the land in accordance with the provisions of the Law of Property Act 1925, and the registered estate shall (without prejudice to any registered charge or any term or subterm created by a charge or by this Act) vest in the person appearing by the register to be entitled to the ultimate equity of redemption.

[237]

29   Priorities of registered charges

Subject to any entry to the contrary on the register, registered charges on the same land shall as between themselves rank according to the order in which they are entered on the register, and not according to the order in which they are created.

[238]

30   Protection of charges for securing further advances

(1)   When a registered charge is made for securing further advances, the registrar shall, before making any entry on the register which would prejudicially affect the priority of any further advance thereunder, give to the proprietor of the charge at his registered address, notice by registered post of the intended entry, and the proprietor of the charge shall not, in respect of any further advance, be affected by such entry, unless the advance is made after the date when the notice ought to have been received in due course of post.

(2)   If, by reason of any failure on the part of the registrar or the post office in reference to the notice, the proprietor of the charge suffers loss in relation to a further

advance, he shall be entitled to be indemnified under this Act in like manner as if a mistake had occurred in the register; but if the loss arises by reason of an omission to register or amend the address for service, no indemnity shall be payable under this Act.

[(3) Where the proprietor of a charge is under an obligation, noted on the register, to make a further advance, a subsequent registered charge shall take effect subject to any further advance made pursuant to the obligation.]

[239]

NOTES

Sub-s (3): inserted by the Law of Property (Amendment) Act 1926, s 5.

---

33   Transfer of charges

(1)   The proprietor of any registered charge may, in the prescribed manner, transfer the charge to another person as proprietor.

(2)   The transfer shall be completed by the registrar entering on the register the transferee as proprietor of the charge transferred, but the transferor shall be deemed to remain proprietor of the charge until the name of the transferee is entered on the register in respect thereof.

(3)   A registered transferee for valuable consideration of a charge and his successors in title shall not be affected by any irregularity or invalidity in the original charge itself of which the transferee did not have notice when it was transferred to him.

(4)   On registration of any transfer of a charge, the term or subterm (if any) granted expressly or by implication by the charge or any deed of alteration shall, without any conveyance or assignment and notwithstanding anything to the contrary in the transfer or any other instrument, vest in the proprietor for the time being of the charge.

(5)   Subject to any entry to the contrary on the register, the vesting of any term or subterm in accordance with this section in the proprietor of a charge shall, subject to the right of redemption, have the same effect as if such proprietor had been registered as the transferee for valuable consideration of the term or subterm.

[240]

34   Powers of proprietor of charge

(1)   Subject to any entry on the register to the contrary, the proprietor of a charge shall have and may exercise all the powers conferred by law on the owner of a legal mortgage.

(2)   Subject to any entry to the contrary on the register and subject to the right of any persons appearing on the register to be prior incumbrancers, the proprietor of a charge may, after entry into possession and after having acquired a title under the Limitation Acts, execute a declaration, in the prescribed form, that the right of redemption is barred, and thereupon he shall be entitled, subject to furnishing any evidence which may be prescribed in support thereof, to be registered as proprietor of the land, with the same consequences as if he had been a purchaser for valuable consideration of the land under the power of sale.

(3)   An order for foreclosure shall be completed by the registration of the proprietor of the charge (or such other person as may be named in the foreclosure order absolute for that purpose) as the proprietor of the land, and by the cancellation of the charge

and of all incumbrances and entries inferior thereto; and such registration shall operate in like manner and with the same consequences as if the proprietor of the charge or other person aforesaid had been a purchaser for valuable consideration of the land under a subsisting power of sale.

(4)   A sale by the court or under the power of sale shall operate and be completed by registration in the same manner, as nearly as may be (but subject to any alterations on the register affecting the priority of the charge), as a transfer for valuable consideration by the proprietor of the land at the time of the registration of the charge would have operated or been completed, and, as respects the land transferred, the charge and all incumbrances and entries inferior thereto shall be cancelled.

(5)   Notwithstanding the creation of a term or subterm, expressly or by implication, under this Act, such transfer shall (subject to any prior incumbrances or other entries on the register) operate to transfer the registered estate, and the mortgage term or subterm shall become merged, and any purported disposition of or dealing with the mortgage term or subterm apart from the charge, and any process or act purporting to keep alive that term or subterm after the cessation of the charge shall be void.

(6)   For the purposes of this section an incumbrance or entry on the register shall not be deemed to be inferior to the charge in right of which title is made if the incumbrance or other interest is given the requisite priority by statute or otherwise.

[241]

NOTES
Limitation Acts: see now the Limitation Act 1980.

35   Discharge of charges

(1)   The registrar shall, on the requisition of the proprietor of any charge, or on due proof of the satisfaction (whole or partial) thereof, notify on the register in the prescribed manner, by cancelling or varying the original entry or otherwise, the cessation (whole or partial) of the charge, and thereupon the charge shall be deemed to have ceased (in whole or in part) accordingly.

(2)   On the notification on the register of the entire cessation of a registered charge, whether as to the whole or part only of the land affected thereby, the term or subterm implied in or granted by the charge or by any deed or alteration, so far as it affects the land to which the discharge extends, shall merge and be extinguished in the registered estate in reversion without any surrender.

[242]

As to Dealings generally

37   Powers of persons entitled to be registered

(1)   Where a person on whom the right to be registered as proprietor of registered land or of a registered charge has devolved by reason of the death of the proprietor, or has been conferred by a disposition or charge, in accordance with this Act, desires to dispose of or charge the land or to deal with the charge before he is himself registered as proprietor, he may do so in the prescribed manner, and subject to the prescribed conditions.

(2)   Subject to the provisions of this Act with regard to registered dealings for valuable consideration, a disposition or charge so made shall have the same effect as if the person making it were registered as proprietor.

(3)   Rules may be made for extending the provisions of this section to the case of any person entitled to be registered as first proprietor, and to any other case for which it may be deemed expedient to prescribe.

[243]

40   Creation and discharge of restrictive covenants

(1)   Subject to any entry to the contrary on the register, and without prejudice to the rights of persons entitled to overriding interests (if any) and to any incumbrances entered on the register, who may not concur therein, the proprietor may in any registered disposition or other instrument by covenant, condition, or otherwise, impose or make binding, so far as the law permits, any obligation or reservation with respect to the building on or other user of the registered land or any part thereof, or with respect to mines and minerals (whether registered separately or as part of the registered land), or with respect to any other thing in like manner as if the proprietor were entitled to the registered land for his own benefit.

(2)   The proprietor may (subject as aforesaid) release or waive any rights arising or which may arise by reason of any covenant or condition, or release any obligation or reservation the benefit of which is annexed or belongs to the registered land, to the same extent and in the same manner as if the rights in respect of the breach or the benefit of the covenant, condition, obligation, or reservation had been vested in him absolutely for his own benefit.

This subsection shall authorise the proprietor in reference to the registered land to give any licence, consent or approval which a tenant for life is by the Settled Land Act 1925 authorised to give in reference to settled land.

(3)   Entries shall be made on the register in the prescribed manner of all obligations and reservations imposed by the proprietor, of the release or waiver of any obligation or reservation, and of all obligations and reservations acquired by him for the benefit of the registered estate.

[244]

Transmissions of Land and Charges on Death and Bankruptcy

41   Transmissions of land and charges on death of proprietor

(1)   On the death of the sole proprietor, or of the survivor of two or more joint proprietors, of any registered land or charge, the personal representative of such sole deceased proprietor, or of the survivor of such joint proprietors, shall be entitled to be registered as proprietor in his place:

Provided that, where a special or additional personal representative is appointed by the court in reference to a registered estate, then on production of the order he shall be registered as proprietor either solely or jointly with any of the other personal representatives, as the case may require, and a copy of the order shall be filed at the registry.

(2)   Pending an application for the appointment of a special or additional personal representative, a caution against dealings may be lodged under this Act by any person intending to apply to the court for the appointment.

(3)   Subject as aforesaid, provision shall be made by rules for the manner in which effect is to be given on the register to transmissions on death.

(4)   An assent by a personal representative shall, in the case of registered land, be in the prescribed form and the production of the assent in that form shall authorise the registrar to register the person named in the assent as the proprietor of the registered land.

[245]

42   Transmissions on bankruptcy of proprietor

(1)   Upon the bankruptcy of the proprietor of any registered land or charge his trustee shall (on production of the prescribed evidence to be furnished by the official receiver or trustee in bankruptcy that the land or charge is [comprised in the bankrupt's estate]) be entitled to be registered as proprietor in his place.

The official receiver shall be entitled to be registered pending the appointment of a trustee.

(2)   Where a trustee in bankruptcy disclaims a registered lease under [sections 315 to 319 of the Insolvency Act 1986], and an order is made by the court vesting the lease in any person, the order shall direct the alteration of the register in favour of the person in whom the lease is so vested, and in such case the registrar shall, on being served with such order, forthwith (without notice to the bankrupt or any other person and without requiring production of the land certificate) alter the register accordingly, and no right to indemnity under this Act shall arise by reason of such alteration.

[246]

NOTES
    Sub-s (1): words in square brackets substituted by the Insolvency Act 1985, s 235(1), Sch 8, para 5(1), (2).
    Sub-s (2): words in square brackets substituted by the Insolvency Act 1986, s 439(2), Sch 14.

PART IV
NOTICES, CAUTIONS, INHIBITIONS, AND RESTRICTIONS

Notices

48   Registration of notice of lease

(1)   Any lessee or other person entitled to or interested in a lease of registered land, where the term granted is not an overriding interest, may apply to the registrar to register notice of such lease in the prescribed manner, and when so registered, every proprietor and the persons deriving title under him shall be deemed to be affected with notice of such lease, as being an incumbrance on the registered land in respect of which the notice is entered:

Provided that a proprietor of a charge or incumbrance registered or protected on the register prior to the registration of such notice shall not be deemed to be so affected by the notice unless such proprietor is, by reason of the lease having been made under a statutory or other power or by reason of his concurrence or otherwise, bound by the terms of the lease.

(2)   In order to register notice of a lease, if the proprietor of the registered land affected does not concur in the registration thereof, the applicant shall obtain an order of the court authorising the registration of notice of the lease, and shall deliver the order to the registrar, accompanied with the original lease or a copy thereof, and thereupon the registrar shall make a notice in the register identifying the lease or copy

so deposited, and the lease or copy so deposited shall be deemed to be the instrument of which notice is given; but if the proprietor concurs in the notice being registered, notice may be entered in such manner as may be agreed upon:

Provided that, where the lease is binding on the proprietor of the land, neither the concurrence of such proprietor nor an order of the court shall be required.

[247]

49   Rules to provide for notices of other rights, interests and claims

(1)   The provisions of the last foregoing section shall be extended by the rules so as to apply to the registration of notices of or of claims in respect of—

(a)   The grant or reservation of any annuity or rentcharge in possession, either perpetual or for a term of years absolute:

(b)   The severance of any mines or minerals from the surface, except where the mines and minerals severed are expressly included in the registration:

(c)   Land charges until the land charge is registered as a registered charge:

(d)   The right of any person interested in the proceeds of sale of land held on trust for sale or in land subject to a settlement to require that (unless a trust corporation is acting as trustee) there shall be at least two trustees of the disposition on trust for sale or of the settlement:

(e)   The rights of any widow in respect of dower or under the Intestates' Estates Act 1890, and any right to free bench or other like right saved by any statute coming into force concurrently with this Act (which rights shall take effect in equity as minor interests):

(f)   Creditors' notices and any other right, interest, or claim which it may be deemed expedient to protect by notice instead of by caution, inhibition, or restriction:

[(g)   charging orders (within the meaning of the Charging Orders Act 1979[, . . . the Criminal Justice Act 1988] [or the Drug Trafficking Act 1994][, or regulations under paragraph 11 of Schedule 4 to the Local Government Finance Act 1988][, or regulations under paragraph 11 of Schedule 4 to the Local Government Finance Act 1992]) which in the case of unregistered land may be protected by registration under the Land Charges Act 1972 and which, notwithstanding section 59 of this Act, it may be deemed expedient to protect by notice instead of by caution:]

[(h)   acquisition orders (within the meaning of Part III of the Landlord and Tenant Act 1987) which in the case of unregistered land may be protected by registration under the Land Charges Act 1972 and which, notwithstanding section 59 of this Act, it may be deemed expedient to protect by notice instead of by caution:]

[(j)   Access orders under the Access to Neighbouring Land Act 1992 which, notwithstanding section 59 of this Act, it may be deemed expedient to protect by notice instead of by caution:]

[(k)   orders made under section 26(1) or 50(1) of the Leasehold Reform, Housing and Urban Development Act 1993 which in the case of unregistered land may be protected by registration under the Land Charges Act 1972 and which, notwithstanding section 59 of this Act, it may be deemed expedient to protect by notice instead of by caution.]

(2)   A notice shall not be registered in respect of any estate, right, or interest which (independently of this Act) is capable of being overridden by the proprietor under a trust for sale or the powers of the Settled Land Act 1925, or any other statute, or of a settlement, and of being protected by a restriction in the prescribed manner:

Provided that notice of such an estate right or interest may be lodged pending the appointment of trustees of a disposition on trust for sale or a settlement, and if so lodged, shall be cancelled if and when the appointment is made and the proper restriction (if any) is entered.

(3)　A notice when registered in respect of a right, interest, or claim shall not affect prejudicially—

(a)　The powers of disposition of the personal representative of the deceased under whose will or by the operation of whose intestacy the right, interest, or claim arose; or

(b)　The powers of disposition (independently of this Act) of a proprietor holding the registered land on trust for sale.

[248]

NOTES

Sub-s (1): para (g) inserted by the Charging Orders Act 1979, s 3(3), words in first pair of square brackets substituted by the Criminal Justice Act 1988, s 170(1), Sch 15, para 6, words omitted repealed and words in second pair of square brackets inserted by the Drug Trafficking Act 1994, ss 65(1), 67(1), Sch 1, para 1, Sch 3, words in third pair of square brackets inserted by the Community Charges (Administration and Enforcement) Regulations 1989, SI 1989/438, reg 45(5), words in fourth pair of square brackets inserted by the Council Tax (Administration and Enforcement) Regulations 1992, SI 1992/613, reg 51(5); para (h) added by the Landlord and Tenant Act 1987, s 61(1), Sch 4, para 1; para (j) added by the Access to Neighbouring Land Act 1992, s 5(2); para (k) added by the Leasehold Reform, Housing and Urban Development Act 1993, s 187(1), Sch 21, para 1.

Intestates' Estates Act 1890: see now the Administration of Estates Act 1925, s 46(1).

50　Notices of restrictive covenants

(1)　Any person entitled to the benefit of a restrictive covenant or agreement (not being a covenant or agreement made between a lessor and lessee) with respect to the building on or other user of registered land may apply to the registrar to enter notice thereof on the register, and where practicable the notice shall be by reference to the instrument, if any, which contains the covenant or agreement, and a copy or abstract of such instrument shall be filed at the registry; and where any such covenant or agreement appears to exist at the time of first registration, notice thereof shall be entered on the register. In the case of registered land the notice aforesaid shall take the place of registration as a land charge.

(2)　When such a notice is entered the proprietor of the land and the persons deriving title under him (except incumbrancers or other persons who at the time when the notice is entered may not be bound by the covenant or agreement) shall be deemed to be affected with notice of the covenant or agreement as being an incumbrance on the land.

(3)　Where the covenant or agreement is discharged [modified or dealt with] by an order under the Law of Property Act 1925, or otherwise, or the court refuses to grant an injunction for enforcing the same, the entry shall either be cancelled or reference made to the order or other instrument and a copy of the order, judgment, or instrument shall be filed at the registry.

(4)　The notice shall, when practicable, refer to the land, whether registered or not, for the benefit of which the restriction was made.

[249]

NOTES

Sub-s (3): words in square brackets substituted by the Law of Property Act 1969, s 28(7).

51 Notice of manorial incidents

Where land is affected by manorial incidents, the registrar may enter a note of that fact on the register, and may cancel such note when extinguishment of the manorial incidents has been proved to his satisfaction.

[250]

52 Effect of notices

(1) A disposition by the proprietor shall take effect subject to all estates, rights, and claims which are protected by way of notice on the register at the date of the registration or entry of notice of the disposition, but only if and so far as such estates, rights, and claims may be valid and are not (independently of this Act) overridden by the disposition.

(2) Where notice of a claim is entered on the register, such entry shall operate by way of notice only, and shall not operate to render the claim valid whether made adversely to or for the benefit of the registered land or charge.

[251]

Cautions

53 Cautions against first registration

(1) Any person having or claiming such an interest in land not already registered as entitles him to object to any disposition thereof being made without his consent, may lodge a caution with the registrar to the effect that the cautioner is entitled to notice in the prescribed form, and to be served in the prescribed manner, of any application that may be made for the registration of an interest in the land affecting the right of the cautioner.

(2) The caution shall be supported by an affidavit or declaration in the prescribed form, stating the nature of the interest of the cautioner, the land and estate therein to be affected by such caution, and such other matters as may be prescribed.

(3) After a caution has been lodged in respect of any estate, which has not already been registered, registration shall not be made of such estate until notice has been served on the cautioner to appear and oppose, if he thinks fit, such registration, and the prescribed time has elapsed since the date of the service of such notice, or the cautioner has entered an appearance, whichever may first happen.

[252]

54 Cautions against dealings

(1) Any person interested under any unregistered instrument, or interested as a judgment creditor, or otherwise howsoever, in any land or charge registered in the name of any other person, may lodge a caution with the registrar to the effect that no dealing with such land or charge on the part of the proprietor is to be registered until notice has been served upon the cautioner:

Provided that a person whose estate, right, interest, or claim has been registered or protected by a notice or restriction shall not be entitled (except with the consent of the registrar) to lodge a caution in respect of such estate, right, interest, or claim, . . .

(2) A caution lodged under this section shall be supported by such evidence as may be prescribed.

[253]

NOTES

Sub-s (1): words omitted repealed by the Land Registration Act 1986, s 5(5)(a).

55 Effect of cautions against dealings

(1) After any such caution against dealings has been lodged in respect of any registered land or charge, the registrar shall not, without the consent of the cautioner, register any dealing or make any entry on the register for protecting the rights acquired under a deposit of a land or charge certificate or other dealing by the proprietor with such land or charge until he has served notice on the cautioner, warning him that his caution will cease to have any effect after the expiration of the prescribed number of days next following the date at which such notice is served; and after the expiration of such time as aforesaid the caution shall cease unless an order to the contrary is made by the registrar, and upon the caution so ceasing the registered land or charge may be dealt with in the same manner as if no caution had been lodged.

(2) If before the expiration of the said period the cautioner, or some person on his behalf, appears before the registrar, and where so required by the registrar gives sufficient security to indemnify every party against any damage that may be sustained by reason of any dealing with the registered land or charge, or the making of any such entry as aforesaid, being delayed, the registrar may thereupon, if he thinks fit to do so, delay registering any dealing with the land or charge or making any such entry for such period as he thinks just.

[254]

56 General provisions as to cautions

(1) Any person aggrieved by any act done by the registrar in relation to a caution under this Act may appeal to the court in the prescribed manner.

(2) A caution lodged in pursuance of this Act shall not prejudice the claim or title of any person and shall have no effect whatever except as in this Act mentioned.

(3) If any person lodges a caution with the registrar without reasonable cause, he shall be liable to make to any person who may have sustained damage by the lodging of the caution such compensation as may be just, and such compensation shall be recoverable as a debt by the person who has sustained damage from the person who lodged the caution.

(4) The personal representative of a deceased cautioner may consent or object to registration or a dealing in the same manner as the cautioner.

[255]

Inhibitions

57 Power for court or registrar to inhibit registered dealings

(1) The court, or, subject to an appeal to the court, the registrar, upon the application of any person interested, made in the prescribed manner, in relation to any registered land or charge, may, after directing such inquiries (if any) to be made and notices to be given and hearing such persons as the court or registrar thinks expedient, issue an order or make an entry inhibiting for a time, or until the occurrence of an event to be named in such order or entry, or generally until further order or entry, the registration or entry of any dealing with any registered land or registered charge.

(2)   The court or registrar may make or refuse to make any such order or entry, and annex thereto any terms or conditions the court or registrar may think fit, and discharge such order or cancel such entry when granted, with or without costs, and generally act in the premises in such manner as the justice of the case requires.

(3)   Any person aggrieved by any act done by the registrar in pursuance of this section may appeal to the court in the prescribed manner.

(4)   The court or the registrar may, in lieu of an inhibition, order a notice or restriction to be placed on the register.

[256]

Restrictions

58   Power to place restrictions on register

(1)   Where the proprietor of any registered land or charge desires to place restrictions on transferring or charging the land or on disposing of or dealing with the land or charge in any manner in which he is by this Act authorised to dispose of or deal with it, or on the deposit by way of security of any certificate, the proprietor may apply to the registrar to make an entry in the register that no transaction to which the application relates shall be effected, unless the following things, or such of them as the proprietor may determine, are done—

(a)   unless notice of any application for the transaction is transmitted by post to such address as he may specify to the registrar;

(b)   unless the consent of some person or persons, to be named by the proprietor, is given to the transaction;

(c)   unless some such other matter or thing is done as may be required by the applicant and approved by the registrar:

Provided that no restriction under this section shall extend or apply to dispositions of or dealings with minor interests.

(2)   The registrar shall thereupon, if satisfied of the right of the applicant to give the directions, enter the requisite restrictions on the register, and no transaction to which the restriction relates shall be effected except in conformity therewith; but it shall not be the duty of the registrar to enter any such restriction, except upon such terms as to payment of fees and otherwise as may be prescribed, or to enter any restriction that the registrar may deem unreasonable or calculated to cause inconvenience.

(3)   In the case of joint proprietors the restriction may be to the effect that when the number of proprietors is reduced below a certain specified number no disposition shall be registered except under an order of the court, or of the registrar after inquiry into title, subject to appeal to the court, and, subject to general rules, such an entry under this subsection as may be prescribed, shall be obligatory unless it is shown to the registrar's satisfaction that the joint proprietors are entitled for their own benefit, or can give valid receipts for capital money, or that one of them is a trust corporation.

(4)   Any such restrictions, except such as are in this section declared to be obligatory, may at any time be withdrawn or modified at the instance of all the persons for the time being appearing by the register to be interested in such directions, and shall also be liable to be set aside by an order of the court.

(5)   Rules may be made to enable applications to be made for the entry of restrictions by persons other than the proprietor.

[257]

Protection of various Interests

59 Writs, orders, deeds of arrangement, pending actions, etc

(1)   A writ, order, deed of arrangement, pending action, or other interest which in the case of unregistered land may be protected by registration under the Land Charges Act 1925, shall, where the land affected or the charge securing the debt affected is registered, be protected only by lodging a creditor's notice, a bankruptcy inhibition or a caution against dealings with the land or the charge.

(2)   Registration of a land charge (other than a local land charge) shall, where the land affected is registered, be effected only by registering under this Act a notice, caution or other prescribed entry:

Provided that before a land charge including a local land charge affecting registered land (being a charge to secure money) is realised, it shall be registered and take effect as a registered charge under this Act in the prescribed manner, without prejudice to the priority conferred by the land charge.

(3)   . . .

(4)   When a land charge protected by notice has been discharged as to all or any part of the land comprised therein, the notices relating thereto and to all devolutions of and dealings therewith shall be vacated as to the registered land affected by the discharge.

(5)   The foregoing provisions of this section shall apply only to writs and orders, deeds of arrangement, pending actions and land charges which if the land were unregistered would for purposes of protection be required to be registered or re-registered after the commencement of this Act under the Land Charges Act 1925; and for the purposes of this section a land charge does not include a puisne mortgage . . .

(6)   Subject to the provisions of this Act relating to fraud and to the title of a trustee in bankruptcy, a purchaser acquiring title under a registered disposition, shall not be concerned with any pending action, writ, order, deed of arrangement, or other document, matter, or claim (not being an overriding interest [or a charge for inheritance tax subject to which the disposition takes effect under section 73 of this Act]) which is not protected by a caution or other entry on the register, whether he has or has not notice thereof, express, implied, or constructive.

(7)   In this section references to registration under the Land Charges Act 1925 apply to any registration made under any other statute which, in the case of unregistered land, is by the Land Charges Act 1925, to have effect as if the registration had been made under that Act.

[258]

NOTES

Sub-s (3): repealed by the Land Registration Act 1988, ss 1(2)(a), 2, Schedule.

Sub-s (5): words omitted repealed by the Finance Act 1975, ss 52(2), 59(5), Sch 13, Pt I.

Sub-s (6): words in square brackets inserted by the Finance Act 1975, s 52(1), Sch 12, paras 2, 5(1), (4).

Inheritance tax: except in relation to a liability to tax arising before 25 July 1986 capital transfer tax is to be known as inheritance tax and the Capital Transfer Tax Act 1984 may be cited as the Inheritance Tax Act 1984, by virtue of the Finance Act 1986, s 100. Accordingly references to capital transfer tax have been changed to references to inheritance tax.

Land Charges Act 1925: see now the Land Charges Act 1972.

60   Notice of incumbrances registered under the Companies Act

(1)   Where a company, registered under the Companies (Consolidation) Act 1908, is registered as proprietor of any estate or charge already registered, the registrar shall not be concerned with any mortgage, charge, debenture, debenture stock, trust deed for securing the same, or other incumbrance created or issued by the company, whether or not registered under that Act, unless the same is registered or protected by caution or otherwise under this Act.

(2)   No indemnity shall be payable under this Act by reason of a purchaser acquiring any interest under a registered disposition from the company free from any such incumbrance.

[259]

NOTES
Companies (Consolidation) Act 1908: see now the Companies Act 1985, ss 395–398.

61   Protection of creditors prior to registration of trustee in bankruptcy

(1)   The registrar shall as soon as practicable after registration of a petition in bankruptcy as a pending action under the Land Charges Act 1925, register a notice (in this Act called a creditors' notice) against the title of any proprietor of any registered land or charge which appears to be affected, and such notice shall protect the rights of all creditors, and unless cancelled by the registrar in the prescribed manner such notice shall remain in force until a bankruptcy inhibition is registered or the trustee in bankruptcy is registered as proprietor.

No fee shall be charged for the registration of the notice.

(2)   . . .

(3)   The registrar shall, as soon as practicable after registration of a [bankruptcy order] under the Land Charges Act 1925, enter an inhibition (in this Act called a bankruptcy inhibition) against the title of any proprietor of any registered land or charge which appears to be affected.

No fee shall be charged for the registration of the inhibition.

(4)   From and after the entry of a bankruptcy inhibition (but without prejudice to dealings with or in right of interests or charges having priority over the estate or charge of the bankrupt proprietor), no dealing affecting the registered land or charge of the proprietor, other than the registration of the trustee in bankruptcy, shall be entered on the register until the inhibition is vacated as to the whole or part of the land or charge dealt with.

(5)   If and when a proprietor of any registered land or charge is adjudged bankrupt, his registered estate or interest, if belonging to him beneficially, and whether acquired before or after the date of adjudication, shall vest in the trustee in bankruptcy in accordance with the statutory provisions relating to bankruptcy for the time being in force.

(6)   Where under a disposition to a purchaser in good faith for money or money's worth such purchaser is registered as proprietor of an estate or a charge, then, [, notwithstanding that the person making the disposition is adjudged bankrupt,] the title of his trustee in bankruptcy acquired after the commencement of this Act shall, as from the date of such disposition, be void as against such purchaser unless at the date of such disposition, either a creditors' notice or a bankruptcy inhibition has been registered, but a purchaser who, at the date of the execution of the registered disposition, has notice of [the bankruptcy petition or the] adjudication, shall not be deemed to take in good faith.

Nothing in this section shall impose on a purchaser a liability to make any search under the Land Charges Act 1925.

(7)   Where the estate or assets of a bankrupt proprietor suffer loss by reason of the omission of the registrar to register a creditors' notice or bankruptcy inhibition, as required by this section, or on account of the execution or registration of a disposition after a petition is registered as a pending action or after [a bankruptcy order] is registered and before the registration of a creditors' notice or bankruptcy inhibition, the trustee in bankruptcy shall be entitled to indemnity as a person suffering loss by reason of an error or omission in the register.

(8)   If neither a creditors' notice nor a bankruptcy inhibition is registered against a bankrupt proprietor, nothing in this section shall prejudicially affect a registered disposition of any registered land or charge acquired by the bankrupt after adjudication . . .

(9)   If and when a bankruptcy inhibition is wholly or partially vacated, for any cause other than by reason of the registration of the trustee in bankruptcy, any registered estate or interest vested in the trustee in bankruptcy shall, as respects the registered land or charge to which the vacation extends, be divested and the same shall vest in the proprietor in whom it would have been vested if there had been no adjudication in bankruptcy.

(10) . . .

[260]

NOTES

Sub-s (2): repealed by the Insolvency Act 1985, s 235(3), Sch 10, Pt III.

Sub-ss (3), (6), (7): words in square brackets substituted by the Insolvency Act 1985, s 235(1), Sch 8, para 5(1), (3).

Sub-s (8): words omitted repealed by the Insolvency Act 1985, s 235(3), Sch 10, Pt III.

Sub-s (10): repealed by the Land Registration Act 1988, ss 1(2)(b), 2, Schedule.

Land Charges Act 1925: see now the Land Charges Act 1972.

---

62   Rules to be made as to certain details

Rules shall be made under this Act—

(a)   For postponing the registration of a creditors' notice or bankruptcy inhibition, where the name, address and description of the debtor [or bankrupt] appearing in the application for the registration of the pending action or [bankruptcy order] are not identical with those stated in the register, until the registrar is satisfied as to the identity of the debtor [or bankrupt];

(b)   For requiring the official receiver to notify to the registrar any mistake occurring in the [bankruptcy order] or any other fact relevant to any proposed amendment in the register; and for enabling the registrar to make any consequential amendment;

(c)   For providing for the whole or partial vacation (subject to notice to the official receiver or trustee in bankruptcy and to his right to appeal to the court) of a bankruptcy inhibition, where . . . the bankruptcy is annulled, or the registrar is satisfied that the bankruptcy proceedings do not affect or have ceased to affect the statutory powers of the bankrupt to deal with the registered land or charge.

[261]

NOTES

Words in square brackets in paras (a) and (b) inserted or substituted by the Insolvency Act 1985, s 235(1), Sch 8, para 5(1), (4); words omitted from para (c) repealed by the Insolvency Act 1985, s 235(3), Sch 10, Pt III.

PART V
LAND AND CHARGE CERTIFICATES

63 Issue of land and charge certificates

(1)   On the first registration of a freehold or leasehold interest in land, and on the registration of a charge, a land certificate, or charge certificate, as the case may be, shall be prepared in the prescribed form; it shall state whether the title is absolute, good leasehold, qualified or possessory, and it shall be either delivered to the proprietor or deposited in the registry as the proprietor may prefer.

(2)   If so deposited in the registry it shall be officially endorsed from time to time, as in this Act provided, with notes of all subsequent entries in the register affecting the registered land or charge to which it relates.

(3)   The proprietor may at any time apply for the delivery of the certificate to himself or to such person as he may direct, and may at any time again deposit it in the land registry.

(4)   The preparation, issue, endorsement, and deposit in the registry of the certificate shall be effected without cost to the proprietor.

[262]

64 Certificates to be produced and noted on dealings

(1)   So long as a land certificate or charge certificate is outstanding, it shall be produced to the registrar—
  (a) on every entry in the register of a disposition by the proprietor of the registered land or charge to which it relates; and
  (b) on every registered transmission; and
  (c) in every case (except as hereinafter mentioned) where under this Act or otherwise notice of any estate right or claim or a restriction is entered or placed on the register, adversely affecting the title of the proprietor of the registered land or charge, but not in the case of the lodgment of a caution or of an inhibition or of a creditors' notice, or of the entry of a notice of a lease at a rent without taking a fine [or a notice of a charge for inheritance tax].

(2)   A note of every such entry or transmission shall be officially entered on the certificate and the registrar shall have the same powers of compelling the production of certificates as are conferred on him by this Act as to the production of maps, surveys, books, and other documents.

(3)   On the completion of the registration of a transferee or grantee of any registered land or charge the registrar shall deliver to him a land certificate or charge certificate, and where part only of the land is dealt with shall also deliver to the transferor or grantor a land certificate containing a description of the land retained by him.

(4)   Where a transfer of land is made by the proprietor of a registered charge in exercise of any power vested in him, it may be registered, and a new land certificate may be issued to the purchaser, without production of the former land certificate (when not deposited at the registry), but the charge certificate, if any, must be produced or accounted for in accordance with this section.

The provisions of this subsection shall be extended in the prescribed manner to the cases of—
  (a) an order for foreclosure absolute;

    (b)   a proprietor of a charge or a mortgagee obtaining a title to the land under the Limitation Acts;

    (c)   title being acquired under a title paramount to the registered estate, including a title acquired pursuant to a vesting or other order of the court or other competent authority.

[(5)   Subsection (1) above shall not require the production of the land certificate when a person applies for the registration of a notice by virtue of [section 2(8) of the Matrimonial Homes Act 1983] (spouse's charge in respect of rights of occupation).]

[(6)   Subsection (1) above shall also not require the production of the land certificate when a person applies for—

    (a)   the registration of a notice of any variation of a lease affected by or in pursuance of an order under section 38 of the Landlord and Tenant Act 1987 (orders by the court varying leases), including any variation as modified by an order under section 39(4) of that Act (effect of orders varying leases: applications by third parties), or

    (b)   the cancellation of any such notice where a variation is cancelled or modified by an order under section 39(4) of that Act.]

[(7)   Subsection (1) above shall also not require the production of the land certificate or of any charge certificate when a person applies for the registration of a notice in respect of an access order under the Access to Neighbouring Land Act 1992.]

                                                                [263]

NOTES

Commencement: 1 January 1926 (sub-ss (1)–(4)); 14 February 1983 (sub-s (5)); 18 April 1988 (sub-s 6)); 31 January 1993 (sub-s (7)).

Sub-s (1): words in square brackets in para (c) added by the Finance Act 1975, s 52(1), Sch 12, paras 2, 5(1), (5).

Sub-s (5): inserted by the Matrimonial Homes and Property Act 1981, s 4(1); words in square brackets substituted by the Matrimonial Homes Act 1983, s 12(1), Sch 2.

Sub-s (6): added by the Landlord and Tenant Act 1987, s 61(1), Sch 4, para 2.

Sub-s (7): added by the Access to Neighbouring Land Act 1992, s 5(3).

Inheritance tax: except in relation to a liability to tax arising before 25 July 1986 capital transfer tax is to be known as inheritance tax and the Capital Transfer Tax Act 1984 may be cited as the Inheritance Tax Act 1984, by virtue of the Finance Act 1986, s 100. Accordingly references to capital transfer tax have been changed to references to inheritance tax.

Limitation Acts: see now the Limitation Act 1980.

65   Deposit at registry of certificate of mortgaged land

Where a charge or mortgage (otherwise than by deposit) is registered, or is protected by a caution in a specially prescribed form, the land certificate shall be deposited at the registry until the charge or mortgage is cancelled.

                                                                [264]

66   Creation of liens by deposit of certificates

The proprietor of any registered land or charge may, subject to the overriding interests, if any, to any entry to the contrary on the register, and to any estates, interests, charges, or rights registered or protected on the register at the date of the deposit, create a lien on the registered land or charge by deposit of the land certificate or charge certificate; and such lien shall, subject as aforesaid, be equivalent to a lien created in the case of unregistered land by the deposit of documents of title or of the mortgage deed by an owner entitled for his own benefit to the registered estate, or a mortgagee beneficially entitled to the mortgage, as the case may be.

                                                                [265]

68 Certificates to be evidence

Any land certificate or charge certificate shall be admissible as evidence of the several matters therein contained.

[266]

PART VI
GENERAL PROVISIONS AS TO REGISTRATION AND THE EFFECT THEREOF

69 Effect of registration on the legal estate

(1) The proprietor of land (whether he was registered before or after the commencement of this Act) shall be deemed to have vested in him without any conveyance, where the registered land is freehold, the legal estate in fee simple in possession, and where the registered land is leasehold the legal term created by the registered lease, but subject to the overriding interests, if any, including any mortgage term or charge by way of legal mortgage created by or under the Law of Property Act 1925 or this Act or otherwise which has priority to the registered estate.

(2) Where any legal estate or term left outstanding at the date of first registration (whether before or after the commencement of this Act), or disposed of or created under section forty-nine of the Land Transfer Act 1875, before the commencement of this Act, becomes satisfied, or the proprietor of the land becomes entitled to require the same to be vested in or surrendered to him, and the entry, if any, for protecting the same on the register has been cancelled, the same shall thereupon, without any conveyance, vest in the proprietor of the land, as if the same had been conveyed or surrendered to him as the case may be.

(3) If and when any person is registered as first proprietor of land in a compulsory area after the commencement of this Act, the provisions of the Law of Property Act 1925 for getting in legal estates shall apply to any legal estate in the land which was expressed to be conveyed or created in favour of a purchaser or lessee before the commencement of this Act but which failed to pass or to be created by reason of the omission of such purchaser or lessee to be registered as proprietor of the land under the Land Transfer Acts 1875 and 1897, and shall operate to vest that legal estate in the person so registered as proprietor on his registration, but subject to any mortgage term or charge by way of legal mortgage having priority thereto.

(4) The estate for the time being vested in the proprietor shall only be capable of being disposed of or dealt with by him in manner authorised by this Act.

(5) Nothing in this section operates to render valid a lease registered with possessory or good leasehold title.

[267]

70 Liability of registered land to overriding interests

(1) All registered land shall, unless under the provisions of this Act the contrary is expressed on the register, be deemed to be subject to such of the following overriding interests as may be for the time being subsisting in reference thereto, and such interests shall not be treated as incumbrances within the meaning of this Act, (that is to say):—

    (a) Rights of common, drainage rights, customary rights (until extinguished), public rights, profits a prendre, rights of sheepwalk, rights of way, watercourses, rights of water, and other easements not being equitable easements required to be protected by notice on the register;

(b) Liability to repair highways by reason of tenure, quit-rents, crown rents, heriots, and other rents and charges (until extinguished) having their origin in tenure;

(c) Liability to repair the chancel of any church;

(d) Liability in respect of embankments, and sea and river walls;

(e) . . . , payments in lieu of tithe, and charges or annuities payable for the redemption of tithe rentcharges;

(f) Subject to the provisions of this Act, rights acquired or in course of being acquired under the Limitation Acts;

(g) The rights of every person in actual occupation of the land or in receipt of the rents and profits thereof, save where enquiry is made of such person and the rights are not disclosed;

(h) In the case of a possessory, qualified, or good leasehold title, all estates, rights, interests, and powers excepted from the effect of registration;

(i) Rights under local land charges unless and until registered or protected on the register in the prescribed manner;

(j) Rights of fishing and sporting, seignorial and manorial rights of all descriptions (until extinguished), and franchises;

[(k) Leases granted for a term not exceeding twenty-one years;]

(l) In respect of land registered before the commencement of this Act, rights to mines and minerals, and rights of entry, search, and user, and other rights and reservations incidental to or required for the purpose of giving full effect to the enjoyment of rights to mines and minerals or of property in mines or minerals, being rights which, where the title was first registered before the first day of January, eighteen hundred and ninety-eight, were created before that date, and where the title was first registered after the thirty-first day of December, eighteen hundred and ninety-seven, were created before the date of first registration:

[(m) any interest or right which is an overriding interest by virtue of paragraph 1(1) of Schedule 9 to the Coal Industry Act 1994:]

Provided that, where it is proved to the satisfaction of the registrar that any land registered or about to be registered is exempt from land tax, or tithe rentcharge or payments in lieu of tithe, or from charges or annuities payable for the redemption of tithe rentcharge, the registrar may notify the fact on the register in the prescribed manner.

(2) Where at the time of first registration any easement, right, privilege, or benefit created by an instrument and appearing on the title adversely affects the land, the registrar shall enter a note thereof on the register.

(3) Where the existence of any overriding interest mentioned in this section is proved to the satisfaction of the registrar or admitted, he may (subject to any prescribed exceptions) enter notice of the same or of a claim thereto on the register, but no claim to an easement, right, or privilege not created by an instrument shall be noted against the title to the servient land if the proprietor of such land (after the prescribed notice is given to him) shows sufficient cause to the contrary.

[(4) Neither subsection (2) nor subsection (3) of this section shall apply in the case of any such interest or right as is mentioned in subsection (1)(m) of this section.]

NOTES

Commencement: 1 January 1926 (sub-ss (1)–(3)); 31 October 1994 (sub-s (4)).

Sub-s (1): words omitted from para (e) repealed by the Finance Act 1963, s 73(8)(b), Sch 14, Pt IV, and by the Tithe Act 1936, s 48(3), Sch 9; para (k) substituted by the Land Registration Act 1986, s 4(1); para (m) inserted by the Coal Industry Act 1994, s 67(1), Sch 9, para 1(2)(a).

Sub-s (4): inserted by the Coal Industry Act 1994, s 67(1), Sch 9, para 1(2)(b).

Limitation Acts: see now the Limitation Act 1980.

71 Dispositions by virtue of overriding interests

Where by virtue of any interest or power which is an overriding interest a mortgagee or other person disposes of any estate, charge, or right in or upon a registered estate, and the disposition is capable of being registered, the registrar shall, if so required, give effect to the disposition on the register.

[269]

72 Appurtenances

If before the registration of any freehold or leasehold interest in land with an absolute or good leasehold title any easement, right, or privilege has been acquired for the benefit thereof, then, on such registration, the easement, right, or privilege shall, subject to any entry to the contrary on the register, become appurtenant to the registered land in like manner as if it had been granted to the proprietor who is registered as aforesaid.

[270]

75 Acquisition of title by possession

(1) The Limitation Acts shall apply to registered land in the same manner and to the same extent as those Acts apply to land not registered, except that where, if the land were not registered, the estate of the person registered as proprietor would be extinguished, such estate shall not be extinguished but shall be deemed to be held by the proprietor for the time being in trust for the person who, by virtue of the said Acts, has acquired title against any proprietor, but without prejudice to the estates and interests of any other person interested in the land whose estate or interest is not extinguished by those Acts.

(2) Any person claiming to have acquired a title under the Limitation Acts to a registered estate in the land may apply to be registered as proprietor thereof.

(3) The registrar shall, on being satisfied as to the applicant's title, enter the applicant as proprietor either with absolute, good leasehold, qualified, or possessory title, as the case may require, but without prejudice to any estate or interest protected by any entry on the register which may not have been extinguished under the Limitation Acts, and such registration shall, subject as aforesaid, have the same effect as the registration of a first proprietor; but the proprietor or the applicant or any other person interested may apply to the court for the determination of any question arising under this section.

(4) . . .

(5) Rules may be made for applying (subject to any necessary modifications) the provisions of this section to cases where an easement, right or privilege has been acquired by prescription.

[271]

NOTES

Sub-s (4): repealed by the Land Registration and Land Charges Act 1971, s 14(1)(b), Sch 2, Pt I.
Limitation Acts: see now the Limitation Act 1980.

76 Description of registered land

Registered land may be described—

    (a) by means of a verbal description and a filed plan or general map, based on the ordnance map; or

    (b) by reference to a deed or other document, a copy or extract whereof is filed at the registry, containing a sufficient description, and a plan or map thereof; or

    (c) otherwise as the applicant for registration may desire, and the registrar, or, if the applicant prefers, the court, may approve,

regard being had to ready identification of parcels, correct descriptions of boundaries, and, so far as may be, uniformity of practice; but the boundaries of all freehold land and all requisite details in relation to the same, shall whenever practicable, be entered on the register or filed plan, or general map, and the filed plan, if any, or general map shall be used for assisting the identification of the land.

[272]

[77 Conversion of title

(1) Where land is registered with a good leasehold title, or satisfies the conditions for such registration under this section, the registrar may, and on application by the proprietor shall, if he is satisfied as to the title to the freehold and the title to any intermediate leasehold, enter the title as absolute.

(2) Where land is registered with a possessory title, the registrar may, and on application by the proprietor shall—

    (a) if he is satisfied as to the title, or

    (b) if the land has been so registered for at least twelve years and he is satisfied that the proprietor is in possession,

enter the title in the case of freehold land as absolute and in the case of leasehold land as good leasehold.

(3) Where land is registered with a qualified title, the registrar may, and on application by the proprietor shall, if he is satisfied as to the title, enter it in the case of freehold land as absolute and in the case of leasehold land as good leasehold.

(4) If any claim adverse to the title of the proprietor has been made, an entry shall not be made in the register under this section unless and until the claim has been disposed of.

(5) No fee shall be charged for the making of an entry in the register under this section at the instance of the registrar or on an application by the proprietor made in connection with a transfer for valuable consideration of the land to which the application relates.

(6) Any person, other than the proprietor, who suffers loss by reason of any entry on the register made by virtue of this section shall be entitled to be indemnified under this Act as if a mistake had been made in the register.]

[273]

NOTES

Substituted by the Land Registration Act 1986, s 1(1).

PART VII
RECTIFICATION OF REGISTER AND INDEMNITY

82 Rectification of the register

(1) The register may be rectified pursuant to an order of the court or by the registrar, subject to an appeal to the court, in any of the following cases, but subject to the provisions of this section:—

(a) Subject to any express provisions of this Act to the contrary, where a court of competent jurisdiction has decided that any person is entitled to any estate right or interest in or to any registered land or charge, and as a consequence of such decision such court is of opinion that a rectification of the register is required, and makes an order to that effect;

(b) Subject to any express provision of this Act to the contrary, where the court, on the application in the prescribed manner of any person who is aggrieved by any entry made in, or by the omission of any entry from, the register, or by any default being made, or unnecessary delay taking place, in the making of any entry in the register, makes an order for the rectification of the register;

(c) In any case and at any time with the consent of all persons interested;

(d) Where the court or the registrar is satisfied that any entry in the register has been obtained by fraud;

(e) Where two or more persons are, by mistake, registered as proprietors of the same registered estate or of the same charge;

(f) Where a mortgagee has been registered as proprietor of the land instead of as proprietor of a charge and a right of redemption is subsisting;

(g) Where a legal estate has been registered in the name of a person who if the land had not been registered would not have been the estate owner; and

(h) In any other case where, by reason of any error or omission in the register, or by reason of any entry made under a mistake, it may be deemed just to rectify the register.

(2) The register may be rectified under this section, notwithstanding that the rectification may affect any estates, rights, charges, or interests acquired or protected by registration, or by any entry on the register, or otherwise.

(3) The register shall not be rectified, except for the purpose of giving effect to an overriding interest [or an order of the court], so as to affect the title of the proprietor who is in possession—

[(a) unless the proprietor has caused or substantially contributed to the error or omission by fraud or lack of proper care; or]

(b) . . .

(c) unless for any other reason, in any particular case, it is considered that it would be unjust not to rectify the register against him.

(4) Where a person is in possession of registered land in right of a minor interest, he shall, for the purposes of this section, be deemed to be in possession as agent for the proprietor.

(5) The registrar shall obey the order of any competent court in relation to any registered land on being served with the order or an official copy thereof.

(6) On every rectification of the register the land certificate and any charge certificate which may be affected shall be produced to the registrar unless an order to the contrary is made by him.

NOTES

Sub-s (3): words in first pair of square brackets inserted, para (a) substituted and para (b) repealed by the Administration of Justice Act 1977, ss 24, 32(4), Sch 5, Pt VI.

83 Right to indemnity in certain cases

(1) Subject to the provisions of this Act to the contrary, any person suffering loss by reason of any rectification of the register under this Act shall be entitled to be indemnified.

(2) Where an error or omission has occurred in the register, but the register is not rectified, any person suffering loss by reason of such error or omission, shall, subject to the provisions of this Act, be entitled to be indemnified.

(3) Where any person suffers loss by reason of the loss or destruction of any document lodged at the registry for inspection or safe custody or by reason of an error in any official search, he shall be entitled to be indemnified under this Act.

(4) Subject as hereinafter provided, a proprietor of any registered land or charge claiming in good faith under a forged disposition shall, where the register is rectified, be deemed to have suffered loss by reason of such rectification and shall be entitled to be indemnified under this Act.

(5) No indemnity shall be payable under this Act in any of the following cases:—
[(a) Where the applicant or a person from whom he derives title (otherwise than under a disposition for valuable consideration which is registered or protected on the register) has caused or substantially contributed to the loss by fraud or lack of proper care;]
(b) On account of any mines or minerals or of the existence of any rights to work or get mines or minerals, unless a note is entered on the register that the mines or minerals are included in the registered title;
(c) On account of costs incurred in taking or defending any legal proceedings without the consent of the registrar.

(6) Where an indemnity is paid in respect of the loss of an estate or interest in or charge on land the amount so paid shall not exceed—
(a) Where the register is not rectified, the value of the estate, interest or charge at the time when the error or omission which caused the loss was made;
(b) Where the register is rectified, the value (if there had been no rectification) of the estate, interest or charge, immediately before the time of rectification.

(7) . . .

[(8) Subject to subsection (5)(c) of this section, as amended by section 2(2) of the Land Registration and Land Charges Act 1971—
(a) an indemnity under any provision of this Act shall include such amount, if any, as may be reasonable in respect of any costs or expenses properly incurred by the applicant in relation to the matter; and
(b) an applicant for an indemnity under any such provision shall be entitled to an indemnity thereunder of such amount, if any, as may be reasonable in respect of any such costs or expenses, notwithstanding that no other indemnity money is payable thereunder.]

(9) Where indemnity is paid for a loss, the registrar, on behalf of the Crown, shall be entitled to recover the amount paid from any person who has caused or substantially contributed to the loss by his fraud.

(10)   The registrar shall be entitled to enforce, on behalf of the Crown, any express or implied covenant or other right which the person who is indemnified would have been entitled to enforce in relation to the matter in respect of which indemnity has been paid.

(11)   A liability to pay indemnity under this Act shall be deemed a simple contract debt; and for the purposes of [the Limitation Act 1980], the cause of action shall be deemed to arise at the time when the claimant knows, or but for his own default might have known, of the existence of his claim:

Provided that, when a claim to indemnity arises in consequence of the registration of an estate in land with an absolute or good leasehold title, the claim shall be enforceable only if made within six years from the date of such registration, except in the following cases:—

(a)   Where at the date of registration the person interested is an infant, the claim by him may be made within six years from the time he attains full age;

(b)   In the case of settled land, or land held on trust for sale, a claim by a person interested in remainder or reversion, may be made within six years from the time when his interest falls into possession;

(c)   Where a claim arises in respect of a restrictive covenant or agreement affecting freehold land which by reason of notice or the registration of a land charge or otherwise was binding on the first proprietor at the time of first registration, the claim shall only be enforceable within six years from the breach of the covenant or agreement;

(d)   Where any person interested is entitled as a proprietor of a charge or as a mortgagee protected by a caution in the specially prescribed form, the claim by him may be made within six years from the last payment in respect of principal or interest.

(12)   This section applies to the Crown in like manner as it applies to a private person.

[275]

NOTES

Sub-s (5): para (a) substituted by the Land Registration and Land Charges Act 1971, s 3(1).
Sub-s (7): repealed by the Land Registration and Land Charges Act 1971, ss 2(4), 14(2)(b), Sch 2, Pt II.
Sub-s (8): substituted by the Land Registration and land Charges Act 1971, s 2(4).
Sub-s (11): words in square brackets substituted by the Limitation Act 1980, s 40(2), Sch 3, para 1.

PART VIII
APPLICATION TO PARTICULAR CLASSES OF LAND

86   Registration of settled land

(1)   Settled land shall be registered in the name of the tenant for life or statutory owner.

(2)   The successive or other interests created by or arising under a settlement shall (save as regards any legal estate which cannot be overridden under the powers of the Settled Land Act 1925, or any other statute) take effect as minor interests and not otherwise; and effect shall be given thereto by the proprietor of the settled land as provided by statute with respect to the estate owner, with such adaptations, if any, as may be prescribed in the case of registered land by rules made under this Act.

(3)   There shall also be entered on the register such restrictions as may be prescribed, or may be expedient, for the protection of the rights of the persons beneficially interested in the land, and such restrictions shall (subject to the provisions

of this Act relating to releases by the trustees of a settlement and to transfers by a tenant for life whose estate has ceased in his lifetime) be binding on the proprietor during his life, but shall not restrain or otherwise affect a disposition by his personal representative.

(4)   Where land already registered is acquired with capital money, the same shall be transferred by a transfer in a specially prescribed form to the tenant for life or statutory owner, and such transfer shall state the names of the persons who are trustees of the settlement for the purposes of the Settled Land Act 1925, and contain an application to register the prescribed restrictions applicable to the case; a transfer made in the specially prescribed form shall be deemed to comply with the requirements of that Act, respecting vesting deeds; and where no capital money is paid but land already registered is to be made subject to a settlement, it shall not be necessary for the trustees of the settlement to concur in the transfer.

(5)   References in this Act to the "tenant for life" shall, where the context admits, be read as referring to the tenant for life, statutory owner, or personal representative who is entitled to be registered.

[276]

87   Changes of ownership of settled land

(1)   On the death of a proprietor, or of the survivor of two or more joint proprietors of settled land (whether the land is settled by his will or by an instrument taking effect on or previously to his death), his personal representative shall hold the settled land subject to payment or to making provision for payment of all death duties and other liabilities affecting the land, and having priority to the settlement, upon trust to transfer the same by an assent in the prescribed manner to the tenant for life or statutory owner, and in the meantime upon trust to give effect to the minor interests under the settlement; but a transfer shall not be made to an infant.

(2)   Rules may be made—
   (a)   for enabling a personal representative or proprietor in proper cases to create legal estates by registered dispositions for giving effect to or creating interests in priority to the settlements;
   (b)   to provide for the cases in which application shall be made by the personal representative or proprietor for the registration of restrictions or notices; and
   (c)   for discharging a personal representative or former proprietor who has complied with the requirements of this Act and rules from all liability in respect of minor interests under a settlement.

(3)   Where a tenant for life or statutory owner who, if the land were not registered, would be entitled to have the settled land vested in him, is not the proprietor, the proprietor shall (notwithstanding any stipulation or provision to the contrary) be bound at the cost of the trust estate to execute such transfers as may be required for giving effect on the register to the rights of such tenant for life or statutory owner.

(4)   Where the trustees of a settlement have in the prescribed manner released the land from the minor interests under such settlement, the registrar shall be entitled to assume that the settlement has determined, and the restrictions for protecting the minor interests thereunder shall be cancelled.

(5)   Where an order is made under the Settled Land Act 1925 authorising the trustees of the settlement to exercise the powers on behalf of a tenant for life who is registered as proprietor, they may in his name and on his behalf do all such acts and

things under this Act as may be requisite for giving effect on the register to the powers authorised to be exercised in like manner as if they were registered as proprietors of the land, but a copy of the order shall be filed at the registry before any such powers are exercised.

(6) Where a proprietor ceases in his lifetime to be a tenant for life, he shall transfer the land to his successor in title, or, if such successor is an infant, to the statutory owner, and on the registration of such successor in title or statutory owner it shall be the duty of the trustees of the settlement, if the same be still subsisting, to apply for such alteration, if any, in the restrictions as may be required for the protection of the minor interests under the settlement.

[277]

95 Restriction on number of trustees

The statutory restrictions affecting the number of persons entitled to hold land on trust for sale and the number of trustees of a settlement apply to registered land.

[278]

PART IX
UNREGISTERED DEALINGS WITH REGISTERED LAND

Powers of dealing with Registered Land off the Register

102 Priorities as between minor interests

(1) If a minor interest subsisting or capable of taking effect at the commencement of this Act, would, if the Law of Property Acts 1922 and 1925 and this Act had not been passed have taken effect as a legal estate, then (subject and without prejudice to the estate and powers of the proprietor whose estate is affected) the conversion thereof into an equitable interest shall not affect its priority over other minor interests.

(2), (3) . . .

[279]

NOTES
Sub-ss (2), (3): repealed by the Land Registration Act 1986, s 5(1), (5)(b).

[106 Creation and protection of mortgages of registered land

(1) The proprietor of any registered land may, subject to any entry to the contrary on the register, mortgage, by deed or otherwise, the land or any part of it in any manner which would have been permissible if the land had not been registered and, subject to this section, with the like effect.

(2) Unless and until the mortgage becomes a registered charge,—
    (a) it shall take effect only in equity, and
    (b) it shall be capable of being overridden as a minor interest unless it is protected as provided by subsection (3) below.

(3) A mortgage which is not a registered charge may be protected on the register by—
    (a) a notice under section 49 of this Act,
    (b) any such other notice as may be prescribed, or
    (c) a caution under section 54 of this Act.

(4)   A mortgage which is not a registered charge shall devolve and may be transferred, discharged, surrendered or otherwise dealt with by the same instruments and in the same manner as if the land had not been registered.]

NOTES
Substituted by the Administration of Justice Act 1977, s 26(1).

PART X
MISCELLANEOUS PROVISIONS

110   Provisions as between vendor and purchaser

On a sale or other disposition of registered land to a purchaser other than a lessee or chargee—

(1)   The vendor shall, notwithstanding any stipulation to the contrary, at his own expense furnish the purchaser . . . , if required, with a copy of the subsisting entries in the register and of any filed plans and copies or abstracts of any documents or any part thereof noted on the register so far as they respectively affect the land to be dealt with (except charges or incumbrances registered or protected on the register which are to be discharged or overridden at or prior to completion):

Provided that—
   (a)   unless the purchase money exceeds one thousand pounds the costs of the copies and abstracts of the said entries plans and documents shall, in the absence of any stipulation to the contrary, be borne by the purchaser requiring the same;
   (b)   nothing in this section shall give a purchaser a right to a copy or abstract of a settlement filed at the registry:

(2)   The vendor shall, subject to any stipulation to the contrary, at his own expense furnish the purchaser with such copies, abstracts and evidence (if any) in respect of any subsisting rights and interests appurtenant to the registered land as to which the register is not conclusive, and of any matters excepted from the effect of registration as the purchaser would have been entitled to if the land had not been registered:

(3)   Except as aforesaid, and notwithstanding any stipulation to the contrary, it shall not be necessary for the vendor to furnish the purchaser with any abstract or other written evidence of title, or any copy or abstract of the land certificate, or of any charge certificate:

(4)   Where the register refers to a filed abstract or copy of or extract from a deed or other document such abstract or extract shall as between vendor and purchaser be assumed to be correct, and to contain all material portions of the original, and no person dealing with any registered land or charge shall have a right to require production of the original, or be affected in any way by any provisions of the said document other than those appearing in such abstract, copy or extract, and any person suffering loss by reason of any error or omission in such abstract, copy or extract shall be entitled to be indemnified under this Act:

(5)   Where the vendor is not himself registered as proprietor of the land or the charge giving a power of sale over the land, he shall, at the request of the purchaser and at his own expense, and notwithstanding any stipulation to the contrary, either procure the registration of himself as proprietor of the land or of the charge, as the case may be, or procure a disposition from the proprietor to the purchaser:

(6) Unless the certificate is deposited at the registry the vendor shall deliver the land certificate, or the charge certificate, as the case may be, to the purchaser on completion of the purchase, or, if only a part of the land comprised in the certificate is dealt with, or only a derivative estate is created, he shall, at his own expense, produce, or procure the production of, the certificate in accordance with this Act for the completion of the purchaser's registration. Where the certificate has been lost or destroyed, the vendor shall, notwithstanding any stipulation to the contrary, pay the costs of the proceedings required to enable the registrar to proceed without it:

(7) The purchaser shall not, by reason of the registration, be affected with notice of any pending action, writ, order, deed of arrangement or land charge (other than a local land charge) to which this subsection applies, which can be protected under this Act by lodging or registering a creditors' notice, restriction, inhibition, caution or other notice, or be concerned to make any search therefor if and so far as they affect registered land.

This subsection applies only to pending actions, writs, orders, deeds of arrangement and land charges (not including local land charges) required to be registered or re-registered after the commencement of this Act, either under the Land Charges Act 1925, or any other statute registration whereunder has effect as if made under that Act.

[281]

NOTES

Sub-s (1): words omitted repealed by the Land Registration Act 1988, s 2, Schedule.
Land Charges Act 1925: see now the Land Charges Act 1972.

[112 Inspection of register and other documents at land registry

(1) Any person may, subject to such conditions as may be prescribed and on payment of any fee payable, inspect and make copies of and extracts from—
  (a) entries on the register, and
  (b) documents referred to in the register which are in the custody of the registrar (other than leases or charges or copies of leases or charges).

(2) Documents in the custody of the registrar relating to any land or charge but not falling within subsection (1)(b) of this section may be inspected, and copies of and extracts from them may be made—
  (a) as of right, in such cases as may be prescribed, and
  (b) at the discretion of the registrar, in any other case,

but subject in all cases to such conditions as may be prescribed and on payment of any fee payable.

(3) References in this section to documents include references to things kept otherwise than in documentary form.]

[282]

NOTES

Commencement: 3 December 1990.
Substituted for original ss 112–112C by the Land Registration Act 1988, s 1(1).

113 Office copies to be evidence

Office copies of and extracts from the register and of and from documents . . . filed in the registry shall be admissible in evidence in all actions and matters, and between all persons or parties, to the same extent as the originals would be admissible, but any person suffering loss by reason of the inaccuracy of any such copy or extract shall be entitled to be indemnified under this Act, and no solicitor, trustee, personal representative, or other person in a fiduciary position shall be answerable in respect of any loss occasioned by relying on any such copy or extract.

[283]

NOTES

Words omitted repealed by the Land Registration Act 1988, s 2, Schedule.

Modified by the Building Societies Act 1986, s 124, Sch 21, paras 9, 12 and by the Administration of Justice Act 1985, ss 9, 34(2), Sch 2, para 37.

PART XI

COMPULSORY REGISTRATION

123   Effect of Act in areas where registration is compulsory

(1)   In any area in which an Order in Council declaring that registration of title to land within that area is to be compulsory on sale is for the time being in force, every conveyance on sale of freehold land and every grant of [a term of years absolute of more than twenty-one years from the date of delivery of the grant], and every assignment on sale of leasehold land held for a term of years absolute [having more than twenty-one years to run from the date of delivery of the assignment], shall (save as hereinafter provided), on the expiration of two months from the date thereof or of any authorised extension of that period, become void so far as regards the grant or conveyance of the legal estate in the freehold or leasehold land comprised in the conveyance, grant, or assignment, or so much of such land as is situated within the area affected, unless the grantee (that is to say, the person who is entitled to be registered as proprietor of the freehold or leasehold land) or his successor in title or assign has in the meantime applied to be registered as proprietor of such land:

Provided that the registrar, or the court on appeal from the registrar, may, on the application of any persons interested in any particular case in which the registrar or the court is satisfied that the application for first registration cannot be made within the said period, or can only be made within that period by incurring unreasonable expense, or that the application has not been made within the said period by reason of some accident or other sufficient cause, make an order extending the said period; and if such order be made, then, upon the registration of the grantee or his successor or assign, a note of the order shall be endorsed on the conveyance, grant or assignment:

In the case of land in an area where, at the date of the commencement of this Act, registration of title is already compulsory on sale, this subsection shall apply to every such conveyance, grant, or assignment, executed on or after that date.

(2)   Rules under this Act may provide for applying the provisions thereof to dealings with the land which may take place between the date of such conveyance, grant, or assignment and the date of application to register as if such dealings had taken place after the date of first registration, and for registration to be effected as of the date of the application to register.

(3)   In this section the expressions "conveyance on sale" and "assignment on sale" mean an instrument made on sale by virtue whereof there is conferred or completed a title under which an application for registration as first proprietor of land may be made under this Act, and include a conveyance or assignment by way of exchange where money is paid for equality of exchange, but do not include an enfranchisement

or extinguishment of manorial incidents, whether under the Law of Property Act 1922, or otherwise, or an assignment or surrender of a lease to the owner of the immediate reversion containing a declaration that the term is to merge in such reversion.

[284]

NOTES

Sub-s (1): words in square brackets substituted by the Land Registration Act 1986, s 2(1), (5), in relation to the grant or assignment of a lease granted after 1 January 1987.

PART XIII
RULES, FEE ORDERS, REGULATIONS, SHORT TITLE, COMMENCEMENT AND EXTENT

148   Short title, commencement and extent

(1)   This Act may be cited as the Land Registration Act 1925.

(2)   This Act shall come into operation on the first day of January nineteen hundred and twenty-six, but shall be deemed to come into operation immediately after the Law of Property Act 1925, the Settled Land Act 1925, the Land Charges Act 1925, the Trustee Act 1925, and the Administration of Estates Act 1925, come into operation.

(3)   This Act extends to England and Wales only.

[285]

ADMINISTRATION OF ESTATES ACT 1925

(C 23)

An Act to consolidate Enactments relating to the Administration of the Estates of Deceased Persons

[9 April 1925]

PART I
DEVOLUTION OF REAL ESTATE

1   Devolution of real estate on personal representative

(1)   Real estate to which a deceased person was entitled for an interest not ceasing on his death shall on his death, and notwithstanding any testamentary disposition thereof, devolve from time to time on the personal representative of the deceased, in like manner as before the commencement of this Act chattels real devolved on the personal representative from time to time of a deceased person.

(2)   The personal representatives for the time being of a deceased person are deemed in law his heirs and assigns within the meaning of all trusts and powers.

(3)   The personal representatives shall be the representative of the deceased in regard to his real estate to which he was entitled for an interest not ceasing on his death as well as in regard to his personal estate.

[286]

2   Application to real estate of law affecting chattels real

(1)   Subject to the provisions of this Act, all enactments and rules of law, and all jurisdiction of any court with respect to the appointment of administrators or to probate or letters of administration, or to dealings before probate in the case of chattels real, and with respect to costs and other matters in the administration of personal estate, in force before the commencement of this Act, and all powers, duties, rights, equities, obligations, and liabilities of a personal representative in force at the commencement of this Act with respect to chattels real, shall apply and attach to the personal representative and shall have effect with respect to real estate vested in him, and in particular all such powers of disposition and dealing as were before the commencement of this Act exercisable as respects chattels real by the survivor or survivors of two or more personal representatives, as well as by a single personal representative, or by all the personal representatives together, shall be exercisable by the personal representatives or representative of the deceased with respect to his real estate.

(2)   Where as respects real estate there are two or more personal representatives, a conveyance of real estate devolving under this Part of this Act [or a contract for such a conveyance] shall not . . . be made without the concurrence therein of all such representatives or an order of the court, but where probate is granted to one or some of two or more persons named as executors, whether or not power is reserved to the other or others to prove, any conveyance of the real estate [or contract for such a conveyance] may be made by the proving executor or executors for the time being, without an order of the court, and shall be as effectual as if all the persons named as executors had concurred therein.

(3)   Without prejudice to the rights and powers of a personal representative, the appointment of a personal representative in regard to real estate shall not, save as hereinafter provided, affect—

(a)   any rule as to marshalling or as to administration of assets;

(b)   the beneficial interest in real estate under any testamentary disposition;

(c)   any mode of dealing with any beneficial interest in real estate, or the proceeds of sale thereof;

(d)   the right of any person claiming to be interested in the real estate to take proceedings for the protection or recovery thereof against any person other than the personal representative.

[287]

NOTES

Sub-s (2): words in square brackets inserted and words omitted repealed by the Law of Property (Miscellaneous Provisions) Act 1994, ss 16, 21(2), Sch 2, in relation to contracts made after 1 July 1995.

3   Interpretation of Part I

(1)   In this Part of this Act "real estate" includes—

(i)   Chattels real, and land in possession, remainder, or reversion, and every interest in or over land to which a deceased person was entitled at the time of his death; and

(ii)   Real estate held on trust (including settled land) or by way of mortgage or security, but not money to arise under a trust for sale of land, nor money secured or charged on land.

(2)   A testator shall be deemed to have been entitled at his death to any interest in real estate passing under any gift contained in his will which operates as an

appointment under a general power to appoint by will, or operates under the testamentary power conferred by statute to dispose of an entailed interest.

(3) An entailed interest of a deceased person shall (unless disposed of under the testamentary power conferred by statute) be deemed an interest ceasing on his death, but any further or other interest of the deceased in the same property in remainder or reversion which is capable of being disposed of by his will shall not be deemed to be an interest so ceasing.

(4) The interest of a deceased person under a joint tenancy where another tenant survives the deceased is an interest ceasing on his death.

(5) On the death of a corporator sole his interest in the corporation's real and personal estate shall be deemed to be an interest ceasing on his death and shall devolve to his successor.

This subsection applies on the demise of the Crown as respects all property, real and personal, vested in the Crown as a corporation sole.

[288]

Part II
Executors and Administrators

General Provisions

5 Cesser of right of executor to prove

Where a person appointed executor by a will—
  (i) survives the testator but dies without having taken out probate of the will; or
  (ii) is cited to take out probate of the will and does not appear to the citation; or
  (iii) renounces probate of the will;

his rights in respect of the executorship shall wholly cease, and the representation to the testator and the administration of his real and personal estate shall devolve and be committed in like manner as if that person had not been appointed executor.

[289]

6 Withdrawal of renunciation

(1) Where an executor who has renounced probate has been permitted, whether before or after the commencement of this Act, to withdraw the renunciation and prove the will, the probate shall take effect and be deemed always to have taken effect without prejudice to the previous acts and dealings of and notices to any other personal representative who has previously proved the will or taken out letters of administration, and a memorandum of the subsequent probate shall be endorsed on the original probate or letters of administration.

(2) This section applies whether the testator died before or after the commencement of this Act.

[290]

7 Executor of executor represents original testator

(1) An executor of a sole or last surviving executor of a testator is the executor of that testator.

This provision shall not apply to an executor who does not prove the will of his testator, and, in the case of an executor who on his death leaves surviving him some other executor of his testator who afterwards proves the will of that testator, it shall cease to apply on such probate being granted.

(2) So long as the chain of such representation is unbroken, the last executor in the chain is the executor of every preceding testator.

(3) The chain of such representation is broken by—
  (a) an intestacy; or
  (b) the failure of a testator to appoint an executor; or
  (c) the failure to obtain probate of a will;

but is not broken by a temporary grant of administration if probate is subsequently granted.

(4) Every person in the chain of representation to a testator—
  (a) has the same rights in respect of the real and personal estate of that testator as the original executor would have had if living; and
  (b) is, to the extent to which the estate whether real or personal of that testator has come to his hands, answerable as if he were an original executor.

[291]

8 Right of proving executors to exercise powers

(1) Where probate is granted to one or some of two or more persons named as executors, whether or not power is reserved to the others or other to prove, all the powers which are by law conferred on the personal representative may be exercised by the proving executor or executors for the time being and shall be as effectual as if all the persons named as executors had concurred therein.

(2) This section applies whether the testator died before or after the commencement of this Act.

[292]

[9 Vesting of estate in Public Trustee where intestacy or lack of executors

(1) Where a person dies intestate, his real and personal estate shall vest in the Public Trustee until the grant of administration.

(2) Where a testator dies and—
  (a) at the time of his death there is no executor with power to obtain probate of the will, or
  (b) at any time before probate of the will is granted there ceases to be any executor with power to obtain probate,

the real and personal estate of which he disposes by the will shall vest in the Public Trustee until the grant of representation.

(3) The vesting of real or personal estate in the Public Trustee by virtue of this section does not confer on him any beneficial interest in, or impose on him any duty, obligation or liability in respect of, the property.]

[293]

NOTES
Commencement: 1 July 1995.
Substituted by the Law of Property (Miscellaneous Provisions) Act 1994, s 14(1).

15   Executor not to act while administration is in force

Where administration has been granted in respect of any real or personal estate of a deceased person, no person shall have power to bring any action or otherwise act as executor of the deceased person in respect of the estate comprised in or affected by the grant until the grant has been recalled or revoked.

[294]

17   Continuance of legal proceedings after revocation of temporary administration

[(1)] If, while any legal proceeding is pending in any court by or against an administrator to whom a temporary administration has been granted, that administration is revoked, that court may order that the proceeding be continued by or against the new personal representative in like manner as if the same had been originally commenced by or against him, but subject to such conditions and variations, if any, as that court directs.

[(2)   The county court has jurisdiction under this section where the proceedings are pending in that court.]

[295]

NOTES
Sub-s (1): numbered as such by the County Courts Act 1984, s 148(1), Sch 2, Pt III, para 11(1).
Sub-s (2): added by the County Courts Act 1984, s 148(1), Sch 2, Pt III, para 11(2).

21   Rights and liabilities of administrator

Every person to whom administration of the real and personal estate of a deceased person is granted, shall, subject to the limitations contained in the grant, have the same rights and liabilities and be accountable in like manner as if he were the executor of the deceased.

[296]

[21A   Debtor who becomes creditor's executor by representation or administrator to account for debt to estate

(1)   Subject to subsection (2) of this section, where a debtor becomes his deceased creditor's executor by representation or administrator—
    (a)   his debt shall thereupon be extinguished; but
    (b)   he shall be accountable for the amount of the debt as part of the creditor's estate in any case where he would be so accountable if he had been appointed as an executor by the creditor's will.

(2)   Subsection (1) of this section does not apply where the debtor's authority to act as executor or administrator is limited to part only of the creditor's estate which does not include the debt; and a debtor whose debt is extinguished by virtue of paragraph (a) shall not be accountable for its amount by virtue of paragraph (b) of that subsection in any case where the debt was barred by the Limitation Act 1939 before he became the creditor's executor or administrator.

(3)   In this section "debt" includes any liability, and "debtor" and "creditor" shall be construed accordingly.]

[297]

NOTES
Inserted by the Limitation Amendment Act 1980, s 10.

Special Provisions as to Settled Land

22 Special executors as respects settled land

(1)   A testator may appoint, and in default of such express appointment shall be deemed to have appointed, as his special executors in regard to settled land, the persons, if any, who are at his death the trustees of the settlement thereof, and probate may be granted to such trustees specially limited to the settled land.

In this subsection "settled land" means land vested in the testator which was settled previously to his death and not by his will.

(2)   A testator may appoint other persons either with or without such trustees as aforesaid or any of them to be his general executors in regard to his other property and assets.

[298]

23 Provisions where, as respects settled land, representation is not granted to the trustees of the settlement

(1)   Where settled land becomes vested in a personal representative, not being a trustee of the settlement, upon trust to convey the land to or assent to the vesting thereof in the tenant for life or statutory owner in order to give effect to a settlement created before the death of the deceased and not by his will, or would, on the grant of representation to him, have become so vested, such representative may—
   (a)   before representation has been granted, renounce his office in regard only to such settled land without renouncing it in regard to other property;
   (b)   after representation has been granted, apply to the court for revocation of the grant in regard to the settled land without applying in regard to other property.

(2)   Whether such renunciation or revocation is made or not, the trustees of the settlement, or any person beneficially interested thereunder, may apply to the High Court for an order appointing a special or additional personal representative in respect of the settled land, and a special or additional personal representative, if and when appointed under the order, shall be in the same position as if representation had originally been granted to him alone in place of the original personal representative, if any, or to him jointly with the original personal representative, as the case may be, limited to the settled land, but without prejudice to the previous acts and dealings, if any, of the personal representative originally constituted or the effect of notices given to such personal representative.

(3)   The court may make such order as aforesaid subject to such security, if any, being given by or on behalf of the special or additional personal representative, as the court may direct, and shall, unless the court considers that special considerations apply, appoint such persons as may be necessary to secure that the persons to act as representatives in respect of the settled land shall, if willing to act, be the same persons as are the trustees of the settlement, and an office copy of the order when made shall be furnished to the [principal registry of the Family Division of the High Court] for entry, and a memorandum of the order shall be endorsed on the probate or administration.

(4)   The person applying for the appointment of a special or additional personal representative shall give notice of the application to the [principal registry of the Family Division of the High Court] in the manner prescribed.

(5)   Rules of court may be made for prescribing for all matters required for giving effect to the provisions of this section, and in particular—

(a)   for notice of any application being given to the proper officer;

(b)   for production of orders, probates, and administration to the registry;

(c)   for the endorsement on a probate or administration of a memorandum of an order, subject or not to any exceptions;

(d)   for the manner in which the costs are to be borne;

(e)   for protecting purchasers and trustees and other persons in a fiduciary position, dealing in good faith with or giving notices to a personal representative before notice of any order has been endorsed on the probate or administration or a pending action has been registered in respect of the proceedings.

[299]

NOTES

Sub-ss (3), (4): words in square brackets substituted by the Administration of Justice Act 1970, s 1(6), Sch 2, para 3.

24   Power for special personal representatives to dispose of settled land

(1)   The special personal representatives may dispose of the settled land without the concurrence of the general personal representatives, who may likewise dispose of the other property and assets of the deceased without the concurrence of the special personal representatives.

(2)   In this section the expression "special personal representatives" means the representatives appointed to act for the purposes of settled land and includes any original personal representative who is to act with an additional personal representative for those purposes.

[300]

Duties, Rights and Obligations

[25   Duty of personal representatives

The personal representative of a deceased person shall be under a duty to—

(a)   collect and get in the real and personal estate of the deceased and administer it according to law;

(b)   when required to do so by the court, exhibit on oath in the court a full inventory of the estate and when so required render an account of the administration of the estate to the court;

(c)   when required to do so by the High Court, deliver up the grant of probate or administration to that court.]

[301]

NOTES

Substituted by the Administration of Estates Act 1971, s 9

26   Distress for rentcharge or rent

(1), (2)   . . .

(3) A personal representative may distrain for arrears of a rentcharge due or accruing to the deceased in his lifetime on the land affected or charged therewith, so long as the land remains in the possession of the person liable to pay the rentcharge or of the persons deriving title under him, and in like manner as the deceased might have done had he been living.

(4) A personal representative may distrain upon land for arrears of rent due or accruing to the deceased in like manner as the deceased might have done had he been living.

Such arrears may be distrained for after the termination of the lease or tenancy as if the term or interest had not determined, if the distress is made—
   (a) within six months after the termination of the lease or tenancy;
   (b) during the continuance of the possession of the lessee or tenant from whom the arrears were due.

The statutory enactments relating to distress for rent apply to any distress made pursuant to this subsection.

(5), (6) . . .

[302]

NOTES
Sub-ss (1), (2), (5), (6): repealed by the Law Reform (Miscellaneous Provisions) Act 1934, s 1(7).

27 Protection of persons on probate or administration

(1) Every person making or permitting to be made any payment or disposition in good faith under a representation shall be indemnified and protected in so doing, notwithstanding any defect or circumstance whatsoever affecting the validity of the representation.

(2) Where a representation is revoked, all payments and dispositions made in good faith to a personal representative under the representation before the revocation thereof are a valid discharge to the person making the same; and the personal representative who acted under the revoked representation may retain and reimburse himself in respect of any payments or dispositions made by him which the person to whom representation is afterwards granted might have properly made.

[303]

28 Liability of person fraudulently obtaining or retaining estate of deceased

If any person, to the defrauding of creditors or without full valuable consideration, obtains, receives or holds any real or personal estate of a deceased person or effects the release of any debt or liability due to the estate of the deceased, he shall be charged as executor in his own wrong to the extent of the real and personal estate received or coming to his hands, or the debt or liability released, after deducting—
   (a) any debt for valuable consideration and without fraud due to him from the deceased person at the time of his death; and
   (b) any payment made by him which might properly be made by a personal representative.

[304]

29 Liability of estate of personal representative

Where a person as personal representative of a deceased person (including an executor in his own wrong) wastes or converts to his own use any part of the real or personal estate of the deceased, and dies, his personal representative shall to the extent of the available assets of the defaulter be liable and chargeable in respect of such waste or conversion in the same manner as the defaulter would have been if living.

[305]

30 Provisions applicable where administration granted to nominee of the Crown

(1)   Where the administration of the real and personal estate of any deceased person is granted to a nominee of the Crown (whether the Treasury Solicitor, or a person nominated by the Treasury Solicitor, or any other person), any legal proceeding by or against that nominee for the recovery of the real or personal estate, or any part or share thereof, shall be of the same character, and be instituted and carried on in the same manner, and be subject to the same rules of law and equity (including, except as otherwise provided by this Act, the rules of limitation under the statutes of limitation or otherwise), in all respects as if the administration had been granted to such nominee as one of the persons interested under this Act in the estate of the deceased.

(2)   An information or other proceeding on the part of His Majesty shall not be filed or instituted, and a petition of right shall not be presented, in respect of the real or personal estate of any deceased person or any part or share thereof, or any claim thereon, except . . . subject to the same rules of law and equity within and subject to which a proceeding for the like purposes might be instituted by or against a subject.

(3)   The Treasury Solicitor shall not be required, when applying for or obtaining administration of the estate of a deceased person for the use or benefit of His Majesty, to deliver, nor shall . . . the High Court or the Commissioners of Inland Revenue be entitled to receive in connexion with any such application or grant of administration, any affidavit, statutory declaration, account, certificate, or other statement verified on oath; but the Treasury Solicitor shall deliver and the said Division and Commissioners respectively shall accept, in lieu thereof, an account or particulars of the estate of the deceased signed by or on behalf of the Treasury Solicitor.

(4)   References in sections two, four . . . and seven of the Treasury Solicitor Act 1876, and in subsection (3) of section three of the Duchy of Lancaster Act 1920, to "personal estate" shall include real estate.

[306]

NOTES
Sub-s (2): words omitted repealed by the Limitation Act 1939, s 34(4), Schedule.
Sub-s (3): words omitted repealed by the Administration of Justice Act 1970, s 54(3), Sch 11.
Sub-s (4): word omitted repealed by the Statute Law (Repeals) Act 1981.

31   Power to make rules

Provision may be made by rules of court for giving effect to the provisions of this Part of this Act so far as relates to real estate and in particular for adapting the procedure and practice on the grant of letters of administration to the case of real estate.

[307]

Part III
Administration of Assets

32   Real and personal estate of deceased are assets for payment of debts

(1)   The real and personal estate, whether legal or equitable, of a deceased person, to the extent of his beneficial interest therein, and the real and personal estate of

which a deceased person in pursuance of any general power (including the statutory power to dispose of entailed interests) disposes by his will, are assets for payment of his debts (whether by specialty or simple contract) and liabilities, and any disposition by will inconsistent with this enactment is void as against the creditors, and the court shall if necessary, administer the property for the purpose of the payment of the debts and liabilities.

This subsection takes effect without prejudice to the rights of incumbrancers.

(2)   If any person to whom any such beneficial interest devolves, or is given, or in whom any such interest vests, disposes thereof in good faith before an action is brought or process is sued out against him, he shall be personally liable for the value of the interest so disposed of by him, but that interest shall not be liable to be taken in execution in the action or under the process.

[308]

33   Trust for sale

(1)   On the death of a person intestate as to any real or personal estate, such estate shall be held by his personal representatives—
  (a)   as to the real estate upon trust to sell the same; and
  (b)   as to the personal estate upon trust to call in sell and convert into money such part thereof as may not consist of money,

with power to postpone such sale and conversion for such a period as the personal representatives, without being liable to account, may think proper, and so that any reversionary interest be not sold until it falls into possession, unless the personal representatives see special reason for sale, and so also that, unless required for purposes of administration owing to want of other assets, personal chattels be not sold except for special reason.

(2)   Out of the net money to arise from the sale and conversion of such real and personal estate (after payment of costs), and out of the ready money of the deceased (so far as not disposed of by his will, if any), the personal representative shall pay all such funeral, testamentary and administration expenses, debts and other liabilities as are properly payable thereout having regard to the rules of administration contained in this Part of this Act, and out of the residue of the said money the personal representative shall set aside a fund sufficient to provide for any pecuniary legacies bequeathed by the will (if any) of the deceased.

(3)   During the minority of any beneficiary or the subsistence of any life interest and pending the distribution of the whole or any part of the estate of the deceased, the personal representatives may invest the residue of the said money, or so much thereof as may not have been distributed, in any investments for the time being authorised by statute for the investment of trust money, with power, at the discretion of the personal representatives, to change such investments for others of a like nature.

(4)   The residue of the said money and any investments for the time being representing the same, including (but without prejudice to the trust for sale) any part of the estate of the deceased which may be retained unsold and is not required for the administration purposes aforesaid, is in this Act referred to as "the residuary estate of the intestate."

(5)   The income (including net rents and profits of real estate and chattels real after payment of rates, taxes, rent, costs of insurance, repairs and other outgoings properly attributable to income) of so much of the real and personal estate of the deceased as

may not be disposed of by his will, if any, or may not be required for the administration purposes aforesaid, may, however such estate is invested, as from the death of the deceased, be treated and applied as income, and for that purpose any necessary apportionment may be made between tenant for life and remainderman.

(6)   Nothing in this section affects the rights of any creditor of the deceased or the rights of the Crown in respect of death duties.

(7)   Where the deceased leaves a will, this section has effect subject to the provisions contained in the will.

[309]

34   Administration of assets

(1), (2)   ...

(3)   Where the estate of a deceased person is solvent his real and personal estate shall, subject to rules of court and the provisions hereinafter contained as to charges on property of the deceased, and to the provisions, if any, contained in his will, be applicable towards the discharge of the funeral, testamentary and administration expenses, debts and liabilities payable thereout in the order mentioned in Part II of the First Schedule to this Act.

[310]

NOTES

Sub-s (1): repealed by the Insolvency Act 1985, s 235(3), Sch 10, Pt III.
Sub-s (2): repealed by the Administration of Estates Act 1971, s 12(2), Sch 2, Pt II.

---

35   Charges on property of deceased to be paid primarily out of the property charged

(1)   Where a person dies possessed of, or entitled to, or, under a general power of appointment (including the statutory power to dispose of entailed interests) by his will disposes of, an interest in property, which at the time of his death is charged with the payment of money, whether by way of legal mortgage, equitable charge or otherwise (including a lien for unpaid purchase money), and the deceased has not by will deed or other document signified a contrary or other intention, the interest so charged shall, as between the different persons claiming through the deceased, be primarily liable for the payment of the charge; and every part of the said interest, according to its value, shall bear a proportionate part of the charge on the whole thereof.

(2)   Such contrary or other intention shall not be deemed to be signified—

    (a)   by a general direction for the payment of debts or of all the debts of the testator out of his personal estate, or his residuary real and personal estate, or his residuary real estate; or

    (b)   by a charge of debts upon any such estate;

unless such intention is further signified by words expressly or by necessary implication referring to all or some part of the charge.

(3)   Nothing in this section affects the right of a person entitled to the charge to obtain payment or satisfaction thereof either out of the other assets of the deceased or otherwise.

[311]

36 Effect of assent or conveyance by personal representative

(1)   A personal representative may assent to the vesting, in any person who (whether by devise, bequest, devolution, appropriation or otherwise) may be entitled thereto, either beneficially or as a trustee or personal representative, of any estate or interest in real estate to which the testator or intestate was entitled or over which he exercised a general power of appointment by his will, including the statutory power to dispose of entailed interests, and which devolved upon the personal representative.

(2)   The assent shall operate to vest in that person the estate or interest to which the assent relates, and, unless a contrary intention appears, the assent shall relate back to the death of the deceased.

(3)   . . .

(4)   An assent to the vesting of a legal estate shall be in writing, signed by the personal representative, and shall name the person in whose favour it is given and shall operate to vest in that person the legal estate to which it relates; and an assent not in writing or not in favour of a named person shall not be effectual to pass a legal estate.

(5)   Any person in whose favour an assent or conveyance of a legal estate is made by a personal representative may require that notice of the assent or conveyance be written or endorsed on or permanently annexed to the probate or letters of administration, at the cost of the estate of the deceased, and that the probate or letters of administration be produced, at the like cost, to prove that the notice has been placed thereon or annexed thereto.

(6)   A statement in writing by a personal representative that he has not given or made an assent or conveyance in respect of a legal estate, shall, in favour of a purchaser, but without prejudice to any previous disposition made in favour of another purchaser deriving title mediately or immediately under the personal representative, be sufficient evidence that an assent or conveyance has not been given or made in respect of the legal estate to which the statement relates, unless notice of a previous assent or conveyance affecting that estate has been placed on or annexed to the probate or administration.

A conveyance by a personal representative of a legal estate to a purchaser accepted on the faith of such a statement shall (without prejudice as aforesaid and unless notice of a previous assent or conveyance affecting that estate has been placed on or annexed to the probate or administration) operate to transfer or create the legal estate expressed to be conveyed in like manner as if no previous assent or conveyance had been made by the personal representative.

A personal representative making a false statement, in regard to any such matter, shall be liable in like manner as if the statement had been contained in a statutory declaration.

(7)   An assent or conveyance by a personal representative in respect of a legal estate shall, in favour of a purchaser, unless notice of a previous assent or conveyance affecting that legal estate has been placed on or annexed to the probate or administration, be taken as sufficient evidence that the person in whose favour the assent or conveyance is given or made is the person entitled to have the legal estate conveyed to him, and upon the proper trusts, if any, but shall not otherwise prejudicially affect the claim of any person rightfully entitled to the estate vested or conveyed or any charge thereon.

(8)   A conveyance of a legal estate by a personal representative to a purchaser shall not be invalidated by reason only that the purchaser may have notice that all the

debts, liabilities, funeral, and testamentary or administration expenses, duties, and legacies of the deceased have been discharged or provided for.

(9) An assent or conveyance given or made by a personal representative shall not, except in favour of a purchaser of a legal estate, prejudice the right of the personal representative or any other person to recover the estate or interest to which the assent or conveyance relates, or to be indemnified out of such estate or interest against any duties, debts, or liability to which such estate or interest would have been subject if there had not been any assent or conveyance.

(10) A personal representative may, as a condition of giving an assent or making a conveyance, require security for the discharge of any such duties, debt, or liability, but shall not be entitled to postpone the giving of an assent merely by reason of the subsistence of any such duties, debt or liability if reasonable arrangements have been made for discharging the same; and an assent may be given subject to any legal estate or charge by way of legal mortgage.

(11) This section shall not operate to impose any stamp duty in respect of an assent, and in this section "purchaser" means a purchaser for money or money's worth.

(12) This section applies to assents and conveyances made after the commencement of this Act, whether the testator or intestate died before of after such commencement.

[312]

NOTES
Sub-s (3): repealed by the Law of Property (Miscellaneous Provisions) Act 1994, s 21(2), Sch 2, in relation to contracts made after 1 July 1995.

37 Validity of conveyance not affected by revocation of representation

(1) All conveyances of any interest in real or personal estate made to a purchaser either before or after the commencement of this Act by a person to whom probate or letters of administration have been granted are valid, notwithstanding any subsequent revocation or variation, either before or after the commencement of this Act, of the probate or administration.

(2) This section takes effect without prejudice to any order of the court made before the commencement of this Act, and applies whether the testator or intestate died before or after such commencement.

[313]

38 Right to follow property and powers of the court in relation thereto

(1) An assent or conveyance by a personal representative to a person other than a purchaser does not prejudice the rights of any person to follow the property to which the assent or conveyance relates, or any property representing the same, into the hands of the person in whom it is vested by the assent or conveyance, or of any other person (not being a purchaser) who may have received the same or in whom it may be vested.

(2) Notwithstanding any such assent or conveyance the court may, on the application of any creditor or other person interested,—
    (a) order a sale, exchange, mortgage, charge, lease, payment, transfer or other transaction to be carried out which the court considers requisite for the purpose of giving effect to the rights of the persons interested;

(b) declare that the person, not being a purchaser, in whom the property is vested is a trustee for those purposes;

(c) give directions respecting the preparation and execution of any conveyance or other instrument or as to any other matter required for giving effect to the order;

(d) make any vesting order, or appoint a person to convey in accordance with the provisions of the Trustee Act 1925.

(3)   This section does not prejudice the rights of a purchaser or a person deriving title under him, but applies whether the testator or intestate died before or after the commencement of this Act.

[(4)   The county court has jurisdiction under this section where the estate in respect of which the application is made does not exceed in amount or value the county court limit.]

[314]

NOTES

Sub-s (4): added by the County Courts Act 1984, s 148(1), Sch 2, Pt III, para 12.

39 Powers of management

(1)   In dealing with the real and personal estate of the deceased his personal representatives shall, for purposes of administration, or during a minority of any beneficiary or the subsistence of any life interest, or until the period of distribution arrives, have—

(i) the same powers and discretions, including power to raise money by mortgage or charge (whether or not by deposit of documents), as a personal representative had before the commencement of this Act, with respect to personal estate vested in him, and such power of raising money by mortgage may in the case of land be exercised by way of legal mortgage; and

(ii) all the powers, discretions and duties conferred or imposed by law on trustees holding land upon an effectual trust for sale (including power to overreach equitable interests and powers as if the same affected the proceeds of sale); and

(iii) all the powers conferred by statute on trustees for sale, and so that every contract entered into by a personal representative shall be binding on and be enforceable against and by the personal representative for the time being of the deceased, and may be carried into effect, or be varied or rescinded by him, and, in the case of a contract entered into by a predecessor, as if it had been entered into by himself.

(2)   Nothing in this section shall affect the right of any person to require an assent or conveyance to be made.

(3)   This section applies whether the testator or intestate died before or after the commencement of this Act.

[315]

40 Powers of personal representative for raising money, etc

(1)   For giving effect to beneficial interests the personal representative may limit or demise land for a term of years absolute, with or without impeachment for waste, to trustees on usual trusts for raising or securing any principal sum and the interest

thereon for which the land, or any part thereof, is liable, and may limit or grant a rentcharge for giving effect to any annual or periodical sum for which the land or the income thereof or any part thereof is liable.

(2)　This section applies whether the testator or intestate died before or after the commencement of this Act.

[316]

41　Powers of personal representative as to appropriation

(1)　The personal representative may appropriate any part of the real or personal estate, including things in action, of the deceased in the actual condition or state of investment thereof at the time of appropriation in or towards satisfaction of any legacy bequeathed by the deceased, or of any other interest or share in his property, whether settled or not, as to the personal representative may seem just and reasonable, according to the respective rights of the persons interested in the property of the deceased:

Provided that—
  (i)　an appropriation shall not be made under this section so as to affect prejudicially any specific devise or bequest;
  (ii)　an appropriation of property, whether or not being an investment authorised by law or by the will, if any, of the deceased for the investment of money subject to the trust, shall not (save as hereinafter mentioned) be made under this section except with the following consents:—
      (a)　when made for the benefit of a person absolutely and beneficially entitled in possession, the consent of that person;
      (b)　when made in respect of any settled legacy share or interest, the consent of either the trustee thereof, if any (not being also the personal representative), or the person who may for the time being be entitled to the income:
      If the person whose consent is so required as aforesaid is an infant or [is incapable by reason of mental disorder within the meaning of [the Mental Health Act 1983], of managing and administering his property and affairs] the consent shall be given on his behalf by his parents or parent, testamentary or other guardian . . . or receiver, or if, in the case of an infant, there is no such parent or guardian, by the court on the application of his next friend;
  (iii)　no consent (save of such trustee as aforesaid) shall be required on behalf of a person who may come into existence after the time of appropriation, or who cannot be found or ascertained at that time;
  (iv)　if no [receiver is acting for a person suffering from mental disorder] then, if the appropriation is of an investment authorised by law or by the will, if any, of the deceased for the investment of money subject to the trust, no consent shall be required on behalf of the [said person];
  (v)　if, independently of the personal representative, there is no trustee of a settled legacy share or interest, and no person of full age and capacity entitled to the income thereof, no consent shall be required to an appropriation in respect of such legacy share or interest, provided that the appropriation is of an investment authorised as aforesaid.

[(1A)　The county court has jurisdiction under proviso (ii) to subsection (1) of this section where the estate in respect of which the application is made does not exceed in amount or value the county court limit.]

(2)   Any property duly appropriated under the powers conferred by this section shall thereafter be treated as an authorised investment, and may be retained or dealt with accordingly.

(3)   For the purposes of such appropriation, the personal representative may ascertain and fix the value of the respective parts of the real and personal estate and the liabilities of the deceased as he may think fit, and shall for that purpose employ a duly qualified valuer in any case where such employment may be necessary; and may make any conveyance (including an assent) which may be requisite for giving effect to the appropriation.

(4)   An appropriation made pursuant to this section shall bind all persons interested in the property of the deceased whose consent is not hereby made requisite.

(5)   The personal representative shall, in making the appropriation, have regard to the rights of any person who may thereafter come into existence, or who cannot be found or ascertained at the time of appropriation, and of any other person whose consent is not required by this section.

(6)   This section does not prejudice any other power of appropriation conferred by law or by the will (if any) of the deceased, and takes effect with any extended powers conferred by the will (if any) of the deceased, and where an appropriation is made under this section, in respect of a settled legacy, share or interest, the property appropriated shall remain subject to all trusts for sale and powers of leasing, disposition, and management or varying investments which would have been applicable thereto or to the legacy, share or interest in respect of which the appropriation is made, if no such appropriation had been made.

(7)   If after any real estate has been appropriated in purported exercise of the powers conferred by this section, the person to whom it was conveyed disposes of it or any interest therein, then, in favour of a purchaser, the appropriation shall be deemed to have been made in accordance with the requirements of this section and after all requisite consents, if any, had been given.

(8)   In this section, a settled legacy, share or interest includes any legacy, share or interest to which a person is not absolutely entitled in possession at the date of the appropriation, also an annuity, and "purchaser" means a purchaser for money or money's worth.

(9)   This section applies whether the deceased died intestate or not, and whether before or after the commencement of this Act, and extends to property over which a testator exercises a general power of appointment, including the statutory power to dispose of entailed interests, and authorises the setting apart of a fund to answer an annuity by means of the income of that fund or otherwise.

[317]

NOTES

Sub-s (1): words in first pair of square brackets in para (ii) substituted by the Mental Health Act 1959, s 149(1), Sch 7, Pt I, words in square brackets therein substituted by the Mental Health Act 1983, s 148(1), Sch 4, para 7; words omitted from para (ii) repealed and words in square brackets in para (iv) substituted by the Mental Health Act 1959, s 149(1), Sch 7, Pt I.

Sub-s (1A): inserted by the County Courts Act 1984, s 148(1), Sch 2, Pt III, para 13.

42   Power to appoint trustees of infants' property

(1)   Where an infant is absolutely entitled under the will or on the intestacy of a person dying before or after the commencement of this Act (in this subsection called

"the deceased") to a devise or legacy, or to the residue of the estate of the deceased, or any share therein, and such devise, legacy, residue or share is not under the will, if any, of the deceased, devised or bequeathed to trustees for the infant, the personal representatives of the deceased may appoint a trust corporation or two or more individuals not exceeding four (whether or not including the personal representatives or one or more of the personal representatives), to be the trustee or trustees of such devise, legacy, residue or share for the infant, and to be trustees of any land devised or any land being or forming part of such residue or share for the purposes of the Settled Land Act 1925, and of the statutory provisions relating to the management of land during a minority, and may execute or do any assurance or thing requisite for vesting such devise, legacy, residue or share in the trustee or trustees so appointed.

On such appointment the personal representatives, as such, shall be discharged from all further liability in respect of such devise, legacy, residue, or share, and the same may be retained in its existing condition or state of investment, or may be converted into money, and such money may be invested in any authorised investment.

(2) Where a personal representative has before the commencement of this Act retained or sold any such devise, legacy, residue or share, and invested the same or the proceeds thereof in any investments in which he was authorised to invest money subject to the trust, then, subject to any order of the court made before such commencement, he shall not be deemed to have incurred any liability on that account, or by reason of not having paid or transferred the money or property into court.

[318]

43 Obligations of personal representative as to giving possession of land and powers of the court

(1) A personal representative, before giving an assent or making a conveyance in favour of any person entitled, may permit that person to take possession of the land, and such possession shall not prejudicially affect the right of the personal representative to take or resume possession nor his power to convey the land as if he were in possession thereof, but subject to the interest of any lessee, tenant or occupier in possession or in actual occupation of the land.

(2) Any person who as against the personal representative claims possession of real estate, or the appointment of a receiver thereof, or a conveyance thereof, or an assent to the vesting thereof, or to be registered as proprietor thereof under the Land Registration Act 1925, may apply to the court for directions with reference thereto, and the court may make such vesting or other order as may be deemed proper, and the provisions of the Trustee Act 1925, relating to vesting orders and to the appointment of a person to convey, shall apply.

(3) This section applies whether the testator or intestate died before or after the commencement of this Act.

[(4) The county court has jurisdiction under this section where the estate in respect of which the application is made does not exceed in amount or value the county court limit.]

[319]

NOTES

Sub-s (4): added by the County Courts Act 1984, s 148(1), Sch 2, Pt III, para 14.

44 Power to postpone distribution

Subject to the foregoing provisions of this Act, a personal representative is not bound to distribute the estate of the deceased before the expiration of one year from the death.

[320]

PART IV
DISTRIBUTION OF RESIDUARY ESTATE

45 Abolition of descent to heir, curtesy, dower and escheat

(1)   With regard to the real estate and personal inheritance of every person dying after the commencement of this Act, there shall be abolished—

  (a) All existing modes rules and canons of descent, and of devolution by special occupancy or otherwise, of real estate, or of a personal inheritance, whether operating by the general law or by the custom of gavelkind or borough english or by any other custom of any county, locality, or manor, or otherwise howsoever; and

  (b) Tenancy by the curtesy and every other estate and interest of a husband in real estate as to which his wife dies intestate, whether arising under the general law or by custom or otherwise; and

  (c) Dower and freebench and every other estate and interest of a wife in real estate as to which her husband dies intestate, whether arising under the general law or by custom or otherwise: Provided that where a right (if any) to freebench or other like right has attached before the commencement of this Act which cannot be barred by a testamentary or other disposition made by the husband, such right shall, unless released, remain in force as an equitable interest; and

  (d) Escheat to the Crown or the Duchy of Lancaster or the Duke of Cornwall or to a mesne lord for want of heirs.

(2)   Nothing in this section affects the descent or devolution of an entailed interest.

[321]

46 Succession to real and personal estate on intestacy

(1)   The residuary estate of an intestate shall be distributed in the manner or be held on the trusts mentioned in this section, namely:—

  [(i) If the intestate leaves a husband or wife, then in accordance with the following Table:

TABLE

If the intestate—

  (1) leaves—   the residuary estate shall be held in trust for the surviving husband or wife absolutely.

    (a) no issue, and

    (b) no   parent,   or
         brother or sister of
         the whole blood,
         or   issue   of a
         brother or sister of
         the whole blood

(2) leaves issue (whether or not persons mentioned in sub-paragraph (b) above also survive) — the surviving husband or wife shall take the personal chattels absolutely and, in addition, the residuary estate of the intestate (other than the personal chattels) shall stand charged with the payment of a [fixed net sum], free of death duties and costs, to the surviving husband or wife with interest thereon from the date of the death . . . [at such rate as the Lord Chancellor may specify by order] until paid or appropriated, and, subject to providing for that sum and the interest thereon, the residuary estate (other than the personal chattels) shall be held—

(a) as to one half upon trust for the surviving husband or wife during his or her life, and, subject to such life interest, on the statutory trusts for the issue of the intestate, and

(b) as to the other half, on the statutory trusts for the issue of the intestate.

(3) leaves one or more of the following, that is to say, a parent, a brother or sister of the whole blood, or issue of a brother or sister of the whole blood, but leaves no issue — the surviving husband or wife shall take the personal chattels absolutely and, in addition, the residuary estate of the intestate (other than the personal chattels) shall stand charged with the payment of a [fixed net sum], free of death duties and costs, to the surviving husband or wife with interest thereon from the date of the death . . . [at such rate as the Lord Chancellor may specify by order] until paid or appropriated, and, subject to providing for that sum and the interest thereon, the residuary estate (other than the personal chattels) shall be held—

(a) as to one half in trust for the surviving husband or wife absolutely, and

(b) as to the other half—

(i) where the intestate leaves one parent or both parents (whether or not brothers or sisters of the intestate or their issue also survive) in trust for the parent absolutely or, as the case may be, for the two parents in equal shares absolutely

(ii) where the intestate leaves no parent, on the statutory trusts for the brothers and sisters of the whole blood of the intestate.]

[The fixed net sums referred to in paragraphs (2) and (3) of this Table shall be of the amounts provided by or under section 1 of the Family Provision Act 1966]]

(ii) If the intestate leaves issue but no husband or wife, the residuary estate of the intestate shall be held on the statutory trusts for the issue of the intestate;

(iii) If the intestate leaves [no husband or wife and] no issue but both parents, then . . . the residuary estate of the intestate shall be held in trust for the father and mother in equal shares absolutely;

   (iv) If the intestate leaves [no husband or wife and] no issue but one parent, then . . . the residuary estate of the intestate shall be held in trust for the surviving father or mother absolutely;

   (v) If the intestate leaves no [husband or wife and no issue and no] parent, then . . . the residuary estate of the intestate shall be held in trust for the following persons living at the death of the intestate, and in the following order and manner, namely:—

      First, on the statutory trusts for the brothers and sisters of the whole blood of the intestate; but if no person takes an absolutely vested interest under such trusts; then

      Secondly, on the statutory trusts for the brothers and sisters of the half blood of the intestate; but if no person takes an absolutely vested interest under such trusts; then

      Thirdly, for the grandparents of the intestate and, if more than one survive the intestate, in equal shares; but if there is no member of this class; then

      Fourthly, on the statutory trusts for the uncles and aunts of the intestate (being brothers or sisters of the whole blood of a parent of the intestate); but if no person takes an absolutely vested interest under such trusts; then

      Fifthly, on the statutory trusts for the uncles and aunts of the intestate (being brothers or sisters of the half blood of a parent of the intestate) . . .

   (vi) In default of any person taking an absolute interest under the foregoing provisions, the residuary estate of the intestate shall belong to the Crown or to the Duchy of Lancaster or to the Duke of Cornwall for the time being, as the case may be, as bona vacantia, and in lieu of any right to escheat.

      The Crown or the said Duchy or the said Duke may (without prejudice to the powers reserved by section nine of the Civil List Act 1910, or any other powers), out of the whole or any part of the property devolving on them respectively, provide, in accordance with the existing practice, for dependents, whether kindred or not, of the intestate, and other persons for whom the intestate might reasonably have been expected to make provision.

[(1A) The power to make orders under subsection (1) above shall be exercisable by statutory instrument subject to annulment in pursuance of a resolution of either House of Parliament; and any such order may be varied or revoked by a subsequent order made under the power.]

(2) A husband and wife shall for all purposes of distribution or division under the foregoing provisions of this section be treated as two persons.

[(3) Where the intestate and the intestate's husband or wife have died in circumstances rendering it uncertain which of them survived the other and the intestate's husband or wife is by virtue of section one hundred and eighty-four of the Law of Property Act 1925, deemed to have survived the intestate, this section shall, nevertheless, have effect as respects the intestate as if the husband or wife had not survived the intestate.

(4) The interest payable on [the fixed net sum] payable to a surviving husband or wife shall be primarily payable out of income.]

NOTES

47   Statutory trusts in favour of issue and other classes of relatives of intestate

(1)   Where under this Part of this Act the residuary estate of an intestate, or any part thereof, is directed to be held on the statutory trusts for the issue of the intestate, the same shall be held upon the following trusts, namely:—

   (i)   In trust, in equal shares if more than one, for all or any the children or child of the intestate, living at the death of the intestate, who attain the age of [eighteen] years or marry under that age, and for all or any of the issue living at the death of the intestate who attain the age of [eighteen] years or marry under that age of any child of the intestate who predeceases the intestate, such issue to take through all degrees, according to their stocks, in equal shares if more than one, the share which their parent would have taken if living at the death of the intestate, and so that no issue shall take whose parent is living at the death of the intestate and so capable of taking;

   (ii)   The statutory power of advancement, and the statutory provisions which relate to maintenance and accumulation of surplus income, shall apply, but when an infant marries such infant shall be entitled to give valid receipts for the income of the infant's share or interest;

   (iii)   Where the property held on the statutory trusts for issue is divisible into shares, then any money or property which, by way of advancement or on the marriage of a child of the intestate, has been paid to such child by the intestate or settled by the intestate for the benefit of such child (including any life or less interest and including property covenanted to be paid or settled) shall, subject to any contrary intention expressed or appearing from the circumstances of the case, be taken as being so paid or settled in or towards satisfaction of the share of such child or the share which such child would have taken if living at the death of the intestate, and shall be brought into account, at a valuation (the value to be reckoned as at the death of the intestate), in accordance with the requirements of the personal representatives;

   (iv)   The personal representatives may permit any infant contingently interested to have the use and enjoyment of any personal chattels in such manner and subject to such conditions (if any) as the personal representatives may consider reasonable, and without being liable to account for any consequential loss.

(2)   If the trusts in favour of the issue of the intestate fail by reason of no child or other issue attaining an absolutely vested interest—

   (a)   the residuary estate of the intestate and the income thereof and all statutory accumulations, if any, of the income thereof, or so much thereof as may not have been paid or applied under any power affecting the same, shall go, devolve and be held under the provisions of this Part of this Act as if the intestate had died without leaving issue living at the death of the intestate;

(b) references in this Part of this Act to the intestate "leaving no issue" shall be construed as "leaving no issue who attain an absolutely vested interest";

(c) references in this Part of this Act to the intestate "leaving issue" or "leaving a child or other issue" shall be construed as "leaving issue who attain an absolutely vested interest."

(3) Where under this Part of this Act the residuary estate of an intestate or any part thereof is directed to be held on the statutory trusts for any class of relatives of the intestate, other than issue of the intestate, the same shall be held on trusts corresponding to the statutory trusts for the issue of the intestate (other than the provision for bringing any money or property into account) as if such trusts (other than as aforesaid) were repeated with the substitution of references to the members or member of that class for references to the children or child of the intestate.

[(4) References in paragraph (i) of subsection (1) of the last foregoing section to the intestate leaving, or not leaving, a member of the class consisting of brothers or sisters of the whole blood of the intestate and issue of brothers or sisters of the whole blood of the intestate shall be construed as references to the intestate leaving, or not leaving, a member of that class who attains an absolutely vested interest.

(5) . . .]

NOTES

Sub-s (1): word in square brackets in para (i) substituted by the Family Law Reform Act 1969, s 3(2).

Sub-s (4): added by the Intestates' Estates Act 1952, s 1(1), (3)(c).

Sub-s (5): added by the Intestates' Estates Act 1952, s 1(1), (3)(c); repealed by the Family Provision Act 1966, ss 9, 10, Sch 2.

[47A Right of surviving spouse to have his own life interest redeemed

(1) Where a surviving husband or wife is entitled to the interest in part of the residuary estate, and so elects, the personal representative shall purchase or redeem the life interest by paying the capital value thereof to the tenant for life, or the persons deriving title under the tenant for life, and the costs of the transaction; and thereupon the residuary estate of the intestate may be dealt with and distributed free from the life interest.

(2) . . .

(3) An election under this section shall only be exercisable if at the time of the election the whole of the said part of the residuary estate consists of property in possession, but, for the purposes of this section, a life interest in property partly in possession and partly not in possession shall be treated as consisting of two separate life interests in those respective parts of the property.

[(3A) The capital value shall be reckoned in such manner as the Lord Chancellor may by order direct, and an order under this subsection may include transitional provisions.

(3B) The power to make orders under subsection (3A) above shall be exercisable by statutory instrument subject to annulment in pursuance of a resolution of either House of Parliament; and any such order may be varied or revoked by a subsequent order made under the power.]

(4)   . . .

(5)   An election under this section shall be exercisable only within the period of twelve months from the date on which representation with respect to the estate of the intestate is first taken out:

Provided that if the surviving husband or wife satisfies the court that the limitation to the said period of twelve months will operate unfairly—

    (a) in consequence of the representation first taken out being probate of a will subsequently revoked on the ground that the will was invalid, or

    (b) in consequence of a question whether a person had an interest in the estate, or as to the nature of an interest in the estate, not having been determined at the time when representation was first taken out, or

    (c) in consequence of some other circumstances affecting the administration or distribution of the estate,

the court may extend the said period.

(6)   An election under this section shall be exercisable, except where the tenant for life is the sole personal representative, by notifying the personal representative (or, where there are two or more personal representatives of whom one is the tenant for life, all of them except the tenant for life) in writing; and a notification in writing under this subsection shall not be revocable except with the consent of the personal representative.

(7)   Where the tenant for life is the sole personal representative an election under this section shall not be effective unless written notice thereof is given to the [[Senior Registrar] of the Family Division of the High Court] within the period within which it must be made; and provision may be made by probate rules for keeping a record of such notices and making that record available to the public.

In this subsection the expression "probate rules" means rules [of court made under section 127 of the Supreme Court Act 1981].

(8)   An election under this section by a tenant for life who is an infant shall be as valid and binding as it would be if the tenant for life were of age; but the personal representative shall, instead of paying the capital value of the life interest to the tenant for life, deal with it in the same manner as with any other part of the residuary estate to which the tenant for life is absolutely entitled.

(9)   In considering for the purposes of the foregoing provisions of this section the question when representation was first taken out, a grant limited to settled land or to trust property shall be left out of account and a grant limited to real estate or to personal estate shall be left out of account unless a grant limited to the remainder of the estate has previously been made or is made at the same time.]

[324]

NOTES

    Added by the Intestates' Estates Act 1952, s 2(b).

    Sub-ss (2), (4): repealed by the Administration of Justice Act 1977, ss 28(2), 32(4), Sch 5, Pt VI.

    Sub-ss (3A), (3B): inserted by the Administration of Justice Act 1977, s 28(3).

    Sub-s (7): words in first (outer) pair of square brackets substituted by the Administration of Justice Act 1970, s 1(6), Sch 2, para 4, words in square brackets therein and word in third pair of square brackets substituted by the Supreme Court Act 1981, s 152(1), Sch 5.

---

48   Powers of personal representative in respect of interests of surviving spouse

(1)   . . .

(2) The personal representatives may raise—

   (a) [the fixed net sum] or any part thereof and the interest thereon payable to the surviving husband or wife of the intestate on the security of the whole or any part of the residuary estate of the intestate (other than the personal chattels), so far as that estate may be sufficient for the purpose of the said sum and interest may not have been satisfied by an appropriation under the statutory power available in that behalf; and

   (b) in like manner the capital sum, if any, required for the purchase or redemption of the life interest of the surviving husband or wife of the intestate, or any part thereof not satisfied by the application for that purpose of any part of the residuary estate of the intestate;

and in either case the amount, if any, properly required for the payment of the costs of the transaction.

[325]

NOTES

Sub-s (1): repealed by the Intestates' Estates Act 1952, s 2(a).

Sub-s (2): words in square brackets substituted by the Family Provision Act 1966, s 1.

49 Application to cases of partial intestacy

[(1)] Where any person dies leaving a will effectively disposing of part of his property, this Part of this Act shall have effect as respects the part of his property not so disposed of subject to the provisions contained in the will and subject to the following modifications:—

   [(aa) where the deceased leaves a husband or wife who acquires any beneficial interests under the will of the deceased (other than personal chattels specifically bequeathed) the references in this Part of this Act to [the fixed net sum] payable to a surviving husband or wife, and to interest on that sum, shall be taken as references to the said sum diminished by the value at the date of death of the said beneficial interests, and to interest on that sum as so diminished, and accordingly, where the said value exceeds the said sum, this Part of this Act shall have effect as if references to the said sum, and interest thereon, were omitted;]

   (a) The requirements [of section forty-seven of this Act] as to bringing property into account shall apply to any beneficial interests acquired by any issue of the deceased under the will of the deceased, but not to beneficial interests so acquired by any other persons;

   (b) The personal representative shall, subject to his rights and powers for the purposes of administration, be a trustee for the persons entitled under this Part of this Act in respect of the part of the estate not expressly disposed of unless it appears by the will that the personal representative is intended to take such part beneficially.

[(2) References in the foregoing provisions of this section to beneficial interests acquired under a will shall be construed as including a reference to a beneficial interest acquired by virtue of the exercise by the will of a general power of appointment (including the statutory power to dispose of entailed interests), but not of a special power of appointment.

(3) For the purposes of paragraph (aa) in the foregoing provisions of this section the personal representative shall employ a duly qualified valuer in any case where such employment may be necessary.

(4)   The references in subsection (3) of section forty-seven A of this Act to property are references to property comprised in the residuary estate and, accordingly, where a will of the deceased creates a life interest in property in possession, and the remaining interest in that property forms part of the residuary estate, the said references are references to that remaining interest (which, until the life interest determines, is property not in possession).]

[326]

NOTES

Sub-s (1): numbered as such by virtue of, and para (aa) inserted by, the Intestates' Estates Act 1952, s 3(2), words in square brackets in para (aa) substituted by the Family Provision Act 1966, s 1; words in square brackets in para (a) inserted by the Intestates' Estates Act 1952, s 3.

Sub-ss (2)–(4): added by the Intestates' Estates Act 1952, s 3(3).

50   Construction of documents

(1)   References to any Statutes of Distribution in an instrument inter vivos made or in a will coming into operation after the commencement of this Act, shall be construed as references to this Part of this Act; and references in such an instrument or will to statutory next of kin shall be construed, unless the context otherwise requires, as referring to the persons who would take beneficially on an intestacy under the foregoing provisions of this Part of this Act.

(2)   Trusts declared in an instrument inter vivos made, or in a will coming into operation, before the commencement of this Act by reference to the Statutes of Distribution, shall, unless the contrary thereby appears, be construed as referring to the enactments (other than the Intestates' Estates Act 1890) relating to the distribution of effects of intestates which were in force immediately before the commencement of this Act.

[(3)   In subsection (1) of this section the reference to this Part of this Act, or the foregoing provisions of this Part of this Act, shall in relation to an instrument inter vivos made, or a will or codicil coming into operation, after the coming into force of section 18 of the Family Law Reform Act 1987 (but not in relation to instruments inter vivos made or wills or codicils coming into operation earlier) be construed as including references to that section.]

[327]

NOTES

Sub-s (3): added by the Family Law Reform Act 1987, s 33(1), Sch 2, para 3.

51   Savings

(1)   Nothing in this Part of this Act affects the right of any person to take beneficially, by purchase, as heir either general or special.

(2)   The foregoing provisions of this Part of this Act do not apply to any beneficial interest in real estate (not including chattels real) to which a [person of unsound mind] or defective living and of full age at the commencement of this Act, and unable, by reason of his incapacity, to make a will, who thereafter dies intestate in respect of such interest without having recovered his testamentary capacity, was entitled at his death, and any such beneficial interest (not being an interest ceasing on his death) shall, without prejudice to any will of the deceased, devolve in accordance with the general law in force before the commencement of this Act applicable to freehold land, and that law shall, notwithstanding any repeal, apply to the case.

For the purposes of this subsection, a [person of unsound mind] or defective who dies intestate as respects any beneficial interest in real estate shall not be deemed to have recovered his testamentary capacity unless his . . . receiver has been discharged.

(3)   Where an infant dies after the commencement of this Act without having been married, and independently of this subsection he would, at his death, have been equitably entitled under a settlement (including a will) to a vested estate in fee simple or absolute interest in freehold land, or in any property settled to devolve therewith or as freehold land, such infant shall be deemed to have had an entailed interest, and the settlement shall be construed accordingly.

(4)   This Part of this Act does not affect the devolution of an entailed interest as an equitable interest.

[328]

NOTES
    Sub-s (2): words in square brackets substituted by the Mental Treatment Act 1930, s 20(5); words omitted repealed by the Mental Health Act 1959, s 149(2), Sch 8, Pt I.

52   Interpretation of Part IV

In this Part of this Act "real and personal estate" means every beneficial interest (including rights of entry and reverter) of the intestate in real and personal estate which (otherwise than in right of a power of appointment or of the testamentary power conferred by statute to dispose of entailed interests) he could, if of full age and capacity, have disposed of by his will [and references (however expressed) to any relationship between two persons shall be construed in accordance with section 1 of the Family Law Reform Act 1987].

[329]

NOTES
    Words in square brackets added by the Family Law Reform Act 1987, s 33(1), Sch 2, para 4.

PART V
SUPPLEMENTAL

53   General savings

(1)   Nothing in this Act shall derogate from the powers of the High Court which exist independently of this Act or alter the distribution of business between the several divisions of the High Court, or operate to transfer any jurisdiction from the High Court to any other court.

(2)   Nothing in this Act shall affect any unrepealed enactment in a public general Act dispensing with probate or administration as respects personal estate not including chattels real.

(3)   . . .

[330]

NOTES
    Sub-s (3): repealed by the Finance Act 1975, ss 52(2), 59(5), Sch 13, Pt I.

54   Application of Act

Save as otherwise expressly provided, this Act does not apply in any case where the death occurred before the commencement of this Act.

[331]

55 Definitions

In this Act, unless the context otherwise requires, the following expressions have the meanings hereby assigned to them respectively, that is to say:—

(1) (i) "Administration" means, with reference to the real and personal estate of a deceased person, letters of administration whether general or limited, or with the will annexed or otherwise:

   (ii) "Administrator" means a person to whom administration is granted:

   (iii) "Conveyance" includes a mortgage, charge by way of legal mortgage, lease, assent, vesting, declaration, vesting instrument, disclaimer, release and every other assurance of property or of an interest therein by any instrument, except a will, and "convey" has a corresponding meaning, and "disposition" includes a "conveyance" also a devise bequest and an appointment of property contained in a will, and "dispose of" has a corresponding meaning:

   [(iiiA) "the County Court limit", in relation to any enactment contained in this Act, means the amount for the time being specified by an Order in Council under section 145 of the County Courts Act 1984 as the county court limit for the purposes of that enactment (or, where no such Order in Council has been made, the corresponding limit specified by Order in Council under section 192 of the County Courts Act 1959);]

   (iv) "the Court" means the High Court and also the county court, where that court has jurisdiction . . .

   (v) "Income" includes rents and profits:

   (vi) "Intestate" includes a person who leaves a will but dies intestate as to some beneficial interest in his real or personal estate:

   (vii) "Legal estates" mean the estates charges and interests in or over land (subsisting or created at law) which are by statute authorised to subsist or to be created at law; and "equitable interests" mean all other interests and charges in or over land or in the proceeds of sale thereof:

   (viii) "[Person of unsound mind]" includes a [person of unsound mind] whether so found or not, and in relation to a [person of unsound mind] not so found; . . . and "defective" includes every person affected by the provisions of section one hundred and sixteen of the Lunacy Act 1890, as extended by section sixty-four of the Mental Deficiency Act 1913, and for whose benefit a receiver has been appointed:

   (ix) "Pecuniary legacy" includes an annuity, a general legacy, a demonstrative legacy so far as it is not discharged out of the designated property, and any other general direction by a testator for the payment of money, including all death duties free from which any devise, bequest, or payment is made to take effect:

   (x) "Personal chattels" mean carriages, horses, stable furniture and effects (not used for business purposes), motor cars and accessories (not used for business purposes), garden effects, domestic animals, plate, plated articles, linen, china, glass, books, pictures, prints, furniture, jewellery, articles of household or personal use or ornament, musical and scientific instruments and apparatus, wines, liquors and consumable stores, but do not include any chattels used at the death of the intestate for business purposes nor money or securities for money:

   (xi) "Personal representative" means the executor, original or by representation, or administrator for the time being of a deceased person, and as regards any liability for the payment of death duties includes any person who takes possession of or intermeddles with the property of a deceased person without the authority of the personal representatives or the court, and "executor" includes a person deemed to be appointed executor as respects settled land:

(xii) "Possession" includes the receipt of rents and profits or the right to receive the same, if any:

(xiii) "Prescribed" means prescribed by rules of court . . . :

(xiv) "Probate" means the probate of a will:

(xv) . . .

(xvi) . . .

(xvii) "Property" includes a thing in action and any interest in real or personal property:

(xviii) "Purchaser" means a lessee, mortgagee, or other person who in good faith acquires an interest in property for valuable consideration, also an intending purchaser and "valuable consideration" includes marriage, but does not include a nominal consideration in money:

(xix) "Real estate" save as provided in Part IV of this Act means real estate, including chattels real, which by virtue of Part I of this Act devolves on the personal representative of a deceased person:

(xx) "Representation" means the probate of a will and administration, and the expression "taking out representation" refers to the obtaining of the probate of a will or of the grant of administration:

(xxi) "Rent" includes a rent service or a rentcharge, or other rent, toll, duty, or annual or periodical payment in money or money's worth, issuing out of or charged upon land, but does not include mortgage interest; and "rentcharge" includes a fee farm rent:

(xxii) . . .

(xxiii) "Securities" include stocks, funds, or shares:

(xxiv) "Tenant for life," "statutory owner," "land," "settled land," "settlement," "trustees of the settlement," "term of years absolute," "death duties," and "legal mortgage," have the same meanings as in the Settled Land Act 1925, and "entailed interest" and "charge by way of legal mortgage" have the same meanings as in the Law of Property Act 1925:

(xxv) "Treasury solicitor" means the solicitor for the affairs of His Majesty's Treasury, and includes the solicitor for the affairs of the Duchy of Lancaster:

(xxvi) "Trust corporation" means the public trustee or a corporation either appointed by the court in any particular case to be a trustee or entitled by rules made under subsection (3) of section four of the Public Trustee Act 1906, to act as custodian trustee:

(xxvii) "Trust for sale," in relation to land, means an immediate binding trust for sale, whether or not exercisable at the request or with the consent of any person, and with or without a power at discretion to postpone the sale; and "power to postpone a sale" means power to postpone in the exercise of a discretion:

(xxviii) "Will" includes codicil.

(2)　References to a child or issue living at the death of any person include child or issue en ventre sa mere at the death.

(3)　References to the estate of a deceased person include property over which the deceased exercises a general power of appointment (including the statutory power to dispose of entailed interests) by his will.

NOTES

Sub-s (1): para (iiiA) inserted by the County Courts Act 1984, s 148(1), Sch 2, Pt III, para 15; words omitted from para (iv) repealed by the Courts Act 1971, s 56(4), Sch 11, Pt II; in para (viii) words omitted repealed by the Mental Health Act 1959, s 149(2), Sch 8, Pt I, words in square brackets substituted by the Mental Treatment Act 1930, s 20(5); words omitted from para (xiii) repealed by the Supreme Court Act 1981, s 152(4), Sch 7; para (xv) repealed by the Law of Property (Miscellaneous Provisions) Act 1994, s 21(2), Sch 2; paras (xvi), (xxii) repealed by the Supreme Court Act 1981, s 152(4), Sch 7.

Modification: definition "Trust corporation" modified in relation to charities by the Charities Act 1993, s 35.

57 Application to Crown

(1)   The provisions of this Act bind the Crown and the Duchy of Lancaster, and the Duke of Cornwall for the time being as respects the estates of persons dying after the commencement of this Act, but not so as to affect the time within which proceedings for the recovery of real or personal estate vesting in or devolving on His Majesty in right of His Crown, to His Duchy of Lancaster, or on the Duke of Cornwall, may be instituted.

(2)   Nothing in this Act in any manner affects or alters the descent or devolution of any property for the time being vested in His Majesty either in right of the Crown or of the Duchy of Lancaster or of any property for the time being belonging to the Duchy of Cornwall.

[333]

58 Short title, commencement and extent

(1)   This Act may be cited as the Administration of Estates Act 1925.

(2)   . . .

(3)   This Act extends to England and Wales only:

[334]

NOTES

Sub-s (2): repealed by the Statute Law Revision Act 1950.

SCHEDULES

FIRST SCHEDULE

Section 34

Part II
Order of Application of Assets where the Estate is Solvent

1.   Property of the deceased undisposed of by will, subject to the retention thereout of a fund sufficient to meet any pecuniary legacies.

2.   Property of the deceased not specifically devised or bequeathed but included (either by a specific or general description) in a residuary gift, subject to the retention out of such property of a fund sufficient to meet any pecuniary legacies, so far as not provided for as aforesaid.

3.   Property of the deceased specifically appropriated or devised or bequeathed (either by a specific or general description) for the payment of debts.

4.   Property of the deceased charged with, or devised or bequeathed (either by a specific or general description) subject to a charge for the payment of debts.

5.   The fund, if any, retained to meet pecuniary legacies.

6.   Property specifically devised or bequeathed, rateably according to value,

7.   Property appointed by will under a general power, including the statutory power to dispose of entailed interests, rateably according to value.

8.   The following provisions shall also apply—
     (a)   The order of application may be varied by the will of the deceased.
     (b)   . . .

NOTES

Para 8: words omitted repealed by the Finance (No 2) Act 1983, s 16(4), Sch 2, Pt II.

[335]

LAW OF PROPERTY (AMENDMENT) ACT 1926

(C 11)

An Act to amend certain enactments relating to the Law of Property and Trustees
[16 June 1926]

1   Conveyances of legal estates subject to certain interests

(1)   Nothing in the Settled Land Act 1925 shall prevent a person on whom the powers of a tenant for life are conferred by paragraph (ix) of subsection (1) of section twenty of that Act from conveying or creating a legal estate subject to a prior interest as if the land had not been settled land.

(2)   In any of the following cases, namely—
     (a)   where a legal estate has been conveyed or created under subsection one of this section, or under section sixteen of the Settled Land Act 1925, subject to any prior interest, or
     (b)   where before the first day of January, nineteen hundred and twenty-six, land has been conveyed to a purchaser for money or money's worth subject to any prior interest whether or not on the purchase the land was expressed to be exonerated from, or the grantor agreed to indemnify the purchaser against, such prior interest,

the estate owner for the time being of the land subject to such prior interest may, notwithstanding any provision contained in the Settled Land Act 1925, but without prejudice to any power whereby such prior interest is capable of being overreached, convey or create a legal estate subject to such prior interest as if the instrument creating the prior interest was not an instrument or one of the instruments constituting a settlement of the land.

(3)   In this section "interest" means an estate, interest, charge or power of charging subsisting, or capable of arising or of being exercised, under a settlement, and, where a prior interest arises under the exercise of a power, "instrument" includes both the instrument conferring the power and the instrument exercising it.

[336]

3   Meaning of "trust corporation"

(1)   For the purposes of the Law of Property Act 1925, the Settled Land Act 1925, the Trustee Act 1925, the Administration of Estates Act 1925, and the [Supreme Court Act 1981], the expression "Trust Corporation" includes the Treasury Solicitor,

the Official Solicitor and any person holding any other official position prescribed by the Lord Chancellor, and, in relation to the property of a bankrupt and property subject to a deed of arrangement, includes the trustee in bankruptcy and the trustee under the deed respectively, and, in relation to charitable ecclesiastical and public trusts, also includes any local or public authority so prescribed, and any other corporation constituted under the laws of the United Kingdom or any part thereof which satisfies the Lord Chancellor that it undertakes the administration of any such trusts without remuneration, or that by its constitution it is required to apply the whole of its net income after payment of outgoings for charitable, ecclesiastical or public purposes, and is prohibited from distributing, directly or indirectly, any part thereof by way of profits amongst any of its members, and is authorised by him to act in relation to such trusts as a trust corporation.

(2)   For the purposes of this provision, the expression "Treasury Solicitor" means the solicitor for the affairs of His Majesty's Treasury, and includes the solicitor for the affairs of the Duchy of Lancaster.

[337]

NOTES

Sub-s (1): words in square brackets substituted by the Supreme Court Act 1981, s 152(1), Sch 5.

8   Short title, construction and commencement

(1)   This Act may be cited as the Law of Property (Amendment) Act 1926, and so far as it amends any Act shall be construed as one with that Act.

(2)   ...

[338]

NOTES

Sub-s (2): repealed by the Statute Law Revision Act 1950.

LANDLORD AND TENANT ACT 1927

(C 36)

An Act to provide for the payment of compensation for improvements and goodwill to tenants of premises used for business purposes, or the grant of a new lease in lieu thereof; and to amend the law of landlord and tenant

[22 December 1927]

PART II
GENERAL AMENDMENTS OF THE LAW OF LANDLORD AND TENANT

18   Provisions as to covenants to repair

(1)   Damages for a breach of a covenant or agreement to keep or put premises in repair during the currency of a lease, or to leave or put premises in repair at the termination of a lease, whether such covenant or agreement is expressed or implied, and whether general or specific, shall in no case exceed the amount (if any) by which the value of the reversion (whether immediate or not) in the premises is diminished owing to the breach of such covenant or agreement as aforesaid; and in particular no damage shall be recovered for a breach of any such covenant or agreement to leave or

put premises in repair at the termination of a lease, if it is shown that the premises, in whatever state of repair they might be, would at or shortly after the termination of the tenancy have been or be pulled down, or such structural alterations made therein as would render valueless the repairs covered by the covenant or agreement.

(2) A right of re-entry or forfeiture for a breach of any such covenant or agreement as aforesaid shall not be enforceable, by action or otherwise, unless the lessor proves that the fact that such a notice as is required by section one hundred and forty-six of the Law of Property Act 1925, had been served on the lessee was known either—

    (a) to the lessee; or

    (b) to an under-lessee holding under an under-lease which reserved a nominal reversion only to the lessee; or

    (c) to the person who last paid the rent due under the lease either on his own behalf or as agent for the lessee or under-lessee;

and that a time reasonably sufficient to enable the repairs to be executed had elapsed since the time when the fact of the service of the notice came to the knowledge of any such person.

Where a notice has been sent by registered post addressed to a person at his last known place of abode in the United Kingdom, then, for the purposes of this subsection, that person shall be deemed, unless the contrary is proved, to have had knowledge of the fact that the notice had been served as from the time at which the letter would have been delivered in the ordinary course of post.

This subsection shall be construed as one with section one hundred and forty-six of the Law of Property Act 1925.

(3) This section applies whether the lease was created before or after the commencement of this Act.

[339]

19 Provisions as to covenants not to assign, etc, without licence or consent

(1) In all leases whether made before or after the commencement of this Act containing a covenant condition or agreement against assigning, under-letting, charging or parting with the possession of demised premises or any part thereof without licence or consent, such covenant condition or agreement shall, notwithstanding any express provision to the contrary, be deemed to be subject—

    (a) to a proviso to the effect that such licence or consent is not to be unreasonably withheld, but this proviso does not preclude the right of the landlord to require payment of a reasonable sum in respect of any legal or other expenses incurred in connection with such licence or consent; and

    (b) (if the lease is for more than forty years, and is made in consideration wholly or partially of the erection, or the substantial improvement, addition or alteration of buildings, and the lessor is not a Government department or local or public authority, or a statutory or public utility company) to a proviso to the effect that in the case of any assignment, under-letting, charging or parting with the possession (whether by the holders of the lease or any under-tenant whether immediate or not) effected more than seven years before the end of the term no consent or licence shall be required, if notice in writing of the transaction is given to the lessor within six months after the transaction is effected.

(2)   In all leases whether made before or after the commencement of this Act containing a covenant condition or agreement against the making of improvements without a licence or consent, such covenant condition or agreement shall be deemed, notwithstanding any express provision to the contrary, to be subject to a proviso that such licence or consent is not to be unreasonably withheld; but this proviso does not preclude the right to require as a condition of such licence or consent the payment of a reasonable sum in respect of any damage to or diminution in the value of the premises or any neighbouring premises belonging to the landlord, and of any legal or other expenses properly incurred in connection with such licence or consent nor, in the case of an improvement which does not add to the letting value of the holding, does it preclude the right to require as a condition of such licence or consent, where such a requirement would be reasonable, an undertaking on the part of the tenant to reinstate the premises in the condition in which they were before the improvement was executed.

(3)   In all leases whether made before or after the commencement of this Act containing a covenant condition or agreement against the alteration of the user of the demised premises, without licence or consent, such covenant condition or agreement shall, if the alteration does not involve any structural alteration of the premises, be deemed, notwithstanding any express provision to the contrary, to be subject to a proviso that no fine or sum of money in the nature of a fine, whether by way of increase of rent or otherwise, shall be payable for or in respect of such licence or consent; but this proviso does not preclude the right of the landlord to require payment of a reasonable sum in respect of any damage to or diminution in the value of the premises or any neighbouring premises belonging to him and of any legal or other expenses incurred in connection with such licence or consent.

Where a dispute as to the reasonableness of any such sum has been determined by a court of competent jurisdiction, the landlord shall be bound to grant the licence or consent on payment of the sum so determined to be reasonable.

(4)   This section shall not apply to leases of agricultural holdings within the meaning of the [Agricultural Holdings Act 1986] [which are leases in relation to which that Act applies, or to farm business tenancies within the meaning of the Agricultural Tenancies Act 1995], and paragraph (b) of subsection (1), subsection (2) and subsection (3) of this section shall not apply to mining leases.

[340]

NOTES
Sub-s (4): words in first pair of square brackets substituted by the Agricultural Holdings Act 1986, s 100, Sch 14, para 15; words in second pair of square brackets inserted by the Agricultural Tenancies Act 1995, s 40, Schedule, para 6.

PART III
GENERAL

23   Service of notices

(1)   Any notice, request, demand or other instrument under this Act shall be in writing and may be served on the person on whom it is to be served either personally, or by leaving it for him at his last known place of abode in England or Wales, or by sending it through the post in a registered letter addressed to him there, or, in the case of a local or public authority or a statutory or a public utility company, to the secretary or other proper officer at the principal office of such authority or company, and in the case of a notice to a landlord, the person on whom it is to be served shall include any agent of the landlord duly authorised in that behalf.

(2)   Unless or until a tenant of a holding shall have received notice that the person theretofore entitled to the rents and profits of the holding (hereinafter referred to as "the original landlord") has ceased to be so entitled, and also notice of the name and address of the person who has become entitled to such rents and profits, any claim, notice, request, demand, or other instrument, which the tenant shall serve upon or deliver to the original landlord shall be deemed to have been served upon or delivered to the landlord of such holding.

[341]

26   Short title, commencement and extent

(1)   This Act may be cited as the Landlord and Tenant Act 1927.

(2)   . . .

(3)   This Act shall extend to England and Wales only.

[342]

NOTES

Sub-s (2): repealed by the Statute Law Revision Act 1950.

LAW OF PROPERTY (AMENDMENT) ACT 1929

(C 9)

An Act to amend the provisions of the Law of Property Act 1925, relating to relief against forfeiture of under-leases

[5 February 1929]

1   Relief of under-lessees against breach of covenant

Nothing in subsection (8), subsection (9) or subsection (10) of section one hundred and forty-six of the Law of Property Act 1925 (which relates to restrictions on and relief against forfeiture of leases and under-leases), shall affect the provisions of subsection (4) of the said section.

[343]

2   Short title

This Act may be cited as the Law of Property (Amendment) Act 1929, and the Law of Property Act 1925, the Law of Property (Amendment) Act 1926, so far as it amends that Act, and this Act may be cited together as the Law of Property Acts 1925 to 1929.

[344]

LEASEHOLD PROPERTY (REPAIRS) ACT 1938

(C 34)

An Act to amend the law as to the enforcement by landlords of obligations to repair and similar obligations arising under leases

[23 June 1938]

1   Restriction on enforcement of repairing covenants in long leases of small houses

(1)   Where a lessor serves on a lessee under sub-section (1) of section one hundred and forty-six of the Law of Property Act 1925, a notice that relates to a breach of a covenant or agreement to keep or put in repair during the currency of the lease [all or

any of the property comprised in the lease], and at the date of the service of the notice [three] years or more of the term of the lease remain unexpired, the lessee may within twenty-eight days from that date serve on the lessor a counter-notice to the effect that he claims the benefit of this Act.

(2) A right to damages for a breach of such a covenant as aforesaid shall not be enforceable by action commenced at any time at which [three] years or more of the term of the lease remain unexpired unless the lessor has served on the lessee not less than one month before the commencement of the action such a notice as is specified in subsection (1) of section one hundred and forty-six of the Law of Property Act 1925, and where a notice is served under this subsection, the lessee may, within twenty-eight days from the date of the service thereof, serve on the lessor a counter-notice to the effect that he claims the benefit of this Act.

(3) Where a counter-notice is served by a lessee under this section, then, notwithstanding anything in any enactment or rule of law, no proceedings, by action or otherwise, shall be taken by the lessor for the enforcement of any right of re-entry or forfeiture under any proviso or stipulation in the lease for breach of the covenant or agreement in question, or for damages for breach thereof, otherwise than with the leave of the court.

(4) A notice served under subsection (1) of section one hundred and forty-six of the Law of Property Act 1925, in the circumstances specified in subsection (1) of this section, and a notice served under subsection (2) of this section shall not be valid unless it contains a statement, in characters not less conspicuous than those used in any other part of the notice, to the effect that the lessee is entitled under this Act to serve on the lessor a counter-notice claiming the benefit of this Act, and a statement in the like characters specifying the time within which, and the manner in which, under this Act a counter-notice may be served and specifying the name and address for service of the lessor.

(5) Leave for the purposes of this section shall not be given unless the lessor proves—
   (a) that the immediate remedying of the breach in question is requisite for preventing substantial diminution in the value of his reversion, or that the value thereof has been substantially diminished by the breach;
   (b) that the immediate remedying of the breach is required for giving effect in relation to the [premises] to the purposes of any enactment, or of any byelaw or other provision having effect under an enactment, [or for giving effect to any order of a court or requirement of any authority under any enactment or any such byelaw or other provision as aforesaid];
   (c) in a case in which the lessee is not in occupation of the whole of the [premises as respects which the covenant or agreement is proposed to be enforced], that the immediate remedying of the breach is required in the interests of the occupier of [those premises] or of part thereof;
   (d) that the breach can be immediately remedied at an expense that is relatively small in comparison with the much greater expense that would probably be occasioned by postponement of the necessary work; or
   (e) special circumstances which in the opinion of the court, render it just and equitable that leave should be given.

(6) The court may, in granting or in refusing leave for the purposes of this section, impose such terms and conditions on the lessor or on the lessee as it may think fit.

[345]

NOTES

Sub-ss (1), (2), (5): words in square brackets substituted by the Landlord and Tenant Act 1954, s 51(2)(a)–(d).

7 Application of certain provisions of 15 and 16 Geo 5 c 20

(1)   In this Act the expressions "lessor", "lessee" and "lease" have the meanings assigned to them respectively by sections one hundred and forty-six and one hundred and fifty-four of the Law of Property Act 1925, except that they do not include any reference to such a grant as is mentioned in the said section one hundred and forty-six, or to the person making, or to the grantee under such a grant, or to persons deriving title under such a person; and "lease" means a lease for a term of [seven years or more, not being a lease of an agricultural holding within the meaning of the [Agricultural Holdings Act 1986]] [which is a lease in relation to which that Act applies and not being a farm business tenancy within the meaning of the Agricultural Tenancies Act 1995].

(2)   The provisions of section one hundred and ninety-six of the said Act (which relate to the service of notices) shall extend to notices and counter-notices required or authorised by this Act.

[346]

NOTES

    Sub-s (1): words in first (outer) pair of square brackets substituted by the Landlord and Tenant Act 1954, s 51(2)(g), words in square brackets therein substituted by the Agricultural Holdings Act 1986, s 100, Sch 14, para 17; words in third pair of square brackets added by the Agricultural Tenancies Act 1995, s 40, Schedule, para 8.

8 Short title and extent

(1)   This Act may be cited as the Leasehold Property (Repairs) Act 1938.

(2)   This Act shall not extend to Scotland or to Northern Ireland.

[347]

INTESTATES' ESTATES ACT 1952

(C 64)

An Act to amend the law of England and Wales, about the property of persons dying intestate; to amend the Inheritance (Family Provision) Act, 1938; and for purposes connected therewith

[30 October 1952]

PART I
AMENDMENTS OF INTESTATE SUCCESSION

5 Rights of surviving spouse as respects the matrimonial home

The Second Schedule to this Act shall have effect for enabling the surviving husband or wife of a person dying intestate after the commencement of this Act to acquire the matrimonial home.

[348]

PART III
GENERAL

9 Short title and commencement

(1)   This Act may be cited as the Intestates' Estates Act 1952.

(2)   This Act shall come into operation on the first day of January, nineteen hundred and fifty-three.

[349]

SECOND SCHEDULE
RIGHTS OF SURVIVING SPOUSE AS RESPECTS THE MATRIMONIAL HOME
Section 5

1.—(1) Subject to the provisions of this Schedule, where the residuary estate of the intestate comprises an interest in a dwelling-house in which the surviving husband or wife was resident at the time of the intestate's death, the surviving husband or wife may require the personal representative, in exercise of the power conferred by section forty-one of the principal Act (and with due regard to the requirements of that section as to valuation) to appropriate the said interest in the dwelling-house in or towards satisfaction of any absolute interest of the surviving husband or wife in the real and personal estate of the intestate.

(2) The right conferred by this paragraph shall not be exercisable where the interest is—
    (a)   a tenancy which at the date of the death of the intestate was a tenancy which would determine within the period of two years from that date; or
    (b)   a tenancy which the landlord by notice given after that date could determine within the remainder of that period.

(3) Nothing in subsection (5) of section forty-one of the principal Act (which requires the personal representative, in making an appropriation to any person under that section, to have regard to the rights of others) shall prevent the personal representative from giving effect to the right conferred by this paragraph.

(4) The reference in this paragraph to an absolute interest in the real and personal estate of the intestate includes a reference to the capital value of a life interest which the surviving husband or wife has under this Act elected to have redeemed.

(5) Where part of a building was, at the date of the death of the intestate, occupied as a separate dwelling, that dwelling shall for the purposes of this Schedule be treated as a dwelling-house.

2. Where—
    (a)   the dwelling-house forms part of a building and an interest in the whole of the building is comprised in the residuary estate; or
    (b)   the dwelling-house is held with agricultural land and an interest in the agricultural land is comprised in the residuary estate; or
    (c)   the whole or part of the dwelling-house was at the time of the intestate's death used as a hotel or lodging house; or
    (d)   a part of the dwelling-house was at the time of the intestate's death used for purposes other than domestic purposes,

the right conferred by paragraph 1 of this Schedule shall not be exercisable unless the court, on being satisfied that the exercise of that right is not likely to diminish the value of assets in the residuary estate (other than the said interest in the dwelling-house) or make them more difficult to dispose of, so orders.

3.—(1) The right conferred by paragraph 1 of this Schedule—
    (a)   shall not be exercisable after the expiration of twelve months from the first taking out of representation with respect to the intestate's estate;
    (b)   shall not be exercisable after the death of the surviving husband or wife
    (c)   shall be exercisable, except where the surviving husband or wife is the sole personal representative, by notifying the personal representative (or, where there are two or more personal representatives of whom one is the surviving husband or wife, all of them except the surviving husband or wife) in writing.

(2) A notification in writing under paragraph (c) of the foregoing sub-paragraph shall not be revocable except with the consent of the personal representative; but the surviving husband or wife may require the personal representative to have the said interest in the dwelling-house valued in accordance with section forty-one of the principal Act and to inform him or her of the result of that valuation before he or she decides whether to exercise the right.

(3) Subsection (9) of the section forty-seven A added to the principal Act by section two of this Act shall apply for the purposes of the construction of the reference in this paragraph to the first taking out of representation, and the proviso to subsection (5) of that section shall apply for the purpose of enabling the surviving husband or wife to apply for an extension of the period of twelve months mentioned in this paragraph.

4.—(1) During the period of twelve months mentioned in paragraph 3 of this Schedule the personal representative shall not without the written consent of the surviving husband or wife sell or otherwise dispose of the said interest in the dwelling-house except in the course of administration owing to want of other assets.

(2) An application to the court under paragraph 2 of this Schedule may be made by the personal representative as well as by the surviving husband or wife, and if, on an application under that paragraph, the court does not order that the right conferred by paragraph 1 of this Schedule shall be exercisable by the surviving husband or wife, the court may authorise the personal representative to dispose of the said interest in the dwelling-house within the said period of twelve months.

(3) Where the court under sub-paragraph (3) of paragraph 3 of this Schedule extends the said period of twelve months, the court may direct that this paragraph shall apply in relation to the extended period as it applied in relation to the original period of twelve months.

(4) This paragraph shall not apply where the surviving husband or wife is the sole personal representative or one of two or more personal representatives.

(5) Nothing in this paragraph shall confer any right on the surviving husband or wife as against a purchaser from the personal representative.

5.—(1) Where the surviving husband or wife is one of two or more personal representatives, the rule that a trustee may not be a purchaser of trust property shall not prevent the surviving husband or wife from purchasing out of the estate of the intestate an interest in a dwelling-house in which the surviving husband or wife was resident at the time of the intestate's death.

(2) The power of appropriation under section forty-one of the principal Act shall include power to appropriate an interest in a dwelling-house in which the surviving husband or wife was resident at the time of the intestate's death partly in satisfaction of an interest of the surviving husband or wife in the real and personal estate of the intestate and partly in return for a payment of money by the surviving husband or wife to the personal representative.

6.—(1) Where the surviving husband or wife is a person of unsound mind or a defective, a requirement or consent under this Schedule may be made or given on his or her behalf by the committee or receiver, if any, or, where there is no committee or receiver, by the court.

(2) A requirement or consent made or given under this Schedule by a surviving husband or wife who is an infant shall be as valid and binding as it would be if he or she were of age; and, as respects an appropriation in pursuance of paragraph 1 of this Schedule, the provisions of section forty-one of the principal Act as to obtaining the consent of the infant's parent or guardian, or of the court on behalf of the infant, shall not apply.

7.—(1) Except where the context otherwise requires, references in this Schedule to a dwelling-house include references to any garden or portion of ground attached to and usually occupied with the dwelling-house or otherwise required for the amenity or convenience of the dwelling-house.

(2) This Schedule shall be construed as one with Part IV of the principal Act.

[350]

NOTES
Principal Act: Administration of Estates Act 1925.

CHARITABLE TRUSTS (VALIDATION) ACT 1954

(C 58)

An Act to validate under the law of England and Wales, and restrict to charitable objects, certain instruments taking effect before the sixteenth day of December, nineteen hundred and fifty-two, and providing for property to be held or applied for objects partly but not exclusively charitable, and to enable corresponding provision to be made by the Parliament of Northern Ireland

[30 July 1954]

1 Validation and modification of imperfect trust instruments

(1) In this Act, "imperfect trust provision" means any provision declaring the objects for which property is to be held or applied, and so describing those objects that, consistently with the terms of the provision, the property could be used exclusively for charitable purposes, but could nevertheless be used for purposes which are not charitable.

(2) Subject to the following provisions of this Act, any imperfect trust provision contained in an instrument taking effect before the sixteenth day of December, nineteen hundred and fifty-two, shall have, and be deemed to have had, effect in relation to any disposition or covenant to which this Act applies—

    (a) as respects the period before the commencement of this Act, as if the whole of the declared objects were charitable; and

    (b) as respects the period after that commencement as if the provision had required the property to be held or applied for the declared objects in so far only as they authorise use for charitable purposes.

(3) A document inviting gifts of property to be held or applied for objects declared by the document shall be treated for the purposes of this section as an instrument taking effect when it is first issued.

(4) In this Act, "covenant" includes any agreement, whether under seal or not, and "covenantor" is to be construed accordingly.

[351]

2 Dispositions and covenants to which the Act applies

(1) Subject to the next following subsection, this Act applies to any disposition of property to be held or applied for objects declared by an imperfect trust provision, and to any covenant to make such a disposition, where apart from this Act the disposition or covenant is invalid under the law of England and Wales, but would be valid if the objects were exclusively charitable.

(2) This Act does not apply to a disposition if before the sixteenth day of December, nineteen hundred and fifty-two, property comprised in, or representing that comprised in, the disposition in question or another disposition made for the objects declared by the same imperfect trust provision, or income arising from any such property, had been paid or conveyed to, or applied for the benefit of, the persons entitled by reason of the invalidity of the disposition in question or of such other disposition as aforesaid, as the case may be.

(3)   A disposition in settlement or other disposition creating more than one interest in the same property shall be treated for the purposes of this Act as a separate disposition in relation to each of the interests created.

3   Savings for adverse claims, etc

(1)   Subject to the next following subsection, where a disposition to which this Act applies was made before, and is not confirmed after, the commencement of this Act, the foregoing sections shall not prejudice a person's right, by reason of the invalidity of the disposition, to property comprised in, or representing that comprised in, the disposition as against the persons administering the imperfect trust provision or the persons on whose behalf they do so, unless the right accrued to him or some person through whom he claims more than six years before the sixteenth day of December, nineteen hundred and fifty-two; but the persons administering the imperfect trust provision, and any trustee for them or for the persons on whose behalf they do so, shall be entitled, as against a person whose right to the property is saved by this subsection, to deal with the property as if this subsection had not been passed, unless they have express notice of a claim by him to enforce his right to the property.

(2)   No proceedings shall be begun by any person to enforce his right to any property by virtue of the foregoing subsection after the expiration of one year beginning with the date of the passing of this Act or the date when the right first accrues to him or to some person through whom he claims, whichever is the later, unless the right (before or after its accrual) either—

   (a)   has been concealed by the fraud of some person administering the imperfect trust provision or his agent; or

   (b)   has been acknowledged by some such person or his agent by means of a written acknowledgment given to the person having the right or his agent and signed by the person making it, or by means of a payment or transfer of property in respect of the right;

and if the period prescribed by this subsection for any person to bring proceedings to recover any property expires without his having recovered the property or begun proceedings to do so, his title to the property shall be extinguished.

   This subsection shall not be taken as extending the time for bringing any proceedings beyond the period of limitation prescribed by any other enactment.

(3)   For the purposes of the foregoing subsections, a right by reason of the invalidity of a disposition to property comprised in, or representing that comprised in, the disposition shall not be deemed to accrue to anyone so long as he is under a disability or has a future interest only, or so long as the disposition is subject to another disposition made by the same person, and the whole of the property or the income arising from it is held or applied for the purposes of that other disposition.

(4)   [Subsections (2) to (6) of section thirty-eight of the Limitation Act 1980] (which define the circumstances in which, for the purposes of that Act, a person is to be deemed to be under a disability or to claim through another person), shall apply for the purposes of the foregoing subsections as they apply for the purposes of that Act.

(5)   Where subsection (1) of this section applies to save a person's right to property comprised in, or representing that comprised in, a disposition, or would have so applied but for some dealing with the property by persons administering the imperfect trust

provision, or by any trustee for them or for the persons on whose behalf they do so, the foregoing sections shall not prejudice the first-mentioned person's right by virtue of his interest in the property to damages or other relief in respect of any dealing with the property by any person administering the imperfect trust provision or by any such trustee as aforesaid, if the person dealing with the property had at the time express notice of a claim by him to enforce his right to the property.

(6)   A covenant entered into before the commencement of this Act shall not be enforceable by virtue of this Act unless confirmed by the covenantor after that commencement, but a disposition made in accordance with such a covenant shall be treated for the purposes of this Act as confirming the covenant and any previous disposition made in accordance with it.

[353]

NOTES

Sub-s (4): words in square brackets substituted by the Limitation Act 1980, s 40(2), Sch 3, para 4.

---

4   Provisions as to pending proceedings and past decisions and tax payments

(1)   Subject to the next following subsection, effect shall be given to the provisions of this Act in legal proceedings begun before its commencement, as well as in those begun afterwards.

(2)   This Act shall not affect any order or judgment made or given before its commencement in legal proceedings begun before the sixteenth day of December, nineteen hundred and fifty-two, or any appeal or other proceedings consequent on any such order or judgment.

(3)   Where in legal proceedings begun on or after the said sixteenth day of December, any order or judgment has been made or given before the commencement of this Act which would not have been made or given after that commencement, the court by which the order or judgment was made or given shall, on the application of any person aggrieved thereby, set it aside in whole or in part and make such further order as the court thinks equitable with a view to placing those concerned as nearly as may be in the position they ought to be in having regard to this Act:

Provided that proceedings to have an order or judgment set aside under this subsection shall not be instituted more than six months after the commencement of this Act.

(4)   This Act shall not, by its operation on any instrument as respects the period before the commencement of the Act, impose or increase any liability to tax nor entitle any person to reclaim any tax paid or borne before that commencement, nor (save as respects taxation) require the objects declared by the instrument to be treated for the purposes of any enactment as having been charitable so as to invalidate anything done or any determination given before that commencement.

[354]

7   Short title

This Act may be cited as the Charitable Trusts (Validation) Act 1954.

[355]

RECREATIONAL CHARITIES ACT 1958

(C 17)

An Act to declare charitable under the law of England and Wales the provision in the interests of social welfare of facilities for recreation or other leisure-time occupation, to make similar provision as to certain trusts heretofore established for carrying out social welfare activities within the meaning of the Miners' Welfare Act 1952, to enable laws for corresponding purposes to be passed by the Parliament of Northern Ireland, and for purposes connected therewith

[13 March 1958]

1   General provision as to recreational and similar trusts, etc

(1)   Subject to the provisions of this Act, it shall be and be deemed always to have been charitable to provide, or assist in the provision of, facilities for recreation or other leisure-time occupation, if the facilities are provided in the interests of social welfare:

Provided that nothing in this section shall be taken to derogate from the principle that a trust or institution to be charitable must be for the public benefit.

(2)   The requirement of the foregoing subsection that the facilities are provided in the interests of social welfare shall not be treated as satisfied unless—
   (a)   the facilities are provided with the object of improving the conditions of life for the persons for whom the facilities are primarily intended; and
   (b)   either—
      (i)   those persons have need of such facilities as aforesaid by reason of their youth, age, infirmity or disablement, poverty or social and economic circumstances; or
      (ii)   the facilities are to be available to the members or female members of the public at large.

(3)   Subject to the said requirement, subsection (1) of this section applies in particular to the provision of facilities at village halls, community centres and women's institutes, and to the provision and maintenance of grounds and buildings to be used for purposes of recreation or leisure-time occupation, and extends to the provision of facilities for those purposes by the organising of any activity.

[356]

6   Short title and extent

(1)   This Act may be cited as the Recreational Charities Act 1958.

(2)   Sections one and two of this Act shall affect the law of Scotland and Northern Ireland only in so far as they affect the operation of the Income Tax Acts or of other enactments in which references to charity are to be construed in accordance with the law of England and Wales [or, without prejudice to the foregoing generality, of the Local Government (Financial Provisions, etc) (Scotland) Act 1962].

[357]

NOTES

   Sub-s (2): words in square brackets added by the Local Government (Financial Provisions, etc) (Scotland) Act 1962, s 12(1), Sch 2, para 5.

VARIATION OF TRUSTS ACT 1958

(C 53)

An Act to extend the jurisdiction of courts of law to vary trusts in the interests of beneficiaries and sanction dealings with trust property

[23 July 1958]

1   Jurisdiction of courts to vary trusts

(1)   Where property, whether real or personal, is held on trusts arising, whether before or after the passing of this Act, under any will, settlement or other disposition, the court may if it thinks fit by order approve on behalf of—

    (a)   any person having, directly or indirectly, an interest, whether vested or contingent, under the trusts who by reason of infancy or other incapacity is incapable of assenting, or

    (b)   any person (whether ascertained or not) who may become entitled, directly or indirectly, to an interest under the trusts as being at a future date or on the happening of a future event a person of any specified description or a member of any specified class of persons, so however that this paragraph shall not include any person who would be of that description, or a member of that class, as the case may be, if the said date had fallen or the said event had happened at the date of the application to the court, or

    (c)   any person unborn, or

    (d)   any person in respect of any discretionary interest of his under protective trusts where the interest of the principal beneficiary has not failed or determined,

any arrangement (by whomsoever proposed, and whether or not there is any other person beneficially interested who is capable of assenting thereto) varying or revoking all or any of the trusts, or enlarging the powers of the trustees of managing or administering any of the property subject to the trusts:

Provided that except by virtue of paragraph (d) of this subsection the court shall not approve an arrangement on behalf of any person unless the carrying out thereof would be for the benefit of that person.

(2)   In the foregoing subsection "protective trusts" means the trusts specified in paragraphs (i) and (ii) of subsection (1) of section thirty-three of the Trustee Act 1925, or any like trusts, "the principal beneficiary" has the same meaning as in the said subsection (1) and "discretionary interest" means an interest arising under the trust specified in paragraph (ii) of the said subsection (1) or any like trust.

(3)   . . . the jurisdiction conferred by subsection (1) of this section shall be exercisable by the High Court, except that the question whether the carrying out of any arrangement would be for the benefit of a person falling within paragraph (a) of the said subsection (1) shall be determined by order of [the authority having jurisdiction under [Part VII of the Mental Health Act 1983], if that person is a patient within the meaning of [the said Part VII]].

(4)   . . .

(5)   Nothing in the foregoing provisions of this section shall apply to trusts affecting property settled by Act of Parliament.

(6)   Nothing in this section shall be taken to limit the powers conferred by section sixty-four of the Settled Land Act 1925, section fifty-seven of the Trustee Act 1925, or [the powers of the authority having jurisdiction under [Part VII of the Mental Health Act 1983]].

[358]

NOTES
  Sub-s (3): words omitted repealed by the County Courts Act 1959, s 204, Sch 3; words in first (outer) pair of square brackets substituted by the Mental Health Act 1959, s 149(1), Sch 7, Pt I, words in square brackets therein substituted by the Mental Health Act 1983, s 148, Sch 4, para 14.
  Sub-s (4): repealed by the County Courts Act 1959, s 204, Sch 3.
  Sub-s (6): words in first (outer) pair of square brackets substituted by the Mental Health Act 1959, s 149(1), Sch 7, Pt I, words in square brackets therein substituted by the Mental Health Act 1983, s 148, Sch 4, para 14.

2   Extent and provisions as to Northern Ireland

(1)   This Act shall not extend to Scotland.

(2)   The foregoing section shall not extend to Northern Ireland . . .

[359]

NOTES
  Sub-s (2): words omitted repealed by the Northern Ireland Constitution Act 1973, s 41(1), Sch 6, Pt I.

3   Short title

This Act may be cited as the Variation of Trusts Act 1958.

[360]–[361]

RIGHTS OF LIGHT ACT 1959

(C 56)

An Act to amend the law relating to rights of light, and for purposes connected therewith
[16 July 1959]

2   Registration of notice in lieu of obstruction of access of light

(1)   For the purpose of preventing the access and use of light from being taken to be enjoyed without interruption, any person who is an owner of land (in this and the next following section referred to as "the servient land") over which light passes to a dwelling-house, workshop or other building (in this and the next following section referred to as "the dominant building") may apply to the local authority in whose area the dominant building is situated for the registration of a notice under this section.

(2)   An application for the registration of a notice under this section shall be in the prescribed form and shall—
    (a)   identify the servient land and the dominant building in the prescribed manner, and
    (b)   state that the registration of a notice in pursuance of the application is intended to be equivalent to the obstruction of the access of light to the dominant building across the servient land which would be caused by the erection, in such position on the servient land as may be specified in the

application, of an opaque structure of such dimensions (including, if the application so states, unlimited height) as may be so specified.

(3)   Any such application shall be accompanied by one or other of the following certificates issued by the Lands Tribunal, that is to say,—

(a)   a certificate certifying that adequate notice of the proposed application has been given to all persons who, in the circumstances existing at the time when the certificate is issued, appear to the Lands Tribunal to be persons likely to be affected by the registration of a notice in pursuance of the application;

(b)   a certificate certifying that, in the opinion of the Lands Tribunal, the case is one of exceptional urgency, and that accordingly a notice should be registered forthwith as a temporary notice for such period as may be specified in the certificate.

(4)   Where application is duly made to a local authority for the registration of a notice under this section, it shall be the duty of [that authority to register the notice in the appropriate local land charges register, and—

(a)   any notice so registered under this section shall be a local land charge; but

(b)   section 5 (1) and (2) and section 10 of the Local Charges Act 1975 shall not apply in relation thereto].

(5)   Provision shall be made by rules under section three of the Lands Tribunal Act 1949, for regulating proceedings before the Lands Tribunal with respect to the issue of certificates for the purposes of this section, and, subject to the approval of the Treasury, the fees chargeable in respect of those proceedings; and, without prejudice to the generality of subsection (6) of that section, any such rules made for the purposes of this section shall include provision—

(a)   for requiring applicants for certificates under paragraph (a) of sub-section (3) of this section to give such notices, whether by way of advertisement or otherwise, and to produce such documents and provide such information, as may be determined by or under the rules;

(b)   for determining the period to be specified in a certificate issued under paragraph (b) of subsection (3) of this section; and

(c)   in connection with any certificate issued under the said paragraph (b), for enabling a further certificate to be issued in accordance (subject to the necessary modifications) with paragraph (a) of subsection (3) of this section.

[362]

NOTES

Sub-s (4): words in square brackets substituted by the Local Land Charges Act 1975, s 17(2), Sch 1.

3   Effect of registered notice and proceedings relating thereto

(1)   Where, in pursuance of an application made in accordance with the last preceding section, a notice is registered thereunder, then, for the purpose of determining whether any person is entitled (by virtue of the Prescription Act 1832, or otherwise) to a right to the access of light to the dominant building across the servient land, the access of light to that building across that land shall be treated as obstructed to the same extent, and with the like consequences, as if an opaque structure, of the dimensions specified in the application,—

(a)   had, on the date of registration of the notice, been erected in the position on the servient land specified in the application, and had been so erected by the person who made the application, and

(b)   had remained in that position during the period for which the notice has effect and had been removed at the end of that period.

(2)   For the purposes of this section a notice registered under the last preceding section shall be taken to have effect until either—

(a)   the registration is cancelled, or

(b)   the period of one year beginning with the date of registration of the notice expires, or

(c)   in the case of a notice registered in pursuance of an application accompanied by a certificate issued under paragraph (b) of subsection (3) of the last preceding section, the period specified in the certificate expires without such a further certificate as is mentioned in paragraph (c) of subsection (5) of that section having before the end of that period been lodged with the local authority,

and shall cease to have effect on the occurrence of any one of those events.

(3)   Subject to the following provisions of this section, any person who, if such a structure as is mentioned in subsection (1) of this section had been erected as therein mentioned, would have had a right of action in any court in respect of that structure, on the grounds that he was entitled to a right to the access of light to the dominant building across the servient land, and that the said right was infringed by that structure, shall have the like right of action in that court in respect of the registration of a notice under the last preceding section:

Provided that an action shall not be begun by virtue of this subsection after the notice in question has ceased to have effect.

(4)   Where, at any time during the period for which a notice registered under the last preceding section has effect, the circumstances are such that, if the access of light to the dominant building had been enjoyed continuously from a date one year earlier than the date on which the enjoyment thereof in fact began, a person would have had a right of action in any court by virtue of the last preceding subsection in respect of the registration of the notice, that person shall have the like right of action in that court by virtue of this subsection in respect of the registration of the notice.

(5)   The remedies available to the plaintiff in an action brought by virtue of subsection (3) or subsection (4) of this section (apart from any order as to costs) shall be such declaration as the court may consider appropriate in the circumstances, and an order directing the registration of the notice to be cancelled or varied, as the court may determine.

(6)   For the purposes of section four of the Prescription Act 1832 (under which a period of enjoyment of any of the rights to which that Act applies is not to be treated as interrupted except by a matter submitted to or acquiesced in for one year after notice thereof)—

(a)   as from the date of registration of a notice under the last preceding section, all persons interested in the dominant building or any part thereof shall be deemed to have notice of the registration thereof and of the person on whose application it was registered;

(b)   until such time as an action is brought by virtue of subsection (3) or subsection (4) of this section in respect of the registration of a notice under the last preceding section, all persons interested in the dominant building or any part thereof shall be deemed to acquiesce in the obstruction which, in accordance with subsection (1) of this section, is to be treated as resulting from the registration of the notice;

(c)   as from the date on which such an action is brought, no person shall be treated as submitting to or acquiescing in that obstruction:

Provided that, if in any such action, the court decides against the claim of the plaintiff, the court may direct that the preceding provisions of this subsection shall apply in relation to the notice as if that action had not been brought.

[363]

8   Short title, commencement and extent

(1)   This Act may be cited as the Rights of Light Act 1959.

(2)   This Act, except sections one and six thereof, shall come into operation at the end of the period of three months beginning with the day on which it is passed.

(3)   This Act shall not extend to Scotland.

(4)   This Act . . . shall not extend to Northern Ireland.

[364]

NOTES

Sub-s (4): words omitted repealed by the Northern Ireland Constitution Act 1973, s 41(1), Sch 6.

TRUSTEE INVESTMENTS ACT 1961

(C 62)

An Act to make fresh provision with respect to investment by trustees and persons having the investment powers of trustees, and by local authorities, and for purposes connected therewith

[3 August 1961]

1   New powers of investment of trustees

(1)   A trustee may invest any property in his hands, whether at the time in a state of investment or not, in any manner specified in Part I or II of the First Schedule to this Act or, subject to the next following section, in any manner specified in Part III of that Schedule, and may also from time to time vary any such investments.

(2)   The supplemental provisions contained in Part IV of that Schedule shall have effect for the interpretation and for restricting the operation of the said Parts I to III.

(3)   No provision relating to the powers of the trustee contained in any instrument (not being an enactment or an instrument made under an enactment) made before the passing of this Act shall limit the powers conferred by this section, but those powers are exerciseable only in so far as a contrary intention is not expressed in any Act or instrument made under an enactment, whenever passed or made, and so relating or in any other instrument so relating which is made after the passing of this Act.

For the purposes of this subsection any rule of the law of Scotland whereby a testamentary writing may be deemed to be made on a date other than that on which it was actually executed shall be disregarded.

(4)   In this Act "narrower-range investment" means an investment falling within Part I or II of the First Schedule to this Act and "wider-range investment" means an investment falling within Part III of that Schedule.

[365]

2 Restrictions on wider-range investment

(1) A trustee shall not have power by virtue of the foregoing section to make or retain any wider-range investment unless the trust fund has been divided into two parts (hereinafter referred to as the narrower-range part and the wider-range part), the parts being, subject to the provisions of this Act, equal in value at the time of the division; and where such a division has been made no subsequent division of the same fund shall be made for the purposes of this section, and no property shall be transferred from one part of the fund to the other unless either—

    (a) the transfer is authorised or required by the following provisions of this Act, or

    (b) a compensating transfer is made at the same time.

In this section "compensating transfer", in relation to any transferred property, means a transfer in the opposite direction of property of equal value.

(2) Property belonging to the narrower-range part of a trust fund shall not by virtue of the foregoing section be invested except in narrower-range investments, and any property invested in any other manner which is or becomes comprised in that part of the trust fund shall either be transferred to the wider-range part of the fund, with a compensating transfer, or be reinvested in narrower-range investments as soon as may be.

(3) Where any property accrues to a trust fund after the fund has been divided in pursuance of subsection (1) of this section, then—

    (a) if the property accrues to the trustee as owner or former owner of property comprised in either part of the fund, it shall be treated as belonging to that part of the fund;

    (b) in any other case, the trustee shall secure, by apportionment of the accruing property or the transfer of property from one part of the fund to the other, or both, that the value of each part of the fund is increased by the same amount.

Where a trustee acquires property in consideration of a money payment the acquisition of the property shall be treated for the purposes of this section as investment and not as the accrual of property to the trust fund, notwithstanding that the amount of the consideration is less than the value of the property acquired; and paragraph (a) of this subsection shall not include the case of a dividend or interest becoming part of a trust fund.

(4) Where in the exercise of any power or duty of a trustee property falls to be taken out of the trust fund, nothing in this section shall restrict his discretion as to the choice of property to be taken out.

[366]

3 Relationship between Act and other powers of investment

(1) The powers conferred by section one of this Act are in addition to and not in derogation from any power conferred otherwise than by this Act of investment or postponing conversion exerciseable by a trustee (hereinafter referred to as a "special power").

(2) Any special power (however expressed) to invest property in any investment for the time being authorised by law for the investment of trust property, being a power conferred on a trustee before the passing of this Act or conferred on him under any enactment passed before the passing of this Act, shall have effect as a power to invest

property in like manner and subject to the like provisions as under the foregoing provisions of this Act.

(3) In relation to property, including wider-range but not including narrower-range investments,—

    (a) which a trustee is authorised to hold apart from—

        (i) the provisions of section one of this Act or any of the provisions of Part I of the Trustee Act 1925, or any of the provisions of the Trusts (Scotland) Act 1921, or

        (ii) any such power to invest in authorised investments as is mentioned in the foregoing subsection, or

    (b) which became part of a trust fund in consequence of the exercise by the trustee, as owner of property falling within this subsection, of any power conferred by subsection (3) or (4) of section ten of the Trustee Act 1925, or paragraph (o) or (p) of subsection (1) of section four of the Trusts (Scotland) Act 1921,

the foregoing section shall have effect subject to the modifications set out in the Second Schedule to this Act.

(4) The foregoing subsection shall not apply where the powers of the trustee to invest or postpone conversion have been conferred or varied—

    (a) by an order of any court made within the period of ten years ending with the passing of this Act, or

    (b) by any enactment passed, or instrument having effect under an enactment made, within that period, being an enactment or instrument relating specifically to the trusts in question; or

    (c) by an enactment contained in a local Act of the present Session;

but the provisions of the Third Schedule to this Act shall have effect in a case falling within this subsection.

[367]

4   Interpretation of references to trust property and trust funds

(1) In this Act "property" includes real or personal property of any description, including money and things in action:

    Provided that it does not include an interest in expectancy, but the falling into possession of such an interest, or the receipt of proceeds of the sale thereof, shall be treated for the purposes of this Act as an accrual of property to the trust fund.

(2) So much of the property in the hands of a trustee shall for the purposes of this Act constitute one trust fund as is held on trusts which (as respects the beneficiaries or their respective interests or the purposes of the trust or as respects the powers of the trustee) are not identical with those on which any other property in his hands is held.

(3) Where property is taken out of a trust fund by way of appropriation so as to form a separate fund, and at the time of the appropriation the trust fund had (as to the whole or a part thereof) been divided in pursuance of subsection (1) of section two of this Act, or that subsection as modified by the Second Schedule to this Act, then if the separate fund is so divided the narrower-range and wider-range parts of the separate fund may be constituted so as either to be equal, or to bear to each other the same proportion as the two corresponding parts of the fund out of which it was so appropriated (the values of those parts of those funds being ascertained as at the time of appropriation), or some intermediate proportion.

(4)   . . .

NOTES
Sub-s (4): not relevant to this work.

5   Certain valuations to be conclusive for purposes of division of trust fund

(1)   If for the purposes of section two or four of this Act or the Second Schedule thereto a trustee obtains, from a person reasonably believed by the trustee to be qualified to make it, a valuation in writing of any property, the valuation shall be conclusive in determining whether the division of the trust fund in pursuance of subsection (1) of the said section two, or any transfer or apportionment of property under that section or the said Second Schedule, has been duly made.

(2)   The foregoing subsection applies to any such valuation notwithstanding that it is made by a person in the course of his employment as an officer or servant.

[369]

6   Duty of trustees in choosing investments

(1)   In the exercise of his powers of investment a trustee shall have regard—
    (a)   to the need for diversification of investments of the trust, in so far as is appropriate to the circumstances of the trust;
    (b)   to the suitability to the trust of investments of the description of investment proposed and of the investment proposed as an investment of that description.

(2)   Before exercising any power conferred by section one of this Act to invest a manner specified in Part II or III of the First Schedule to this Act, or before investing in any such manner in the exercise of a power falling within subsection (2) of section three of this Act, a trustee shall obtain and consider proper advice on the question whether the investment is satisfactory having regard to the matters mentioned in paragraphs (a) and (b) of the foregoing subsection.

(3)   A trustee retaining any investment made in the exercise of such a power and in such a manner as aforesaid shall determine at what intervals the circumstances, and in particular the nature of the investment, make it desirable to obtain such advice as aforesaid, and shall obtain and consider such advice accordingly.

(4)   For the purposes of the two foregoing subsections, proper advice is the advice of a person who is reasonably believed by the trustee to be qualified by his ability in and practical experience of financial matters; and such advice may be given by a person notwithstanding that he gives it in the course of his employment as an officer or servant.

(5)   A trustee shall not be treated as having complied with subsection (2) or (3) of this section unless the advice was given or has been subsequently confirmed in writing.

(6)   Subsections (2) and (3) of this section shall not apply to one of two or more trustees where he is the person giving the advice required by this section to his co-trustee or co-trustees, and shall not apply where powers of a trustee are lawfully exercised by an officer or servant competent under subsection (4) of this section to give proper advice.

(7)   Without prejudice to section eight of the Trustee Act 1925, or section thirty of the Trusts (Scotland) Act 1921 (which relate to valuation, and the proportion of the value to be lent, where a trustee lends on the security of property) the advice required by this section shall not include, in the case of a loan on the security of freehold or leasehold property in England and Wales or Northern Ireland or on heritable security in Scotland, advice on the suitability of the particular loan.

[370]

7   Application of ss 1–6 to persons, other than trustees, having trustee investment powers

(1)   Where any persons, not being trustees, have a statutory power of making investments which is or includes power—
   (a)   to make the like investments as are authorised by section one of the Trustee Act 1925, or section ten of the Trusts (Scotland) Act 1921, or
   (b)   to make the like investments as trustees are for the time being by law authorised to make,

however the power is expressed, the foregoing provisions of this Act shall with the necessary modifications apply in relation to them as if they were trustees:

Provided that property belonging to a Consolidated Loans Fund or any other fund applicable wholly or partly for the redemption of debt shall not by virtue of the foregoing provisions of this Act be invested or held invested in any manner specified in paragraph 6 of Part II of the First Schedule to this Act or in wider-range investments.

(2)   Where, in the exercise of powers conferred by any enactment, an authority to which paragraph 9 of Part II of the First Schedule to this Act applies uses money belonging to any fund for a purpose for which the authority has power to borrow, the foregoing provisions of this Act, as applied by the foregoing subsection, shall apply as if there were comprised in the fund (in addition to the actual content thereof) property, being narrower-range investments, having a value equal to so much of the said money as for the time being has not been repaid to the fund, and accordingly any repayment of such money to the fund shall not be treated for the said purposes as the accrual of property to the fund:

Provided that nothing in this subsection shall be taken to require compliance with any of the provisions of section six of this Act in relation to the exercise of such powers as aforesaid.

(3)   In this section "Consolidated Loans Fund" means a fund established under section fifty-five of the Local Government Act 1958, and includes a loans fund established under [Schedule 3 to the Local Government (Scotland) Act 1975], and "statutory power" means a power conferred by an enactment passed before the passing of this Act or by any instrument made under any such enactment.

[371]

NOTES
Sub-s (3): words in square bracket substituted by the Local Government and Planning (Scotland) Act 1982, s 66(1), Sch 3, para 4.
Local Government Act 1958: see now the Local Government Act 1972.

8   Application of ss 1–6 in special cases

(1)   In relation to persons to whom this section applies—
   (a)   notwithstanding anything in subsection (3) of section one of this Act, no provision of any enactment passed, or instrument having effect under an

enactment and made, before the passing of this Act shall limit the powers conferred by the said section one;

(b) subsection (1) of the foregoing section shall apply where the power of making investments therein mentioned is or includes a power to make some only of the investments mentioned in paragraph (a) or (b) of that subsection.

(2) This section applies to—

(a) the persons for the time being authorised to invest funds of the Duchy of Lancaster;

(b) any persons specified in an order made by the Treasury by statutory instrument, being persons (whether trustees or not) whose power to make investments is conferred by or under any enactment contained in a local or private Act.

(3) An order of the Treasury made under the foregoing subsection may provide that the provisions of sections one to six of this Act (other than the provisions of subsection (3) of section one) shall, in their application to any persons specified therein, have effect subject to such exceptions and modifications as may be specified.

[372]

9 Supplementary provisions as to investments

(1) . . .

(2) It is hereby declared that the power to subscribe for securities conferred by subsection (4) of the said section ten includes power to retain them for any period for which the trustee has power to retain the holding in respect of which the right to subscribe for the securities was offered, but subject to any conditions subject to which the trustee has that power.

[373]

NOTES
Sub-s (1): inserts the Trustee Act 1925, s 10(3)(bb).

11 Local Authority investment schemes

(1) Without prejudice to powers conferred by or under any other enactment, any authority to which this section applies may invest property held by the authority in accordance with a scheme submitted to the Treasury by any association of local authorities . . . and approved by the Treasury as enabling investments to be made collectively without in substance extending the scope of powers of investment.

(2) A scheme under this section may apply to a specified authority or to a specified class of authorities, may make different provisions as respects different authorities or different classes of authorities or as respects different descriptions of property or property held for different purposes, and may impose restrictions on the extent to which the power controlled by the foregoing subsection shall be exerciseable.

(3) In approving a scheme under this section, the Treasury may direct that [the Financial Services Act 1986] shall not apply to dealings undertaken or documents issued for the purposes of the scheme, or to such dealings or documents of such descriptions as may be specified in the direction.

(4) The authorities to which this section applies are—

(a) in England and Wales, the council of a county, [a county borough,] a . . . borough . . . a district or a [parish, the Common] Council of the City of

London [the Broads Authority][, a police authority established under section 3 of the Police Act 1964][, . . . a joint authority established by Part IV of the Local Government Act 1985] . . . and the Council of the Isles of Scilly;

(b) in Scotland, a local authority within the meaning of the Local Government (Scotland) Act 1947;

(c) in any part of Great Britain, a joint board or joint committee constituted to discharge or advise on the discharge of the functions of any two or more of the authorities mentioned in the foregoing paragraphs (including a joint committee established by [those authorities acting in combination in accordance with regulations made under section 7 of the Superannuation Act 1972];

(d) in Northern Ireland, [a district council established under the Local Government Act (Northern Ireland) 1972] and the Northern Ireland Local Government Officers' Superannuation Committee established under the Local Government (Superannuation) Act (Northern Ireland) 1950.

[374]

NOTES

Sub-s (1): words omitted repealed by the London Government Act 1963, s 93(1), Sch 8, Pt II and by the Local Government Act 1985, s 102, Sch 17.

Sub-s (3): words in square brackets substituted by the Financial Services Act 1986, s 212(2), Sch 16, para 2(a).

Sub-s (4): in para (a) words in first pair of square brackets inserted by the Local Government (Wales) Act 1994, s 66(6), Sch 16, para 19(1), as from a day to be appointed, first words omitted repealed by the London Government Act 1963, s 93(1), Sch 18, Pt II, second words omitted repealed by the Local Government Act 1972, s 272(1), Sch 30, third words omitted repealed by the Education Reform Act 1988, s 237, Sch 13, Pt I, fourth words omitted repealed by the Local Government Act 1985, s 102, Sch 17, words in second pair of square brackets substituted by the Water Act 1989, s 190, Sch 25, para 29(1), words in third pair of square brackets inserted by the Norfolk and Suffolk Broads Act 1988, s 21, Sch 6, para 3, words in fourth pair of square brackets inserted by the Police and Magistrates' Courts Act 1994, s 43, Sch 4, Pt II, para 46, words in fifth pair of square brackets inserted by the Local Government Act 1985, s 84, Sch 14, Pt II, para 38; words in square brackets in para (c) substituted by the Superannuation Act 1972, s 29(1), Sch 6, para 40; words in square brackets in para (d) substituted by the Transfer of Functions (Local Government, etc) (Northern Ireland) Order 1973, SR & O (NI) 1973/256, art 3, Sch 2.

Modified by the Waste Regulation and Disposal (Authorities) Order 1985, SI 1985/1884, art 10, Sch 3.

Local Government (Scotland) Act 1947: see now the Local Government (Scotland) Act 1973, s 235(1).

12   Power to confer additional powers of investment

(1) Her Majesty may by Order in Council extend the powers of investment conferred by section one of this Act by adding to Part I, Part II or Part III of the First Schedule to this Act any manner of investment specified in the Order.

(2)   Any Order under this section shall be subject to annulment in pursuance of a resolution of either House of Parliament.

[375]

13   Power to modify provisions as to division of trust fund

(1)   The Treasury may by order made by statutory instrument direct that, subject to subsection (3) of section four of this Act, any division of a trust fund made in pursuance of subsection (1) of section two of this Act during the continuance in force of the order shall be made so that the value of the wider-range part at the time of the division bears to the then value of the narrower-range part such proportion, greater than one but not greater than three to one, as may be prescribed by the order; and in

this Act "the prescribed proportion" means the proportion for the time being prescribed under this subsection.

(2)   A fund which has been divided in pursuance of subsection (1) of section two of this Act before the coming into operation of an order under the foregoing subsection may notwithstanding anything in that subsection be again divided (once only) in pursuance of the said subsection (1) during the continuance in force of the order.

(3)   If an order is made under subsection (1) of this section, then as from the coming into operation of the order—

(a)   paragraph (b) of subsection (3) of section two of this Act and sub-paragraph (b) of paragraph 3 of the Second Schedule thereto shall have effect with the substitution, for the words from "each" to the end, of the words "the wider-range part of the fund is increased by an amount which bears the prescribed proportion to the amount by which the value of the narrower-range part of the fund is increased";

(b)   subsection (3) of section four of this Act shall have effect as if for the words "so as either" to "each other" there were substituted the words "so as to bear to each other either the prescribed proportion or".

(4)   An order under this section may be revoked by a subsequent order thereunder prescribing a greater proportion.

(5)   An order under this section shall not have effect unless approved by a resolution of each House of Parliament.

[376]

15   Saving for powers of court

The enlargement of the investment powers of trustees by this Act shall not lessen any power of a court to confer wider powers of investment on trustees, or affect the extent to which any such power is to be exercised.

[377]

16   Minor and consequential amendments and repeals

(1)   The provisions of the Fourth Schedule to this Act (which contain minor amendments and amendments consequential on the foregoing provisions of this Act) shall have effect.

(2)   . . .

[378]

NOTES

Sub-s (2): repealed by the Statute Law (Repeals) Act 1974.

17   Short title, extent and construction

(1)   This Act may be cited as the Trustee Investments Act 1961.

(2), (3)   . . .

(4)   Except where the context otherwise requires, in this Act, in its application to trusts the execution of which is governed by the law in force in England and Wales, expressions have the same meaning as in the Trustee Act 1925.

(5)   . . .

[379]

SCHEDULES

FIRST SCHEDULE
MANNER OF INVESTMENT

Section 1

PART I
NARROWER-RANGE INVESTMENTS NOT REQUIRING ADVICE

1. In Defence Bonds, National Savings Certificates, Ulster Savings Certificates, [Ulster Development Bonds] [National Development Bonds], [British Savings Bonds], [National Savings Income Bonds] [National Savings Deposit Bonds] [National Savings Indexed-Income Bonds], [National Savings Capital Bonds] [National Savings FIRST Option Bonds] [National Savings Pensioners Guaranteed Income Bonds].

2. In deposits in [the National Savings Bank], . . . and deposits in a bank or department thereof certified under subsection (3) of section nine of the Finance Act 1956.

[380]

NOTES

Para 1: words in square brackets added by the Trustee Investments (Additional Powers) (No 2) Order 1962, SI 1962/2611, the Trustee Investments (Additional Powers) Order 1964, SI 1964/703, the Trustee Investments (Additional Powers) Order 1968, SI 1968/470, the Trustee Investments (Additional Powers) Order 1982, SI 1982/1086, the Trustee Investments (Additional Powers) (No 2) Order 1983, SI 1983/1525, the Trustee Investments (Additional Powers) Order 1985, SI 1985/1780, the Trustee Investments (Additional Powers) Order 1988, SI 1988/2254, art 2, the Trustee Investments (Additional Powers) Order 1992, SI 1992/1738, art 2 and the Trustee Investments (Additional Powers) Order 1994, SI 1994/265, art 2.

Para 2: words in square brackets added by the Post Office Act 1969, ss 94, 114, Sch 6, Pt III; words omitted repealed by the Trustee Savings Banks Act 1976, s 36(2), Sch 6.

PART II
NARROWER-RANGE OF INVESTMENTS REQUIRING ADVICE

1. In securities issued by Her Majesty's Government in the United Kingdom, the Government of Northern Ireland or the Government of the Isle of Man, not being securities falling within Part I of this Schedule and being fixed-interest securities registered in the United Kingdom or the Isle of Man, Treasury Bills or Tax Reserve Certificates [or any variable interest securities issued by Her Majesty's Government in the United Kingdom and registered in the United Kingdom].

2. In any securities the payment of interest on which is guaranteed by Her Majesty's Government in the United Kingdom or the Government of Northern Ireland.

3. In fixed-interest securities issued in the United Kingdom by any public authority or nationalised industry or undertaking in the United Kingdom.

4. In fixed-interest securities issued in the United Kingdom by the government of any overseas territory within the Commonwealth or by any public or local authority within such a territory, being securities registered in the United Kingdom.

References in this paragraph to an overseas territory or to the government of such a territory shall be construed as if they occurred in the Overseas Service Act, 1958.

[4A. In securities issued in the United Kingdom by the government of an overseas territory

within the Commonwealth or by any public or local authority within such a territory, being securities registered in the United Kingdom and in respect of which the rate of interest is variable by reference to one or more of the following:—
    (a)   the Bank of England's minimum lending rate;
    (b)   the average rate of discount on allotment on 91-day Treasury bills;
    (c)   a yield on 91-day Treasury bills;
    (d)   a London sterling inter-bank offered rate;
    (e)   a London sterling certificate of deposit rate.

    References in this paragraph to an overseas territory or to the government of such a territory shall be construed as if they occurred in the Overseas Service Act 1958.]

5.   In fixed-interest securities issued in the United Kingdom by [the African Development Bank, the Asian Development Bank, the Caribbean Development Bank, [the European Bank for Reconstruction and Development,] the International Finance Corporation, the International Monetary Fund or by] the International Bank for Reconstruction and Development, being securities registered in the United Kingdom.

[In fixed-interest securities issued in the United Kingdom by the Inter-American Development Bank],

[In fixed interest securities issued in the United Kingdom by [the European Atomic Energy Community, the European Economic Community,] the European Investment Bank or by the European Coal and Steel Community, being securities registered in the United Kingdom.]

[5A.   In securities issued in the United Kingdom by
    (i)   the International Bank for Reconstruction and Development or by the European Investment Bank or by the European Coal and Steel Community, being securities registered in the United Kingdom or
    (ii)   the Inter-American Development Bank

being securities in respect of which the rate of interest is variable by reference to one or more of the following:—
    (a)   the Bank of England's minimum lending rate;
    (b)   the average rate of discount on allotment on 91-day Treasury bills;
    (c)   a yield on 91-day Treasury bills;
    (d)   a London sterling inter-bank offered rate;
    (e)   a London sterling certificate of deposit rate.]

[5B.   In securities issued in the United Kingdom by the African Development Bank, the Asian Development Bank, the Caribbean Development Bank, the European Atomic Energy Community, [the European Bank for Reconstruction and Development,] the European Economic Community, the International Finance Corporation or by the International Monetary Fund, being securities registered in the United Kingdom and in respect of which the rate of interest is variable by reference to one or more of the following:—
    (a)   The average rate of discount on allotment on 91-day Treasury Bills;
    (b)   a yield on 91-day Treasury Bills;
    (c)   a London sterling inter-bank offered rate;
    (d)   a London sterling certificate of deposit rate.]

6.   In debentures issued in the United Kingdom by a company incorporated in the United Kingdom, being debentures registered in the United Kingdom.

7.   In stock of the Bank of Ireland.

[In Bank of Ireland 7 per cent. Loan Stock 1968/91].

8.   . . .

9.   In loans to any authority to which this paragraph applies charged on all or any of the revenues of the authority or on a fund into which all or any of those revenues are payable, in any fixed-interest securities issued in the United Kingdom by any such authority for the purpose of

borrowing money so charged, and in deposits with any such authority by way of temporary loan made on the giving of a receipt for the loan by the treasurer or other similar officer of the authority and on the giving of an undertaking by the authority that, if requested to charge the loan as aforesaid, it will either comply with the request or repay the loan.

This paragraph applies to the following authorities, that is to say—
- (a) any local authority in the United Kingdom;
- (b) any authority all the members of which are appointed or elected by one or more local authorities in the United Kingdom;
- (c) any authority the majority of the members of which are appointed or elected by one or more local authorities in the United Kingdom, being an authority which by virtue of any enactment has power to issue a precept to a local authority in England and Wales, or a requisition to a local authority in Scotland, or to the expenses of which, by virtue of any enactment, a local authority in the United Kingdom is or can be required to contribute;
- (d) the Receiver for the Metropolitan Police District or [a police authority established under section 3 of the Police Act 1964];
- (e) the Belfast City and District Water Commissioners.
- [(f) the Great Ouse Water Authority].
- [(g) any district council in Northern Ireland.]
- [(h) . . .
- (i) any residuary body established by section 57 of the Local Government Act 1985.]

[9A. In any securities issued in the United Kingdom by any authority to which paragraph 9 applies for the purpose of borrowing money charged on all or any of the revenues of the authority or on a fund into which all or any of those revenues are payable and being securities in respect of which the rate of interest is variable by reference to one or more of the following:—
- (a) the Bank of England's minimum lending rate;
- (b) the average rate of discount on allotment on 91-day Treasury bills;
- (c) a yield on 91-day Treasury bills;
- (d) a London sterling inter-bank offered rate;
- (e) a London sterling certificate of deposit rate.]

10. . . .

[10A. In any units of a gilt unit trust scheme.

References in this Schedule to a gilt unit trust scheme are references to a collective investment scheme—
- (a) which is an authorised unit trust scheme within the meaning of the Financial Services Act 1986, a recognised scheme within the meaning of that Act or a UCITS; and
- (b) whose objective is to invest not less than 90% of the property of the scheme in loan stock, bonds and other instruments creating or acknowledging indebtedness which are transferable and which are issued or guaranteed by—
  - (i) the government of the United Kingdom or elsewhere,
  - (ii) by a local authority in the United Kingdom or in a relevant state, or
  - (iii) by an international organisation the members of which include the United Kingdom or a relevant state;

and, in respect of the remainder of the property of the scheme, whose objective is to invest in any instrument falling within any of paragraphs 1 to 3, 5 or 6 of Schedule 1 to the Financial Services Act 1986.]

11. . . .

[12. In deposits with a building society within the meaning of the Building Societies Act 1986.]

13. In mortgages of freehold property in England and Wales or Northern Ireland and of leasehold property in those countries of which the unexpired term at the time of investment is not less than sixty years, and in loans on heritable security in Scotland.

14. In perpetual rent-charges charged on land in England and Wales or Northern Ireland and fee-farm rents (not being rent-charges) issuing out of such land, and in feu-duties or ground annuals in Scotland.

[15. In Certificates of Tax Deposit.]

[16. In fixed-interest or variable interest securities issued by the government of a relevant state.

17. In any securities the payment of interest on which is guaranteed by the government of a relevant state.

18. In fixed-interest securities issued in any relevant state by any public authority or nationalised industry or undertaking in that state.

19. In fixed-interest or variable interest securities issued in a relevant state by the government of any overseas territory within the Commonwealth or by any public or local authority within such a territory.

References in this paragraph to an overseas territory or to the government of such a territory shall be construed as if they occurred in the Overseas Development and Co-operation Act 1980.

20. In fixed-interest or variable interest securities issued in a relevant state by—
    (a)   the African Development Bank;
    (b)   the Asian Development Bank;
    (c)   the Caribbean Development Bank;
    (d)   the International Finance Corporation;
    (e)   the International Monetary Fund;
    (f)   the International Bank for Reconstruction and Development;
    (g)   the Inter-American Development Bank;
    (h)   the European Atomic Energy Community;
    (i)   the European Bank for Reconstruction and Development;
    (j)   the European Economic Community;
    (k)   the European Investment Bank; or
    (l)   the European Coal and Steel Community.

21. In debentures issued in any relevant state by a company incorporated in that state.

22. In loans to any authority to which this paragraph applies secured on all or any of the revenues of the authority or on a fund into which all or any of those revenues are payable, in fixed-interest or variable interest securities issued in a relevant state by any such authority in that state for the purpose of borrowing money so secured, and in deposits with any authority to which this paragraph applies by way of temporary loan made on the giving of a receipt for the loan by the treasurer or other similar officer of the authority and on the giving of an undertaking by the authority that, if requested to charge the loan as aforesaid, it will either comply with the request or repay the loan.

This paragraph applies to the following authorities, that is to say—
    (a)   any local authority in a relevant state; or
    (b)   any authority all the members of which are appointed or elected by one or more local authorities in any such state.

23. In deposits with a mutual investment society whose head office is located in a relevant state.

24. In loans secured on any interest in property in a relevant state which corresponds to an interest in property falling within paragraph 13 of this Part of this Schedule.]

[381]

NOTES

Commencement: 3 August 1961 (paras 1–4, 5, 6–9, 10, 11, 13, 14); 19 November 1975 (para 15); 14 December 1977 (paras 4A, 5A, 9A); 6 July 1983 (para 5B); 1 January 1987 (para 12); 22 August 1994 (paras 10A, 16–24).
Para 1: words in square brackets added by the Trustee Investments (Additional Powers) Order 1977, SI 1977/831, art 3.

Paras 4A, 5A, 9A: inserted by the Trustee Investments (Additional Powers) (No 2) Order 1977, SI 1977/1878, art 3.

Para 5: words in first (outer) pair of square brackets inserted by the Trustee Investments (Additional Powers) Order 1983, SI 1983/772, art 2(a), words in square brackets therein inserted by the Trustee Investments (Additional Powers) Order 1991, SI 1991/999, art 2; words in third pair of square brackets inserted by the Trustee Investments (Additional Powers) (No 2) Order 1964 SI 1964/1404, art 1; words in fourth (outer) pair of square brackets inserted by the Trustee Investments (Additional Powers) Order 1972, SI 1972/1818, art 3, words in square brackets therein inserted by the Trustee Investments (Additional Powers) Order 1983, SI 1983/772, art 2(b).

Para 5B: inserted by the Trustee Investments (Additional Powers) Order 1983, SI 1983/772, art 2(c); words in square brackets added by the Trustee Investments (Additional Powers) Order 1991, SI 1991/999, art 2.

Para 7: words in square brackets added by the Trustee Investments (Additional Powers) Order 1966, SI 1966/401, art 1.

Para 8: repealed by the Agriculture and Forestry (Financial Provisions) Act 1991, s 1, Schedule, Pt IV.

Para 9: words in square brackets in sub-para (d) substituted by the Police and Magistrates' Courts Act 1994, s 43, Sch 4, Pt II, para 47; sub-para (f) inserted by Trustee Investments (Additional Powers) Order 1962, SI 1962/658; sub-para (g) inserted by Trustee Investments (Additional Powers) Order 1973, SI 1973/1332; sub-paras (h), (i) inserted by the Trustee Investments (Additional Powers) Order 1986, SI 1986/601, art 2, sub-para (h) repealed by the Education Reform Act 1988, s 237, Sch 1, Sch 13, Pt I.

Para 10: repealed by the Water Act 1989, s 190(1), Sch 25, para 29(2), (3).

Para 10A: inserted by the Finance Act 1982, s 150; substituted by the Trustee Investments (Additional Powers) (No 2) Order 1994, SI 1994/1908, art 2(1).

Para 11: repealed by the Trustee Savings Bank Act 1976, s 36(2), Sch 6.

Para 12: substituted by the Building Societies Act 1986, s 120, Sch 18, Pt I, para 4(2).

Para 15: inserted by the Trustee Investments (Additional Powers) Order 1975, SI 1975/1710.

Paras 16–24: inserted by the Trustee Investments (Additional Powers) (No 2) Order 1994, SI 1994/1908, art 2(2).

PART III
WIDER-RANGE INVESTMENTS

1. In any securities issued in the United Kingdom by a company incorporated in the United Kingdom, being securities registered in the United Kingdom and not being securities falling within Part II of this Schedule.

[2. In shares in a building society within the meaning of the Building Societies Act 1986.]

[3. In any units of an authorised unit trust scheme within the meaning of the Financial Services Act 1986.]

[4. In any securities issued in any relevant state by a company incorporated in that state or by any unincorporated body constituted under the law of that state, not being (in either case) securities falling within Part II of this Schedule or paragraph 6 of this Part of this Schedule.

5. In shares in a mutual investment society whose head office is located in a relevant state.

6. In any units of a collective investment scheme which is—
    (a)   a recognised scheme within the meaning of the Financial Services Act 1986 which is constituted in a relevant state; or
    (b)   a UCITS;

and which does not fall within Part II of this Schedule.]

[382]

NOTES

Commencement: 3 August 1961 (para 1); 1 January 1987 (para 2); 29 April 1988 (para 3); 24 August 1994 (paras 4–6).

Para 2: substituted by the Building Societies Act 1986, s 120(1), Sch 18, Pt I, para 4(3).

Para 3: substituted by the Financial Services Act 1986, s 212(2), Sch 16, para 2(b).

Paras 4–6: inserted by the Trustee Investments (Additional Powers) (No 2) Order 1994, SI 1994/1908, art 2(3).

Part IV
Supplemental

1.   The securities mentioned in Parts I to III of this Schedule do not include any securities where the holder can be required to accept repayment of the principal, or the payment of any interest, otherwise than in sterling[, in the currency of a relevant state or in the seuropean currency unit (as defined in article 1 of Council Regulation No 3180/78/EEC)].

2.   The securities mentioned in paragraphs 1 to 8 of Part II, other than Treasury Bills or Tax Reserve Certificates, securities issued before the passing of this Act by the Government of the Isle of Man, securities falling within paragraph 4 of the said Part II issued before the passing of this Act or securities falling within paragraph 9 of that Part, and the securities mentioned in paragraph 1 of Part III of this Schedule, do not include—
- (a)   securities the price of which is not quoted on [a recognised investment exchange within the meaning of the Financial Services Act 1986] [or on an investment exchange which constitutes the principal or only market established in a relevant state on which securities admitted to official listing are dealt in or traded]
- (b)   shares or debenture stock not fully paid up (except shares or debenture stock which by the terms of issue are required to be fully paid up within nine months of the date of issue).

[2A.   The securities mentioned in paragraphs 16 to 21 of Part II of this Schedule, other than securities traded on a relevant money market or securities falling within paragraph 22 of Part II of this Schedule, and the securities mentioned in paragraph 4 of Part III of this Schedule do not include—
- (a)   securities the price for which is not quoted on a recognised investment exchange within the meaning of the Financial Services Act 1986 or on an investment exchange which constitutes the principal or only market established in a relevant state on which securities admitted to official listing are dealt in or traded;
- (b)   shares or debenture stock not fully paid up (except shares or debenture stock which by the terms of issue are required to be fully paid up within nine months of the date of issue or shares issued with no nominal value).]

3.   The securities mentioned in paragraph 6 [and 21] of Part II and paragraph 1 [or 4] of Part III of this Schedule do not include—
- (a)   shares or debentures of an incorporated company of which the total issued and paid up share capital is less than one million pounds;
- [(ab)   shares or debentures of an incorporated company of which the total issued and paid up share capital at any time on the business day before the investment is made is less than the equivalent of one million pounds in the currency of a relevant state (at the exchange rate prevailing in the United Kingdom at the close of business on the day before the investment is made);]
- (b)   shares or debentures of an incorporated company which has not in each of the five years immediately preceding the calendar year in which the investment is made paid a dividend on all the shares issued by the company, excluding any shares issued after the dividend was declared and any shares which by their terms of issue did not rank for the dividend for that year.

For the purposes of sub-paragraph (b) of this paragraph a company formed—
- (i)   to take over the business of another company or other companies, or
- (ii)   to acquire the securities of, or control of, another company or other companies,

or for either of those purposes and for other purposes shall be deemed to have paid a dividend as mentioned in that sub-paragraph in any year in which such a dividend has been paid by the other company or all the other companies, as the case may be.

[For the purposes of sub-paragraph (b) of this paragraph in relation to investment in shares or debentures of a successor company within the meaning of the Electricity (Northern Ireland) Order 1992 the company shall be deemed to have paid a dividend as mentioned in that sub-paragraph—

(iii) in every year preceding the calendar year in which the transfer date within the meaning of Part III of that Order of 1992 falls ("the first investment year") which is included in the relevant five years; and

(iv) in the first investment year, if that year is included in the relevant five years and that company does not in fact pay such a dividend in that year; and

"the relevant five years" means the five years immediately preceding the year in which the investment in question is made or proposed to be made.]

[3A. . . .]

4.   In this Schedule, unless the context otherwise requires, the following expressions have the meanings hereby respectively assigned to them, that is to say—

   "debenture" includes debenture stock and bonds, whether constituting a charge on assets or not, and loan stock or notes;

   "enactment" includes an enactment of the Parliament of Northern Ireland;

   "fixed-interest securities" means securities which under their terms of issue bear a fixed rate of interest;

   "local authority" in relation to the United Kingdom, means any of the following authorities—

   (a) in England and Wales, the council of a county, [a county borough] a . . . borough . . . an urban or rural district or a parish, the Common Council of the City of London [the Greater London Council] and the Council of the Isles of Scilly;

   (b) in Scotland, a local authority within the meaning of the Local Government (Scotland) Act 1947;

   (c) . . .

   ["mutual investment society" means a credit institution which operates on mutual principles and which is authorised by the appropriate supervisory authority of a relevant state;

   "relevant money market" means a money market which is supervised by the central bank, or a government agency, of a relevant state;

   "relevant state" means Austria, Finland, Iceland, Norway, Sweden or a member state other than the United Kingdom;]

   . . . . . .

   "securities" includes shares, debentures [units within paragraph 3 [or 6] of Part III of this Schedule], Treasury Bills and Tax Reserve Certificates;

   "shares" includes stock;

   "Treasury Bills" includes . . . bills issued by Her Majesty's Government in the United Kingdom and Northern Ireland Treasury Bills.

5.   It is hereby declared that in this Schedule "mortgage", in relation to freehold or leasehold property in Northern Ireland, includes a registered charge which, by virtue of subsection (4) of section forty of the Local Registration of Title (Ireland) Act 1891, or any other enactment, operates as a mortgage by deed.

6.   [In relation to the United Kingdom,] references in this Schedule to an incorporated company are references to a company incorporated by or under any enactment and include references to a body of persons established for the purpose of trading for profit and incorporated by Royal Charter.

[6A.   References in this Schedule to a UCITS are references to a collective investment scheme which is constituted in a relevant state and which complies with the conditions necessary for it to enjoy the rights conferred by Council Directive 85/611/EEC co-ordinating the laws, regulations and administrative provisions relating to undertakings for collective investment in transferable securities; and section 86(8) of the Financial Services Act 1986 (meaning of "constituted in a member state") shall apply for the purposes of this paragraph as it applies for the purposes of that section but as if for references in that section to a member state there were substituted references to a relevant state.]

7.   . . .

NOTES

Para 1: words in square brackets inserted by the Trustee Investments (Additional Powers) (No 2) Order 1994, SI 1994/1908, art 3(1), (2).

Para 2: in sub-para (a) words in first pair of square brackets substituted by the Financial Services Act 1986, s 212(2), Sch 16, para 2(c), words in second pair of square brackets inserted by the Trustee Investments (Additional Powers) (No 2) Order 1994, SI 1994/1908, art 3(1), (3).

Para 2A: inserted by the Trustee Investments (Additional Powers) (No 2) Order 1994, SI 1994/1908, art 3(1), (4).

Para 3: words in first and second pairs of square brackets, and sub-para (ab) inserted by the Trustee Investments (Additional Powers) (No 2) Order 1994, SI 1994/1908, art 3(1), (5); words in final pair of square brackets inserted by the Electricity (Northern Ireland Consequential Amendments) Order 1992, SI 1992/232, art 4.

Para 3A: inserted by the Housing (Consequential Provisions) Act 1985, s 4, Sch 2, para 5; repealed by the Building Societies Act 1986, s 120(2), Sch 19, Pt I.

Para 4: in definition "local authority" words in first pair of square brackets insesrted by the Local Government (Wales) Act 1994, s 66(6), Sch 16, para 19(2), as from a day to be appointed, first words omitted repealed by the London Government Act 1963, s 93(1), Sch 18, Pt II, second words omitted repealed by the Local Government Act 1972, s 272(1), Sch 30, para (c) repealed by the Statute Law (Repeals) Act 1981, words in second pair of square brackets substituted by the London Government Act 1963, s 83(1), Sch 17, para 25; definitions "mutual investment society", "relevant money market" and "relevant state" inserted by the Trustee Investments (Additional Powers) (No 2) Order 1994, SI 1994/1908, art 3(1), (6)(a); definitions "ordinary deposits" and "special investment" repealed by the Trustee Savings Banks Act 1976, s 36(2), Sch 6; in definition "securities" words in first (outer) pair of square brackets inserted by the Financial Services Act 1986, s 212(2), Sch 16, para 2(d), words in square brackets therein inserted by the Trustee Investments (Additional Powers) (No 2) Order 1994, SI 1994/1908, art 3(1), (6)(b); in definition "Treasury Bills", words omitted repealed by the National Loans Act 1968, s 24(2), Sch 6, Pt I.

Para 6: words in square brackets inserted by the Trustee Investments (Additional Powers) (No 2) Order 1994, SI 1994/1908, art 3(1), (7).

Para 6A: inserted by the Trustee Investments (Additional Powers) (No 2) Order 1994, SI 1994/1908, art 3(1), (8).

Para 7: repealed by the Building Societies Act 1986, s 120(2), Sch 19, Pt I.

SECOND SCHEDULE
Modification of S 2 in relation to Property Falling within S 3(3)
Section 3

1.   In this Schedule "special-range property" means property falling within subsection (3) of section three of this Act.

2.—(1)   Where a trust fund includes special-range property, subsection (1) of section two of this Act shall have effect as if references to the trust fund were references to so much thereof as does not consist of special-range property, and the special-range property shall be carried to a separate part of the fund.

(2)   Any property which—

    (a)   being property belonging to the narrower-range or wider-range part of a trust fund, is converted into special-range property, or

    (b)   being special-range property, accrues to a trust fund after the division of the fund or part thereof in pursuance of subsection (1) of section two of this Act or of that subsection as modified by sub-paragraph (1) of this paragraph,

shall be carried to such a separate part of the fund as aforesaid; and subsections (2) and (3) of the said section two shall have effect subject to this sub-paragraph.

3.   Where property carried to such a separate part as aforesaid is converted into property other than special-range property,—

(a)   it shall be transferred to the narrower-range part of the fund or the wider-range part of the fund or apportioned between them, and

(b)   any transfer of property from one of those parts to the other shall be made which is necessary to secure that the value of each of those parts of the fund is increased by the same amount.

[384]

THIRD SCHEDULE
PROVISIONS SUPPLEMENTARY TO S 3(4)

Section 3

1.   Where in a case falling within subsection (4) of section three of this Act, property belonging to the narrower-range part of a trust fund—

(a)   is invested otherwise than in a narrower-range investment, or

(b)   being so invested, is retained and not transferred or as soon as may be reinvested as mentioned in subsection (2) of section two of this Act.

then, so long as the property continues so invested and comprised in the narrower-range part of the fund, section one of this Act shall not authorise the making or retention of any wider-range investment.

2.   Section four of the Trustee Act 1925, or section thirty-three of the Trusts (Scotland) Act 1921 (which relieve a trustee from liability for retaining an investment which has ceased to be authorised), shall not apply where an investment ceased to be authorised in consequence of the foregoing paragraph.

[385]

FOURTH SCHEDULE
MINOR AND CONSEQUENTIAL AMENDMENTS

Section 16

1.—(1)   References in the Trustee Act 1925, except in subsection (2) of section sixty-nine of that Act, to section one of that Act or to provisions which include that section shall be construed respectively as references to section one of this Act and as including references to section one of this Act.

(2) References in the Trusts (Scotland) Act 1921, to section ten or eleven of that Act, or to provisions which include either of those sections, shall be construed respectively as references to section one of this Act and as including references to that section.

2–6.   . . .

[386]

NOTES

Para 2: repealed by the Building Societies Act 1962, s 131, Sch 10, Pt I.

Para 3: repealed by the Water Act 1989, s 190(3), Sch 27, Pt II.

Paras 4, 5: repealed by the National Savings Bank Act 1971, s 28, Sch 2.

Para 6: repealed by the Housing (Consequential Provisions) Act 1985, s 3, Sch 1, Pt I.

RECORDED DELIVERY SERVICE ACT 1962

(C 27)

An Act to authorise the sending by the recorded delivery service of certain documents and other things required or authorised to be sent by registered post; and for purposes connected therewith
[3 July 1962]

1 Recorded delivery service to be an alternative to registered post

(1) Any enactment which requires or authorises a document or other thing to be sent by registered post (whether or not it makes any other provision in relation thereto) shall have effect as if it required or, as the case may be, authorised that thing to be sent by registered post or the recorded delivery service; and any enactment which makes any other provision in relation to the sending of a document or other thing by registered post or to a thing so sent shall have effect as if it made the like provision in relation to the sending of that thing by the recorded delivery service or, as the case may be, to a thing sent by that service.

(2) The Schedule to this Act shall have effect for the purpose of making consequential adaptations of the enactments therein mentioned.

(3) Subject to the following subsection the Postmaster General may by order make such amendments of any enactment contained in a local or private Act (being an enactment to which this Act applies) as appear to him to be necessary or expedient in consequence of subsection (1) of this section.

(4) Before making an order under this section, the Postmaster General shall, unless it appears to him to be impracticable to do so, consult with the person who promoted the Bill for the Act to which the order relates, or where it appears to the Postmaster General that some other person has succeeded to the promoter's interest in that Act, that other person.

(5) Any order under this section may be varied or revoked by a subsequent order thereunder, and the power to make any such order shall be exercisable by statutory instrument which shall be subject to annulment in pursuance of a resolution of either House of Parliament.

(6) This section shall not be construed as authorising the sending by the recorded delivery service of anything which under the Post Office Act 1953 or any instrument thereunder is not allowed to be sent by that service.

[387]

2 Application and interpretation

(1) Subject to the next following subsection, this Act applies to the following enactments, that is to say,—

  (a) the provisions of any Act (whether public general, local or private) passed before or in the same Session as this Act;
  (b) the provisions of any Church Assembly Measure so passed;
  (c) the provisions of any agricultural marketing scheme made under the Agricultural Marketing Act 1958 before the passing of this Act or having effect as if made under that Act;

and, in the case of a provision which has been applied by or under any other enactment passed, or any instrument made under any enactment passed, before or in the same Session as this Act, applies to that provision as so applied, subject, however, in the case of an instrument made after the passing of this Act to any contrary intention appearing therein; and references in this Act (except this section) to any enactment shall be construed accordingly.

(2)   This Act does not apply—

(a)   to subsection (2) of section nine of the Crown Proceedings Act 1947 (which enables proceedings to be brought against the Crown for loss of or damage to registered inland postal packets);

(b)   to any enactment which, either as originally enacted or as amended by any subsequent enactment, requires or authorises a thing to be sent by the recorded delivery service as an alternative to registered post or makes provision in relation to a thing sent by that service;

(c)   to the provisions of any Act of the Parliament of Northern Ireland or of any local or private Act which extends only to Northern Ireland.

(3)   In this Act—

references to sending a document or other thing include references to serving, executing, giving or delivering it or doing any similar thing;

references to sending any thing by registered post include references to sending it by or in a registered letter or packet, whether the references are expressed in those terms or terms having the like effect and whether or not there is any mention of the post or pre-payment;

references to any thing sent by registered post or the recorded delivery service shall be construed accordingly; and

references to a local Act include references to any Act confirming a provisional order or scheme.

[388]

4   Short title

This Act may be cited as the Recorded Delivery Service Act 1962.

[389]

WILLS ACT 1963

(C 44)

An Act to repeal the Wills Act 1861 and make new provision in lieu thereof; and to provide that certain testamentary instruments shall be probative for the purpose of the conveyance of heritable property in Scotland

[31 July 1963]

1   General rule as to formal validity

A will shall be treated as properly executed if its execution conformed to the internal law in force in the territory where it was executed, or in the territory where, at the time of its execution or of the testator's death, he was domiciled or had his habitual residence, or in a state of which, at either of those times, he was a national.

[390]

2   Additional rules

(1)   Without prejudice to the preceding section, the following shall be treated as
properly executed—
   (a)   a will executed on board a vessel or aircraft of any description, if the
         execution of the will conformed to the internal law in force in the
         territory with which, having regard to its registration (if any) and other
         relevant circumstances, the vessel or aircraft may be taken to have been
         most closely connected;
   (b)   a will so far as it disposes of immovable property, if its execution
         conformed to the internal law in force in the territory where the property
         was situated;
   (c)   a will so far as it revokes a will which under this Act would be treated as
         properly executed or revokes a provision which under this Act would be
         treated as comprised in a properly executed will, if the execution of the
         later will conformed to any law by reference to which the revoked will or
         provision would be so treated;
   (d)   a will so far as it exercises a power of appointment, if the execution of the
         will conformed to the law governing the essential validity of the power.

(2)   A will so far as it exercises a power of appointment shall not be treated as
improperly executed by reason only that its execution was not in accordance with any
formal requirements contained in the instrument creating the power.

[391]

3   Certain requirements to be treated as formal

Where (whether in pursuance of this Act or not) a law in force outside the United
Kingdom falls to be applied in relation to a will, any requirement of that law whereby
special formalities are to be observed by testators answering a particular description, or
witnesses to the execution of a will are to possess certain qualifications, shall be treated,
notwithstanding any rule of that law to the contrary, as a formal requirement only.

[392]

4   Construction of wills

The construction of a will shall not be altered by reason of any change in the testator's
domicile after the execution of the will.

[393]

6   Interpretation

(1)   In this Act—
         "internal law" in relation to any territory or state means the law which would
            apply in a case where no question of the law in force in any other territory
            or state arose;
         "state" means a territory or group of territories having its own law of
            nationality;
         "will" includes any testamentary instrument or act, and "testator" shall be
            construed accordingly.

(2)   Where under this Act the internal law in force in any territory or state is to be
applied in the case of a will, but there are in force in that territory or state two or
more systems of internal law relating to the formal validity of wills, the system to be
applied shall be ascertained as follows—

(a) if there is in force throughout the territory or state a rule indicating which of those systems can properly be applied in the case in question, that rule shall be followed; or

(b) if there is no such rule, the system shall be that with which the testator was most closely connected at the relevant time, and for this purpose the relevant time is the time of the testator's death where the matter is to be determined by reference to circumstances prevailing at his death, and the time of execution of the will in any other case.

(3) In determining for the purposes of this Act whether or not the execution of a will conformed to a particular law, regard shall be had to the formal requirements of that law at the time of execution, but this shall not prevent account being taken of an alteration of law affecting wills executed at that time if the alteration enables the will to be treated as properly executed.

[394]

7 Short title, commencement, repeal and extent

(1) This Act may be cited as the Wills Act 1963.

(2) This Act shall come into operation on 1st January 1964.

(3) . . .

(4) This Act shall not apply to a will of a testator who died before the time of the commencement of this Act and shall apply to a will of a testator who dies after that time whether the will was executed before or after that time, but so that the repeal of the Wills Act 1861 shall not invalidate a will executed before that time.

(5) It is hereby declared that this Act extends to Northern Ireland . . .

[395]

NOTES
Sub-s (3): repeals the Wills Act 1861.
Sub-s (5): words omitted repealed by the Northern Ireland Constitution Act 1973, s 41(1), Sch 6, Pt I.

PERPETUITIES AND ACCUMULATIONS ACT 1964

(C 55)

An Act to modify the law of England and Wales relating to the avoidance of future interests in property on grounds of remoteness and governing accumulations of income from property
[16 July 1964]

Perpetuities

1 Power to specify perpetuity period

(1) Subject to section 9(2) of this Act and subsection (2) below, where the instrument by which any disposition is made so provides, the perpetuity period applicable to the disposition under the rule against perpetuities, instead of being of any other duration, shall be of a duration equal to such number of years not exceeding eighty as is specified in that behalf in the instrument.

(2)   Subsection (1) above shall not have effect where the disposition is made in exercise of a special power of appointment, but where a period is specified under that subsection in the instrument creating such a power the period shall apply in relation to any disposition under the power as it applies in relation to the power itself.

[396]

2   Presumptions and evidence as to future parenthood

(1)   Where in any proceedings there arises on the rule against perpetuities a question which turns on the ability of a person to have a child at some future time, then—

(a)   subject to paragraph (b) below, it shall be presumed that a male can have a child at the age of fourteen years or over, but not under that age, and that a female can have a child at the age of twelve years or over, but not under that age or over the age of fifty-five years; but

(b)   in the case of a living person evidence may be given to show that he or she will or will not be able to have a child at the time in question.

(2)   Where any such question is decided by treating a person as unable to have a child at a particular time, and he or she does so, the High Court may make such order as it thinks fit for placing the persons interested in the property comprised in the disposition, so far as may be just, in the position they would have held if the question had not been so decided.

(3)   Subject to subsection (2) above, where any such question is decided in relation to a disposition by treating a person as able or unable to have a child at a particular time, then he or she shall be so treated for the purpose of any question which may arise on the rule against perpetuities in relation to the same disposition in any subsequent proceedings.

(4)   In the foregoing provisions of this section references to having a child are references to begetting or giving birth to a child, but those provisions (except subsection (1)(b)) shall apply in relation to the possibility that a person will at any time have a child by adoption, legitimation or other means as they apply to his or her ability at that time to beget or give birth to a child.

[397]

3   Uncertainty as to remoteness

(1)   Where, apart from the provisions of this section and sections 4 and 5 of this Act, a disposition would be void on the ground that the interest disposed of might not become vested until too remote a time, the disposition shall be treated, until such time (if any) as it becomes established that the vesting must occur, if at all, after the end of the perpetuity period, as if the disposition were not subject to the rule against perpetuities; and its becoming so established shall not affect the validity of anything previously done in relation to the interest disposed of by way of advancement, application of intermediate income or otherwise.

(2)   Where, apart from the said provisions, a disposition consisting of the conferring of a general power of appointment would be void on the ground that the power might not become exercisable until too remote a time, the disposition shall be treated, until such time (if any) as it becomes established that the power will not be exercisable within the perpetuity period, as if the disposition were not subject to the rule against perpetuities.

(3)   Where, apart from the said provisions, a disposition consisting of the conferring of any power, option or other right would be void on the ground that the right might be exercised at too remote a time, the disposition shall be treated as regards any exercise of the right within the perpetuity period as if it were not subject to the rule against perpetuities and, subject to the said provisions, shall be treated as void for remoteness only if, and so far as, the right is not fully exercised within that period.

(4)   Where this section applies to a disposition and the duration of the perpetuity period is not determined by virtue of section 1 or 9(2) of this Act, it shall be determined as follows:—

(a)   where any persons falling within subsection (5) below are individuals in being and ascertainable at the commencement of the perpetuity period the duration of the period shall be determined by reference to their lives and no others, but so that the lives of any description of persons falling within paragraph (b) or (c) of that subsection shall be disregarded if the number of persons of that description is such as to render it impracticable to ascertain the date of death of the survivor;

(b)   where there are no lives under paragraph (a) above the period shall be twenty-one years.

(5)   The said persons are as follows:—

(a)   the person by whom the disposition was made;

(b)   a person to whom or in whose favour the disposition was made, that is to say—

(i)   in the case of a disposition to a class of persons, any member or potential member of the class;

(ii)   in the case of an individual disposition to a person taking only on certain conditions being satisfied, any person as to whom some of the conditions are satisfied and the remainder may in time be satisfied;

(iii)   in the case of a special power of appointment exercisable in favour of members of a class, any member or potential member of the class;

(iv)   in the case of a special power of appointment exercisable in favour of one person only, that person or, where the object of the power is ascertainable only on certain conditions being satisfied, any person as to whom some of the conditions are satisfied and the remainder may in time be satisfied;

(v)   in the case of any power, option or other right, the person on whom the right is conferred;

(c)   a person having a child or grandchild within sub-paragraphs (i) to (iv) of paragraph (b) above, or any of whose children or grandchildren, if subsequently born, would by virtue of his or her descent fall within those sub-paragraphs;

(d)   any person on the failure or determination of whose prior interest the disposition is limited to take effect.

[398]

4   Reduction of age and exclusion of class members to avoid remoteness

(1)   Where a disposition is limited by reference to the attainment by any person or persons of a specified age exceeding twenty-one years, and it is apparent at the time the disposition is made or becomes apparent at a subsequent time—

(a)   that the disposition would, apart from this section, be void for remoteness, but

(b)   that it would not be so void if the specified age had been twenty-one years, the disposition shall be treated for all purposes as if, instead of being limited by reference to the age in fact specified, it had been limited by reference to the age nearest to that age which would, if specified instead, have prevented the disposition from being so void.

(2)   Where in the case of any disposition different ages exceeding twenty-one years are specified in relation to different persons—

    (a)   the reference in paragraph (b) of subsection (1) above to the specified age shall be construed as a reference to all the specified ages, and

    (b)   that subsection shall operate to reduce each such age so far as is necessary to save the disposition from being void for remoteness.

(3)   Where the inclusion of any persons, being potential members of a class or unborn persons who at birth would become members or potential members of the class, prevents the foregoing provisions of this section from operating to save a disposition from being void for remoteness, those persons shall thenceforth be deemed for all the purposes of the disposition to be excluded from the class, and the said provisions shall thereupon have effect accordingly.

(4)   Where, in the case of a disposition to which subsection (3) above does not apply, it is apparent at the time the disposition is made or becomes apparent at a subsequent time that, apart from this subsection, the inclusion of any persons, being potential members of a class or unborn persons who at birth would become members or potential members of the class, would cause the disposition to be treated as void for remoteness, those persons shall, unless their exclusion would exhaust the class, thenceforth be deemed for all the purposes of the disposition to be excluded from the class.

(5)   Where this section has effect in relation to a disposition to which section 3 above applies, the operation of this section shall not affect the validity of anything previously done in relation to the interest disposed of by way of advancement, application of intermediate income or otherwise.

(6)   . . .

[(7)   For the avoidance of doubt it is hereby declared that a question arising under section 3 of this Act or subsection (1)(a) above of whether a disposition would be void apart from this section is to be determined as if subsection (6) above had been a separate section of this Act.]

[399]

NOTES

    Sub-s (6): repeals the Law of Property Act 1925, s 163.

    Sub-s (7): inserted by the Children Act 1975, s 108(1)(a), Sch 3, para 43.

---

5   Condition relating to death of surviving spouse

Where a disposition is limited by reference to the time of death of the survivor of a person in being at the commencement of the perpetuity period and any spouse of that person, and that time has not arrived at the end of the perpetuity period, the disposition shall be treated for all purposes, where to do so would save it from being void for remoteness, as if it had instead been limited by reference to the time immediately before the end of that period.

[400]

6   Saving and acceleration of expectant interests

A disposition shall not be treated as void for remoteness by reason only that the interest disposed of is ulterior to and dependent upon an interest under a disposition which is so void, and the vesting of an interest shall not be prevented from being accelerated on the failure of a prior interest by reason only that the failure arises because of remoteness.

[401]

7   Powers of appointment

For the purposes of the rule against perpetuities, a power of appointment shall be treated as a special power unless—

(a)   in the instrument creating the power it is expressed to be exercisable by one person only, and

(b)   it could, at all times during its currency when that person is of full age and capacity, be exercised by him so as immediately to transfer to himself the whole of the interest governed by the power without the consent of any other person or compliance with any other condition, not being a formal condition relating only to the mode of exercise of the power:

Provided that for the purpose of determining whether a disposition made under a power of appointment exercisable by will only is void for remoteness, the power shall be treated as a general power where it would have fallen to be so treated if exercisable by deed.

[402]

8   Administrative powers of trustees

(1)   The rule against perpetuities shall not operate to invalidate a power conferred on trustees or other persons to sell, lease, exchange or otherwise dispose of any property for full consideration, or to do any other act in the administration (as opposed to the distribution) of any property, and shall not prevent the payment to trustees or other persons of reasonable remuneration for their services.

(2)   Subsection (1) above shall apply for the purpose of enabling a power to be exercised at any time after the commencement of this Act notwithstanding that the power is conferred by an instrument which took effect before that commencement.

[403]

9   Options relating to land

(1)   The rule against perpetuities shall not apply to a disposition consisting of the conferring of an option to acquire for valuable consideration an interest reversionary (whether directly or indirectly) on the term of a lease if—

(a)   the option is exercisable only by the lessee or his successors in title, and

(b)   it ceases to be exercisable at or before the expiration of one year following the determination of the lease.

This subsection shall apply in relation to an agreement for a lease as it applies in relation to a lease, and "lessee" shall be construed accordingly.

(2)   In the case of a disposition consisting of the conferring of an option to acquire for valuable consideration any interest in land, the perpetuity period under the rule against perpetuities shall be twenty-one years, and section 1 of this Act shall not apply:

Provided that this subsection shall not apply to a right of pre-emption conferred on a public or local authority in respect of land used or to be used for religious purposes where the right becomes exercisable only if the land ceases to be used for such purposes.

[404]

10   Avoidance of contractual and other rights in cases of remoteness

Where a disposition inter vivos would fall to be treated as void for remoteness if the rights and duties thereunder were capable of transmission to persons other than the original parties and had been so transmitted, it shall be treated as void as between the person by whom it was made and the person to whom or in whose favour it was made or any successor of his, and no remedy shall lie in contract or otherwise for giving effect to it or making restitution for its lack of effect.

[405]

11   Rights for enforcement of rentcharges

(1)   The rule against perpetuities shall not apply to any powers or remedies for recovering or compelling the payment of an annual sum to which section 121 or 122 of the Law of Property Act 1925 applies, or otherwise becoming exercisable or enforceable on the breach of any condition or other requirement relating to that sum.

(2)   . . .

[406]

NOTES
Sub-s (2): amends the Law of Property Act 1925, s 121(6).

12   Possibilities of reverter, conditions subsequent, exceptions and reservations

(1)   In the case of—
   (a)   a possibility of reverter on the determination of a determinable fee simple, or
   (b)   a possibility of a resulting trust on the determination of any other determinable interest in property,

the rule against perpetuities shall apply in relation to the provision causing the interest to be determinable as it would apply if that provision were expressed in the form of a condition subsequent giving rise, on breach thereof, to a right of re-entry or an equivalent right in the case of property other than land, and where the provision falls to be treated as void for remoteness the determinable interest shall become an absolute interest.

(2)   Where a disposition is subject to any such provision, or to any such condition subsequent, or to any exception or reservation, the disposition shall be treated for the purposes of this Act as including a separate disposition of any rights arising by virtue of the provision, condition subsequent, exception or reservation.

[407]

Accumulations

13   Amendment of s 164 of Law of Property Act 1925

(1)   The periods for which accumulations of income under a settlement or other disposition are permitted by section 164 of the Law of Property Act 1925 shall include—

    (a) a term of twenty-one years from the date of the making of the disposition, and

    (b) the duration of the minority or respective minorities of any person or persons in being at that date.

(2)   It is hereby declared that the restrictions imposed by the said section 164 apply in relation to a power to accumulate income whether or not there is a duty to exercise that power, and that they apply whether or not the power to accumulate extends to income produced by the investment of income previously accumulated.

[408]

14 Right to stop accumulations

Section 2 above shall apply to any question as to the right of beneficiaries to put an end to accumulations of income under any disposition as it applies to questions arising on the rule against perpetuities.

[409]

Supplemental

15 Short title, interpretation and extent

(1)   This Act may be cited as the Perpetuities and Accumulations Act 1964.

(2)   In this Act—

    "disposition" includes the conferring of a power of appointment and any other disposition of an interest in or right over property, and references to the interest disposed of shall be construed accordingly;

    "in being" means living or en ventre sa mere;

    "power of appointment" includes any discretionary power to transfer a beneficial interest in property without the furnishing of valuable consideration;

    "will" includes a codicil;

and for the purposes of this Act a disposition contained in a will shall be deemed to be made at the death of the testator.

(3)   For the purposes of this Act a person shall be treated as a member of a class if in his case all the conditions identifying a member of the class are satisfied, and shall be treated as a potential member if in his case some only of those conditions are satisfied but there is a possibility that the remainder will in time be satisfied.

(4)   Nothing in this Act shall affect the operation of the rule of law rendering void for remoteness certain dispositions under which property is limited to be applied for purposes other than the benefit of any person or class of persons in cases where the property may be so applied after the end of the perpetuity period.

(5)   The foregoing sections of this Act shall apply (except as provided in section 8(2) above) only in relation to instruments taking effect after the commencement of this Act, and in the case of an instrument made in the exercise of a special power of appointment shall apply only where the instrument creating the power takes effect after that commencement;

    Provided that section 7 above shall apply in all cases for construing the foregoing reference to a special power of appointment.

(6)   This Act shall apply in relation to a disposition made otherwise than by an instrument as if the disposition had been contained in an instrument taking effect when the disposition was made.

(7)   This Act binds the Crown.

(8)   Except in so far as the contrary intention appears, any enactment of the Parliament of Northern Ireland passed for purposes similar to the purposes of this Act shall bind the Crown.

(9)   This Act shall not extend to Scotland or (apart from subsection (8) above) to Northern Ireland.

[410]

LAW OF PROPERTY (JOINT TENANTS) ACT 1964

(C 63)

An Act to amend the law with respect to land vested in joint tenants

[31 July 1964]

1   Assumptions on sale of land by survivor of joint tenants

(1)   For the purposes of section 36 (2) of the Law of Property Act 1925, as amended by section 7 of and the Schedule to the Law of Property (Amendment) Act 1926, the survivor of two or more joint tenants shall, in favour of a purchaser of the legal estate, be deemed to be solely and beneficially interested if . . . the conveyance includes a statement that he is so interested.

Provided that the foregoing provisions of this subsection shall not apply if, at any time before the date of the conveyance by the survivor—

(a)   a memorandum of severance (that is to say a note or memorandum signed by the joint tenants or one of them and recording that the joint tenancy was severed in equity on a date therein specified) had been endorsed on or annexed to the conveyance by virtue of which the legal estate was vested in the joint tenants; or

(b)   [a bankruptcy order] made against any of the joint tenants, or a petition for such an order, had been registered under the Land Charges Act 1925, being an order or petition of which the purchaser has notice, by virtue of the registration, on the date of the conveyance by the survivor.

(2)   The foregoing provisions of this section shall apply with the necessary modifications in relation to a conveyance by the personal representatives of the survivor of joint tenants as they apply in relation to a conveyance by such a survivor.

[411]

NOTES

Sub-s (1): words omitted repealed by the Law of Property (Miscellaneous Provisions) Act 1994, s 21(1), (2), Sch 1, para 3, Sch 2, subject to transitional provisions in s 21(4) thereof; words in square brackets in para (b) substituted by the Insolvency Act 1985, s 235(1), Sch 8, para 13.

2   Retrospective and transitional provisions

Section 1 of this Act shall be deemed to have come into force on 1st January 1926, and for the purposes of that section in its application to a conveyance executed before the passing of this Act a statement signed by the vendor or by his personal representatives that he was solely and beneficially interested shall be treated as if it had been included in the conveyance.

[412]

3 Exclusion of registered land

This Act shall not apply to any land the title of which has been registered under the provisions of the Land Registration Acts 1925 and 1936.

[413]

4 Short title, construction, citation and extent

(1) This Act may be cited as the Law of Property (Joint Tenants) Act 1964, and shall be construed as one with the Law of Property Act 1925.

(2) The Law of Property Acts 1925 to 1932, and this Act, may be cited together as the Law of Property Acts 1925 to 1964.

(3) This Act extends to England and Wales only.

[414]

MISREPRESENTATION ACT 1967

(C 7)

An Act to amend the law relating to innocent misrepresentations and to amend sections 11 and 35 of the Sale of Goods Act 1893

[22 March 1967]

1 Removal of certain bars to rescission for innocent misrepresentation

Where a person has entered into a contract after a misrepresentation has been made to him, and—

(a) the misrepresentation has become a term of the contract; or

(b) the contract has been performed;

or both, then, if otherwise he would be entitled to rescind the contract without alleging fraud, he shall be so entitled, subject to the provisions of this Act, notwithstanding the matters mentioned in paragraphs (a) and (b) of this section.

[415]

2 Damages for misrepresentation

(1) Where a person has entered into a contract after a misrepresentation has been made to him by another party thereto and as a result thereof he has suffered loss, then, if the person making the misrepresentation would be liable to damages in respect thereof had the misrepresentation been made fraudulently, that person shall be so liable notwithstanding that the misrepresentation was not made fraudulently, unless he proves that he had reasonable ground to believe and did believe up to the time the contract was made that the facts represented were true.

(2) Where a person has entered into a contract after a misrepresentation has been made to him otherwise than fraudulently, and he would be entitled, by reason of the misrepresentation, to rescind the contract, then, if it is claimed, in any proceedings arising out of the contract, that the contract ought to be or has been rescinded the court or arbitrator may declare the contract subsisting and award damages in lieu of rescission, if of opinion that it would be equitable to do so, having regard to the nature of the misrepresentation and the loss that would be caused by it if the contract were upheld, as well as to the loss that rescission would cause to the other party.

(3)   Damages may be awarded against a person under subsection (2) of this section whether or not he is liable to damages under subsection (1) thereof, but where he is so liable any award under the said subsection (2) shall be taken into account in assessing his liability under the said subsection (1).

[416]

[3   Avoidance of provision excluding liability for misrepresentation

If a contract contains a term which would exclude or restrict—

    (a)   any liability to which a party to a contract may be subject by reason of any misrepresentation made by him before the contract was made; or

    (b)   any remedy available to another party to the contract by reason of such a misrepresentation,

that term shall be of no effect except in so far as it satisfies the requirement of reasonableness as stated in section 11(1) of the Unfair Contract Terms Act 1977; and it is for those claiming that the term satisfies that requirement to show that it does.]

[417]

NOTES

Substituted by the Unfair Contract Terms Act 1977, s 8(1).

5   Saving for past transactions

Nothing in this Act shall apply in relation to any misrepresentation or contract of sale which is made before the commencement of this Act.

[418]

6   Short title, commencement and extent

(1)   This Act may be cited as the Misrepresentation Act 1967.

(2)   This Act shall come into operation at the expiration of the period of one month beginning with the date on which it is passed.

(3)   . . .

(4)   This Act does not extend to Northern Ireland.

[419]

NOTES

Sub-s (3): not relevant to this work.

WILLS ACT 1968

(C 28)

An Act to restrict the operation of section 15 of the Wills Act 1837

[30 May 1968]

1   Restriction of operation of Wills Act 1837, s 15

(1)   For the purposes of section 15 of the Wills Act 1837 (avoidance of gifts to attesting witnesses and their spouses) the attestation of a will by a person to whom or to whose spouse there is given or made any such disposition as is described in that section shall be disregarded if the will is duly executed without his attestation and without that of any other such person.

(2)   This section applies to the will of any person dying after the passing of this Act, whether executed before or after the passing of this Act.

[420]

2   Short title and extent

(1)   This Act may be cited as the Wills Act 1968.

(2)   This Act does not extend to Scotland or Northern Ireland.

[421]

FAMILY LAW REFORM ACT 1969

(C 46)

An Act to amend the law relating to the age of majority, to persons who have not attained that age and to the time when a particular age is attained; to amend the law relating to the property rights of illegitimate children and of other persons whose relationship is traced through an illegitimate link; to make provision for the use of blood tests for the purpose of determining the paternity of any person in civil proceedings; to make provision with respect to the evidence required to rebut a presumption of legitimacy and illegitimacy; to make further provision, in connection with the registration of the birth of an illegitimate child, for entering the name of the father; and for connected purposes

[25 July 1969]

PART I
REDUCTION OF AGE OF MAJORITY AND RELATED PROVISIONS

1   Reduction of age of majority from 21 to 18

(1)   As from the date on which this section comes into force a person shall attain full age on attaining the age of eighteen instead of on attaining the age of twenty-one; and a person shall attain full age on that date if he has then already attained the age of eighteen but not the age of twenty-one.

(2)   The foregoing subsection applies for the purposes of any rule of law, and, in the absence of a definition or of any indication of a contrary intention, for the construction of "full age", "infant", "infancy", "minor", "minority" and similar expressions in—

    (a)   any statutory provision, whether passed or made before, on or after the date on which this section comes into force; and

    (b)   any deed, will or other instrument of whatever nature (not being a statutory provision) made on or after that date.

(3)   In the statutory provisions specified in Schedule 1 to this Act for any reference to the age of twenty-one years there shall be substituted a reference to the age of eighteen years; but the amendment by this subsection of the provisions specified in Part II of that Schedule shall be without prejudice to any power of amending or revoking those provisions.

(4)   This section does not affect the construction of any such expression as is referred to in subsection (2) of this section in any of the statutory provisions described in Schedule 2 to this Act, and the transitional provisions and savings contained in Schedule 3 to this Act shall have effect in relation to this section.

(5)   The Lord Chancellor may by order made by statutory instrument amend any provision in any local enactment passed on or before the date on which this section comes into force (not being a provision described in paragraph 2 of Schedule 2 to this Act) by substituting a reference to the age of eighteen years for any reference therein to the age of twenty-one years; and any statutory instrument containing an order under this subsection shall be subject to annulment in pursuance of a resolution of either House of Parliament.

(6)   In this section "statutory provision" means any enactment (including, except where the context otherwise requires, this Act) and any order, rule, regulation, byelaw or other instrument made in the exercise of a power conferred by any enactment.

(7)   Notwithstanding any rule of law, a will or codicil executed before the date on which this section come into force shall not be treated for the purposes of this section as made on or after that date by reason only that the will or codicil is confirmed by a codicil executed on or after that date.

[422]

3   Provisions relating to wills and intestacy

(1), (2)   . . .

(3)   Any will which—
    (a)   has been made, whether before or after the coming into force of this section, by a person under the age of eighteen; and
    (b)   is valid by virtue of the provisions of section 11 of the said Act of 1837 and the said Act of 1918,

may be revoked by that person notwithstanding that he is still under that age whether or not the circumstances are then such that he would be entitled to make a valid will under those provisions.

(4)   In this section "will" has the same meaning as in the said Act of 1837 and "intestate" has the same meaning as in the said Act of 1925.

[423]

NOTES

    Sub-s (1): amends the Wills Act 1837, s 7, and the Wills (Soldiers and Sailors) Act 1918, ss 1, 3(1).
    Sub-s (2): amends the Administration of Estates Act 1925, s 47(1)(i).

9   Time at which a person attains a particular age

(1)   The time at which a person attains a particular age expressed in years shall be the commencement of the relevant anniversary of the date of his birth.

(2)   This section applies only where the relevant anniversary falls on a date after that on which this section comes into force, and, in relation to any enactment, deed, will or other instrument, has effect subject to any provision therein.

[424]

PART IV
MISCELLANEOUS AND GENERAL

28   Short title, interpretation, commencement and extent

(1)   This Act may be cited as the Family Law Reform Act 1969.

(2)　Except where the context otherwise requires, any reference in this Act to any enactment shall be construed as a reference to that enactment as amended, extended or applied by or under any other enactment, including this Act.

(3)　This Act shall come into force on such date as the Lord Chancellor may appoint by order made by statutory instrument, and different dates may be appointed for the coming into force of different provisions.

(4)　In this Act—

(a)　. . .

(b)　section 2, so far as it amends any provision of . . . the Marriage with Foreigners Act 1906, has the same extent as that provision;

(c)　sections . . . 6(7), so far as they affect Part II of the Maintenance Orders Act 1950, extend to Scotland and Northern Ireland;

(d)　section 10, so far as it relates to the Civil List Act 1952, extends to Scotland and Northern Ireland;

(e)–(g)　. . .

but, save as aforesaid, this Act shall extend to England and Wales only.

[425]

NOTES

　Sub-s (4): para (a) repealed by the British Nationality Act 1981, s 52(8), Sch 9; words omitted from para (b) repealed by the Foreign Marriage (Amendment) Act 1988, s 7(2), Schedule; words omitted from para (c) repealed by the Guardianship of Minors Act 1971, s 18(2), (4), Sch 2; paras (e), (g) not relevant to this work; para (f) repealed by the Northern Ireland Constitution Act 1973, s 41(1), Sch 6, Pt I.

SCHEDULES

SCHEDULE 2
STATUTORY PROVISIONS UNAFFECTED BY SECTION 1

Section 1(4)

1.　The Regency Acts 1937 to 1953.

2.　. . . , section 7 of the Parliamentary Elections Act 1695, . . .

3.　. . .

[426]

NOTES

　Para 2: words omitted repealed by the Representation of the People Act 1983, s 206, Sch 9, Pt I and the Statute Law (Repeals) Act 1993.

　Para 3: repealed by the Finance Act 1969, ss 16(1), 61(6), Sch 21, Pt IV.

SCHEDULE 3
TRANSITIONAL PROVISIONS AND SAVINGS

Section 1(4)

Interpretation

1.—(1) In this Schedule "the principal section" means section 1 of this Act and "the commencement date" means the date on which that section comes into force.

(2)　Subsection (7) of the principal section shall apply for the purposes of this Schedule as it applies for the purposes of that section.

Funds in court

2.   Any order or directions in force immediately before the commencement date by virtue of—

(a)   any rules of court or other statutory provision (including, in particular, section 174 of the County Courts Act 1959) relating to the control of money recovered by or otherwise payable to an infant in any proceedings; or

(b)   section 19 of the Administration of Justice Act 1965 (control of money recovered by widow in fatal accident proceedings which are also brought for the benefit of an infant),

shall have effect as if any reference therein to the infant's attaining the age of twenty-one were a reference to his attaining the age of eighteen or, in relation to a person who by virtue of the principal section attains full age on the commencement date, to that date.

Wardship and custody orders

3.—(1) Any order in force immediately before the commencement date—

(a)   making a person a ward of court; or

(b)   under the Guardianship of Infants Acts 1886 and 1925, or under the Matrimonial Causes Act 1965 or any enactment repealed by that Act, for the custody of, or access to, any person,

which is expressed to continue in force until the person who is the subject of the order attains the age of twenty-one, or any age between eighteen and twenty-one, shall have effect as if the reference to his attaining that age were a reference to his attaining the age of eighteen or, in relation to a person who by virtue of the principal section attains full age on the commencement date, to that date.

(2)   This paragraph is without prejudice to so much of any order as makes provision for the maintenance or education of a person after he has attained the age of eighteen.

Adoption orders

4.   The principal section shall not prevent the making of an adoption order or provisional adoption order under the Adoption Act 1958 in respect of a person who has attained the age of eighteen if the application for the order was made before the commencement date, and in relation to any such case that Act shall have effect as if the principal section had not been enacted.

Power of trustees to apply income for maintenance of minor

5.—(1)   The principal section shall not affect section 31 of the Trustee Act 1925—

(a)   in its application to any interest under an instrument made before the commencement date; or

(b)   in its application, by virtue of section 47(1)(ii) of the Administration of Estates Act 1925, to the estate of an intestate (within the meaning of that Act) dying before that date.

(2)   In any case in which (whether by virtue of this paragraph or paragraph 9 of this Schedule) trustees have power under subsection (1)(i) of the said section 31 to pay income to the parent or guardian of any person who has attained the age of eighteen, or to apply it for or towards the maintenance, education or benefit of any such person, they shall also have power to pay it to that person himself.

Personal representatives' powers during minority of beneficiary

6.   The principal section shall not affect the meaning of "minority" in sections 33(3) and 39(1) of the Administration of Estates Act 1925 in the case of a beneficiary whose interest arises under a will or codicil made before the commencement date or on the death before that date of an intestate (within the meaning of that Act).

Accumulation periods

7.　The change by virtue of the principal section, in the construction of—

    (a)　sections 164 to 166 of the Law of Property Act 1925;

    (b)　section 13(1) of the Perpetuities and Accumulations Act 1964,

(which lay down permissible periods for the accumulation of income under settlements and other dispositions) shall not invalidate any direction for accumulation in a settlement or other disposition made by a deed, will or other instrument which was made before the commencement date.

Limitation of actions

8.　The change, by virtue of the principal section, in the construction of section 31(2) of the Limitation Act 1939 (limitation in case of person under disability) shall not affect the time for bringing proceedings in respect of a cause of action which arose before the commencement date.

Statutory provisions incorporated in deeds, wills, etc

9.　The principal section shall not affect the construction of any statutory provision where it is incorporated in and has effect as part of any deed, will or other instrument the construction of which is not affected by that section.

[427]

LAW OF PROPERTY ACT 1969

(C 59)

An Act to amend Part II of the Landlord and Tenant Act 1954; to provide for the closing of the Yorkshire deeds registries; to amend the law relating to dispositions of estates and interests in land and to land charges; to make further provision as to the powers of the Lands Tribunal and court in relation to restrictive covenants affecting land; and for purposes connected with those matters

[22 October 1969]

PART III
AMENDMENT OF LAW RELATING TO DISPOSITIONS OF ESTATES AND INTERESTS IN LAND

23　Reduction of statutory period of title

Section 44(1) of the Law of Property Act 1925 (under which the period of commencement of title which may be required under a contract expressing no contrary intention is thirty years except in certain cases) shall have effect, in its application to contracts made after the commencement of this Act, as if it specified fifteen years instead of thirty years as the period of commencement of title which may be so required.

[428]

24　Contracts for purchase of land affected by land charge, etc

(1)　Where under a contract for the sale or other disposition of any estate or interest in land the title to which is not registered under the Land Registration Act 1925 or any enactment replaced by it any question arises whether the purchaser had knowledge, at the time of entering into the contract, of a registered land charge, that question shall be determined by reference to his actual knowledge and without regard to the provisions of section 198 of the Law of Property Act 1925 (under which registration under the Land Charges Act 1925 or any enactment replaced by it is deemed to constitute actual notice).

(2)   Where any estate or interest with which such a contract is concerned is affected by a registered land charge and the purchaser, at the time of entering into the contract, had not received notice and did not otherwise actually know that the estate or interest was affected by the charge, any provision of the contract shall be void so far as it purports to exclude the operation of subsection (1) above or to exclude or restrict any right or remedy that might otherwise be exercisable by the purchaser on the ground that the estate or interest is affected by the charge.

(3)   In this section—
    "purchaser" includes a lessee, mortgagee or other person acquiring or intending to acquire an estate or interest in land; and
    "registered land charge" means any instrument or matter registered, otherwise than in a register of local land charges, under the Land Charges Act 1925 or any Act replaced by it.

(4)   For the purposes of this section any knowledge acquired in the course of a transaction by a person who is acting therein as counsel, or as solicitor or other agent, for another shall be treated as the knowledge of that other.

(5)   This section does not apply to contracts made before the commencement of this Act.

[429]

NOTES
    Modification: any reference to solicitor(s) etc modified to include references to bodies recognised under the Administration of Justice Act 1985, s 9, by the Solicitors' Incorporated Practices Order 1991, SI 1991/2684, arts 4, 5, Sch 1.
    Land Charges Act 1925: see now the Land Charges Act 1972.

---

25   Compensation in certain cases for loss due to undisclosed land charges

(1)   Where a purchaser of any estate or interest in land under a disposition to which this section applies has suffered loss by reason that the estate or interest is affected by a registered land charge, then if—
    (a)   the date of completion was after the commencement of this Act; and
    (b)   on that date the purchaser had no actual knowledge of the charge; and
    (c)   the charge was registered against the name of an owner of an estate in the land who was not as owner of any such estate a party to any transaction, or concerned in any event, comprised in the relevant title;

the purchaser shall be entitled to compensation for the loss.

(2)   For the purposes of subsection (1)(b) above, the question whether any person had actual knowledge of a charge shall be determined without regard to the provisions of section 198 of the Law of Property Act 1925 (under which registration under the Land Charges Act 1925 or any enactment replaced by it is deemed to constitute actual notice).

(3)   Where a transaction comprised in the relevant title was effected or evidenced by a document which expressly provided that it should take effect subject to an interest or obligation capable of registration in any of the relevant registers, the transaction which created that interest or obligation shall be treated for the purposes of subsection (1)(c) above as comprised in the relevant title.

(4)   Any compensation for loss under this section shall be paid by the Chief Land Registrar, and where the purchaser of the estate or interest in question has incurred expenditure for the purpose—
(a)   of securing that the estate or interest is no longer affected by the registered land charge or is so affected to a less extent; or
(b)   of obtaining compensation under this section;

the amount of the compensation shall include the amount of the expenditure (so far as it would not otherwise fall to be treated as compensation for loss) reasonably incurred by the purchaser for that purpose.

(5)   In the case of an action to recover compensation under this section, the cause of action shall be deemed for the purposes of [the Limitation Act 1980] to accrue at the time when the registered land charge affecting the estate or interest in question comes to the notice of the purchaser.

(6)   Any proceedings for the recovery of compensation under this section shall be commenced in the High Court; and if in such proceedings the High Court dismisses a claim to compensation it shall not order the purchaser to pay the Chief Land Registrar's costs unless it considers that it was unreasonable for the purchaser to commence the proceedings.

(7)   . . .

(8)   Where compensation under this section has been paid in a case where the purchaser would have had knowledge of the registered land charge but for the fraud of any person, the Chief Land Registrar, on behalf of the Crown, may recover the amount paid from that person.

(9)   This section applies to the following dispositions, that is to say—
(a)   any sale or exchange and, subject to the following provisions of this subsection, any mortgage of an estate or interest in land;
(b)   any grant of a lease for a term of years derived out of a leasehold interest;
(c)   any compulsory purchase, by whatever procedure, of land; and
(d)   any conveyance of a fee simple in land under Part I of the Leasehold Reform Act 1967;

but does not apply to the grant of a term of years derived out of the freehold or the mortgage of such a term by the lessee; and references in this section to a purchaser shall be construed accordingly.

(10) In this section—
"date of completion", in relation to land which vests in the Land Commission or another acquiring authority by virtue of a general vesting declaration under the Land Commission Act 1967 or the Town and Country Planning Act 1968, means the date on which it so vests;
"mortgage" includes any charge;
"registered land charge" means any instrument or matter registered, otherwise than in a register of local land charges, under the Land Charges Act 1925 or any Act replaced by it, except that—
(a)   in relation to an assignment of a lease or underlease or a mortgage by an assignee under such an assignment, it does not include any instrument or matter affecting the title to the freehold or to any relevant leasehold reversion; and
(b)   in relation to the grant of an underlease or the mortgage by the underlessee of the term of years created by an underlease, it does not include any instrument or matter affecting the title to the freehold or

to any leasehold reversion superior to the leasehold interest out of
which the term of years is derived;

"relevant registers" means the registers kept under section 1 of the Land
Charges Act 1925;

"relevant title" means—

(a) in relation to a disposition made under a contract, the title which the
purchaser was, apart from any acceptance by him (by agreement or
otherwise) of a shorter or an imperfect title, entitled to require; or

(b) in relation to any other disposition, the title which he would have
been entitled to require if the disposition had been made under a
contract to which section 44(1) of the Law of Property Act 1925
applied and that contract had been made on the date of completion.

(11) For the purposes of this section any knowledge acquired in the course of a
transaction by a person who is acting therein as counsel, or as solicitor or other agent,
for another shall be treated as the knowledge of that other.

[430]

NOTES

Sub-s (5): words in square brackets substituted by the Limitation Act 1980, s 40(2), Sch 3, para 9.

Sub-s (7): repealed by the Land Charges Act 1972, s 18(3), Sch 5.

Modification: any reference to solicitor(s) etc modified to include references to bodies recognised
under the Administration of Justice Act 1985, s 9, by the Solicitors' Incorporated Practices Order 1991,
SI 1991/2684, arts 4, 5, Sch 1.

Land Charges Act 1925: see now the Land Charges Act 1972.

PART V
SUPPLEMENTARY PROVISIONS

31   Short title, commencement and extent

(1)   This Act may be cited as the Law of Property Act 1969.

(2)   This Act, except section 28(6), shall come into force on 1st January 1970.

(3)   This Act does not extend to Scotland or Northern Ireland.

[431]

ADMINISTRATION OF JUSTICE ACT 1970

(C 31)

*An Act to make further provision about the courts (including assizes), their business, jurisdiction
and procedure; to enable a High Court judge to accept appointment as arbitrator or umpire
under an arbitration agreement; to amend the law respecting the enforcement of debt and other
liabilities; to amend section 106 of the Rent Act 1968; and for miscellaneous purposes
connected with the administration of justice*

[29 May 1970]

PART IV
ACTIONS BY MORTGAGEES FOR POSSESSION

36   Additional powers of court in action by mortgagee for possession of dwelling-house

(1)   Where the mortgagee under a mortgage of land which consists of or includes a
dwelling-house brings an action in which he claims possession of the mortgaged

property, not being an action for foreclosure in which a claim for possession of the mortgaged property is also made, the court may exercise any of the powers conferred on it by subsection (2) below if it appears to the court that in the event of its exercising the power the mortgagor is likely to be able within a reasonable period to pay any sums due under the mortgage or to remedy a default consisting of a breach of any other obligation arising under or by virtue of the mortgage.

(2)   The court—
   (a)   may adjourn the proceedings, or
   (b)   on giving judgment, or making an order, for delivery of possession of the mortgaged property, or at any time before the execution of such judgment or order, may—
      (i)   stay or suspend execution of the judgment or order, or
      (ii)   postpone the date for delivery of possession,

for such period or periods as the court thinks reasonable.

(3)   Any such adjournment, stay, suspension or postponement as is referred to in subsection (2) above may be made subject to such conditions with regard to payment by the mortgagor of any sum secured by the mortgage or the remedying of any default as the court thinks fit.

(4)   The court may from time to time vary or revoke any condition imposed by virtue of this section.

(5)   This section shall have effect in relation to such an action as is referred to in subsection (1) above begun before the date on which this section comes into force unless in that action judgment has been given, or an order made, for delivery of possession of the mortgaged property and that judgment or order was executed before that date.

(6)   In the application of this section to Northern Ireland, "the court" means a judge of the High Court in Northern Ireland, and in subsection (1) the words from "not being" to "made" shall be omitted.

[432]

Part VI
General

54   Citation, interpretation, repeals, commencement and extent

(1)   This Act may be cited as the Administration of Justice Act 1970.

(2)   References in this Act to any enactment include references to that enactment as amended or extended by or under any other enactment, including this Act.

(3)   The enactments specified in Schedule 11 to this Act are hereby repealed to the extent specified in the third column of that Schedule.

(4)   This Act shall come into force on such day as the Lord Chancellor may appoint by order made by statutory instrument, and different days may be so appointed for different provisions of this Act, or for different purposes.

(5)   . . .

(6)   This section (except subsection (3)) and the following provisions only of this Act extend to Northern Ireland, that is to say—

(a) sections 1(6) . . . and Schedules 2 . . . , so far as they relate to any enactment which extends to Northern Ireland, and section 2(5);

(b) Part III; and

(c) sections 36, [38A], 39, 43(6) . . . ;

. . . . .

[433]

NOTES

Sub-s (5): not relevant to this work.

Sub-s (6): first and second words omitted repealed by the Attachment of Earnings Act 1971, s 29(2), Sch 6; figure in square brackets in para (c) inserted by the Consumer Credit Act 1974, s 192(3)(a), Sch 4, Pt I, para 31; third words omitted repealed by the Northern Ireland Constitution Act 1973, s 41(1), Sch 6, Pt I; final words omitted repealed by the Administration of Estates Act 1971, s 12(1), Sch 2, Pt I.

MATRIMONIAL PROCEEDINGS AND PROPERTY ACT 1970

(C 45)

An Act to make fresh provision for empowering the court in matrimonial proceedings to make orders ordering either spouse to make financial provision for, or transfer property to, the other spouse or a child of the family, orders for the variation of ante-nuptial and post-nuptial settlements, orders for the custody and education of children and orders varying, discharging or suspending orders made in such proceedings; to make other amendments of the law relating to matrimonial proceedings; to abolish the right to claim restitution of conjugal rights; to declare what interest in property is acquired by a spouse who contributes to its improvement; to make provision as to a spouse's rights of occupation under section 1 of the Matrimonial Homes Act 1967 in certain cases; to extend section 17 of the Married Women's Property Act 1882 and section 7 of the Matrimonial Causes (Property and Maintenance) Act 1958; to amend the law about the property of a person whose marriage is the subject of a decree of judicial separation dying intestate; to abolish the agency of necessity of a wife; and for purposes connected with the matters aforesaid

[29 May 1970]

PART II
MISCELLANEOUS PROVISIONS

Provisions relating to property of married persons

37 Contributions by spouse in money or money's worth to the improvement of property

It is hereby declared that where a husband or wife contributes in money or money's worth to the improvement of real or personal property in which or in the proceeds of sale of which either or both of them has or have a beneficial interest, the husband or wife so contributing shall, if the contribution is of a substantial nature and subject to any agreement between them to the contrary express or implied, be treated as having then acquired by virtue of his or her contribution a share or an enlarged share, as the case may be, in that beneficial interest of such an extent as may have been then agreed or, in default of such agreement, as may seem in all the circumstances just to any court before which the question of the existence or extent of the beneficial interest of the husband or wife arises (whether in proceedings between them or in any other proceedings).

[434]

Part III
Supplementary

43　Citation, commencement and extent

(1)　This Act may be cited as the Matrimonial Proceedings and Property Act 1970.

(2)　...

(3)　Any reference in any provision of this Act, or in any enactment amended by a provision of this Act, to the commencement of this Act shall be construed as a reference to the date on which that provision comes into force.

(4)　... this Act does not extend to Scotland or Northern Ireland.

[435]

POWERS OF ATTORNEY ACT 1971

(C 27)

An Act to make new provision in relation to powers of attorney and the delegation by trustees of their trusts, powers and discretions

[12 May 1971]

1　Execution of powers of attorney

(1)　An instrument creating a power of attorney shall be [executed as a deed by] the donor of the power.

(2)　...

(3)　This section is without prejudice to any requirement in, or having effect under, any other Act as to the witnessing of instruments creating powers of attorney and does not affect the rules relating to the execution of instruments by bodies corporate.

[436]

3　Proof of instruments creating powers of attorney

(1)　The contents of an instrument creating a power of attorney may be proved by means of a copy which—

(a)　is a reproduction of the original made with a photographic or other device for reproducing documents in facsimile; and

(b)　contains the following certificate or certificates signed by the donor of the power or by a solicitor [duly certificated notary public] or stockbroker, that is to say—

(i) a certificate at the end to the effect that the copy is a true and complete copy of the original; and

(ii) if the original consists of two or more pages, a certificate at the end of each page of the copy to the effect that it is a true and complete copy of the corresponding page of the original.

(2)   Where a copy of an instrument creating a power of attorney has been made which complies with subsection (1) of this section, the contents of the instrument may also be proved by means of a copy of that copy if the further copy itself complies with that subsection, taking references in it to the original as references to the copy from which the further copy is made.

(3)   In this section ["duly certificated notary public" has the same meaning as it has in the Solicitors Act 1974 by virtue of section 87(1) of that Act and] "stockbroker" means a member of any stock exchange within the meaning of the Stock Transfer Act 1963 or the Stock Transfer Act (Northern Ireland) 1963.

(4)   This section is without prejudice to section 4 of the Evidence and Powers of Attorney Act 1940 (proof of deposited instruments by office copy) and to any other method of proof authorised by law.

(5)   For the avoidance of doubt, in relation to an instrument made in Scotland the references to a power of attorney in this section and in section 4 of the Evidence and Powers of Attorney Act 1940 include references to a factory and commission.

[437]

NOTES

Sub-ss (1), (3): words in square brackets inserted by the Courts and Legal Services Act 1990, s 125(2), Sch 17, para 4.

Modification: any reference to solicitor(s) etc modified to include references to bodies recognised under the Administration of Justice Act 1985, s 9, by the Solicitors' Incorporated Practices Order 1991, SI 1991/2684, arts 4, 5, Sch 1.

4   Powers of attorney given as security

(1)   Where a power of attorney is expressed to be irrevocable and is given to secure—

(a)   a proprietary interest of the donee of the power; or

(b)   the performance of an obligation owed to the donee,

then, so long as the donee has that interest or the obligation remains undischarged, the power shall not be revoked—

(i) by the donor without the consent of the donee; or

(ii) by the death, incapacity or bankruptcy of the donor or, if the donor is a body corporate, by its winding up or dissolution.

(2)   A power of attorney given to secure a proprietary interest may be given to the person entitled to the interest and persons deriving title under him to that interest, and those persons shall be duly constituted donees of the power for all purposes of the power but without prejudice to any right to appoint substitutes given by the power.

(3)   This section applies to powers of attorney whenever created.

[438]

5   Protection of donee and third persons where power of attorney is revoked

(1)   A donee of a power of attorney who acts in pursuance of the power at a time when it has been revoked shall not, by reason of the revocation, incur any liability

(either to the donor or to any other person) if at that time he did not know that the power had been revoked.

(2)   Where a power of attorney has been revoked and a person, without knowledge of the revocation, deals with the donee of the power, the transaction between them shall, in favour of that person, be as valid as if the power had then been in existence.

(3)   Where the power is expressed in the instrument creating it to be irrevocable and to be given by way of security then, unless the person dealing with the donee knows that it was not in fact given by way of security, he shall be entitled to assume that the power is incapable of revocation except by the donor acting with the consent of the donee and shall accordingly be treated for the purposes of subsection (2) of this section as having knowledge of the revocation only if he knows that it has been revoked in that manner.

(4)   Where the interest of a purchaser depends on whether a transaction between the donee of a power of attorney and another person was valid by virtue of subsection (2) of this section, it shall be conclusively presumed in favour of the purchaser that that person did not at the material time know of the revocation of the power if—
  (a)   the transaction between that person and the donee was completed within twelve months of the date on which the power came into operation; or
  (b)   that person makes a statutory declaration, before or within three months after the completion of the purchase, that he did not at the material time know of the revocation of the power.

(5)   Without prejudice to subsection (3) of this section, for the purposes of this section knowledge of the revocation of power of attorney includes knowledge of the occurrence of any event (such as the death of the donor) which has the effect of revoking the power.

(6)   In this section "purchaser" and "purchase" have the meanings specified in section 205(1) of the Law of Property Act 1925.

(7)   This section applies whenever the power of attorney was created but only to acts and transactions after the commencement of this Act.

[439]

6   Additional protection for transferees under stock exchange transactions

(1)   Without prejudice to section 5 of this Act, where—
  (a)   the donee of a power of attorney executes, as transferor, an instrument transferring registered securities; and
  (b)   the instrument is executed for the purposes of a stock exchange transaction,

it shall be conclusively presumed in favour of the transferee that the power had not been revoked at the date of the instrument if a statutory declaration to that effect is made by the donee of the power on or within three months after that date.

(2)   In this section "registered securities" and "stock exchange transaction" have the same meanings as in the Stock Transfer Act 1963.

[440]

7   Execution of instruments etc by donee of power of attorney

[(1)   If the donee of a power of attorney is an individual, he may, if he thinks fit—
  (a)   execute any instrument with his own signature, and]
  (b)   do any other thing in his own name,

by the authority of the donor of the power; and any document executed or thing done in that manner shall be as effective as if executed or done by the donee with the signature . . . , or, as the case may be, in the name, of the donor of the power.

(2)   For the avoidance of doubt it is hereby declared that an instrument to which subsection (3) . . . of section 74 of the Law of Property Act 1925 applies may be executed either as provided in [that subsection] or as provided in this section.

(3)   This section is without prejudice to any statutory direction requiring an instrument to be executed in the name of an estate owner within the meaning of the said Act of 1925.

(4)   This section applies whenever the power of attorney was created.

[441]

NOTES

    Sub-ss (1), (2): words in square brackets substituted and words omitted repealed by the Law of Property (Miscellaneous Provisions) Act 1989, ss 1, 4, Sch 1, para 7, Sch 2.

9   Power to delegate trusts etc by power of attorney

(1)   Section 25 of the Trustee Act 1925 (power to delegate trusts etc, during absence abroad) shall be amended as follows:

(2), (3) . . .

(4)   This section applies whenever the trusts, powers or discretions in question arose but does not invalidate anything done by virtue of the said section 25 as in force at the commencement of this Act.

[442]

NOTES

    Sub-ss (2), (3): amend the Trustee Act 1925, s 25.

10   Effect of general power of attorney in specified form

(1)   Subject to subsection (2) of this section, a general power of attorney in the form set out in Schedule 1 to this Act, or in a form to the like effect but expressed to be made under this Act, shall operate to confer—

    (a)   on the donee of the power; or

    (b)   if there is more than one donee, on the donees acting jointly or acting jointly or severally, as the case may be,

authority to do on behalf of the donor anything which he can lawfully do by an attorney.

(2)   This section does not apply to functions which the donor has as a trustee or personal representative or as a tenant for life or statutory owner within the meaning of the Settled Land Act 1925.

[443]

11   Short title, repeals, consequential amendments, commencement and extent

(1)   This Act may be cited as the Powers of Attorney Act 1971.

(2)   The enactments specified in Schedule 2 to this Act are hereby repealed to the extent specified in the third column of that Schedule.

(3) . . .

(4)   This Act shall come into force on 1st October 1971.

(5)   Section 3 of this Act extends to Scotland and Northern Ireland but, save as aforesaid, this Act extends to England and Wales only.

[444]

NOTES

Sub-s (3): in part amends the Law of Property Act 1925, s 125(2); remainder repealed by the Supreme Court Act 1981, s 152(4), Sch 7.

SCHEDULE 1
FORM OF GENERAL POWER OF ATTORNEY FOR PURPOSES OF SECTION 10
Section 10

THIS GENERAL POWER OF ATTORNEY is made this   day of   19   by AB of

I   appoint   CD
of

[*or* CD of   and

EF of   jointly *or*

jointly and severally] to be my attorney[s] in accordance with section 10 of the Powers of Attorney Act 1971.

   IN WITNESS etc,

[445]

DEFECTIVE PREMISES ACT 1972

(C 35)

An Act to impose duties in connection with the provision of dwellings and otherwise to amend the law of England and Wales as to liability for injury or damage caused to persons through defects in the state of premises

[29 June 1972]

1   Duty to build dwellings properly

(1)   A person taking on work for or in connection with the provision of a dwelling (whether the dwelling is provided by the erection or by the conversion or enlargement of a building) owes a duty—
   (a)   if the dwelling is provided to the order of any person, to that person; and
   (b)   without prejudice to paragraph (a) above, to every person who acquires an interest (whether legal or equitable) in the dwelling;

to see that the work which he takes on is done in a workmanlike or, as the case may be, professional manner, with proper materials and so that as regards that work the dwelling will be fit for habitation when completed.

(2)   A person who takes on any such work for another on terms that he is to do it in accordance with instructions given by or on behalf of that other shall, to the extent to which he does it properly in accordance with those instructions, be treated for the

purposes of this section as discharging the duty imposed on him by subsection (1) above except where he owes a duty to that other to warn him of any defects in the instructions and fails to discharge that duty.

(3) A person shall not be treated for the purposes of subsection (2) above as having given instructions for the doing of work merely because he has agreed so the work being done in a specified manner, with specified materials or to a specified design.

(4) A person who—
    (a) in the course of a business which consists of or includes providing or arranging for the provision of dwellings or installations in dwellings; or
    (b) in the exercise of a power of making such provision or arrangements conferred by or by virtue of any enactment;

arranges for another to take on work for or in connection with the provision of a dwelling shall be treated for the purposes of this section as included among the persons who have taken on the work.

(5) Any cause of action in respect of a breach of the duty imposed by this section shall be deemed, for the purposes of the Limitation Act 1939, the Law Reform (Limitation of Actions, &c.) Act 1954 and the Limitation Act 1963, to have accrued at the time when the dwelling was completed, but if after that time a person who has done work for or in connection with the provision of the dwelling does further work to rectify the work he has already done, any such cause of action in respect of that further work shall be deemed for those purposes to have accrued at the time when the further work was finished.

2 Cases excluded from the remedy under section 1

(1) Where—
    (a) in connection with the provision of a dwelling or its first sale or letting for habitation any rights in respect of defects in the state of the dwelling are conferred by an approved scheme to which this section applies on a person having or acquiring an interest in the dwelling; and
    (b) it is stated in a document of a type approved for the purposes of this section that the requirements as to design or construction imposed by or under the scheme have, or appear to have, been substantially complied with in relation to the dwelling;

no action shall be brought by any person having or acquiring an interest in the dwelling for breach of the duty imposed by section 1 above in relation to the dwelling.

(2) A scheme to which this section applies—
    (a) may consist of any number of documents and any number of agreements or other transactions between any number of persons; but
    (b) must confer, by virtue of agreements entered into with persons having or acquiring an interest in the dwellings to which the scheme applies, rights on such persons in respect of defects in the state of the dwellings.

(3) In this section "approved" means approved by the Secretary of State, and the power of the Secretary of State to approve a scheme or document for the purposes of this section shall be exercisable by order, except that any requirements as to construction or design imposed under a scheme to which this section applies may be approved by him without making any order or, if he thinks fit, by order.

(4)   The Secretary of State—
    (a)   may approve a scheme or document for the purposes of this section with or without limiting the duration of his approval; and
    (b)   may by order revoke or vary a previous order under this section or, without such an order, revoke or vary a previous approval under this section given otherwise than by order.

(5)   The production of a document purporting to be a copy of an approval given by the Secretary of State otherwise than by order and certified by an officer of the Secretary of State to be a true copy of the approval shall be conclusive evidence of the approval, and without proof of the handwriting or official position of the person purporting to sign the certificate.

(6)   The power to make an order under this section shall be exercisable by statutory instrument which shall be subject to annulment in pursuance of a resolution by either House of Parliament.

(7)   Where an interest in a dwelling is compulsorily acquired—
    (a)   no action shall be brought by the acquiring authority for breach of the duty imposed by section 1 above in respect of the dwelling; and
    (b)   if any work for or in connection with the provision of the dwelling was done otherwise than in the course of a business by the person in occupation of the dwelling at the time of the compulsory acquisition, the acquiring authority and not that person shall be treated as the person who took on the work and accordingly as owing that duty.

[447]

3 Duty of care with respect to work done on premises not abated by disposal of premises

(1)   Where work of construction, repair, maintenance or demolition or any other work is done on or in relation to premises, any duty of care owed, because of the doing of the work, to persons who might reasonably be expected to be affected by defects in the state of the premises created by the doing of the work shall not be abated by the subsequent disposal of the premises by the person who owed the duty.

(2)   This section does not apply—
    (a)   in the case of premises which are let, where the relevant tenancy of the premises commenced, or the relevant tenancy agreement of the premises was entered into, before the commencement of this Act;
    (b)   in the case of premises disposed of in any other way, when the disposal of the premises was completed, or a contract for their disposal was entered into, before the commencement of this Act; or
    (c)   in either case, where the relevant transaction disposing of the premises is entered into in pursuance of an enforceable option by which the consideration for the disposal was fixed before the commencement of this Act.

[448]

7 Short title, commencement and extent

(1)   This Act may be cited as the Defective Premises Act 1972.

(2)   This Act shall come into force on 1st January 1974.

(3)   This Act does not extend to Scotland or Northern Ireland.

[449]

LAND CHARGES ACT 1972

(C 61)

An Act to consolidate certain enactments relating to the registration of land charges and other instruments and matters affecting land

[9 August 1972]

Preliminary

1 The registers and the index

(1) The registrar shall continue to keep at the registry in the prescribed manner the following registers, namely—

(a) a register of land charges;
(b) a register of pending actions;
(c) a register of writs and orders affecting land;
(d) a register of deeds of arrangement affecting land;
(e) a register of annuities,

and shall also continue to keep there an index whereby all entries made in any of those registers can readily be traced.

(2) Every application to register shall be in the prescribed form and shall contain the prescribed particulars.

[(3) Where any charge or other matter is registrable in more than one of the registers kept under this Act, it shall be sufficient if it is registered in one such register, and if it is so registered the person entitled to the benefit of it shall not be prejudicially affected by any provision of this Act as to the effect of non-registration in any other such register.

(3A) Where any charge or other matter is registrable in a register kept under this Act and was also, before the commencement of the Local Land Charges Act 1975, registrable in a local land charges register, then, if before the commencement of the said Act it was registered in the appropriate local land charges register, it shall be treated for the purposes of the provisions of this Act as to the effect of non-registration as if it had been registered in the appropriate register under this Act; and any certificate setting out the result of an official search of the appropriate local land charges register shall, in relation to it, have effect as if it were a certificate setting out the result of an official search under this Act.]

(4) Schedule 1 to this Act shall have effect in relation to the register of annuities.

(5) An office copy of an entry in any register kept under this section shall be admissible in evidence in all proceedings and between all parties to the same extent as the original would be admissible.

(6) Subject to the provisions of this Act, registration may be vacated pursuant to an order of the court.

[(6A) The county courts have jurisdiction under subsection (6) above—

(a) in the case of a land charge of Class C(i), C(ii) or D(i), if the amount does not exceed £30,000;
(b) in the case of a land charge of Class C(iii), if it is for a specified capital sum of money not exceeding £30,000 or, where it is not for a specified capital sum, if the capital value of the land affected does not exceed £30,000;

(c) in the case of a land charge of Class A, Class B, Class C(iv), Class D(ii), Class D(iii) or Class E if the capital value of the land affected does not exceed £30,000;

(d) in the case of a land charge of Class F, if the land affected by it is the subject of an order made by the court under section 1 of the Matrimonial Homes Act 1983 or an application for an order under that section relating to that land has been made to the court;

(e) in a case where an application under section 23 of the Deeds of Arrangement Act 1914 could be entertained by the court.]

[(6B) . . .]

(7) In this section "index" includes any device or combination of devices serving the purpose of an index.

[450]

NOTES

Commencement: 29 January 1973 (sub-ss (1), (2), (4)–(6), (7)); 1 August 1977 (sub-ss (3), (3A)); 1 July 1991 (sub-ss (6A)).

Sub-ss (3), (3A): substituted for existing sub-s (3) by the Local Land Charges Act 1975, s 17(1)(a).

Sub-s (6A): inserted by the County Courts Act 1984, s 148(1), Sch 2, Pt IV, para 16; substituted by the High Court and County Courts Jurisdiction Order 1991, SI 1991/724, art 2(6), (8), Schedule, Pt I.

Sub-s (6B): inserted by the County Courts Act 1984, s 148(1), Sch 2, Pt IV, para 16; repealed by the High Court and County Courts Jurisdiction Order 1991, SI 1991/724, art 2(6), (8), Schedule, Pt I.

Registration in register of land charges

2 The register of land charges

(1) If a charge on or obligation affecting land falls into one of the classes described in this section, it may be registered in the register of land charges as a land charge of that class.

(2) A Class A land charge is—

(a) a rent or annuity or principal money payable by instalments or otherwise, with or without interest, which is not a charge created by deed but is a charge upon land (other than a rate) created pursuant to the application of some person under the provisions of any Act of Parliament, for securing to any person either the money spent by him or the costs, charges and expenses incurred by him under such Act, or the money advanced by him for repaying the money spent or the costs, charges and expenses incurred by another person under the authority of an Act of Parliament; or

(b) a rent or annuity or principal money payable as mentioned in paragraph (a) above which is not a charge created by deed but is a charge upon land (other than a rate) created pursuant to the application of some person under any of the enactments mentioned in Schedule 2 to this Act.

(3) A Class B land charge is a charge on land (not being a local land charge . . .) of any of the kinds described in paragraph (a) of subsection (2) above, created otherwise than pursuant to the application of any person.

(4) A Class C land charge is any of the following [(not being a local land charge)], namely—

(i) a puisne mortgage;

(ii) a limited owner's charge;

(iii) a general equitable charge;

(iv) an estate contract;

and for this purpose—

    (i)   a puisne mortgage is a legal mortgage which is not protected by a deposit of documents relating to the legal estate affected;

    (ii)   a limited owner's charge is an equitable charge acquired by a tenant for life or statutory owner under [[the Inheritance Tax Act 1984] or under] any other statute by reason of the discharge by him of any [inheritance tax] or other liabilities and to which special priority is given by the statute;

    (iii)   a general equitable charge is any equitable charge which—

        (a)   is not secured by a deposit of documents relating to the legal estate affected; and

        (b)   does not arise or affect an interest arising under a trust for sale or a settlement; and

        (c)   is not a charge given by way of indemnity against rents equitably apportioned or charged exclusively on land in exoneration of other land and against the breach or non-observance of covenants or conditions; and

        (d)   is not included in any other class of land charge;

    (iv)   an estate contract is a contract by an estate owner or by a person entitled at the date of the contract to have a legal estate conveyed to him to convey or create a legal estate, including a contract conferring either expressly or by statutory implication a valid option to purchase, a right of pre-emption or any other like right.

(5)   A Class D land charge is any of the following [(not being a local land charge)], namely—

    (i)   an Inland Revenue charge;

    (ii)   a restrictive covenant;

    (iii)   an equitable easement;

and for this purpose—

    (i)   an Inland Revenue charge is a charge on land, being a charge acquired by the Board under [the Inheritance Tax Act 1984];

    (ii)   a restrictive covenant is a covenant or agreement (other than a covenant or agreement between a lessor and a lessee) restrictive of the user of land and entered into on or after 1st January 1926;

    (iii)   an equitable easement is an easement, right or privilege over or affecting land created or arising on or after 1st January 1926, and being merely an equitable interest.

(6)   A Class E land charge is an annuity created before 1st January 1926 and not registered in the register of annuities.

(7)   A Class F land charge is a charge affecting any land by virtue of the [Matrimonial Homes Act 1983].

(8)   A charge or obligation created before 1st January 1926 can only be registered as a Class B land charge or a Class C land charge if it is acquired under a conveyance made on or after that date.

(9)   . . .

NOTES

    Sub-s (3): words omitted repealed by the Local Land Charges Act 1975, s 19(1), Sch 2.

    Sub-s (4): words in first pair of square brackets inserted by the Local Land Charges Act 1975, s 17(1)(b); words in second (outer) pair of square brackets substituted by the Finance Act 1975, s 52(1), Sch 12, paras 2, 18(1), (2), words in square brackets therein substituted by the Inheritance Tax Act 1984, s 276, Sch 8, para 3(1)(a); words in final pair of square brackets substituted by the Finance Act 1975, s 52(1), Sch 12, paras 2, 18(1), (2).

Sub-s (5): words in first pair of square brackets inserted by the Local Land Charges Act 1975, s 17(1)(b); words in second pair of square brackets substituted by the Inheritance Tax Act 1984, s 276, Sch 8, para 3(1)(b).

Sub-s (7): words in square brackets substituted by the Matrimonial Homes Act 1983, s 12(1), Sch 2.

Sub-s (9): repealed by the Finance Act 1977, s 59, Sch 9, Pt V.

Inheritance tax: except in relation to a liability to tax arising before 25 July 1986 capital transfer tax shall be known as inheritance tax and the Capital Transfer Tax Act 1984 may be cited as the Inheritance Tax Act 1984, by virtue of the Finance Act 1986, s 100. Accordingly references to capital transfer tax have been changed to references to inheritance tax throughout this Act.

---

3 Registration of land charges

(1)   A land charge shall be registered in the name of the estate owner whose estate is intended to be affected.

[(1A)   Where a person has died and a land charge created before his death would apart from his death have been registered in his name, it shall be so registered notwithstanding his death.]

(2)   A land charge registered before 1st January 1926 under any enactment replaced by the Land Charges Act 1925 in the name of a person other than the estate owner may remain so registered until it is registered in the name of the estate owner in the prescribed manner.

(3)   A puisne mortgage created before 1st January 1926 may be registered as a land charge before any transfer of the mortgage is made.

(4)   The expenses incurred by the person entitled to the charge in registering a land charge of Class A, Class B or Class C (other than an estate contract) or by the Board in registering an Inland Revenue charge shall be deemed to form part of the land charge, and shall be recoverable accordingly on the day for payment of any part of the land charge next after such expenses are incurred.

(5)   Where a land charge is not created by an instrument, short particulars of the effect of the charge shall be furnished with the application to register the charge.

(6)   An application to register an Inland Revenue charge shall state the [tax] in respect of which the charge is claimed and, so far as possible, shall define the land affected, and such particulars shall be entered or referred to in the register.

(7)   In the case of a land charge for securing money created by a company before 1st January 1970 or so created at any time as a floating charge, registration under *any of the enactments mentioned in subsection (8) below* shall be sufficient in place of registration under this Act, and shall have effect as if the land charge had been registered under this Act.

(8)   *The enactments* referred to in subsection (7) above are section 93 of the Companies (Consolidation) Act 1908, section 79 of the Companies Act 1929 . . . section 95 of the Companies Act 1948 [and sections 395 to 398 of the Companies Act 1985] [as originally enacted].

[452]

NOTES

Commencement: 29 January 1973 (sub-ss (1), (2)–(8)); 1 July 1995 (sub-s (1A)).

Sub-s (1A): inserted by the Law of Property (Miscellaneous Provisions) Act 1994, s 15(1), (2), in relation to applications for registration made after 1 July 1995.

Sub-s (6): words in square brackets substituted by the Finance Act 1975, s 52, Sch 12, paras 2, 18(1), (4).

Sub-s (7): words in italics substituted by the words "Part XII, or Chapter III of Part XXIII, of the Companies Act 1985 (or corresponding earlier enactments)" by the Companies Act 1989, s 107, Sch 16, para 1(1), (2), as from a day to be appointed.

Sub-s (8): words in italics substituted by the words "The corresponding earlier enactments" and words in second pair of square brackets inserted by the Companies Act 1989, s 107, Sch 16, para 1(1), (3), as from a day to be appointed; word omitted repealed, and words in first pair of square brackets substituted by the Companies Consolidation (Consequential Provisions) Act 1985, s 30, Sch 2.

4 Effect of land charges and protection of purchasers

(1)   A land charge of Class A (other than a land improvement charge registered after 31st December 1969) or of Class B shall, when registered, take effect as if it had been created by a deed of charge by way of legal mortgage, but without prejudice to the priority of the charge.

(2)   A land charge of Class A created after 31st December 1888 shall be void as against a purchaser of the land charged with it or of any interest in such land, unless the land charge is registered in the register of land charges before the completion of the purchase.

(3)   After the expiration of one year from the first conveyance occurring on or after 1st January 1889 of a land charge of Class A created before that date the person entitled to the land charge shall not be able to recover the land charge or any part of it as against a purchaser of the land charged with it or of any interest in the land, unless the land charge is registered in the register of land charges before the completion of the purchase.

(4)   If a land improvement charge was registered as a land charge of Class A before 1st January 1970, any body corporate which, but for the charge, would have power to advance money on the security of the estate or interest affected by it shall have that power notwithstanding the charge.

(5)   A land charge of Class B and a land charge of Class C (other than an estate contract) created or arising on or after 1st January 1926 shall be void as against a purchaser of the land charged with it, or of any interest in such land, unless the land charge is registered in the appropriate register before the completion of the purchase.

(6)   An estate contract and a land charge of Class D created or entered into on or after 1st January 1926 shall be void as against a purchaser for money or money's worth [(or, in the case of an Inland Revenue charge, a purchaser within the meaning of [the Inheritance Tax Act 1984)]] of a legal estate in the land charged with it, unless the land charge is registered in the appropriate register before the completion of the purchase.

(7)   After the expiration of one year from the first conveyance occurring on or after 1st January 1926 of a land charge of Class B or Class C created before that date the person entitled to the land charge shall not be able to enforce or recover the land charge or any part of it as against a purchaser of the land charged with it, or of any interest in the land, unless the land charge is registered in the appropriate register before the completion of the purchase.

(8)   A land charge of Class F shall be void as against a purchaser of the land charged with it, or of any interest in such land, unless the land charge is registered in the appropriate register before the completion of the purchase.

[453]

NOTES

Sub-s (6): words in first (outer) pair of square brackets inserted by the Finance Act 1975, s 52, Sch 12, paras 2, 18(1), (5), words in square brackets therein substituted by the Inheritance Tax Act 1984, s 276, Sch 8, para 3(2).

Inheritance tax: except in relation to a liability to tax arising before 25 July 1986 capital transfer tax shall be known as inheritance tax and the Capital Transfer Tax Act 1984 may be cited as the Inheritance Tax Act 1984, by virtue of the Finance Act 1986, s 100. Accordingly references to capital transfer tax have been changed to references to inheritance tax throughout this Act.

Registration in registers of pending actions, writs and orders and deeds of arrangement

5   The register of pending actions

(1)   There may be registered in the register of pending actions—
    (a)   a pending land action;
    (b)   a petition in bankruptcy filed on or after 1st January 1926.

(2)   Subject to general rules under section 16 of this Act, every application for registration under this section shall contain particulars of the title of the proceedings and the name, address and description of the estate owner or other person whose estate or interest is intended to be affected.

(3)   An application for registration shall also state—
    (a)   if it relates to a pending land action, the court in which and the day on which the action was commenced; and
    (b)   if it relates to a petition in bankruptcy, the court in which and the day on which the petition was filed.

(4)   The registrar shall forthwith enter the particulars in the register, in the name of the estate owner or other person whose estate or interest is intended to be affected.

[(4A)   Where a person has died and a pending land action would apart from his death have been registered in his name, it shall be so registered notwithstanding his death.]

(5)   An application to register a petition in bankruptcy against a firm shall state the names and addresses of the partners, and the registration shall be effected against each partner as well as against the firm.

(6)   No fee shall be charged for the registration of a petition in bankruptcy if the application for registration is made by the registrar of the court in which the petition is filed.

(7)   A pending land action shall not bind a purchaser without express notice of it unless it is for the time being registered under this section.

(8)   A petition in bankruptcy shall not bind a purchaser of a legal estate in good faith, for money or money's worth, . . . , unless it is for the time being registered under this section.

(9)   . . .

(10)   The court, if it thinks fit, may upon the determination of the proceedings, or during the pendency of the proceedings if satisfied that they are not prosecuted in good faith, make an order vacating a registration under this section, and direct the party on whose behalf it was made to pay all or any of the costs and expenses occasioned by the registration and by its vacation.

[(11) The county court has jurisdiction under subsection (10) of this section where the action was brought or the petition in bankruptcy was filed in that court.]

NOTES

Commencement: 29 January 1973 (sub-ss (1)–(4), (5)–(10)); 1 August 1984 (sub-s (11)); 1 July 1995 (sub-s (4A)).

Sub-s (4A): inserted by the Law of Property (Miscellaneous Provisions) Act 1994, s 15(1), (3), in relation to applications for registration made on or after 1 July 1995.

Sub-s (8): words omitted repealed by the Insolvency Act 1985, s 235, Sch 8, para 21(2), Sch 10, Pt III.

Sub-s (9): repealed by the Insolvency Act 1985, s 235, Sch 10, Pt III.

Sub-s (11): added by the County Courts Act 1984, s 148(1), Sch 2, Pt IV, para 17.

6   The register of writs and orders affecting land

(1)   There may be registered in the register of writs and orders affecting land—

    (a)   any writ or order affecting land issued or made by any court for the purpose of enforcing a judgment or recognisance;

    (b)   any order appointing a receiver or sequestrator of land;

    [(c)   any bankruptcy order, whether or not the bankrupt's estate is known to include land.]

    [(d)   any access order under the Access to Neighbouring Land Act 1992.]

(2)   Every entry made pursuant to this section shall be made in the name of the estate owner or other person whose land, if any, is affected by the writ or order registered.

[(2A)   Where a person has died and any such writ or order as is mentioned in subsection (1)(a) or (b) above would apart from his death have been registered in his name, it shall be so registered notwithstanding his death.]

(3)   No fee shall be charged for the registration of a [bankruptcy order] if the application for registration is made by an official receiver.

(4)   Except as provided by subsection (5) below and by [section 37(5) of the Supreme Court Act 1981] and [section 107(3) of the County Courts Act 1984] (which make special provision as to receiving orders in respect of land of judgment debtors) every such writ and order as is mentioned in subsection (1) above, and every delivery in execution or other proceeding taken pursuant to any such writ or order, or in obedience to any such writ or order, shall be void as against a purchaser of the land unless the writ or order is for the time being registered under this section.

[(5)   Subject to subsection (6) below, the title of a trustee in bankruptcy shall be void as against a purchaser of a legal estate in good faith for money or money's worth unless the bankruptcy order is for the time being registered under this section.]

(6)   Where a petition in bankruptcy has been registered under section 5 above, the title of the trustee in bankruptcy shall be void as against a purchaser of a legal estate in good faith for money or money's worth . . . claiming under a conveyance made after the date of registration, unless at the date of the conveyance either the registration of the petition is in force or a receiving order on the petition is registered under this section.

NOTES

Commencement: 29 January 1973 (sub-ss (1), (2), (3), (4), (6)); 29 December 1986 (sub-s (5)); 1 July 1995 (sub-s (2A)).

Sub-s (1): para (c) substituted by the Insolvency Act 1985, s 235(1), Sch 8, para 21(3)(a); para (d) added by the Access to Neighbouring Land Act 1992, s 5(1).

Sub-s (2A): inserted by the Law of Property (Miscellaneous Provisions) Act 1994, s 15(1), (4), in relation to applications for registration made after 1 July 1995.

Sub-s (3): words in square brackets substituted by the Insolvency Act 1985, s 235(1), Sch 8, para 21(3)(b).

Sub-s (4): words in first pair of square brackets substituted by the Supreme Court Act 1981, s 152(1), Sch 5; words in second pair of square brackets substituted by the County Courts Act 1984, s 148(1), Sch 2, Pt IV, para 18.

Sub-s (5): substituted by the Insolvency Act 1985, s 235(1), Sch 8, para 21(3)(c).

Sub-s (6): words omitted repealed by the Insolvency Act 1985, s 235, Sch 8, para 21(3)(d), Sch 10, Pt III.

7   The register of deeds of arrangement affecting land

(1)   The deed of arrangement affecting land may be registered in the register of deeds of arrangement affecting land, in the name of the debtor, on the application of a trustee of the deed or a creditor assenting to or taking the benefit of the deed.

(2)   Every deed of arrangement shall be void as against a purchaser of any land comprised in it or affected by it unless it is for the time being registered under this section.

[456]

8   Expiry and renewal of registrations

A registration under section 5, section 6 or section 7 of this Act shall cease to have effect at the end of the period of five years from the date on which it is made, but may be renewed from time to time and, if so renewed, shall have effect for five years from the date of renewal.

[457]

Searches and official searches

10   Official searches

(1)   Where any person requires search to be made at the registry for entries of any matters or documents, entries of which are required or allowed to be made in the registry by this Act, he may make a requisition in that behalf to the registrar, which may be either—

(a)   a written requisition delivered at or sent by post to the registry; or

(b)   a requisition communicated by teleprinter, telephone or other means in such manner as may be prescribed in relation to the means in question, in which case it shall be treated as made to the registrar if, but only if, he accepts it;

and the registrar shall not accept a requisition made in accordance with paragraph (b) above unless it is made by a person maintaining a credit account at the registry, and may at his discretion refuse to accept it notwithstanding that it is made by such a person.

(2)   The prescribed fee shall be payable in respect of every requisition made under this section; and that fee—

(a)   in the case of a requisition made in accordance with subsection (1)(a) above, shall be paid in such manner as may be prescribed for the purposes of this paragraph unless the requisition is made by a person maintaining a credit account at the registry and the fee is debited to that account;

(b)   in the case of a requisition made in accordance with subsection (1)(b) above, shall be debited to the credit account of the person by whom the requisition is made.

(3)   Where a requisition is made under subsection (1) above and the fee payable in respect of it is paid or debited in accordance with subsection (2) above, the registrar shall thereupon make the search required and—

(a) shall issue a certificate setting out the result of the search; and

(b) without prejudice to paragraph (a) above, may take such other steps as he considers appropriate to communicate that result to the person by whom the requisition was made.

(4) In favour of a purchaser or an intending purchaser, as against persons interested under or in respect of matters or documents entries of which are required or allowed as aforesaid, the certificate, according to its tenor, shall be conclusive, affirmatively or negatively, as the case may be.

(5) If any officer, clerk or person employed in the registry commits, or is party or privy to, any act of fraud or collusion, or is wilfully negligent, in the making of or otherwise in relation to any certificate under this section, he shall be guilty of an offence and shall be liable on conviction on indictment to imprisonment for a term not exceeding two years, or on summary conviction to imprisonment for a term not exceeding three months or to a fine not exceeding [the prescribed sum], or to both such imprisonment and fine.

(6) Without prejudice to subsection (5) above, no officer, clerk or person employed in the registry shall, in the absence of fraud on his part, be liable for any loss which may be suffered—

(a) by reason of any discrepancy between—

(i) the particulars which are shown in a certificate under this section as being the particulars in respect of which the search for entries was made, and

(ii) the particulars in respect of which a search for entries was required by the person who made the requisition; or

(b) by reason of any communication of the result of a search under this section made otherwise than by issuing a certificate under this section.

[458]

NOTES

Sub-s (5): words in square brackets substituted by virtue of the Magistrates' Courts Act 1980, s 32(2).

Miscellaneous and supplementary

11 Date of effective registration and priority notices

(1) Any person intending to make an application for the registration of any contemplated charge, instrument or other matter in pursuance of this Act or any rule made under this Act may give a priority notice in the prescribed form at least the relevant number of days before the registration is to take effect.

(2) Where a notice is given under subsection (1) above, it shall be entered in the register to which the intended application when made will relate.

(3) If the application is presented within the relevant number of days thereafter and refers in the prescribed manner to the notice, the registration shall take effect as if the registration had been made at the time when the charge, instrument or matter was created, entered into, made or arose, and the date at which the registration so takes effect shall be deemed to be the date of registration.

(4) Where—

(a) any two charges, instruments or matters are contemporaneous; and

(b)   one of them (whether or not protected by a priority notice) is subject to or dependent on the other; and

(c)   the latter is protected by a priority notice,

the subsequent or dependent charge, instrument or matter shall be deemed to have been created, entered into or made, or to have arisen, after the registration of the other.

(5)   Where a purchaser has obtained a certificate under section 10 above, any entry which is made in the register after the date of the certificate and before the completion of the purchase, and is not made pursuant to a priority notice entered on the register on or before the date of the certificate, shall not affect the purchaser if the purchase is completed before the expiration of the relevant number of days after the date of the certificate.

(6)   The relevant number of days is—
(a)   for the purposes of subsections (1) and (5) above, fifteen;
(b)   for the purposes of subsection (3) above, thirty;

or such other number as may be prescribed; but in reckoning the relevant number of days for any of the purposes of this section any days when the registry is not open to the public shall be excluded.

[459]

12   Protection of solicitors, trustees, etc

A solicitor, or a trustee, personal representative, agent or other person in a fiduciary position, shall not be answerable—
(a)   in respect of any loss occasioned by reliance on an office copy of an entry in any register kept under this Act;
(b)   for any loss that may arise from error in a certificate under section 10 above obtained by him.

[460]

13   Saving for overreaching powers

(1)   The registration of any charge, annuity or other interest under this Act shall not prevent the charge, annuity or interest being overreached under any other Act, except where otherwise provided by that other Act.

(2)   The registration as a land charge of a puisne mortgage or charge shall not operate to prevent that mortgage or charge being overreached in favour of a prior mortgagee or a person deriving title under him where, by reason of a sale or foreclosure, or otherwise, the right of the puisne mortgagee or subsequent chargee to redeem is barred.

[461]

17   Interpretation

(1)   In this Act, unless the context otherwise requires,—

"annuity" means a rentcharge or an annuity for a life or lives or for any term of years or greater estate determinable on a life or on lives and created after 25th April 1855 and before 1st January 1926, but does not include an annuity created by a marriage settlement or will;

"the Board" means the Commissioners of Inland Revenue;

"conveyance" includes a mortgage, charge, lease, assent, vesting declaration, vesting instrument, release and every other assurance of property, or of an interest in property, by any instrument except a will, and "convey" has a corresponding meaning;

"court" means the High Court, or the county court in a case where that court has jurisdiction;

"deed of arrangement" has the same meaning as in the Deeds of Arrangement Act 1914;

"estate owner", "legal estate", "equitable interest", "trust for sale", "charge by way of legal mortgage", [and "will"] have the same meanings as in the Law of Property Act 1925;

"judgment" includes any order or decree having the effect of a judgment;

"land" includes land of any tenure and mines and minerals, whether or not severed from the surface, buildings or parts of buildings (whether the division is horizontal, vertical or made in any other way) and other corporeal hereditaments, also a manor, an advowson and a rent and other incorporeal hereditaments, and an easement, right, privilege or benefit in, over or derived from land, but not an undivided share in land, and "hereditament" means real property which, on an intestacy occurring before 1st January 1926, might have devolved on an heir;

"land improvement charge" means any charge under the Improvement of Land Act 1864 or under any special improvement Act within the meaning of the Improvement of Land Act 1899;

"pending land action" means any action or proceeding pending in court relating to land or any interest in or charge on land;

"prescribed" means prescribed by rules made pursuant to this Act;

"purchaser" means any person (including a mortgagee or lessee) who, for valuable consideration, takes any interest in land or in a charge on land, and "purchase" has a corresponding meaning;

"registrar" means the Chief Land Registrar, "registry" means Her Majesty's Land Registry, and "registered land" has the same meaning as in the Land Registration Act 1925;

"tenant for life", "statutory owner", "vesting instrument" and "settlement" have the same meanings as in the Settled Land Act 1925.

(2)   For the purposes of any provision in this Act requiring or authorising anything to be done at or delivered or sent to the registry, any reference to the registry shall, if the registrar so directs, be read as a reference to such office of the registry (whether in London or elsewhere) as may be specified in the direction.

(3)   Any reference in this Act to any enactment is a reference to it as amended by or under any other enactment, including this Act.

[462]

NOTES

Sub-s (1): words in square brackets substituted by the Finance Act 1975, s 52(1), Sch 12, paras 2, 18(1), (6).

---

19   Short title, commencement and extent

(1)   This Act may be cited as the Land Charges Act 1972.

(2)   This Act shall come into force on such day as the Lord Chancellor may by order made by statutory instrument appoint; and different days may be so appointed for different purposes.

(3)   This Act extends to England and Wales only.

[463]

SCHEDULE 1
ANNUITIES

Section 1

1.   No further entries shall be made in the register of annuities.

2.   An entry of an annuity made in the register of annuities before 1st January 1926 may be vacated in the prescribed manner on the prescribed evidence as to satisfaction, cesser or discharge being furnished.

3.   The register shall be closed when all the entries in it have been vacated or the prescribed evidence of the satisfaction, cesser or discharge of all the annuities has been furnished.

4.   An annuity which before 1st January 1926 was capable of being registered in the register of annuities shall be void as against a creditor or a purchaser of any interest in the land charged with the annuity unless the annuity is for the time being registered in the register of annuities or in the register of land charges.

[464]

ADMINISTRATION OF JUSTICE ACT 1973

(C 15)

An Act to amend the law relating to justices of the peace and to make further provision with respect to the administration of justice and matters connected therewith

[18 April 1973]

PART II
MISCELLANEOUS

8   Extension of powers of court in action by mortgagee of dwelling-house

(1)   Where by a mortgage of land which consists of or includes a dwelling-house, or by any agreement between the mortgagee under such a mortgage and the mortgagor, the mortgagor is entitled or is to be permitted to pay the principal sum secured by instalments or otherwise to defer payment of it in whole or in part, but provision is also made for earlier payment in the event of any default by the mortgagor or of a demand by the mortgagee or otherwise, then for purposes of section 36 of the Administration of Justice Act 1970 (under which a court has power to delay giving a mortgagee possession of the mortgaged property so as to allow the mortgagor a reasonable time to pay any sums due under the mortgage) a court may treat as due under the mortgage on account of the principal sum secured and of interest on it only such amounts as the mortgagor would have expected to be required to pay if there had been no such provision for earlier payment.

(2)   A court shall not exercise by virtue of subsection (1) above the powers conferred by section 36 of the Administration of Justice Act 1970 unless it appears to the court not only that the mortgagor is likely to be able within a reasonable period to pay any amounts regarded (in accordance with subsection (1) above) as due on account of the principal sum secured, together with the interest on those amounts, but also that he is likely to be able by the end of that period to pay any further amounts that he would have expected to be required to pay by then on account of that sum and of interest on it if there had been no such provision as is referred to in subsection (1) above for earlier payment.

(3)   Where subsection (1) above would apply to an action in which a mortgagee only claimed possession of the mortgaged property, and the mortgagee brings an action for foreclosure (with or without also claiming possession of the property), then section 36 of the Administration of Justice Act 1970 together with subsections (1) and (2) above shall apply as they would apply if it were an action in which the mortgagee only claimed possession of the mortgaged property, except that—

    (a)   section 36(2)(b) shall apply only in relation to any claim for possession; and

    (b)   section 36(5) shall not apply.

(4)   For purposes of this section the expressions "dwelling-house", "mortgage", "mortgagee" and "mortgagor" shall be construed in the same way as for the purposes of Part IV of the Administration of Justice Act 1970.

(5)   This section shall have effect in relation to an action begun before the date on which this section comes into force if before that date judgment has not been given, nor an order made, in that action for delivery of possession of the mortgaged property and, where it is a question of subsection (3) above, an order *nisi* for foreclosure has not been made in that action.

(6)   In the application of this section to Northern Ireland, subsection (3) shall be omitted.

[465]

PART III
SUPPLEMENTARY

21 Short title and extent

(1)   This Act may be cited as the Administration of Justice Act 1973.

(2)   The foregoing sections of this Act shall not extend to Scotland or to Northern Ireland except to the following extent, that is to say—

    (a)   sections 9 to 12 of this Act, and the repeals made by Parts IV and V of Schedule 5, shall extend to Scotland or to Northern Ireland in so far as they affect the law of Scotland or of Northern Ireland; and

    (b)   sections 8, 14 and 18 of this Act (together with so much of section 20(1) as relates to those sections) shall extend to Northern Ireland.

[466]

CONSUMER CREDIT ACT 1974

(C 39)

An Act to establish for the protection of consumers a new system, administered by the Director General of Fair Trading, of licensing and other control of traders concerned with the provision of credit, or the supply of goods on hire or hire-purchase, and their transactions, in place of the present enactments regulating moneylenders, pawnbrokers and hire-purchase traders and their transactions, and for related matters

[31 July 1974]

PART II
CREDIT AGREEMENTS, HIRE AGREEMENTS AND LINKED TRANSACTIONS

8 Consumer credit agreements

(1)   A personal credit agreement is an agreement between an individual ("the

debtor") and any other person ("the creditor") by which the creditor provides the debtor with credit of any amount.

(2) A consumer credit agreement is a personal credit agreement by which the creditor provides the debtor with credit not exceeding [£15,000].

(3) A consumer credit agreement is a regulated agreement within the meaning of this Act if it is not an agreement (an "exempt agreement") specified in or under section 16.

[467]

NOTES

    Sub-s (2): sum in square brackets substituted by the Consumer Credit (Increase of Monetary Limits) Order 1983, SI 1983/1878, art 4, Schedule, Pt II.

15   Consumer hire agreements

(1) A consumer hire agreement is an agreement made by a person with an individual (the "hirer") for the bailment or (in Scotland) the hiring of goods to the hirer, being an agreement which—

    (a)   is not a hire-purchase agreement, and
    (b)   is capable of subsisting for more than three months, and
    (c)   does not require the hirer to make payments exceeding [£15,000].

(2) A consumer hire agreement is a regulated agreement if it is not an exempt agreement.

[468]

NOTES

    Sub-s (1): sum in square brackets in para (c) substituted by the Consumer Credit (Increase of Monetary Limits) Order 1983, SI 1983/1878, art 4, Schedule, Pt II.

16   Exempt agreements

(1) This Act does not regulate a consumer credit agreement where the creditor is a local authority . . . , or a body specified, or of a description specified, in an order made by the Secretary of State, being—

    (a)   an insurance company,
    (b)   a friendly society,
    (c)   an organisation of employers or organisation of workers,
    (d)   a charity,
    (e)   a land improvement company, . . .
    (f)   a body corporate named or specifically referred to in any public general Act
    [(ff)   a body corporate named or specifically referred to in an order made under—
        section 156(4), 444(1) or 447(2)(a) of the Housing Act 1985,
        section 2 of the Home Purchase Assistance and Housing Corporation Guarantee Act 1978 or section 31 of the Tenants' Rights, &c. (Scotland) Act 1980, or
        Article 154(1)(a) or 156AA of the Housing (Northern Ireland) Order 1981 or Article 10(6A) of the Housing (Northern Ireland) Order 1983; or]
    [(g)   a building society][, or
    (h)   an authorised institution or wholly-owned subsidiary (within the meaning of the Companies Act 1985) of such an institution].

(2)   Subsection (1) applies only where the agreement is—
    (a)   a debtor-creditor-supplier agreement financing—
        (i)   the purchase of land, or
        (ii)   the provision of dwellings on any land,
        and secured by a land mortgage on that land; or
    (b)   a debtor-creditor agreement secured by any land mortgage; or
    (c)   a debtor-creditor-supplier agreement financing a transaction which is a linked transaction in relation to—
        (i)   an agreement falling within paragraph (a), or
        (ii)   an agreement falling within paragraph (b) financing—
            (aa)   the purchase of any land, or
            (bb)   the provision of dwellings on any land,
        and secured by a land mortgage on the land referred to in paragraph (a) or, as the case may be, the land referred to in sub-paragraph (ii).

(3)   The Secretary of State shall not make, vary or revoke an order—
    (a)   under subsection (1)(a) without consulting the Minister of the Crown responsible for insurance companies,
    (b)   under subsection (1)(b) . . . without consulting the Chief Registrar of Friendly Societies,
    (c)   under subsection (1)(d) without consulting the Charity Commissioners, . . .
    (d)   under subsection (1)(e)[, (f) or (ff)] without consulting any Minister of the Crown with responsibilities concerning the body in question [or
    (e)   under subsection (1)(g) without consulting the Building Societies Commission and the Treasury] [or
    (f)   under subsection (1)(h) without consulting the Treasury and the Bank of England].

(4)   An order under subsection (1) relating to a body may be limited so as to apply only to agreements by that body of a description specified in the order.

(5)   The Secretary of State may by order provide that this Act shall not regulate other consumer credit agreements where—
    (a)   the number of payments to be made by the debtor does not exceed the number specified for that purpose in the order, or
    (b)   the rate of the total charge for credit does not exceed the rate so specified, or
    (c)   an agreement has a connection with a country outside the United Kingdom.

(6)   The Secretary of State may by order provide that this Act shall not regulate consumer hire agreements of a description specified in the order where—
    (a)   the owner is a body corporate authorised by or under any enactment to supply electricity, gas or water, and
    (b)   the subject of the agreement is a meter or metering equipment,

[or where the owner is a public telecommunications operator specified in the order].

[(6A)   This Act does not regulate a consumer credit agreement where the creditor is a housing authority and the agreement is secured by a land mortgage of a dwelling.

(6B)   In subsection (6A) "housing authority" means—
    (a)   as regards England and Wales, [the Housing Corporation, Housing for Wales and] an authority or body within section 80(1) of the Housing Act 1985 (the landlord condition for secure tenancies), other than a housing association or a housing trust which is a charity;

(b) as regards Scotland, a development corporation established under an order made, or having effect as if made under the New Towns (Scotland) Act 1968, the Scottish Special Housing Association or the Housing Corporation;

(c) as regards Northern Ireland, the Northern Ireland Housing Executive.]

(7) Nothing in this section affects the application of sections 137 to 140 (extortionate credit bargains).

(8) . . .

(9) In the application of this section to Northern Ireland subsection (3) shall have effect as if any reference to a Minister of the Crown were a reference to a Northern Ireland department, any reference to the Chief Registrar of Friendly Societies were a reference to the Registrar of Friendly Societies for Northern Ireland, and any reference to the Charity Commissioners were a reference to the Department of Finance for Northern Ireland.

[469]

NOTES

Sub-s (1): words omitted from para (b) repealed and para (g) inserted by the Building Societies Act 1986, s 120, Sch 18, Pt I, para 10(2), Sch 19, Pt I; para (ff) inserted by the Housing and Planning Act 1986, s 22(2), (4), in relation to agreements made after 7 January 1987; para (h) added by the Banking Act 1987, s 88(2).

Sub-s (3): words omitted from para (b) repealed by the Employment Protection Act 1975, s 125(3), Sch 18, in relation to England and Wales; word omitted from para (c) repealed and para (e) inserted by the Building Societies Act 1986, s 120, Sch 18, Pt I, para 10(3), Sch 19, Pt I; words in square brackets in para (d) substituted by the Housing and Planning Act 1986, s 22(2), (4), in relation to agreements made after 7 January 1987; para (f) added by the Banking Act 1987, s 88.

Sub-s (6): words in square brackets substituted by the Telecommunications Act 1984, s 109, Sch 4, para 60(1).

Sub-s (6A): inserted, together with sub-s (6B) by the Housing and Planning Act 1986, s 22(3), (4), in relation to agreements made after 7 January 1987.

Sub-s (6B): inserted, together with sub-s (6A) by the Housing and Planning Act 1986, s 22(3), (4), in relation to agreements made after 7 January 1987; words in square brackets inserted by the Housing Act 1988, s 140, Sch 17, Pt I, para 20.

Sub-s (8): not relevant to this work.

PART V
ENTRY INTO CREDIT OR HIRE AGREEMENTS

Preliminary matters

58 Opportunity for withdrawal from prospective land mortgage

(1) Before sending to the debtor or hirer, for his signature, an unexecuted agreement in a case where the prospective regulated agreement is to be secured on land (the "mortgaged land"), the creditor or owner shall give the debtor or hirer a copy of the unexecuted agreement which contains a notice in the prescribed form indicating the right of the debtor or hirer to withdraw from the prospective agreement, and how and when the right is exercisable, together with a copy of any other document referred to in the unexecuted agreement.

(2) Subsection (1) does not apply to—

(a) a restricted-use credit agreement to finance the purchase of the mortgaged land, or

(b) an agreement for a bridging loan in connection with the purchase of the mortgaged land or other land.

[470]

Part VII
Default and Termination

Further restriction of remedies for default

92   Recovery of possession of goods or land

(1)   Except under an order of the court, the creditor or owner shall not be entitled to enter any premises to take possession of goods subject to a regulated hire-purchase agreement, regulated conditional sale agreement or regulated consumer hire agreement.

(2)   At any time when the debtor is in breach of a regulated conditional sale agreement relating to land, the creditor is entitled to recover possession of the land from the debtor, or any person claiming under him, on an order of the court only.

(3)   An entry in contravention of subsection (1) or (2) is actionable as a breach of statutory duty.

[471]

Part VIII
Security

Land mortgages

126   Enforcement of land mortgages

A land mortgage securing a regulated agreement is enforceable (so far as provided in relation to the agreement) on an order of the court only.

[472]

Part IX
Judicial Control

Extortionate credit bargains

137   Extortionate credit bargains

(1)   If the court finds a credit bargain extortionate it may reopen the credit agreement so as to do justice between the parties.

(2)   In this section and sections 138 to 140—

    (a)   "credit agreement" means any agreement between an individual (the "debtor") and any other person (the "creditor") by which the creditor provides the debtor with credit of any amount, and

    (b)   "credit bargain"—

        (i)   where no transaction other than the credit agreement is to be taken into account in computing the total charge for credit, means the credit agreement, or

        (ii)   where one or more other transactions are to be so taken into account, means the credit agreement and those other transactions, taken together.

[473]

140   Interpretation of sections 137 to 139

Where the credit agreement is not a regulated agreement, expressions used in sections 137 to 139 which, apart from this section, apply only to regulated agreements, shall be construed as nearly as may be as if the credit agreement were a regulated agreement.

[474]

PART XII
SUPPLEMENTAL

Miscellaneous

192   Transitional and commencement provisions, amendments and repeals

(1)   The provisions of Schedule 3 shall have effect for the purposes of this Act.

(2)   The appointment of a day for the purposes of any provision of Schedule 3 shall be effected by an order of the Secretary of State made by statutory instrument; and any such order shall include a provision amending Schedule 3 so as to insert an express reference to the day appointed.

(3)   Subject to subsection (4)—
   (a)   the enactments specified in Schedule 4 shall have effect subject to the amendments specified in that Schedule (being minor amendments or amendments consequential on the preceding provisions of this Act), and
   (b)   the enactments specified in Schedule 5 are hereby repealed to the extent shown in column 3 of that Schedule.

(4)   The Secretary of State shall by order made by statutory instrument provide for the coming into operation of the amendments contained in Schedule 4 and the repeals contained in Schedule 5, and those amendments and repeals shall have effect only as provided by an order so made.

[475]

193   Short title and extent

(1)   This Act may be cited as the Consumer Credit Act 1974.

(2)   This Act extends to Northern Ireland.

[476]

INHERITANCE (PROVISION FOR FAMILY AND DEPENDANTS) ACT 1975

(C 63)

An Act to make fresh provisions for empowering the court to make orders for the making out of the estate of a deceased person of provision for the spouse, former spouse, child, child of the family or dependant of that person; and for matters connected therewith

[12 November 1975]

1   Application for financial provision from deceased's estate

(1)   Where after the commencement of this Act a person dies domiciled in England and Wales and is survived by any of the following persons:—

(a)   the wife or husband of the deceased;

(b)   a former wife or former husband of the deceased who has not remarried;

(c)   a child of the deceased;

(d)   any person (not being a child of the deceased) who, in the case of any marriage to which the deceased was at any time a party, was treated by the deceased as a child of the family in relation to that marriage;

(e)   any person (not being a person included in the foregoing paragraphs of this subsection) who immediately before the death of the deceased was being maintained, either wholly or partly, by the deceased;

that person may apply to the court for an order under section 2 of this Act on the ground that the disposition of the deceased's estate effected by his will or the law relating to intestacy, or the combination of his will and that law, is not such as to make reasonable financial provision for the applicant.

(2)   In this Act "reasonable financial provision"—

(a)   in the case of an application made by virtue of subsection (1)(a) above by the husband or wife of the deceased (except where the marriage with the deceased was the subject of a decree of judicial separation and at the date of death the decree was in force and the separation was continuing), means such financial provision as it would be reasonable in all the circumstances of the case for a husband or wife to receive, whether or not that provision is required for his or her maintenance;

(b)   in the case of any other application made by virtue of subsection (1) above, means such financial provision as it would be reasonable in all the circumstances of the case for the applicant to receive for his maintenance.

(3)   For the purposes of subsection (1)(e) above, a person shall be treated as being maintained by the deceased, either wholly or partly, as the case may be, if the deceased, otherwise than for full valuable consideration, was making a substantial contribution in money or money's worth towards the reasonable needs of that person.

[477]

2   Powers of court to make orders

(1)   Subject to the provisions of this Act, where an application is made for an order under this section, the court may, if it is satisfied that the disposition of the deceased's estate effected by his will or the law relating to intestacy, or the combination of his will and that law, is not such as to make reasonable financial provision for the applicant, make any one or more of the following orders—

(a)   an order for the making to the applicant out of the net estate of the deceased of such periodical payments and for such term as may be specified in the order;

(b)   an order for the payment to the applicant out of that estate of a lump sum of such amount as may be so specified;

(c)   an order for the transfer to the applicant of such property comprised in that estate as may be so specified;

(d)   an order for the settlement for the benefit of the applicant of such property comprised in that estate as may be so specified;

(e)   an order for the acquisition out of property comprised in that estate of such property as may be so specified and for the transfer of the property so acquired to the applicant or for the settlement thereof for his benefit;

(f)   an order varying any ante-nuptial or post-nuptial settlement (including such a settlement made by will) made on the parties to a marriage to which the deceased was one of the parties, the variation being for the benefit of the surviving party to that marriage, or any child of that marriage, or any person who was treated by the deceased as a child of the family in relation to that marriage.

(2)   An order under subsection (1)(a) above providing for the making out of the net estate of the deceased of periodical payments may provide for—

(a)   payments of such amount as may be specified in the order,

(b)   payments equal to the whole of the income of the net estate or of such portion thereof as may be so specified,

(c)   payments equal to the whole of the income of such part of the net estate as the court may direct to be set aside or appropriated for the making out of the income thereof of payments under this section,

or may provide for the amount of the payments or any of them to be determined in any other way the court thinks fit.

(3)   Where an order under subsection (1)(a) above provides for the making of payments of an amount specified in the order, the order may direct that such part of the net estate as may be so specified shall be set aside or appropriated for the making out of the income thereof of those payments; but no larger part of the net estate shall be so set aside or appropriated than is sufficient, at the date of the order, to produce by the income thereof the amount required for the making of those payments.

(4)   An order under this section may contain such consequential and supplemental provisions as the court thinks necessary or expedient for the purpose of giving effect to the order or for the purpose of securing that the order operates fairly as between one beneficiary of the estate of the deceased and another and may, in particular, but without prejudice to the generality of this subsection—

(a)   order any person who holds any property which forms part of the net estate of the deceased to make such payment or transfer such property as may be specified in the order;

(b)   varying the disposition of the deceased's estate effected by the will or the law relating to intestacy, or by both the will and the law relating to intestacy, in such manner as the court thinks fair and reasonable having regard to the provisions of the order and all the circumstances of the case;

(c)   confer on the trustees of any property which is the subject of an order under this section such powers as appear to the court to be necessary or expedient.

[478]

3   Matters to which court is to have regard in exercising powers under s 2

(1)   Where an application is made for an order under section 2 of this Act, the court shall, in determining whether the disposition of the deceased's estate effected by his will or the law relating to intestacy, or the combination of his will and that law, is such as to make reasonable financial provision for the applicant and, if the court considers that reasonable financial provision has not been made, in determining whether and in what manner it shall exercise its powers under that section, have regard to the following matters, that is to say—

(a)   the financial resources and financial needs which the applicant has or is likely to have in the foreseeable future;

(b)   the financial resources and financial needs which any other applicant for an order under section 2 of this Act has or is likely to have in the foreseeable future;

(c) the financial resources and financial needs which any beneficiary of the estate of the deceased has or is likely to have in the foreseeable future;

(d) any obligations and responsibilities which the deceased had towards any applicant for an order under the said section 2 or towards any beneficiary of the estate of the deceased;

(e) the size and nature of the net estate of the deceased;

(f) any physical or mental disability of any applicant for an order under the said section 2 or any beneficiary of the estate of the deceased;

(g) any other matter, including the conduct of the applicant or any other person, which in the circumstances of the case the court may consider relevant.

(2) Without prejudice to the generality of paragraph (g) of subsection (1) above, where an application for an order under section 2 of this Act is made by virtue of section 1(1)(a) or 1(1)(b) of this Act, the court shall, in addition to the matters specifically mentioned in paragraphs (a) to (f) of that subsection, have regard to—

(a) the age of the applicant and the duration of the marriage;

(b) the contribution made by the applicant to the welfare of the family of the deceased, including any contribution made by looking after the home or caring for the family;

and, in the case of an application by the wife or husband of the deceased, the court shall also, unless at the date of death a decree of judicial separation was in force and the separation was continuing, have regard to the provision which the applicant might reasonably have expected to receive if on the day on which the deceased died the marriage, instead of being terminated by death, had been terminated by a decree of divorce.

(3) Without prejudice to the generality of paragraph (g) of subsection (1) above, where an application for an order under section 2 of this Act is made by virtue of section 1(1)(c) or 1(1)(d) of this Act, the court shall, in addition to the matters specifically mentioned in paragraphs (a) to (f) of that subsection, have regard to the manner in which the applicant was being or in which he might expect to be educated or trained, and where the application is made by virtue of section 1(1)(d) the court shall also have regard—

(a) to whether the deceased had assumed any responsibility for the applicant's maintenance and, if so, to the extent to which and the basis upon which the deceased assumed that responsibility and to the length of time for which the deceased discharged that responsibility;

(b) to whether in assuming and discharging that responsibility the deceased did so knowing that the applicant was not his own child;

(c) to the liability of any other person to maintain the applicant.

(4) Without prejudice to the generality of paragraph (g) of subsection (1) above, where an application for an order under section 2 of this Act is made by virtue of section 1(1)(e) of this Act, the court shall, in addition to the matters specifically mentioned in paragraphs (a) to (f) of that subsection, have regard to the extent to which and the basis upon which the deceased assumed responsibility for the maintenance of the applicant, and to the length of time for which the deceased discharged that responsibility.

(5) In considering the matters to which the court is required to have regard under this section, the court shall take into account the facts as known to the court at the date of the hearing.

(6)   In considering the financial resources of any person for the purposes of this section the court shall take into account his earning capacity and in considering the financial needs of any person for the purposes of this section the court shall take into account his financial obligations and responsibilities.

[479]

4   Time-limit for applications

An application for an order under section 2 of this Act shall not, except with the permission of the court, be made after the end of the period of six months from the date on which representation with respect to the estate of the deceased is first taken out.

[480]

5   Interim orders

(1)   Where on an application for an order under section 2 of this Act it appears to the court—
- (a)   that the applicant is in immediate need of financial assistance, but it is not yet possible to determine what order (if any) should be made under that section; and
- (b)   that property forming part of the net estate of the deceased is or can be made available to meet the need of the applicant;

the court may order that, subject to such conditions or restrictions, if any, as the court may impose and to any further order of the court, there shall be paid to the applicant out of the net estate of the deceased such sum or sums and (if more than one) at such intervals as the court thinks reasonable; and the court may order that, subject to the provisions of this Act, such payments are to be made until such date as the court may specify, not being later than the date on which the court either makes an order under the said section 2 or decides not to exercise its powers under that section.

(2)   Subsections (2), (3) and (4) of section 2 of this Act shall apply in relation to an order under this section as they apply in relation to an order under that section.

(3)   In determining what order, if any, should be made under this section the court shall, so far as the urgency of the case admits, have regard to the same matters as those to which the court is required to have regard under section 3 of this Act.

(4)   An order made under section 2 of this Act may provide that any sum paid to the applicant by virtue of this section shall be treated to such an extent and in such manner as may be provided by that order as having been paid on account of any payment provided for by that order.

[481]

6   Variation, discharge, etc of orders for periodical payments

(1)   Subject to the provisions of this Act, where the court has made an order under section 2(1)(a) of this Act (in this section referred to as "the original order") for the making of periodical payments to any person (in this section referred to as "the original recipient"), the court, on an application under this section, shall have power by order to vary or discharge the original order or to suspend any provision of it temporarily and to revive the operation of any provision so suspended.

(2)   Without prejudice to the generality of subsection (1) above, an order made on an application for the variation of the original order may—

    (a) provide for the making out of any relevant property of such periodical payments and for such term as may be specified in the order to any person who has applied, or would but for section 4 of this Act be entitled to apply, for an order under section 2 of this Act (whether or not, in the case of any application, an order was made in favour of the applicant);

    (b) provide for the payment out of any relevant property of a lump sum of such amount as may be so specified to the original recipient or to any such person as is mentioned in paragraph (a) above;

    (c) provide for the transfer of the relevant property, or such part thereof as may be so specified, to the original recipient or to any such person as is so mentioned.

(3)   Where the original order provides that any periodical payments payable thereunder to the original recipient are to cease on the occurrence of an event specified in the order (other than the remarriage of a former wife or former husband) or on the expiration of a period so specified, then, if, before the end of the period of six months from the date of the occurrence of that event or of the expiration of that period, an application is made for an order under this section, the court shall have power to make any order which it would have had power to make if the application had been made before the date (whether in favour of the original recipient or any such person as is mentioned in subsection (2)(a) above and whether having effect from that date or from such later date as the court may specify).

(4)   Any reference in this section to the original order shall include a reference to an order made under this section and any reference in this section to the original recipient shall include a reference to any person to whom periodical payments are required to be made by virtue of an order under this section.

(5)   An application under this section may be made by any of the following persons, that is to say—

    (a) any person who by virtue of section 1(1) of this Act has applied, or would but for section 4 of this Act be entitled to apply, for an order under section 2 of this Act,

    (b) the personal representatives of the deceased,

    (c) the trustees of any relevant property, and

    (d) any beneficiary of the estate of the deceased.

(6)   An order under this section may only affect—

    (a) property the income of which is at the date of the order applicable wholly or in part for the making of periodical payments to any person who has applied for an order under this Act, or

    (b) in the case of an application under subsection (3) above in respect of payments which have ceased to be payable on the occurrence of an event or the expiration of a period, property the income of which was so applicable immediately before the occurrence of that event or the expiration of that period, as the case may be,

and any such property as is mentioned in paragraph (a) or (b) above is in subsections (2) and (5) above referred to as "relevant property".

(7)   In exercising the powers conferred by this section the court shall have regard to all the circumstances of the case, including any change in any of the matters to which the court was required to have regard when making the order to which the application relates.

(8)   Where the court makes an order under this section, it may give such consequential directions as it thinks necessary or expedient having regard to the provisions of the order.

(9)   No such order as is mentioned in sections 2(1)(d), (e) or (f), 9, 10 or 11 of this Act shall be made on an application under this section.

(10) For the avoidance of doubt it is hereby declared that, in relation to an order which provides for the making of periodical payments which are to cease on the occurrence of an event specified in the order (other than the remarriage of a former wife or former husband) or on the expiration of a period so specified, the power to vary an order includes power to provide for the making of periodical payments after the expiration of that period or the occurrence of that event.

[482]

7   Payment of lump sums by instalments

(1)   An order under section 2(1)(b) or 6(2)(b) of this Act for the payment of a lump sum may provide for the payment of that sum by instalments of such amount as may be specified in the order.

(2)   Where an order is made by virtue of subsection (1) above, the court shall have power, on an application made by the person to whom the lump sum is payable, by the personal representatives of the deceased or by the trustees of the property out of which the lump sum is payable, to vary that order by varying the number of instalments payable, the amount of any instalment and the date on which any instalment becomes payable.

[483]

Property available for financial provision

8   Property treated as part of "net estate"

(1)   Where a deceased person has in accordance with the provisions of any enactment nominated any person to receive any sum of money or other property on his death and that nomination is in force at the time of his death, that sum of money, after deducting therefrom any inheritance tax payable in respect thereof, or that other property, to the extent of the value thereof at the date of the death of the deceased after deducting therefrom any inheritance tax so payable, shall be treated for the purposes of this Act as part of the net estate of the deceased; but this subsection shall not render any person liable for having paid that sum or transferred that other property to the person named in the nomination in accordance with the directions given in the nomination.

(2)   Where any sum of money or other property is received by any person as a donatio mortis causa made by a deceased person, that sum of money, after deducting therefrom any inheritance tax payable thereon, or that other property, to the extent of the value thereof at the date of the death of the deceased after deducting therefrom any inheritance tax so payable, shall be treated for the purposes of this Act as part of the net estate of the deceased; but this subsection shall not render any person liable for having paid that sum or transferred that other property in order to give effect to that donatio mortis causa.

(3)   The amount of inheritance tax to be deducted for the purposes of this section shall not exceed the amount of that tax which has been borne by the person

nominated by the deceased or, as the case may be, the person who has received a sum of money or other property as a donatio mortis causa.

[484]

NOTES

Capital transfer tax: except in relation to a liability to tax arising before 25 July 1986 capital transfer tax shall be known as inheritance tax and the Capital Transfer Tax Act 1984 may be cited as the Inheritance Tax Act 1984, by virtue of the Finance Act 1986, s 100.

9 Property held on a joint tenancy

(1)   Where a deceased person was immediately before his death beneficially entitled to a joint tenancy of any property, then, if, before the end of the period of six months from the date on which representation with respect to the estate of the deceased was first taken out, an application is made for an order under section 2 of this Act, the court for the purpose of facilitating the making of financial provision for the applicant under this Act may order that the deceased's severable share of that property, at the value thereof immediately before his death, shall, to such extent as appears to the court to be just in all the circumstances of the case, be treated for the purposes of this Act as part of the net estate of the deceased.

(2)   In determining the extent to which any severable share is to be treated as part of the net estate of the deceased by virtue of an order under subsection (1) above, the court shall have regard to any inheritance tax payable in respect of that severable share.

(3)   Where an order is made under subsection (1) above, the provisions of this section shall not render any person liable for anything done by him before the order was made.

(4)   For the avoidance of doubt it is hereby declared that for the purposes of this section there may be a joint tenancy of a chose in action.

[485]

NOTES

Capital transfer tax: except in relation to a liability to tax arising before 25 July 1986 capital transfer tax shall be known as inheritance tax and the Capital Transfer Tax Act 1984 may be cited as the Inheritance Tax Act 1984, by virtue of the Finance Act 1986, s 100.

Powers of court in relation to transactions intended to defeat applications for financial provision

10 Dispositions intended to defeat applications for financial provision

(1)   Where an application is made to the court for an order under section 2 of this Act, the applicant may, in the proceedings on that application, apply to the court for an order under subsection (2) below.

(2)   Where on an application under subsection (1) above the court is satisfied—

    (a)   that, less than six years before the date of the death of the deceased, the deceased with the intention of defeating an application for financial provision under this Act made a disposition, and

    (b)   that full valuable consideration for that disposition was not given by the person to whom or for the benefit of whom the disposition was made (in this section referred to as "the donee") or by any other person, and

    (c)   that the exercise of the powers conferred by this section would facilitate the making of financial provision for the applicant under this Act, then, subject to the provisions of this section and of sections 12 and 13 of this Act, the court may order the donee (whether or not at the date of the order he holds any interest in the property disposed of to him or for his benefit by the deceased) to provide, for the purpose of the making of that financial provision, such sum of money or other property as may be specified in the order.

(3)   Where an order is made under subsection (2) above as respects any disposition made by the deceased which consisted of the payment of money to or for the benefit of the donee, the amount of any sum of money or the value of any property ordered to be provided under that subsection shall not exceed the amount of the payment made by the deceased after deducting therefrom any inheritance tax borne by the donee in respect of that payment.

(4)   Where an order is made under subsection (2) above as respects any disposition made by the deceased which consisted of the transfer of property (other than a sum of money) to or for the benefit of the donee, the amount of any sum of money or the value of any property ordered to be provided under that subsection shall not exceed the value at the date of the death of the deceased of the property disposed of by him to or for the benefit of the donee (or if that property has been disposed of by the person to whom it was transferred by the deceased, the value at the date of that disposal thereof) after deducting therefrom any inheritance tax borne by the donee in respect of the transfer of that property by the deceased.

(5)   Where an application (in this subsection referred to as "the original application") is made for an order under subsection (2) above in relation to any disposition, then, if on an application under this subsection by the donee or by any applicant for an order under section 2 of this Act the court is satisfied—

(a)   that, less than six years before the date of the death of the deceased, the deceased with the intention of defeating an application for financial provision under this Act made a disposition other than the disposition which is the subject of the original application, and

(b)   that full valuable consideration for that other disposition was not given by the person to whom or for the benefit of whom that other disposition was made or by any other person,

the court may exercise in relation to the person to whom or for the benefit of whom that other disposition was made the powers which the court would have had under subsection (2) above if the original application had been made in respect of that other disposition and the court had been satisfied as to the matters set out in paragraphs (a), (b) and (c) of that subsection; and where any application is made under this subsection, any reference in this section (except in subsection (2)(b)) to the donee shall include a reference to the person to whom or for the benefit of whom that other disposition was made.

(6)   In determining whether and in what manner to exercise its powers under this section, the court shall have regard to the circumstances in which any disposition was made and any valuable consideration which was given therefor, the relationship, if any, of the donee to the deceased, the conduct and financial resources of the donee and all the other circumstances of the case.

(7)   In this section "disposition" does not include—

(a)   any provision in a will, any such nomination as is mentioned in section 8(1) of this Act or any donatio mortis causa, or

(b)   any appointment of property made, otherwise than by will, in the exercise of a special power of appointment, but, subject to these exceptions, includes any payment of money (including the payment of a premium under a policy of assurance) and any conveyance, assurance, appointment or gift of property of any description, whether made by an instrument or otherwise.

(8) The provisions of this section do not apply to any disposition made before the commencement of this Act.

NOTES

Capital transfer tax: except in relation to a liability to tax arising before 25 July 1986 capital transfer tax shall be known as inheritance tax and the Capital Transfer Tax Act 1984 may be cited as the Inheritance Tax Act 1984, by virtue of the Finance Act 1986, s 100.

11 Contracts to leave property by will

(1) Where an application is made to a court for an order under section 2 of this Act, the applicant may, in the proceedings on that application, apply to the court for an order under this section.

(2) Where on an application under subsection (1) above the court is satisfied—

    (a) that the deceased made a contract by which he agreed to leave by his will a sum of money or other property to any person or by which he agreed that a sum of money or other property would be paid or transferred to any person out of his estate, and

    (b) that the deceased made that contract with the intention of defeating an application for financial provision under this Act, and

    (c) that when the contract was made full valuable consideration for that contract was not given or promised by the person with whom or for the benefit of whom the contract was made (in this section referred to as "the donee") or by any other person, and

    (d) that the exercise of the powers conferred by this section would facilitate the making of financial provision for the applicant under this Act,

then, subject to the provisions of this section and of sections 12 and 13 of this Act, the court may make any one or more of the following orders, that is to say—

    (i) if any money has been paid or any other property has been transferred to or for the benefit of the donee in accordance with the contract, an order directing the donee to provide, for the purpose of the making of that financial provision, such sum of money or other property as may be specified in the order;

    (ii) if the money or all the money has not been paid or the property or all the property has not been transferred in accordance with the contract, an order directing the personal representatives not to make any payment or transfer any property, or not to make any further payment or transfer any further property, as the case may be, in accordance therewith or directing the personal representatives only to make such payment or transfer such property as may be specified in the order.

(3) Notwithstanding anything in subsection (2) above, the court may exercise its powers thereunder in relation to any contract made by the deceased only to the extent that the court considers that the amount of any sum of money paid or to be paid or the value of any property transferred or to be transferred in accordance with the contract exceeds the value of any valuable consideration given or to be given for that contract, and for this purpose the court shall have regard to the value of property at the date of the hearing.

(4)   In determining whether and in what manner to exercise its powers under this section, the court shall have regard to the circumstances in which the contract was made, the relationship, if any, of the donee to the deceased, the conduct and financial resources of the donee and all the other circumstances of the case.

(5)   Where an order has been made under subsection (2) above in relation to any contract, the rights of any person to enforce that contract or to recover damages or to obtain other relief for the breach thereof shall be subject to any adjustment made by the court under section 12(3) of this Act and shall survive to such extent only as is consistent with giving effect to the terms of that order.

(6)   The provisions of this section do not apply to a contract made before the commencement of this Act.

[487]

12   Provisions supplementary to ss 10 and 11

(1)   Where the exercise of any of the powers conferred by section 10 or 11 of this Act is conditional on the court being satisfied that a disposition or contract was made by a deceased person with the intention of defeating an application for financial provision under this Act, that condition shall be fulfilled if the court is of the opinion that, on a balance of probabilities, the intention of the deceased (though not necessarily his sole intention) in making the disposition or contract was to prevent an order for financial provision being made under this Act or to reduce the amount of the provision which might otherwise be granted by an order thereunder.

(2)   Where an application is made under section 11 of this Act with respect to any contract made by the deceased and no valuable consideration was given or promised by any person for that contract then, notwithstanding anything in subsection (1) above, it shall be presumed, unless the contrary is shown, that the deceased made that contract with the intention of defeating an application for financial provision under this Act.

(3)   Where the court makes an order under section 10 or 11 of this Act it may give such consequential directions as it thinks fit (including directions requiring the making of any payment or the transfer of any property) for giving effect to the order or for securing a fair adjustment of the rights of the persons affected thereby.

(4)   Any power conferred on the court by the said section 10 or 11 to order the donee, in relation to any disposition or contract, to provide any sum of money or other property shall be exercisable in like manner in relation to the personal representative of the donee, and—

(a)   any reference in section 10(4) to the disposal of property by the donee shall include a reference to disposal by the personal representative of the donee, and

(b)   any reference in section 10(5) to an application by the donee under that subsection shall include a reference to an application by the personal representative of the donee;

but the court shall not have power under the said section 10 or 11 to make an order in respect of any property forming part of the estate of the donee which has been distributed by the personal representative; and the personal representative shall not be liable for having distributed any such property before he has notice of the making of an application under the said section 10 or 11 on the ground that he ought to have taken into account the possibility that such an application would be made.

[488]

13   Provisions as to trustees in relation to ss 10 and 11

(1)   Where an application is made for—
- (a) an order under section 10 of this Act in respect of a disposition made by the deceased to any person as a trustee, or
- (b) an order under section 11 of this Act in respect of any payment made or property transferred, in accordance with a contract made by the deceased, to any person as a trustee,

the powers of the court under the said section 10 or 11 to order that trustee to provide a sum of money or other property shall be subject to the following limitation (in addition, in a case of an application under section 10, to any provision regarding the deduction of inheritance tax) namely, that the amount of any sum of money or the value of any property ordered to be provided—
- (i) in the case of an application in respect of a disposition which consisted of the payment of money or an application in respect of the payment of money in accordance with a contract, shall not exceed the aggregate of so much of that money as is at the date of the order in the hands of the trustee and the value at that date of any property which represents that money or is derived therefrom and is at that date in the hands of the trustee;
- (ii) in the case of an application in respect of a disposition which consisted of the transfer of property (other than a sum of money) or an application in respect of the transfer of property (other than a sum of money) in accordance with a contract, shall not exceed the aggregate of the value at the date of the order of so much of that property as is at that date in the hands of the trustee and the value at that date of any property which represents the first-mentioned property or is derived therefrom and is at that date in the hands of the trustee.

(2)   Where any such application is made in respect of a disposition made to any person as a trustee or in respect of any payment made or property transferred in pursuance of a contract to any person as a trustee, the trustee shall not be liable for having distributed any money or other property on the ground that he ought to have taken into account the possibility that such an application would be made.

(3)   Where any such application is made in respect of a disposition made to any person as a trustee or in respect of any payment made or property transferred in accordance with a contract to any person as a trustee, any reference in the said section 10 or 11 to the donee shall be construed as including a reference to the trustee or trustees for the time being of the trust in question and any reference in subsection (1) or (2) above to a trustee shall be construed in the same way.

[489]

NOTES

Capital transfer tax: except in relation to a liability to tax arising before 25 July 1986 capital transfer tax shall be known as inheritance tax and the Capital Transfer Tax Act 1984 may be cited as the Inheritance Tax Act 1984, by virtue of the Finance Act 1986, s 100.

Special provisions relating to cases of divorce, separation, etc

14   Provision as to cases where no financial relief was granted in divorce proceedings, etc

(1)   Where, within twelve months from the date on which a decree of divorce or nullity of marriage has been made absolute or a decree of judicial separation has been granted, a party to the marriage dies and—

(a) an application for a financial provision order under section 23 of the Matrimonial Causes Act 1973 or a property adjustment order under section 24 of that Act has not been made by the other party to that marriage, or

(b) such an application has been made but the proceedings thereon have not been determined at the time of the death of the deceased,

then, if an application for an order under section 2 of this Act is made by that other party, the court shall, notwithstanding anything in section 1 or section 3 of this Act, have power, if it thinks it just to do so, to treat that party for the purposes of that application as if the decree of divorce or nullity of marriage had not been made absolute or the decree of judicial separation had not been granted, as the case may be.

(2) This section shall not apply in relation to a decree of judicial separation unless at the date of the death of the deceased the decree was in force and the separation was continuing.

[490]

15 Restriction imposed in divorce proceedings, etc on application under this Act

[(1) On the grant of a decree of divorce, a decree of nullity of marriage or a decree of judicial separation or at any time thereafter the court, if it considers it just to do so, may, on the application of either party to the marriage, order that the other party to the marriage shall not on the death of the applicant be entitled to apply for an order under section 2 of this Act.

In this subsection "the court" means the High Court or, where a county court has jurisdiction by virtue of Part V of the Matrimonial and Family Proceedings Act 1984, a county court.]

(2) In the case of a decree of divorce or nullity of marriage an order may be made under subsection (1) above before or after the decree is made absolute, but if it is made before the decree is made absolute it shall not take effect unless the decree is made absolute.

(3) Where an order made under subsection (1) above on the grant of a decree of divorce or nullity of marriage has come into force with respect to a party to a marriage, then, on the death of the other party to that marriage, the court shall not entertain any application for an order under section 2 of this Act made by the first-mentioned party.

(4) Where an order made under subsection (1) above on the grant of a decree of judicial separation has come into force with respect to any party to a marriage, then, if the other party to that marriage dies while the decree is in force and the separation is continuing, the court shall not entertain any application for an order under section 2 of this Act made by the first-mentioned party.

[491]

NOTES

Sub-s (1): substituted by the Matrimonial and Family Proceedings Act 1984, s 8(1).

[15A Restriction imposed in proceedings under Matrimonial and Family Proceedings Act 1984 on application under this Act

(1) On making an order under section 17 of the Matrimonial and Family Proceedings Act 1984 (orders for financial provision and property adjustment

following overseas divorces, etc) the court, if it considers it just to do so, may, on the application of either party to the marriage, order that the other party to the marriage shall not on the death of the applicant be entitled to apply for an order under section 2 of this Act.

In this subsection "the court" means the High Court or, where a county court has jurisdiction by virtue of Part V of the Matrimonial and Family Proceedings Act 1984, a county court.

(2)   Where an order under subsection (1) above has been made with respect to a party to a marriage which has been dissolved or annulled, then, on the death of the other party to that marriage, the court shall not entertain an application under section 2 of this Act made by the first-mentioned party.

(3)   Where an order under subsection (1) above has been made with respect to a party to a marriage the parties to which have been legally separated, then, if the other party to the marriage dies while the legal separation is in force, the court shall not entertain an application under section 2 of this Act made by the first-mentioned party.]

[492]

NOTES
Inserted by the Matrimonial and Family Proceedings Act 1984, s 25(3).

16   Variation and discharge of secured periodical payments orders made under Matrimonial Causes Act 1973

(1)   Where an application for an order under section 2 of this Act is made to the court by any person who was at the time of the death of the deceased entitled to payments from the deceased under a secured periodical payments order made under the Matrimonial Causes Act 1973, then, in the proceedings on that application, the court shall have power, if an application is made under this section by that person or by the personal representative of the deceased, to vary or discharge that periodical payments order or to revive the operation of any provision thereof which has been suspended under section 31 of that Act.

(2)   In exercising the powers conferred by this section the court shall have regard to all the circumstances of the case, including any order which the court proposes to make under section 2 or section 5 of this Act and any change (whether resulting from the death of the deceased or otherwise) in any of the matters to which the court was required to have regard when making the secured periodical payments order.

(3)   The powers exercisable by the court under this section in relation to an order shall be exercisable also in relation to any instrument executed in pursuance of the order.

[493]

17   Variation and revocation of maintenance agreements

(1)   Where an application for an order under section 2 of this Act is made to the court by any person who was at the time of the death of the deceased entitled to payments from the deceased under a maintenance agreement which provided for the continuation of payments under the agreement after the death of the deceased, then, in the proceedings on that application, the court shall have power, if an application is made under this section by that person or by the personal representative of the deceased, to vary or revoke that agreement.

(2)   In exercising the powers conferred by this section the court shall have regard to all the circumstances of the case, including any order which the court proposes to make under section 2 or section 5 of this Act and any change (whether resulting from the death of the deceased or otherwise) in any of the circumstances in the light of which the agreement was made.

(3)   If a maintenance agreement is varied by the court under this section the like consequences shall ensue as if the variation had been made immediately before the death of the deceased by agreement between the parties and for valuable consideration.

(4)   In this section "maintenance agreement", in relation to a deceased person, means any agreement made, whether in writing or not and whether before or after the commencement of this Act, by the deceased with any person with whom he entered into a marriage, being an agreement which contained provisions governing the rights and liabilities towards one another when living separately of the parties to that marriage (whether or not the marriage has been dissolved or annulled) in respect of the making or securing of payments or the disposition or use of any property, including such rights and liabilities with respect to the maintenance or education of any child, whether or not a child of the deceased or a person who was treated by the deceased as a child of the family in relation to that marriage.

[494]

18   Availability of court's powers under this Act in applications under ss 31 and 36 of the Matrimonial Causes Act 1973

(1)   Where—
   (a) a person against whom a secured periodical payments order was made under the Matrimonial Causes Act 1973 has died and an application is made under section 31(6) of that Act for the variation or discharge of that order or for the revival of the operation of any provision thereof which has been suspended, or
   (b) a party to a maintenance agreement within the meaning of section 34 of that Act has died, the agreement being one which provides for the continuation of payments thereunder after the death of one of the parties, and an application is made under section 36(1) of that Act for the alteration of the agreement under section 35 thereof.

the court shall have power to direct that the application made under the said section 31(6) or 36(1) shall be deemed to have been accompanied by an application for an order under section 2 of this Act.

(2)   Where the court gives a direction under subsection (1) above it shall have power, in the proceedings on the application under the said section 31(6) or 36(1), to make any order which the court would have had power to make under the provisions of this Act if the application under the said section 31(6) or 36(1), as the case may be, had been made jointly with an application for an order under the said section 2; and the court shall have power to give such consequential directions as may be necessary for enabling the court to exercise any of the powers available to the court under this Act in the case of an application for an order under section 2.

(3)   Where an order made under section 15(1) of this Act is in force with respect to a party to a marriage, the court shall not give a direction under subsection (1) above with respect to any application made under the said section 31(6) or 36(1) by that party on the death of the other party.

[495]

Miscellaneous and supplementary provisions

19 Effect, duration and form of orders

(1)   Where an order is made under section 2 of this Act then for all purposes, including the purposes of the enactments relating to inheritance tax, the will or the law relating to intestacy, or both the will and the law relating to intestacy, as the case may be, shall have effect and be deemed to have had effect as from the deceased's death subject to the provisions of the order.

(2)   Any order made under section 2 or 5 of this Act in favour of—
   (a)   an applicant who was the former husband or former wife of the deceased, or
   (b)   an applicant who was the husband or wife of the deceased in a case where the marriage with the deceased was the subject of a decree of judicial separation and at the date of death the decree was in force and the separation was continuing,

shall, in so far as it provides for the making of periodical payments, cease to have effect on the remarriage of the applicant, except in relation to any arrears due under the order on the date of the remarriage.

(3)   A copy of every order made under this Act [other than an order made under section 15(1) of this Act] shall be sent to the principal registry of the Family Division for entry and filing, and a memorandum of the order shall be endorsed on, or permanently annexed to, the probate or letters of administration under which the estate is being administered.

[496]

NOTES

Sub-s (3): words in square brackets inserted by the Administration of Justice Act 1982, s 52.

Capital transfer tax: except in relation to a liability to tax arising before 25 July 1986 capital transfer tax shall be known as inheritance tax and the Capital Transfer Tax Act 1984 may be cited as the Inheritance Tax Act 1984, by virtue of the Finance Act 1986, s 100.

20 Provisions as to personal representatives

(1)   The provisions of this Act shall not render the personal representative of a deceased person liable for having distributed any part of the estate of the deceased, after the end of the period of six months from the date on which representation with respect to the estate of the deceased is first taken out, on the ground that he ought to have taken into account the possibility—
   (a)   that the court might permit the making of an application for an order under section 2 of this Act after the end of that period, or
   (b)   that, where an order has been made under the said section 2, the court might exercise in relation thereto the powers conferred on it by section 6 of this Act,

but this subsection shall not prejudice any power to recover, by reason of the making of an order under this Act, any part of the estate so distributed.

(2)   Where the personal representative of a deceased person pays any sum directed by an order under section 5 of this Act to be paid out of the deceased's net estate, he shall not be under any liability by reason of that estate not being sufficient to make the payment, unless at the time of making the payment he has reasonable cause to believe that the estate is not sufficient.

(3)   Where a deceased person entered into a contract by which he agreed to leave by his will any sum of money or other property to any person or by which he agreed that a sum of money or other property would be paid or transferred to any person out of his estate, then, if the personal representative of the deceased has reason to believe that the deceased entered into the contract with the intention of defeating an application for financial provision under this Act, he may, notwithstanding anything in that contract, postpone the payment of that sum of money or the transfer of that property until the expiration of the period of six months from the date on which representation with respect to the estate of the deceased is first taken out or, if during that period an application is made for an order under section 2 of this Act, until the determination of the proceedings on that application.

[497]

21   Admissibility as evidence of statements made by deceased

In any proceedings under this Act a statement made by the deceased, whether orally or in a document or otherwise, shall be admissible under section 2 of the Civil Evidence Act 1968 as evidence of any fact stated therein in like manner as if the statement were a statement falling within section 2(1) of that Act; and any reference in that Act to a statement admissible, or given or proposed to be given, in evidence under section 2 thereof or to the admissibility or the giving in evidence of a statement by virtue of that section or to any statement falling within section 2(1) of that Act shall be construed accordingly.

[498]

23   Determination of date on which representation was first taken out

In considering for the purposes of this Act when representation with respect to the estate of a deceased person was first taken out, a grant limited to settled land or to trust property shall be left out of account, and a grant limited to real estate or to personal estate shall be left out of account unless a grant limited to the remainder of the estate has previously been made or is made at the same time.

[499]

24   Effect of this Act on s 46(1)(vi) of Administration of Estates Act 1925

Section 46(1)(vi) of the Administration of Estates Act 1925, in so far as it provides for the devolution of property on the Crown, the Duchy of Lancaster or the Duke of Cornwall as bona vacantia, shall have effect subject to the provisions of this Act.

[500]

25   Interpretation

(1)   In this Act—
    "beneficiary", in relation to the estate of a deceased person, means—
        (a)   a person who under the will of the deceased or under the law relating to intestacy is beneficially interested in the estate or would be so interested if an order had not been made under this Act, and
        (b)   a person who has received any sum of money or other property which by virtue of section 8(1) or 8(2) of this Act is treated as part of the net estate of the deceased or would have received that sum or other property if an order had not been made under this Act;
    "child" includes an illegitimate child and a child en ventre sa mere at the death of the deceased;

"the court" [unless the context otherwise requires] means the High Court, or where a county court has jurisdiction by virtue of section 22 of this Act, a county court;

["former wife" or "former husband" means a person whose marriage with the deceased was during the lifetime of the deceased either—

    (a) dissolved or annulled by a decree of divorce or a decree of nullity of marriage granted under the law of any part of the British Islands, or

    (b) dissolved or annulled in any country or territory outside the British Islands by a divorce or annulment which is entitled to be recognised as valid by the law of England and Wales;]

"net estate", in relation to a deceased person, means—

    (a) all property of which the deceased had power to dispose by his will (otherwise than by virtue of a special power of appointment) less the amount of his funeral, testamentary and administration expenses, debts and liabilities, including any inheritance tax payable out of his estate on his death;

    (b) any property in respect of which the deceased held a general power of appointment (not being a power exercisable by will) which has not been exercised;

    (c) any sum of money or other property which is treated for the purposes of this Act as part of the net estate of the deceased by virtue of section 8(1) or (2) of this Act;

    (d) any property which is treated for the purposes of this Act as part of the net estate of the deceased by virtue of an order made under section 9 of the Act;

    (e) any sum of money or other property which is, by reason of a disposition or contract made by the deceased, ordered under section 10 or 11 of this Act to be provided for the purpose of the making of financial provision under this Act;

"property" includes any chose in action;

"reasonable financial provision" has the meaning assigned to it by section 1 of this Act;

"valuable consideration" does not include marriage or a promise of marriage;

"will" includes codicil.

(2) For the purposes of paragraph (a) of the definition of "net estate" in subsection (1) above a person who is not of full age and capacity shall be treated as having power to dispose by will of all property of which he would have had power to dispose by will if he had been of full age and capacity.

(3) Any reference in this Act to provision out of the net estate of a deceased person includes a reference to provision extending to the whole of that estate.

(4) For the purposes of this Act any reference to a wife or husband shall be treated as including a reference to a person who in good faith entered into a void marriage with the deceased unless either—

    (a) the marriage of the deceased and that person was dissolved or annulled during the lifetime of the deceased and the dissolution or annulment is recognised by the law of England and Wales, or

    (b) that person has during the lifetime of the deceased entered into a later marriage.

(5) Any reference in this Act to remarriage or to a person who has remarried includes a reference to a marriage which is by law void or voidable or to a person

who has entered into such a marriage, as the case may be, and a marriage shall be treated for the purposes of this Act as a remarriage, in relation to any party thereto, notwithstanding that the previous marriage of that party was void or voidable.

(6)   Any reference in this Act to an order or decree made under the Matrimonial Causes Act 1973 or under any section of that Act shall be construed as including a reference to an order or decree which is deemed to have been made under that Act or under that section thereof, as the case may be.

(7)   Any reference in this Act to any enactment is a reference to that enactment as amended by or under any subsequent enactment.

[501]

NOTES

Sub-s (1): in definition "the court" words in square brackets inserted and definition "former wife" or "former husband" substituted by the Matrimonial and Family Proceedings Act 1984, ss 8(2), 25(2).

Capital transfer tax: except in relation to a liability to tax arising before 25 July 1986 capital transfer tax shall be known as inheritance tax and the Capital Transfer Tax Act 1984 may be cited as the Inheritance Tax Act 1984, by virtue of the Finance Act 1986, s 100.

26   Consequential amendments, repeals and transitional provisions

(1)   . . .

(2)   Subject to the provisions of this section, the enactments specified in the Schedule to this Act are hereby repealed to the extent specified in the third column of the Schedule; . . .

(3)   The repeal of the said enactment shall not affect their operation in relation to any application made thereunder (whether before or after the commencement of this Act) with reference to the death of any person who died before the commencement of this Act.

(4)   Without prejudice to the provisions of section 38 of the Interpretation Act 1889 (which relates to the effect of repeals) nothing in any repeal made by this Act shall affect any order made or direction given under any enactment repealed by this Act, and, subject to the provisions of this Act, every such order or direction (other than an order made under section 4A of the Inheritance Family Provision Act 1938 or section 28A of the Matrimonial Causes Act 1965) shall, if it is in force at the commencement of this Act or is made by virtue of subsection (3) above, continue in force as if it had been made under section 2(1)(a) of this Act, and for the purposes of section 6(7) of this Act the court in exercising its powers under that section in relation to an order continued in force by this subsection shall be required to have regard to any change in any of the circumstances to which the court would have been required to have regard when making that order if the order had been made with reference to the death of any person who died after the commencement of this Act.

[502]

NOTES

Sub-ss (1), (2): words omitted amend the Matrimonial Causes Act 1973, s 36, Sch 2, para 5(2).

27   Short title, commencement and extent

(1)   This Act may be cited as the Inheritance (Provision for Family and Dependants) Act 1975.

(2)   This Act does not extend to Scotland or Northern Ireland.

(3)   This Act shall come into force on 1st April 1976.

[503]

LOCAL LAND CHARGES ACT 1975

(C 76)

An Act to make fresh provision for and in connection with the keeping of local land charges registers and the registration of matters therein

[12 November 1975]

Compensation for non-registration or defective official search certificate

10   Compensation for non-registration or defective official search certificate

(1)   Failure to register a local land charge in the appropriate local land charges register shall not affect the enforceability of the charge but where a person has purchased any land affected by a local land charge, then—

    (a) in a case where a material personal search of the appropriate local land charges register was made in respect of the land in question before the relevant time, if at the time of the search the charge was in existence but not registered in that register; or

    [(aa) in a case where the appropriate local land charges register kept otherwise than in documentary form and a material personal search of that register was made in respect of the land in question before the relevant time, if the entitlement to search in that register conferred by section 8 above was not satisfied as mentioned in subsection (1A) of that section; or]

    (b) in a case where a material official search of the appropriate local land charges register was made in respect of the land in question before the relevant time, if the charge was in existence at the time of the search but (whether registered or not) was not shown by the official search certificate as registered in that register,

the purchaser shall (subject to section 11(1) below) be entitled to compensation for any loss suffered by him [in consequence].

(2)   At any time when rules made under this Act make provision for local land charges registers to be divided into parts then, for the purposes of subsection (1) above—

    (a) a search (whether personal or official) of a part or parts only of any such register shall not constitute a search of that register in relation to any local land charge registrable in a part of the register not searched; and

    (b) a charge shall not be taken to be registered in the appropriate local land charges register unless registered in the appropriate part of the register.

(3)   For the purposes of this section—

    (a) a person purchases land where, for valuable consideration, he acquires any interest in land or the proceeds of sale of land, and this includes cases where he acquires as lessee or mortgagee and shall be treated as including cases where an interest is conveyed or assigned at his direction to another person;

    (b) the relevant time—

        (i) where the acquisition of the interest in question was preceded by a contract for its acquisition, other than a qualified liability contract, is the time when that contract was made;

(ii) in any other case, is the time when the purchaser acquired the interest in question or, if he acquired it under a disposition which took effect only when registered under the Land Registration Act 1925, the time when that disposition was made; [and for the purposes of sub-paragraph (i) above, a qualified liability contract is a contract containing a term the effect of which is to make the liability of the purchaser dependent upon, or avoidable by reference to, the outcome of a search for local land charges affecting the land to be purchased;

(c) a personal search is material if, but only if—
  (i) it is made after the commencement of this Act, and
  (ii) it is made by or on behalf of the purchaser or, before the relevant time, the purchaser or his agent has knowledge of the result of it;

(d) an official search is material if, but only if—
  (i) it is made after the commencement of this Act, and
  (ii) it is requisitioned by or on behalf of the purchaser or, before the relevant time, the purchaser or his agent has knowledge of the contents of the official search certificate.

(4) Any compensation for loss under this section shall be paid by the registering authority in whose area the land affected is situated; and where the purchaser has incurred expenditure for the purpose of obtaining compensation under this section, the amount of the compensation shall include the amount of the expenditure reasonably incurred by him for that purpose (so far as that expenditure would not otherwise fall to be treated as loss for which he is entitled to compensation under this section).

(5) Where any compensation for loss under this section is paid by a registering authority in respect of a local land charge as respects which they are not the originating authority, then, unless an application for registration of the charge was made to the registering authority by the originating authority in time for it to be practicable for the registering authority to avoid incurring liability to pay that compensation, an amount equal thereto shall be recoverable from the originating authority by the registering authority.

(6) Where any compensation for loss under this section is paid by a registering authority, no part of the amount paid, or of any corresponding amount paid to that authority by the originating authority under subsection (5) above, shall be recoverable by the registering authority or the originating authority from any other person except as provided by subsection (5) above or under a policy of insurance or on grounds of fraud.

(7) In the case of an action to recover compensation under this section the cause of action shall be deemed for the purposes of the Limitation Act 1939 to accrue at the time when the local land charge comes to the notice of the purchaser; and for the purposes of this subsection the question when the charge came to his notice shall be determined without regard to the provisions of section 198 of the Law of Property Act 1925 (under which registration under certain enactments is deemed to constitute actual notice).

[(8) Where the amount claimed by way of compensation under this section does not exceed £5,000, proceedings for the recovery of such compensation may be begun in a county court.]

(9) If in any proceedings for the recovery of compensation under this section the court dismisses a claim to compensation, it shall not order the purchaser to pay the

registering authority's costs unless it considers that it was unreasonable for the purchaser to commence the proceedings.

NOTES

Commencement: 1 August 1977 (sub-ss (1)–(7), (9)); 1 July 1991 (sub-s (8)).

Sub-s (1): para (aa) inserted and words in square brackets therein substituted by the Local Government (Miscellaneous Provisions) Act 1982, s 34(d)(i), (ii).

Sub-s (8): substituted for existing sub-ss (8), (8A) by the High Court and County Courts Jurisdiction Order 1991, SI 1991/724, art 2(2)(a), (8), Schedule, Pt I.

Miscellaneous and supplementary

20   Short title etc

(1)   This Act may be cited as the Local Land Charges Act 1975.

(2)   This Act binds the Crown, but nothing in this Act shall be taken to render land owned by or occupied for the purposes of the Crown subject to any charge to which, independently of this Act, it would not be subject.

(3)   This Act shall come into force on such day as the Lord Chancellor may by order made by statutory instrument appoint.

(4)   This Act extends to England and Wales only.

RENTCHARGES ACT 1977

(C 30)

An Act to prohibit the creation, and provide for the extinguishment, apportionment and redemption, of certain rentcharges

[22 July 1977]

Prohibition and extinguishment

1   Meaning of "rentcharge"

For the purposes of this Act "rentcharge" means any annual or other periodic sum charged on or issuing out of land, except—
    (a)   rent reserved by a lease or tenancy, or
    (b)   any sum payable by way of interest.

2   Creation of rentcharges prohibited

(1)   Subject to this section, no rentcharge may be created whether at law or in equity after the coming into force of this section.

(2)   Any instrument made after the coming into force of this section shall, to the extent that it purports to create a rentcharge the creation of which is prohibited by this section, be void.

(3)   This section does not prohibit the creation of a rentcharge—
    (a)   which has the effect of making the land on which the rent is charged settled land by virtue of section 1(1)(v) of the Settled Land Act 1925;

(b) which would have that effect but for the fact that the land on which the rent is charged is already settled land or is held on trust for sale;

(c) which is an estate rentcharge;

(d) under any Act of Parliament providing for the creation of rentcharges in connection with the execution of works on land (whether by way of improvements, repairs or otherwise) or the commutation of any obligation to do any such work; or

(e) by, or in accordance with the requirements of, any order of a court.

(4) For the purposes of this section "estate rentcharge" means (subject to subsection (5) below) a rentcharge created for the purpose—

(a) of making covenants to be performed by the owner of the land affected by the rentcharge enforceable by the rent owner against the owner for the time being of the land; or

(b) of meeting, or contributing towards, the cost of the performance by the rent owner of covenants for the provision of services, the carrying out of maintenance or repairs, the effecting of insurance or the making of any payment by him for the benefit of the land affected by the rentcharge or for the benefit of that and other land.

(5) A rentcharge of more than a nominal amount shall not be treated as an estate rentcharge for the purposes of this section unless it represents a payment for the performance by the rent owner of any such covenant as is mentioned in subsection (4)(b) above which is reasonable in relation to that covenant.

[507]

3 Extinguishment of rentcharges

(1) Subject to this section, every rentcharge shall (if it has not then ceased to have effect) be extinguished at the expiry of the period of 60 years beginning—

(a) with the passing of this Act, or

(b) with the date on which the rentcharge first became payable,

whichever is the later; and accordingly the land on which it was charged or out of which it issued shall, at the expiration of that period, be discharged and freed from the rentcharge.

(2) The extinguishment of a rentcharge under this section shall not affect the exercise by any person of any right or remedy for the recovery of any rent which accrues before the rentcharge is so extinguished.

(3) This section shall not have the effect of extinguishing any rentcharge—

(a) which is, by virtue of any enactment or agreement or by custom, charged on or otherwise payable in relation to land wholly or partly in lieu of tithes; or

(b) which is of a kind referred to in subsection (3) of section 2 above (disregarding subsection (5) of that section).

(4) Subsection (1) above shall not apply to a variable rentcharge; but where such a rentcharge ceases to be variable, subsection (1) above shall apply as if the date on which the rentcharge first became payable were the date on which it ceased to be variable.

(5) For the purposes of subsection (4) above, a rentcharge shall (at any time) be treated as variable if at any time thereafter the amount of the rentcharge will, or may, vary in accordance with the provisions of the instrument under which it is payable.

[508]

Apportionment

4 Application for apportionment

(1) The owner of any land which is affected by a rentcharge which also affects land which is not in his ownership may, subject to this section, apply to the Secretary of State for an order apportioning the rentcharge between that land and the remaining land affected by the rentcharge.

(2) The owner of any land which is affected by a rentcharge which does not affect land not in his ownership may apply to the Secretary of State for an order apportioning the rentcharge between such parts of his land as may be specified in the application.

(3) No application for apportionment may be made under this section in respect of—
(a) a rentcharge of a kind mentioned in section 2(3)(d) or 3(3)(a) above, or
(b) land affected by a rentcharge which also affects other land, if the whole of that other land is exonerated or indemnified from the whole of the rentcharge by means of a charge on the first mentioned land.

(4) Every application—
(a) under subsection (1) above, shall specify the amount (if any) equitably apportioned to the applicant's land, and
(b) under subsection (2) above, shall specify the applicant's proposal for apportioning the rentcharge between the parts of his land specified in the application.

(5) Subject to subsection (4) above, every application under this section shall be in such form and shall contain such information and be accompanied by such documents as may be prescribed by regulations.

(6) In any case where the Secretary of State considers that any additional document or information ought to be furnished by the applicant he may require the applicant—
(a) to deliver to him such documents (including documents of title and, in the case of registered land, an authority to inspect the register), and
(b) to furnish him with such information,

as the Secretary of State may specify.

(7) Where an applicant's documents of title are in the custody of a mortgagee the mortgagee shall, if requested to do so by the Secretary of State for the purpose of an application made under this section, deliver those documents to the Secretary of State on such terms as to their custody and return as the mortgagee may reasonably require.

[509]

5 Apportionment

(1) Where an application for apportionment is made under section 4 above and the Secretary of State is satisfied that he is in a position to do so, he shall prepare a draft order for apportionment of the rentcharge.

(2) If the application is made under section 4(1) above, the amount specified in the draft order as being that part of the rentcharge apportioned to the applicant's land shall be—
(a) the amount specified in the application as the amount equitably apportioned to that land; or
(b) where no amount has been equitably apportioned to that land, such amount as the Secretary of State considers appropriate.

(3)   If the application is made under section 4(2) above, the amounts specified in the draft order as apportioned between the parts of the applicant's land specified in the application shall be those proposed in the application.

(4)   A copy of the draft order shall be served by the Secretary of State on the person appearing to him to be the rent owner or his agent, and, in a case falling within subsection (2)(b) above, on such persons as appear to him to be the owners of the land affected by the rentcharge.

(5)   After service of a draft order on the rent owner or his agent under subsection (4) above, the rent owner may, before the expiry of the period of 21 days beginning with the date on which the draft order is served (or such longer period, not exceeding the period of 42 days beginning with that date, as the Secretary of State may in a particular case allow)—

    (a)   object to it on the ground that such an apportionment would provide insufficient security for any part of the rentcharge;

    (b)   make an application to the effect that in the event of the apportionment not exceeding the sum mentioned in section 7(2) below, a condition should be imposed under that section.

(6)   Where a draft order is served under subsection (4) above on a person who is the owner of any land affected by the rentcharge, that person may, before the expiry of the period of 21 days beginning with the date on which the draft order is served (or such longer period, not exceeding the period of 42 days beginning with that date, as the Secretary of State may in a particular case allow), make representations to the Secretary of State concerning the apportionment specified in the draft order.

(7)   Any objection, application or representations under subsection (5) or (6) above shall be made in writing.

(8)   An objection under subsection (5) above shall state what apportionment (if any) would in the opinion of the rent owner provide sufficient security for the rentcharge or, as the case may be, part of the rentcharge.

(9)   The Secretary of State shall consider any objection duly made under subsection (5) above and any representations duly made under subsection (6) above and, if he is satisfied that the draft order should be modified—

    (a)   in the case of an objection, in order to preserve for the rent owner sufficient security for each apportioned part of the rentcharge, or

    (b)   to take account of any such representations,

he shall make such modifications in the draft order as appear to him to be appropriate.

(10)   Where—

    (a)   the relevant period has expired without any objection or representation having been duly made, or

    (b)   an objection has, or any representations have, been duly made and the objection has, or, as the case may be, all the representations have, been considered by the Secretary of State,

the Secretary of State shall, if the applicant has not then withdrawn his application and the Secretary of State is satisfied that it is appropriate to do so, make an order (an "apportionment order") in the form of the draft but incorporating—

    (i)   any modifications made by the Secretary of State in accordance with subsection (9) above, and

    (ii)   where appropriate, a condition imposed by virtue of section 7(2) below.

(11) Immediately after making an apportionment order the Secretary of State shall serve copies of the order on the applicant and on the person appearing to him to be the rent owner or his agent, and, in a case falling within subsection (2)(b) above, on those persons on whom copies of the draft order were served under subsection (4) above.

(12) In a case where modifications have been made in a draft order under subsection (9) above, the Secretary of State shall not make an apportionment order without giving the applicant an opportunity to withdraw his application.

[510]

6 Appeal

(1) Where the applicant or the rent owner or, in a case falling within section 5(2)(b) above, any other person who is the owner of any land affected by the rentcharge, is aggrieved by the terms of an apportionment order, he may appeal to the Lands Tribunal.

(2) Where an appeal has been duly made to the Lands Tribunal under this section, the Tribunal shall—
  (a) confirm the order, or
  (b) set it aside, and, subject to section 7(2) below, make such other order apportioning the rentcharge as it thinks fit.

[511]

7 Effect of apportionment order

(1) An apportionment order shall, subject to subsection (2) below, have effect—
  (a) on the expiry of the period of 28 days beginning with the day on which it is made, or
  (b) where an appeal against the order has been duly made under section 6 above, on such day as the Lands Tribunal shall specify.

(2) If—
  (a) in the case of an application made under section 4(1) above, the part of the rentcharge apportioned to the applicant's land, or
  (b) in the case of an application under section 4(2) above, any apportioned part of the rentcharge,

does not exceed the annual sum of £5, then, subject to subsection (3) below, it shall, where an application has been duly made under section 5(5)(b) above, be made a condition of the apportionment order that it shall have effect only for the purpose of the redemption of that part of the rentcharge in accordance with the following provisions of this Act.

(3) The Secretary of State shall not impose a condition under subsection (2) above in any case where he considers that, having regard to all the circumstances, to do so would cause the applicant to suffer financial hardship.

(4) In the case of an application under section 4(1) above, the effect of an apportionment order shall (subject to subsection (2) above) be to release the applicant's land from any part of the rentcharge not apportioned to it and to release the remaining land affected by the rentcharge from such part (if any) of the rentcharge as is apportioned to the applicant's land.

(5) In the case of an application under section 4(2) above, the effect of an apportionment order shall (subject to subsection (2) above) be to release each part of the applicant's land from any part of the rentcharge not apportioned to it.

(6)   The Secretary of State may by regulations specify, in substitution for the sum mentioned in subsection (2) above, such other annual sum as he considers appropriate.

[512]

Redemption

8   Application for redemption certificate

(1)   The owner of any land affected by a rentcharge may apply to the Secretary of State, in accordance with this section, for a certificate (in this Act referred to as a "redemption certificate") certifying that the rentcharge has been redeemed.

(2)   Every application under this section shall be in such form and shall contain such information and be accompanied by such documents as may be prescribed by regulations.

(3)   In any case where the Secretary of State considers that any additional document or information ought to be furnished by the applicant he may require the applicant—
   (a)   to deliver to him such documents (including documents of title and, in the case of registered land, an authority to inspect the register), and
   (b)   to furnish him with such information.

as the Secretary of State may specify.

(4)   No application may be made under this section in respect of a rentcharge of a kind mentioned in section 2(3) or 3(3)(a) above.

(5)   An application under this section may only be made—
   (a)   if the period for which the rentcharge concerned would remain payable if it were not redeemed is ascertainable, and
   (b)   in the case of a rentcharge which has at any time been a variable rentcharge, if it has ceased to be variable at the time of making the application.

For the purposes of this section a rentcharge shall (at any time) be treated as variable if at any time thereafter the amount of the rentcharge will, or may, vary in accordance with the provisions of the instrument under which it is payable.

(6)   Where an applicant's documents of title are in the custody of a mortgagee the mortgagee shall, if requested to do so by the Secretary of State for the purpose of an application made under this section, deliver those documents to the Secretary of State on such terms as to their custody and return as the mortgagee may reasonably require.

[513]

9   Issue of redemption certificate

(1)   Where an application for a redemption certificate has been duly made under section 8 above, the Secretary of State shall serve notice of the application ("notice of application") on the person appearing to him to be the rent owner in relation to the rentcharge to which the application relates or his agent.

(2)   A notice of application shall require the person on whom it is served to notify the Secretary of State, before the expiry of the period of 21 days beginning with the date on which the notice of application is served, whether or not he is the rent owner in relation to that rentcharge.

(3)   Notification under subsection (2) above shall be given in the form prescribed by regulations and shall contain such information, and be accompanied by such documents, as may be so prescribed.

(4)   Where the Secretary of State has been duly notified under subsection (2) above, or the period mentioned in that subsection has expired without his being so notified, he shall serve a notice ("instructions for redemption") on the applicant for the redemption certificate—

   (a)   specifying the sum required to redeem the rentcharge (the "redemption price") calculated in accordance with section 10(1) below, and

   (b)   naming the person (determined in accordance with section 10(2) below), if any, appearing to the Secretary of State to be the person to whom the redemption price should be paid by the applicant.

(5)   After service of instructions for redemption, the Secretary of State shall issue the applicant with a redemption certificate on proof—

   (a)   that the applicant has, before the expiry of the period of 28 days beginning with the date on which the instructions are served—

      (i)   paid the amount specified as the redemption price to the person named in the instructions as the person to whom payment should be made, or

      (ii) where no person is so named, paid that amount into court in accordance with section 10(4) below, or

   (b)   in a case where the applicant has been authorised to do so under subsection (6) below, that he has paid that amount into court in accordance with section 10(4) below before the expiry of that period, (or such longer period as the Secretary of State may allow).

(6)   For the purposes of subsection (5)(b) above, the Secretary of State may authorise payment into court in any case where he is satisfied that the applicant is unable to effect payment in accordance with the instructions for redemption or that it would be unreasonable to require him to do so.

[514]

10   Provisions supplemental to section 9

(1)   For the purposes of section 9 above, the redemption price shall be calculated by applying the formula:—

where:—

$$P = £\frac{R}{Y} - \frac{R}{Y(1+Y)^n}$$

P=the redemption price;

R=the annual amount of the rentcharge to be redeemed;

Y=the yield, expressed as a decimal fraction, from $2\frac{1}{2}$ per cent Consolidated Stock; and

n=the period, expressed in years (taking any part of a year as a whole year), for which the rentcharge would remain payable if it were not redeemed.

   In calculating the yield from $2\frac{1}{2}$ per cent Consolidated Stock, the price of that stock shall be taken to be the middle market price at the close of business on the last trading day in the week before that in which instructions for redemption are served under section 9(4) above.

(2)   For the purposes of section 9(4)(b) above, the person to whom the redemption price should be paid is—

(a)   in a case where the rentcharge was subject to a mortgage, the mortgagee or, if there is more than one mortgagee, the first mortgagee;

(b)   in a case where the rentcharge was not subject to a mortgage but was settled land or was subject to a trust for sale, the trustees;

(c)   in any other case, the rent owner.

(3)   Where a redemption certificate has been issued under section 9 above—

(a)   it shall have the effect of releasing the applicant's land from the rentcharge concerned, but

(b)   it shall not affect the exercise by the rent owner of any right or remedy for the recovery of any rent which accrues before the date on which it was issued.

(4)   Where a payment is made into court for the purposes of section 9 above, the sum concerned shall—

(a)   if it does not exceed [£5,000], be paid into the county court, and

(b)   in any other case, be paid into the High Court.

[(4A)   . . .]

(5)   Any person who, in notifying the Secretary of State under section 9(2) above, makes a statement which he knows to be false in a material particular, or recklessly makes any statement which is so false, shall be guilty of an offence punishable on summary conviction by a fine not exceeding [level 5 on the standard scale].

[515]

NOTES

Sub-s (4): sum in square brackets substituted by the High Court and County Courts Jurisdiction Order 1991, SI 1991/724, art 2(2)(b), (8), Schedule, Pt I.

Sub-s (4A): inserted by the County Courts Act 1984, s 148(1), Sch 2, Pt V, para 63(b); repealed by the High Court and County Courts Jurisdiction Order 1991, SI 1991/724, art 2(2)(b), (8), Schedule, Pt I.

Sub-s (5): maximum fine converted to a level on the standard scale by the Criminal Justice Act 1982, ss 37, 46.

Miscellaneous and general

11   Implied covenants

(1)   Where any land affected by a rentcharge created after the passing of this Act by virtue of section 2(3)(a) or (b) above—

(a)   is conveyed for consideration in money or money's worth, and

(b)   remains affected by the rentcharge or by any part of it,

the following provisions of this section shall have effect in place of those of section 77 of the Law of Property Act 1925, in respect of the covenants deemed to be included and implied in the conveyance.

(2)   In addition to the covenants implied under [Part I of the Law of Property (Miscellaneous Provisions) Act 1994], there shall be deemed to be included and implied in the conveyance covenants by the conveying party or joint and several covenants by the conveying parties (if more than one) with the grantee (or with each of the grantees) in the following terms:—

(a) that the conveying party will at all times from the date of the conveyance duly pay the rentcharge (or part of the rentcharge) and keep the grantee and those deriving title under him and their respective estates and effects indemnified against all claims and demands whatsoever in respect of the rentcharge; and

(b) that the conveying party will (at his expense), in the event of the rentcharge (or part of the rentcharge) ceasing to affect the land conveyed, furnish evidence of that fact to the grantee and those deriving title under him.

(3) The benefit of the covenants deemed to be included and implied in a conveyance, by virtue of subsection (2) above, shall be annexed and incident to and shall go with the estate or interest of the implied covenantee and shall be capable of being enforced by every person in whom the estate or interest is from time to time vested.

(4) Any stipulation which is contained in an agreement and which is inconsistent with, or designed to prevent the operation of, the said covenants (or any part of them) shall be void.

[516]

NOTES

Sub-s (2): words in square brackets substituted by the Law of Property (Miscellaneous Provisions) Act 1994, s 21(1), Sch 1, para 7, subject to transitional provisions in s 21(4) thereof.

12 Regulations

(1) Regulations under any provision of this Act shall be made by the Secretary of State and shall be contained in a statutory instrument, which shall be subject to annulment in pursuance of a resolution of either House of Parliament.

(2) Regulations under any provision of this Act may contain such incidental and supplemental provisions as the Secretary of State considers appropriate, and may make different provisions in relation to different cases or classes of case and in relation to different circumstances.

[517]

13 Interpretation

(1) In this Act—

"apportionment", in relation to a rentcharge, includes an apportionment which provides for the amount apportioned to any part of the land affected by the rentcharge to be nil;

"apportionment order" means an order made under section 5(10) above or, where appropriate, an order made by the Lands Tribunal under section 6(2)(b) above;

"conveyance" has the same meaning as in section 205(1) of the Law of Property Act 1925;

"land" has the same meaning as in section 205(1) of the Law of Property Act 1925;

"legal apportionment" and "equitable apportionment" in relation to a rentcharge mean, respectively—

(a) any apportionment of the rentcharge which is binding on the rent owner, and

(b) any apportionment or exoneration of the rentcharge which is not binding on the rent owner;

"owner", in relation to any land, means a person, other than a mortgagee not in possession, who is for the time being entitled to dispose of the fee simple of the land, whether in possession or in reversion, and includes a person holding or entitled to the rents and profits of the land under a lease or agreement;

"redemption certificate" has the meaning given in section 8(1) above;

"rent owner", in relation to a rentcharge, means the person entitled to the rentcharge or empowered to dispose of it absolutely or to give an absolute discharge for the capital value thereof.

(2) The provisions of this Act relating to the redemption and apportionment of rentcharges shall apply equally to the redemption and further apportionment of legally apportioned parts of rentcharges.

(3) Subject to section 3(4) above, a rentcharge shall be treated for the purposes of this Act as becoming payable on the first day of the first period in respect of which it is to be paid.

[518]

14 Application to Crown

(1) This Act shall apply in relation to any land in which there subsists a Crown interest as it applies in relation to land in which no such interest subsists.

(2) In this section "Crown interest" means an interest which belongs to Her Majesty in right of the Crown or of the Duchy of Lancaster or to the Duchy of Cornwall or to a government department, or which is held in trust for Her Majesty for the purposes of a government department.

[519]

15 Expenses

(1) Any expenses incurred by the Secretary of State in consequence of this Act shall be paid out of money provided by Parliament.

(2) Subject to any provision made by regulations, any expenses incurred by any person in connection with an application for an apportionment order or for a redemption certificate under this Act shall be borne by that person.

(3) Regulations under subsection (2) above shall, in particular, provide for the reasonable expenses of a mortgagee, incurred in complying with a request under section 4(7) or 8(6) above, to be borne by the applicant.

[520]

16 Service of notices, etc

(1) Any document required to be served under this Act may be served on the person to be served either by delivering it to him, or by leaving it at his proper address, or by sending it by post.

(2) Any such document required to be served on a body corporate or a firm shall be duly served if it is served on the secretary or clerk of that body or a partner of that firm.

(3) For the purposes of this section, and of section 26 of the Interpretation Act 1889, in its application to this section, the proper address of a person shall be—

(a) in the case of a secretary or clerk of a body corporate, that of the registered or principal office of that body;

(b)   in the case of a partner of a firm, that of the principal office of the firm;

(c)   in any other case, the last known address of the person to be served.

[521]

18   Short title etc

(1)   This Act may be cited as the Rentcharges Act 1977.

(2)   The following provisions shall come into force on the expiry of the period of one month beginning with the date on which this Act is passed:—

(a)   sections 1 to 3;

(b)   sections 12 to 15, in section 17, subsection (1)(so far as it relates to paragraph 2 of Schedule 1), subsection (2) (except as it applies to the entries in Schedule 2 relating to section 10 of the Inclosure Act 1854 and section 191 of the Law of Property Act 1925) and subsections (3) and (6), and this section;

and the remaining provisions of this Act shall come into force on such day as the Secretary of State may by order appoint.

(3)   This Act does not extend to Scotland or Northern Ireland.

[522]

PROTECTION FROM EVICTION ACT 1977

(C 43)

An Act to consolidate section 16 of the Rent Act 1957 and Part III of the Rent Act 1965, and related enactments

[29 July 1977]

PART I
UNLAWFUL EVICTION AND HARASSMENT

1   Unlawful eviction and harassment of occupier

(1)   In this section "residential occupier", in relation to any premises, means a person occupying the premises as a residence, whether under a contract or by virtue of any enactment or rule of law giving him the right to remain in occupation or restricting the right of any other person to recover possession of the premises.

(2)   If any person unlawfully deprives the residential occupier of any premises of his occupation of the premises or any part thereof, or attempts to do so, he shall be guilty of an offence unless he proves that he believed, and had reasonable cause to believe, that the residential occupier had ceased to reside in the premises.

(3)   If any person with intent to cause the residential occupier of any premises—

(a)   to give up the occupation of the premises or any part thereof; or

(b)   to refrain from exercising any right or pursuing any remedy in respect of the premises or part thereof;

does acts [likely] to interfere with the peace or comfort of the residential occupier or members of his household, or persistently withdraws or withholds services reasonably required for the occupation of the premises as a residence, he shall be guilty of an offence.

[(3A)   Subject to subsection (3B) below, the landlord of a residential occupier or an agent of the landlord shall be guilty of an offence if—

(a)   he does acts likely to interfere with the peace or comfort of the residential occupier or members of his household, or

(b)   he persistently withdraws or withholds services reasonably required for the occupation of the premises in question as a residence,

and (in either case) he knows, or has reasonable cause to believe, that that conduct is likely to cause the residential occupier to give up the occupation of the whole or part of the premises or to refrain from exercising any right or pursuing any remedy in respect of the whole or part of the premises.

(3B) A person shall not be guilty of an offence under subsection (3A) above if he proves that he had reasonable grounds for doing the acts or withdrawing or withholding the services in question.

(3C) In subsection (3A) above "landlord", in relation to a residential occupier of any premises, means the person who, but for—

(a)   the residential occupier's right to remain in occupation of the premises, or

(b)   a restriction on the person's right to recover possession of the premises,

would be entitled to occupation of the premises and any superior landlord under whom that person derives title.]

(4)   A person guilty of an offence under this section shall be liable—

(a)   on summary conviction, to a fine not exceeding [the prescribed sum] or to imprisonment for a term not exceeding 6 months or to both;

(b)   on conviction on indictment, to a fine or to imprisonment for a term not exceeding 2 years or to both.

(5)   Nothing in this section shall be taken to prejudice any liability or remedy to which a person guilty of an offence thereunder may be subject in civil proceedings.

(6)   Where an offence under this section committed by a body corporate is proved to have been committed with the consent or connivance of, or to be attributable to any neglect on the part of, any director, manager or secretary or other similar officer of the body corporate or any person who was purporting to act in any such capacity, he as well as the body corporate shall be guilty of that offence and shall be liable to be proceeded against and punished accordingly.

[523]

NOTES

Sub-s (3): word in square brackets substituted by the Housing Act 1988, s 29(1), in relation to acts done after 15 January 1989.

Sub-ss (3A)–(3C): inserted by the Housing Act 1988, s 29(2).

Sub-s (4): words in square brackets substituted by virtue of the Magistrates' Courts Act 1980, s 32(2).

---

2   Restriction on re-entry without due process of law

Where any premises are let as a dwelling on a lease which is subject to a right of re-entry or forfeiture it shall not be lawful to enforce that right otherwise than by proceedings in the court while any person is lawfully residing in the premises or part of them.

[524]

3 Prohibition of eviction without due process of law

(1) Where any premises have been let as a dwelling under a tenancy which is [neither a statutorily protected tenancy nor an excluded tenancy] and—

    (a) the tenancy (in this section referred to as the former tenancy) has come to an end, but

    (b) the occupier continues to reside in the premises or part of them,

it shall not be lawful for the owner to enforce against the occupier, otherwise than by proceedings in the court, his right to recover possession of the premises.

(2) In this section "the occupier", in relation to any premises, means any person lawfully residing in the premises or part of them at the termination of the former tenancy.

[(2A) Subsections (1) and (2) above apply in relation to any restricted contract (within the meaning of the Rent Act 1977) which—

    (a) creates a licence; and

    (b) is entered into after the commencement of section 69 of the Housing Act 1980;

as they apply in relation to a restricted contract which creates a tenancy.]

[(2B) Subsections (1) and (2) above apply in relation to any premises occupied as a dwelling under a licence, other than an excluded licence, as they apply in relation to premises let as a dwelling under a tenancy, and in those subsections the expressions "let" and "tenancy" shall be construed accordingly.

(2C) References in the preceding provisions of this section and section 4(2A) below to an excluded tenancy do not apply to—

    (a) a tenancy entered into before the date on which the Housing Act 1988 came into force, or

    (b) a tenancy entered into on or after that date but pursuant to a contract made before that date,

but, subject to that, "excluded tenancy" and "excluded licence" shall be construed in accordance with section 3A below.]

(3) This section shall, with the necessary modifications, apply where the owner's right to recover possession arises on the death of the tenant under a statutory tenancy within the meaning of the Rent Act 1977 or the Rent (Agriculture) Act 1976.

[525]

NOTES

    Sub-s (1): words in square brackets substituted by the Housing Act 1988, s 30(1).
    Sub-s (2A): inserted by the Housing Act 1980, s 69(1).
    Sub-ss (2B), (2C): inserted by the Housing Act 1988, s 30(2).

[3A Excluded tenancies and licences

(1) Any reference in this Act to an excluded tenancy or an excluded licence is a reference to a tenancy or licence which is excluded by virtue of any of the following provisions of this section.

(2) A tenancy or licence is excluded if—

    (a) under its terms the occupier shares any accommodation with the landlord or licensor; and

   (b) immediately before the tenancy or licence was granted and also at the time it comes to an end, the landlord or licensor occupied as his only or principal home premises of which the whole or part of the shared accommodation formed part.

(3) A tenancy or licence is also excluded if—

   (a) under its terms the occupier shares any accommodation with a member of the family of the landlord or licensor;

   (b) immediately before the tenancy or licence was granted and also at the time it comes to an end, the member of the family of the landlord or licensor occupied as his only or principal home premises of which the whole or part of the shared accommodation formed part; and

   (c) immediately before the tenancy or licence was granted and also at the time it comes to an end, the landlord or licensor occupied as his only or principal home premises in the same building as the shared accommodation and that building is not a purpose-built block of flats.

(4) For the purposes of subsections (2) and (3) above, an occupier shares accommodation with another person if he has the use of it in common with that person (whether or not also in common with others) and any reference in those subsections to shared accommodation shall be construed accordingly, and if, in relation to any tenancy or licence, there is at any time more than one person who is the landlord or licensor, any reference in those subsections to the landlord or licensor shall be construed as a reference to any one of those persons.

(5) In subsections (2) to (4) above—

   (a) "accommodation" includes neither an area used for storage nor a staircase, passage, corridor or other means of access;

   (b) "occupier" means, in relation to a tenancy, the tenant and, in relation to a licence, the licensee; and

   (c) "purpose-built block of flats" has the same meaning as in Part III of Schedule 1 to the Housing Act 1988;

and section 113 of the Housing Act 1985 shall apply to determine whether a person is for the purposes of subsection (3) above a member of another's family as it applies for the purposes of Part IV of that Act.

(6) A tenancy or licence is excluded if it was granted as a temporary expedient to a person who entered the premises in question or any other premises as a trespasser (whether or not, before the beginning of that tenancy or licence, another tenancy or licence to occupy the premises or any other premises had been granted to him).

(7) A tenancy or licence is excluded if—

   (a) it confers on the tenant or licensee the right to occupy the premises for a holiday only; or

   (b) it is granted otherwise than for money or money's worth.

(8) A licence is excluded if it confers rights of occupation in a hostel, within the meaning of the Housing Act 1985, which is provided by—

   (a) the council of a county, [county borough,] district or London Borough, the Common Council of the City of London, the Council of the Isles of Scilly, the Inner London Education Authority, a joint authority within the meaning of the Local Government Act 1985 or a residuary body within the meaning of that Act;

   (b) a development corporation within the meaning of the New Towns Act 1981;

    (c) the Commission for the New Towns;

    (d) an urban development corporation established by an order under section 135 of the Local Government, Planning and Land Act 1980;

    (e) a housing action trust established under Part III of the Housing Act 1988;

    (f) the Development Board for Rural Wales;

    (g) the Housing Corporation or Housing for Wales;

    (h) a housing trust which is a charity or a registered housing association, within the meaning of the Housing Associations Act 1985; or

    (i) any other person who is, or who belongs to a class of person which is, specified in an order made by the Secretary of State.

(9)   The power to make an order under subsection (8)(i) above shall be exercisable by statutory instrument which shall be subject to annulment in pursuance of a resolution of either House of Parliament.]

[526]

NOTES

Inserted by the Housing Act 1988, s 31.

Sub-s (8): words in square brackets inserted by the Local Government (Wales) Act 1994, s 22(2), Sch 8, para 4(1), as from a day to be appointed.

PART II
NOTICE TO QUIT

5   Validity of notices to quit

(1)   [Subject to subsection (1B) below] no notice by a landlord or a tenant to quit any premises let (whether before or after the commencement of this Act) as a dwelling shall be valid unless—

    (a) it is in writing and contains such information as may be prescribed, and

    (b) it is given not less than 4 weeks before the date on which it is to take effect.

[(1A)   Subject to subsection (1B) below, no notice by a licensor or licensee to determine a periodic licence to occupy premises as a dwelling (whether the licence was granted before or after the passing of this Act) shall be valid unless—

    (a) it is in writing and contains such information as may be prescribed, and

    (b) it is given not less than 4 weeks before the date on which it is to take effect.

(1B) Nothing in subsection (1) or subsection (1A) above applies to—

    (a) premises let on an excluded tenancy which is entered into on or after the date on which the Housing Act 1988 came into force unless it is entered into pursuant to a contract made before that date; or

    (b) premises occupied under an excluded licence.]

(2)   In this section "prescribed" means prescribed by regulations made by the Secretary of State by statutory instrument, and a statutory instrument containing any such regulations shall be subject to annulment in pursuance of a resolution of either House of Parliament.

(3)   Regulations under this section may make different provision in relation to different descriptions of lettings and different circumstances.

[527]

PART III
SUPPLEMENTAL PROVISIONS

13   Short title, etc

(1)   This Act may be cited as the Protection from Eviction Act 1977.

(2)   This Act shall come into force on the expiry of the period of one month beginning with the date on which it is passed.

(3)   This Act does not extend to Scotland or Northern Ireland.

(4)   References in this Act to any enactment are references to that enactment as amended, and include references thereto as applied by any other enactment including, except where the context otherwise requires, this Act.

[528]

CHARGING ORDERS ACT 1979

(C 53)

An Act to make provision for imposing charges to secure payment of money due, or to become due, under judgments or orders of court; to provide for restraining and prohibiting dealings with, and the making of payments in respect of, certain securities; and for connected purposes

[6 December 1979]

Charging orders

1   Charging orders

(1)   Where, under a judgment or order of the High Court or a county court, a person (the "debtor") is required to pay a sum of money to another person (the "creditor") then, for the purpose of enforcing that judgment or order, the appropriate court may make an order in accordance with the provisions of this Act imposing on any such property of the debtor as may be specified in the order a charge for securing the payment of any money due or to become due under the judgment or order.

(2)   The appropriate court is—

    (a)   in a case where the property to be charged is a fund in court, the court in which that fund is lodged;

    (b)   in a case where paragraph (a) above does not apply and the order to be enforced is a maintenance order of the High Court, the High Court or a county court;

    (c)   in a case where neither paragraph (a) nor paragraph (b) above applies and the judgment or order to be enforced is a judgment or order of the High Court for a sum exceeding [the county court limit], the High Court [or a county court]; and

    (d)   in any other case, a county court.

In this section ["county court limit" means the county court limit for the time being specified in an Order in Council under [section 145 of the County Courts Act 1984], as the county court limit for the purposes of this section and] "maintenance order" has the same meaning as in section 2(a) of the Attachment of Earnings Act 1971.

(3)   An order under subsection (1) above is referred to in this Act as a "charging order".

(4)   Where a person applies to the High Court for a charging order to enforce more than one judgment or order, that court shall be the appropriate court in relation to the application if it would be the appropriate court, apart from this subsection, on an application relating to one or more of the judgments or orders concerned.

(5)   In deciding whether to make a charging order the court shall consider all the circumstances of the case and, in particular, any evidence before it as to—
    (a)   the personal circumstances of the debtor, and
    (b)   whether any other creditor of the debtor would be likely to be unduly prejudiced by the making of the order.

[529]

NOTES
Sub-s (2): words in first pair of square brackets substituted and words in second pair of square brackets inserted by the Administration of Justice Act 1982, ss 34(3), 37, Sch 3, Pt II, paras 2, 3; words in third (outer) pair of square brackets inserted by the Administration of Justice Act 1982, s 37, Sch 3, Pt II, para 6, words in square brackets therein substituted by the County Courts Act 1984, s 148(1), Sch 2, Pt V, para 71.

2   Property which may be charged

(1)   Subject to subsection (3) below, a charge may be imposed by a charging order only on—
    (a)   any interest held by the debtor beneficially—
        (i)   in any asset of a kind mentioned in subsection (2) below, or
        (ii)   under any trust; or
    (b)   any interest held by a person as trustee of a trust ("the trust"), if the interest is in such an asset or is an interest under another trust and—
        (i)   the judgment or order in respect of which a charge is to be imposed was made against that person as trustee of the trust, or
        (ii)   the whole beneficial interest under the trust is held by the debtor unencumbered and for his own benefit, or
        (iii)   in a case where there are two or more debtors all of whom are liable to the creditor for the same debt, they together hold the whole beneficial interest under the trust unencumbered and for their own benefit.

(2)   The assets referred to in subsection (1) above are—
    (a)   land,
    (b)   securities of any of the following kinds—
        (i)   government stock,
        (ii)   stock of any body (other than a building society) incorporated within England and Wales,
        (iii)   stock of any body incorporated outside England and Wales or of any state or territory outside the United Kingdom, being stock registered in a register kept at any place within England and Wales,
        (iv)   units of any unit trust in respect of which a register of the unit holders is kept at any place within England and Wales, or
    (c)   funds in court.

(3)   In any case where a charge is imposed by a charging order on any interest in an asset of a kind mentioned in paragraph (b) or (c) of subsection (2) above, the court making the order may provide for the charge to extend to any interest or dividend payable in respect of the asset.

[530]

3   Provisions supplementing sections 1 and 2

(1)   A charging order may be made either absolutely or subject to conditions as to notifying the debtor or as to the time when the charge is to become enforceable, or as to other matters.

(2)   The Land Charges Act 1972 and the Land Registration Act 1925 shall apply in relation to charging orders as they apply in relation to other orders or writs issued or made for the purpose of enforcing judgments.

(3)   . . .

(4)   Subject to the provisions of this Act, a charge imposed by a charging order shall have the like effect and shall be enforceable in the same courts and in the same manner as an equitable charge created by the debtor by writing under his hand.

(5)   The court by which a charging order was made may at any time, on the application of the debtor or of any person interested in any property to which the order relates, make an order discharging or varying the charging order.

(6)   Where a charging order has been protected by an entry registered under the Land Charges Act 1972 or the Land Registration Act 1925, an order under subsection (5) above discharging the charging order may direct that the entry be cancelled.

(7)   The Lord Chancellor may by order made by statutory instrument amend section 2(2) of this Act by adding to, or removing from, the kinds of asset for the time being referred to there, any asset of a kind which in his opinion ought to be so added or removed.

(8)   Any order under subsection (7) above shall be subject to annulment in pursuance of a resolution of either House of Parliament.

[531]

NOTES
Sub-s (3): amends the Land Registration Act 1925, s 49.

Stop orders and notices

5   Stop orders and notices

(1)   In this section—
   "stop order" means an order of the court prohibiting the taking, in respect of any of the securities specified in the order, of any of the steps mentioned in subsection (5) below;
   "stop notice" means a notice requiring any person or body on whom it is duly served to refrain from taking, in respect of any of the securities specified in the notice, any of those steps without first notifying the person by whom, or on whose behalf, the notice was served; and
   "prescribed securities" means securities (including funds in court) of a kind prescribed by rules of court made under this section.

(2)   The power to make rules of court under section [84 of the Supreme Court Act 1981] shall include power by any such rules to make provision—
  (a) for the court to make a stop order on the application of any person claiming to be entitled to an arrest in prescribed securities;
  (b) for the service of a stop notice by any person claiming to be entitled to an interest in prescribed securities.

(3)   The power to make rules of court under [section 75 of the County Courts Act 1984] shall include power by any such rules to make provision for the service of a stop notice by any person entitled to an interest in any securities by virtue of a charging order made by a county court.

(4)   Rules of court made by virtue of subsection (2) or (3) above shall prescribe the person or body on whom a copy of any stop order or a stop notice is to be served.

(5)   The steps mentioned in subsection (1) above are—
  (a) the registration of any transfer of the securities;
  (b) in the case of funds in court, the transfer, sale, delivery out, payment or other dealing with the funds, or of the income thereon;
  (c) the making of any payment by way of dividend, interest or otherwise in respect of the securities; and
  (d) in the case of a unit trust, any acquisition of or other dealing with the units by any person or body exercising functions under the trust.

(6)   Any rules of court made by virtue of this section may include such incidental, supplemental and consequential provisions as the authority making them consider necessary or expedient, and may make different provision in relation to different cases or classes of case.

[532]

NOTES
  Sub-s (2): words in square brackets substituted by the Supreme Court Act 1981, s 152(1), Sch 5.
  Sub-s (3): words in square brackets substituted by the County Courts Act 1984, s 148(1), Sch 2, Pt V, para 72.

Supplemental

6   Interpretation

(1)   In this Act—
  "building society" has the same meaning as in the Building Societies Act [1986];
  "charging order" means an order made under section 1(1) of this Act:
  "debtor" and "creditor" have the meanings given by section 1(1) of this Act;
  "dividend" includes any distribution in respect of any unit of a unit trust;
  "government stock" means any stock issued by Her Majesty's government in the United Kingdom or any funds of, or annuity granted by, that government;
  "stock" includes shares, debentures and any securities of the body concerned, whether or not constituting a charge on the assets of that body;
  "unit trust" means any trust established for the purpose, or having the effect, of providing, for persons having funds available for investment, facilities for the participation by them, as beneficiaries under the trust, in any profits or income arising from the acquisition, holding, management or disposal of any property whatsoever.

(2) For the purposes of section 1 of this Act references to a judgment or order of the High Court or a county court shall be taken to include references to a judgment, order, decree or award (however called) of any court or arbitrator (including any foreign court or arbitrator) which is or has become enforceable (whether wholly or to a limited extent) as if it were a judgment or order of the High Court or a county court.

(3) References in section 2 of this Act to any securities include references to any such securities standing in the name of the Accountant General.

[533]

NOTES

Sub-s (1): date in square brackets substituted by the Building Societies Act 1986, s 120, Sch 18, Pt I, para 14.

7 Consequential amendment, repeals and transitional provisions

(1), (2) . . .

(3) Any order made or notice given under any enactment repealed by this Act or under any rules of court revoked by rules of court made under this Act (the "new rules") shall, if still in force when the provisions of this Act or, as the case may be, the new rules come into force, continue to have effect as if made under this Act or, as the case may be, under the new rules.

(4) Any notice of such an order registered in the register maintained under the Land Registration Act 1925 which would have been registrable by virtue of the paragraph inserted in section 49(1) of that Act by section 3(3) of this Act, if section 3(3) had been in force when the notice was registered, shall have effect as if registered by virtue of that paragraph.

[534]

NOTES

Sub-s (1): repealed by the County Courts Act 1984, s 148(3), Sch 4.

Sub-s (2): repealed in part by the Supreme Court Act 1981, s 152(4), Sch 7; remainder repealed by the County Courts Act 1984, s 148(3), Sch 4.

8 Short title, commencement and extent

(1) This Act may be cited as the Charging Orders Act 1979.

(2) This Act comes into force on such day as the Lord Chancellor may appoint by order made by statutory instrument.

(3) This Act does not extend to Scotland or Northern Ireland.

[535]

LIMITATION ACT 1980

(C 58)

An Act to consolidate the Limitation Acts 1939 to 1980

[13 November 1980]

PART I
ORDINARY TIME LIMITS FOR DIFFERENT CLASSES OF ACTION

Actions founded on simple contract

5 Time limit for actions founded on simple contract

An action founded on simple contract shall not be brought after the expiration of six years from the date on which the cause of action accrued.

[536]

Actions to recover land and rent

15 Time limit for actions to recover land

(1) No action shall be brought by any person to recover any land after the expiration of twelve years from the date on which the right of action accrued to him or, if it first accrued to some person through whom he claims, to that person.

(2) Subject to the following provisions of this section, where—
 (a) the estate or interest claimed was an estate or interest in reversion or remainder or any other future estate or interest and the right of action to recover the land accrued on the date on which the estate or interest fell into possession by the determination of the preceding estate or interest; and
 (b) the person entitled to the preceding estate or interest (not being a term of years absolute) was not in possession of the land on that date;

no action shall be brought by the person entitled to the succeeding estate or interest after the expiration of twelve years from the date on which the right of action accrued to the person entitled to the preceding estate or interest or six years from the date on which the right of action accrued to the person entitled to the succeeding estate or interest, whichever period last expires.

(3) Subsection (2) above shall not apply to any estate or interest which falls into possession on the determination of an entailed interest and which might have been barred by the person entitled to the entailed interest.

(4) No person shall bring an action to recover any estate or interest in land under an assurance taking effect after the right of action to recover the land had accrued to the person by whom the assurance was made or some person through whom he claimed or some person entitled to a preceding estate or interest, unless the action is brought within the period during which the person by whom the assurance was made could have brought such an action.

(5) Where any person is entitled to any estate or interest in land in possession and, while so entitled, is also entitled to any future estate or interest in that land, and his right to recover the estate or interest in possession is barred under this Act, no action shall be brought by that person, or by any person claiming through him, in respect of

the future estate or interest, unless in the meantime possession of the land has been recovered by a person entitled to an intermediate estate or interest.

(6)   Part I of Schedule 1 to this Act contains provisions for determining the date of accrual of rights of action to recover land in the cases there mentioned.

(7)   Part II of that Schedule contains provisions modifying the provisions of this section in their application to actions brought by, or by a person claiming through, the Crown or any spiritual or eleemosynary corporation sole.

[537]

16   Time limit for redemption actions

When a mortgagee of land has been in possession of any of the mortgaged land for a period of twelve years, no action to redeem the land of which the mortgagee has been so in possession shall be brought after the end of that period by the mortgagor or any person claiming through him.

[538]

17   Extinction of title to land after expiration of time limit

Subject to—
  (a)   section 18 of this Act; and
  (b)   section 75 of the Land Registration Act 1925;

at the expiration of the period prescribed by this Act for any person to bring an action to recover land (including a redemption action) the title of that person to the land shall be extinguished.

[539]

18   Settled land and land held on trust

(1)   Subject to section 21(1) and (2) of this Act, the provisions of this Act shall apply to equitable interests in land, including interests in the proceeds of the sale of land held upon trust for sale, as they apply to legal estates.

Accordingly a right of action to recover the land shall, for the purposes of this Act but not otherwise, be treated as accruing to a person entitled in possession to such an equitable interest in the like manner and circumstances, and on the same date, as it would accrue if his interest were a legal estate in the land (and any relevant provision of Part I of Schedule 1 to this Act shall apply in any such case accordingly).

(2)   Where the period prescribed by this Act has expired for the bringing of an action to recover land by a tenant for life or a statutory owner of settled land—
  (a)   his legal estate shall not be extinguished if and so long as the right of action to recover the land of any person entitled to a beneficial interest in the land either has not accrued or has not been barred by this Act; and
  (b)   the legal estate shall accordingly remain vested in the tenant for life or statutory owner and shall devolve in accordance with the Settled Land Act 1925;

but if and when every such right of action has been barred by this Act, his legal estate shall be extinguished.

(3)   Where any land is held upon trust (including a trust for sale) and the period prescribed by this Act has expired for the bringing of an action to recover the land by the trustees, the estate of the trustees shall not be extinguished if and so long as the right of action to recover the land of any person entitled to a beneficial interest in the

land or in the proceeds of sale either has not accrued or has not been barred by this Act; but if and when every such right of action has been so barred the estate of the trustees shall be extinguished.

(4)   Where—
    (a)   any settled land is vested in a statutory owner; or
    (b)   any land is held upon trust (including a trust for sale);

an action to recover the land may be brought by the statutory owner or trustees on behalf of any person entitled to a beneficial interest in possession in the land or in the proceeds of sale whose right of action has not been barred by this Act, notwithstanding that the right of action of the statutory owner or trustees would apart from this provision have been barred by this Act.

[540]

19   Time limit for actions to recover rent

No action shall be brought, or distress made, to recover arrears of rent, or damages in respect of arrears of rent, after the expiration of six years from the date on which the arrears became due.

[541]

Actions to recover money secured by a mortgage or charge or to recover proceeds of the sale of land

20   Time limit for actions to recover money secured by a mortgage or charge or to recover proceeds of the sale of land

(1)   No action shall be brought to recover—
    (a)   any principal sum of money secured by a mortgage or other charge on property (whether real or personal); or
    (b)   proceeds of the sale of land;

after the expiration of twelve years from the date on which the right to receive the money accrued.

(2)   No foreclosure action in respect of mortgaged personal property shall be brought after the expiration of twelve years from the date on which the right to foreclose accrued.

But if the mortgagee was in possession of the mortgaged property after that date, the right to foreclose on the property which was in his possession shall not be treated as having accrued for the purposes of this subsection until the date on which his possession discontinued.

(3)   The right to receive any principal sum of money secured by a mortgage or other charge and the right to foreclose on the property subject to the mortgage or charge shall not be treated as accruing so long as that property comprises any future interest or any life insurance policy which has not matured or been determined.

(4)   Nothing in this section shall apply to a foreclosure action in respect of mortgaged land, but the provisions of this Act relating to actions to recover land shall apply to such an action.

(5)   Subject to subsections (6) and (7) below, no action to recover arrears of interest payable in respect of any sum of money secured by a mortgage or other charge or payable in respect of proceeds of the sale of land, or to recover damages in respect of such arrears shall be brought after the expiration of six years from the date on which the interest became due.

(6)   Where—

(a)   a prior mortgagee or other incumbrancer has been in possession of the property charged; and

(b)   an action is brought within one year of the discontinuance of that possession by the subsequent incumbrancer;

the subsequent incumbrancer may recover by that action all the arrears of interest which fell due during the period of possession by the prior incumbrancer or damages in respect of those arrears, notwithstanding that the period exceeded six years.

(7)   Where—

(a)   the property subject to the mortgage or charge comprises any future interest or life insurance policy; and

(b)   it is a term of the mortgage or charge that arrears of interest shall be treated as part of the principal sum of money secured by the mortgage or charge;

interest shall not be treated as becoming due before the right to recover the principal sum of money has accrued or is treated as having accrued.

[542]

Actions in respect of trust property or the personal estate of deceased persons

21   Time limit for actions in respect of trust property

(1)   No period of limitation prescribed by this Act shall apply to an action by a beneficiary under a trust, being an action—

(a)   in respect of any fraud or fraudulent breach of trust to which the trustee was a party or privy; or

(b)   to recover from the trustee trust property or the proceeds of trust property in the possession of the trustee, or previously received by the trustee and converted to his use.

(2)   Where a trustee who is also a beneficiary under the trust receives or retains trust property or its proceeds as his share on a distribution of trust property under the trust, his liability in any action brought by virtue of subsection (1)(b) above to recover that property or its proceeds after the expiration of the period of limitation prescribed by this Act for bringing an action to recover trust property shall be limited to the excess over his proper share.

This subsection only applies if the trustee acted honestly and reasonably in making the distribution.

(3)   Subject to the preceding provisions of this section, an action by a beneficiary to recover trust property or in respect of any breach of trust, not being an action for which a period of limitation is prescribed by any other provision of this Act, shall not be brought after the expiration of six years from the date on which the right of action accrued.

For the purposes of this subsection, the right of action shall not be treated as having accrued to any beneficiary entitled to a future interest in the trust property until the interest fell into possession.

(4)   No beneficiary as against whom there would be a good defence under this Act shall derive any greater or other benefit from a judgment or order obtained by any other beneficiary than he could have obtained if he had brought the action and this Act had been pleaded in defence.

PART II
EXTENSION OR EXCLUSION OF ORDINARY TIME LIMITS

Disability

28 Extension of limitation period in case of disability

(1)   Subject to the following provisions of this section, if on the date when any right of action accrued for which a period of limitation is prescribed by this Act, the person to whom it accrued was under a disability, the action may be brought at any time before the expiration of six years from the date when he ceased to be under a disability or died (whichever first occurred) notwithstanding that the period of limitation has expired.

(2)   This section shall not affect any case where the right of action first accrued to some person (not under a disability) through whom the person under a disability claims.

(3)   When a right of action which has accrued to a person under a disability accrues, on the death of that person while still under a disability, to another person under a disability, no further extension of time shall be allowed by reason of the disability of the second person.

(4)   No action to recover land or money charged on land shall be brought by virtue of this section by any person after the expiration of thirty years from the date on which the right of action accrued to that person or some person through whom he claims.

[(4A)   If the action is one to which section 4A of this Act applies, subsection (1) above shall have effect as if for the words from "at any time" to "occurred)" there were substituted the words "by him at any time before the expiration of three years from the date when he ceased to be under a disability".]

(5)   If the action is one to which section 10 of this Act applies, subsection (1) above shall have effect as if for the words "six years" there were substituted the words "two years".

(6)   If the action is one to which section 11 or 12(2) of this Act applies, subsection (1) above shall have effect as if for the words "six years" there were substituted the words "three years".

[(7)   If the action is one to which section 11A of this Act applies or one by virtue of section 6(1)(a) of the Consumer Protection Act 1987 (death caused by defective product), subsection (1) above—

(a)   shall not apply to the time limit prescribed by subsection (3) of the said section 11A or to that time limit as applied by virtue of section 12(1) of this Act; and

(b)   in relation to any other time limit prescribed by this Act shall have effect as if for the words "six years" there were substituted the words "three years".]

[544]

NOTES
   Sub-s (4A): inserted by the Administration of Justice Act 1985, s 57(3).
   Sub-s (7): added by the Consumer Protection Act 1987, s 6, Sch 1, Pt I, para 4.

[28A Extension for cases where the limitation period is the period under section 14A(4)(b)

(1)   Subject to subsection (2) below, if in the case of any action for which a period of limitation is prescribed by section 14A of this Act—

    (a) the period applicable in accordance with subsection (4) of that section is the period mentioned in paragraph (b) of that subsection;

    (b) on the date which is for the purposes of that section the starting date for reckoning that period the person by reference to whose knowledge that date fell to be determined under subsection (5) of that section was under a disability; and

    (c) section 28 of this Act does not apply to the action;

the action may be brought at any time before the expiration of three years from the date when he ceased to be under a disability or died (whichever first occurred) notwithstanding that the period mentioned above has expired.

(2)   An action may not be brought by virtue of subsection (1) above after the end of the period of limitation prescribed by section 14B of this Act.]

[545]

NOTES

Inserted by the Latent Damage Act 1986, s 2(1).

<hr>

Acknowledgment and part payment

29   Fresh accrual of action on acknowledgment or part payment

(1)   Subsections (2) and (3) below apply where any right of action (including a foreclosure action) to recover land or an advowson or any right of a mortgagee of personal property to bring a foreclosure action in respect of the property has accrued.

(2)   If the person in possession of the land, benefice or personal property in question acknowledges the title of the person to whom the right of action has accrued—

    (a) the right shall be treated as having accrued on and not before the date of the acknowledgment; and

    (b) in the case of a right of action to recover land which has accrued to a person entitled to an estate or interest taking effect on the determination of an entailed interest against whom time is running under section 27 of this Act, section 27 shall thereupon cease to apply to the land.

(3)   In the case of a foreclosure or other action by a mortgagee, if the person in possession of the land, benefice or personal property in question or the person liable for the mortgage debt makes any payment in respect of the debt (whether of principal or interest) the right shall be treated as having accrued on and not before the date of the payment.

(4)   Where a mortgagee is by virtue of the mortgage in possession of any mortgaged land and either—

    (a) receives any sum in respect of the principal or interest of the mortgage debt; or

    (b) acknowledges the title of the mortgagor, or his equity of redemption;

an action to redeem the land in his possession may be brought at any time before the expiration of twelve years from the date of the payment or acknowledgment.

(5)   Subject to subsection (6) below, where any right of action has accrued to recover—

    (a) any debt or other liquidated pecuniary claim; or

    (b) any claim to the personal estate of a deceased person or to any share or interest in any such estate;

and the person liable or accountable for the claim acknowledges the claim or makes any payment in respect of it the right shall be treated as having accrued on and not before the date of the acknowledgment or payment.

(6)   A payment of a part of the rent or interest due at any time shall not extend the period for claiming the remainder then due, but any payment of interest shall be treated as a payment in respect of the principal debt.

(7)   Subject to subsection (6) above, a current period of limitation may be repeatedly extended under this section by further acknowledgments or payments, but a right of action, once barred by this Act, shall not be revived by any subsequent acknowledgment or payment.

[546]

30   Formal provisions as to acknowledgments and part payments

(1)   To be effective for the purposes of section 29 of this Act, an acknowledgment must be in writing and signed by the person making it.

(2)   For the purposes of section 29, any acknowledgment or payment—
     (a)   may be made by the agent of the person by whom it is required to be made under that section; and
     (b)   shall be made to the person, or to an agent of the person, whose title or claim is being acknowledged or, as the case may be, in respect of whose claim the payment is being made.

[547]

31   Effect of acknowledgment or part payment on persons other than the maker or recipient

(1)   An acknowledgment of the title to any land, benefice, or mortgaged personalty by any person in possession of it shall bind all other persons in possession during the ensuing period of limitation.

(2)   A payment in respect of a mortgage debt by the mortgagor or any other person liable for the debt, or by any person in possession of the mortgaged property, shall, so far as any right of the mortgagee to foreclose or otherwise to recover the property is concerned, bind all other persons in possession of the mortgaged property during the ensuing period of limitation.

(3)   Where two or more mortgagees are by virtue of the mortgage in possession of the mortgaged land, an acknowledgment of the mortgagor's title or of his equity of redemption by one of the mortgagees shall only bind him and his successors and shall not bind any other mortgagee or his successors.

(4)   Where in a case within subsection (3) above the mortgagee by whom the acknowledgment is given is entitled to a part of the mortgaged land and not to any ascertained part of the mortgage debt the mortgagor shall be entitled to redeem that part of the land on payment, with interest, of the part of the mortgage debt which bears the same proportion to the whole of the debt as the value of the part of the land bears to the whole of the mortgaged land.

(5)   Where there are two or more mortgagors, and the title or equity of redemption of one of the mortgagors is acknowledged as mentioned above in this section, the acknowledgment shall be treated as having been made to all the mortgagors.

(6)   An acknowledgment of any debt or other liquidated pecuniary claim shall bind the acknowledgor and his successors but not any other person.

(7)   A payment made in respect of any debt or other liquidated pecuniary claim shall bind all persons liable in respect of the debt or claim.

(8)   An acknowledgment by one of several personal representatives of any claim to the personal estate of a deceased person or to any share or interest in any such estate, or a payment by one of several personal representatives in respect of any such claim, shall bind the estate of the deceased person.

(9)   In this section "successor", in relation to any mortgagee or person liable in respect of any debt or claim, means his personal representatives and any other person on whom the rights under the mortgage or, as the case may be, the liability in respect of the debt or claim devolve (whether on death or bankruptcy or the disposition of property or the determination of a limited estate or interest in settled property or otherwise).

[548]

Fraud, concealment and mistake

32   Postponement of limitation period in case of fraud, concealment or mistake

(1)   Subject to [subsections (3) and (4A)] below, where in the case of any action for which a period of limitation is prescribed by this Act, either—
- (a)   the action is based upon the fraud of the defendant; or
- (b)   any fact relevant to the plaintiff's right of action has been deliberately concealed from him by the defendant; or
- (c)   the action is for relief from the consequences of a mistake;

the period of limitation shall not begin to run until the plaintiff has discovered the fraud, concealment or mistake (as the case may be) or could with reasonable diligence have discovered it.

References in this subsection to the defendant include references to the defendant's agent and to any person through whom the defendant claims and his agent.

(2)   For the purposes of subsection (1) above, deliberate commission of a breach of duty in circumstances in which it is unlikely to be discovered for some time amounts to deliberate concealment of the facts involved in that breach of duty.

(3)   Nothing in this section shall enable any action—
- (a)   to recover, or recover the value of, any property; or
- (b)   to enforce any charge against, or set aside any transaction affecting, any property;

to be brought against the purchaser of the property or any person claiming through him in any case where the property has been purchased for valuable consideration by an innocent third party since the fraud or concealment or (as the case may be) the transaction in which the mistake was made took place.

(4)   A purchaser is an innocent third party for the purposes of this section—
- (a)   in the case of fraud or concealment of any fact relevant to the plaintiff's right of action, if he was not a party to the fraud or (as the case may be) to the concealment of that fact and did not at the time of the purchase know or have reason to believe that the fraud or concealment had taken place; and

(b) in the case of mistake, if he did not at the time of the purchase know or have reason to believe that the mistake had been made.

[(4A) Subsection (1) above shall not apply in relation to the time limit prescribed by section 11A(3) of this Act or in relation to that time limit as applied by virtue of section 12(1) of this Act].

[(5) Sections 14A and 14B of this Act shall not apply to any action to which subsection (1)(b) above applies (and accordingly the period of limitation referred to in that subsection, in any case to which either of those sections would otherwise apply, is the period applicable under section 2 of this Act).]

[549]

NOTES

Sub-s (1): words in square brackets substituted by the Consumer Protection Act 1987, s 6, Sch 1, Pt I, para 5(a).

Sub-s (4A): inserted by the Consumer Protection Act 1987, s 6, Sch 1, Pt I, para 5(b).

Sub-s (5): added by the Latent Damage Act 1986, s 2(2).

PART III
MISCELLANEOUS AND GENERAL

36 Equitable jurisdiction and remedies

(1) The following time limits under this Act, that is to say—
  (a) the time limit under section 2 for actions founded on tort;
  [(aa) the time limit under section 4A for actions for libel or slander;]
  (b) the time limit under section 5 for actions founded on simple contract;
  (c) the time limit under section 7 for actions to enforce awards where the submission is not by an instrument under seal;
  (d) the time limit under section 8 for actions on a specialty;
  (e) the time limit under section 9 for actions to recover a sum recoverable by virtue of any enactment; and
  (f) the time limit under section 24 for actions to enforce a judgment;

shall not apply to any claim for specific performance of a contract or for an injunction or for other equitable relief, except in so far as any such time limit may be applied by the court by analogy in like manner as the corresponding time limit under any enactment repealed by the Limitation Act 1939 was applied before 1st July 1940.

(2) Nothing in this Act shall affect any equitable jurisdiction to refuse relief on the ground of acquiescence or otherwise.

[550]

NOTES

Sub-s (1): para (aa) inserted by the Administration of Justice Act 1985, s 57(5).

38 Interpretation

(1) In this Act, unless the context otherwise requires—
  "action" includes any proceeding in a court of law, including an ecclesiastical court;
  "land" includes corporeal hereditaments, tithes and rentcharges and any legal or equitable estate or interest therein, including an interest in the proceeds of the sale of land held upon trust for sale, but except as provided above in this definition does not include any incorporeal hereditament;

"personal estate" and "personal property" do not include chattels real;

"personal injuries" includes any disease and any impairment of a person's physical or mental condition, and "injury" and cognate expressions shall be construed accordingly;

"rent" includes a rentcharge and a rentservice;

"rentcharge" means any annuity or periodical sum of money charged upon or payable out of land, except a rent service or interest on a mortgage on land;

"settled land", "statutory owner" and "tenant for life" have the same meanings respectively as in the Settled Land Act 1925;

"trust" and "trustee" have the same meanings respectively as in the Trustee Act 1925; and

"trust for sale" has the same meaning as in the Law of Property Act 1925.

(2) For the purposes of this Act a person shall be treated as under a disability while he is an infant, or of unsound mind.

(3) For the purposes of subsection (2) above a person is of unsound mind if he is a person who, by reason of mental disorder within the meaning of the [Mental Health Act 1983], is incapable of managing and administering his property and affairs.

(4) Without prejudice to the generality of subsection (3) above, a person shall be conclusively presumed for the purposes of subsection (2) above to be of unsound mind—

(a) while he is liable to be detained or subject to guardianship under [the Mental Health Act 1983 (otherwise than by virtue of section 35 or 89)]; and

[(b) while he is receiving treatment as an in-patient in any hospital within the meaning of the Mental Health Act 1983 or mental nursing home within the meaning of the Nursing Homes Act 1975 without being liable to be detained under the said Act of 1983 (otherwise than by virtue of section 35 or 89), being treatment which follows without any interval a period during which he was liable to be detained or subject to guardianship under the Mental Health Act 1959, or the said Act of 1983 (otherwise than by virtue of section 35 or 89) or by virtue of any enactment repealed or excluded by the Mental Health Act 1959].

(5) Subject to subsection (6) below, a person shall be treated as claiming through another person if he became entitled by, through, under, or by the act of that other person to the right claimed, and any person whose estate or interest might have been barred by a person entitled to an entailed interest in possession shall be treated as claiming through the person so entitled.

(6) A person becoming entitled to any estate or interest by virtue of a special power of appointment shall not be treated as claiming through the appointor.

(7) References in this Act to a right of action to recover land shall include references to a right to enter into possession of the land or, in the case of rentcharges and tithes, to distrain for arrears of rent or tithe, and references to the bringing of such an action shall include references to the making of such an entry or distress.

(8) References in this Act to the possession of land shall, in the case of tithes and rentcharges, be construed as references to the receipt of the tithe or rent, and references to the date of dispossession or discontinuance of possession of land shall, in the case of rent charges, be construed as references to the date of the last receipt of rent.

(9)   References in Part II of this Act to a right of action shall include references to—
    (a)   a cause of action;
    (b)   a right to receive money secured by a mortgage or charge on any property;
    (c)   a right to recover proceeds of the sale of land; and
    (d)   a right to receive a share or interest in the personal estate of a deceased person.

(10)   References in Part II to the date of the accrual of a right of action shall be construed—
    (a)   in the case of an action upon a judgment, as references to the date on which the judgment became enforceable; and
    (b)   in the case of an action to recover arrears of rent or interest, or damages in respect of arrears of rent or interest, as references to the date on which the rent or interest became due.

[551]

NOTES

Sub-ss (3), (4): words in square brackets substituted by the Mental Health Act 1983, s 148, Sch 4, para 55.

---

41   Short title, commencement and extent

(1)   This Act may be cited as the Limitation Act 1980.

(2)   This Act, except section 35, shall come into force on 1st May 1981.

(3)   Section 35 of this Act shall come into force on 1st May 1981 to the extent (if any) that the section substituted for section 28 of the Limitation Act 1939 by section 8 of the Limitation Amendment Act 1980 is in force immediately before that date; but otherwise section 35 shall come into force on such day as the Lord Chancellor may by order made by statutory instrument appoint, and different days may be appointed for different purposes of that section (including its application in relation to different courts or proceedings).

(4)   The repeal by this Act of section 14(1) of the Limitation Act 1963 and the corresponding saving in paragraph 2 of Schedule 2 to this Act shall extend to Northern Ireland, but otherwise this Act does not extend to Scotland or to Northern Ireland.

[552]

SCHEDULE 1
PROVISIONS WITH RESPECT TO ACTIONS TO RECOVER LAND
Section 15(6), (7)

PART I
ACCRUAL OF RIGHTS OF ACTION TO RECOVER LAND

Accrual of right of action in case of present interests in land

1.   Where the person bringing an action to recover land, or some person through whom he claims, has been in possession of the land, and has while entitled to the land been dispossessed or discontinued his possession, the right of action shall be treated as having accrued on the date of the dispossession or discontinuance.

2.   Where any person brings an action to recover any land of a deceased person (whether under a will or on intestacy) and the deceased person—
    (a)   was on the date of his death in possession of the land or, in the case of a rentcharge created by will or taking effect upon his death, in possession of the land charged; and
    (b)   was the last person entitled to the land to be in possession of it;

the right of action shall be treated as having accrued on the date of his death.

3. Where any person brings an action to recover land, being an estate or interest in possession assured otherwise than by will to him, or to some person through whom he claims, and—

    (a) the person making the assurance was on the date when the assurance took effect in possession of the land or, in the case of a rentcharge created by the assurance, in possession of the land charged; and

    (b) no person has been in possession of the land by virtue of the assurance;

the right of action shall be treated as having accrued on the date when the assurance took effect.

Accrual of right of action in case of future interests

4. The right of action to recover any land shall, in a case where—

    (a) the estate or interest claimed was an estate or interest in reversion or remainder or any other future estate or interest; and

    (b) no person has taken possession of the land by virtue of the estate or interest claimed;

be treated as having accrued on the date on which the estate or interest fell into possession by the determination of the preceding estate or interest.

5.—(1) Subject to sub-paragraph (2) below, a tenancy from year to year or other period, without a lease in writing, shall for the purposes of this Act be treated as being determined at the expiration of the first year or other period; and accordingly the right of action of the person entitled to the land subject to the tenancy shall be treated as having accrued at the date on which in accordance with this sub-paragraph the tenancy is determined.

(2) Where any rent has subsequently been received in respect of the tenancy, the right of action shall be treated as having accrued on the date of the last receipt of rent.

6.—(1) Where—

    (a) any person is in possession of land by virtue of a lease in writing by which a rent of not less than ten pounds a year is reserved; and

    (b) the rent is received by some person wrongfully claiming to be entitled to the land in reversion immediately expectant on the determination of the lease; and

    (c) no rent is subsequently received by the person rightfully so entitled;

the right of action to recover the land of the person rightfully so entitled shall be treated as having accrued on the date when the rent was first received by the person wrongfully claiming to be so entitled and not on the date of the determination of the lease.

(2) Sub-paragraph (1) above shall not apply to any lease granted by the Crown.

Accrual of right of action in case of forfeiture or breach of condition

7.—(1) Subject to sub-paragraph (2) below, a right of action to recover land by virtue of a forfeiture or breach of condition shall be treated as having accrued on the date on which the forfeiture was incurred or the condition broken.

(2) If any such right has accrued to a person entitled to an estate or interest in reversion or remainder and the land was not recovered by virtue of that right, the right of action to recover the land shall not be treated as having accrued to that person until his estate or interest fell into possession, as if no such forfeiture or breach of condition had occurred.

Right of action not to accrue or continue unless there is adverse possession

8.—(1) No right of action to recover land shall be treated as accruing unless the land is in the possession of some person in whose favour the period of limitation can run (referred to below in this paragraph as "adverse possession"); and where under the preceding provisions of this Schedule any such right of action is treated as accruing on a certain date and no person is in adverse possession on that date, the right of action shall not be treated as accruing unless and until adverse possession is taken of the land.

(2)   Where a right of action to recover land has accrued and after its accrual, before the right is barred, the land ceases to be in adverse possession, the right of action shall no longer be treated as having accrued and no fresh right of action shall be treated as accruing unless and until the land is again taken into adverse possession.

(3)   For the purposes of this paragraph—
  (a)   possession of any land subject to a rentcharge by a person (other than the person entitled to the rentcharge) who does not pay the rent shall be treated as adverse possession of the rentcharge; and
  (b)   receipt of rent under a lease by a person wrongfully claiming to be entitled to the land in reversion immediately expectant on the determination of the lease shall be treated as adverse possession of the land.

(4)   For the purpose of determining whether a person occupying any land is in adverse possession of the land it shall not be assumed by implication of law that his occupation is by permission of the person entitled to the land merely by virtue of the fact that his occupation is not inconsistent with the latter's present or future enjoyment of the land.

This provision shall not be taken as prejudicing a finding to the effect that a person's occupation of any land is by implied permission of the person entitled to the land in any case where such a finding is justified on the actual facts of the case.

Possession of beneficiary not adverse to others interested in settled land or land held on trust for sale

9.   Where any settled land or any land held on trust for sale is in the possession of a person entitled to a beneficial interest in the land or in the proceeds of sale (not being a person solely or absolutely entitled to the land or the proceeds), no right of action to recover the land shall be treated for the purposes of this Act as accruing during that possession to any person in whom the land is vested as tenant for life, statutory owner or trustee, or to any other person entitled to a beneficial interest in the land or the proceeds of sale.

[553]

Part II
Modifications of Section 15 where Crown or Certain Corporations Sole are Involved

10.   Subject to paragraph 11 below, section 15(1) of this Act shall apply to the bringing of an action to recover any land by the Crown or by any spiritual or eleemosynary corporation sole with the substitution for the reference to twelve years of a reference to thirty years.

11.—(1) An action to recover foreshore may be brought by the Crown at any time before the expiration of sixty years from the date mentioned in section 15(1) of this Act.

(2)   Where any right of action to recover land which has ceased to be foreshore but remains in the ownership of the Crown accrued when the land was foreshore, the action may be brought at any time before the expiration of—
  (a)   sixty years from the date of accrual of the right of action; or
  (b)   thirty years from the date when the land ceased to be foreshore;
whichever period first expires.

(3)   In this paragraph "foreshore" means the shore and bed of the sea and of any tidal water, below the line of the medium high tide between the spring tides and the neap tides.

12. Notwithstanding section 15(1) of this Act, where in the case of any action brought by a person other than the Crown or a spiritual or eleemosynary corporation sole the right of action first accrued to the Crown or any such corporation sole through whom the person in question claims, the action may be brought at any time before the expiration of—
  (a)   the period during which the action could have been brought by the Crown or the corporation sole; or
  (b)   twelve years from the date on which the right of action accrued to some person other than the Crown or the corporation sole;
whichever period first expires.

13. Section 15(2) of this Act shall apply in any case where the Crown or a spiritual or eleemosynary corporation sole is entitled to the succeeding estate or interest with the substitution—

(a)   for the reference to twelve years of a reference to thirty years; and

(b)   for the reference to six years of a reference to twelve years.

[554]

SUPREME COURT ACT 1981

(C 54)

An Act to consolidate with amendments the Supreme Court of Judicature (Consolidation) Act 1925 and other enactments relating to the Supreme Court in England and Wales and the administration of justice therein; to repeal certain obsolete or unnecessary enactments so relating; to amend Part VIII of the Mental Health Act 1959, the Courts-Martial (Appeals) Act 1968, the Arbitration Act 1979 and the law relating to county courts; and for connected purposes

[28 July 1981]

PART II
JURISDICTION

THE HIGH COURT

Powers

38   Relief against forfeiture for non-payment of rent

(1)   In any action in the High Court for the forfeiture of a lease for non-payment of rent, the court shall have power to grant relief against forfeiture in a summary manner, and may do so subject to the same terms and conditions as to the payment of rent, costs or otherwise as could have been imposed by it in such an action immediately before the commencement of this Act.

(2)   Where the lessee or a person deriving title under him is granted relief under this section, he shall hold the demised premises in accordance with the terms of the lease without the necessity for a new lease.

[555]

PART VI
MISCELLANEOUS AND SUPPLEMENTARY

Supplementary

153   Citation, commencement and extent

(1)   This Act may be cited as the Supreme Court Act 1981.

(2)   This Act, except the provisions mentioned in subsection (3), shall come into force on 1st January 1982; and references to the commencement of this Act shall be construed as references to the beginning of that day.

(3)–(5)   . . .

[556]

NOTES

Sub-ss (3)–(5): not relevant to this work.

ADMINISTRATION OF JUSTICE ACT 1982

(C 53)

An Act to make further provision with respect to the administration of justice and matters connected therewith; to amend the law relating to actions for damages for personal injuries, including injuries resulting in death, and to abolish certain actions for loss of services; to amend the law relating to wills; to make further provision with respect to funds in court, statutory deposits and schemes for the common investment of such funds and deposits and certain other funds; to amend the law relating to deductions by employers under attachment of earnings orders; to make further provision with regard to penalties that may be awarded by the Solicitors' Disciplinary Tribunal under section 47 of the Solicitors Act 1974; to make further provision for the appointment of justices of the peace in England and Wales and in relation to temporary vacancies in the membership of the Law Commission; to enable the title register kept by the Chief Land Registrar to be kept otherwise than in documentary form; and to authorise the payment of travelling, subsistence and financial loss allowances for justices of the peace in Northern Ireland

[28 October 1982]

PART IV
WILLS

Rectification and interpretation of wills

20   Rectification

(1)   If a court is satisfied that a will is so expressed that it fails to carry out the testator's intentions, in consequence—

    (a)   of a clerical error; or

    (b)   of a failure to understand his instructions,

it may order that the will shall be rectified so as to carry out his intentions.

(2)   An application for an order under this section shall not, except with the permission of the court, be made after the end of the period of six months from the date on which representation with respect to the estate of the deceased is first taken out.

(3)   The provisions of this section shall not render the personal representatives of a deceased person liable for having distributed any part of the estate of the deceased, after the end of the period of six months from the date on which representation with respect to the estate of the deceased is first taken out, on the ground that they ought to have taken into account the possibility that the court might permit the making of an application for an order under this section after the end of that period; but this subsection shall not prejudice any power to recover, by reason of the making of an order under this section, any part of the estate so distributed.

(4)   In considering for the purposes of this section when representation with respect to the estate of a deceased person was first taken out, a grant limited to settled land or to trust property shall be left out of account, and a grant limited to real estate or to personal estate shall be left out of account unless a grant limited to the remainder of the estate has previously been made or is made at the same time.

Registration of wills

25 Regulations as to deposit and registration of wills

(1) Regulations may make provision—
  (a) as to the conditions for the deposit of a will;
  (b) as to the manner of and procedure for—
    (i) the deposit and registration of a will; and
    (ii) the withdrawal of a will which has been deposited; and
    (iii) the cancellation of the registration of a will; and
  (c) as to the manner in which the Principal Registry of the Family Division is to perform its functions as the national body under the Registration Convention.

(2) Regulations under this section may contain such incidental or supplementary provisions as the authority making the regulations considers appropriate.

(3) Any such regulations are to be made—
  (a) for England and Wales, by the President of the Family Division of the High Court of Justice, with the concurrence of the Lord Chancellor;
  (b) for Scotland, by the Secretary of State after consultation with the Lord President of the Court of Session; and
  (c) for Northern Ireland, by the Northern Ireland Supreme Court Rules Committee, with the concurrence of the Lord Chancellor.

(4) Regulations made by virtue of subsection (1)(c) above shall be made by the Lord Chancellor.

(5) Subject to subsection (6) below, regulations under this section shall be made by statutory instrument and shall be laid before Parliament after being made.

(6) Regulations for Northern Ireland shall be statutory rules for the purposes of the Statutory Rules (Northern Ireland) Order 1979; and any such statutory rule shall be laid before Parliament after being made in like manner as a statutory instrument and section 4 of the Statutory Instruments Act 1946 shall apply accordingly.

(7) The Statutory Instruments Act 1946 shall apply to a statutory instrument containing regulations made in accordance with subsection (3)(a) or (c) above as if the regulations had been made by a Minister of the Crown.

(8) Any regulations made under section 172 of the Supreme Court of Judicature (Consolidation) Act 1925 or section 126 of the Supreme Court Act 1981 shall have effect for the purposes of this Part of this Act as they have effect for the purposes of the enactment under which they were made.

[558]

NOTES

Commencement: to be appointed.

PART IX
GENERAL AND SUPPLEMENTARY

76 Commencement

(1) The provisions of this Act specified in subsection (2) below shall come into operation on such day as the Lord Chancellor may by order appoint.

(2)　...

(3)　The provisions of this Act specified in subsection (4) below shall come into operation on such day as the Secretary of State may by order appoint.

(4)–(6)　...

(7)　Any order under this section shall be made by statutory instrument.

(8)　Any such order may appoint different days for different provisions and for different purposes.

(9)　The provisions of this Act specified in subsection (10) below shall come into operation on the day this Act is passed.

(10)　...

(11)　Subject to the foregoing provisions of this section, this Act shall come into operation on 1st January 1983.

[559]

NOTES

Sub-ss (2), (4)–(6), (10): not relevant to this work.

78　Citation

This Act may be cited as the Administration of Justice Act 1982.

[560]

MATRIMONIAL HOMES ACT 1983

(C 19)

An Act to consolidate certain enactments relating to the rights of a husband or wife to occupy a dwelling house that has been a matrimonial home

[9 May 1983]

1　Rights concerning matrimonial home where one spouse has no estate, etc

(1)　Where one spouse is entitled to occupy a dwelling house by virtue of a beneficial estate or interest or contract or by virtue of any enactment giving him or her the right to remain in occupation, and the other spouse is not so entitled, then, subject to the provisions of this Act, the spouse not so entitled shall have the following rights (in this Act referred to as "rights of occupation")—

    (a)　if in occupation, a right not to be evicted or excluded from the dwelling house or any part thereof by the other spouse except with the leave of the court given by an order under this section;

    (b)　if not in occupation, a right with the leave of the court so given to enter into and occupy the dwelling house.

(2)　So long as one spouse has rights of occupation, either of the spouses may apply to the court for an order—

    (a)　declaring, enforcing, restricting or terminating those rights, or

    (b)　prohibiting, suspending or restricting the exercise by either spouse of the right to occupy the dwelling house, or

    (c)　requiring either spouse to permit the exercise by the other of that right.

(3)   On an application for an order under this section, the court may make such order as it thinks just and reasonable having regard to the conduct of the spouses in relation to each other and otherwise, to their respective needs and financial resources, to the needs of any children and to all the circumstances of the case, and, without prejudice to the generality of the foregoing provision—

  (a) may except part of the dwelling house from a spouse's rights of occupation (and in particular a part used wholly or mainly for or in connection with the trade, business or profession of the other spouse),

  (b) may order a spouse occupying the dwelling house or any part thereof by virtue of this section to make periodical payments to the other in respect of the occupation,

  (c) may impose on either spouse obligations as to the repair and maintenance of the dwelling house or the discharge of any liabilities in respect of the dwelling house.

(4)   Orders under this section may, in so far as they have a continuing effect, be limited so as to have effect for a period specified in the order or until further order.

(5)   Where a spouse is entitled under this section to occupy a dwelling house or any part thereof, any payment or tender made or other thing done by that spouse in or towards satisfaction of any liability of the other spouse in respect of rent, rates, mortgage payments or other outgoings affecting the dwelling house shall, whether or not it is made or done in pursuance of an order under this section, be as good as if made or done by the other spouse.

(6)   A spouse's occupation by virtue of this section shall, for the purposes of the Rent (Agriculture) Act 1976, and of the Rent Act 1977 (other than Part V and sections 103 to 106), be treated as possession by the other spouse and [for the purposes of Part IV of the Housing Act 1985 [and Part I of the Housing Act 1988] (secure tenancies)] be treated as occupation by the other spouse.

(7)   Where a spouse is entitled under this section to occupy a dwelling house or any part thereof and makes any payment in or towards satisfaction of any liability of the other spouse in respect of mortgage payments affecting the dwelling house, the person to whom the payment is made may treat it as having been made by that other spouse, but the fact that that person has treated any such payment as having been so made shall not affect any claim of the first-mentioned spouse against the other to an interest in the dwelling house by virtue of the payment.

(8)   Where a spouse is entitled under this section to occupy a dwelling house or part thereof by reason of an interest of the other spouse under a trust, all the provisions of subsections (5) to (7) above shall apply in relation to the trustees as they apply in relation to the other spouse.

(9)   The jurisdiction conferred on the court by this section shall be exercisable by the High Court or by a county court, and shall be exercisable by a county court notwithstanding that by reason of the amount of the net annual value for rating of the dwelling house or otherwise the jurisdiction would not but for this subsection be exercisable by a county court.

(10)   This Act shall not apply to a dwelling house which has at no time been a matrimonial home of the spouses in question; and a spouse's rights of occupation shall continue only so long as the marriage subsists and the other spouse is entitled as mentioned in subsection (1) above to occupy the dwelling house, except where provision is made by section 2 of this Act for those rights to be a charge on an estate or interest in the dwelling house.

(11) It is hereby declared that a spouse who has an equitable interest in a dwelling house or in the proceeds of sale thereof, not being a spouse in whom is vested (whether solely or as a joint tenant) a legal estate in fee simple or a legal term of years absolute in the dwelling house, is to be treated for the purpose only of determining whether he or she has rights of occupation under this section as not being entitled to occupy the dwelling house by virtue of that interest.

[561]

NOTES

Sub-s (6): words in first (outer) pair of square brackets substituted by the Housing (Consequential Provisions) Act 1985, s 4, Sch 2, para 56, words in square brackets therein inserted by the Housing Act 1988, s 140(1), Sch 17, Pt I, para 33.

Modified for certain purposes by the Insolvency Act 1986, ss 336, 337.

2   Effect of rights of occupation as charge on dwelling house

(1)   Where, at any time during the subsistence of a marriage, one spouse is entitled to occupy a dwelling house by virtue of a beneficial estate or interest, then the other spouse's rights of occupation shall be a charge on that estate or interest, having the like priority as if it were an equitable interest created at whichever is the latest of the following dates, that is to say—

    (a)   the date when the spouse so entitled acquires the estate or interest,

    (b)   the date of the marriage, and

    (c)   the 1st January 1968 (which is the date of commencement of the Act of 1967).

(2)   If, at any time when a spouse's rights of occupation are a charge on an interest of the other spouse under a trust, there are, apart from either of the spouses, no persons, living or unborn, who are or could become beneficiaries under the trust, then those rights shall be a charge also on the estate or interest of the trustees for the other spouse, having the like priority as if it were an equitable interest created (under powers overriding the trusts) on the date when it arises.

(3)   In determining for purposes of subsection (2) above whether there are any persons who are not, but could become, beneficiaries under the trust, there shall be disregarded any potential exercise of a general power of appointment exercisable by either or both of the spouses alone (whether or not the exercise of it requires the consent of another person).

(4)   Notwithstanding that a spouse's rights of occupation are a charge on an estate or interest in the dwelling house, those rights shall be brought to an end by—

    (a)   the death of the other spouse, or

    (b)   the termination (otherwise than by death) of the marriage,

unless in the event of a matrimonial dispute or estrangement the court sees fit to direct otherwise by an order made under section 1 above during the subsistence of the marriage.

(5)   Where a spouse's rights of occupation are a charge on the estate or interest of the other spouse or of trustees for the other spouse—

    (a)   any order under section 1 above against the other spouse shall, except in so far as the contrary intention appears, have the like effect against persons deriving title under the other spouse or under the trustees and affected by the charge, and

    (b)   subsections (2) to (8) of section 1 above shall apply in relation to any person deriving title under the other spouse or under the trustees and affected by the charge as they apply in relation to the other spouse.

(6) Where—
    (a)   a spouse's rights of occupation are a charge on an estate or interest in the dwelling house, and
    (b)   that estate or interest is surrendered so as to merge in some other estate or interest expectant thereon in such circumstances that, but for the merger, the person taking the estate or interest surrendered would be bound by the charge,

the surrender shall have effect subject to the charge and the persons thereafter entitled to the other estate or interest shall, for so long as the estate or interest surrendered would have endured if not so surrendered, be treated for all purposes of this Act as deriving title to the other estate or interest under the other spouse or, as the case may be, under the trustees for the other spouse, by virtue of the surrender.

(7)   . . .

(8)   Where the title to the legal estate by virtue of which a spouse is entitled to occupy a dwelling house (including any legal estate held by trustees for that spouse) is registered under the Land Registration Act 1925 or any enactment replaced by that Act—
    (a)   registration of a land charge affecting the dwelling house by virtue of this Act shall be effected by registering a notice under that Act, and
    (b)   a spouse's rights of occupation shall not be an overriding interest within the meaning of that Act affecting the dwelling house notwithstanding that the spouse is in actual occupation of the dwelling house.

(9)   A spouse's rights of occupation (whether or not constituting a charge) shall not entitle that spouse to lodge a caution under section 54 of the Land Registration Act 1925.

(10) Where—
    (a)   a spouse's rights of occupation are a charge on the estate of the other spouse or of trustees for the other spouse, and
    (b)   that estate is the subject of a mortgage within the meaning of the Law of Property Act 1925,

then, if, after the date of creation of the mortgage, the charge is registered under section 2 of the Land Charges Act 1972, the charge shall, for the purposes of section 94 of that Act of 1925 (which regulates the rights of mortgagees to make further advances ranking in priority to subsequent mortgages), be deemed to be a mortgage subsequent in date to the first-mentioned mortgage.

(11) It is hereby declared that a charge under subsection (1) or (2) above is not registrable under section 2 of the Land Charges Act 1972 or subsection (8) above unless it is a charge on a legal estate.

[562]

NOTES
Sub-s (7): repealed by the Insolvency Act 1985, s 235(3), Sch 10, Pt III.

4   Contract for sale of house affected by registered charge to include term requiring cancellation of registration before completion

(1)   Where one spouse is entitled by virtue of section 2 above to a charge on an estate in a dwelling house and the charge is registered under section 2 of the Land Charges Act 1972 or section 2(8) above, it shall be a term of any contract for the sale

of that estate whereby the vendor agrees to give vacant possession of the dwelling house on completion of the contract that the vendor will before such completion procure the cancellation of the registration of the charge at his expense.

(2)   Subsection (1) above shall not apply to any such contract made by a vendor who is entitled to sell the estate in the dwelling house freed from any such charge.

(3)   If, on the completion of such a contract as is referred to in subsection (1) above, there is delivered to the purchaser or his solicitor an application by the spouse entitled to the charge for the cancellation of the registration of that charge, the term of the contract for which subsection (1) above provides shall be deemed to have been performed.

(4)   This section applies only if and so far as a contrary intention is not expressed in the contract.

(5)   This section shall apply to a contract for exchange as it applies to a contract for sale.

(6)   This section shall, with the necessary modifications, apply to a contract for the grant of a lease or underlease of a dwelling house as it applies to a contract for the sale of an estate in a dwelling house.

[563]

NOTES
Modified by the Building Societies Act 1986, s 124, Sch 21, paras 9, 12.

13   Short title, commencement and extent

(1)   This Act may be cited as the Matrimonial Homes Act 1983.

(2)   This Act shall come into force at the end of the period of three months beginning with the day on which it is passed.

(3)   This Act does not extend to Scotland or Northern Ireland.

[564]

COUNTY COURTS ACT 1984

(C 28)

An Act to consolidate certain enactments relating to county courts

[26 June 1984]

PART IX
MISCELLANEOUS AND GENERAL

Forfeiture for non-payment of rent

138   Provisions as to forfeiture for non-payment of rent

(1)   This section has effect where a lessor is proceeding by action in a county court (being an action in which the county court has jurisdiction) to enforce against a lessee a right of re-entry or forfeiture in respect of any land for non-payment of rent.

(2)   If the lessee pays into court [or to the lessor] not less than 5 clear days before the return day all the rent in arrear and the costs of the action, the action shall cease, and the lessee shall hold the land according to the lease without any new lease.

(3)   If—
(a)   the action does not cease under subsection (2); and
(b)   the court at the trial is satisfied that the lessor is entitled to enforce the right of re-entry or forfeiture,

the court shall order possession of the land to be given to the lessor at the expiration of such period, not being less than 4 weeks from the date of the order, as the court thinks fit, unless within that period the lessee pays into court [or to the lessor] all the rent in arrear and the costs of the action.

(4)   The court may extend the period specified under subsection (3) at any time before possession of the land is recovered in pursuance of the order under that subsection.

(5)   . . . if—
(a)   within the period specified in the order; or
(b)   within that period as extended under subsection (4),

the lessee pays into court [or to the lessor]—
(i)   all the rent in arrear; and
(ii)   the costs of the action,

he shall hold the land according to the lease without any new lease.

(6)   Subsection (2) shall not apply where the lessor is proceeding in the same action to enforce a right of re-entry or forfeiture on any other ground as well as for non-payment of rent, or to enforce any other claim as well as the right of re-entry or forfeiture and the claim for arrears of rent.

(7)   If the lessee does not—
(a)   within the period specified in the order; or
(b)   within that period as extended under subsection (4),

pay into court [or to the lessor]—
(i)   all the rent in arrear; and
(ii)   the costs of the action,

the order shall be [enforceable] in the prescribed manner and so long as the order remains unreversed the lessee shall[, subject to subsections (8) and (9A),] be barred from all relief.

(8)   The extension under subsection (4) of a period fixed by a court shall not be treated as relief from which the lessee is barred by subsection (7) if he fails to pay into court [or to the lessor] all the rent in arrear and the costs of the action within that period.

(9)   Where the court extends a period under subsection (4) at a time when—
(a)   that period has expired; and
(b)   a warrant has been issued for the possession of the land,

the court shall suspend the warrant for the extended period; and, if, before the expiration of the extended period, the lessee pays into court [or to the lessor] all the rent in arrear and all the costs of the action, the court shall cancel the warrant.

[(9A)   Where the lessor recovers possession of the land at any time after the making of the order under subsection (3) (whether as a result of the enforcement of the order or otherwise) the lessee may, at any time within six months from the date on which the lessor recovers possession, apply to the court for relief; and on any such application the court may, if it thinks fit, grant to the lessee such relief, subject to such terms and conditions, as it thinks fit.

(9B)   Where the lessee is granted relief on an application under subsection (9A) he shall hold the land according to the lease without any new lease.

(9C)   An application under subsection (9A) may be made by a person with an interest under a lease of the land derived (whether immediately or otherwise) from the lessee's interest therein in like manner as if he were the lessee; and on any such application the court may make an order which (subject to such terms and conditions as the court thinks fit) vests the land in such a person, as lessee of the lessor, for the remainder of the term of the lease under which he has any such interest as aforesaid, or for any lesser term.

In this subsection any reference to the land includes a reference to a part of the land.]

(10)   Nothing in this section or section 139 shall be taken to affect—

    (a)   the power of the court to make any order which it would otherwise have power to make as respects a right of re-entry or forfeiture on any ground other than non-payment of rent; or

    (b)   section 146(4) of the Law of Property Act 1925 (relief against forfeiture).

[565]

NOTES

Sub-ss (2), (3), (8), (9): words in square brackets inserted by the Courts and Legal Services Act 1990, s 125(2), Sch 17, para 17.

Sub-s (5): words omitted repealed by the Administration of Justice Act 1985, ss 55(2), 67(2), Sch 8, Pt III; words in square brackets inserted by the Courts and Legal Services Act 1990, s 125(2), Sch 17, para 17.

Sub-s (7): words in first pair of square brackets inserted by the Courts and Legal Services Act 1990, s 125(2), Sch 17, para 17; words in second pair of square brackets substituted and words in third pair of square brackets inserted by the Administration of Justice Act 1985, s 55(3).

Sub-ss (9A)–(9C): inserted by the Administration of Justice Act 1985, s 55(4).

---

139   Service of summons and re-entry

(1)   In a case where section 138 has effect, if—

    (a)   one-half-year's rent is in arrear at the time of the commencement of the action; and

    (b)   the lessor has a right to re-enter for non-payment of that rent; and

    (c)   no sufficient distress is to be found on the premises countervailing the arrears then due,

the service of the summons in the action in the prescribed manner shall stand in lieu of a demand and re-entry.

(2)   Where a lessor has enforced against a lessee, by re-entry without action, a right of re-entry or forfeiture as respects any land for non-payment of rent, the lessee may . . . at any time within six months from the date on which the lessor re-entered apply to the county court for relief, and on any such application the court may, if it thinks fit, grant to the lessee such relief as the High Court could have granted.

[(3) Subsections (9B) and (9C) of section 138 shall have effect in relation to an application under subsection (2) of this section as they have effect in relation to an application under subsection (9A) of that section.]

[566]

<hr>

NOTES

Sub-s (2): words omitted repealed by the High Court and County Courts Jurisdiction Order 1991, SI 1991/724, art 2(1)(l), (8), Schedule, Pt I.

Sub-s (3): inserted by the Administration of Justice Act 1985, s 55(5).

<hr>

140 Interpretation of sections 138 and 139

For the purposes of sections 138 and 139—
   "lease" includes—
    (a) an original or derivative under-lease;
    (b) an agreement for a lease where the lessee has become entitled to have his lease granted; and
    (c) a grant at a fee farm rent, or under a grant securing a rent by condition;
   "lessee" includes—
    (a) an original or derivative under-lessee;
    (b) the persons deriving title under a lessee;
    (c) a grantee under a grant at a fee farm rent, or under a grant securing a rent by condition; and
    (d) the persons deriving title under such a grantee;
   "lessor" includes—
    (a) an original or derivative under-lessor;
    (b) the persons deriving title under a lessor;
    (c) a person making a grant at a fee farm rent, or a grant securing a rent by condition; and
    (d) the persons deriving title under such a grantor;
   "under-lease" includes an agreement for an under-lease where the under-lessee has become entitled to have his underlease granted; and
   "under-lessee" includes any person deriving title under an under-lessee.

[567]

General

149 Extent

(1) Section 148(1) and Schedule 2 extend to Scotland so far as they amend enactments extending to Scotland.

(2) Section 148(1) and Schedule 2 extend to Northern Ireland so far as they amend enactments extending to Northern Ireland.

(3) Subject to subsections (1) and (2), this Act extends to England and Wales only.

[568]

150 Commencement

This Act shall come into force on 1st August 1984.

[569]

151 Short title

This Act may be cited as the County Courts Act 1984.

[570]

COMPANIES ACT 1985

(C 6)

An Act to consolidate the greater part of the Companies Acts

[11 March 1985]

PART XII
REGISTRATION OF CHARGES

CHAPTER I
REGISTRATION OF CHARGES (ENGLAND AND WALES)

395   Certain charges void if not registered

(1)   Subject to the provisions of this Chapter, a charge created by a company registered in England and Wales and being a charge to which this section applies is, so far as any security on the company's property or undertaking is conferred by the charge, void against the liquidator [or administrator] and any creditor of the company, unless the prescribed particulars of the charge together with the instrument (if any) by which the charge is created or evidenced, are delivered to or received by the registrar of companies for registration in the manner required by this Chapter within 21 days after the date of the charge's creation.

(2)   Subsection (1) is without prejudice to any contract or obligation for repayment of the money secured by the charge; and when a charge becomes void under this section, the money secured by it immediately becomes payable.

[571]

NOTES

New ss 395, 396 inserted by the Companies Act 1989, s 93, as from a day to be appointed, as follows:

"Registration in the company charges register

395   Introductory provisions
(1) The purpose of this Part is to secure the registration of charges on a company's property.
(2) In this Part—
    "charge" means any form of security interest (fixed or floating) over property, other than an
        interest arising by operation of law; and
    "property", in the context of what is the subject of a charge, includes future property.
(3) It is immaterial for the purposes of this Part where the property subject to a charge is situated.
(4) References in this Part to "the registrar" are—
    (a)   in relation to a company registered in England and Wales, to the registrar of companies
         for England and Wales, and
    (b)   in relation to a company registered in Scotland, to the registrar of companies for
         Scotland;
and references to registration, in relation to a charge, are to registration in the register kept by him under this Part.

396   Charges requiring registration
(1)   The charges requiring registration under this Part are—
    (a)   a charge on land or any interest in land, other than—
        (i)   in England and Wales, a charge for rent or any other periodical sum issuing out of
           the land,
        (ii) in Scotland, a charge for any rent, ground annual or other periodical sum payable
           in respect of the land;
    (b)   a charge on goods or any interest in goods, other than a charge under which the chargee
         is entitled to possession either of the goods or of a document of title to them;
    (c)   a charge on intangible movable property (in Scotland, incorporeal moveable property) of
         any of the following descriptions—

      (i)   goodwill,
      (ii) intellectual property,
      (iii) book debts (whether book debts of the company or assigned to the company),
      (iv) uncalled share capital of the company or calls made but not paid;
  (d)   a charge for securing an issue of debentures; or
  (e)   a floating charge on the whole or part of the company's property.

(2) The descriptions of charge mentioned in subsection (1) shall be construed as follows—

  (a)   a charge on a debenture forming part of an issue or series shall not be treated as falling within paragraph (a) or (b) by reason of the fact that the debenture is secured by a charge on land or goods (or on an interest in land or goods);

  (b)   in paragraph (b) "goods" means any tangible movable property (in Scotland, corporeal moveable property) other than money;

  (c)   a charge is not excluded from paragraph (b) because the chargee is entitled to take possession in case of default or on the occurrence of some other event;

  (d)   in paragraph (c)(ii) "intellectual property" means—

      (i)   any patent, trade mark, service mark, registered design, copyright or design right, or
      (ii) any licence under or in respect of any such right;

  (e)   a debenture which is part of an issue or series shall not be treated as a book debt for the purposes of paragraph (c)(iii);

  (f)   the deposit by way of security of a negotiable instrument given to secure the payment of book debts shall not be treated for the purposes of paragraph (c)(iii) as a charge on book debts;

  (g)   a shipowner's lien on subfreights shall not be treated as a charge on book debts for the purposes of paragraph (c)(iii) or as a floating charge for the purposes of paragraph (e).

(3) Whether a charge is one requiring registration under this Part shall be determined—

  (a)   in the case of a charge created by a company, as at the date the charge is created, and

  (b)   in the case of a charge over property acquired by a company, as at the date of the acquisition.

(4) The Secretary of State may by regulations amend subsections (1) and (2) so as to add any description of charge to, or remove any description of charge from, the charges requiring registration under this Part.

(5) Regulations under this section shall be made by statutory instrument which shall be subject to annulment in pursuance of a resolution of either House of Parliament.

(6) In the following provisions of this Part references to a charge are, unless the context otherwise requires, to a charge requiring registration under this Part.

Where a charge not otherwise requiring registration relates to property by virtue of which it requires to be registered and to other property, the references are to the charge so far as it relates to property of the former description."

Sub-s (1): words in square brackets added by the Insolvency Act 1985, s 109, Sch 6, para 10.

---

396 Charges which have to be registered

(1)   Section 395 applies to the following charges—

  (a)   a charge for the purpose of securing any issue of debentures,

  (b)   a charge on uncalled share capital of the company,

  (c)   a charge created or evidenced by an instrument which, if executed by an individual, would require registration as a bill of sale,

  (d)   a charge on land (wherever situated) or any interest in it, but not including a charge for any rent or other periodical sum issuing out of the land,

  (e)   a charge on book debts of the company,

  (f)   a floating charge on the company's undertaking or property,

  (g)   a charge on calls made but not paid,

  (h)   a charge on a ship or aircraft, or any share in a ship,

  (j)   a charge on goodwill, [or on any intellectual property].

(2)   Where a negotiable instrument has been given to secure the payment of any book debts of a company, the deposit of the instrument for the purpose of securing an advance to the company is not, for purposes of section 395, to be treated as a charge on those book debts.

(3)   The holding of debentures entitling the holder to a charge on land is not for purposes of this section deemed to be an interest in land.

[(3A)   The following are "intellectual property" for the purposes of this section—

      (a)   any patent, trade mark, . . . registered design, copyright or design right;

      (b)   any licence under or in respect of any such right.]

(4)   In this Chapter, "charge" includes mortgage.

[572]

NOTES

    New ss 395, 396 inserted by the Companies Act 1989, s 93, as from a day to be appointed, as set out in the notes to para **[571]** above.

    Sub-s (1): in para (j), words in square brackets substituted by the Copyright, Designs and Patents Act 1988, s 303(1), Sch 7, para 31(2).

    Sub-s (3A): inserted by the Copyright, Designs and Patents Act 1988, s 303(1), Sch 7, para 31(2); words omitted repealed by the Trade Marks Act 1994, s 106(1), Sch 4, para 1.

PART XXVII

FINAL PROVISIONS

746 Commencement

. . . this Act comes into force on 1st July 1985.

[573]

NOTES

    Words omitted repealed by the Companies Act 1989, s 212, Sch 24.

747   Citation

This Act may be cited as the Companies Act 1985.

[574]

ENDURING POWERS OF ATTORNEY ACT 1985

(C 29)

An Act to enable powers of attorney to be created which will survive any subsequent mental incapacity of the donor and to make provision in connection with such powers.

[26 June 1985]

Enduring powers of attorney

1   Enduring power of attorney to survive mental incapacity of donor

(1)   Where an individual creates a power of attorney which is an enduring power within the meaning of this Act then—

      (a)   the power shall not be revoked by any subsequent mental incapacity of his; but

      (b)   upon such incapacity supervening the donee of the power may not do anything under the authority of the power except as provided by subsection (2) below or as directed or authorised by the court under section 5 unless or, as the case may be, until the instrument creating the power is registered by the court under section 6; and

(c) section 5 of the Powers of Attorney Act 1971 (protection of donee and third persons) so far as applicable shall apply if and so long as paragraph (b) above operates to suspend the donee's authority to act under the power as if the power had been revoked by the donor's mental incapacity.

(2) Notwithstanding subsection (1)(b) above, where the attorney has made an application for registration of the instrument then, until the application has been initially determined, the attorney may take action under the power—

(a) to maintain the donor or prevent loss to his estate; or

(b) to maintain himself or other persons in so far as section 3(4) permits him to do so.

(3) Where the attorney purports to act as provided by subsection (2) above then, in favour of a person who deals with him without knowledge that the attorney is acting otherwise than in accordance with paragraph (a) or (b) of that subsection, the transaction between them shall be as valid as if the attorney were acting in accordance with paragraph (a) or (b).

[575]

2 Characteristics of an enduring power

(1) Subject to subsections (7) to (9) below and section 11, a power of attorney is an enduring power within the meaning of this Act if the instrument which creates the power—

(a) is in the prescribed form; and

(b) was executed in the prescribed manner by the donor and the attorney; and

(c) incorporated at the time of execution by the donor the prescribed explanatory information.

(2) The Lord Chancellor shall make regulations as to the form and execution of instruments creating enduring powers and the regulations shall contain such provisions as appear to him to be appropriate for securing—

(a) that no document is used to create an enduring power which does not incorporate such information explaining the general effect of creating or accepting the power as may be prescribed; and

(b) that such instruments include statements to the following effect—

(i) by the donor, that he intends the power to continue in spite of any intervening mental incapacity of his;

(ii) by the donor, that he read or had read to him the information explaining the effect of creating the power;

(iii) by the attorney, that he understands the duty of registration imposed by this Act.

(3) Regulations under subsection (2) above—

(a) may include different provision for cases where more than one attorney is to be appointed by the instrument than for cases where only one attorney is to be appointed; and

(b) may, if they amend or revoke any regulations previously made under that subsection, include saving and transitional provisions.

(4) Regulations under subsection (2) above shall be made by statutory instrument which shall be subject to annulment in pursuance of a resolution of either House of Parliament.

(5) An instrument in the prescribed form purporting to have been executed in the prescribed manner shall be taken, in the absence of evidence to the contrary, to be a

document which incorporated at the time of execution by the donor the prescribed explanatory information.

(6)   Where an instrument differs in an immaterial respect in form or mode of expression from the prescribed form the instrument shall be treated as sufficient in point of form and expression.

(7)   A power of attorney cannot be an enduring power unless, when he executes the instrument creating it, the attorney is—

> (a)   an individual who has attained eighteen years and is not bankrupt; or
> (b)   a trust corporation.

(8)   A power of attorney under section 25 of the Trustee Act 1925 (power to delegate trusts etc by power of attorney) cannot be an enduring power.

(9)   A power of attorney which gives the attorney a right to appoint a substitute or successor cannot be an enduring power.

(10)   An enduring power shall be revoked by the bankruptcy of the attorney whatever the circumstances of the bankruptcy.

(11)   An enduring power shall be revoked on the exercise by the court of any of its powers under Part VII of the Mental Health Act 1983 if, but only if, the court so directs.

(12)   No disclaimer of an enduring power, whether by deed or otherwise, shall be valid unless and until the attorney gives notice of it to the donor or, where section 4(6) or 7(1) applies, to the court.

(13)   In this section "prescribed" means prescribed under subsection (2) above.

[576]

3   Scope of authority etc of attorney under enduring power

(1)   An enduring power may confer general authority (as defined in subsection (2) below) on the attorney to act on the donor's behalf in relation to all or a specified part of the property and affairs of the donor or may confer on him authority to do specified things on the donor's behalf and the authority may, in either case, be conferred subject to conditions and restrictions.

(2)   Where an instrument is expressed to confer general authority on the attorney it operates to confer, subject to the restriction imposed by subsection (5) below and to any conditions or restrictions contained in the instrument, authority to do on behalf of the donor anything which the donor can lawfully do by an attorney.

(3)   Subject to any conditions or restrictions contained in the instrument, an attorney under an enduring power, whether general or limited, may (without obtaining any consent) execute or exercise all or any of the trusts, powers or discretions vested in the donor as trustee and may (without the concurrence of any other person) give a valid receipt for capital or other money paid.

(4)   Subject to any conditions or restrictions contained in the instrument, an attorney under an enduring power, whether general or limited, may (without obtaining any consent) act under the power so as to benefit himself or other persons than the donor to the following extent but no further, that is to say—

> (a)   he may so act in relation to himself or in relation to any other person if the donor might be expected to provide for his or that person's needs respectively; and
> (b)   he may do whatever the donor might be expected to do to meet those needs.

(5) Without prejudice to subsection (4) above but subject to any conditions or restrictions contained in the instrument, an attorney under an enduring power, whether general or limited, may (without obtaining any consent) dispose of the property of the donor by way of gift to the following extent but no further, that is to say—

    (a) he may make gifts of a seasonal nature or at a time, or on an anniversary, of a birth or marriage, to persons (including himself) who are related to or connected with the donor, and

    (b) he may make gifts to any charity to whom the donor made or might be expected to make gifts,

provided that the value of each such gift is not unreasonable having regard to all the circumstances and in particular the size of the donor's estate.

[577]

Action on actual or impending incapacity of donor

4   Duties of attorney in event of actual or impending incapacity of donor

(1) If the attorney under an enduring power has reason to believe that the donor is or is becoming mentally incapable subsections (2) to (6) below shall apply.

(2) The attorney shall, as soon as practicable, make an application to the court for the registration of the instrument creating the power.

(3) Before making an application for registration the attorney shall comply with the provisions as to notice set out in Schedule 1.

(4) An application for registration shall be made in the prescribed form and shall contain such statements as may be prescribed.

(5) The attorney may, before making an application for the registration of the instrument, refer to the court for its determination any question as to the validity of the power and he shall comply with any direction given to him by the court on that determination.

(6) No disclaimer of the power shall be valid unless and until the attorney gives notice of it to the court.

(7) Any person who, in an application for registration, makes a statement which he knows to be false in a material particular shall be liable—

    (a) on conviction on indictment, to imprisonment for a term not exceeding two years or to a fine, or both; and

    (b) on summary conviction, to imprisonment for a term not exceeding six months or to a fine not exceeding the statutory maximum, or both.

(8) In this section and Schedule 1 "prescribed" means prescribed by rules of the court.

[578]

5   Functions of court prior to registration

Where the court has reason to believe that the donor of an enduring power may be, or may be becoming, mentally incapable and the court is of the opinion that it is necessary, before the instrument creating the power is registered, to exercise any power with respect to the power of attorney or the attorney appointed to act under it which would become exercisable under section 8(2) on its registration, the court may exercise that power under this section and may do so whether the attorney has or has not made an application to the court for the registration of the instrument.

[579]

6   Functions of court on application for registration

(1)   In any case where—
    (a)   an application for registration is made in accordance with section 4(3) and (4), and
    (b)   neither subsection (2) nor subsection (4) below applies,

the court shall register the instrument to which the application relates.

(2)   Where it appears to the court that there is in force under Part VII of the Mental Health Act 1983 an order appointing a receiver for the donor but the power has not also been revoked then, unless it directs otherwise, the court shall not exercise or further exercise its functions under this section but shall refuse the application for registration.

(3)   Where it appears from an application for registration that notice of it has not been given under Schedule 1 to some person entitled to receive it (other than a person in respect of whom the attorney has been dispensed or is otherwise exempt from the requirement to give notice) the court shall direct that the application be treated for the purposes of this Act as having been made in accordance with section 4(3), if the court is satisfied that, as regards each such person—
    (a)   it was undesirable or impracticable for the attorney to give him notice; or
    (b)   no useful purpose is likely to be served by giving him notice.

(4)   If, in the case of an application for registration—
    (a)   a valid notice of objection to the registration is received by the court before the expiry of the period of five weeks beginning with the date or, as the case may be, the latest date on which the attorney gave notice to any person under Schedule 1, or
    (b)   it appears from the application that there is no one to whom notice has been given under paragraph 1 of that Schedule, or
    (c)   the court has reason to believe that appropriate inquiries might bring to light evidence on which the court could be satisfied that one of the grounds of objection set out in subsection (5) below was established,

the court shall neither register the instrument nor refuse the application until it has made or caused to be made such inquiries (if any) as it thinks appropriate in the circumstances of the case.

(5)   For the purposes of this Act a notice of objection to the registration of an instrument is valid if the objection is made on one or more of the following grounds, namely—
    (a)   that the power purported to have been created by the instrument was not valid as an enduring power of attorney;
    (b)   that the power created by the instrument no longer subsists;
    (c)   that the application is premature because the donor is not yet becoming mentally incapable;
    (d)   that fraud or undue pressure was used to induce the donor to create the power;
    (e)   that, having regard to all the circumstances and in particular the attorney's relationship to or connection with the donor, the attorney is unsuitable to be the donor's attorney.

(6)   If, in a case where subsection (4) above applies, any of the grounds of objection in subsection (5) above is established to the satisfaction of the court, the court shall refuse the application but if, in such a case, it is not so satisfied, the court shall register the instrument to which the application relates.

(7)   Where the court refuses an application for registration on ground (d) or (e) in subsection (5) above it shall by order revoke the power created by the instrument.

(8)   Where the court refuses an application for registration on any ground other than that specified in subsection (5)(c) above the instrument shall be delivered up to be cancelled, unless the court otherwise directs.

[580]

Legal position after registration

7   Effect and proof of registration etc

(1)   The effect of the registration of an instrument under section 6 is that—
    (a)   no revocation of the power by the donor shall be valid unless and until the court confirms the revocation under section 8(3);
    (b)   no disclaimer of the power shall be valid unless and until the attorney gives notice of it to the court;
    (c)   the donor may not extend or restrict the scope of the authority conferred by the instrument and no instruction or consent given by him after registration shall, in the case of a consent, confer any right and, in the case of an instruction, impose or confer any obligation or right on or create any liability of the attorney or other persons having notice of the instruction or consent.

(2)   Subsection (1) above applies for so long as the instrument is registered under section 6 whether or not the donor is for the time being mentally incapable.

(3)   A document purporting to be an office copy of an instrument registered under this Act [or under the Enduring Powers of Attorney (Northern Ireland) Order 1987] shall, in any part of the United Kingdom, be evidence of the contents of the instrument and of the fact that it has been so registered.

(4)   Subsection (3) above is without prejudice to section 3 of the Powers of Attorney Act 1971 (proof by certified copies) and to any other method of proof authorised by law.

[581]

NOTES
    Sub-s (2): words in square brackets inserted by the Enduring Powers of Attorney (Northern Ireland) Consequential Amendment) Order 1987, SI 1987/1628, art 2.

8   Functions of court with respect to registered power

(1)   Where an instrument has been registered under section 6, the court shall have the following functions with respect to the power and the donor of and the attorney appointed to act under the power.

(2)   The court may—
    (a)   determine any question as to the meaning or effect of the instrument;
    (b)   give directions with respect to—
        (i)   the management or disposal by the attorney of the property and affairs of the donor;
        (ii)   the rendering of accounts by the attorney and the production of the records kept by him for the purpose;
        (iii)   the remuneration or expenses of the attorney, whether or not in default of or in accordance with any provision made by the

instrument, including directions for the repayment of excessive or the payment of additional remuneration;

    (c)   require the attorney to furnish information or produce documents or things in his possession as attorney;

    (d)   give any consent or authorisation to act which the attorney would have to obtain from a mentally capable donor;

    (e)   authorise the attorney to act so as to benefit himself or other persons than the donor otherwise than in accordance with section 3(4) and (5) (but subject to any conditions or restrictions contained in the instrument);

    (f)   relieve the attorney wholly or partly from any liability which he has or may have incurred on account of a breach of his duties as attorney.

(3)   On application made for the purpose by or on behalf of the donor, the court shall confirm the revocation of the power if satisfied that the donor has done whatever is necessary in law to effect an express revocation of the power and was mentally capable of revoking a power of attorney when he did so (whether or not he is so when the court considers the application).

(4)   The court shall cancel the registration of an instrument registered under section 6 in any of the following circumstances, that is to say—

    (a)   on confirming the revocation of the power under subsection (3) above or receiving notice of disclaimer under section 7(1)(b);

    (b)   on giving a direction revoking the power on exercising any of its powers under Part VII of the Mental Health Act 1983;

    (c)   on being satisfied that the donor is and is likely to remain mentally capable;

    (d)   on being satisfied that the power has expired or has been revoked by the death or bankruptcy of the donor or the death, mental incapacity or bankruptcy of the attorney or, if the attorney is a body corporate, its winding up or dissolution;

    (e)   on being satisfied that the power was not a valid and subsisting enduring power when registration was effected;

    (f)   on being satisfied that fraud or undue pressure was used to induce the donor to create the power; or

    (g)   on being satisfied that, having regard to all the circumstances and in particular the attorney's relationship to or connection with the donor, the attorney is unsuitable to be the donor's attorney.

(5)   Where the court cancels the registration of an instrument on being satisfied of the matters specified in paragraph (f) or (g) of subsection (4) above it shall by order revoke the power created by the instrument.

(6)   On the cancellation of the registration of an instrument under subsection (4) above except paragraph (c) the instrument shall be delivered up to be cancelled, unless the court otherwise directs.

[582]

Protection of attorney and third parties

9 Protection of attorney and third persons where power invalid or revoked

(1)   Subsections (2) and (3) below apply where an instrument which did not create a valid power of attorney has been registered under section 6 (whether or not the registration has been cancelled at the time of the act or transaction in question).

(2)   An attorney who acts in pursuance of the power shall not incur any liability (either to the donor or to any other person) by reason of the non-existence of the power unless at the time of acting he knows—

(a)   that the instrument did not create a valid enduring power; or

(b)   that an event has occurred which, if the instrument had created a valid enduring power, would have had the effect of revoking the power; or

(c)   that, if the instrument had created a valid enduring power, the power would have expired before that time.

(3)   Any transaction between the attorney and another person shall, in favour of that person, be as valid as if the power had then been in existence, unless at the time of the transaction that person has knowledge of any of the matters mentioned in subsection (2) above.

(4)   Where the interest of a purchaser depends on whether a transaction between the attorney and another person was valid by virtue of subsection (3) above, it shall be conclusively presumed in favour of the purchaser that the transaction was valid if—

(a)   the transaction between that person and the attorney was completed within twelve months of the date on which the instrument was registered; or

(b)   that person makes a statutory declaration, before or within three months after the completion of the purchase, that he had no reason at the time of the transaction to doubt that the attorney had authority to dispose of the property which was the subject of the transaction.

(5)   For the purposes of section 5 of the Powers of Attorney Act 1971 (protection of attorney and third persons where action is taken under the power of attorney in ignorance of its having been revoked) in its application to an enduring power the revocation of which by the donor is by virtue of section 7(1)(a) above invalid unless and until confirmed by the court under section 8(3) above, knowledge of the confirmation of the revocation is, but knowledge of the unconfirmed revocation is not, knowledge of the revocation of the power.

(6)   Schedule 2 shall have effect to confer protection in cases where the instrument failed to create a valid enduring power and the power has been revoked by the donor's mental incapacity.

(7)   In this section "purchaser" and "purchase" have the meanings specified in section 205(1) of the Law of Property Act 1925.

[583]

Supplementary

10   Application of Mental Health Act provisions relating to the court

(1)   The provisions of Part VII of the Mental Health Act 1983 (relating to the Court of Protection) specified below shall apply to persons within and proceedings under this Act in accordance with the following paragraphs of this subsection and subsection (2) below, that is to say—

(a)   section 103 (functions of Visitors) shall apply to persons within this Act as it applies to the persons mentioned in that section;

(b)   section 104 (powers of judge) shall apply to proceedings under this Act with respect to persons within this Act as it applies to the proceedings mentioned in subsection (1) of that section;

(c) section 105(1) (appeals to nominated judge) shall apply to any decision of the Master of the Court of Protection or any nominated officer in proceedings under this Act as it applies to any decision to which that subsection applies and an appeal shall lie to the Court of Appeal from any decision of a nominated judge whether given in the exercise of his original jurisdiction or on the hearing of an appeal under section 105(1) as extended by this paragraph;

(d) section 106 except subsection (4) (rules of procedure) shall apply to proceedings under this Act and persons within this Act as it applies to the proceedings and persons mentioned in that section.

(2)   Any functions conferred or imposed by the provisions of the said Part VII applied by subsection (1) above shall be exercisable also for the purposes of this Act and the persons who are "within this Act" are the donors of and attorneys under enduring powers of attorney whether or not they would be patients for the purposes of the said Part VII.

(3)   In this section "nominated judge" and "nominated officer" have the same meanings as in Part VII of the Mental Health Act 1983.

[584]

11   Application to joint and joint and several attorneys

(1)   An instrument which appoints more than one person to be an attorney cannot create an enduring power unless the attorneys are appointed to act jointly or jointly and severally.

(2)   This Act, in its application to joint attorneys, applies to them collectively as it applies to a single attorney but subject to the modifications specified in Part I of Schedule 3.

(3)   This Act, in its application to joint and several attorneys, applies with the modifications specified in subsections (4) to (7) below and in Part II of Schedule 3.

(4)   A failure, as respects any one attorney, to comply with the requirements for the creation of enduring powers, shall prevent the instrument from creating such a power in his case without however affecting its efficacy for that purpose as respects the other or others or its efficacy in his case for the purpose of creating a power of attorney which is not an enduring power.

(5)   Where one or more but not both or all the attorneys makes or joins in making an application for registration of the instrument then—

(a) an attorney who is not an applicant as well as one who is may act pending the initial determination of the application as provided in section 1(2) (or under section 5);

(b) notice of the application shall also be given under Schedule 1 to the other attorney or attorneys; and

(c) objection may validly be taken to the registration on a ground relating to an attorney or to the power of an attorney who is not an applicant as well as to one or the power of one who is an applicant.

(6)   The court shall not refuse under section 6(6) to register an instrument because a ground of objection to an attorney or power is established if an enduring power subsists as respects some attorney who is not affected thereby but shall give effect to it by the prescribed qualification of the registration.

(7)   The court shall not cancel the registration of an instrument under section 8(4) for any of the causes vitiating registration specified in that subsection if an enduring power subsists as respects some attorney who is not affected thereby but shall give effect to it by the prescribed qualification of the registration.

(8)   In this section—

   "prescribed" means prescribed by rules of the court; and

   "the requirements for the creation of enduring powers" means the provisions of section 2 other than subsections (10) to (12) and of regulations under subsection (2) of that section.

[585]

12   Power of Lord Chancellor to modify pre-registration requirements in certain cases

(1)   The Lord Chancellor may by order exempt attorneys of such descriptions as he thinks fit from the requirements of this Act to give notice to relatives prior to registration.

(2)   Subject to subsection (3) below, where an order is made under this section with respect to attorneys of a specified description then, during the currency of the order, this Act shall have effect in relation to any attorney of that description with the omission of so much of section 4(3) and Schedule 1 as requires notice of an application for registration to be given to relatives.

(3)   Notwithstanding that an attorney under a joint or joint and several power is of a description specified in a current order under this section, subsection (2) above shall not apply in relation to him if any of the other attorneys under the power is not of a description specified in that or another current order under this section.

(4)   The power to make an order under this section shall be exercisable by statutory instrument which shall be subject to annulment in pursuance of a resolution of either House of Parliament.

[586]

13   Interpretation

(1)   In this Act—

   "the court", in relation to any functions under this Act, means the authority having jurisdiction under Part VII of the Mental Health Act 1983;

   "enduring power" is to be construed in accordance with section 2;

   "mentally incapable" or "mental incapacity", except where it refers to revocation at common law, means, in relation to any person, that he is incapable by reason of mental disorder of managing and administering his property and affairs and "mentally capable" and "mental capacity" shall be construed accordingly;

   "mental disorder" has the same meaning as it has in the Mental Health Act 1983;

   "notice" means notice in writing;

   "rules of the court" means rules under Part VII of the Mental Health Act 1983 as applied by section 10;

. . . . .

   "trust corporation" means the Public Trustee or a corporation either appointed by the High Court or a county court (according to their respective jurisdictions) in any particular case to be a trustee or entitled by rules under section 4(3) of the Public Trustee Act 1906 to act as custodian trustee.

(2)   Any question arising under or for the purposes of this Act as to what the donor of the power might at any time be expected to do shall be determined by assuming that he had full mental capacity at the time but otherwise by reference to the circumstances existing at that time.

[587]

NOTES

Sub-s (1): definition omitted repealed by the Statute Law (Repeals) Act 1993.

14   Short title, commencement and extent

(1)   This Act may be cited as the Enduring Powers of Attorney Act 1985.

(2)   This Act shall come into force on such day as the Lord Chancellor appoints by order made by statutory instrument.

(3)   This Act extends to England and Wales only except that section 7(3) and section 10(1)(b) so far as it applies section 104(4) of the Mental Health Act 1983 extend also to Scotland and Northern Ireland.

[588]

SCHEDULE 1
NOTIFICATION PRIOR TO REGISTRATION

Section 4(3)

PART I
DUTY TO GIVE NOTICE TO RELATIVES AND DONOR
Duty to give notice to relatives

1.   Subject to paragraph 3 below, before making an application for registration the attorney shall give notice of his intention to do so to all those persons (if any) who are entitled to receive notice by virtue of paragraph 2 below.

2.—(1) Subject to the limitations contained in sub-paragraphs (2) to (4) below, persons of the following classes (referred to in this Act as "relatives") are entitled to receive notice under paragraph 1 above—

   (a)   the donor's husband or wife;
   (b)   the donor's children;
   (c)   the donor's parents;
   (d)   the donor's brothers and sisters, whether of the whole or half blood;
   (e)   the widow or widower of a child of the donor;
   (f)   the donor's grandchildren;
   (g)   the children of the donor's brothers and sisters of the whole blood;
   (h)   the children of the donor's brothers an sisters of the half blood;
   (i)   the donor's uncles and aunts of the whole blood; and
   (j)   the children of the donor's uncles and aunts of the whole blood.

(2)   A person is not entitled to receive notice under paragraph 1 above if—

   (a)   his name or address is not known to the attorney and cannot be reasonably ascertained by him; or
   (b)   the attorney has reason to believe that he has not attained eighteen years or is mentally incapable.

(3)   Except where sub-paragraph (4) below applies, no more than three persons are entitled to receive notice under paragraph 1 above and, in determining the persons who are so entitled, persons falling within class (a) of sub-paragraph (1) above are to be preferred to persons falling with class (b) of that sub-paragraph, persons falling within class (b) are to be preferred to persons falling within class (c) of that sub-paragraph; and so on.

(4) Notwithstanding the limit of three specified in sub-paragraph (3) above, where—
  - (a) there is more than one person falling within any of classes (a) to (j) of sub-paragraph (1) above, and
  - (b) at least one of those persons would be entitled to receive notice under paragraph 1 above,

then, subject to sub-paragraph (2) above, all the persons falling within that class are entitled to receive notice under paragraph 1 above.

3.—(1) An attorney shall not be required to give notice under paragraph 1 above to himself or to any other attorney under the power who is joining in making the application, notwithstanding that he or, as the case may be, the other attorney is entitled to receive notice by virtue of paragraph 2 above.

(2) In the case of any person who is entitled to receive notice under paragraph 1 above, the attorney, before applying for registration, may make an application to the court to be dispensed from the requirement to give him notice; and the court shall grant the application if it is satisfied—
  - (a) that it would be undesirable or impracticable for the attorney to give him notice; or
  - (b) that no useful purpose is likely to be served by giving him notice.

Duty to give notice to donor

4.—(1) Subject to sub-paragraph (2) below, before making an application for registration the attorney shall give notice of his intention to do so to the donor.

(2) Paragraph 3(2) above shall apply in relation to the donor as it applies in relation to a person who is entitled to receive notice under paragraph 1 above.

[589]

PART II
CONTENTS OF NOTICES

5. A notice to relatives under this Schedule—
  - (a) shall be in the prescribed form;
  - (b) shall state that the attorney proposes to make an application to the Court of Protection for the registration of the instrument creating the enduring power in question;
  - (c) shall inform the person to whom it is given that he may object to the proposed registration by notice in writing to the Court of Protection before the expiry of the period of four weeks beginning with the day on which the notice under this Schedule was given to him;
  - (d) shall specify, as the grounds on which an objection to registration may be made, the grounds set out in section 6(5).

6. A notice to the donor under this Schedule—
  - (a) shall be in the prescribed form;
  - (b) shall contain the statement mentioned in paragraph 5(b) above; and
  - (c) shall inform the donor that, whilst the instrument remains registered, any revocation of the power by him will be ineffective unless and until the revocation is confirmed by the Court of Protection.

[590]

PART III
DUTY TO GIVE NOTICE TO OTHER ATTORNEYS

7.—(1) Subject to sub-paragraph (2) below, before making an application for registration an attorney under a joint and several power shall give notice of his intention to do so to any other attorney under the power who is not joining in making the application; and paragraphs 3(2) and 5 above shall apply in relation to attorneys entitled to receive notice by virtue of this paragraph as they apply in relation to persons entitled to receive notice by virtue of paragraph 2 above.

(2)   An attorney is not entitled to receive notice by virtue of this paragraph if—

    (a)   his address is not known to the applying attorney and cannot reasonably be ascertained by him; or

    (b)   the applying attorney has reason to believe that he has not attained eighteen years or is mentally incapable.

[591]

PART IV
SUPPLEMENTARY

8.—(1) For the purposes of this Schedule an illegitimate child shall be treated as if he were the legitimate child of his mother and father.

(2)   Notwithstanding anything in section 7 of the Interpretation Act 1978 (construction of references to service by post), for the purposes of this Schedule a notice given by post shall be regarded as given on the date on which it was posted.

[592]

SCHEDULE 2
FURTHER PROTECTION OF ATTORNEY AND THIRD PERSONS
Section 9(6)

1.   Where—

    (a)   an instrument framed in a form prescribed under section 2(2) creates a power which is not a valid enduring power; and

    (b)   the power is revoked by the mental incapacity of the donor, paragraphs 2 and 3 below shall apply, whether or not the instrument has been registered.

2.   An attorney who acts in pursuance of the power shall not, by reason of the revocation, incur any liability (either to the donor or to any other person) unless at the time of acting he knows—

    (a)   that the instrument did not create a valid enduring power; and

    (b)   that the donor has become mentally incapable.

3.   Any transaction between the attorney and another person shall, in favour of that person, be as valid as if the power had then been in existence, unless at the time of the transaction that person knows—

    (a)   that the instrument did not create a valid enduring power; and

    (b)   that the donor has become mentally incapable.

4.   Section 9(4) shall apply for the purpose of determining whether a transaction was valid by virtue of paragraph 3 above as it applies for the purpose of determining whether a transaction was valid by virtue of section 9(3).

[593]

SCHEDULE 3
JOINT AND JOINT AND SEVERAL ATTORNEYS
Section 11(2), (3)

PART I
JOINT ATTORNEYS

1.   In section 2(7), the reference to the time when the attorney executes the instrument shall be read as a reference to the time when the second or last attorney executes the instrument.

2.   In section 2(9) and (10), the reference to the attorney shall be read as a reference to any attorney under the power.

3.   In section 5, references to the attorney shall be read as including references to any attorney under the power.

4.   Section 6 shall have effect as if the ground of objection to the registration of the instrument specified in subsection (5)(e) applied to any attorney under the power.

5.   In section 8(2), references to the attorney shall be read as including references to any attorney under the power.

6.   In section 8(4), references to the attorney shall be read as including references to any attorney under the power.

[594]

PART II
JOINT AND SEVERAL ATTORNEYS

7.   In section 2(10), the reference to the bankruptcy of the attorney shall be construed as a reference to the bankruptcy of the last remaining attorney under the power; and the bankruptcy of any other attorney under the power shall cause that person to cease to be attorney, whatever the circumstances of the bankruptcy.

8.   The restriction upon disclaimer imposed by section 4(6) applies only to those attorneys who have reason to believe that the donor is or is becoming mentally incapable.

[595]

LANDLORD AND TENANT ACT 1985

(C 70)

An Act to consolidate certain provisions of the law of landlord and tenant formerly found in the Housing Acts, together with the Landlord and Tenant Act 1962, with amendments to give effect to recommendations of the Law Commission

[30 October 1985]

Implied terms as to fitness for human habitation

8   Implied terms as to fitness for human habitation

(1)   In a contract to which this section applies for the letting of a house for human habitation there is implied, notwithstanding any stipulation to the contrary—

   (a)   a condition that the house is fit for human habitation at the commencement of the tenancy, and

   (b)   an undertaking that the house will be kept by the landlord fit for human habitation during the tenancy.

(2)   The landlord, or a person authorised by him in writing, may at reasonable times of the day, on giving 24 hours' notice in writing to the tenant or occupier, enter premises to which this section applies for the purpose of viewing their state and condition.

(3)   This section applies to a contract if—

   (a)   the rent does not exceed the figure applicable in accordance with subsection (4), and

   (b)   the letting is not on such terms as to the tenant's responsibility as are mentioned in subsection (5).

(4)   The rent limit for the application of this section is shown by the following Table, by reference to the date of making of the contract and the situation of the premises;

TABLE

Date of making of contract	Rent limit
Before 31st July 1923.	In London: £40. Elsewhere: £26 or £16 (see Note 1).
On or after 31st July 1923 and before 6th July 1957.	In London: £40. Elsewhere: £26.
On or after 6th July 1957.	In London: £80. Elsewhere: £52.

NOTES

1.   The applicable figure for contracts made before 31st July 1923 is £26 in the case of premises situated in a borough or urban district which at the date of the contract had according to the last published census a population of 50,000 or more. In the case of a house situated elsewhere, the figure is £16.

2.   The references to "London" are, in relation to contracts made before 1st April 1965, to the administrative county of London and, in relation to contracts made on or after that date, to Greater London exclusive of the outer London boroughs.

(5)   This section does not apply where a house is let for a term of three years or more (the lease not being determinable at the option of either party before the expiration of three years) upon terms that the tenant puts the premises into a condition reasonably fit for human habitation.

(6)   In this section "house" includes—

   (a)   a part of a house, and
   (b)   any yard, garden, outhouses and appurtenances belonging to the house or usually enjoyed with it.

[596]

10   Fitness for human habitation

In determining for the purposes of this Act whether a house is unfit for human habitation, regard shall be had to its condition in respect of the following matters—

   repair,
   stability,
   freedom from damp,
   internal arrangement,
   natural lighting,
   ventilation,
   water supply,
   drainage and sanitary conveniences,
   facilities for preparation and cooking of food and for the disposal of waste water;

and the house shall be regarded as unfit for human habitation if, and only if, it is so far defective in one or more of those matters that it is not reasonably suitable for occupation in that condition.

[597]

Repairing obligations

11   Repairing obligations in short leases

(1)   In a lease to which this section applies (as to which, see sections 13 and 14) there is implied a covenant by the lessor—

    (a)   to keep in repair the structure and exterior of the dwelling-house (including drains, gutters and external pipes),

    (b)   to keep in repair and proper working order the installations in the dwelling-house for the supply of water, gas and electricity and for sanitation (including basins, sinks, baths and sanitary conveniences, but not other fixtures, fittings and appliances for making use of the supply of water, gas or electricity), and

    (c)   to keep in repair and proper working order the installations in the dwelling-house for space heating and heating water.

[(1A)   If a lease to which this section applies is a lease of a dwelling-house which forms part only of a building, then, subject to subsection (1B), the covenant implied by subsection (1) shall have effect as if—

    (a)   the reference in paragraph (a) of that subsection to the dwelling-house included a reference to any part of the building in which the lessor has an estate or interest; and

    (b)   any reference in paragraphs (b) and (c) of that subsection to an installation in the dwelling-house included a reference to an installation which, directly or indirectly, serves the dwelling-house and which either—

        (i)   forms part of any part of a building in which the lessor has an estate or interest; or

        (ii)   is owned by the lessor or under his control.

(1B)   Nothing in subsection (1A) shall be construed as requiring the lessor to carry out any works or repairs unless the disrepair (or failure to maintain in working order) is such as to affect the lessee's enjoyment of the dwelling-house or of any common parts, as defined in section 60(1) of the Landlord and Tenant Act 1987, which the lessee, as such, is entitled to use.]

(2)   The covenant implied by subsection (1) ("the lessor's repairing covenant") shall not be construed as requiring the lessor—

    (a)   to carry out works or repairs for which the lessee is liable by virtue of his duty to use the premises in a tenant-like manner, or would be so liable but for an express covenant on his part,

    (b)   to rebuild or reinstate the premises in the case of destruction or damage by fire, or by tempest, flood or other inevitable accident, or

    (c)   to keep in repair or maintain anything which the lessee is entitled to remove from the dwelling-house.

(3)   In determining the standard of repair required by the lessor's repairing covenant, regard shall be had to the age, character and prospective life of the dwelling-house and the locality in which it is situated.

[(3A)   In any case where—

    (a)   the lessor's repairing covenant has effect as mentioned in subsection (1A), and

    (b)   in order to comply with the covenant the lessor needs to carry out works or repairs otherwise than in, or to an installation in, the dwelling-house, and

(c) the lessor does not have a sufficient right in the part of the building or the installation concerned to enable him to carry out the required works or repairs,

then, in any proceedings relating to a failure to comply with the lessor's repairing covenant, so far as it requires the lessor to carry out the works or repairs in question, it shall be a defence for the lessor to prove that he used all reasonable endeavours to obtain, but was unable to obtain, such rights as would be adequate to enable him to carry out the works or repairs.]

(4) A covenant by the lessee for the repair of the premises is of no effect so far as it relates to the matters mentioned in subsection (1)(a) to (c), except so far as it imposes on the lessee any of the requirements mentioned in subsection (2)(a) or (c).

(5) The reference in subsection (4) to a covenant by the lessee for the repair of the premises includes a covenant—
(a) to put in repair or deliver up in repair,
(b) to paint, point or render,
(c) to pay money in lieu of repairs by the lessee, or
(d) to pay money on account of repairs by the lessor.

(6) In a lease in which the lessor's repairing covenant is implied there is also implied a covenant by the lessee that the lessor, or any person authorised by him in writing, may at reasonable times of the day and on giving 24 hours' notice in writing to the occupier, enter the premises comprised in the lease for the purpose of viewing their condition and state of repair.

[598]

NOTES

Sub-ss (1A), (1B), (3A): inserted by the Housing Act 1988, s 116(1), (2), (4), except with respect to leases entered into before 15 January 1989 or a lease entered into pursuant to a contract made before that date.

12 Restriction on contracting out of s 11

(1) A covenant or agreement, whether contained in a lease to which section 11 applies or in an agreement collateral to such a lease, is void in so far as it purports—
(a) to exclude or limit the obligations of the lessor or the immunities of the lessee under that section, or
(b) to authorise any forfeiture or impose on the lessee any penalty, disability or obligation in the event of his enforcing or relying upon those obligations or immunities,

unless the inclusion of the provision was authorised by the county court.

(2) The county court may, by order made with the consent of the parties, authorise the inclusion in a lease, or in an agreement collateral to a lease, of provisions excluding or modifying in relation to the lease, the provisions of section 11 with respect to the repairing obligations of the parties if it appears to the court that it is reasonable to do so, having regard to all the circumstances of the case, including the other terms and conditions of the lease.

[599]

13 Leases to which s 11 applies: general rule

(1) Section 11 (repairing obligations) applies to a lease of a dwelling-house granted on or after 24th October 1961 for a term of less than seven years.

(2)   In determining whether a lease is one to which section 11 applies—
   (a)   any part of the term which falls before the grant shall be left out of account and the lease shall be treated as a lease for a term commencing with the grant,
   (b)   a lease which is determinable at the option of the lessor before the expiration of seven years from the commencement of the term shall be treated as a lease for a term of less than seven years, and
   (c)   a lease (other than a lease to which paragraph (b) applies) shall not be treated as a lease for a term of less than seven years if it confers on the lessee an option for renewal for a term which, together with the original term, amounts to seven years or more.

(3)   This section has effect subject to—
   section 14 (leases to which section 11 applies: exceptions), and
   section 32(2) (provisions not applying to tenancies within Part II of the Landlord and Tenant Act 1954).

[600]

14   Leases to which s 11 applies: exceptions

(1)   Section 11 (repairing obligations) does not apply to a new lease granted to an existing tenant, or to a former tenant still in possession, if the previous lease was not a lease to which section 11 applied (and, in the case of a lease granted before 24th October 1961, would not have been if it had been granted on or after that date).

(2)   In subsection (1)—
   "existing tenant" means a person who is when, or immediately before, the new lease is granted, the lessee under another lease of the dwelling-house;
   "former tenant still in possession" means a person who—
   (a)   was the lessee under another lease of the dwelling-house which terminated at some time before the new lease was granted, and
   (b)   between the termination of that other lease and the grant of the new lease was continuously in possession of the dwelling-house or of the rents and profits of the dwelling-house; and
   "the previous lease" means the other lease referred to in the above definitions.

(3)   Section 11 does not apply to a lease of a dwelling-house which is a tenancy of an agricultural holding within the meaning of the [Agricultural Holdings Act 1986] [and in relation to which that Act applies or to a farm business tenancy within the meaning of the Agricultural Tenancies Act 1995].

(4)   Section 11 does not apply to a lease granted on or after 3rd October 1980 to—
   a local authority,
   a new town corporation,
   an urban development corporation,
   the Development Board for Rural Wales,
   a registered housing association,
   a co-operative housing association, or
   an educational institution or other body specified, or of a class specified, by regulations under section 8 of the Rent Act 1977 [or paragraph 8 of Schedule 1 to the Housing Act 1988] (bodies making student lettings)
   [a housing action trust established under Part III of the Housing Act 1988].

(5)   Section 11 does not apply to a lease granted on or after 3rd October 1980 to—
   (a)   Her Majesty in right of the Crown (unless the lease is under the management of the Crown Estate Commissioners), or
   (b)   a government department or a person holding in trust for Her Majesty for the purposes of a government department.

[601]

NOTES

Sub-s (3): words in first pair of square brackets substituted by the Agricultural Holdings Act 1986, s 100, Sch 14, para 64; words in second pair of square brackets added by the Agricultural Tenancies Act 1995, s 40, Schedule, para 31.

Sub-s (4): words in first pair of square brackets inserted by the Local Government and Housing Act 1989, s 194(1), Sch 11, para 89; words in second pair of square brackets added by the Housing Act 1988, s 116(3), (4), except with respect to leases entered into before 15 January 1989 or a lease entered into pursuant to a contract made before that date.

15 Jurisdiction of county court

The county court has jurisdiction to make a declaration that section 11 (repairing obligations) applies, or does not apply, to a lease—

    (a) whatever the net annual value of the property in question, and

    (b) notwithstanding that no other relief is sought than a declaration.

[602]

16 Meaning of "lease" and related expressions

In sections 11 to 15 (repairing obligations in short leases)—

    (a) "lease" does not include a mortgage term;

    (b) "lease of a dwelling-house" means a lease by which a building or part of a building is let wholly or mainly as a private residence, and "dwelling-house" means that building or part of a building;

    (c) "lessee" and "lessor" mean, respectively, the person for the time being entitled to the term of a lease and to the reversion expectant on it.

[603]

17 Specific performance of landlord's repairing obligations

(1) In proceedings in which a tenant of a dwelling alleges a breach on the part of his landlord of a repairing covenant relating to any part of the premises in which the dwelling is comprised, the court may order specific performance of the covenant whether or not the breach relates to a part of the premises let to the tenant and notwithstanding any equitable rule restricting the scope of the remedy, whether on the basis of a lack of mutuality or otherwise.

(2) In this section—

    (a) "tenant" includes a statutory tenant,

    (b) in relation to a statutory tenant the reference to the premises let to him is to the premises of which he is a statutory tenant,

    (c) "landlord", in relation to a tenant, includes any person against whom the tenant has a right to enforce a repairing covenant, and

    (d) "repairing covenant" means a covenant to repair, maintain, renew, construct or replace any property.

[604]

Final provisions

40 Short title, commencement and extent

(1) This Act may be cited as the Landlord and Tenant Act 1985.

(2) This Act comes into force on 1st April 1986.

(3) This Act extends to England and Wales.

[605]

INSOLVENCY ACT 1986

(C 45)

An Act to consolidate the enactments relating to company insolvency and winding up (including the winding up of companies that are not insolvent, and of unregistered companies); enactments relating to the insolvency and bankruptcy of individuals; and other enactments bearing on those two subject matters, including the functions and qualification of insolvency practitioners, the public administration of insolvency, the penalisation and redress of malpractice and wrongdoing, and the avoidance of certain transactions at an undervalue

[25 July 1986]

THE FIRST GROUP OF PARTS
COMPANY INSOLVENCY; COMPANY WINDING UP

PART II
ADMINISTRATION ORDERS

Administrators

19 Vacation of office

(1) The administrator of a company may at any time be removed from office by order of the court and may, in the prescribed circumstances, resign his office by giving notice of his resignation to the court.

(2) The administrator shall vacate office if—

    (a) he ceases to be qualified to act as an insolvency practitioner in relation to the company, or

    (b) the administration order is discharged.

(3) Where at any time a person ceases to be administrator, the [following] subsections apply.

(4) His remuneration and any expenses properly incurred by him shall be charged on and paid out of any property of the company which is in his custody or under his control at that time in priority to any security to which section 15(1) then applies.

(5) Any sums payable in respect of debts or liabilities incurred, while he was administrator, under contracts entered into . . . by him or a predecessor of his in the carrying out of his or the predecessor's functions shall be charged on and paid out of any such property as is mentioned in subsection (4) in priority to any charge arising under that subsection.

[(6) Any sums payable in respect of liabilities incurred, while he was administrator, under contracts of employment adopted by him or a predecessor of his in the carrying out of his or the predecessor's functions shall, to the extent that the liabilities are qualifying liabilities, be charged on and paid out of any such property as is mentioned in subsection (4) and enjoy the same priority as any sums to which subsection (5) applies.]

For this purpose, the administrator is not to be taken to have adopted a contract of employment by reason of anything done or omitted to be done within 14 days after his appointment.

[(7)   For the purposes of subsection (6), a liability under a contract of employment is a qualifying liability if—

(a)   it is a liability to pay a sum by way of wages or salary or contribution to an occupational pension scheme, and

(b)   it is in respect of services rendered wholly or partly after the adoption of the contract.

(8)   There shall be disregarded for the purposes of subsection (6) so much of any qualifying liability as represents payment in respect of services rendered before the adoption of the contract.

(9)   For the purposes of subsections (7) and (8)—

(a)   wages or salary payable in respect of a period of holiday or absence from work through sickness or other good cause are deemed to be wages or (as the case may be) salary in respect of services rendered in that period, and

(b)   a sum payable in lieu of holiday is deemed to be wages or (as the case may be) salary in respect of services rendered in the period by reference to which the holiday entitlement arose.

(10)   In subsection (9)(a), the reference to wages or salary payable in respect of a period of holiday includes any sums which, if they had been paid, would have been treated for the purposes of the enactments relating to social security as earnings in respect of that period.]

[605A]

NOTES

Commencement: 29 December 1986 (sub-ss (1)–(6)); 15 March 1994 (sub-ss (7)–(10)).

Sub-s (3): word in square brackets substituted by the Insolvency Act 1994, s 1(1), (2), in relation to contracts of employment adopted on or after 15 March 1994.

Sub-s (5): words omitted repealed by the Insolvency Act 1994, s 1(1), (3), in relation to contracts of employment adopted on or after 15 March 1994.

Sub-s (6): words in square brackets inserted by the Insolvency Act 1994, s 1(1), (4), in relation to contracts of employment adopted on or after 15 March 1994.

Sub-ss (7)–(10): added by the Insolvency Act 1994, s 1(1), (6), in relation to contracts of employment adopted on or after 15 March 1994.

PART III
RECEIVERSHIP

CHAPTER I
RECEIVERS AND MANAGERS (ENGLAND AND WALES)

Administrative receivers; general

44   Agency and liability for contracts

(1)   The administrative receiver of a company—

(a)   is deemed to be the company's agent, unless and until the company goes into liquidation;

(b)   is personally liable on any contract entered into by him in the carrying out of his functions (except in so far as the contract otherwise provides) and[, to the extent of any qualifying liability,] on any contract of employment adopted by him in the carrying out of those functions; and

(c)   is entitled in respect of that liability to an indemnity out of the assets of the company.

(2) For the purposes of subsection (1)(b) the administrative receiver is not to be taken to have adopted a contract of employment by reason of anything done or omitted to be done within 14 days after his appointment.

[(2A) For the purposes of subsection (1)(b), a liability under a contract of employment is a qualifying liability if—

  (a) it is a liability to pay a sum by way of wages or salary or contribution to an occupational pension scheme,

  (b) it is incurred while the administrative receiver is in office, and

  (c) it is in respect of services rendered wholly or partly after the adoption of the contract.

(2B) Where a sum payable in respect of a liability which is a qualifying liability for the purposes of subsection (1)(b) is payable in respect of services rendered partly before and partly after the adoption of the contract, liability under subsection (1)(b) shall only extend to so much of the sum as is payable in respect of services rendered after the adoption of the contract.

(2C) For the purposes of subsections (2A) and (2B)—

  (a) wages or salary payable in respect of a period of holiday or absence from work through sickness or other good cause are deemed to be wages or (as the case may be) salary in respect of services rendered in that period, and

  (b) a sum payable in lieu of holiday is deemed to be wages or (as the case may be) salary in respect of services rendered in the period by reference to which the holiday entitlement arose.

(2D) In subsection (2C)(a), the reference to wages or salary payable in respect of a period of holiday includes any sums which, if they had been paid, would have been treated for the purposes of the enactments relating to social security as earnings in respect of that period.]

(3) This section does not limit any right to indemnity which the administrative receiver would have apart from it, nor limit his liability on contracts entered into or adopted without authority, nor confer any right to indemnity in respect of that liability.

[605B]

NOTES

Commencement: 29 December 1986 (sub-ss (1), (2), (3)); 24 March 1994 (sub-ss (2A)–(2D)).

Sub-s (1): words in square brackets inserted by the Insolvency Act 1994, s 2(1), (2), in relation to contracts of employment adopted on or after 15 March 1994.

Sub-ss (2A)–(2D): inserted by the Insolvency Act 1994, s 2(1), (3), in relation to contracts of employment adopted on or after 15 March 1994.

THE SECOND GROUP OF PARTS
INSOLVENCY OF INDIVIDUALS; BANKRUPTCY

PART IX
BANKRUPTCY

CHAPTER IV
ADMINISTRATION BY TRUSTEE

Acquisition, control and realisation of bankrupt's estate

314 Powers of trustee

(1) The trustee may—

(a) with the permission of the creditors' committee or the court, exercise any of the powers specified in Part I of Schedule 5 to this Act, and

(b) without that permission, exercise any of the general powers specified in Part II of that Schedule.

(2) With the permission of the creditors' committee or the court, the trustee may appoint the bankrupt—

(a) to superintend the management of his estate or any part of it,

(b) to carry on his business (if any) for the benefit of his creditors, or

(c) in any other respect to assist in administering the estate in such manner and on such terms as the trustee may direct.

(3) A permission given for the purposes of subsection (1)(a) or (2) shall not be a general permission but shall relate to a particular proposed exercise of the power in question; and a person dealing with the trustee in good faith and for value is not to be concerned to enquire whether any permission required in either case has been given.

(4) Where the trustee has done anything without the permission required by subsection (1)(a) or (2), the court or the creditors' committee may, for the purpose of enabling him to meet his expenses out of the bankrupt's estate, ratify what the trustee has done.

But the committee shall not do so unless it is satisfied that the trustee has acted in a case of urgency and has sought its ratification without undue delay.

(5) Part III of Schedule 5 to this Act has effect with respect to the things which the trustee is able to do for the purposes of, or in connection with, the exercise of any of his powers under any of this Group of Parts.

(6) Where the trustee (not being the official receiver) in exercise of the powers conferred on him by any provision in this Group of Parts—

(a) disposes of any property comprised in the bankrupt's estate to an associate of the bankrupt, or

(b) employs a solicitor,

he shall, if there is for the time being a creditors' committee, give notice to the committee of that exercise of his powers.

(7) Without prejudice to the generality of subsection (5) and Part III of Schedule 5, the trustee may, if he thinks fit, at any time summon a general meeting of the bankrupt's creditors.

Subject to the preceding provisions in this Group of Parts, he shall summon such a meeting if he is requested to do so by a creditor of the bankrupt and the request is made with the concurrence of not less than one-tenth, in value, of the bankrupt's creditors (including the creditor making the request).

(8) Nothing in this Act is to be construed as restricting the capacity of the trustee to exercise any of his powers outside England and Wales.

[606]

NOTES

Modification: any reference to solicitor(s) etc modified to include references to bodies recognised under the Administration of Justice Act 1985, s 9, by the Solicitors' Incorporated Practices Order 1991, SI 1991/2684, arts 4, 5, Sch 1.

Disclaimer of onerous property

315 Disclaimer (general powers)

(1) Subject as follows, the trustee may, by the giving of the prescribed notice, disclaim any onerous property and may do so notwithstanding that he has taken possession of it, endeavoured to sell it or otherwise exercised rights of ownership in relation to it.

(2) The following is onerous property for the purposes of this section, that is to say—
   (a) any unprofitable contract, and
   (b) any other property comprised in the bankrupt's estate which is unsaleable or not readily saleable, or is such that it may give rise to a liability to pay money or perform any other onerous act.

(3) A disclaimer under this section—
   (a) operates so as to determine, as from the date of the disclaimer, the rights, interests and liabilities of the bankrupt and his estate in or in respect of the property disclaimed, and
   (b) discharges the trustee from all personal liability in respect of that property as from the commencement of his trusteeship,

but does not, except so far as is necessary for the purpose of releasing the bankrupt, the bankrupt's estate and the trustee from any liability, affect the rights or liabilities of any other person.

(4) A notice of disclaimer shall not be given under this section in respect of any property that has been claimed for the estate under section 307 (after-acquired property) or 308 (personal property of bankrupt exceeding reasonable replacement value) [or 308A], except with the leave of the court.

(5) Any person sustaining loss or damage in consequence of the operation of a disclaimer under this section is deemed to be a creditor of the bankrupt to the extent of the loss or damage and accordingly may prove for the loss or damage as a bankruptcy debt.

[607]

NOTES
Sub-s (4): words in square brackets inserted by the Housing Act 1988, s 117(4).

Chapter V
Effect of Bankruptcy on Certain Rights, Transactions, etc

Rights of occupation

336 Rights of occupation etc of bankrupt's spouse

(1) Nothing occurring in the initial period of the bankruptcy (that is to say, the period beginning with the day of the presentation of the petition for the bankruptcy order and ending with the vesting of the bankrupt's estate in a trustee) is to be taken as having given rise to any rights of occupation under the Matrimonial Homes Act 1983 in relation to a dwelling house comprised in the bankrupt's estate.

(2) Where a spouse's rights of occupation under the Act of 1983 are a charge on the estate or interest of the other spouse, or of trustees for the other spouse, and the other spouse is adjudged bankrupt—
   (a) the charge continues to subsist notwithstanding the bankruptcy and, subject to the provisions of that Act, binds the trustee of the bankrupt's estate and persons deriving title under that trustee, and

(b)   any application for an order under section 1 of that Act shall be made to the court having jurisdiction in relation to the bankruptcy.

(3)   Where a person and his spouse or former spouse are trustees for sale of a dwelling house and that person is adjudged bankrupt, any application by the trustee of the bankrupt's estate for an order under section 30 of the Law of Property Act 1925 (powers of court where trustees for sale refuse to act) shall be made to the court having jurisdiction in relation to the bankruptcy.

(4)   On such an application as is mentioned in subsection (2) or (3) the court shall make such order under section 1 of the Act of 1983 or section 30 of the Act of 1925 as it thinks just and reasonable having regard to—
   (a)   the interests of the bankrupt's creditors,
   (b)   the conduct of the spouse or former spouse, so far as contributing to the bankruptcy,
   (c)   the needs and financial resources of the spouse or former spouse,
   (d)   the needs of any children, and
   (e)   all the circumstances of the case other than the needs of the bankrupt.

(5)   Where such an application is made after the end of the period of one year beginning with the first vesting under Chapter IV of this Part of the bankrupt's estate in a trustee, the court shall assume, unless the circumstances of the case are exceptional, that the interests of the bankrupt's creditors outweigh all other considerations.

[608]

The Third Group of Parts
Miscellaneous Matters Bearing on Both Company and Individual Insolvency; General Interpretation

Part XIX
Final Provisions

443   Commencement

This Act comes into force on the day appointed under section 236(2) of the Insolvency Act 1985 for the coming into force of Part III of that Act (individual insolvency and bankruptcy), immediately after that Part of that Act comes into force for England and Wales.

[609]

444   Citation

This Act may be cited as the Insolvency Act 1986.

[610]

SCHEDULE 5
Powers of Trustee in Bankruptcy

Section 314

Part I
Powers Exercisable with Sanction

1.   Power to carry on any business of the bankrupt so far as may be necessary for winding it up beneficially and so far as the trustee is able to do so without contravening any requirement imposed by or under any enactment.

2. Power to bring, institute or defend any action or legal proceedings relating to the property comprised in the bankrupt's estate.

3. Power to accept as the consideration for the sale of any property comprised in the bankrupt's estate a sum of money payable at a future time subject to such stipulations as to security or otherwise as the creditors' committee or the court thinks fit.

4. Power to mortgage or pledge any part of the property comprised in the bankrupt's estate for the purpose of raising money for the payment of his debts.

5. Power, where any right, option or other power forms part of the bankrupt's estate, to make payments or incur liabilities with a view to obtaining, for the benefit of the creditors, any property which is the subject of the right, option or power.

6. Power to refer to arbitration, or compromise on such terms as may be agreed on, any debts, claims or liabilities subsisting or supposed to subsist between the bankrupt and any person who may have incurred any liability to the bankrupt.

7. Power to make such compromise or other arrangement as may be thought expedient with creditors, or persons claiming to be creditors, in respect of bankruptcy debts.

8. Power to make such compromise or other arrangement as may be thought expedient with respect to any claim arising out of or incidental to the bankrupt's estate made or capable of being made on the trustee by any person or by the trustee on any person.

[611]

PART II
GENERAL POWERS

9. Power to sell any part of the property for the time being comprised in the bankrupt's estate, including the goodwill and book debts of any business.

10. Power to give receipts for any money received by him, being receipts which effectually discharge the person paying the money from all responsibility in respect of its application.

11. Power to prove, rank, claim and draw a dividend in respect of such debts due to the bankrupt as are comprised in his estate.

12. Power to exercise in relation to any property comprised in the bankrupt's estate any powers the capacity to exercise which is vested in him under Parts VIII to XI of this Act.

13. Power to deal with any property comprised in the estate to which the bankrupt is beneficially entitled as tenant in tail in the same manner as the bankrupt might have dealt with it.

[612]

PART III
ANCILLARY POWERS

14. For the purposes of, or in connection with, the exercise of any of his powers under Parts VIII to XI of this Act, the trustee may, by his official name—
    (a) hold property of every description,
    (b) make contracts,
    (c) sue and be sued,
    (d) enter into engagements binding on himself and, in respect of the bankrupt's estate, on his successors in office,
    (e) employ an agent,
    (f) execute any power of attorney, deed or other instrument;

and he may do any other act which is necessary or expedient for the purposes of or in connection with the exercise of those powers.

[613]

BUILDING SOCIETIES ACT 1986

(C 53)

An Act to make fresh provision with respect to building societies and further provision with respect to conveyancing services

[25 July 1986]

PART III
ADVANCES, LOANS AND OTHER ASSETS

Class 1 advances and class 2 advances secured on land

13   Security for advances: valuation and supplementary and related provisions

(1)–(6)   . . .

(7)   Schedule 4 to this Act, which contains supplementary provisions as to mortgages, shall have effect.

[614]

NOTES

Sub-ss (1)–(6): not relevant to this work.

PART XI
MISCELLANEOUS AND SUPPLEMENTARY CONVEYANCING SERVICES

General

125   Short title

This Act may be cited as the Building Societies Act 1986.

[615]

126   Commencement

(1)   This Act shall come into operation as follows.

(2)   Part I (and Schedule 1) shall come into operation at the end of the period of two months beginning with the day on which this Act is passed.

(3)   The remaining provisions of this Act, except sections 121, 124, 125, this section, in Schedule 20, paragraph 7 (and section 120(4) so far as it relates to that paragraph) and Schedule 21, shall come into operation on such day as the Treasury may appoint by order made by statutory instrument and different days may be appointed for different provisions or different purposes.

(4), (5)   . . .

[616]

NOTES

Sub-ss (4), (5): not relevant to this work.

SCHEDULE 4
ADVANCES: SUPPLEMENTARY PROVISIONS

Section 13(7)

Provisions as to sale of mortgaged property

1.—(1) Where any land has been mortgaged to a building society as security for an advance and a person sells the land in the exercise of a power (whether statutory or express) exercisable by virtue of the mortgage, it shall be his duty—

    (a) in exercising that power, to take reasonable care to ensure that the price at which the land is sold is the best price that can reasonably be obtained, and

    (b) within 28 days from the completion of the sale, to send to the mortgagor at his last-known address by the recorded delivery service a notice containing the prescribed particulars of the sale.

(2) In so far as any agreement relieves, or may have the effect of relieving, a building society or any other person from the obligation imposed by sub-paragraph (1)(a) above, the agreement shall be void.

(3) Breach by a building society or any other person of the duty imposed by sub-paragraph (1)(b) above, if without reasonable excuse, shall be an offence.

(4) Any person guilty of an offence under sub-paragraph (3) above shall be liable on summary conviction—

    (a) to a fine not exceeding level 2 on the standard scale, and

    (b) to an additional fine for each week during which the offence continues not exceeding £10,

and, in relation to such an offence on the part of a building society, so shall any officer who is also guilty of the offence.

(5) Nothing in this section shall affect the operation of any rule of law relating to the duty of a mortgagee to account to his mortgagor.

(6) In sub-paragraph (1) above "mortgagor", in relation to a mortgage in favour of a building society, includes any person to whom, to the knowledge of the person selling the land, any of the rights or liabilities of the mortgagor under the mortgage have passed, whether by operation of law or otherwise.

Discharge of mortgages

2.—(1) When all money intended to be secured by a mortgage given to a building society has been fully paid or discharged, the society may endorse on or annex to the mortgage one or other of the following—

    (a) a receipt in the prescribed form under the society's seal, countersigned by any person acting under the authority of the board of directors;

    (b) a reconveyance of the mortgaged property to the mortgagor;

    (c) a reconveyance of the mortgaged property to such person of full age, and on such trusts (if any), as the mortgagor may direct.

(2) Where in pursuance of sub-paragraph (1) above a receipt is endorsed on or annexed to a mortgage, not being a charge or incumbrance registered under the Land Registration Act 1925, the receipt shall operate in accordance with section 115(1), (3), (6) and (8) of the Law of Property Act 1925 (discharge of mortgages by receipt) in the like manner as a receipt which fulfils all the requirements of subsection (1) of that section.

(3) Section 115(9) of the Law of Property Act 1925 shall not apply to a receipt in the prescribed form endorsed or annexed by a building society in pursuance of sub-paragraph (1) above; and in the application of that subsection to a receipt so endorsed or annexed which is not in that form, the receipt shall be taken to be executed in the manner required by the statute relating to the society if it is under the society's seal and countersigned as mentioned in sub-paragraph (1)(a) above.

(4) The foregoing sub-paragraphs shall, in the case of a mortgage of registered land, have effect without prejudice to the operation of the Land Registration Act 1925 or any rules in force under it.

(5) In this paragraph—

"mortgage" includes a further charge;

"the mortgagor", in relation to a mortgage, means the person for the time being entitled to the equity of redemption; and

"registered land" has the same meaning as in the Land Registration Act 1925.

(6) This paragraph does not apply to Scotland.

(7) In the application of this paragraph to Northern Ireland—

(a) in sub-paragraph (1) for the words "on such trusts" there shall be substituted the words "on such uses";

(b) in sub-paragraph (2)—

(i) for the words from "charge" to "Property Act 1925" there shall be substituted the words "on registered land, the receipt to operate in accordance with Article 3(1), (7) and (9) of the Property (Discharge of Mortgage by Receipt) (Northern Ireland) Order 1983"; and

(ii) for the words "subsection (1) of that section" there shall be substituted the words "paragraph (1) of that Article";

(c) for sub-paragraphs (3) and (4) there shall be substituted—

"(3) If the mortgage is registered in accordance with the Registration of Deeds Act (Northern Ireland) 1970, the registrar under that Act shall—

(a) on production of the receipt mentioned in sub-paragraph (1) above make a note in the Abstract Book against the entry relating to the mortgage that the mortgage is satisfied; and

(b) grant a certificate, either on the mortgage or separately, that the mortgage is satisfied.

(4) The certificate granted under sub-paragraph (3)(b) above shall—

(a) be received in all courts and proceedings without further proof; and

(b) have the effect of clearing the register of the mortgage.";

(d) in sub-paragraph (5) for the definition of "registered land" there shall be substituted the following definition—

"registered land" means land the title to which is registered under Part III of the Land Registration Act (Northern Ireland) 1970;".

Power to prescribe form of documents

3.—(1) The Chief Registrar may make rules for prescribing anything authorised or required by any provision of this Schedule to be prescribed; and in this Schedule "prescribed" means prescribed by rules made under this paragraph.

(2) The power to make rules under this paragraph shall be exercisable by statutory instrument.

FAMILY LAW REFORM ACT 1987

(C 42)

An Act to reform the law relating to the consequences of birth outside marriage; to make further provision with respect to the rights and duties of parents and the determination of parentage; and for connected purposes

[15 May 1987]

PART I
GENERAL PRINCIPLE

1 General principle

(1)   In this Act and enactments passed and instruments made after the coming into force of this section, references (however expressed) to any relationship between two persons shall, unless the contrary intention appears, be construed without regard to whether or not the father and mother of either of them, or the father and mother of any person through whom the relationship is deduced, have or had been married to each other at any time.

(2)   In this Act and enactments passed after the coming into force of this section, unless the contrary intention appears—

  (a)   references to a person whose father and mother were married to each other at the time of his birth include; and

  (b)   references to a person whose father and mother were not married to each other at the time of his birth do not include,

references to any person whom subsection (3) below applies, and cognate references shall be construed accordingly.

(3)   This subsection applies to any person who—

  (a)   is treated as legitimate by virtue of section 1 of the Legitimacy Act 1976;

  (b)   is a legitimated person within the meaning of section 10 of that Act;

  (c)   is an adopted child within the meaning of Part IV of that Act 1976; or

  (d)   is otherwise treated in law as legitimate.

(4)   For the purpose of construing references falling within subsection (2) above, the time of a person's birth shall be taken to include any time during the period beginning with—

  (a)   the insemination resulting in his birth; or

  (b)   where there was no such insemination, his conception,

and (in either case) ending with his birth.

[618]

PART III
PROPERTY RIGHTS

18 Succession on intestacy

(1)   In Part IV of the Administration of Estates Act 1925 (which deals with the distribution of the estate of an intestate), references (however expressed) to any relationship between two persons shall be construed in accordance with section 1 above.

(2)   For the purposes of subsection (1) above and that Part of that Act, a person whose father and mother were not married to each other at the time of his birth shall be presumed not to have been survived by his father, or by any person related to him only through his father, unless the contrary is shown.

(3)   In section 50(1) of that Act (which relates to the construction of documents), the reference to Part IV of that Act, or to the foregoing provisions of that Part, shall in relation to an instrument inter vivos made, or a will or codicil coming into operation, after the coming into force of this section (but not in relation to instruments inter vivos made or wills or codicils coming into operation earlier) be construed as including references to this section.

(4)   This section does not affect any rights under the intestacy of a person dying before the coming into force of this section.

[619]

19   Dispositions of property

(1)   In the following dispositions, namely—
   (a)   dispositions inter vivos made on or after the date on which this section comes into force; and
   (b)   dispositions by will or codicil where the will or codicil is made on or after that date,

references (whether express or implied) to any relationship between two persons shall be construed in accordance with section 1 above.

(2)   It is hereby declared that the use, without more, of the word "heir" or "heirs" or any expression which is used to create an entailed interest in real or personal property does not show a contrary intention for the purposes of section 1 as applied by subsection (1) above.

(3)   In relation to the dispositions mentioned in subsection (1) above, section 33 of the Trustee Act 1925 (which specifies the trust implied by a direction that income is to be held on protective trusts for the benefit of any person) shall have effect as if any reference (however expressed) to any relationship between two persons were constructed in accordance with section 1 above.

(4)   Where under any disposition of real or personal property, any interest in such property is limited (whether subject to any preceding limitation or charge or not) in such a way that it would, apart from this section, devolve (as nearly as the law permits) along with a dignity or title of honour, then—
   (a)   whether or not the disposition contains an express reference to the dignity or title of honour; and
   (b)   whether or not the property or some interest in the property may in some event become severed from it,

nothing in this section shall operate to sever the property or any interest in it from the dignity or title, but the property or interest shall devolve in all respects as if this section had not been enacted.

(5)   This section is without prejudice to section 42 of the Adoption Act 1976 (construction of dispositions in cases of adoption).

(6)   In this section "disposition" means a disposition, including an oral disposition, of real or personal property whether inter vivos or by will or codicil.

(7)   Notwithstanding any rule of law, a disposition made by will or codicil executed before the date on which this section comes into force shall not be treated for the purposes of this section as made on or after that date by reason only that the will or codicil is confirmed by a codicil executed on or after that date.

[620]

21   Entitlement to grant of probate etc

(1)   For the purpose of determining the person or persons who would in accordance with probate rules be entitled to a grant of probate or administration in respect of the estate of a deceased person, the deceased shall be presumed, unless the contrary is shown, not to have been survived—

     (a)   by any person related to him whose father and mother were not married to each other at the time of his birth; or

     (b)   by any person whose relationship with him is deduced through such a person as is mentioned in paragraph (a) above.

(2)   In this section "probate rules" means rules of court made under section 127 of the Supreme Court Act 1981.

(3)   This section does not apply in relation to the estate of a person dying before the coming into force of this section.

[621]

Part VI
Miscellaneous and Supplemental

Supplemental

34   Short title, commencement and extent

(1)   This Act may be cited as the Family Law Reform Act 1987.

(2)   This Act shall come into force on such day as the Lord Chancellor may by order made by statutory instrument appoint; and different days may be so appointed for different provisions or different purposes.

(3), (4). . .

(5)   Subject to subsection (4) above, this Act extends to England and Wales only.

[622]

NOTES
     Sub-ss (3), (4): not relevant to this work.

LANDLORD AND TENANT ACT 1988

(C 26)

An Act to make new provision for imposing statutory duties in connection with covenants in tenancies against assigning, underletting, charging or parting with the possession of premises without consent

[29 July 1988]

1   Qualified duty to consent to assigning, underletting etc of premises

(1)   This section applies in any case where—

    (a)   a tenancy includes a covenant on the part of the tenant not to enter into one or more of the following transactions, that is—
        (i)   assigning,
        (ii)   underletting,
        (iii)   charging, or
        (iv)   parting with the possession of,
      the premises comprised in the tenancy or any part of the premises without the consent of the landlord or some other person, but
    (b)   the covenant is subject to the qualification that the consent is not to be unreasonably withheld (whether or not it is also subject to any other qualification).

(2)   In this section and section 2 of this Act—
    (a)   references to a proposed transaction are to any assignment, underletting, charging or parting with possession to which the covenant relates, and
    (b)   references to the person who may consent to such a transaction are to the person who under the covenant may consent to the tenant entering into the proposed transaction.

(3)   Where there is served on the person who may consent to a proposed transaction a written application by the tenant for consent to the transaction, he owes a duty to the tenant within a reasonable time—
    (a)   to give consent, except in a case where it is reasonable not to give consent,
    (b)   to serve on the tenant written notice of his decision whether or not to give consent specifying in addition—
        (i)   if the consent is given subject to conditions, the conditions,
        (ii)   if the consent is withheld, the reasons for withholding it.

(4)   Giving consent subject to any condition that is not a reasonable condition does not satisfy the duty under subsection (3)(a) above.

(5)   For the purposes of this Act it is reasonable for a person not to give consent to a proposed transaction only in a case where, if he withheld consent and the tenant completed the transaction, the tenant would be in breach of a covenant.

(6)   It is for the person who owed any duty under subsection (3) above—
    (a)   if he gave consent and the question arises whether he gave it within a reasonable time, to show that he did,
    (b)   if he gave consent subject to any condition and the question arises whether the condition was a reasonable condition, to show that it was,
    (c)   if he did not give consent and the question arises whether it was reasonable for him not to do so, to show that it was reasonable,

and, if the question arises whether he served notice under that subsection within a reasonable time, to show that he did.

[623]

2   Duty to pass on applications

(1)   If, in a case where section 1 of this Act applies, any person receives a written application by the tenant for consent to a proposed transaction and that person—
    (a)   is a person who may consent to the transaction or (though not such a person) is the landlord, and
    (b)   believes that another person, other than a person who he believes has received the application or a copy of it, is a person who may consent to the transaction,

he owes a duty to the tenant (whether or not he owes him any duty under section 1 of this Act) to take such steps as are reasonable to secure the receipt within a reasonable time by the other person of a copy of the application.

(2)　The reference in section 1(3) of this Act to the service of an application on a person who may consent to a proposed transaction includes a reference to the receipt by him of an application or a copy of an application (whether it is for his consent or that of another).

[624]

3　Qualified duty to approve consent by another

(1)　This section applies in any case where—
- (a)　a tenancy includes a covenant on the part of the tenant not without the approval of the landlord to consent to the sub-tenant—
  - (i)　assigning,
  - (ii)　underletting,
  - (iii)　charging, or
  - (iv)　parting with the possession of,
  - the premises comprised in the sub-tenancy or any part of the premises, but
- (b)　the covenant is subject to the qualification that the approval is not to be unreasonably withheld (whether or not it is also subject to any other qualification).

(2)　Where there is served on the landlord a written application by the tenant for approval or a copy of a written application to the tenant by the sub-tenant for consent to a transaction to which the covenant relates the landlord owes a duty to the sub-tenant within a reasonable time—
- (a)　to give approval, except in a case where it is reasonable not to give approval,
- (b)　to serve on the tenant and the sub-tenant written notice of his decision whether or not to give approval specifying in addition—
  - (i)　if approval is given subject to conditions, the conditions,
  - (ii)　if approval is withheld, the reasons for withholding it.

(3)　Giving approval subject to any condition that is not a reasonable condition does not satisfy the duty under subsection (2)(a) above.

(4)　For the purposes of this section it is reasonable for the landlord not to give approval only in a case where, if he withheld approval and the tenant gave his consent, the tenant would be in breach of covenant.

(5)　It is for a landlord who owed any duty under subsection (2) above—
- (a)　if he gave approval and the question arises whether he gave it within a reasonable time, to show that he did,
- (b)　if he gave approval subject to any condition and the question arises whether the condition was a reasonable condition, to show that it was,
- (c)　if he did not give approval and the question arises whether it was reasonable for him not to do so, to show that it was reasonable,

and, if the question arises whether he served notice under that subsection within a reasonable time, to show that he did.

[625]

4   Breach of duty

A claim that a person has broken any duty under this Act may be made the subject of civil proceedings in like manner as any other claim in tort for breach of statutory duty.

[626]

7   Short title, commencement and extent

(1)   This Act may be cited as the Landlord and Tenant Act 1988.

(2)   This Act shall come into force at the end of the period of two months beginning with the day on which it is passed.

(3)   This Act extends to England and Wales only.

[627]

HOUSING ACT 1988

(C 50)

An Act to make further provision with respect to dwelling-houses let on tenancies or occupied under licences; to amend the Rent Act 1977 and the Rent (Agriculture) Act 1976; to establish a body, Housing for Wales, having functions relating to housing associations; to amend the Housing Associations Act 1985 and to repeal and re-enact with amendments certain provisions of Part II of that Act; to make provision for the establishment of housing action trusts for areas designated by the Secretary of State; to confer on persons approved for the purpose the right to acquire from public sector landlords certain dwelling-houses occupied by secure tenants; to make further provision about rent officers, the administration of housing benefit and rent allowance subsidy, the right to buy, repair notices and certain disposals of land and the application of capital money arising thereon; to make provision consequential upon the Housing (Scotland) Act 1988; and for connected purposes

[15 November 1988]

PART I
RENTED ACCOMMODATION

CHAPTER IV
PROTECTION FROM EVICTION

27   Damages for unlawful eviction

(1)   This section applies if, at any time after 9th June 1988, a landlord (in this section referred to as "the landlord in default") or any person acting on behalf of the landlord in default unlawfully deprives the residential occupier of any premises of his occupation of the whole or part of the premises.

(2)   This section also applies if, at any time after 9th June 1988, a landlord (in this section referred to as "the landlord in default") or any person acting on behalf of the landlord in default—

    (a)   attempts unlawfully to deprive the residential occupier of any premises of his occupation of the whole or part of the premises, or

    (b)   knowing or having reasonable cause to believe that the conduct is likely to cause the residential occupier of any premises—

       (i)   to give up his occupation of the premises or any part thereof, or

       (ii) to refrain from exercising any right or pursuing any remedy in respect of the premises or any part thereof,

does acts likely to interfere with the peace or comfort of the residential occupier or members of his household, or persistently withdraws or withholds services reasonably required for the occupation of the premises as a residence,

and, as a result, the residential occupier gives up his occupation of the premises as a residence.

(3)   Subject to the following provisions of this section, where this section applies, the landlord in default shall, by virtue of this section, be liable to pay to the former residential occupier, in respect of his loss of the right to occupy the premises in question as his residence, damages assessed on the basis set out in section 28 below.

(4)   Any liability arising by virtue of subsection (3) above—

    (a)   shall be in the nature of a liability in tort; and

    (b)   subject to subsection (5) below, shall be in addition to any liability arising apart from this section (whether in tort, contract or otherwise).

(5)   Nothing in this section affects the right of a residential occupier to enforce any liability which arises apart from this section in respect of his loss of the right to occupy premises as his residence; but damages shall not be awarded both in respect of such a liability and in respect of a liability arising by virtue of this section on account of the same loss.

(6)   No liability shall arise by virtue of subsection (3) above if—

    (a)   before the date on which proceedings to enforce the liability are finally disposed of, the former residential occupier is reinstated in the premises in question in such circumstances that he becomes again the residential occupier of them; or

    (b)   at the request of the former residential occupier, a court makes an order (whether in the nature of an injunction or otherwise) as a result of which he is reinstated as mentioned in paragraph (a) above;

and, for the purposes of paragraph (a) above, proceedings to enforce a liability are finally disposed of on the earliest date by which the proceedings (including any proceedings on or in consequence of an appeal) have been determined and any time for appealing or further appealing has expired, except that if any appeal is abandoned, the proceedings shall be taken to be disposed of on the date of the abandonment.

(7)   If, in proceedings to enforce a liability arising by virtue of subsection (3) above, it appears to the court—

    (a)   that, prior to the event which gave rise to the liability, the conduct of the former residential occupier or any person living with him in the premises concerned was such that it is reasonable to mitigate the damages for which the landlord in default would otherwise be liable, or

    (b)   that, before the proceedings were begun, the landlord in default offered to reinstate the former residential occupier in the premises in question and either it was unreasonable of the former residential occupier to refuse that offer or, if he had obtained alternative accommodation before the offer was made, it would have been unreasonable of him to refuse that offer if he had not obtained that accommodation,

the court may reduce the amount of damages which would otherwise be payable to such amount as it thinks appropriate.

(8)   In proceedings to enforce a liability arising by virtue of subsection (3) above, it shall be a defence for the defendant to prove that he believed, and had reasonable cause to believe—

   (a)   that the residential occupier had ceased to reside in the premises in question at the time when he was deprived of occupation as mentioned in subsection (1) above or, as the case may be, when the attempt was made or the acts were done as a result of which he gave up his occupation of those premises; or

   (b)   that, where the liability would otherwise arise by virtue only of the doing of acts or the withdrawal or withholding of services, he had reasonable grounds for doing the acts or withdrawing or withholding the services in question.

(9)   In this section—

   (a)   "residential occupier", in relation to any premises, has the same meaning as in section 1 of the 1977 Act;

   (b)   "the right to occupy", in relation to a residential occupier, includes any restriction on the right of another person to recover possession of the premises in question;

   (c)   "landlord", in relation to a residential occupier, means the person who, but for the occupier's right to occupy, would be entitled to occupation of the premises and any superior landlord under whom that person derives title;

   (d)   "former residential occupier", in relation to any premises, means the person who was the residential occupier until he was deprived of or gave up his occupation as mentioned in subsection (1) or subsection (2) above (and, in relation to a former residential occupier, "the right to occupy" and "landlord" shall be construed accordingly).

                                                                            [628]

28   The measure of damages

(1)   The basis for the assessment of damages referred to in section 27(3) above is the difference in value, determined as at the time immediately before the residential occupier ceased to occupy the premises in question as his residence, between—

   (a)   the value of the interest of the landlord in default determined on the assumption that the residential occupier continues to have the same right to occupy the premises as before that time; and

   (b)   the value of that interest determined on the assumption that the residential occupier has ceased to have that right.

(2)   In relation to any premises, any reference in this section to the interest of the landlord in default is a reference to his interest in the building in which the premises in question are comprised (whether or not that building contains any other premises) together with its curtilage.

(3)   For the purposes of the valuations referred to in subsection (1) above, it shall be assumed—

   (a)   that the landlord in default is selling his interest on the open market to a willing buyer;

   (b)   that neither the residential occupier nor any member of his family wishes to buy; and

   (c)   that it is unlawful to carry out any substantial development of any of the land in which the landlord's interest subsists or to demolish the whole or part of any building on that land.

(4)   In this section "the landlord in default" has the same meaning as in section 27 above and subsection (9) of that section applies in relation to this section as it applies in relation to that.

(5)   Section 113 of the Housing Act 1985 (meaning of "members of a person's family") applies for the purposes of subsection (3)(b) above.

(6)   The reference in subsection (3)(c) above to substantial development of any of the land in which the landlord's interest subsists is a reference to any development other than—

    (a)   development for which planning permission is granted by a general development order for the time being in force and which is carried out so as to comply with any condition or limitation subject to which planning permission is so granted; or

    (b)   a change of use resulting in the building referred to in subsection (2) above or any part of it being used as, or as part of, one or more dwelling-houses;

and in this subsection "general development order" [has the meaning given in section 56(6) of the Town and Country Planning Act 1990] and other expressions have the same meaning as in that Act.

[629]

NOTES

    Sub-s (6): words in square brackets substituted by the Planning (Consequential Provisions) Act 1990, s 4, Sch 2, para 79(1).

    The Act: Protection from Eviction Act 1977.

PART V
MISCELLANEOUS AND GENERAL

Supplementary

141   Short title, commencement and extent

(1)   This Act may be cited as the Housing Act 1988.

(2)   The provisions of Parts II and IV of this Act and sections 119, 122, 124, 128, 129, 135 and 140 above shall come into force on such day as the Secretary of State may by order made by statutory instrument appoint, and different days may be so appointed for different provisions or for different purposes.

(3)   Part I and this Part of this Act, other than sections 119, 122, 124, 128, 129, 132, 133, 134, 135 and 138 onwards, shall come into force at the expiry of the period of two months beginning on the day it is passed; and any reference in those provisions to the commencement of this Act shall be construed accordingly.

(4)   An order under subsection (2) above may make such transitional provisions as appear to the Secretary of State necessary or expedient in connection with the provisions brought into force by the order.

(5)   Parts I, III and IV of this Act and this Part, except sections 118, 128, 132, 134, 135 and 137 onwards, extend to England and Wales only.

(6)   This Act does not extend to Northern Ireland.

[630]

LAW OF PROPERTY (MISCELLANEOUS PROVISIONS) ACT 1989

(C 34)

An Act to make new provision with respect to deeds and their execution and contracts for the sale or other disposition of interests in land; and to abolish the rule of law known as the rule in Bain v Fothergill

[27 July 1989]

1 Deeds and their execution

(1) Any rule of law which—
    (a) restricts the substances on which a deed may be written;
    (b) requires a seal for the valid execution of an instrument as a deed by an individual; or
    (c) requires authority by one person to another to deliver an instrument as a deed on his behalf to be given by deed,

is abolished.

(2) An instrument shall not be a deed unless—
    (a) it makes it clear on its face that it is intended to be a deed by the person making it or, as the case may be, by the parties to it (whether by describing itself as a deed or expressing itself to be executed or signed as a deed or otherwise); and
    (b) it is validly executed as a deed by that person or, as the case may be, one or more of those parties.

(3) An instrument is validly executed as a deed by an individual if, and only if—
    (a) it is signed—
      (i) by him in the presence of a witness who attests the signature; or
      (ii) at his direction and in his presence and the presence of two witnesses who each attest the signature; and
    (b) it is delivered as a deed by him or a person authorised to do so on his behalf.

(4) In subsections (2) and (3) above "sign", in relation to an instrument, includes making one's mark on the instrument and "signature" is to be construed accordingly.

(5) Where a solicitor[, duly certificated notary public] or licensed conveyancer, or an agent or employee of a solicitor[, duly certificated notary public] or licensed conveyancer, in the course of or in connection with a transaction involving the disposition or creation of an interest in land, purports to deliver an instrument as a deed on behalf of a party to the instrument, it shall be conclusively presumed in favour of a purchaser that he is authorised so to deliver the instrument.

(6) In subsection (5) above—
    "disposition" and "purchaser" have the same meanings as in the Law of Property Act 1925;
    ["duly certificated notary public" has the same meaning as it has in the Solicitors Act 1974 by virtue of section 87 of that Act;] and
    "interest in land" means any estate, interest or charge in or over land or in or over the proceeds of sale of land.

(7) Where an instrument under seal that constitutes a deed is required for the purposes of an Act passed before this section comes into force, this section shall have effect as to signing, sealing or delivery of an instrument by an individual in place of any provision of that Act as to signing, sealing or delivery.

(8) The enactments mentioned in Schedule 1 to this Act (which in consequence of this section require amendments other than those provided by subsection (7) above) shall have effect with the amendments specified in that Schedule.

(9) Nothing in subsection (1)(b), (2), (3), (7) or (8) above applies in relation to deeds required or authorised to be made under—
    (a) the seal of the county palatine of Lancaster;
    (b) the seal of the Duchy of Lancaster; or
    (c) the seal of the Duchy of Cornwall.

(10) The references in this section to the execution of a deed by an individual do not include execution by a corporation sole and the reference in subsection (7) above to signing, sealing or delivery by an individual does not include signing, sealing or delivery by such a corporation.

(11) Nothing in this section applies in relation to instruments delivered as deeds before this section comes into force.

[631]

NOTES
    Commencement: 31 July 1990.
    Sub-ss (5), (6): words in square brackets inserted by the Courts and Legal Services Act 1990, s 125(2), Sch 17, para 20.

2   Contracts for sale etc of land to be made by signed writing

(1) A contract for the sale or other disposition of an interest in land can only be made in writing and only by incorporating all the terms which the parties have expressly agreed in one document or, where contracts are exchanged, in each.

(2) The terms may be incorporated in a document either by being set out in it or by reference to some other document.

(3) The document incorporating the terms or, where contracts are exchanged, one of the documents incorporating them (but not necessarily the same one) must be signed by or on behalf of each party to the contract.

(4) Where a contract for the sale or other disposition of an interest in land satisfies the conditions of this section by reason only of the rectification of one or more documents in pursuance of an order of a court, the contract shall come into being, or be deemed to have come into being, at such time as may be specified in the order.

(5) This section does not apply in relation to—
    (a) a contract to grant such a lease as is mentioned in section 54(2) of the Law of Property Act 1925 (short leases);
    (b) a contract made in the course of a public auction; or
    (c) a contract regulated under the Financial Services Act 1986;

and nothing in this section affects the creation or operation of resulting, implied or constructive trusts.

(6) In this section—
    "disposition" has the same meaning as in the Law of Property Act 1925;

"interest in land" means any estate, interest or charge in or over land or in or over the proceeds of sale of land.

(7) Nothing in this section shall apply in relation to contracts made before this section comes into force.

(8) . . .

[632]

_____

NOTES

Sub-s (8): repeals the Law of Property Act 1925, s 40.

_____

5 Commencement

(1) The provisions of this Act to which this subsection applies shall come into force on such day as the Lord Chancellor may by order made by statutory instrument appoint.

(2) The provisions to which subsection (1) above applies are—
  (a) section 1 above; and
  (b) section 4 above, except so far as it relates to section 40 of the Law of Property Act 1925.

(3) The provisions of this Act to which this subsection applies shall come into force at the end of the period of two months beginning with the day on which this Act is passed.

(4) The provisions of this Act to which subsection (3) above applies are–
  (a) sections 2 and 3 above; and
  (b) section 4 above, so far as it relates to section 40 of the Law of Property Act 1925.

[633]

6 Citation

(1) This Act may be cited as the Law of Property (Miscellaneous Provisions) Act 1989.

(2) This Act extends to England and Wales only.

[634]

ACCESS TO NEIGHBOURING LAND ACT 1992

(C 23)

An Act to enable persons who desire to carry out works to any land which are reasonably necessary for the preservation of that land to obtain access to neighbouring land in order to do so; and for purposes connected therewith

[16 March 1992]

1 Access orders

(1) A person—
  (a) who, for the purpose of carrying out works to any land (the "dominant land"), desires to enter upon any adjoining or adjacent land (the "servient land"), and

(b) who needs, but does not have, the consent of some other person to that entry,

may make an application to the court for an order under this section ("an access order") against that other person.

(2) On an application under this section, the court shall make an access order if, and only if, it is satisfied—

    (a) that the works are reasonably necessary for the preservation of the whole or any part of the dominant land; and

    (b) that they cannot be carried out, or would be substantially more difficult to carry out, without entry upon the servient land;

but this subsection is subject to subsection (3) below.

(3) The court shall not make an access order in any case where it is satisfied that, were it to make such an order—

    (a) the respondent or any other person would suffer interference with, or disturbance of, his use or enjoyment of the servient land, or

    (b) the respondent, or any other person (whether of full age or capacity or not) in occupation of the whole or any part of the servient land, would suffer hardship,

to such a degree by reason of the entry (notwithstanding any requirement of this Act or any term or condition that may be imposed under it) that it would be unreasonable to make the order.

(4) Where the court is satisfied on an application under this section that it is reasonably necessary to carry out any basic preservation works to the dominant land, those works shall be taken for the purposes of this Act to be reasonably necessary for the preservation of the land; and in this subsection "basic preservation works" means any of the following, that is to say—

    (a) the maintenance, repair or renewal of any part of a building or other structure comprised in, or situate on, the dominant land;

    (b) the clearance, repair or renewal of any drain, sewer, pipe or cable so comprised or situate;

    (c) the treatment, cutting back, felling, removal or replacement of any hedge, tree, shrub or other growing thing which is so comprised and which is, or is in danger of becoming, damaged, diseased, dangerous, insecurely rooted or dead;

    (d) the filling in, or clearance, of any ditch so comprised;

but this subsection is without prejudice to the generality of the works which may, apart from it, be regarded by the court as reasonably necessary for the preservation of any land.

(5) If the court considers it fair and reasonable in all the circumstances of the case, works may be regarded for the purposes of this Act as being reasonably necessary for the preservation of any land (or, for the purposes of subsection (4) above, as being basic preservation works which it is reasonably necessary to carry out to any land) notwithstanding that the works incidentally involve—

    (a) the making of some alteration, adjustment or improvement to the land, or

    (b) the demolition of the whole or any part of a building or structure comprised in or situate upon the land.

(6) Where any works are reasonably necessary for the preservation of the whole or any part of the dominant land, the doing to the dominant land of anything which is requisite for, incidental to, or consequential on, the carrying out of those works shall

be treated for the purposes of this Act as the carrying out of works which are reasonably necessary for the preservation of that land; and references in this Act to works, or to the carrying out of works, shall be construed accordingly.

(7) Without prejudice to the generality of subsection (6) above, if it is reasonably necessary for a person to inspect the dominant land—

   (a) for the purpose of ascertaining whether any works may be reasonably necessary for the preservation of the whole or any part of that land,

   (b) for the purpose of making any map or plan, or ascertaining the course of any drain, sewer, pipe or cable, in preparation for, or otherwise in connection with, the carrying out of works which are so reasonably necessary, or

   (c) otherwise in connection with the carrying out of any such works,

the making of such an inspection shall be taken for the purposes of this Act to be the carrying out to the dominant land of works which are reasonably necessary for the preservation of that land; and references in this Act to works, or to the carrying out of works, shall be construed accordingly.

[634A]

NOTES

Commencement: 31 January 1993.

2　Terms and conditions of access orders

(1) An access order shall specify—

   (a) the works to the dominant land that may be carried out by entering upon the servient land in pursuance of the order;

   (b) the particular area of servient land that may be entered upon by virtue of the order for the purpose of carrying out those works to the dominant land; and

   (c) the date on which, or the period during which, the land may be so entered upon;

and in the following provisions of this Act any reference to the servient land is a reference to the area specified in the order in pursuance of paragraph (b) above.

(2) An access order may impose upon the applicant or the respondent such terms and conditions as appear to the court to be reasonably necessary for the purpose of avoiding or restricting—

   (a) any loss, damage, or injury which might otherwise be caused to the respondent or any other person by reason of the entry authorised by the order; or

   (b) any inconvenience or loss of privacy that might otherwise be so caused to the respondent or any other person.

(3) Without prejudice to the generality of subsection (2) above, the terms and conditions which may be imposed under that subsection include provisions with respect to—

   (a) the manner in which the specified works are to be carried out;

   (b) the days on which, and the hours between which, the work involved may be executed;

   (c) the persons who may undertake the carrying out of the specified works or enter upon the servient land under or by virtue of the order;

   (d) the taking of any such precautions by the applicant as may be specified in the order.

(4)   An access order may also impose terms and conditions—

     (a)   requiring the applicant to pay, or to secure that such person connected with him as may be specified in the order pays, compensation for—

        (i)   any loss, damage or injury, or

        (ii)   any substantial loss of privacy or other substantial inconvenience,

       which will, or might, be caused to the respondent or any other person by reason of the entry authorised by the order;

     (b)   requiring the applicant to secure that he, or such person connected with him as may be specified in the order, is insured against any such risks as may be so specified; or

     (c)   requiring such a record to be made of the condition of the servient land, or of such part of it as may be so specified, as the court may consider expedient with a view to facilitating the determination of any question that may arise concerning damage to that land.

(5)   An access order may include provision requiring the applicant to pay the respondent such sum by way of consideration for the privilege of entering the servient land in pursuance of the order as appears to the court to be fair and reasonable having regard to all the circumstances of the case, including, in particular—

     (a)   the likely financial advantage of the order to the applicant and any persons connected with him; and

     (b)   the degree of inconvenience likely to be caused to the respondent or any other person by the entry;

but no payment shall be ordered under this subsection if and to the extent that the works which the applicant desires to carry out by means of the entry are works to residential land.

(6)   For the purposes of subsection (5)(a) above, the likely financial advantage of an access order to the applicant and any persons connected with him shall in all cases be taken to be a sum of money equal to the greater of the following amounts, that is to say—

     (a)   the amount (if any) by which so much of any likely increase in the value of any land—

        (i)   which consists of or includes the dominant land, and

        (ii)   which is owned or occupied by the same person as the dominant land,

       as may reasonably be regarded as attributable to the carrying out of the specified works exceeds the likely cost of carrying out those works with the benefit of the access order; and

     (b)   the difference (if it would have been possible to carry out the specified works without entering upon the servient land) between—

        (i)   the likely cost of carrying out those works without entering upon the servient land; and

        (ii)   the likely cost of carrying them out with the benefit of the access order.

(7)   For the purposes of subsection (5) above, "residential land" means so much of any land as consists of—

     (a)   a dwelling or part of a dwelling;

     (b)   a garden, yard, private garage or outbuilding which is used and enjoyed wholly or mainly with a dwelling; or

     (c)   in the case of a building which includes one or more dwellings, any part of the building which is used and enjoyed wholly or mainly with those dwellings or any of them.

(8)   The persons who are to be regarded for the purposes of this section as "connected with" the applicant are—

  (a)   the owner of any estate or interest in, or right over, the whole or any part of the dominant land;

  (b)   the occupier of the whole or any part of the dominant land; and

  (c)   any person whom the applicant may authorise under section 3(7) below to exercise the power of entry conferred by the access order.

(9)   The court may make provision—

  (a)   for the reimbursement by the applicant of any expenses reasonably incurred by the respondent in connection with the application which are not otherwise recoverable as costs;

  (b)   for the giving of security by the applicant for any sum that might become payable to the respondent or any other person by virtue of this section or section 3 below.

[634B]

NOTES
Commencement: 31 January 1993.

3   Effect of access order

(1)   An access order requires the respondent, so far as he has power to do so, to permit the applicant or any of his associates to do anything which the applicant or associate is authorised or required to do under or by virtue of the order or this section.

(2)   Except as otherwise provided by or under this Act, an access order authorises the applicant or any of his associates, without the consent of the respondent,—

  (a)   to enter upon the servient land for the purpose of carrying out the specified works;

  (b)   to bring on to that land, leave there during the period permitted by the order and, before the end of that period, remove, such materials, plant and equipment as are reasonably necessary for the carrying out of those works; and

  (c)   to bring on to that land any waste arising from the carrying out of those works, if it is reasonably necessary to do so in the course of removing it from the dominant land;

but nothing in this Act or in any access order shall authorise the applicant or any of his associates to leave anything in, on or over the servient land (otherwise than in discharge of their duty to make good that land) after their entry for the purpose of carrying out works to the dominant land ceases to be authorised under or by virtue of the order.

(3)   An access order requires the applicant—

  (a)   to secure that any waste arising from the carrying out of the specified works is removed from the servient land forthwith;

  (b)   to secure that, before the entry ceases to be authorised under or by virtue of the order, the servient land is, so far as reasonably practicable, made good; and

  (c)   to indemnify the respondent against any damage which may be caused to the servient land or any goods by the applicant or any of his associates which would not have been so caused had the order not been made;

but this subsection is subject to subsections (4) and (5) below.

(4)   In making an access order, the court may vary or exclude, in whole or in part,—

  (a)   any authorisation that would otherwise be conferred by subsection (2)(b) or (c) above; or

  (b)   any requirement that would otherwise be imposed by subsection (3) above.

(5)   Without prejudice to the generality of subsection (4) above, if the court is satisfied that it is reasonably necessary for any such waste as may arise from the carrying out of the specified works to be left on the servient land for some period before removal, the access order may, in place of subsection (3)(a) above, include provision—

  (a)   authorising the waste to be left on that land for such period as may be permitted by the order; and

  (b)   requiring the applicant to secure that the waste is removed before the end of that period.

(6)   Where the applicant or any of his associates is authorised or required under or by virtue of an access order or this section to enter, or do any other thing, upon the servient land, he shall not (as respects that access order) be taken to be a trespasser from the beginning on account of his, or any other person's, subsequent conduct.

(7)   For the purposes of this section, the applicant's "associates" are such number of persons (whether or not servants or agents of his) whom he may reasonably authorise under this subsection to exercise the power of entry conferred by the access order as may be reasonably necessary for carrying out the specified works.

[634C]

NOTES
Commencement: 31 January 1993.

4   Persons bound by access order, unidentified persons and bar on contracting out

(1)   In addition to the respondent, an access order shall, subject to the provisions of the Land Charges Act 1972 and the Land Registration Act 1925, be binding on—

  (a)   any of his successors in title to the servient land; and

  (b)   any person who has an estate or interest in, or right over, the whole or any part of the servient land which was created after the making of the order and who derives his title to that estate, interest or right under the respondent;

and references to the respondent shall be construed accordingly.

(2)   If and to the extent that the court considers it just and equitable to allow him to do so, a person on whom an access order becomes binding by virtue of subsection (1)(a) or (b) above shall be entitled, as respects anything falling to be done after the order becomes binding on him, to enforce the order or any of its terms or conditions as if he were the respondent, and references to the respondent shall be construed accordingly.

(3)   Rules of court may—

  (a)   provide a procedure which may be followed where the applicant does not know, and cannot reasonably ascertain, the name of any person whom he desires to make respondent to the application; and

  (b)   make provision enabling such an applicant to make such a person respondent by description instead of by name;

and in this subsection "applicant" includes a person who proposes to make an application for an access order.

(4)   Any agreement, whenever made, shall be void if and to the extent that it would, apart from this subsection, prevent a person from applying for an access order or restrict his right to do so.

[634D]

NOTES
Commencement: 31 January 1993.

5   Registration of access orders and of applications for such orders

(1)–(3)   . . .

(4)   In any case where—
    (a)   an access order is discharged under section 6(1)(a) below, and
    (b)   the order has been protected by an entry registered under the Land Charges Act 1972 or by a notice or caution under the Land Registration Act 1925,

the court may by order direct that the entry, notice or caution shall be cancelled.

(5)   The rights conferred on a person by or under an access order are not capable of constituting an overriding interest within the meaning of the Land Registration Act 1925, notwithstanding that he or any other person is in actual occupation of the whole or any part of the servient land in question.

(6)   An application for an access order shall be regarded as a pending land action for the purposes of the Land Charges Act 1972 and the Land Registration Act 1925.

[634E]

NOTES
Commencement: 31 January 1993.
Sub-s (1): amends the Land Charges Act 1972, s 6(1).
Sub-ss (2), (3): amend the Land Registration Act 1925, s 49(1) and add s 64(7).

6   Variation of orders and damages for breach

(1)   Where an access order or an order under this subsection has been made, the court may, on the application of any party to the proceedings in which the order was made or of any other person on whom the order is binding—
    (a)   discharge or vary the order or any of its terms or conditions;
    (b)   suspend any of its terms or conditions; or
    (c)   revive any term or condition suspended under paragraph (b) above;

and in the application of subsections (1) and (2) of section 4 above in relation to an access order, any order under this subsection which relates to the access order shall be treated for the purposes of those subsections as included in the access order.

(2)   If any person contravenes or fails to comply with any requirement, term or condition imposed upon him by or under this Act, the court may, without prejudice to any other remedy available, make an order for the payment of damages by him to any other person affected by the contravention or failure who makes an application for relief under this subsection.

[634F]

NOTES
Commencement: 31 January 1993.

7   Jurisdiction over, and allocation of, proceedings

(1)   The High Court and the county courts shall both have jurisdiction under this Act.

(2)   ...

(3)   The amendment by subsection (2) above of provisions contained in an order shall not be taken to have prejudiced any power to make further orders revoking or amending those provisions.

[634G]

NOTES

    Commencement: 31 January 1993.

    Sub-s (2): amends the High Court and County Courts Jurisdiction Order 1991, SI 1991/724, art 4 and adds art 6A.

8   Interpretation and application

(1)   Any reference in this Act to an "entry" upon any servient land includes a reference to the doing on that land of anything necessary for carrying out the works to the dominant land which are reasonably necessary for its preservation; and "enter" shall be construed accordingly.

(2)   This Act applies in relation to any obstruction of, or other interference with, a right over, or interest in, any land as it applies in relation to an entry upon that land; and "enter" and "entry" shall be construed accordingly.

(3)   In this Act—

    "access order" has the meaning given by section 1(1) above;

    "applicant" means a person making an application for an access order and, subject to section 4 above, "the respondent" means the respondent, or any of the respondents, to such an application;

    "the court" means the High Court or a county court;

    "the dominant land" and "the servient land" respectively have the meanings given by section 1(1) above, but subject, in the case of servient land, to section 2(1) above;

    "land" does not include a highway;

    "the specified works" means the works specified in the access order in pursuance of section 2(1)(a) above.

[634H]

NOTES

    Commencement: 31 January 1993.

9   Short title, commencement and extent

(1)   This Act may be cited as the Access to Neighbouring Land Act 1992.

(2)   This Act shall come into force on such day as the Lord Chancellor may by order made by statutory instrument appoint.

(3)   This Act extends to England and Wales only.

[634I]

NOTES

    Commencement: 31 January 1993.

CHARITIES ACT 1993

(C 10)

An Act to consolidate the Charitable Trustees Incorporation Act 1872 and, except for certain spent or transitional provisions, the Charities Act 1960 and Part I of the Charities Act 1992
[27 May 1993]

PART I
THE CHARITY COMMISSIONERS AND THE OFFICIAL CUSTODIAN FOR CHARITIES

1   The Charity Commissioners

(1)   There shall continue to be a body of Charity Commissioners for England and Wales, and they shall have such functions as are conferred on them by this Act in addition to any functions under any other enactment for the time being in force.

(2)   The provisions of Schedule 1 to this Act shall have effect with respect to the constitution and proceedings of the Commissioners and other matters relating to the Commissioners and their officers and employees.

(3)   The Commissioners shall (without prejudice to their specific powers and duties under other enactments) have the general function of promoting the effective use of charitable resources by encouraging the development of better methods of administration, by giving charity trustees information or advice on any matter affecting the charity and by investigating and checking abuses.

(4)   It shall be the general object of the Commissioners so to act in the case of any charity (unless it is a matter of altering its purposes) as best to promote and make effective the work of the charity in meeting the needs designated by its trusts; but the Commissioners shall not themselves have power to act in the administration of a charity.

(5)   The Commissioners shall, as soon as possible after the end of every year, make to the Secretary of State a report on their operations during that year, and he shall lay a copy of the report before each House of Parliament.

[635]

NOTES
Commencement: 1 August 1993.

2   The official custodian for charities

(1)   There shall continue to be an officer known as the official custodian for charities (in this Act referred to as "the official custodian") whose function it shall be to act as trustee for charities in the cases provided for by this Act; and the official custodian shall be by that name a corporation sole having perpetual succession and using an official seal which shall be officially and judicially noticed.

(2)   Such officer of the Commissioners as they may from time to time designate shall be the official custodian.

(3)   The official custodian shall perform his duties in accordance with such general or special directions as may be given him by the Commissioners, and his expenses (except those re-imbursed to him or recovered by him as trustee for any charity) shall be defrayed by the Commissioners.

(4)   Anything which is required to or may be done by, to or before the official custodian may be done by, to or before any officer of the Commissioners generally or specially authorised by them to act for him during a vacancy in his office or otherwise.

(5)   The official custodian shall not be liable as trustee for any charity in respect of any loss or of the mis-application of any property unless it is occasioned by or through the wilful neglect or default of the custodian or of any person acting for him; but the Consolidated Fund shall be liable to make good to a charity any sums for which the custodian may be liable by reason of any such neglect or default.

(6)   The official custodian shall keep such books of account and such records in relation thereto as may be directed by the Treasury and shall prepare accounts in such form, in such manner and at such times as may be so directed.

(7)   The accounts so prepared shall be examined and certified by the Comptroller and Auditor General, and the report to be made by the Commissioners to the Secretary of State for any year shall include a copy of the accounts so prepared for any period ending in or with the year and of the certificate and report of the Comptroller and Auditor General with respect to those accounts.

[636]

NOTES
Commencement: 1 August 1993.

PART II
REGISTRATION AND NAMES OF CHARITIES

Registration of charities

3   The register of charities

(1)   The Commissioners shall continue to keep a register of charities, which shall be kept by them in such manner as they think fit.

(2)   There shall be entered in the register every charity not excepted by subsection (5) below; and a charity so excepted (other than one excepted by paragraph (a) of that subsection) may be entered in the register at the request of the charity, but (whether or not it was excepted at the time of registration) may at any time, and shall at the request of the charity, be removed from the register.

(3)   The register shall contain—
   (a)   the name of every registered charity; and
   (b)   such other particulars of, and such other information relating to, every such charity as the Commissioners think fit.

(4)   Any institution which no longer appears to the Commissioners to be a charity shall be removed from the register, with effect, where the removal is due to any change in its purposes or trusts, from the date of that change; and there shall also be removed from the register any charity which ceases to exist or does not operate.

(5)   The following charities are not required to be registered—
   (a)   any charity comprised in Schedule 2 to this Act (in this Act referred to as an "exempt charity");
   (b)   any charity which is excepted by order or regulations;
   (c)   any charity which has neither—

(i) any permanent endowment, nor
(ii) the use or occupation of any land,
and whose income from all sources does not in aggregate amount to more than £1,000 a year;

and no charity is required to be registered in respect of any registered place of worship.

(6) With any application for a charity to be registered there shall be supplied to the Commissioners copies of its trusts (or, if they are not set out in any extant document, particulars of them), and such other documents or information as may be prescribed by regulations made by the Secretary of State or as the Commissioners may require for the purpose of the application.

(7) It shall be the duty—
(a) of the charity trustees of any charity which is not registered nor excepted from registration to apply for it to be registered, and to supply the documents and information required by subsection (6) above; and
(b) of the charity trustees (or last charity trustees) of any institution which is for the time being registered to notify the Commissioners if it ceases to exist, or if there is any change in its trusts or in the particulars of it entered in the register, and to supply to the Commissioners particulars of any such change and copies of any new trusts or alterations of the trusts.

(8) The register (including the entries cancelled when institutions are removed from the register) shall be open to public inspection at all reasonable times; and copies (or particulars) of the trusts of any registered charity as supplied to the Commissioners under this section shall, so long as it remains on the register, be kept by them and be open to public inspection at all reasonable times, except in so far as regulations made by the Secretary of State otherwise provide.

(9) Where any information contained in the register is not in documentary form, subsection (8) above shall be construed as requiring the information to be available for public inspection in legible form at all reasonable times.

(10) If the Commissioners so determine, subsection (8) above shall not apply to any particular information contained in the register and specified in their determination.

(11) Nothing in the foregoing subsections shall require any person to supply the Commissioners with copies of schemes for the administration of a charity made otherwise than by the court, or to notify the Commissioners of any change made with respect to a registered charity by such a scheme, or require a person, if he refers the Commissioners to a document or copy already in the possession of the Commissioners, to supply a further copy of the document; but where by virtue of this subsection a copy of any document need not be supplied to the Commissioners, a copy of it, if it relates to a registered charity, shall be open to inspection under subsection (8) above as if supplied to the Commissioners under this section.

(12) If the Secretary of State thinks it expedient to do so—
(a) in consequence of changes in the value of money, or
(b) with a view to extending the scope of the exception provided for by subsection (5)(c) above,

he may by order amend subsection (5)(c) by substituting a different sum for the sum for the time being specified there.

(13) The reference in subsection (5)(b) above to a charity which is excepted by order or regulations is to a charity which—

(a) is for the time being permanently or temporarily excepted by order of the Commissioners; or

(b) is of a description permanently or temporarily excepted by regulations made by the Secretary of State,

and which complies with any conditions of the exception.

(14) In this section "registered place of worship" means any land or building falling within section 9 of the Places of Worship Registration Act 1855 (that is to say, the land and buildings which if the Charities Act 1960 had not been passed, would by virtue of that section as amended by subsequent enactments be partially exempted from the operation of the Charitable Trusts Act 1853), and for the purposes of this subsection "building" includes part of a building.

[637]

NOTES
Commencement: 1 August 1993.

4 Effect of, and claims and objections to, registration

(1) An institution shall for all purposes other than rectification of the register be conclusively presumed to be or to have been a charity at any time when it is or was on the register of charities.

(2) Any person who is or may be affected by the registration of an institution as a charity may, on the ground that it is not a charity, object to its being entered by the Commissioners in the register, or apply to them for it to be removed from the register; and provision may be made by regulations made by the Secretary of State as to the manner in which any such objection or application is to be made, prosecuted or dealt with.

(3) An appeal against any decision of the Commissioners to enter or not to enter an institution in the register of charities, or to remove or not to remove an institution from the register, may be brought in the High Court by the Attorney General, or by the persons who are or claim to be the charity trustees of the institution, or by any person whose objection or application under subsection (2) above is disallowed by the decision.

(4) If there is an appeal to the High Court against any decision of the Commissioners to enter an institution in the register, or not to remove an institution from the register, then until the Commissioners are satisfied whether the decision of the Commissioners is or is not to stand, the entry in the register shall be maintained, but shall be in suspense and marked to indicate that it is in suspense; and for the purposes of subsection (1) above an institution shall be deemed not to be on the register during any period when the entry relating to it is in suspense under this subsection.

(5) Any question affecting the registration or removal from the register of an institution may, notwithstanding that it has been determined by a decision on appeal under subsection (3) above, be considered afresh by the Commissioners and shall not be concluded by that decision, if it appears to the Commissioners that there has been a change of circumstances or that the decision is inconsistent with a later judicial decision, whether given on such an appeal or not.

[638]

NOTES
Commencement: 1 August 1993.

5 Status of registered charity (other than small charity) to appear on official publications etc

(1) This section applies to a registered charity if its gross income in its last financial year exceeded £5,000.

(2) Where this section applies to a registered charity, the fact that it is a registered charity shall be stated . . . in legible characters—

    (a) in all notices, advertisements and other documents issued by or on behalf of the charity and soliciting money or other property for the benefit of the charity;

    (b) in all bills of exchange, promissory notes, endorsements, cheques and orders for money or goods purporting to be signed on behalf of the charity; and

    (c) in all bills rendered by it and in all its invoices, receipts and letters of credit.

[(2A) The statement required by subsection (2) above shall be in English, except that, in the case of a document which is otherwise wholly in Welsh, the statement may be in Welsh if it consists of or includes the words "elusen cofrestredig" (the Welsh equivalent of "registered charity").]

(3) Subsection (2)(a) above has effect whether the solicitation is express or implied, and whether the money or other property is to be given for any consideration or not.

(4) If, in the case of a registered charity to which this section applies, any person issues or authorises the issue of any document falling within paragraph (a) or (c) of subsection (2) above [which does not contain the statement] required by that subsection, he shall be guilty of an offence and liable on summary conviction to a fine not exceeding level 3 on the standard scale.

(5) If, in the case of any such registered charity, any person signs any document falling within paragraph (b) of subsection (2) above [which does not contain the statement] required by that subsection, he shall be guilty of an offence and liable on summary conviction to a fine not exceeding level 3 on the standard scale.

(6) The Secretary of State may by order amend subsection (1) above by substituting a different sum for the sum for the time being specified there.

[639]

NOTES

Commencement: 1 August 1993. (sub-ss (1), (2), (3)–(6)); 21 December 1993 (sub-s (2A)).
Sub-s (2): words omitted repealed by the Welsh Language Act 1993, ss 32(1), (2), 35(1), Sch 2.
Sub-s (2A): inserted by the Welsh Language Act 1993, s 32(1), (3).
Sub-ss (4), (5): words in square brackets substituted by the Welsh Language Act 1993, s 32(1), (4), (5).

Charity names

6 Power of Commissioners to require charity's name to be changed

(1) Where this subsection applies to a charity, the Commissioners may give a direction requiring the name of the charity to be changed, within such period as is specified in the direction, to such other name as the charity trustees may determine with the approval of the Commissioners.

(2) Subsection (1) above applies to a charity if—

    (a) it is a registered charity and its name ("the registered name")—

        (i) is the same as, or

        (ii) is in the opinion of the Commissioners too like,

the name, at the time when the registered name was entered in the register in respect of the charity, of any other charity (whether registered or not);

(b) the name of the charity is in the opinion of the Commissioners likely to mislead the public as to the true nature—

    (i) of the purposes of the charity as set out in its trusts, or

    (ii) of the activities which the charity carries on under its trusts in pursuit of those purposes;

(c) the name of the charity includes any word or expression for the time being specified in regulations made by the Secretary of State and the inclusion in its name of that word or expression is in the opinion of the Commissioners likely to mislead the public in any respect as to the status of the charity;

(d) the name of the charity is in the opinion of the Commissioners likely to give the impression that the charity is connected in some way with Her Majesty's Government or any local authority, or with any other body of persons or any individual, when it is not so connected; or

(e) the name of the charity is in the opinion of the Commissioners offensive;

and in this subsection any reference to the name of a charity is, in relation to a registered charity, a reference to the name by which it is registered.

(3) Any direction given by virtue of subsection (2)(a) above must be given within twelve months of the time when the registered name was entered in the register in respect of the charity.

(4) Any direction given under this section with respect to a charity shall be given to the charity trustees; and on receiving any such direction the charity trustees shall give effect to it notwithstanding anything in the trusts of the charity.

(5) Where the name of any charity is changed under this section, then (without prejudice to section 3(7)(b) above) it shall be the duty of the charity trustees forthwith to notify the Commissioners of the charity's new name and of the date on which the change occurred.

(6) A change of name by a charity under this section does not affect any rights or obligations of the charity; and any legal proceedings that might have been continued or commenced by or against it in its former name may be continued or commenced by or against it in its new name.

(7) Section 26(3) of the Companies Act 1985 (minor variations in names to be disregarded) shall apply for the purposes of this section as if the reference to section 26(1)(c) of that Act were a reference to subsection (2)(a) above.

(8) Any reference in this section to the charity trustees of a charity shall, in relation to a charity which is a company, be read as a reference to the directors of the company.

(9) Nothing in this section applies to an exempt charity.

[640]

NOTES

Commencement: 1 August 1993.

7   Effect of direction under s 6 where charity is a company

(1) Where any direction is given under section 6 above with respect to a charity which is a company, the direction shall be taken to require the name of the charity to be changed by resolution of the directors of the company.

(2)   Section 380 of the Companies Act 1985 (registration etc of resolutions and agreements) shall apply to any resolution passed by the directors in compliance with any such direction.

(3)   Where the name of such a charity is changed in compliance with any such direction, the registrar of companies—

    (a)   shall, subject to section 26 of the Companies Act 1985 (prohibition on registration of certain names), enter the new name on the register of companies in place of the former name, and

    (b)   shall issue a certificate of incorporation altered to meet the circumstances of the case;

and the change of name has effect from the date on which the altered certificate is issued.

[641]

NOTES
Commencement: 1 August 1993.

Part III
Commissioners' Information Powers

8   General power to institute inquiries

(1)   The Commissioners may from time to time institute inquiries with regard to charities or a particular charity or class of charities, either generally or for particular purposes, but no such inquiry shall extend to any exempt charity.

(2)   The Commissioners may either conduct such an inquiry themselves or appoint a person to conduct it and make a report to them.

(3)   For the purposes of any such inquiry the Commissioners, or a person appointed by them to conduct it, may direct any person (subject to the provisions of this section)—

    (a)   to furnish accounts and statements in writing with respect to any matter in question at the inquiry, being a matter on which he has or can reasonably obtain information, or to return answers in writing to any questions or inquiries addressed to him on any such matter, and to verify any such accounts, statements or answers by statutory declaration;

    (b)   to furnish copies of documents in his custody or under his control which relate to any matter in question at the inquiry, and to verify any such copies by statutory declaration;

    (c)   to attend at a specified time and place and give evidence or produce any such documents.

(4)   For the purposes of any such inquiry evidence may be taken on oath, and the person conducting the inquiry may for that purpose administer oaths, or may instead of administering an oath require the person examined to make and subscribe a declaration of the truth of the matters about which he is examined.

(5)   The Commissioners may pay to any person the necessary expenses of his attendance to give evidence or produce documents for the purpose of an inquiry under this section, and a person shall not be required in obedience to a direction under paragraph (c) of subsection (3) above to go more than ten miles from his place of residence unless those expenses are paid or tendered to him.

(6)   Where an inquiry has been held under this section, the Commissioners may either—

    (a)   cause the report of the person conducting the inquiry, or such other statement of the results of the inquiry as they think fit, to be printed and published, or

    (b)   publish any such report or statement in some other way which is calculated in their opinion to bring it to the attention of persons who may wish to make representations to them about the action to be taken.

(7)   The council of a county or district, the Common Council of the City of London and the council of a London borough may contribute to the expenses of the Commissioners in connection with inquiries under this section into local charities in the council's area.

                                                                             [642]

NOTES

Commencement: 1 August 1993.

9   Power to call for documents and search records

(1)   The Commissioners may by order—

    (a)   require any person to furnish them with any information in his possession which relates to any charity and is relevant to the discharge of their functions or of the functions of the official custodian;

    (b)   require any person who has in his custody or under his control any document which relates to any charity and is relevant to the discharge of their functions or of the functions of the official custodian—

        (i)   to furnish them with a copy of or extract from the document, or

        (ii)   (unless the document forms part of the records or other documents of a court or of a public or local authority) to transmit the document itself to them for their inspection.

(2)   Any officer of the Commissioners, if so authorised by them, shall be entitled without payment to inspect and take copies of or extracts from the records or other documents of any court, or of any public registry or office of records, for any purpose connected with the discharge of the functions of the Commissioners or of the official custodian.

(3)   The Commissioners shall be entitled without payment to keep any copy or extract furnished to them under subsection (1) above; and where a document transmitted to them under that subsection for their inspection relates only to one or more charities and is not held by any person entitled as trustee or otherwise to the custody of it, the Commissioners may keep it or may deliver it to the charity trustees or to any other person who may be so entitled.

(4)   No person properly having the custody of documents relating only to an exempt charity shall be required under subsection (1) above to transmit to the Commissioners any of those documents, or to furnish any copy of or extract from any of them.

(5)   The rights conferred by subsection (2) above shall, in relation to information recorded otherwise than in legible form, include the right to require the information to be made available in legible form for inspection or for a copy or extract to be made of or from it.

                                                                             [643]

NOTES

Commencement: 1 August 1993.

10 Disclosure of information to and by Commissioners

(1)   Subject to subsection (2) below and to any express restriction imposed by or under any other enactment, a body or person to whom this section applies may disclose to the Charity Commissioners any information received by that body or person under or for the purposes of any enactment, where the disclosure is made by the body or person for the purpose of enabling or assisting the Commissioners to discharge any of their functions.

(2)   Subsection (1) above shall not have effect in relation to the Commissioners of Customs and Excise or the Commissioners of Inland Revenue; but either of those bodies of Commissioners ("the relevant body") may disclose to the Charity Commissioners the following information—

    (a)   the name and address of any institution which has for any purpose been treated by the relevant body as established for charitable purposes;

    (b)   information as to the purposes of an institution and the trusts under which it is established or regulated, where the disclosure is made by the relevant body in order to give or obtain assistance in determining whether the institution ought for any purpose to be treated as established for charitable purposes; and

    (c)   information with respect to an institution which has for any purpose been treated as so established but which appears to the relevant body—

        (i)   to be, or to have been, carrying on activities which are not charitable, or

        (ii)   to be, or to have been, applying any of its funds for purposes which are not charitable.

(3)   In subsection (2) above, any reference to an institution shall, in relation to the Commissioners of Inland Revenue, be construed as a reference to an institution in England and Wales.

(4)   Subject to subsection (5) below, the Charity Commissioners may disclose to a body or person to whom this section applies any information received by them under or for the purposes of any enactment, where the disclosure is made by the Commissioners—

    (a)   for any purpose connected with the discharge of their functions, and

    (b)   for the purpose of enabling or assisting that body or person to discharge any of its or his functions.

(5)   Where any information disclosed to the Charity Commissioners under subsection (1) or (2) above is so disclosed subject to any express restriction on the disclosure of the information by the Commissioners, the Commissioners' power of disclosure under subsection (4) above shall, in relation to the information, be exercisable by them subject to any such restriction.

(6)   This section applies to the following bodies and persons—

    (a)   any government department (including a Northern Ireland department);

    (b)   any local authority;

    (c)   any constable; and

    (d)   any other body or person discharging functions of a public nature (including a body or person discharging regulatory functions in relation to any description of activities).

(7)   In subsection (6)(d) above the reference to any such body or person as is there mentioned shall, in relation to a disclosure by the Charity Commissioners under

subsection (4) above, be construed as including a reference to any such body or person in a country or territory outside the United Kingdom.

(8) Nothing in this section shall be construed as affecting any power of disclosure exercisable apart from this section.

(9) In this section "enactment" includes an enactment comprised in subordinate legislation (within the meaning of the Interpretation Act 1978).

[644]

NOTES

Commencement: 1 August 1993.

11 Supply of false or misleading information to Commissioners, etc

(1) Any person who knowingly or recklessly provides the Commissioners with information which is false or misleading in a material particular shall be guilty of an offence if the information—

(a) is provided in purported compliance with a requirement imposed by or under this Act; or

(b) is provided otherwise than as mentioned in paragraph (a) above but in circumstances in which the person providing the information intends, or could reasonably be expected to know, that it would be used by the Commissioners for the purpose of discharging their functions under this Act.

(2) Any person who wilfully alters, suppresses, conceals or destroys any document which he is or is liable to be required, by or under this Act, to produce to the Commissioners shall be guilty of an offence.

(3) Any person guilty of an offence under this section shall be liable—

(a) on summary conviction, to a fine not exceeding the statutory maximum;

(b) on conviction on indictment, to imprisonment for a term not exceeding two years or to a fine, or both.

(4) In this section references to the Commissioners include references to any person conducting an inquiry under section 8 above.

[645]

NOTES

Commencement: 1 August 1993.

12 Data protection

An order under section 30 of the Data Protection Act 1984 (exemption from subject access provisions of data held for the purpose of discharging designated functions in connection with the regulation of financial services etc) may designate for the purposes of that section, as if they were functions conferred by or under such an enactment as is there mentioned, any functions of the Commissioners appearing to the Secretary of State to be—

(a) connected with the protection of charities against misconduct or mismanagement (whether by trustees or other persons) in their administration; or

(b) connected with the protection of the property of charities from loss or misapplication or with the recovery of such property.

[646]

NOTES

Commencement: 1 August 1993.

PART IV
APPLICATION OF PROPERTY CY-PRES AND ASSISTANCE AND SUPERVISION OF CHARITIES BY COURT AND COMMISSIONERS

Extended powers of court and variation of charters

13 Occasions for applying property cy-pres.

(1) Subject to subsection (2) below, the circumstances in which the original purposes of a charitable gift can be altered to allow the property given or part of it to be applied cy-pres shall be as follows—

(a) where the original purposes, in whole or in part—
  (i) have been as far as may be fulfilled; or
  (ii) cannot be carried out, or not according to the directions given and to the spirit of the gift; or

(b) where the original purposes provide a use for part only of the property available by virtue of the gift; or

(c) where the property available by virtue of the gift and other property applicable for similar purposes can be more effectively used in conjunction, and to that end can suitably, regard being had to the spirit of the gift, be made applicable to common purposes; or

(d) where the original purposes were laid down by reference to an area which then was but has since ceased to be a unit for some other purpose, or by reference to a class of persons or to an area which has for any reason since ceased to be suitable, regard being had to the spirit of the gift, or to be practical in administering the gift; or

(e) where the original purposes, in whole or in part, have, since they were laid down,—
  (i) been adequately provided for by other means; or
  (ii) ceased, as being useless or harmful to the community or for other reasons, to be in law charitable; or
  (iii) ceased in any other way to provide a suitable and effective method of using the property available by virtue of the gift, regard being had to the spirit of the gift.

(2) Subsection (1) above shall not affect the conditions which must be satisfied in order that property given for charitable purposes may be applied cy-pres except in so far as those conditions require a failure of the original purposes.

(3) References in the foregoing subsections to the original purposes of a gift shall be construed, where the application of the property given has been altered or regulated by a scheme or otherwise, as referring to the purposes for which the property is for the time being applicable.

(4) Without prejudice to the power to make schemes in circumstances falling within subsection (1) above, the court may by scheme made under the court's jurisdiction with respect to charities, in any case where the purposes for which the property is held are laid down by reference to any such area as is mentioned in the first column in Schedule 3 to this Act, provide for enlarging the area to any such area as is mentioned in the second column in the same entry in that Schedule.

(5) It is hereby declared that a trust for charitable purposes places a trustee under a duty, where the case permits and requires the property or some part of it to be

applied cy-pres, to secure its effective use for charity by taking steps to enable it to be so applied.

[647]

NOTES
Commencement: 1 August 1993.

14 Application cy-pres of gifts of donors unknown or disclaiming

(1) Property given for specific charitable purposes which fail shall be applicable cy-pres as if given for charitable purposes generally, where it belongs—

(a) to a donor who after—
   (i) the prescribed advertisements and inquiries have been published and made, and
   (ii) the prescribed period beginning with the publication of those advertisements has expired,
   cannot be identified or cannot be found; or
(b) to a donor who has executed a disclaimer in the prescribed form of his right to have the property returned.

(2) Where the prescribed advertisements and inquiries have been published and made by or on behalf of trustees with respect to any such property, the trustees shall not be liable to any person in respect of the property if no claim by him to be interested in it is received by them before the expiry of the period mentioned in subsection (1)(a)(ii) above.

(3) For the purposes of this section property shall be conclusively presumed (without any advertisement or inquiry) to belong to donors who cannot be identified, in so far as it consists—

(a) of the proceeds of cash collections made by means of collecting boxes or by other means not adapted for distinguishing one gift from another; or
(b) of the proceeds of any lottery, competition, entertainment, sale or similar money-raising activity, after allowing for property given to provide prizes or articles for sale or otherwise to enable the activity to be undertaken.

(4) The court may by order direct that property not falling within subsection (3) above shall for the purposes of this section be treated (without any advertisement or inquiry) as belonging to donors who cannot be identified where it appears to the court either—

(a) that it would be unreasonable, having regard to the amounts likely to be returned to the donors, to incur expense with a view to returning the property; or
(b) that it would be unreasonable, having regard to the nature, circumstances and amounts of the gifts, and to the lapse of time since the gifts were made, for the donors to expect the property to be returned.

(5) Where property is applied cy-pres by virtue of this section, the donor shall be deemed to have parted with all his interest at the time when the gift was made; but where property is so applied as belonging to donors who cannot be identified or cannot be found, and is not so applied by virtue of subsection (3) or (4) above—

(a) the scheme shall specify the total amount of that property; and
(b) the donor of any part of that amount shall be entitled, if he makes a claim not later than six months after the date on which the scheme is made, to recover from the charity for which the property is applied a sum equal to

that part, less any expenses properly incurred by the charity trustees after that date in connection with claims relating to his gift; and

(c) the scheme may include directions as to the provision to be made for meeting any such claim.

(6) Where—

(a) any sum is, in accordance with any such directions, set aside for meeting any such claims, but

(b) the aggregate amount of any such claims actually made exceeds the relevant amount,

then, if the Commissioners so direct, each of the donors in question shall be entitled only to such proportion of the relevant amount as the amount of his claim bears to the aggregate amount referred to in paragraph (b) above; and for this purpose "the relevant amount" means the amount of the sum so set aside after deduction of any expenses properly incurred by the charity trustees in connection with claims relating to the donors' gifts.

(7) For the purposes of this section, charitable purposes shall be deemed to "fail" where any difficulty in applying property to those purposes makes that property or the part not applicable cy-pres available to be returned to the donors.

(8) In this section "prescribed" means prescribed by regulations made by the Commissioners; and such regulations may, as respects the advertisements which are to be published for the purposes of subsection (1)(a) above, make provision as to the form and content of such advertisements as well as the manner in which they are to be published.

(9) Any regulations made by the Commissioners under this section shall be published by the Commissioners in such manner as they think fit.

(10) In this section, except in so far as the context otherwise requires, references to a donor include persons claiming through or under the original donor, and references to property given include the property for the time being representing the property originally given or property derived from it.

(11) This section shall apply to property given for charitable purposes, notwithstanding that it was so given before the commencement of this Act.

[648]

NOTES
Commencement: 1 August 1993.

15 Charities governed by charter, or by or under statute

(1) Where a Royal charter establishing or regulating a body corporate is amendable by the grant and acceptance of a further charter, a scheme relating to the body corporate or to the administration of property held by the body (including a scheme for the cy-pres application of any such property) may be made by the court under the court's jurisdiction with respect to charities notwithstanding that the scheme cannot take effect without the alteration of the charter, but shall be so framed that the scheme, or such part of it as cannot take effect without the alteration of the charter, does not purport to come into operation unless or until Her Majesty thinks fit to amend the charter in such manner as will permit the scheme or that part of it to have effect.

(2) Where under the court's jurisdiction with respect to charities or the corresponding jurisdiction of a court in Northern Ireland, or under powers conferred by this Act or by any Northern Ireland legislation relating to charities, a scheme is

made with respect to a body corporate, and it appears to Her Majesty expedient, having regard to the scheme, to amend any Royal charter relating to that body, Her Majesty may, on the application of that body, amend the charter accordingly by Order in Council in any way in which the charter could be amended by the grant and acceptance of a further charter; and any such Order in Council may be revoked or varied in like manner as the charter it amends.

(3)   The jurisdiction of the court with respect to charities shall not be excluded or restricted in the case of a charity of any description mentioned in Schedule 4 to this Act by the operation of the enactments or instruments there mentioned in relation to that description, and a scheme established for any such charity may modify or supersede in relation to it the provision made by any such enactment or instrument as if made by a scheme of the court, and may also make any such provision as is authorised by that Schedule.

[649]

NOTES

Commencement: 1 August 1993.

Powers of Commissioners to make schemes and act for protection of charities etc

16   Concurrent jurisdiction with High Court for certain purposes

(1)   Subject to the provisions of this Act, the Commissioners may by order exercise the same jurisdiction and powers as are exercisable by the High Court in charity proceedings for the following purposes—

    (a)   establishing a scheme for the administration of a charity;

    (b)   appointing, discharging or removing a charity trustee or trustee for a charity, or removing an officer or employee;

    (c)   vesting or transferring property, or requiring or entitling any person to call for or make any transfer of property or any payment.

(2)   Where the court directs a scheme for the administration of a charity to be established, the court may by order refer the matter to the Commissioners for them to prepare or settle a scheme in accordance with such directions (if any) as the court sees fit to give, and any such order may provide for the scheme to be put into effect by order of the Commissioners as if prepared under subsection (1) above and without any further order of the court.

(3)   The Commissioners shall not have jurisdiction under this section to try or determine the title at law or in equity to any property as between a charity or trustee for a charity and a person holding or claiming the property or an interest in it adversely to the charity, or to try or determine any question as to the existence or extent of any charge or trust.

(4)   Subject to the following subsections, the Commissioners shall not exercise their jurisdiction under this section as respects any charity, except—

    (a)   on the application of the charity; or

    (b)   on an order of the court under subsection (2) above; or

    (c)   in the case of a charity other than an exempt charity, on the application of the Attorney General.

(5)   In the case of a charity which is not an exempt charity and whose income from all sources does not in aggregate exceed £500 a year, the Commissioners may exercise their jurisdiction under this section on the application—

(a) of any one or more of the charity trustees; or

(b) of any person interested in the charity; or

(c) of any two or more inhabitants of the area of the charity if it is a local charity.

(6)   Where in the case of a charity, other than an exempt charity, the Commissioners are satisfied that the charity trustees ought in the interests of the charity to apply for a scheme, but have unreasonably refused or neglected to do so and the Commissioners have given the charity trustees an opportunity to make representations to them, the Commissioners may proceed as if an application for a scheme had been made by the charity but the Commissioners shall not have power in a case where they act by virtue of this subsection to alter the purposes of a charity, unless forty years have elapsed from the date of its foundation.

(7)   Where—

(a) a charity cannot apply to the Commissioners for a scheme by reason of any vacancy among the charity trustees or the absence or incapacity of any of them, but

(b) such an application is made by such number of the charity trustees as the Commissioners consider appropriate in the circumstances of the case,

the Commissioners may nevertheless proceed as if the application were an application made by the charity.

(8)   The Commissioners may on the application of any charity trustee or trustee for a charity exercise their jurisdiction under this section for the purpose of discharging him from his trusteeship.

(9)   Before exercising any jurisdiction under this section otherwise than on an order of the court, the Commissioners shall give notice of their intention to do so to each of the charity trustees, except any that cannot be found or has no known address in the United Kingdom or who is party or privy to an application for the exercise of the jurisdiction; and any such notice may be given by post, and, if given by post, may be addressed to the recipient's last known address in the United Kingdom.

(10)   The Commissioners shall not exercise their jurisdiction under this section in any case (not referred to them by order of the court) which, by reason of its contentious character, or of any special question of law or of fact which it may involve, or for other reasons, the Commissioners may consider more fit to be adjudicated on by the court.

(11)   An appeal against any order of the Commissioners under this section may be brought in the High Court by the Attorney General.

(12)   An appeal against any order of the Commissioners under this section may also, at any time within the three months beginning with the day following that on which the order is published, be brought in the High Court by the charity or any of the charity trustees, or by any person removed from any office or employment by the order (unless he is removed with the concurrence of the charity trustees or with the approval of the special visitor, if any, of the charity).

(13)   No appeal shall be brought under subsection (12) above except with a certificate of the Commissioners that it is a proper case for an appeal or with the leave of one of the judges of the High Court attached to the Chancery Division.

(14)   Where an order of the Commissioners under this section establishes a scheme for the administration of a charity, any person interested in the charity shall have the

like right of appeal under subsection (12) above as a charity trustee, and so also, in the case of a charity which is a local charity in any area, shall any two or more inhabitants of the area and the council of any parish or (in Wales) any community comprising the area or any part of it.

(15) If the Secretary of State thinks it expedient to do so—
    (a) in consequence of changes in the value of money, or
    (b) with a view to increasing the number of charities in respect of which the Commissioners may exercise their jurisdiction under this section in accordance with subsection (5) above,

he may by order amend that subsection by substituting a different sum for the sum for the time being specified there.

[650]

NOTES
Commencement: 1 August 1993.

17 Further powers to make schemes or alter application of charitable property

(1) Where it appears to the Commissioners that a scheme should be established for the administration of a charity, but also that it is necessary or desirable for the scheme to alter the provision made by an Act of Parliament establishing or regulating the charity or to make any other provision which goes or might go beyond the powers exercisable by them apart from this section, or that it is for any reason proper for the scheme to be subject to parliamentary review, then (subject to subsection (6) below) the Commissioners may settle a scheme accordingly with a view to its being given effect under this section.

(2) A scheme settled by the Commissioners under this section may be given effect by order of the Secretary of State, and a draft of the order shall be laid before Parliament.

(3) Without prejudice to the operation of section 6 of the Statutory Instruments Act 1946 in other cases, in the case of a scheme which goes beyond the powers exercisable apart from this section in altering a statutory provision contained in or having effect under any public general Act of Parliament, the order shall not be made unless the draft has been approved by resolution of each House of Parliament.

(4) Subject to subsection (5) below, any provision of a scheme brought into effect under this section may be modified or superseded by the court or the Commissioners as if it were a scheme brought into effect by order of the Commissioners under section 16 above.

(5) Where subsection (3) above applies to a scheme, the order giving effect to it may direct that the scheme shall not be modified or superseded by a scheme brought into effect otherwise than under this section, and may also direct that that subsection shall apply to any scheme modifying or superseding the scheme to which the order gives effect.

(6) The Commissioners shall not proceed under this section without the like application and the like notice to the charity trustees, as would be required if they were proceeding (without an order of the court) under section 16 above; but on any application for a scheme, or in a case where they act by virtue of subsection (6) or (7) of that section, the Commissioners may proceed under this section or that section as appears to them appropriate.

(7)   Notwithstanding anything in the trusts of a charity, no expenditure incurred in preparing or promoting a Bill in Parliament shall without the consent of the court or the Commissioners be defrayed out of any moneys applicable for the purposes of a charity but this subsection shall not apply in the case of an exempt charity.

(8)   Where the Commissioners are satisfied—
   (a)   that the whole of the income of a charity cannot in existing circumstances be effectively applied for the purposes of the charity; and
   (b)   that, if those circumstances continue, a scheme might be made for applying the surplus cy-pres; and
   (c)   that it is for any reason not yet desirable to make such a scheme;

then the Commissioners may by order authorise the charity trustees at their discretion (but subject to any conditions imposed by the order) to apply any accrued or accruing income for any purposes for which it might be made applicable by such a scheme, and any application authorised by the order shall be deemed to be within the purposes of the charity.

(9)   An order under subsection (8) above shall not extend to more than £300 out of income accrued before the date of the order, nor to income accruing more than three years after that date, nor to more than £100 out of the income accruing in any of those three years.

                                                                              [651]

NOTES
Commencement: 1 August 1993.

18   Power to act for protection of charities

(1)   Where, at any time after they have instituted an inquiry under section 8 above with respect to any charity, the Commissioners are satisfied—
   (a)   that there is or has been any misconduct or mismanagement in the administration of the charity; or
   (b)   that it is necessary or desirable to act for the purpose of protecting the property of the charity or securing a proper application for the purposes of the charity of that property or of property coming to the charity,

the Commissioners may of their own motion do one or more of the following things—
   (i)   by order suspend any trustee, charity trustee, officer, agent or employee of the charity from the exercise of his office or employment pending consideration being given to his removal (whether under this section or otherwise);
   (ii)   by order appoint such number of additional charity trustees as they consider necessary for the proper administration of the charity;
   (iii) by order vest any property held by or in trust for the charity in the official custodian, or require the persons in whom any such property is vested to transfer it to him, or appoint any person to transfer any such property to him;
   (iv)   order any person who holds any property on behalf of the charity, or of any trustee for it, not to part with the property without the approval of the Commissioners;
   (v)   order any debtor of the charity not to make any payment in or towards the discharge of his liability to the charity without the approval of the Commissioners;

    (vi) by order restrict (notwithstanding anything in the trusts of the charity) the transactions which may be entered into, or the nature or amount of the payments which may be made, in the administration of the charity without the approval of the Commissioners;

   (vii) by order appoint (in accordance with section 19 below) a receiver and manager in respect of the property and affairs of the charity.

(2)   Where, at any time after they have instituted an inquiry under section 8 above with respect to any charity, the Commissioners are satisfied—

    (a) that there is or has been any misconduct or mismanagement in the administration of the charity; and

    (b) that it is necessary or desirable to act for the purpose of protecting the property of the charity or securing a proper application for the purposes of the charity of that property or of property coming to the charity,

the Commissioners may of their own motion do either or both of the following things—

    (i) by order remove any trustee, charity trustee, officer, agent or employee of the charity who has been responsible for or privy to the misconduct or mismanagement or has by his conduct contributed to it or facilitated it;

   (ii) by order establish a scheme for the administration of the charity.

(3)   The references in subsection (1) or (2) above to misconduct or mismanagement shall (notwithstanding anything in the trusts of the charity) extend to the employment for the remuneration or reward of persons acting in the affairs of the charity, or for other administrative purposes, of sums which are excessive in relation to the property which is or is likely to be applied or applicable for the purposes of the charity.

(4)   The Commissioners may also remove a charity trustee by order made of their own motion—

    (a) where, within the last five years, the trustee—

      (i) having previously been adjudged bankrupt or had his estate sequestrated, has been discharged, or

     (ii) having previously made a composition or arrangement with, or granted a trust deed for, his creditors, has been discharged in respect of it;

    (b) where the trustee is a corporation in liquidation;

    (c) where the trustee is incapable of acting by reason of mental disorder within the meaning of the Mental Health Act 1983;

    (d) where the trustee has not acted, and will not declare his willingness or unwillingness to act;

    (e) where the trustee is outside England and Wales or cannot be found or does not act, and his absence or failure to act impedes the proper administration of the charity.

(5)   The Commissioners may by order made of their own motion appoint a person to be a charity trustee—

    (a) in place of a charity trustee removed by them under this section or otherwise;

    (b) where there are no charity trustees, or where by reason of vacancies in their number or the absence or incapacity of any of their number the charity cannot apply for the appointment;

    (c) where there is a single charity trustee, not being a corporation aggregate, and the Commissioners are of opinion that it is necessary to increase the number for the proper administration of the charity;

    (d)   where the Commissioners are of opinion that it is necessary for the proper administration of the charity to have an additional charity trustee because one of the existing charity trustees who ought nevertheless to remain a charity trustee either cannot be found or does not act or is outside England and Wales.

(6)   The powers of the Commissioners under this section to remove or appoint charity trustees of their own motion shall include power to make any such order with respect to the vesting in or transfer to the charity trustees of any property as the Commissioners could make on the removal or appointment of a charity trustee by them under section 16 above.

(7)   Any order under this section for the removal or appointment of a charity trustee or trustee for a charity, or for the vesting or transfer of any property, shall be of the like effect as an order made under section 16 above.

(8)   Subject to subsection (9) below, subsections (11) to (13) of section 16 above shall apply to orders under this section as they apply to orders under that section.

(9)   The requirement to obtain any such certificate or leave as is mentioned in section 16(13) above shall not apply to—

    (a)   an appeal by a charity or any of the charity trustees of a charity against an order under subsection (1)(vii) above appointing a receiver and manager in respect of the charity's property and affairs, or

    (b)   an appeal by a person against an order under subsection (2)(i) or (4)(a) above removing him from his office or employment.

(10)   Subsection (14) of section 16 above shall apply to an order under this section which establishes a scheme for the administration of a charity as it applies to such an order under that section.

(11)   The power of the Commissioners to make an order under subsection (1)(i) above shall not be exercisable so as to suspend any person from the exercise of his office or employment for a period of more than twelve months; but (without prejudice to the generality of section 89(1) below), any such order made in the case of any person may make provision as respects the period of his suspension for matters arising out of it, and in particular for enabling any person to execute any instrument in his name or otherwise act for him and, in the case of a charity trustee, for adjusting any rules governing the proceedings of the charity trustees to take account of the reduction in the number capable of acting.

(12)   Before exercising any jurisdiction under this section otherwise than by virtue of subsection (1) above, the Commissioners shall give notice of their intention to do so to each of the charity trustees, except any that cannot be found or has no known address in the United Kingdom; and any such notice may be given by post and, if given by post, may be addressed to the recipient's last known address in the United Kingdom.

(13)   The Commissioners shall, at such intervals as they think fit, review any order made by them under paragraph (i), or any of paragraphs (iii) to (vii), of subsection (1) above; and, if on any such review it appears to them that it would be appropriate to discharge the order in whole or in part, they shall so discharge it (whether subject to any savings or other transitional provisions or not).

(14)   If any person contravenes an order under subsection (1)(iv), (v) or (vi) above, he shall be guilty of an offence and liable on summary conviction to a fine not exceeding level 5 on the standard scale.

(15) Subsection (14) above shall not be taken to preclude the bringing of proceedings for breach of trust against any charity trustee or trustee for a charity in respect of a contravention of an order under subsection (1)(iv) or (vi) above (whether proceedings in respect of the contravention are brought against him under subsection (14) above or not).

(16) This section shall not apply to an exempt charity.

[652]

NOTES
Commencement: 1 August 1993.

19 Supplementary provisions relating to receiver and manager appointed for a charity

(1) The Commissioners may under section 18(1)(vii) above appoint to be receiver and manager in respect of the property and affairs of a charity such person (other than an officer or employee of theirs) as they think fit.

(2) Without prejudice to the generality of section 89(1) below, any order made by the Commissioners under section 18(1)(vii) above may make provision with respect to the functions to be discharged by the receiver and manager appointed by the order; and those functions shall be discharged by him under the supervision of the Commissioners.

(3) In connection with the discharge of those functions any such order may provide—
  (a) for the receiver and manager appointed by the order to have such powers and duties of the charity trustees of the charity concerned (whether arising under this Act or otherwise) as are specified in the order;
  (b) for any powers or duties exercisable or falling to be performed by the receiver and manager by virtue of paragraph (a) above to be exercisable or performed by him to the exclusion of those trustees.

(4) Where a person has been appointed receiver and manager by any such order—
  (a) section 29 below shall apply to him and to his functions as a person so appointed as it applies to a charity trustee of the charity concerned and to his duties as such; and
  (b) the Commissioners may apply to the High Court for directions in relation to any particular matter arising in connection with the discharge of those functions.

(5) The High Court may on an application under subsection (4)(b) above—
  (a) give such directions, or
  (b) make such orders declaring the rights of any persons (whether before the court or not),

as it thinks just; and the costs of any such application shall be paid by the charity concerned.

(6) Regulations made by the Secretary of State may make provision with respect to—
  (a) the appointment and removal of persons appointed in accordance with this section;
  (b) the remuneration of such persons out of the income of the charities concerned;
  (c) the making of reports to the Commissioners by such persons.

(7)   Regulations under subsection (6) above may, in particular, authorise the Commissioners—

    (a) to require security for the due discharge of his functions to be given by a person so appointed;

    (b) to determine the amount of such a person's remuneration;

    (c) to disallow any amount of remuneration in such circumstances as are prescribed by the regulations.

[653]

NOTES

Commencement: 1 August 1993.

20   Publicity for proceedings under ss 16 to 18

(1)   The Commissioners shall not make any order under this Act to establish a scheme for the administration of a charity, or submit such a scheme to the court or the Secretary of State for an order giving it effect, unless not less than one month previously there has been given public notice of their proposals, inviting representations to be made to them within a time specified in the notice, being not less than one month from the date of such notice, and, in the case of a scheme relating to a local charity, other than on ecclesiastical charity, in a parish or (in Wales) a community, a draft of the scheme has been communicated to the parish or community council or, in the case of a parish not having a council, to the chairman of the parish meeting.

(2)   The Commissioners shall not make any order under this Act to appoint, discharge or remove a charity trustee or trustee for a charity (other than the official custodian), unless not less than one month previously there has been given the like public notice as is required by subsection (1) above for an order establishing a scheme but this subsection shall not apply in the case of—

    (a) an order under section 18(1)(ii) above; or

    (b) an order discharging or removing a trustee if the Commissioners are of opinion that it is unnecessary and not in his interest to give publicity to the proposal to discharge or remove him.

(3)   Before the Commissioners make an order under this Act to remove without his consent a charity trustee or trustee for a charity, or an officer, agent or employee of a charity, the Commissioners shall, unless he cannot be found or has no known address in the United Kingdom, give him not less than one month's notice of their proposal, inviting representations to be made to them within a time specified in the notice.

(4)   Where notice is given of any proposals as required by subsections (1) to (3) above, the Commissioners shall take into consideration any representations made to them about the proposals within the time specified in the notice, and may (without further notice) proceed with the proposals either without modification or with such modifications as appear to them to be desirable.

(5)   Where the Commissioners make an order which is subject to appeal under subsection (12) of section 16 above the order shall be published either by giving public notice of it or by giving notice of it to all persons entitled to appeal against it under that subsection, as the Commissioners think fit.

(6)   Where the Commissioners make an order under this Act to establish a scheme for the administration of a charity, a copy of the order shall, for not less than one month after the order is published, be available for public inspection at all reasonable

times at the Commissioners' office and also at some convenient place in the area of the charity, if it is a local charity.

(7)　Any notice to be given under this section of any proposals or order shall give such particulars of the proposals or order, or such directions for obtaining information about them, as the Commissioners think sufficient and appropriate, and any public notice shall be given in such manner as they think sufficient and appropriate.

(8)　Any notice to be given under this section, other than a public notice, may be given by post and, if given by post, may be addressed to the recipient's last known address in the United Kingdom.

[654]

NOTES
Commencement: 1 August 1993.

Property vested in official custodian

21　Entrusting charity property to official custodian, and termination of trust

(1)　The court may by order—
　(a)　vest in the official custodian any land held by or in trust for a charity;
　(b)　authorise or require the persons in whom any such land is vested to transfer it to him; or
　(c)　appoint any person to transfer any such land to him;

but this subsection does not apply to any interest in land by way of mortgage or other security.

(2)　Where property is vested in the official custodian in trust for a charity, the court may make an order discharging him from the trusteeship as respects all or any of that property.

(3)　Where the official custodian is discharged from his trusteeship of any property, or the trusts on which he holds any property come to an end, the court may make such vesting orders and give such directions as may seem to the court to be necessary or expedient in consequence.

(4)　No person shall be liable for any loss occasioned by his acting in conformity with an order under this section or by his giving effect to anything done in pursuance of such an order, or be excused from so doing by reason of the order having been in any respect improperly obtained.

[655]

NOTES
Commencement: 1 August 1993.

22　Supplementary provisions as to property vested in official custodian

(1)　Subject to the provisions of this Act, where property is vested in the official custodian in trust for a charity, he shall not exercise any powers of management, but he shall as trustee of any property have all the same powers, duties and liabilities, and be entitled to the same rights and immunities, and be subject to the control and orders of the court, as a corporation appointed custodian trustee under section 4 of the Public Trustee Act 1906 except that he shall have no power to charge fees.

(2) Subject to subsection (3) below, where any land is vested in the official custodian in trust for a charity, the charity trustees shall have power in his name and on his behalf to execute and do all assurances and things which they could properly execute or do in their own name and on their own behalf if the land were vested in them.

(3) If any land is so vested in the official custodian by virtue of an order under section 18 above, the power conferred on the charity trustees by subsection (2) above shall not be exercisable by them in relation to any transaction affecting the land, unless the transaction is authorised by order of the court or of the Commissioners.

(4) Where any land is vested in the official custodian in trust for a charity, the charity trustees shall have the like power to make obligations entered into by them binding on the land as if it were vested in them; and any covenant, agreement or condition which is enforceable by or against the custodian by reason of the land being vested in him shall be enforceable by or against the charity trustees as if the land were vested in them.

(5) In relation to a corporate charity, subsections (2), (3) and (4) above shall apply with the substitution of references to the charity for references to the charity trustees.

(6) Subsections (2), (3) and (4) above shall not authorise any charity trustees or charity to impose any personal liability on the official custodian.

(7) Where the official custodian is entitled as trustee for a charity to the custody of securities or documents of title relating to the trust property, he may permit them to be in the possession or under the control of the charity trustees without thereby incurring any liability.

[656]

NOTES

Commencement: 1 August 1993.

---

23 Divestment in the case of land subject to Reverter of Sites Act 1987

(1) Where—
   (a) any land is vested in the official custodian in trust for a charity, and
   (b) it appears to the Commissioners that section 1 of the Reverter of Sites Act 1987 (right of reverter replaced by trust for sale) will, or is likely to, operate in relation to the land at a particular time or in particular circumstances,

the jurisdiction which, under section 16 above, is exercisable by the Commissioners for the purpose of discharging a trustee for a charity may, at any time before section 1 of that Act ("the 1987 Act") operates in relation to the land, be exercised by them of their own motion for the purpose of—
   (i) making an order discharging the official custodian from his trusteeship of the land, and
   (ii) making such vesting orders and giving such directions as appear to them to be necessary or expedient in consequence.

(2) Where—
   (a) section 1 of the 1987 Act has operated in relation to any land which, immediately before the time when that section so operated, was vested in the official custodian in trust for a charity, and

(b) the land remains vested in him but on the trust arising under that section,

the court or the Commissioners (of their own motion) may—

    (i) make an order discharging the official custodian from his trusteeship of the land, and

    (ii) (subject to the following provisions of this section) make such vesting orders and give such directions as appear to it or them to be necessary or expedient in consequence.

(3) Where any order discharging the official custodian from his trusteeship of any land—

    (a) is made by the court under section 21(2) above, or by the Commissioners under section 16 above, on the grounds that section 1 of the 1987 Act will, or is likely to, operate in relation to the land, or

    (b) is made by the court or the Commissioners under subsection (2) above,

the persons in whom the land is to be vested on the discharge of the official custodian shall be the relevant charity trustees (as defined in subsection (4) below), unless the court or (as the case may be) the Commissioners is or are satisfied that it would be appropriate for it to be vested in some other persons.

(4) In subsection (3) above "the relevant charity trustees" means—

    (a) in relation to an order made as mentioned in paragraph (a) of that subsection, the charity trustees of the charity in trust for which the land is vested in the official custodian immediately before the time when the order takes effect, or

    (b) in relation to an order made under subsection (2) above, the charity trustees of the charity in trust for which the land was vested in the official custodian immediately before the time when section 1 of the 1987 Act operated in relation to the land.

(5) Where—

    (a) section 1 of the 1987 Act has operated in relation to any such land as is mentioned in subsection (2)(a) above, and

    (b) the land remains vested in the official custodian as mentioned in subsection (2)(b) above,

then (subject to subsection (6) below), all the powers, duties and liabilities that would, apart from this section, be those of the official custodian as trustee for sale of the land shall instead be those of the charity trustees of the charity concerned; and those trustees shall have power in his name and on his behalf to execute and do all assurances and things which they could properly execute or do in their own name and on their own behalf if the land were vested in them.

(6) Subsection (5) above shall not be taken to require or authorise those trustees to sell the land at a time when it remains vested in the official custodian.

(7) Where—

    (a) the official custodian has been discharged from his trusteeship of any land by an order under subsection (2) above, and

    (b) the land has, in accordance with subsection (3) above, been vested in the charity trustees concerned or (as the case may be) in any persons other than those trustees,

the land shall be held by those trustees, or (as the case may be) by those persons, as trustees for sale on the terms of the trust arising under section 1 of the 1987 Act.

(8)   The official custodian shall not be liable to any person in respect of any loss or misapplication of any land vested in him in accordance with that section unless it is occasioned by or through any wilful neglect or default of his or of any person acting for him; but the Consolidated Fund shall be liable to make good to any person any sums for which the official custodian may be liable by reason of any such neglect or default.

(9)   In this section any reference to section 1 of the 1987 Act operating in relation to any land is a reference to a trust for sale arising in relation to the land under that section.

[657]

NOTES
Commencement: 1 August 1993.

Establishment of common investment or deposit funds

24   Schemes to establish common investment funds

(1)   The court or the Commissioners may by order make and bring into effect schemes (in this section referred to as "common investment schemes") for the establishment of common investment funds under trusts which provide—

(a)   for property transferred to the fund by or on behalf of a charity participating in the scheme to be invested under the control of trustees appointed to manage the fund; and

(b)   for the participating charities to be entitled (subject to the provisions of the scheme) to the capital and income of the fund in shares determined by reference to the amount or value of the property transferred to it by or on behalf of each of them and to the value of the fund at the time of the transfers.

(2)   The court or the Commissioners may make a common investment scheme on the application of any two or more charities.

(3)   A common investment scheme may be made in terms admitting any charity to participate, or the scheme may restrict the right to participate in any manner.

(4)   A common investment scheme may make provision for, and for all matters connected with, the establishment, investment, management and winding up of the common investment fund, and may in particular include provision—

(a)   for remunerating persons appointed trustees to hold or manage the fund or any part of it, with or without provision authorising a person to receive the remuneration notwithstanding that he is also a charity trustee of or trustee for a participating charity;

(b)   for restricting the size of the fund, and for regulating as to time, amount or otherwise the right to transfer property to or withdraw it from the fund, and for enabling sums to be advanced out of the fund by way of loan to a participating charity pending the withdrawal of property from the fund by the charity;

(c)   for enabling income to be withheld from distribution with a view to avoiding fluctuations in the amounts distributed, and generally for regulating distributions of income;

(d)   for enabling money to be borrowed temporarily for the purpose of meeting payments to be made out of the funds;

(e)   for enabling questions arising under the scheme as to the right of a charity to participate, or as to the rights of participating charities, or as to any other matter, to be conclusively determined by the decision of the trustees managing the fund or in any other manner;

(f)	for regulating the accounts and information to be supplied to participating charities.

(5)	A common investment scheme, in addition to the provision for property to be transferred to the fund on the basis that the charity shall be entitled to a share in the capital and income of the fund, may include provision for enabling sums to be deposited by or on behalf of a charity on the basis that (subject to the provisions of the scheme) the charity shall be entitled to repayment of the sums deposited and to interest thereon at a rate determined by or under the scheme; and where a scheme makes any such provision it shall also provide for excluding from the amount of capital and income to be shared between charities participating otherwise than by way of deposit such amounts (not exceeding the amounts properly attributable to the making of deposits) as are from time to time reasonably required in respect of the liabilities of the fund for the repayment of deposits and for the interest on deposits, including amounts required by way of reserve.

(6)	Except in so far as a common investment scheme provides to the contrary, the rights under it of a participating charity shall not be capable of being assigned or charged, nor shall any trustee or other person concerned in the management of the common investment fund be required or entitled to take account of any trust or other equity affecting a participating charity or its property or rights.

(7)	The powers of investment of every charity shall include power to participate in common investment schemes unless the power is excluded by a provision specifically referring to common investment schemes in the trusts of the charity.

(8)	A common investment fund shall be deemed for all purposes to be a charity; and if the scheme admits only exempt charities, the fund shall be an exempt charity for the purposes of this Act.

(9)	Subsection (8) above shall apply not only to common investment funds established under the powers of this section, but also to any similar fund established for the exclusive benefit of charities by or under any enactment relating to any particular charities or class of charity.

[658]

NOTES
Commencement: 1 August 1993.

## 25	Schemes to establish common deposit funds

(1)	The court or the Commissioners may by order make and bring into effect schemes (in this section referred to as "common deposit schemes") for the establishment of common deposit funds under trusts which provide—

(a)	for sums to be deposited by or on behalf of a charity participating in the scheme and invested under the control of trustees appointed to manage the fund; and

(b)	for any such charity to be entitled (subject to the provisions of the scheme) to repayment of any sums so deposited and to interest thereon at a rate determined under the scheme.

(2)	Subject to subsection (3) below, the following provisions of section 24 above, namely—

(a)	subsections (2) to (4), and

(b)	subsections (6) to (9),

shall have effect in relation to common deposit schemes and common deposit funds as they have effect in relation to common investment schemes and common investment funds.

(3) In its application in accordance with subsection (2) above, subsection (4) of that section shall have effect with the substitution for paragraphs (b) and (c) of the following paragraphs—

"(b) for regulating as to time, amount or otherwise the right to repayment of sums deposited in the fund;

(c) for authorising a part of the income for any year to be credited to a reserve account maintained for the purpose of counteracting any losses accruing to the fund, and generally for regulating the manner in which the rate of interest on deposits is to be determined from time to time;".

[659]

NOTES

Commencement: 1 August 1993.

Additional powers of Commissioners

26 Power to authorise dealings with charity property etc

(1) Subject to the provisions of this section, where it appears to the Commissioners that any action proposed or contemplated in the administration of a charity is expedient in the interests of the charity, they may by order sanction that action, whether or not it would otherwise be within the powers exercisable by the charity trustees in the administration of the charity; and anything done under the authority of such an order shall be deemed to be properly done in the exercise of those powers.

(2) An order under this section may be made so as to authorise a particular transaction, compromise or the like, or a particular application of property, or so as to give a more general authority, and (without prejudice to the generality of subsection (1) above) may authorise a charity to use common premises, or employ a common staff, or otherwise combine for any purpose of administration, with any other charity.

(3) An order under this section may give directions as to the manner in which any expenditure is to be borne and as to other matters connected with or arising out of the action thereby authorised; and where anything is done in pursuance of an authority given by any such order, any directions given in connection therewith shall be binding on the charity trustees for the time being as if contained in the trusts of the charity; but any such directions may on the application of the charity be modified or superseded by a further order.

(4) Without prejudice to the generality of subsection (3) above, the directions which may be given by an order under this section shall in particular include directions for meeting any expenditure out of a specified fund, for charging any expenditure to capital or to income, for requiring expenditure charged to capital to be recouped out of income within a specified period, for restricting the costs to be incurred at the expense of the charity, or for the investment of moneys arising from any transaction.

(5) An order under this section may authorise any act notwithstanding that it is prohibited by any of the disabling Acts mentioned in subsection (6) below or that the trusts of the charity provide for the act to be done by or under the authority of the court; but no such order shall authorise the doing of any act expressly prohibited by

Act of Parliament other than the disabling Acts or by the trusts of the charity or shall extend or alter the purposes of the charity.

(6)   The Acts referred to in subsection (5) above as the disabling Acts are the Ecclesiastical Leases Act 1571, the Ecclesiastical Leases Act 1572, the Ecclesiastical Leases Act 1575 and the Ecclesiastical Leases Act 1836.

(7)   An order under this section shall not confer any authority in relation to a building which has been consecrated and of which the use or disposal is regulated, and can be further regulated, by a scheme having effect under the Union of Benefices Measures 1923 to 1952, the Reorganisation Areas Measures 1944 and 1954, the Pastoral Measure 1968 or the Pastoral Measure 1983, the reference to a building being taken to include part of a building and any land which under such a scheme is to be used or disposed of with a building to which the scheme applies.

[660]

NOTES
Commencement: 1 August 1993.

27   Power to authorise ex gratia payments etc

(1)   Subject to subsection (3) below, the Commissioners may by order exercise the same power as is exercisable by the Attorney General to authorise the charity trustees of a charity—
    (a)   to make any application of property of the charity, or
    (b)   to waive to any extent, on behalf of the charity, its entitlement to receive any property,

in a case where the charity trustees—
    (i)   (apart from this section) have no power to do so, but
    (ii)   in all the circumstances regard themselves as being under a moral obligation to do so.

(2)   The power conferred on the Commissioners by subsection (1) above shall be exercisable by them under the supervision of, and in accordance with such directions as may be given by, the Attorney General; and any such directions may in particular require the Commissioners, in such circumstances as are specified in the directions—
    (a)   to refrain from exercising that power; or
    (b)   to consult the Attorney General before exercising it.

(3)   Where—
    (a)   an application is made to the Commissioners for them to exercise that power in a case where they are not precluded from doing so by any such directions, but
    (b)   they consider that it would nevertheless be desirable for the application to be entertained by the Attorney General rather than by them,

they shall refer the application to the Attorney General.

(4)   It is hereby declared that where, in the case of any application made to them as mentioned in subsection (3)(a) above, the Commissioners determine the application by refusing to authorise charity trustees to take any action falling within subsection (1)(a) or (b) above, that refusal shall not preclude the Attorney General, on an application subsequently made to him by the trustees, from authorising the trustees to take that action.

[661]

NOTES
Commencement: 1 August 1993.

28 Power to give directions about dormant bank accounts of charities

(1) Where the Commissioners—

    (a) are informed by a relevant institution—

        (i) that it holds one or more accounts in the name of or on behalf of a particular charity ("the relevant charity"), and

        (ii) that the account, or (if it so holds two or more accounts) each of the accounts, is dormant, and

    (b) are unable, after making reasonable inquiries, to locate that charity or any of its trustees,

they may give a direction under subsection (2) below.

(2) A direction under this subsection is a direction which—

    (a) requires the institution concerned to transfer the amount, or (as the case may be) the aggregate amount, standing to the credit of the relevant charity in the account or accounts in question to such other charity as is specified in the direction in accordance with subsection (3) below; or

    (b) requires the institution concerned to transfer to each of two or more other charities so specified in the direction such part of that amount or aggregate amount as is there specified in relation to that charity.

(3) The Commissioners may specify in a direction under subsection (2) above such other charity or charities as they consider appropriate, having regard, in a case where the purposes of the relevant charity are known to them, to those purposes and to the purposes of the other charity or charities; but the Commissioners shall not so specify any charity unless they have received from the charity trustees written confirmation that those trustees are willing to accept the amount proposed to be transferred to the charity.

(4) Any amount received by a charity by virtue of this section shall be received by the charity on terms that—

    (a) it shall be held and applied by the charity for the purposes of the charity, but

    (b) it shall, as property of the charity, nevertheless be subject to any restrictions on expenditure to which it was subject as property of the relevant charity.

(5) Where—

    (a) the Commissioners have been informed as mentioned in subsection (1)(a) above by any relevant institution, and

    (b) before any transfer is made by the institution in pursuance of a direction under subsection (2) above, the institution has, by reason of any circumstances, cause to believe that the account, or (as the case may be) any of the accounts, held by it in the name of or on behalf of the relevant charity is no longer dormant,

the institution shall forthwith notify those circumstances in writing to the Commissioners; and, if it appears to the Commissioners that the account or accounts in question is or are no longer dormant, they shall revoke any direction under subsection (2) above which has previously been given by them to the institution with respect to the relevant charity.

(6)   The receipt of any charity trustees or trustee for a charity in respect of any amount received from a relevant institution by virtue of this section shall be a complete discharge of the institution in respect of that amount.

(7)   No obligation as to secrecy or other restriction on disclosure (however imposed) shall preclude a relevant institution from disclosing any information to the Commissioners for the purpose of enabling them to discharge their functions under this section.

(8)   For the purposes of this section—
-    (a)   an account is dormant if no transaction, other than—
     -    (i)   a transaction consisting in a payment into the account, or
     -    (ii)   a transaction which the institution holding the account has itself caused to be effected,

     has been effected in relation to the account within the period of five years immediately preceding the date when the Commissioners are informed as mentioned in paragraph (a) of subsection (1) above;
-    (b)   a "relevant institution" means—
     -    (i)   the Bank of England;
     -    (ii)   an institution which is authorised by the Bank of England to operate a deposit-taking business under Part I of the Banking Act 1987;
     -    (iii)   a European deposit-taker as defined in regulation 82(3) of the Banking Coordination (Second Council Directive) Regulations 1992;
     -    (iv)   a building society which is authorised by the Building Societies Commission under section 9 of the Building Societies Act 1986 to raise money from its members; or
     -    (v)   such other institution mentioned in Schedule 2 to the Banking Act 1987 as the Secretary of State may prescribe by regulations; and
-    (c)   references to the transfer of any amount to a charity are references to its transfer—
     -    (i)   to the charity trustees, or
     -    (ii)   to any trustee for the charity,

     as the charity trustees may determine (and any reference to any amount received by a charity shall be construed accordingly).

(9)   For the purpose of determining the matters in respect of which any of the powers conferred by section 8 or 9 above may be exercised it shall be assumed that the Commissioners have no functions under this section in relation to accounts to which this subsection applies (with the result that, for example, a relevant institution shall not, in connection with the functions of the Commissioners under this section, be required under section 8(3)(a) above to furnish any statements, or answer any questions or inquiries, with respect to any such accounts held by the institution).

This subsection applies to accounts which are dormant accounts by virtue of subsection (8)(a) above but would not be such accounts if sub-paragraph (i) of that provision were omitted.

(10)   Subsection (1) above shall not apply to any account held in the name of or on behalf of an exempt charity.

[662]

NOTES

Commencement: 1 August 1993.

---

29 Power to advise charity trustees

(1) The Commissioners may on the written application of any charity trustee give him their opinion or advice on any matter affecting the performance of his duties as such.

(2) A charity trustee or trustee for a charity acting in accordance with the opinion or advice of the Commissioners given under this section with respect to the charity shall be deemed, as regards his responsibility for so acting, to have acted in accordance with his trust, unless, when he does so, either—

 (a) he knows or has reasonable cause to suspect that the opinion or advice was given in ignorance of material facts; or

 (b) the decision of the court has been obtained on the matter or proceedings are pending to obtain one.

[663]

NOTES

Commencement: 1 August 1993.

30 Powers for preservation of charity documents

(1) The Commissioners may provide books in which any deed, will or other document relating to a charity may be enrolled.

(2) The Commissioners may accept for safe keeping any document of or relating to a charity, and the charity trustees or other persons having the custody of documents of or relating to a charity (including a charity which has ceased to exist) may with the consent of the Commissioners deposit them with the Commissioners for safe keeping, except in the case of documents required by some other enactment to be kept elsewhere.

(3) Where a document is enrolled by the Commissioners or is for the time being deposited with them under this section, evidence of its contents may be given by means of a copy certified by any officer of the Commissioners generally or specially authorised by them to act for this purpose; and a document purporting to be such a copy shall be received in evidence without proof of the official position, authority or handwriting of the person certifying it or of the original document being enrolled or deposited as aforesaid.

(4) Regulations made by the Secretary of State may make provision for such documents deposited with the Commissioners under this section as may be prescribed by the regulations to be destroyed or otherwise disposed of after such period or in such circumstances as may be so prescribed.

(5) Subsections (3) and (4) above shall apply to any document transmitted to the Commissioners under section 9 above and kept by them under subsection (3) of that section, as if the document had been deposited with them for safe keeping under this section.

[664]

NOTES

Commencement: 1 August 1993.

31 Power to order taxation of solicitor's bill

(1) The Commissioners may order that a solicitor's bill of costs for business done for a charity, or for charity trustees or trustees for a charity, shall be taxed, together

with the costs of the taxation, by a taxing officer in such division of the High Court as may be specified in the order, or by the taxing officer of any other court having jurisdiction to order the taxation of the bill.

(2) On any order under this section for the taxation of a solicitor's bill the taxation shall proceed, and the taxing officer shall have the same powers and duties, and the costs of the taxation shall be borne, as if the order had been made, on the application of the person chargeable with the bill, by the court in which the costs are taxed.

(3) No order under this section for the taxation of a solicitor's bill shall be made after payment of the bill unless the Commissioners are of opinion that it contains exorbitant charges; and no such order shall in any case be made where the solicitor's costs are not subject to taxation on an order of the High Court by reason either of an agreement as to his remuneration or the lapse of time since payment of the bill.

[665]

NOTES
Commencement: 1 August 1993.

Legal proceedings relating to charities

32 Proceedings by Commissioners

(1) Subject to subsection (2) below, the Commissioners may exercise the same powers with respect to—
  (a) the taking of legal proceedings with reference to charities or the property or affairs of charities, or
  (b) the compromise of claims with a view to avoiding or ending such proceedings,
as are exercisable by the Attorney General acting ex officio.

(2) Subsection (1) above does not apply to the power of the Attorney General under section 63(1) below to present a petition for the winding up of a charity.

(3) The practice and procedure to be followed in relation to any proceedings taken by the Commissioners under subsection (1) above shall be the same in all respects (and in particular as regards costs) as if they were proceedings taken by the Attorney General acting ex officio.

(4) No rule of law or practice shall be taken to require the Attorney General to be a party to any such proceedings.

(5) The powers exercisable by the Commissioners by virtue of this section shall be exercisable by them of their own motion, but shall be exercisable only with the agreement of the Attorney General on each occasion.

[666]

NOTES
Commencement: 1 August 1993.

33 Proceedings by other persons

(1) Charity proceedings may be taken with reference to a charity either by the charity, or by any of the charity trustees, or by any person interested in the charity, or by any two or more inhabitants of the area of the charity if it is a local charity, but not by any other person.

(2) Subject to the following provisions of this section, no charity proceedings relating to a charity (other than an exempt charity) shall be entertained or proceeded with in any court unless the taking of the proceedings is authorised by order of the Commissioners.

(3) The Commissioners shall not, without special reasons, authorise the taking of charity proceedings where in their opinion the case can be dealt with by them under the powers of this Act other than those conferred by section 32 above.

(4) This section shall not require any order for the taking of proceedings in a pending cause or matter or for the bringing of any appeal.

(5) Where the foregoing provisions of this section require the taking of charity proceedings to be authorised by an order of the Commissioners, the proceedings may nevertheless be entertained or proceeded with if, after the order had been applied for and refused, leave to take the proceedings was obtained from one of the judges of the High Court attached to the Chancery Division.

(6) Nothing in the foregoing subsections shall apply to the taking of proceedings by the Attorney General, with or without a relator, or to the taking of proceedings by the Commissioners in accordance with section 32 above.

(7) Where it appears to the Commissioners, on an application for an order under this section or otherwise, that it is desirable for legal proceedings to be taken with reference to any charity (other than an exempt charity) or its property or affairs, and for the proceedings to be taken by the Attorney General, the Commissioners shall so inform the Attorney General, and send him such statements and particulars as they think necessary to explain the matter.

(8) In this section "charity proceedings" means proceedings in any court in England or Wales brought under the court's jurisdiction with respect to charities, or brought under the court's jurisdiction with respect to trusts in relation to the administration of a trust for charitable purposes.

[667]

NOTES
Commencement: 1 August 1993.

34 Report of s 8 inquiry to be evidence in certain proceedings

(1) A copy of the report of the person conducting an inquiry under section 8 above shall, if certified by the Commissioners to be a true copy, be admissible in any proceedings to which this section applies—
  (a) as evidence of any fact stated in the report; and
  (b) as evidence of the opinion of that person as to any matter referred to in it.

(2) This section applies to—
  (a) any legal proceedings instituted by the Commissioners under this Part of this Act; and
  (b) any legal proceedings instituted by the Attorney General in respect of a charity.

(3) A document purporting to be a certificate issued for the purposes of subsection (1) above shall be received in evidence and be deemed to be such a certificate, unless the contrary is proved.

[668]

NOTES
    Commencement: 1 August 1993.

Meaning of "trust corporation"

35   Application of provisions to trust corporations appointed under s 16 or 18

(1)   In the definition of "trust corporation" contained in the following provisions—
    (a)   section 117(xxx) of the Settled Land Act 1925,
    (b)   section 68(18) of the Trustee Act 1925,
    (c)   section 205(xxviii) of the Law of Property Act 1925,
    (d)   section 55(xxvi) of the Administration of Estates Act 1925, and
    (e)   section 128 of the Supreme Court Act 1981,

the reference to a corporation appointed by the court in any particular case to be a trustee includes a reference to a corporation appointed by the Commissioners under this Act to be a trustee.

(2)   This section shall be deemed always to have had effect; but the reference to section 128 of the Supreme Court Act 1981 shall, in relation to any time before 1st January 1982, be construed as a reference to section 175(1) of the Supreme Court of Judicature (Consolidation) Act 1925.

[669]

NOTES
    Commencement: 1 August 1993 (for effect see sub-s (2) above).

PART V
CHARITY LAND

36   Restrictions on dispositions

(1)   Subject to the following provisions of this section and section 40 below, no land held by or in trust for a charity shall be sold, leased or otherwise disposed of without an order of the court or of the Commissioners.

(2)   Subsection (1) above shall not apply to a disposition of such land if—
    (a)   the disposition is made to a person who is not—
        (i)   a connected person (as defined in Schedule 5 to this Act), or
        (ii)   a trustee for, or nominee of, a connected person; and
    (b)   the requirements of subsection (3) or (5) below have been complied with in relation to it.

(3)   Except where the proposed disposition is the granting of such a lease as is mentioned in subsection (5) below, the charity trustees must, before entering into an agreement for the sale, or (as the case may be) for a lease or other disposition, of the land—
    (a)   obtain and consider a written report on the proposed disposition from a qualified surveyor instructed by the trustees and acting exclusively for the charity;
    (b)   advertise the proposed disposition for such period and in such manner as the surveyor has advised in his report (unless he has there advised that it would not be in the best interests of the charity to advertise the proposed disposition); and

(c)   decide that they are satisfied, having considered the surveyor's report, that the terms on which the disposition is proposed to be made are the best that can reasonably be obtained for the charity.

(4)   For the purposes of subsection (3) above a person is a qualified surveyor if—

(a)   he is a fellow or professional associate of the Royal Institution of Chartered Surveyors or of the Incorporated Society of Valuers and Auctioneers or satisfies such other requirement or requirements as may be prescribed by regulations made by the Secretary of State; and

(b)   he is reasonably believed by the charity trustees to have ability in, and experience of, the valuation of land of the particular kind, and in the particular area, in question;

and any report prepared for the purposes of that subsection shall contain such information, and deal with such matters, as may be prescribed by regulations so made.

(5)   Where the proposed disposition is the granting of a lease for a term ending not more than seven years after it is granted (other than one granted wholly or partly in consideration of a fine), the charity trustees must, before entering into an agreement for the lease—

(a)   obtain and consider the advice on the proposed disposition of a person who is reasonably believed by the trustees to have the requisite ability and practical experience to provide them with competent advice on the proposed disposition; and

(b)   decide that they are satisfied, having considered that person's advice, that the terms on which the disposition is proposed to be made are the best that can reasonably be obtained for the charity.

(6)   Where—

(a)   any land is held by or in trust for a charity, and

(b)   the trusts on which it is so held stipulate that it is to be used for the purposes, or any particular purposes, of the charity,

then (subject to subsections (7) and (8) below and without prejudice to the operation of the preceding provisions of this section) the land shall not be sold, leased or otherwise disposed of unless the charity trustees have previously—

(i)   given public notice of the proposed disposition, inviting representations to be made to them within a time specified in the notice, being not less than one month from the date of the notice; and

(ii)   taken into consideration any representations made to them within that time about the proposed disposition.

(7)   Subsection (6) above shall not apply to any such disposition of land as is there mentioned if—

(a)   the disposition is to be effected with a view to acquiring by way of replacement other property which is to be held on the trusts referred to in paragraph (b) of that subsection; or

(b)   the disposition is the granting of a lease for a term ending not more than two years after it is granted (other than one granted wholly or partly in consideration of a fine).

(8)   The Commissioners may direct—

(a)   that subsection (6) above shall not apply to dispositions of land held by or in trust for a charity or class of charities (whether generally or only in the case of a specified class of dispositions or land, or otherwise as may be provided in the direction), or

(b) that that subsection shall not apply to a particular disposition of land held by or in trust for a charity,

if, on an application made to them in writing by or on behalf of the charity or charities in question, the Commissioners are satisfied that it would be in the interests of the charity or charities for them to give the direction.

(9) The restrictions on disposition imposed by this section apply notwithstanding anything in the trusts of a charity; but nothing in this section applies—

  (a) to any disposition for which general or special authority is expressly given (without the authority being made subject to the sanction of an order of the court) by any statutory provision contained in or having effect under an Act of Parliament or by any scheme legally established; or

  (b) to any disposition of land held by or in trust for a charity which—
    (i) is made to another charity otherwise than for the best price that can reasonably be obtained, and
    (ii) is authorised to be so made by the trusts of the first-mentioned charity; or

  (c) to the granting, by or on behalf of a charity and in accordance with its trusts, of a lease to any beneficiary under those trusts where the lease—
    (i) is granted otherwise than for the best rent that can reasonably be obtained; and
    (ii) is intended to enable the demised premises to be occupied for the purposes, or any particular purposes, of the charity.

(10) Nothing in this section applies—

  (a) to any disposition of land held by or in trust for an exempt charity;
  (b) to any disposition of land by way of mortgage or other security; or
  (c) to any disposition of an advowson.

(11) In this section "land" means land in England or Wales.

[670]

NOTES

Commencement: 1 August 1993.

37 Supplementary provisions relating to dispositions

(1) Any of the following instruments, namely—

  (a) any contract for the sale, or for a lease or other disposition, of land which is held by or in trust for a charity, and

  (b) any conveyance, transfer, lease or other instrument effecting a disposition of such land,

shall state—

  (i) that the land is held by or in trust for a charity,
  (ii) whether the charity is an exempt charity and whether the disposition is one falling within paragraph (a), (b) or (c) of subsection (9) of section 36 above, and
  (iii) if it is not an exempt charity and the disposition is not one falling within any of those paragraphs, that the land is land to which the restrictions on disposition imposed by that section apply.

(2) Where any land held by or in trust for a charity is sold, leased or otherwise disposed of by a disposition to which subsection (1) or (2) of section 36 above applies, the charity trustees shall certify in the instrument by which the disposition is effected—

(a) (where subsection (1) of that section applies) that the disposition has been sanctioned by an order of the court or of the Commissioners (as the case may be), or

(b) (where subsection (2) of that section applies) that the charity trustees have power under the trusts of the charity to effect the disposition, and that they have complied with the provisions of that section so far as applicable to it.

(3)   Where subsection (2) above has been complied with in relation to any disposition of land, then in favour of a person who (whether under the disposition or afterwards) acquires an interest in the land for money or money's worth, it shall be conclusively presumed that the facts were as stated in the certificate.

(4)   Where—

(a) any land held by or in trust for a charity is sold, leased or otherwise disposed of by a disposition to which subsection (1) or (2) of section 36 above applies, but

(b) subsection (2) above has not been complied with in relation to the disposition,

then in favour of a person who (whether under the disposition or afterwards) in good faith acquires an interest in the land for money or money's worth, the disposition shall be valid whether or not—

(i) the disposition has been sanctioned by an order of the court or of the Commissioners, or

(ii) the charity trustees have power under the trusts of the charity to effect the disposition and have complied with the provisions of that section so far as applicable to it.

(5)   Any of the following instruments, namely—

(a) any contract for the sale, or for a lease or other disposition, of land which will, as a result of the disposition, be held by or in trust for a charity, and

(b) any conveyance, transfer, lease or other instrument effecting a disposition of such land,

shall state—

(i) that the land will, as a result of the disposition, be held by or in trust for a charity,

(ii) whether the charity is an exempt charity, and

(iii) if it is not an exempt charity, that the restrictions on disposition imposed by section 36 above will apply to the land (subject to subsection (9) of that section).

(6)   In section 29(1) of the Settled Land Act 1925 (charitable and public trusts)—

(a) the requirement for a conveyance of land held on charitable, ecclesiastical or public trusts to state that it is held on such trusts shall not apply to any instrument to which subsection (1) above applies; and

(b) the requirement imposed on a purchaser, in the circumstances mentioned in section 29(1) of that Act, to see that any consents or orders requisite for authorising a transaction have been obtained shall not apply in relation to any disposition in relation to which subsection (2) above has been complied with;

and expressions used in this subsection which are also used in that Act have the same meaning as in that Act.

(7)   Where—
  (a)   the disposition to be effected by any such instrument as is mentioned in subsection (1)(b) or (5)(b) above will be a registered disposition, or
  (b)   any such instrument will on taking effect be an instrument to which section 123(1) of the Land Registration Act 1925 (compulsory registration of title) applies,

the statement which, by virtue of subsection (1) or (5) above, is to be contained in the instrument shall be in such form as may be prescribed.

(8)   Where—
  (a)   an application is duly made—
     (i)   for registration of a disposition of registered land, or
     (ii)   for registration of a person's title under a disposition of unregistered land, and
  (b)   the instrument by which the disposition is effected contains a statement complying with subsections (5) and (7) above, and
  (c)   the charity by or in trust for which the land is held as a result of the disposition is not an exempt charity,

the registrar shall enter in the register, in respect of the land, a restriction in such form as may be prescribed.

(9)   Where—
  (a)   any such restriction is entered in the register in respect of any land, and
  (b)   the charity by or in trust for which the land is held becomes an exempt charity,

the charity trustees shall apply to the registrar for the restriction to be withdrawn; and on receiving any application duly made under this subsection the registrar shall withdraw the restriction.

(10)   Where—
  (a)   any registered land is held by or in trust for an exempt charity and the charity ceases to be an exempt charity, or
  (b)   any registered land becomes, as a result of a declaration of trust by the registered proprietor, land held in trust for a charity (other than an exempt charity),

the charity trustees shall apply to the registrar for such a restriction as is mentioned in subsection (8) above to be entered in the register in respect of the land; and on receiving any application duly made under this subsection the registrar shall enter such a restriction in the register in respect of the land.

(11)   In this section—
  (a)   references to a disposition of land do not include references to—
     (i)   a disposition of land by way of mortgage or other security,
     (ii)   any disposition of an advowson, or
     (iii)   any release of a rentcharge failing within section 40(1) below; and
  (b)   "land" means land in England or Wales;

and subsections (7) to (10) above shall be construed as one with the Land Registration Act 1925.

38 Restrictions on mortgaging

(1)   Subject to subsection (2) below, no mortgage of land held by or in trust for a charity shall be granted without an order of the court or of the Commissioners.

(2)   Subsection (1) above shall not apply to a mortgage of any such land by way of security for the repayment of a loan where the charity trustees have, before executing the mortgage, obtained and considered proper advice, given to them in writing, on the matters mentioned in subsection (3) below.

(3)   Those matters are—
    (a)   whether the proposed loan is necessary in order for the charity trustees to be able to pursue the particular course of action in connection with which the loan is sought by them;
    (b)   whether the terms of the proposed loan are reasonable having regard to the status of the charity as a prospective borrower; and
    (c)   the ability of the charity to repay on those terms the sum proposed to be borrowed.

(4)   For the purposes of subsection (2) above proper advice is the advice of a person—
    (a)   who is reasonably believed by the charity trustees to be qualified by his ability in and practical experience of financial matters; and
    (b)   who has no financial interest in the making of the loan in question;

and such advice may constitute proper advice for those purposes notwithstanding that the person giving it does so in the course of his employment as an officer or employee of the charity or of the charity trustees.

(5)   This section applies notwithstanding anything in the trusts of a charity; but nothing in this section applies to any mortgage for which general or special authority is given as mentioned in section 36(9)(a) above.

(6)   In this section—
    "land" means land in England or Wales;
    "mortgage" includes a charge.

(7)   Nothing in this section applies to an exempt charity.

39 Supplementary provisions relating to mortgaging

(1)   Any mortgage of land held by or in trust for a charity shall state—
    (a)   that the land is held by or in trust for a charity,
    (b)   whether the charity is an exempt charity and whether the mortgage is one falling within subsection (5) of section 38 above, and
    (c)   if it is not an exempt charity and the mortgage is not one falling within that subsection, that the mortgage is one to which the restrictions imposed by that section apply;

and where the mortgage will be a registered disposition any such statement shall be in such form as may be prescribed.

(2)   Where subsection (1) or (2) of section 38 above applies to any mortgage of land held by or in trust for a charity, the charity trustees shall certify in the mortgage—

    (a)   (where subsection (1) of that section applies) that the mortgage has been sanctioned by an order of the court or of the Commissioners (as the case may be), or

    (b)   (where subsection (2) of that section applies) that the charity trustees have power under the trusts of the charity to grant the mortgage, and that they have obtained and considered such advice as is mentioned in that subsection.

(3)   Where subsection (2) above has been complied with in relation to any mortgage, then in favour of a person who (whether under the mortgage or afterwards) acquires an interest in the land in question for money or money's worth, it shall be conclusively presumed that the facts were as stated in the certificate.

(4)   Where—

    (a)   subsection (1) or (2) of section 38 above applies to any mortgage of land held by or in trust for a charity, but

    (b)   subsection (2) above has not been complied with in relation to the mortgage,

then in favour of a person who (whether under the mortgage or afterwards) in good faith acquires an interest in the land for money or money's worth, the mortgage shall be valid whether or not—

    (i)   the mortgage has been sanctioned by an order of the court or of the Commissioners, or

    (ii)   the charity trustees have power under the trusts of the charity to grant the mortgage and have obtained and considered such advice as is mentioned in subsection (2) of that section.

(5)   In section 29(1) of the Settled Land Act 1925 (charitable and public trusts)—

    (a)   the requirement for a mortgage of land held on charitable, ecclesiastical or public trusts (as a "conveyance" of such land for the purposes of that Act) to state that it is held on such trusts shall not apply to any mortgage to which subsection (1) above applies; and

    (b)   the requirement imposed on a mortgagee (as a "purchaser" for those purposes), in the circumstances mentioned in section 29(1) of that Act, to see that any consents or orders requisite for authorising a transaction have been obtained shall not apply in relation to any mortgage in relation to which subsection (2) above has been complied with;

and expressions used in this subsection which are also used in that Act have the same meaning as in that Act.

(6)   In this section—

    "mortgage" includes a charge, and "mortgagee" shall be construed accordingly;

    "land" means land in England or Wales;

    "prescribed" and "registered disposition" have the same meaning as in the Land Registration Act 1925.

[673]

NOTES

Commencement: 1 August 1993.

40 Release of charity rentcharges

(1)   Section 36(1) above shall not apply to the release by a charity of a rentcharge which it is entitled to receive if the release is given in consideration of the payment of an amount which is not less than ten times the annual amount of the rentcharge.

(2)   Where a charity which is entitled to receive a rentcharge releases it in consideration of the payment of an amount not exceeding £500, any costs incurred by the charity in connection with proving its title to the rentcharge shall be recoverable by the charity from the person or persons in whose favour the rentcharge is being released.

(3)   Neither section 36(1) nor subsection (2) above applies where a rentcharge which a charity is entitled to receive is redeemed under sections 8 to 10 of the Rentcharges Act 1977.

(4)   The Secretary of State may by order amend subsection (2) above by substituting a different sum for the sum for the time being specified there.

[674]

NOTES
Commencement: 1 August 1993.

PART VI
CHARITY ACCOUNTS, REPORTS AND RETURNS

41 Duty to keep accounting records

(1)   The charity trustees of a charity shall ensure that accounting records are kept in respect of the charity which are sufficient to show and explain all the charity's transactions, and which are such as to—
  (a)   disclose at any time, with reasonable accuracy, the financial position of the charity at that time, and
  (b)   enable the trustees to ensure that, where any statements of accounts are prepared by them under section 42(1) below, those statements of accounts comply with the requirements of regulations under that provision.

(2)   The accounting records shall in particular contain—
  (a)   entries showing from day to day all sums of money received and expended by the charity, and the matters in respect of which the receipt and expenditure takes place; and
  (b)   a record of the assets and liabilities of the charity.

(3)   The charity trustees of a charity shall preserve any accounting records made for the purposes of this section in respect of the charity for at least six years from the end of the financial year of the charity in which they are made.

(4)   Where a charity ceases to exist within the period of six years mentioned in subsection (3) above as it applies to any accounting records, the obligation to preserve those records in accordance with that subsection shall continue to be discharged by the last charity trustees of the charity, unless the Commissioners consent in writing to the records being destroyed or otherwise disposed of.

(5)   Nothing in this section applies to a charity which is a company.

[675]

NOTES
Commencement: to be appointed.

42   Annual statements of accounts

(1)   The charity trustees of a charity shall (subject to subsection (3) below) prepare in respect of each financial year of the charity a statement of accounts complying with such requirements as to its form and contents as may be prescribed by regulations made by the Secretary of State.

(2)   Without prejudice to the generality of subsection (1) above, regulations under that subsection may make provision—

     (a)   for any such statement to be prepared in accordance with such methods and principles as are specified or referred to in the regulations;

     (b)   as to any information to be provided by way of notes to the accounts;

and regulations under that subsection may also make provision for determining the financial years of a charity for the purposes of this Act and any regulations made under it.

(3)   Where a charity's gross income in any financial year does not exceed £25,000, the charity trustees may, in respect of that year, elect to prepare the following, namely—

     (a)   a receipts and payments account, and

     (b)   a statement of assets and liabilities,

instead of a statement of accounts under subsection (1) above.

(4)   The charity trustees of a charity shall preserve—

     (a)   any statement of accounts prepared by them under subsection (1) above, or

     (b)   any account and statement prepared by them under subsection (3) above,

for at least six years from the end of the financial year to which any such statement relates or (as the case may be) to which any such account and statement relate.

(5)   Subsection (4) of section 41 above shall apply in relation to the preservation of any such statement or account and statement as it applies in relation to the preservation of any accounting records (the references to subsection (3) of that section being read as references to subsection (4) above).

(6)   The Secretary of State may by order amend subsection (3) above by substituting a different sum for the sum for the time being specified there.

(7)   Nothing in this section applies to a charity which is a company.

                                                                  [676]

NOTES

Commencement: to be appointed.

43   Annual audit or examination of charity accounts

(1)   Subsection (2) below applies to a financial year of a charity ("the relevant year") if the charity's gross income or total expenditure in any of the following, namely—

     (a)   the relevant year,

     (b)   the financial year of the charity immediately preceding the relevant year (if any), and

     (c)   the financial year of the charity immediately preceding the year specified in paragraph (b) above (if any),

exceeds £100,000.

(2)   If this subsection applies to a financial year of a charity, the accounts of the charity for that year shall be audited by a person who—

(a) is, in accordance with section 25 of the Companies Act 1989 (eligibility for appointment), eligible for appointment as a company auditor, or

(b) is a member of a body for the time being specified in regulations under section 44 below and is under the rules of that body eligible for appointment as auditor of the charity.

(3) If subsection (2) above does not apply to a financial year of a charity [and its gross income or total expenditure in that year exceeds £10,000], then (subject to subsection (4) below) the accounts of the charity for that year shall, at the election of the charity trustees, either—

(a) be examined by an independent examiner, that is to say an independent person who is reasonably believed by the trustees to have the requisite ability and practical experience to carry out a competent examination of the accounts, or

(b) be audited by such a person as is mentioned in subsection (2) above.

(4) Where it appears to the Commissioners—

(a) that subsection (2), or (as the case may be) subsection (3) above, has not been complied with in relation to a financial year of a charity within ten months from the end of that year, or

(b) that, although subsection (2) above does not apply to a financial year of a charity, it would nevertheless be desirable for the accounts of the charity for that year to be audited by such a person as is mentioned in that subsection,

the Commissioners may by order require the accounts of the charity for that year to be audited by such a person as is mentioned in that subsection.

(5) If the Commissioners make an order under subsection (4) above with respect to a charity, then unless—

(a) the order is made by virtue of paragraph (b) of that subsection, and

(b) the charity trustees themselves appoint an auditor in accordance with the order,

the auditor shall be a person appointed by the Commissioners.

(6) The expenses of any audit carried out by an auditor appointed by the Commissioners under subsection (5) above, including the auditor's remuneration, shall be recoverable by the Commissioners—

(a) from the charity trustees of the charity concerned, who shall be personally liable, jointly and severally, for those expenses; or

(b) to the extent that it appears to the Commissioners not to be practical to seek recovery of those expenses in accordance with paragraph (a) above, from the funds of the charity.

(7) The Commissioners may—

(a) give guidance to charity trustees in connection with the selection of a person for appointment as an independent examiner;

(b) give such directions as they think appropriate with respect to the carrying out of an examination in pursuance of subsection (3)(a) above;

and any such guidance or directions may either be of general application or apply to a particular charity only.

(8) The Secretary of State may by order amend subsection (1) [or (3)] above by substituting a different sum for the sum for the time being specified there.

(9)   Nothing in this section applies to a charity which is a company.

[677]

NOTES
Commencement: to be appointed.
    Sub-ss (3), (8): words in square brackets inserted by the Deregulation and Contracting Out Act 1994, s 28.

44   Supplementary provisions relating to audits etc

(1)   The Secretary of State may by regulations make provision—
    (a)   specifying one or more bodies for the purposes of section 43(2)(b) above;
    (b)   with respect to the duties of an auditor carrying out an audit under section 43 above, including provision with respect to the making by him of a report on—
        (i)   the statement of accounts prepared for the financial year in question under section 42(1) above, or
        (ii)   the account and statement so prepared under section 42(3) above, as the case may be;
    (c)   with respect to the making by an independent examiner of a report in respect of an examination carried out by him under section 43 above;
    (d)   conferring on such an auditor or on an independent examiner a right of access with respect to books, documents and other records (however kept) which relate to the charity concerned;
    (e)   entitling such an auditor or an independent examiner to require, in the case of a charity, information and explanations from past or present charity trustees or trustees for the charity, or from past or present officers or employees of the charity;
    (f)   enabling the Commissioners, in circumstances specified in the regulations, to dispense with the requirements of section 43(2) or (3) above in the case of a particular charity or in the case of any particular financial year of a charity.

(2)   If any person fails to afford an auditor or an independent examiner any facility to which he is entitled by virtue of subsection (1)(d) or (e) above, the Commissioners may by order give—
    (a)   to that person, or
    (b)   to the charity trustees for the time being of the charity concerned,

such directions as the Commissioners think appropriate for securing that the default is made good.

(3)   Section 727 of the Companies Act 1985 (power of court to grant relief in certain cases) shall have effect in relation to an auditor or independent examiner appointed by a charity in pursuance of section 43 above as it has effect in relation to a person employed as auditor by a company within the meaning of that Act.

[678]

NOTES
Commencement: to be appointed.

45   Annual reports

(1)   The charity trustees of a charity shall prepare in respect of each financial year of the charity an annual report containing—
    (a)   such a report by the trustees on the activities of the charity during that year, and

(b) such other information relating to the charity or to its trustees or officers,

as may be prescribed by regulations made by the Secretary of State.

(2) Without prejudice to the generality of subsection (1) above, regulations under that subsection may make provision—

    (a) for any such report as is mentioned in paragraph (a) of that subsection to be prepared in accordance with such principles as are specified or referred to in the regulations;

    (b) enabling the Commissioners to dispense with any requirement prescribed by virtue of subsection (1)(b) above in the case of a particular charity or a particular class of charities, or in the case of a particular financial year of a charity or of any class of charities.

(3) [Where in any financial year of a charity its gross income or total expenditure exceeds £10,000, the annual report required to be prepared under this section in respect of that year] shall be transmitted to the Commissioners by the charity trustees—

    (a) within ten months from the end of that year, or

    (b) within such longer period as the Commissioners may for any special reason allow in the case of that report.

[(3A) Where in any financial year of a charity neither its gross income nor its total expenditure exceeds £10,000, the annual report required to be prepared under this section in respect of that year shall, if the Commissioners so request, be transmitted to them by the charity trustees—

    (a) in the case of a request made before the end of seven months from the end of the financial year to which the report relates, within ten months from the end of that year, and

    (b) in the case of a request not so made, within three months from the date of the request,

or, in either case, within such longer period as the Commissioners may for any special reason allow in the case of that report.]

(4) Subject to subsection (5) below, [any annual report transmitted to the Commissioners under this section] shall have attached to it the statement of accounts prepared for the financial year in question under section 42(1) above or (as the case may be) the account and statement so prepared under section 42(3) above, together with—

    (a) where the accounts of the charity for that year have been audited under section 43 above, a copy of the report made by the auditor on that statement of accounts or (as the case may be) on that account and statement;

    (b) where the accounts of the charity for that year have been examined under section 43 above, a copy of the report made by the independent examiner in respect of the examination carried out by him under that section.

(5) Subsection (4) above does not apply to a charity which is a company, and any annual report transmitted by the charity trustees of such a charity under [this section] shall instead have attached to it a copy of the charity's annual accounts prepared for the financial year in question under Part VII of the Companies Act 1985, together with a copy of [any auditors' report or report made for the purposes of section 249A(2) of that Act] on those accounts.

(6) Any annual report transmitted to the Commissioners under [this section], together with the documents attached to it, shall be kept by the Commissioners for such period as they think fit.

[(7)   The charity trustees of a charity shall preserve, for at least six years from the end of the financial year to which it relates, any annual report prepared by them under subsection (1) above which they have not been required to transmit to the Commissioners.

(8)   Subsection (4) of section 41 above shall apply in relation to the preservation of any such annual report as it applies in relation to the preservation of any accounting records (the references in subsection (3) of that section being read as references to subsection (7) above).

(9)   The Secretary of State may by order amend subsection (3) or (3A) above by substituting a different sum for the sum for the time being specified there.]

[679]

NOTES

Commencement: to be appointed.

Sub-ss (3), (4), (6): words in square brackets substituted by the Deregulation and Contracting Out Act 1994, s 29(1), (3), (5).

Sub-ss (3A), (7)–(9): inserted by the Deregulation and Contracting Out Act 1994, s 29(2), (6).

Sub-s (5): words in first pair of square brackets substituted by the Deregulation and Contracting Out Act 1994, s 29(4); words in second pair of square brackets substituted by the Companies Act 1985 (Audit Exemption) Regulations 1994, SI 1994/1935, reg 4, Sch 1, Pt II, para 6.

46   Special provision as respects accounts and annual reports of exempt and other excepted charities

(1)   Nothing in sections 41 to 45 above applies to any exempt charity; but the charity trustees of an exempt charity shall keep proper books of account with respect to the affairs of the charity, and if not required by or under the authority of any other Act to prepare periodical statements of account shall prepare consecutive statements of account consisting on each occasion of an income and expenditure account relating to a period of not more than fifteen months and a balance sheet relating to the end of that period.

(2)   The books of accounts and statements of account relating to an exempt charity shall be preserved for a period of six years at least unless the charity ceases to exist and the Commissioners consent in writing to their being destroyed or otherwise disposed of.

(3)   Nothing in sections 43 to 45 above applies to any charity which—
   (a)   falls within section 3(5)(c) above, and
   (b)   is not registered.

(4)   Except in accordance with subsection (7) below, nothing in section 45 above applies to any charity (other than an exempt charity or a charity which falls within section 3(5)(c) above) which—
   (a)   is excepted by section 3(5) above, and
   (b)   is not registered.

(5)   If requested to do so by the Commissioners, the charity trustees of any such charity as is mentioned in subsection (4) above shall prepare an annual report in respect of such financial year of the charity as is specified in the Commissioners' request.

(6)   Any report prepared under subsection (5) above shall contain—
   (a)   such a report by the charity trustees on the activities of the charity during the year in question, and
   (b)   such other information relating to the charity or to its trustees or officers,

as may be prescribed by regulations made under section 45(1) above in relation to annual reports prepared under that provision.

(7)   Subsections (3) to (6) of section 45 [(as originally enacted)] above shall apply to any report required to be prepared under subsection (5) above as if it were an annual report required to be prepared under subsection (1) of that section.

(8)   Any reference in this section to a charity which falls within section 3(5)(c) above includes a reference to a charity which falls within that provision but is also excepted from registration by section 3(5)(b) above.

[680]

NOTES

Commencement: to be appointed.

Sub-s (7): words in square brackets inserted by the Deregulation and Contracting Out Act 1994, s 29(7).

47   Public inspection of annual reports etc

(1)   Any annual report or other document kept by the Commissioners in pursuance of section 45(6) above shall be open to public inspection at all reasonable times—
  (a)   during the period for which it is so kept; or
  (b)   if the Commissioners so determine, during such lesser period as they may specify.

(2)   Where any person—
  (a)   requests the charity trustees of a charity in writing to provide him with a copy of the charity's most recent accounts, and
  (b)   pays them such reasonable fee (if any) as they may require in respect of the costs of complying with the request,

those trustees shall comply with the request within the period of two months beginning with the date on which it is made.

(3)   In subsection (2) above the reference to a charity's most recent accounts is—
  (a)   . . . ;
  (b)   in the case of [a charity other than one falling within paragraph (c) or (d) below], a reference to the statement of accounts or account and statement prepared in pursuance of section 42(1) or (3) above in respect of the last financial year of the charity in respect of which a statement of accounts or account and statement has or have been so prepared;
  [(c)   in the case of a charity which is a company, a reference to the most recent annual accounts of the company prepared under Part VII of the Companies Act 1985 in relation to which any of the following conditions is satisfied—
     (i)   they have been audited;
     (ii) a report required for the purposes of section 249A(2) of that Act has been made in respect of them; or
     (iii) they relate to a year in respect of which the company is exempt from audit by virtue of section 249A(1) of that Act; and]
  (d)   in the case of an exempt charity, a reference to the accounts of the charity most recently audited in pursuance of any statutory or other requirement or, if its accounts are not required to be audited, the accounts most recently prepared in respect of the charity.

[681]

NOTES

Commencement: to be appointed.

Sub-s (3): para (a) repealed and words in square brackets in para (b) substituted by the Deregulation and Contracting Out Act 1994, ss 39, 81(1), Sch 11, para 12, Sch 17; para (c) substituted by the Companies Act 1985 (Audit Exemption) Regulations 1994, SI 1994/1935, reg 4, Sch 1, Pt II, para 7.

48 Annual returns by registered charities

(1) [Subject to subsection (1A) below] every registered charity shall prepare in respect of each of its financial years an annual return in such form, and containing such information, as may be prescribed by regulations made by the Commissioners.

[(1A) Subsection (1) above shall not apply in relation to any financial year of a charity in which neither the gross income nor the total expenditure of the charity exceeds £10,000.]

(2) Any such return shall be transmitted to the Commissioners by the date by which the charity trustees are, by virtue of section 45(3) above, required to transmit to them the annual report required to be prepared in respect of the financial year in question.

(3) The Commissioners may dispense with the requirements of subsection (1) above in the case of a particular charity or a particular class of charities, or in the case of a particular financial year of a charity or of any class of charities.

[(4) The Secretary of State may by order amend subsection (1A) above by substituting a different sum for the sum for the time being specified there.]

[682]

NOTES
Commencement: to be appointed.

Sub-s (1): words in square brackets inserted by the Deregulation and Contracting Out Act 1994, s 30(1), (2).

Sub-ss (1A), (4): inserted by the Deregulation and Contracting Out Act 1994, s 30(1), (3), (4).

49 Offences

Any person who, without reasonable excuse, is persistently in default in relation to any requirement imposed—

    (a) by section 45(3) [or (3A)] above (taken with section 45(4) or (5), as the case may require), or

    (b) by section 47(2) or 48(2) above,

shall be guilty of an offence and liable on summary conviction to a fine not exceeding level 4 on the standard scale.

[683]

NOTES
Commencement: to be appointed.

Words in square brackets inserted by the Deregulation and Contracting Out Act 1994, s 29(8).

PART VII
INCORPORATION OF CHARITY TRUSTEES

50 Incorporation of trustees of a charity

(1) Where—

    (a) the trustees of a charity, in accordance with section 52 below, apply to the Commissioners for a certificate of incorporation of the trustees as a body corporate, and

    (b) the Commissioners consider that the incorporation of the trustees would be in the interests of the charity,

the Commissioners may grant such a certificate, subject to such conditions or directions as they think fit to insert in it.

(2)   The Commissioners shall not, however, grant such a certificate in a case where the charity appears to them to be required to be registered under section 3 above but is not so registered.

(3)   On the grant of such a certificate—
- (a)   the trustees of the charity shall become a body corporate by such name as is specified in the certificate; and
- (b)   (without prejudice to the operation of section 54 below) any relevant rights or liabilities of those trustees shall become rights or liabilities of that body.

(4)   After their incorporation the trustees—
- (a)   may sue and be sued in their corporate name; and
- (b)   shall have the same powers, and be subject to the same restrictions and limitations, as respects the holding, acquisition and disposal of property for or in connection with the purposes of the charity as they had or were subject to while unincorporated;

and any relevant legal proceedings that might have been continued or commenced by or against the trustees may be continued or commenced by or against them in their corporate name.

(5)   A body incorporated under this section need not have a common seal.

(6)   In this section—
"relevant rights or liabilities" means rights or liabilities in connection with any property vesting in the body in question under section 51 below; and
"relevant legal proceedings" means legal proceedings in connection with any such property.

[684]

NOTES

Commencement: 1 August 1993.

---

51   Estate to vest in body corporate

The certificate of incorporation shall vest in the body corporate all real and personal estate, of whatever nature or tenure, belonging to or held by any person or persons in trust for the charity, and thereupon any person or persons in whose name or names any stocks, funds or securities are standing in trust for the charity, shall transfer them into the name of the body corporate, except that the foregoing provisions shall not apply to property vested in the official custodian.

[685]

NOTES

Commencement: 1 August 1993.

---

52   Applications for incorporation

(1)   Every application to the Commissioners for a certificate of incorporation under this Part of this Act shall—
- (a)   be in writing and signed by the trustees of the charity concerned; and
- (b)   be accompanied by such documents or information as the Commissioners may require for the purpose of the application.

(2)   The Commissioners may require—
- (a)   any statement contained in any such application, or
- (b)   any document or information supplied under subsection (1)(b) above,

to be verified in such manner as they may specify.

[686]

NOTES
Commencement: 1 August 1993.

53   Nomination of trustees, and filling up vacancies

(1)   Before a certificate of incorporation is granted under this Part of this Act, trustees of the charity must have been effectually appointed to the satisfaction of the Commissioners.

(2)   Where a certificate of incorporation is granted vacancies in the number of the trustees of the charity shall from time to time be filled up so far as required by the constitution or settlement of the charity, or by any conditions or directions in the certificate, by such legal means as would have been available for the appointment of new trustees of the charity if no certificate of incorporation had been granted, or otherwise as required by such conditions or directions.

[687]

NOTES
Commencement: 1 August 1993.

54   Liability of trustees and others, notwithstanding incorporation

After a certificate of incorporation has been granted under this Part of this Act all trustees of the charity, notwithstanding their incorporation, shall be chargeable for such property as shall come into their hands, and shall be answerable and accountable for their own acts, receipts, neglects, and defaults, and for the due administration of the charity and its property, in the same manner and to the same extent as if no such incorporation had been effected.

[688]

NOTES
Commencement: 1 August 1993.

55   Certificate to be evidence of compliance with requirements for incorporation

A certificate of incorporation granted under this Part of this Act shall be conclusive evidence that all the preliminary requirements for incorporation under this Part of this Act have been complied with, and the date of incorporation mentioned in the certificate shall be deemed to be the date at which incorporation has taken place.

[689]

NOTES
Commencement: 1 August 1993.

56   Power of Commissioners to amend certificate of incorporation

(1)   The Commissioners may amend a certificate of incorporation either on the application of the incorporated body to which it relates or of their own motion.

(2)   Before making any such amendment of their own motion, the Commissioners shall by notice in writing—
    (a)   inform the trustees of the relevant charity of their proposals, and
    (b)   invite those trustees to make representations to them within a time specified in the notice, being not less than one month from the date of the notice.

(3)   The Commissioners shall take into consideration any representations made by those trustees within the time so specified, and may then (without further notice) proceed with their proposals either without modification or with such modifications as appear to them to be desirable.

(4)   The Commissioners may amend a certificate of incorporation either—
    (a) by making an order specifying the amendment; or
    (b) by issuing a new certificate of incorporation taking account of the amendment.

[690]

NOTES
Commencement: 1 August 1993.

57   Records of applications and certificates

(1)   The Commissioners shall keep a record of all applications for, and certificates of, incorporation under this Part of this Act and shall preserve all documents sent to them under this Part of this Act.

(2)   Any person may inspect such documents, under the direction of the Commissioners, and any person may require a copy or extract of any such document to be certified by a certificate signed by the secretary of the Commissioners.

[691]

NOTES
Commencement: 1 August 1993.

58   Enforcement of orders and directions

All conditions and directions inserted in any certificate of incorporation shall be binding upon and performed or observed by the trustees as trusts of the charity, and section 88 below shall apply to any trustee who fails to perform or observe any such condition or direction as it applies to a person guilty of disobedience to any such order of the Commissioners as is mentioned in that section.

[692]

NOTES
Commencement: 1 August 1993.

59   Gifts to charity before incorporation to have same effect afterwards

After the incorporation of the trustees of any charity under this Part of this Act every donation, gift and disposition of property, real or personal, lawfully made before the incorporation but not having actually taken effect, or thereafter lawfully made, by deed, will or otherwise to or in favour of the charity, or the trustees of the charity, or otherwise for the purposes of the charity, shall take effect as if made to or in favour of the incorporated body or otherwise for the like purposes.

[693]

NOTES
Commencement: 1 August 1993.

60   Execution of documents by incorporated body

(1)   This section has effect as respects the execution of documents by an incorporated body.

(2)   If an incorporated body has a common seal, a document may be executed by the body by the affixing of its common seal.

(3)   Whether or not it has a common seal, a document may be executed by an incorporated body either—

   (a) by being signed by a majority of the trustees of the relevant charity and expressed (in whatever form of words) to be executed by the body; or

   (b) by being executed in pursuance of an authority given under subsection (4) below.

(4)   For the purposes of subsection (3)(b) above the trustees of the relevant charity in the case of an incorporated body may, subject to the trusts of the charity, confer on any two or more of their number—

   (a) a general authority, or

   (b) an authority limited in such manner as the trustees think fit,

to execute in the name and on behalf of the body documents for giving effect to transactions to which the body is a party.

(5)   An authority under subsection (4) above—

   (a) shall suffice for any document if it is given in writing or by resolution of a meeting of the trustees of the relevant charity, notwithstanding the want of any formality that would be required in giving an authority apart from that subsection;

   (b) may be given so as to make the powers conferred exercisable by any of the trustees, or may be restricted to named persons or in any other way;

   (c) subject to any such restriction, and until it is revoked, shall, notwithstanding any change in the trustees of the relevant charity, have effect as a continuing authority given by the trustees from time to time of the charity and exercisable by such trustees.

(6)   In any authority under subsection (4) above to execute a document in the name and on behalf of an incorporated body there shall, unless the contrary intention appears, be implied authority also to execute it for the body in the name and on behalf of the official custodian or of any other person, in any case in which the trustees could do so.

(7)   A document duly executed by an incorporated body which makes it clear on its face that it is intended by the person or persons making it to be a deed has effect, upon delivery, as a deed; and it shall be presumed, unless a contrary intention is proved, to be delivered upon its being so executed.

(8)   In favour of a purchaser a document shall be deemed to have been duly executed by such a body if it purports to be signed—

   (a) by a majority of the trustees of the relevant charity, or

   (b) by such of the trustees of the relevant charity as are authorised by the trustees of that charity to execute it in the name and on behalf of the body,

and, where the document makes it clear on its face that it is intended by the person or persons making it to be a deed, it shall be deemed to have been delivered upon its being executed.

For this purpose "purchaser" means a purchaser in good faith for valuable consideration and includes a lessee, mortgagee or other person who for valuable consideration acquires an interest in property.

NOTES
Commencement: 1 August 1993.

61 Power of Commissioners to dissolve incorporated body

(1) Where the Commissioners are satisfied—

(a) that an incorporated body has no assets or does not operate, or

(b) that the relevant charity in the case of an incorporated body has ceased to exist, or

(c) that the institution previously constituting, or treated by them as constituting, any such charity has ceased to be, or (as the case may be) was not at the time of the body's incorporation, a charity, or

(d) that the purposes of the relevant charity in the case of an incorporated body have been achieved so far as is possible or are in practice incapable of being achieved,

they may of their own motion make an order dissolving the body as from such date as is specified in the order.

(2) Where the Commissioners are satisfied, on the application of the trustees of the relevant charity in the case of an incorporated body, that it would be in the interests of the charity for that body to be dissolved, the Commissioners may make an order dissolving the body as from such date as is specified in the order.

(3) Subject to subsection (4) below, an order made under this section with respect to an incorporated body shall have the effect of vesting in the trustees of the relevant charity, in trust for that charity, all property for the time being vested—

(a) in the body, or

(b) in any other person (apart from the official custodian),

in trust for that charity.

(4) If the Commissioners so direct in the order—

(a) all or any specified part of that property shall, instead of vesting in the trustees of the relevant charity, vest—

(i) in a specified person as trustee for, or nominee of, that charity, or

(ii) in such persons (other than the trustees of the relevant charity) as may be specified;

(b) any specified investments, or any specified class or description of investments, held by any person in trust for the relevant charity shall be transferred—

(i) to the trustees of that charity, or

(ii) to any such person or persons as is or are mentioned in paragraph (a)(i) or (ii) above;

and for this purpose "specified" means specified by the Commissioners in the order.

(5) Where an order to which this subsection applies is made with respect to an incorporated body—

(a) any rights or liabilities of the body shall become rights or liabilities of the trustees of the relevant charity; and

(b) any legal proceedings that might have been continued or commenced by or against the body may be continued or commenced by or against those trustees.

(6) Subsection (5) above applies to any order under this section by virtue of which—

(a) any property vested as mentioned in subsection (3) above is vested—
:   (i) in the trustees of the relevant charity, or
:   (ii) in any person as trustee for, or nominee of, that charity; or
(b) any investments held by any person in trust for the relevant charity are required to be transferred—
:   (i) to the trustees of that charity, or
:   (ii) to any person as trustee for, or nominee of, that charity.

(7) Any order made by the Commissioners under this section may be varied or revoked by a further order so made.

[695]

NOTES
Commencement: 1 August 1993.

62 Interpretation of Part VII

In this Part of this Act—
:   "incorporated body" means a body incorporated under section 50 above;
:   "the relevant charity", in relation to an incorporated body, means the charity the trustees of which have been incorporated as that body;
:   "the trustees", in relation to a charity, means the charity trustees.

[696]

NOTES
Commencement: 1 August 1993.

PART VIII
CHARITABLE COMPANIES

63 Winding up

(1) Where a charity may be wound up by the High Court under the Insolvency Act 1986, a petition for it to be wound up under that Act by any court in England or Wales having jurisdiction may be presented by the Attorney General, as well as by any person authorised by that Act.

(2) Where a charity may be so wound up by the High Court, such a petition may also be presented by the Commissioners if, at any time after they have instituted an inquiry under section 8 above with respect to the charity, they are satisfied as mentioned in section 18(1)(a) or (b) above.

(3) Where a charitable company is dissolved, the Commissioners may make an application under section 651 of the Companies Act 1985 (power of court to declare dissolution of company void) for an order to be made under that section with respect to the company; and for this purpose subsection (1) of that section shall have effect in relation to a charitable company as if the reference to the liquidator of the company included a reference to the Commissioners.

(4) Where a charitable company's name has been struck off the register of companies under section 652 of the Companies Act 1985 (power of registrar to strike defunct company off register), the Commissioners may make an application under section 653(2) of that Act (objection to striking off by person aggrieved) for an order restoring the company's name to that register; and for this purpose section 653(2) shall have effect in relation to a charitable company as if the reference to any such person aggrieved as is there mentioned included a reference to the Commissioners.

(5)   The powers exercisable by the Commissioners by virtue of this section shall be exercisable by them of their own motion, but shall be exercisable only with the agreement of the Attorney General on each occasion.

(6)   In this section "charitable company" means a company which is a charity.

[697]

NOTES
Commencement: 1 August 1993.

64   Alteration of objects clause

(1)   Where a charity is a company or other body corporate having power to alter the instruments establishing or regulating it as a body corporate, no exercise of that power which has the effect of the body ceasing to be a charity shall be valid so as to affect the application of—

    (a)   any property acquired under any disposition or agreement previously made otherwise than for full consideration in money or money's worth, or any property representing property so acquired,

    (b)   any property representing income which has accrued before the alteration is made, or

    (c)   the income from any such property as aforesaid.

(2)   Where a charity is a company, any alteration by it—

    (a)   of the objects clause in its memorandum of association, or

    (b)   of any other provision in its memorandum of association, or any provision in its articles of association, which is a provision directing or restricting the manner in which property of the company may be used or applied,

is ineffective without the prior written consent of the Commissioners.

(3)   Where a company has made any such alteration in accordance with subsection (2) above and—

    (a)   in connection with the alteration is required by virtue of—

        (i)   section 6(1) of the Companies Act 1985 (delivery of documents following alteration of objects), or

        (ii)   that provision as applied by section 17(3) of that Act (alteration of condition in memorandum which could have been contained in articles),

    to deliver to the registrar of companies a printed copy of its memorandum, as altered, or

    (b)   is required by virtue of section 380(1) of that Act (registration etc of resolutions and agreements) to forward to the registrar a printed or other copy of the special resolution effecting the alteration,

the copy so delivered or forwarded by the company shall be accompanied by a copy of the Commissioner's consent.

(4)   Section 6(3) of that Act (offences) shall apply to any default by a company in complying with subsection (3) above as it applies to any such default as is mentioned in that provision.

[698]

NOTES
Commencement: 1 August 1993.

65   Invalidity of certain transactions

(1)   Sections 35 and 35A of the Companies Act 1985 (capacity of company not limited by its memorandum; power of directors to bind company) do not apply to the acts of a company which is a charity except in favour of a person who—

    (a)   gives full consideration in money or money's worth in relation to the act in question, and

    (b)   does not know that the act is not permitted by the company's memorandum or, as the case may be, is beyond the powers of the directors,

or who does not know at the time the act is done that the company is a charity.

(2)   However, where such a company purports to transfer or grant an interest in property, the fact that the act was not permitted by the company's memorandum or, as the case may be, that the directors in connection with the act exceeded any limitation on their powers under the company's constitution, does not affect the title of a person who subsequently acquires the property or any interest in it for full consideration without actual notice of any such circumstances affecting the validity of the company's act.

(3)   In any proceedings arising out of subsection (1) above the burden of proving—

    (a)   that a person knew that an act was not permitted by the company's memorandum or was beyond the powers of the directors, or

    (b)   that a person knew that the company was a charity,

lies on the person making that allegation.

(4)   Where a company is a charity, the ratification of an act under section 35(3) of the Companies Act 1985, or the ratification of a transaction to which section 322A of that Act applies (invalidity of certain transactions to which directors or their associates are parties), is ineffective without the prior written consent of the Commissioners.

                                                              [699]

NOTES

Commencement: 1 August 1993.

66   Requirement of consent of Commissioners to certain acts

(1)   Where a company is a charity—

    (a)   any approval given by the company for the purposes of any of the provisions of the Companies Act 1985 specified in subsection (2) below, and

    (b)   any affirmation by it for the purposes of section 322(2)(c) of that Act (affirmation of voidable arrangements under which assets are acquired by or from a director or person connected with him),

is ineffective without the prior written consent of the Commissioners.

(2)   The provisions of the Companies Act 1985 referred to in subsection (1)(a) above are—

    (a)   section 312 (payment to director in respect of loss of office or retirement);

    (b)   section 313(1) (payment to director in respect of loss of office or retirement made in connection with transfer of undertaking or property of company);

    (c)   section 319(3) (incorporation in director's service contract of term whereby his employment will or may continue for a period of more than five years);

    (d) section 320(1) (arrangement whereby assets are acquired by or from director or person connected with him);

    (e) section 337(3)(a) (provision of funds to meet certain expenses incurred by director).

            [700]

NOTES
Commencement: 1 August 1993.

67   Name to appear on correspondence etc

Section 30(7) of the Companies Act 1985 (exemption from requirements relating to publication of name etc) shall not, in its application to any company which is a charity, have the effect of exempting the company from the requirements of section 349(1) of that Act (company's name to appear in its correspondence etc).

            [701]

NOTES
Commencement: 1 August 1993.

68   Status to appear on correspondence etc

(1)   Where a company is a charity and its name does not include the word "charity" or the word "charitable" [then, subject to subsection (1A)], the fact that the company is a charity shall be stated . . . in legible characters—

    (a) in all business letters of the company,

    (b) in all its notices and other official publications,

    (c) in all bills of exchange, promissory notes, endorsements, cheques and orders for money or goods purporting to be signed on behalf of the company,

    (d) in all conveyances purporting to be executed by the company, and

    (e) in all bills rendered by it and in all its invoices, receipts, and letters of credit.

[(1A)   Where a company's name includes the word "elusen" or the word "elusennol" (the Welsh equivalents of the words "charity" and "charitable"), subsection (1) above shall not apply in relation to any document which is wholly in Welsh.

(1B) The statement required by subsection (1) above shall be in English, except that, in the case of a document which is otherwise wholly in Welsh, the statement may be in Welsh if it consists of or includes the word "elusen" or the word "elusennol".]

(2)   In subsection (1)(d) above "conveyance" means any instrument creating, transferring, varying or extinguishing an interest in land.

(3)   Subsections (2) to (4) of section 349 of the Companies Act 1985 (offences in connection with failure to include required particulars in business letters etc.) shall apply in relation to a contravention of subsection (1) above, taking the reference in subsection (3)(b) of that section to a bill of parcels as a reference to any such bill as is mentioned in subsection (1)(e) above.

            [702]

NOTES
Commencement: 1 August 1993 (sub-ss (1), (2), (3)); 21 December 1993 (sub-ss (1A), (1B)).

Sub-s (1): words in square brackets inserted and words omitted repealed by the Welsh Language Act 1993, ss 33(1), (2), 35(1), Sch 2.

Sub-ss (1A), (1B): inserted by the Welsh Language Act 1993, s 33(1), (3).

69   Investigation of accounts

(1)   In the case of a charity which is a company the Commissioners may by order require that the condition and accounts of the charity for such period as they think fit shall be investigated and audited by an auditor appointed by them, being a person eligible for appointment as a company auditor under section 25 of the Companies Act 1989.

(2)   An auditor acting under subsection (1) above—

     (a)   shall have a right of access to all books, accounts and documents relating to the charity which are in the possession or control of the charity trustees or to which the charity trustees have access;

     (b)   shall be entitled to require from any charity trustee, past or present, and from any past or present officer or employee of the charity such information and explanation as he thinks necessary for the performance of his duties;

     (c)   shall at the conclusion or during the progress of the audit make such reports to the Commissioners about the audit or about the accounts or affairs of the charity as he thinks the case requires, and shall send a copy of any such report to the charity trustees.

(3)   The expenses of any audit under subsection (1) above, including the remuneration of the auditor, shall be paid by the Commissioners.

(4)   If any person fails to afford an auditor any facility to which he is entitled under subsection (2) above the Commissioners may by order give to that person or to the charity trustees for the time being such directions as the Commissioners think appropriate for securing that the default is made good.

                                                                     [703]

NOTES

Commencement: to be appointed.

PART IX
MISCELLANEOUS

Powers of investment

70   Relaxation of restrictions on wider-range investments

(1)   The Secretary of State may by order made with the consent of the Treasury—

     (a)   direct that, in the case of a trust fund consisting of property held by or in trust for a charity, any division of the fund in pursuance of section 2(1) of the Trustee Investments Act 1961 (trust funds to be divided so that wider-range and narrower-range investments are equal in value) shall be made so that the value of the wider-range part at the time of the division bears to the then value of the narrower-range part such proportion as is specified in the order;

     (b)   provide that, in its application in relation to such a trust fund, that Act shall have effect subject to such modifications so specified as the Secretary of State considers appropriate in consequence of, or in connection with, any such direction.

(2)   Where, before the coming into force of an order under this section, a trust fund consisting of property held by or in trust for a charity has already been divided in

pursuance of section 2(1) of that Act, the fund may, notwithstanding anything in that provision, be again divided (once only) in pursuance of that provision during the continuance in force of the order.

(3)   No order shall be made under this section unless a draft of the order has been laid before and approved by a resolution of each House of Parliament.

(4)   Expressions used in this section which are also used in the Trustee Investments Act 1961 have the same meaning as in that Act.

(5)   In the application of this section to Scotland, "charity" means a recognised body within the meaning of section 1(7) of the Law Reform (Miscellaneous Provisions) (Scotland) Act 1990.

[704]

NOTES
Commencement: 1 August 1993.

71   Extension of powers of investment

(1)   The Secretary of State may by regulations made with the consent of the Treasury make, with respect to property held by or in trust for a charity, provision authorising a trustee to invest such property in any manner specified in the regulations, being a manner of investment not for the time being included in any Part of Schedule 1 to the Trustee Investments Act 1961.

(2)   Regulations under this section may make such provision—
   (a)   regulating the investment of property in any manner authorised by virtue of subsection (1) above, and
   (b)   with respect to the variation and retention of investments so made,

as the Secretary of State considers appropriate.

(3)   Such regulations may, in particular, make provision—
   (a)   imposing restrictions with respect to the proportion of the property held by or in trust for a charity which may be invested in any manner authorised by virtue of subsection (1) above, being either restrictions applying to investment in any such manner generally or restrictions applying to investment in any particular such manner;
   (b)   imposing the like requirements with respect to the obtaining and consideration of advice as are imposed by any of the provisions of section 6 of the Trustee Investments Act 1961 (duty of trustees in choosing investments).

(4)   Any power of investment conferred by any regulations under this section—
   (a)   shall be in addition to, and not in derogation from, any power conferred otherwise than by such regulations; and
   (b)   shall not be limited by the trusts of a charity (in so far as they are not contained in any Act or instrument made under an enactment) unless it is excluded by those trusts in express terms;

but any such power shall only be exercisable by a trustee in so far as a contrary intention is not expressed in any Act or in any instrument made under an enactment and relating to the powers of the trustee.

(5)   No regulations shall be made under this section unless a draft of the regulations has been laid before and approved by a resolution of each House of Parliament.

(6) In this section "property"—

(a) in England and Wales, means real or personal property of any description, including money and things in action, but does not include an interest in expectancy; and

(b) in Scotland, means property of any description (whether heritable or moveable, corporeal or incorporeal) which is presently enjoyable, but does not include a future interest, whether vested or contingent;

and any reference to property held by or in trust for a charity is a reference to property so held, whether it is for the time being in a state of investment or not.

(7) In the application of this section to Scotland, "charity" means a recognised body within the meaning of section 1(7) of the Law Reform (Miscellaneous Provisions) (Scotland) Act 1990.

[705]

NOTES

Commencement: 1 August 1993.

Disqualification for acting as charity trustee

72 Persons disqualified for being trustees of a charity

(1) Subject to the following provisions of this section, a person shall be disqualified for being a charity trustee or trustee for a charity if—

(a) he has been convicted of any offence involving dishonesty or deception;

(b) he has been adjudged bankrupt or sequestration of his estate has been awarded and (in either case) he has not been discharged;

(c) he has made a composition or arrangement with, or granted a trust deed for, his creditors and has not been discharged in respect of it;

(d) he has been removed from the office of charity trustee or trustee for a charity by an order made—

(i) by the Commissioners under section 18(2)(i) above, or

(ii) by the Commissioners under section 20(1A)(i) of the Charities Act 1960 (power to act for protection of charities) or under section 20(1)(i) of that Act (as in force before the commencement of section 8 of the Charities Act 1992), or

(iii) by the High Court,

on the grounds of any misconduct or mismanagement in the administration of the charity for which he was responsible or to which he was privy, or which he by his conduct contributed to or facilitated;

(e) he has been removed, under section 7 of the Law Reform (Miscellaneous Provisions) (Scotland) Act 1990 (powers of Court of Session to deal with management of charities), from being concerned in the management or control of any body;

(f) he is subject to a disqualification order under the Company Directors Disqualification Act 1986 or to an order made under section 429(2)(b) of the Insolvency Act 1986 (failure to pay under county court administration order).

(2) In subsection (1) above—

(a) paragraph (a) applies whether the conviction occurred before or after the commencement of that subsection, but does not apply in relation to any conviction which is a spent conviction for the purposes of the Rehabilitation of Offenders Act 1974;

(b) paragraph (b) applies whether the adjudication of bankruptcy or the sequestration occurred before or after the commencement of that subsection;

(c) paragraph (c) applies whether the composition or arrangement was made, or the trust deed was granted, before or after the commencement of that subsection; and

(d) paragraphs (d) to (f) apply in relation to orders made and removals effected before or after the commencement of that subsection.

(3)   Where (apart from this subsection) a person is disqualified under subsection (1)(b) above for being a charity trustee or trustee for any charity which is a company, he shall not be so disqualified if leave has been granted under section 11 of the Company Directors Disqualification Act 1986 (undischarged bankrupts) for him to act as director of the charity; and similarly a person shall not be disqualified under subsection (1)(f) above for being a charity trustee or trustee for such a charity if—

(a) in the case of a person subject to a disqualification order, leave under the order has been granted for him to act as director of the charity, or

(b) in the case of a person subject to an order under section 429(2)(b) of the Insolvency Act 1986, leave has been granted by the court which made the order for him to so act.

(4)   The Commissioners may, on the application of any person disqualified under subsection (1) above, waive his disqualification either generally or in relation to a particular charity or a particular class of charities; but no such waiver may be granted in relation to any charity which is a company if—

(a) the person concerned is for the time being prohibited, by virtue of—

(i) a disqualification order under the Company Directors Disqualification Act 1986, or

(ii) section 11(1) or 12(2) of that Act (undischarged bankrupts; failure to pay under county court administration order),

from acting as director of the charity; and

(b) leave has not been granted for him to act as director of any other company.

(5)   Any waiver under subsection (4) above shall be notified in writing to the person concerned.

(6)   For the purposes of this section the Commissioners shall keep, in such manner as they think fit, a register of all persons who have been removed from office as mentioned in subsection (1)(d) above either—

(a) by an order of the Commissioners made before or after the commencement of subsection (1) above, or

(b) by an order of the High Court made after the commencement of section 45(1) of the Charities Act 1992;

and, where any person is so removed from office by an order of the High Court, the court shall notify the Commissioners of his removal.

(7)   The entries in the register kept under subsection (6) above shall be available for public inspection in legible form at all reasonable times.

                                                                                                    [706]

NOTES

Commencement: 1 August 1993.

73   Persons acting as charity trustee while disqualified

(1)   Subject to subsection (2) below, any person who acts as a charity trustee or trustee for a charity while he is disqualified for being such a trustee by virtue of section 72 above shall be guilty of an offence and liable—
   (a)   on summary conviction, to imprisonment for a term not exceeding six months or to a fine not exceeding the statutory maximum, or both;
   (b)   on conviction on indictment, to imprisonment for a term not exceeding two years or to a fine, or both.

(2)   Subsection (1) above shall not apply where—
   (a)   the charity concerned is a company; and
   (b)   the disqualified person is disqualified by virtue only of paragraph (b) or (f) of section 72(1) above.

(3)   Any acts done as charity trustee or trustee for a charity by a person disqualified for being such a trustee by virtue of section 72 above shall not be invalid by reason only of that disqualification.

(4)   Where the Commissioners are satisfied—
   (a)   that any person has acted as charity trustee or trustee for a charity (other than an exempt charity) while disqualified for being such a trustee by virtue of section 72 above, and
   (b)   that, while so acting, he has received from the charity any sums by way of remuneration or expenses, or any benefit in kind, in connection with his acting as charity trustee or trustee for the charity,

they may by order direct him to repay to the charity the whole or part of any such sums, or (as the case may be) to pay to the charity the whole or part of the monetary value (as determined by them) of any such benefit.

(5)   Subsection (4) above does not apply to any sums received by way of remuneration or expenses in respect of any time when the person concerned was not disqualified for being a charity trustee or trustee for the charity.

[707]

NOTES
Commencement: 1 August 1993.

Small charities

74   Power to transfer all property, modify objects etc

(1)   This section applies to a charity if—
   (a)   its gross income in its last financial year did not exceed £5,000, and
   (b)   it does not hold any land on trusts which stipulate that the land is to be used for the purposes, or any particular purposes, of the charity,

and it is neither an exempt charity nor a charitable company.

(2)   Subject to the following provisions of this section, the charity trustees of a charity to which this section applies may resolve for the purposes of this section—
   (a)   that all the property of the charity should be transferred to such other charity as is specified in the resolution, being either a registered charity or a charity which is not required to be registered;
   (b)   that all the property of the charity should be divided, in such manner as is specified in the resolution, between such two or more other charities as are

so specified, being in each case either a registered charity or a charity which is not required to be registered;

(c) that the trusts of the charity should be modified by replacing all or any of the purposes of the charity with such other purposes, being in law charitable, as are specified in the resolution;

(d) that any provision of the trusts of the charity—
    (i) relating to any of the powers exercisable by the charity trustees in the administration of the charity, or
    (ii) regulating the procedure to be followed in any respect in connection with its administration,

should be modified in such manner as is specified in the resolution.

(3) Any resolution passed under subsection (2) above must be passed by a majority of not less than two-thirds of such charity trustees as vote on the resolution.

(4) The charity trustees of a charity to which this section applies ("the transferor charity") shall not have power to pass a resolution under subsection (2)(a) or (b) above unless they are satisfied—

(a) that the existing purposes of the transferor charity have ceased to be conducive to a suitable and effective application of the charity's resources; and

(b) that the purposes of the charity or charities specified in the resolution are as similar in character to the purposes of the transferor charity as is reasonably practicable;

and before passing the resolution they must have received from the charity trustees of the charity, or (as the case may be) of each of the charities, specified in the resolution written confirmation that those trustees are willing to accept a transfer of property under this section.

(5) The charity trustees of any such charity shall not have power to pass a resolution under subsection (2)(c) above unless they are satisfied—

(a) that the existing purposes of the charity (or, as the case may be, such of them as it is proposed to replace) have ceased to be conducive to a suitable and effective application of the charity's resources; and

(b) that the purposes specified in the resolution are as similar in character to those existing purposes as is practical in the circumstances.

(6) Where charity trustees have passed a resolution under subsection (2) above, they shall—

(a) give public notice of the resolution in such manner as they think reasonable in the circumstances; and

(b) send a copy of the resolution to the Commissioners, together with a statement of their reasons for passing it.

(7) The Commissioners may, when considering the resolution, require the charity trustees to provide additional information or explanation—

(a) as to the circumstances in and by reference to which they have determined to act under this section, or

(b) relating to their compliance with this section in connection with the resolution;

and the Commissioners shall take into account any representations made to them by persons appearing to them to be interested in the charity where those representations are made within the period of six weeks beginning with the date when the Commissioners receive a copy of the resolution by virtue of subsection (6)(b) above.

(8)   Where the Commissioners have so received a copy of a resolution from any charity trustees and it appears to them that the trustees have complied with this section in connection with the resolution, the Commissioners shall, within the period of three months beginning with the date when they receive the copy of the resolution, notify the trustees in writing either—

    (a)   that the Commissioners concur with the resolution; or

    (b)   that they do not concur with it.

(9)   Where the Commissioners so notify their concurrence with the resolution, then—

    (a)   if the resolution was passed under subsection (2)(a) or (b) above, the charity trustees shall arrange for all the property of the transferor charity to be transferred in accordance with the resolution and on terms that any property so transferred—

        (i)   shall be held and applied by the charity to which it is transferred ("the transferee charity") for the purposes of that charity, but

        (ii)   shall, as property of the transferee charity, nevertheless be subject to any restrictions on expenditure to which it is subject as property of the transferor charity,

    and those trustees shall arrange for it to be so transferred by such date as may be specified in the notification; and

    (b)   if the resolution was passed under subsection (2)(c) or (d) above, the trusts of the charity shall be deemed, as from such date as may be specified in the notification, to have been modified in accordance with the terms of the resolution.

(10)   For the purpose of enabling any property to be transferred to a charity under this section, the Commissioners shall have power, at the request of the charity trustees of that charity, to make orders vesting any property of the transferor charity—

    (a)   in the charity trustees of the first-mentioned charity or in any trustee for that charity, or

    (b)   in any other person nominated by those charity trustees to hold the property in trust for that charity.

(11)   The Secretary of State may by order amend subsection (1) above by substituting a different sum for the sum for the time being specified there.

(12)   In this section—

    (a)   "charitable company" means a charity which is a company or other body corporate; and

    (b)   references to the transfer of property to a charity are references to its transfer—

        (i)   to the charity trustees, or

        (ii)   to any trustee for the charity, or

        (iii)   to a person nominated by the charity trustees to hold it in trust for the charity,

    as the charity trustees may determine.

[708]

NOTES

Commencement: 1 August 1993.

75   Power to spend capital

(1)   This section applies to a charity if—

    (a)   it has a permanent endowment which does not consist of or comprise any land, and

(b) its gross income in its last financial year did not exceed £1,000,

and it is neither an exempt charity nor a charitable company.

(2) Where the charity trustees of a charity to which this section applies are of the opinion that the property of the charity is too small, in relation to its purposes, for any useful purpose to be achieved by the expenditure of income alone, they may resolve for the purposes of this section that the charity ought to be freed from the restrictions with respect to expenditure of capital to which its permanent endowment is subject.

(3) Any resolution passed under subsection (2) above must be passed by a majority of not less than two-thirds of such charity trustees as vote on the resolution.

(4) Before passing such a resolution the charity trustees must consider whether any reasonable possibility exists of effecting a transfer or division of all the charity's property under section 74 above (disregarding any such transfer or division as would, in their opinion, impose on the charity an unacceptable burden of costs).

(5) Where charity trustees have passed a resolution under subsection (2) above, they shall—

(a) give public notice of the resolution in such manner as they think reasonable in the circumstances; and

(b) send a copy of the resolution to the Commissioners, together with a statement of their reasons for passing it.

(6) The Commissioners may, when considering the resolution, require the charity trustees to provide additional information or explanation—

(a) as to the circumstances in and by reference to which they have determined to act under this section, or

(b) relating to their compliance with this section in connection with the resolution;

and the Commissioners shall take into account any representations made to them by persons appearing to them to be interested in the charity where those representations are made within the period of six weeks beginning with the date when the Commissioners receive a copy of the resolution by virtue of subsection (5)(b) above.

(7) Where the Commissioners have so received a copy of a resolution from any charity trustees and it appears to them that the trustees have complied with this section in connection with the resolution, the Commissioners shall, within the period of three months beginning with the date when they receive the copy of the resolution, notify the trustees in writing either—

(a) that the Commissioners concur with the resolution; or

(b) that they do not concur with it.

(8) Where the Commissioners so notify their concurrence with the resolution, the charity trustees shall have, as from such date as may be specified in the notification, power by virtue of this section to expend any property of the charity without regard to any such restrictions as are mentioned in subsection (2) above.

(9) The Secretary of State may by order amend subsection (1) above by substituting a different sum for the sum for the time being specified there.

(10) In this section "charitable company" means a charity which is a company or other body corporate.

NOTES

Commencement: 1 August 1993.

Local charities

76 Local authority's index of local charities

(1) The council of a county [or county borough] or of a district or London borough and the Common Council of the City of London may maintain an index of local charities or of any class of local charities in the council's area, and may publish information contained in the index, or summaries or extracts taken from it.

(2) A council proposing to establish or maintaining under this section an index of local charities or of any class of local charities shall, on request, be supplied by the Commissioners free of charge with copies of such entries in the register of charities as are relevant to the index or with particulars of any changes in the entries of which copies have been supplied before; and the Commissioners may arrange that they will without further request supply a council with particulars of any such changes.

(3) An index maintained under this section shall be open to public inspection at all reasonable times.

(4) A council may employ any voluntary organisation as their agent for the purposes of this section, on such terms and within such limits (if any) or in such cases as they may agree; and for this purpose "voluntary organisation" means any body of which the activities are carried on otherwise than for profit, not being a public or local authority.

(5) A joint board discharging any of a council's functions shall have the same powers under this section as the council as respects local charities in the council's area which are established for purposes similar or complementary to any services provided by the board.

[710]

NOTES

Commencement: 1 August 1993.

Sub-s (1): words in square brackets inserted by the Local Government (Wales) Act 1994, s 66(6), Sch 16, para 101(1), as from a day to be appointed.

77 Reviews of local charities by local authority

(1) The council of a county [or county borough] or of a district or London borough and the Common Council of the City of London may, subject to the following provisions of this section, initiate, and carry out in co-operation with the charity trustees, a review of the working of any group of local charities with the same or similar purposes in the council's area, and may make to the Commissioners such report on the review and such recommendations arising from it as the council after consultation with the trustees think fit.

(2) A council having power to initiate reviews under this section may co-operate with other persons in any review by them of the working of local charities in the council's area (with or without other charities), or may join with other persons in initiating and carrying out such a review.

(3) No review initiated by a council under this section shall extend to any charity without the consent of the charity trustees, nor to any ecclesiastical charity.

(4) No review initiated under this section by the council of a district shall extend to

the working in any county of a local charity established for purposes similar or complementary to any services provided by county councils unless the review so extends with the consent of the council of that county.

[(4A)   Subsection (4) above does not apply in relation to Wales.]

(5)   Subsections (4) and (5) of section 76 above shall apply for the purposes of this section as they apply for the purposes of that section.

[711]

NOTES

Commencement: 1 August 1993.

Sub-s (1): words in square brackets inserted by the Local Government (Wales) Act 1994, s 66(6), Sch 16, para 101(2), as from a day to be appointed.

Sub-s (4A): inserted by the Local Government (Wales) Act 1994, s 66(6), Sch 16, para 101(2), as from a day to be appointed.

78   Co-operation between charities, and between charities and local authorities

(1)   Any local council and any joint board discharging any functions of such a council—

(a)   may make, with any charity established for purposes similar or complementary to services provided by the council or board, arrangements for co-ordinating the activities of the council or board and those of the charity in the interests of persons who may benefit from those services or from the charity; and

(b)   shall be at liberty to disclose to any such charity in the interests of those persons any information obtained in connection with the services provided by the council or board, whether or not arrangements have been made with the charity under this subsection.

In this subsection "local council" means[, in relation to England,] the council of a county, or of a district, London borough, *parish or (in Wales) community,* and includes also the Common Council of the City of London and the Council of the Isles of Scilly [and, in relation to Wales, the council of a county, county borough or community].

(2)   Charity trustees shall, notwithstanding anything in the trusts of the charity, have power by virtue of this subsection to do all or any of the following things, where it appears to them likely to promote or make more effective the work of the charity, and may defray the expense of so doing out of any income or money applicable as income of the charity, that is to say—

(a)   they may co-operate in any review undertaken under section 77 above or otherwise of the working of charities or any class of charities;

(b)   they may make arrangements with an authority acting under subsection (1) above or with another charity for co-ordinating their activities and those of the authority or of the other charity;

(c)   they may publish information of other charities with a view to bringing them to the notice of those for whose benefit they are intended.

[712]

NOTES

Commencement: 1 August 1993.

Sub-s (1): words in square brackets inserted, and words in italics substituted by the words "or parish", by the Local Government (Wales) Act 1994, s 66(6), Sch 16, para 101(3), as from a day to be appointed.

79   Parochial charities

(1)   Where trustees hold any property for the purposes of a public recreation ground, or of allotments (whether under inclosure Acts or otherwise), for the benefit of inhabitants of a parish having a parish council, or for other charitable purposes connected with such a parish, except for an ecclesiastical charity, they may with the approval of the Commissioners and with the consent of the parish council transfer the property to the parish council or to persons appointed by the parish council; and the council or their appointees shall hold the property on the same trusts and subject to the same conditions as the trustees did.

This subsection shall apply to property held for any public purposes as it applies to property held for charitable purposes.

(2)   Where the charity trustees of a parochial charity in a parish, not being an ecclesiastical charity nor a charity founded within the preceding forty years, do not include persons elected by the local government electors, ratepayers or inhabitants of the parish or appointed by the parish council or parish meeting, the parish council or parish meeting may appoint additional charity trustees, to such number as the Commissioners may allow; and if there is a sole charity trustee not elected or appointed as aforesaid of any such charity, the number of the charity trustees may, with the approval of the Commissioners, be increased to three of whom one may be nominated by the person holding the office of the sole trustee and one by the parish council or parish meeting.

(3)   Where, under the trusts of a charity other than an ecclesiastical charity, the inhabitants of a rural parish (whether in vestry or not) or a select vestry were formerly (in 1894) entitled to appoint charity trustees for, or trustees or beneficiaries of, the charity, then—

    (a)   in a parish having a parish council, the appointment shall be made by the parish council or, in the case of beneficiaries, by persons appointed by the parish council; and

    (b)   in a parish not having a parish council, the appointment shall be made by the parish meeting.

(4)   Where overseers as such or, except in the case of an ecclesiastical charity, churchwardens as such were formerly (in 1894) charity trustees of or trustees for a parochial charity in a rural parish, either alone or jointly with other persons, then instead of the former overseer or church warden trustees there shall be trustees (to a number not greater than that of the former overseer or churchwarden trustees) appointed by the parish council or, if there is no parish council, by the parish meeting.

(5)   Where, outside Greater London (other than the outer London boroughs), overseers of a parish as such were formerly (in 1927) charity trustees of or trustees for any charity, either alone or jointly with other persons, then instead of the former overseer trustees there shall be trustees (to a number not greater than that of the former overseer trustees) appointed by the parish council or, if there is no parish council, by the parish meeting.

(6)   In the case of an urban parish existing immediately before the passing of the Local Government Act 1972 which after 1st April 1974 is not comprised in a parish, the power of appointment under subsection (5) above shall be exercisable by the district council.

(7)   In the application of the foregoing provisions of this section to Wales—

    (a) for references in subsections (1) and (2) to a parish or a parish council there shall be substituted respectively references to a community or a community council;

    (b) for references in subsections (3)(a) and (b) to a parish, a parish council or a parish meeting there shall be substituted respectively references to a community, a community council or the *district council*;

    (c) for references in subsections (4) and (5) to a parish council or a parish meeting there shall be substituted respectively references to a community council or the *district council*.

(8)   Any appointment of a charity trustee or trustee for a charity which is made by virtue of this section shall be for a term of four years, and a retiring trustee shall be eligible for re-appointment but—

    (a) on an appointment under subsection (2) above, where no previous appointments have been made by virtue of that subsection or of the corresponding provision of the Local Government Act 1894 or the Charities Act 1960, and more than one trustee is appointed, half of those appointed (or as nearly as may be) shall be appointed for a term of two years; and

    (b) an appointment made to fill a casual vacancy shall be for the remainder of the term of the previous appointment.

(9)   This section shall not affect the trusteeship, control or management of any voluntary school within the meaning of the Education Act 1944 or of any grant-maintained school.

(10)   The provisions of this section shall not extend to the Isles of Scilly, and shall have effect subject to any order (including any future order) made under any enactment relating to local government with respect to local government areas or the powers of local authorities.

(11)   In this section the expression "formerly (in 1894)" relates to the period immediately before the passing of the Local Government Act 1894, and the expression "formerly (in 1927)" to the period immediately before 1st April 1927; and the word "former" shall be construed accordingly.

[713]

NOTES

    Commencement: 1 August 1993.

    Sub-s (7): in paras (b), (c) words in italics substituted by the words "council of the county or (as the case may be) county borough" by the Local Government (Wales) Act 1994, s 66(6), Sch 16, para 101(4), as from a day to be appointed.

Administrative provisions about charities

81   Manner of giving notice of charity meetings, etc

(1)   All notices which are required or authorised by the trusts of a charity to be given to a charity trustee, member or subscriber may be sent by post, and, if sent by post, may be addressed to any address given as his in the list of charity trustees, members or subscribers for the time being in use at the office or principal office of the charity.

(2)   Where any such notice required to be given as aforesaid is given by post, it shall be deemed to have been given by the time at which the letter containing it would be delivered in the ordinary course of post.

(3)   No notice required to be given as aforesaid of any meeting or election need be given to any charity trustee, member or subscriber, if in the list above mentioned he has no address in the United Kingdom.

[714]

NOTES
Commencement: 1 August 1993.

82   Manner of executing instruments

(1)   Charity trustees may, subject to the trusts of the charity, confer on any of their body (not being less than two in number) a general authority, or an authority limited in such manner as the trustees think fit, to execute in the names and on behalf of the trustees assurances or other deeds or instruments for giving effect to transactions to which the trustees are a party; and any deed or instrument executed in pursuance of an authority so given shall be of the same effect as if executed by the whole body.

(2)   An authority under subsection (1) above—
   (a)   shall suffice for any deed or instrument if it is given in writing or by resolution of a meeting of the trustees, notwithstanding the want of any formality that would be required in giving an authority apart from that subsection;
   (b)   may be given so as to make the powers conferred exercisable by any of the trustees, or may be restricted to named persons or in any other way;
   (c)   subject to any such restriction, and until it is revoked, shall, notwithstanding any change in the charity trustees, have effect as a continuing authority given by the charity trustees from time to time of the charity and exercisable by such trustees.

(3)   In any authority under this section to execute a deed or instrument in the names and on behalf of charity trustees there shall, unless the contrary intention appears, be implied authority also to execute it for them in the name and on behalf of the official custodian or of any other person, in any case in which the charity trustees could do so.

(4)   Where a deed or instrument purports to be executed in pursuance of this section, then in favour of a person who (then or afterwards) in good faith acquires for money or money's worth an interest in or charge on property or the benefit of any covenant or agreement expressed to be entered into by the charity trustees, it shall be conclusively presumed to have been duly executed by virtue of this section.

(5)   The powers conferred by this section shall be in addition to and not in derogation of any other powers.

[715]

NOTES
Commencement: 1 August 1993.

83   Transfer and evidence of title to property vested in trustees

(1)   Where, under the trusts of a charity, trustees of property held for the purposes of the charity may be appointed or discharged by resolution of a meeting of the charity trustees, members or other persons, a memorandum declaring a trustee to have been so appointed or discharged shall be sufficient evidence of that fact if the memorandum is signed either at the meeting by the person presiding or in some other manner directed by the meeting and is attested by two persons present at the meeting.

(2)   A memorandum evidencing the appointment or discharge of a trustee under subsection (1) above, if executed as a deed, shall have the like operation under section 40 of the Trustee Act 1925 (which relates to vesting declarations as respects trust property in deeds appointing or discharging trustees) as if the appointment or discharge were effected by the deed.

(3)   For the purposes of this section, where a document purports to have been signed and attested as mentioned in subsection (1) above, then on proof (whether by evidence or as a matter of presumption) of the signature the document shall be presumed to have been so signed and attested, unless the contrary is shown.

(4)   This section shall apply to a memorandum made at any time, except that subsection (2) shall apply only to those made after the commencement of the Charities Act 1960.

(5)   This section shall apply in relation to any institution to which the Literary and Scientific Institutions Act 1854 applies as it applies in relation to a charity.

[716]

NOTES

Commencement: 1 August 1993.

PART X
SUPPLEMENTARY

84   Supply by Commissioners of copies of documents open to public inspection

The Commissioners shall, at the request of any person, furnish him with copies of, or extracts from, any document in their possession which is for the time being open to inspection under Parts II to VI of this Act.

[717]

NOTES

Commencement: 1 August 1993.

85   Fees and other amounts payable to Commissioners

(1)   The Secretary of State may by regulations require the payment to the Commissioners of such fees as may be prescribed by the regulations in respect of—
- (a) the discharge by the Commissioners of such functions under the enactments relating to charities as may be so prescribed;
- (b) the inspection of the register of charities or of other material kept by them under those enactments, or the furnishing of copies of or extracts from documents so kept.

(2)   Regulations under this section may—
- (a) confer, or provide for the conferring of, exemptions from liability to pay a prescribed fee;
- (b) provide for the remission or refunding of a prescribed fee (in whole or in part) in circumstances prescribed by the regulations.

(3)   Any regulations under this section which require the payment of a fee in respect of any matter for which no fee was previously payable shall not be made unless a draft of the regulations has been laid before and approved by a resolution of each House of Parliament.

(4)   The Commissioners may impose charges of such amounts as they consider reasonable in respect of the supply of any publications produced by them.

(5)   Any fees and other payments received by the Commissioners by virtue of this section shall be paid into the Consolidated Fund.

[718]

NOTES
Commencement: 1 August 1993.

86   Regulations and orders

(1)   Any regulations or order of the Secretary of State under this Act—
   (a)   shall be made by statutory instrument; and
   (b)   (subject to subsection (2) below) shall be subject to annulment in pursuance of a resolution of either House of Parliament.

(2)   Subsection (1)(b) above does not apply—
   (a)   to an order under section 17(2), 70 or 99(2);
   (b)   to any regulations under section 71; or
   (c)   to any regulations to which section 85(3) applies.

(3)   Any regulations of the Secretary of State or the Commissioners and any order of the Secretary of State under this Act may make—
   (a)   different provision for different cases; and
   (b)   such supplemental, incidental, consequential or transitional provision or savings as the Secretary of State or, as the case may be, the Commissioners consider appropriate.

(4)   Before making any regulations under section 42, 44 or 45 above the Secretary of State shall consult such persons or bodies of persons as he considers appropriate.

[719]

NOTES
Commencement: 1 August 1993.

87   Enforcement of requirements by order of Commissioners

(1)   If a person fails to comply with any requirement imposed by or under this Act then (subject to subsection (2) below) the Commissioners may by order give him such directions as they consider appropriate for securing that the default is made good.

(2)   Subsection (1) above does not apply to any such requirement if—
   (a)   a person who fails to comply with, or is persistently in default in relation to, the requirement is liable to any criminal penalty; or
   (b)   the requirement is imposed—
      (i)   by an order of the Commissioners to which section 88 below applies, or
      (ii)   by a direction of the Commissioners to which that section applies by virtue of section 90(2) below.

[720]

NOTES
Commencement: 1 August 1993.

88   Enforcement of orders of Commissioners

A person guilty of disobedience—

- (a)   to an order of the Commissioners under section 9(1), 44(2), 61, 73 or 80 above; or
- (b)   to an order of the Commissioners under section 16 or 18 above requiring a transfer of property or payment to be called for or made; or
- (c)   to an order of the Commissioners requiring a default under this Act to be made good;

may on the application of the Commissioners to the High Court be dealt with as for disobedience to an order of the High Court.

[721]

_____

NOTES

Commencement: 1 August 1993.

_____

89   Other provisions as to orders of Commissioners

(1)   Any order made by the Commissioners under this Act may include such incidental or supplementary provisions as the Commissioners think expedient for carrying into effect the objects of the order, and where the Commissioners exercise any jurisdiction to make such an order on an application or reference to them, they may insert any such provisions in the order notwithstanding that the application or reference does not propose their insertion.

(2)   Where the Commissioners make an order under this Act, then (without prejudice to the requirements of this Act where the order is subject to appeal) they may themselves give such public notice as they think fit of the making or contents of the order, or may require it to be given by any person on whose application the order is made or by any charity affected by the order.

(3)   The Commissioners at any time within twelve months after they have made an order under any provision of this Act other than section 61 if they are satisfied that the order was made by mistake or on misrepresentation or otherwise than in conformity with this Act, may with or without any application or reference to them discharge the order in whole or in part, and subject or not to any savings or other transitional provisions.

(4)   Except for the purposes of subsection (3) above or of an appeal under this Act, an order made by the Commissioners under this Act shall be deemed to have been duly and formally made and not be called in question on the ground only of irregularity or informality, but (subject to any further order) have effect according to its tenor.

[722]

_____

NOTES

Commencement: 1 August 1993.

_____

90   Directions of the Commissioners

(1)   Any direction given by the Commissioners under any provision contained in this Act—

- (a)   may be varied or revoked by a further direction given under that provision; and
- (b)   shall be given in writing.

(2) Sections 88 and 89(1), (2) and (4) above shall apply to any such directions as they apply to an order of the Commissioners.

(3) In subsection (1) above the reference to the Commissioners includes, in relation to a direction under subsection (3) of section 8 above, a reference to any person conducting an inquiry under that section.

(4) Nothing in this section shall be read as applying to any directions contained in an order made by the Commissioners under section 87(1) above.

[723]

NOTES

Commencement: 1 August 1993.

91 Service of orders and directions

(1) This section applies to any order or direction made or given by the Commissioners under this Act.

(2) An order or direction to which this section applies may be served on a person (other than a body corporate)—
    (a) by delivering it to that person;
    (b) by leaving it at his last known address in the United Kingdom; or
    (c) by sending it by post to him at that address.

(3) An order or direction to which this section applies may be served on a body corporate by delivering it or sending it by post—
    (a) to the registered or principal office of the body in the United Kingdom, or
    (b) if it has no such office in the United Kingdom, to any place in the United Kingdom where it caries on business or conducts its activities (as the case may be).

(4) Any such order or direction may also be served on a person (including a body corporate) by sending it by post to that person at an address notified by that person to the Commissioners for the purposes of this subsection.

(5) In this section any reference to the Commissioners includes, in relation to a direction given under subsection (3) of section 8 above, a reference to any person conducting an inquiry under that section.

[724]

NOTES

Commencement: 1 August 1993.

92 Appeals from Commissioners

(1) Provision shall be made by rules of court for regulating appeals to the High Court under this Act against orders or decisions of the Commissioners.

(2) On such an appeal the Attorney General shall be entitled to appear and be heard, and such other persons as the rules allow or as the court may direct.

[725]

NOTES

Commencement: 1 August 1993.

93   Miscellaneous provisions as to evidence

(1)   Where, in any proceedings to recover or compel payment of any rentcharge or other periodical payment claimed by or on behalf of a charity out of land or of the rents, profits or other income of land, otherwise than as rent incident to a reversion, it is shown that the rentcharge or other periodical payment has at any time been paid for twelve consecutive years to or for the benefit of the charity, that shall be prima facie evidence of the perpetual liability to it of the land or income, and no proof of its origin shall be necessary.

(2)   In any proceedings, the following documents, that is to say,—

     (a)   the printed copies of the reports of the Commissioners for enquiring concerning charities, 1818 to 1837, who were appointed under the Act 58 Geo 3 c 91 and subsequent Acts; and

     (b)   the printed copies of the reports which were made for various counties and county boroughs to the Charity Commissioners by their assistant commissioners and presented to the House of Commons as returns to orders of various dates beginning with 8th December 1890, and ending with 9th September 1909,

shall be admissible as evidence of the documents and facts stated in them.

(3)   Evidence of any order, certificate or other document issued by the Commissioners may be given by means of a copy retained by them, or taken from a copy so retained, and certified to be a true copy by any officer of the Commissioners generally or specially authorised by them to act for this purpose; and a document purporting to be such a copy shall be received in evidence without proof of the official position, authority or handwriting of the person certifying it.

[726]

NOTES

Commencement: 1 August 1993.

94   Restriction on institution of proceedings for certain offences

(1)   No proceedings for an offence under this Act to which this section applies shall be instituted except by or with the consent of the Director of Public Prosecutions.

(2)   This section applies to any offence under—

     (a)   section 5;

     (b)   section 11;

     (c)   section 18(14);

     (d)   section 49; or

     (e)   section 73(1).

[727]

NOTES

Commencement: 1 August 1993.

95   Offences by bodies corporate

Where any offence under this Act is committed by a body corporate and is proved to have been committed with the consent or connivance of, or to be attributable to any neglect on the part of, any director, manager, secretary or other similar officer of the body corporate, or any person who was purporting to act in any such capacity, he as well as the body corporate shall be guilty of that offence and shall be liable to be proceeded against and punished accordingly.

In relation to a body corporate whose affairs are managed by its members, "director" means a member of the body corporate.

NOTES

Commencement: 1 August 1993.

96 Construction of references to a "charity" or to particular classes of charity

(1) In this Act, except in so far as the context otherwise requires—

"charity" means any institution, corporate or not, which is established for charitable purposes and is subject to the control of the High Court in the exercise of the court's jurisdiction with respect to charities;

"ecclesiastical charity" has the same meaning as in the Local Government Act 1894;

"exempt charity" means (subject to section 24(8) above) a charity comprised in Schedule 2 to this Act;

"local charity" means, in relation to any area, a charity established for purposes which are by their nature or by the trusts of the charity directed wholly or mainly to the benefit of that area or of part of it;

"parochial charity" means, in relation to any parish or (in Wales) community, a charity the benefits of which are, or the separate distribution of the benefits of which is, confined to inhabitants of the parish or community, or of a single ancient ecclesiastical parish which included that parish or community or part of it, or of an area consisting of that parish or community with not more than four neighbouring parishes or communities.

(2) The expression "charity" is not in this Act applicable—

(a) to any ecclesiastical corporation (that is to say, any corporation in the Church of England, whether sole or aggregate, which is established for spiritual purposes) in respect of the corporate property of the corporation, except to a corporation aggregate having some purposes which are not ecclesiastical in respect of its corporate property held for those purposes; or

(b) to any Diocesan Board of Finance within the meaning of the Endowments and Glebe Measure 1976 for any diocese in respect of the diocesan glebe land of that diocese within the meaning of that Measure; or

(c) to any trust of property for purposes for which the property has been consecrated.

(3) A charity shall be deemed for the purposes of this Act to have a permanent endowment unless all property held for the purposes of the charity may be expended for those purposes without distinction between capital and income, and in this Act "permanent endowment" means, in relation to any charity, property held subject to a restriction on its being expended for the purposes of the charity.

(4) References in this Act to a charity whose income from all sources does not in aggregate amount to more than a specified amount shall be construed—

(a) by reference to the gross revenues of the charity, or

(b) if the Commissioners so determine, by reference to the amount which they estimate to be the likely amount of those revenues,

but without (in either case) bringing into account anything for the yearly value of land occupied by the charity apart from the pecuniary income (if any) received from that land; and any question as to the application of any such reference to a charity shall be determined by the Commissioners, whose decision shall be final.

(5)   The Commissioners may direct that for all or any of the purposes of this Act an institution established for any special purposes of or in connection with a charity (being charitable purposes) shall be treated as forming part of that charity or as forming a distinct charity.

[729]

NOTES
Commencement: 1 August 1993.

97   General interpretation

(1)   In this Act, except in so far as the context otherwise requires—

"charitable purposes" means purposes which are exclusively charitable according to the law of England and Wales;

"charity trustees" means the persons having the general control and management of the administration of a charity;

"the Commissioners" means the Charity Commissioners for England and Wales;

"company" means a company formed and registered under the Companies Act 1985 or to which the provisions of that Act apply as they apply to such a company;

"the court" means the High Court and, within the limits of its jurisdiction, any other court in England and Wales having a jurisdiction in respect of charities concurrent (within any limit of area or amount) with that of the High Court, and includes any judge or officer of the court exercising the jurisdiction of the court;

"financial year"—

(a)   in relation to a charity which is a company, shall be construed in accordance with section 223 of the Companies Act 1985; and

(b)   in relation to any other charity, shall be construed in accordance with regulations made by virtue of section 42(2) above;

but this definition is subject to the transitional provisions in section 99(4) below and Part II of Schedule 8 to this Act;

"gross income", in relation to charity, means its gross recorded income from all sources including special trusts;

"independent examiner", in relation to a charity, means such a person as is mentioned in section 43(3)(a) above;

"institution" includes any trust or undertaking;

"the official custodian" means the official custodian for charities;

"permanent endowment" shall be construed in accordance with section 96(3) above;

"the register" means the register of charities kept under section 3 above and "registered" shall be construed accordingly;

"special trust" means property which is held and administered by or on behalf of a charity for any special purposes of the charity, and is so held and administered on separate trusts relating only to that property but a special trust shall not, by itself, constitute a charity for the purposes of Part VI of this Act;

"trusts" in relation to a charity, means the provisions establishing it as a charity and regulating its purposes and administration, whether those provisions take effect by way of trust or not, and in relation to other institutions has a corresponding meaning.

(2)   In this Act, except in so far as the context otherwise requires, "document" includes information recorded in any form, and, in relation to information recorded otherwise than in legible form—

  (a)   any reference to its production shall be construed as a reference to the furnishing of a copy of it in legible form; and

  (b)   any reference to the furnishing of a copy of, or extract from, it shall accordingly be construed as a reference to the furnishing of a copy of, or extract from, it in legible form.

(3)   No vesting or transfer of any property in pursuance of any provision of Part IV or IX of this Act shall operate as a breach of a covenant or condition against alienation or give rise to a forfeiture.

[730]

NOTES
Commencement: 1 August 1993.

98   Consequential amendments and repeals

(1)   The enactments mentioned in Schedule 6 to this Act shall be amended as provided in that Schedule.

(2)   The enactments mentioned in Schedule 7 to this Act are hereby repealed to the extent specified in the third column of the Schedule.

[731]

NOTES
Commencement: 1 August 1993 (sub-s (1) certain purposes, sub-s (2)); to be appointed (sub-s (1), remaining purposes).

99   Commencement and transitional provisions

(1)   Subject to subsection (2) below this Act shall come into force on 1st August 1993.

(2)   Part VI, section 69 and paragraph 21(3) of Schedule 6 shall not come into force until such day as the Secretary of State may by order appoint; and different days may be appointed for different provisions or different purposes.

(3)   Until the coming into force of all the provisions mentioned in subsection (2) above the provisions mentioned in Part I of Schedule 8 to this Act shall continue in force notwithstanding their repeal.

(4)   Part II of Schedule 8 to this Act shall have effect until the coming into force of the first regulations made by virtue of section 42(2) above for determining the financial year of a charity for the purposes of the provisions mentioned in that Part.

[732]

NOTES
Commencement: 1 August 1993.

100   Short title and extent

(1)   This Act may be cited as the Charities Act 1993.

(2)   Subject to subsection (3) to (6) below, this Act extends only to England and Wales.

(3)   Section 10 above and this section extend to the whole of the United Kingdom.

(4)   Section 15(2) extends also to Northern Ireland.

(5)   Sections 70 and 71 and so much of section 86 as relates to those sections extend also to Scotland.

(6)   The amendments in Schedule 6 and the repeals in Schedule 7 have the same extent as the enactments to which they refer and section 98 above extends accordingly.

[733]

NOTES

Commencement: 1 August 1993.

SCHEDULE 2
EXEMPT CHARITIES

Sections 3, 96

The following institutions, so far as they are charities, are exempt charities within the meaning of this Act, that is to say—

  (a)   any institution which, if the Charities Act 1960 had not been passed, would be exempted from the powers and jurisdiction, under the Charitable Trusts Acts 1853 to 1939, of the Commissioners or Minister of Education (apart from any power of the Commissioners or Minister to apply those Acts in whole or in part to charities otherwise exempt) by the terms of any enactment not contained in those Acts other than section 9 of the Places of Worship Registration Act 1855;

  (b)   the universities of Oxford, Cambridge, London, Durham and Newcastle, the colleges and halls in the universities of Oxford, Cambridge, Durham and Newcastle, Queen Mary and Westfield College in the University of London and the colleges of Winchester and Eton;

  (c)   any university, university college, or institution connected with a university or university college, which Her Majesty declares by Order in Council to be an exempt charity for the purposes of this Act;

  (d)   a grant-maintained school;

 [(da)   the School Curriculum and Assessment Authority;]

  (e)   *the National Curriculum Council;*

 [(f)   the Curriculum and Assessment Authority for Wales;]

  (g)   *the School Examinations and Assessment Council;*

  (h)   a higher education corporation;

  (i)   a successor company to a higher education corporation (within the meaning of section 129(5) of the Education Reform Act 1988) at a time when an institution conducted by the company is for the time being designated under that section;

  (j)   a further education corporation;

  (k)   the Board of Trustees of the Victoria and Albert Museum;

  (l)   the Board of Trustees of the Science Museum;

  (m)   the Board of Trustees of the Armouries;

  (n)   the Board of Trustees of the Royal Botanic Gardens, Kew;

  (o)   the Board of Trustees of the National Museums and Galleries on Merseyside;

  (p)   the trustees of the British Museum and the trustees of the Natural History Museum;

  (q)   the Board of Trustees of the National Gallery;

  (r)   the Board of Trustees of the Tate Gallery;

  (s)   the Board of Trustees of the National Portrait Gallery;

  (t)   the Board of Trustees of the Wallace Collection;

  (u)   the Trustees of the Imperial War Museum;

  (v)   the Trustees of the National Maritime Museum;

  (w)   any institution which is administered by or on behalf of an institution included above and is established for the general purposes of, or for any special purpose of or in connection with, the last-mentioned institution;

  (x)   the Church Commissioners and any institution which is administered by them;

(y) any registered society within the meaning of the Industrial and Provident Societies Act 1965 and any registered society or branch within the meaning of the Friendly Societies Act 1974;

(z) the Board of Governors of the Museum of London;

(za) the British Library Board;

[(zb) the National Lottery Charities Board.]

[734]

NOTES
Commencement: 1 August 1993.

Para (da) inserted and para (f) substituted, and paras (e), (g) repealed, as from a day to be appointed, by the Education Act 1993, ss 253(2), 307(1), (3), Sch 15, para 5, Sch 19, para 175, Sch 21, Pt II; para (zb) inserted by the National Lottery etc Act 1993, s 37, Sch 4, para 12.

SCHEDULE 5
MEANING OF "CONNECTED PERSON" FOR PURPOSES OF SECTION 36(2)
Section 36(2)

1. In section 36(2) of this Act "connected person", in relation to a charity, means—

(a) a charity trustee or trustee for the charity;

(b) a person who is the donor of any land to the charity (whether the gift was made on or after the establishment of the charity);

(c) a child, parent, grandchild, grandparent, brother or sister of any such trustee or donor;

(d) an officer, agent or employee of the charity;

(e) the spouse of any person falling within any of sub-paragraphs (a) to (d) above;

(f) an institution which is controlled—

    (i) by any person failing within any of sub-paragraphs (a) to (e) above, or

    (ii) by two or more such persons taken together; or

(g) a body corporate in which—

    (i) any connected person falling within any of sub-paragraphs (a) to (f) above has a substantial interest, or

    (ii) two or more such persons, taken together, have a substantial interest.

2.—(1) In paragraph 1(c) above "child" includes a stepchild and an illegitimate child.

(2) For the purposes of paragraph 1(e) above a person living with another as that person's husband or wife shall be treated as that person's spouse.

3. For the purposes of paragraph 1(f) above a person controls an institution if he is able to secure that the affairs of the institution are conducted in accordance with his wishes.

4.—(1) For the purposes of paragraph 1(g) above any such connected person as is there mentioned has a substantial interest in a body corporate if the person or institution in question—

(a) is interested in shares comprised in the equity share capital of that body of a nominal value of more than one-fifth of that share capital, or

(b) is entitled to exercise, or control the exercise of, more than one-fifth of the voting power at any general meeting of that body.

(2) The rules set out in Part I of Schedule 13 to the Companies Act 1985 (rules for interpretation of certain provisions of that Act) shall apply for the purposes of sub-paragraph (1) above as they apply for the purposes of section 346(4) of that Act ("connected persons" etc).

(3) In this paragraph "equity share capital" and "share" have the same meaning as in that Act.

[735]

NOTES
Commencement: 1 August 1993.

LEASEHOLD REFORM, HOUSING AND URBAN DEVELOPMENT ACT 1993

(C 28)

An Act to confer rights to collective enfranchisement and lease renewal on tenants of flats; to make further provision with respect to enfranchisement by tenants of houses; to make provision for auditing the management, by landlords or other persons, of residential property and for the approval of codes of practice relating thereto; to amend Parts III and IV of the Landlord and Tenant Act 1987; to confer jurisdiction on leasehold valuation tribunals as respects Crown land; to make provision for rendering void agreements preventing the occupation of leasehold property by persons with mental disorders; to amend Parts II, IV and V of the Housing Act 1985, Schedule 2 to the Housing Associations Act 1985, Parts I and III and sections 248 and 299 of the Housing (Scotland) Act 1987, Part III of the Housing Act 1988, and Part VI of the Local Government and Housing Act 1989; to make provision with respect to certain disposals requiring consent under Part II of the Housing Act 1985, including provision for the payment of a levy; to alter the basis of certain contributions by the Secretary of State under section 569 of that Act; to establish and confer functions on a body to replace the English Industrial Estates Corporation and to be known as the Urban Regeneration Agency; to provide for the designation of certain urban and other areas and to make provision as to the effect of such designation; to amend section 23 of the Land Compensation Act 1961, section 98 of the Local Government, Planning and Land Act 1980 and section 27 of the Housing and Planning Act 1986; to make further provision with respect to urban development corporations and urban development areas; and for connected purposes

[20 July 1993]

PART I
LANDLORD AND TENANT

CHAPTER VI
MISCELLANEOUS

Codes of practice

87   Approval by Secretary of State of codes of management practice

(1)   The Secretary of State may, if he considers it appropriate to do so, by order—

    (a)   approve any code of practice—

        (i)   which appears to him to be designed to promote desirable practices in relation to any matter or matters directly or indirectly concerned with the management of residential property by relevant persons; and

        (ii)   which has been submitted to him for his approval;

    (b)   approve any modifications of any such code which have been so submitted; or

    (c)   withdraw his approval for any such code or modifications.

(2)   The Secretary of State shall not approve any such code or any modifications of any such code unless he is satisfied that arrangements have been made for the text of the code or the modifications to be published in such manner as he considers appropriate for bringing the provisions of the code or the modifications to the notice of those likely to be affected by them (which, in the case of modifications of a code, may include publication of a text of the code incorporating the modifications).

(3)   The power of the Secretary of State under this section to approve a code of practice which has been submitted to him for his approval includes power to approve a part of any such code; and references in this section to a code of practice may accordingly be read as including a reference to a part of a code of practice.

(4)   At any one time there may be two or more codes of practice for the time being approved under this section.

(5)   A code of practice approved under this section may make different provision with respect to different cases or descriptions of cases, including different provision for different areas.

(6)   Without prejudice to the generality of subsections (1) and (5)—

   (a)   a code of practice approved under this section may, in relation to any such matter as is referred to in subsection (1), make provision in respect of relevant persons who are under an obligation to discharge any function in connection with that matter as well as in respect of relevant persons who are not under such an obligation; and

   (b)   any such code may make provision with respect to—

      (i)   the resolution of disputes with respect to residential property between relevant persons and the tenants of such property;

      (ii)   competitive tendering for works in connection with such property; and

      (iii)   the administration of trusts in respect of amounts paid by tenants by way of service charges.

(7)   A failure on the part of any person to comply with any provision of a code of practice for the time being approved under this section shall not of itself render him liable to any proceedings; but in any proceedings before a court or tribunal—

   (a)   any code of practice approved under this section shall be admissible in evidence; and

   (b)   any provision of any such code which appears to the court or tribunal to be relevant to any question arising in the proceedings shall be taken into account in determining that question.

(8)   For the purposes of this section—

   (a)   "relevant person" means any landlord of residential property or any person who discharges management functions in respect of such property, and for this purpose "management functions" includes functions with respect to the provision of services or the repair, maintenance or insurance of such property;

   (b)   "residential property" means any building or part of a building which consists of one or more dwellings let on leases, but references to residential property include—

      (i)   any garage, outhouse, garden, yard and appurtenances belonging to or usually enjoyed with such dwellings,

      (ii)   any common parts of any such building or part, and

      (iii)   any common facilities which are not within any such building or part; and

   (c)   "service charge" means an amount payable by a tenant of a dwelling as part of or in addition to the rent—

      (i)   which is payable, directly or indirectly, for services, repairs, maintenance or insurance or any relevant person's costs of management, and

(ii) the whole or part of which varies or may vary according to the costs or estimated costs incurred or to be incurred by any relevant person in connection with the matters mentioned in sub-paragraph (i).

(9) This section applies in relation to dwellings let on licences to occupy as it applies in relation to dwellings let on leases, and references in this section to landlords and tenants of residential property accordingly include references to licensors and licensees of such property.

[736]

NOTES
Commencement: 1 November 1993.

Provision of accommodation for persons with mental disorders

89 Avoidance of provisions preventing occupation of leasehold property by persons with mental disorders

(1) Any agreement relating to a lease of any property which comprises or includes a dwelling (whether contained in the instrument creating the lease or not and whether made before the creation of the lease or not) shall be void in so far as it would otherwise have the effect of prohibiting or imposing any restriction on—
   (a) the occupation of the dwelling, or of any part of the dwelling, by persons with mental disorders (within the meaning of the Mental Health Act 1983), or
   (b) the provision of accommodation within the dwelling for such persons.

(2) Subsection (1) applies to any agreement made after the coming into force of this section.

[737]

NOTES
Commencement: 1 November 1993.

PART IV
SUPPLEMENTAL

188 Short title, commencement and extent

(1) This Act may be cited as the Leasehold Reform, Housing and Urban Development Act 1993.

(2) This Act, except—
   (a) this section;
   (b) sections 126 and 127, 135 to 140, 149 to 151, 181(1), (2) and (4) and 186; and
   (c) the repeal in section 80(1) of the Local Government and Housing Act 1989,

shall come into force on such day as the Secretary of State may by order made by statutory instrument appoint; and different days may be so appointed for different provisions or for different purposes.

(3)–(7) . . .

[738]

NOTES
Sub-ss (3)–(7): not relevant to this work.

LAW OF PROPERTY (MISCELLANEOUS PROVISIONS) ACT 1994

(C 36)

An Act to provide for new covenants for title to be implied on dispositions of property; to amend the law with respect to certain matters arising in connection with the death of the owner of property; and for connected purposes

[3 November 1994]

PART I
IMPLIED COVENANTS FOR TITLE

The covenants

1 Covenants to be implied on a disposition of property

(1) In an instrument effecting or purporting to effect a disposition of property there shall be implied on the part of the person making the disposition, whether or not the disposition is for valuable consideration, such of the covenants specified in sections 2 to 5 as are applicable to the disposition.

(2) Of those sections—
  (a) sections 2, 3(1) and (2), 4 and 5 apply where dispositions are expressed to be made with full title guarantee; and
  (b) sections 2, 3(3), 4 and 5 apply where dispositions are expressed to be made with limited title guarantee.

(3) Sections 2 to 4 have effect subject to section 6 (no liability under covenants in certain cases); and sections 2 to 5 have effect subject to section 8(1) (limitation or extension of covenants by instrument effecting the disposition).

(4) In this Part—
  "disposition" includes the creation of a term of years;
  "instrument" includes an instrument which is not a deed; and
  "property" includes a thing in action, and any interest in real or personal property.

[739]

NOTES
Commencement: 1 July 1995.

---

2 Right to dispose and further assurance

(1) If the disposition is expressed to be made with full title guarantee or with limited title guarantee there shall be implied the following covenants—
  (a) that the person making the disposition has the right (with the concurrence of any other person conveying the property) to dispose of the property as he purports to, and
  (b) that that person will at his own cost do all that he reasonably can to give the person to whom he disposes of the property the title he purports to give.

(2) The latter obligation includes—
  (a) in relation to a disposition of an interest in land the title to which is registered, doing all that he reasonably can to ensure that the person to whom the disposition is made is entitled to be registered as proprietor with at least the class of title registered immediately before the disposition; and

(b) in relation to a disposition of an interest in land the title to which is required to be registered by virtue of the disposition, giving all reasonable assistance fully to establish to the satisfaction of the Chief Land Registrar the right of the person to whom the disposition is made to registration as proprietor.

(3)   In the case of a disposition of an existing legal interest in land, the following presumptions apply, subject to the terms of the instrument, in ascertaining for the purposes of the covenants implied by this section what the person making the disposition purports to dispose of—

(a) where the title to the interest is registered, it shall be presumed that the disposition is of the whole of that interest;

(b) where the title to the interest is not registered, then—

(i) if it appears from the instrument that the interest is a leasehold interest, it shall be presumed that the disposition is of the property for the unexpired portion of the term of years created by the lease; and

(ii) in any other case, it shall be presumed that what is disposed of is the fee simple.

[740]

NOTES
Commencement: 1 July 1995.

3   Charges, incumbrances and third party rights

(1)   If the disposition is expressed to be made with full title guarantee there shall be implied a covenant that the person making the disposition is disposing of the property free—

(a) from all charges and incumbrances (whether monetary or not), and

(b) from all other rights exercisable by third parties,

other than any charges, incumbrances or rights which that person does not and could not reasonably be expected to know about.

(2)   In its application to charges, incumbrances and other third party rights subsection (1) extends to liabilities imposed and rights conferred by or under any enactment, except to the extent that such liabilities and rights are, by reason of—

(a) being, at the time of the disposition, only potential liabilities and rights in relation to the property, or

(b) being liabilities and rights imposed or conferred in relation to property generally,

not such as to constitute defects in title.

(3)   If the disposition is expressed to be made with limited title guarantee there shall be implied a covenant that the person making the disposition has not since the last disposition for value—

(a) charged or incumbered the property by means of any charge or incumbrance which subsists at the time when the disposition is made, or granted third party rights in relation to the property which so subsist, or

(b) suffered the property to be so charged or incumbered or subjected to any such rights,

and that he is not aware that anyone else has done so since the last disposition for value.

[741]

NOTES
Commencement: 1 July 1995.

4   Validity of lease

(1)   Where the disposition is of leasehold land and is expressed to be made with full title guarantee or with limited title guarantee, the following covenants shall also be implied—

(a)   that the lease is subsisting at the time of the disposition, and

(b)   that there is no subsisting breach of a condition or tenant's obligation, and nothing which at that time would render the lease liable to forfeiture.

(2)   If the disposition is the grant of an underlease, the references to "the lease" in subsection (1) are references to the lease out of which the underlease is created.

[742]

NOTES
Commencement: 1 July 1995.

5   Discharge of obligations where property subject to rentcharge or leasehold land

(1)   Where the disposition is a mortgage of property subject to a rentcharge, or of leasehold land, and is expressed to be made with full title guarantee or with limited title guarantee, the following covenants shall also be implied.

(2)   If the property is subject to a rentcharge, there shall be implied a covenant that the mortgagor will fully and promptly observe and perform all the obligations under the instrument creating the rentcharge that are for the time being enforceable with respect to the property by the owner of the rentcharge in his capacity as such.

(3)   If the property is leasehold land, there shall be implied a covenant that the mortgagor will fully and promptly observe and perform all the obligations under the lease subject to the mortgage that are for the time being imposed on him in his capacity as tenant under the lease.

(4)   In this section "mortgage" includes charge, and "mortgagor" shall be construed accordingly.

[743]

NOTES
Commencement: 1 July 1995.

Effect of covenants

6   No liability under covenants in certain cases

(1)   The person making the disposition is not liable under the covenants implied by virtue of—

(a)   section 2(1)(a) (right to dispose),

(b)   section 3 (charges, incumbrances and third party rights), or

(c)   section 4 (validity of lease),

in respect of any particular matter to which the disposition is expressly made subject.

(2)   Furthermore that person is not liable under any of those covenants for anything (not falling within subsection (1))—

(a)   which at the time of the disposition is within the actual knowledge, or

(b)   which is a necessary consequence of facts that are then within the actual knowledge,

of the person to whom the disposition is made.

(3)   For this purpose section 198 of the Law of Property Act 1925 (deemed notice by virtue of registration) shall be disregarded.

[744]

NOTES
Commencement: 1 July 1995.

7   Annexation of benefit of covenants

The benefit of a covenant implied by virtue of this Part shall be annexed and incident to, and shall go with, the estate or interest of the person to whom the disposition is made, and shall be capable of being enforced by every person in whom that estate or interest is (in whole or in part) for the time being vested.

[745]

NOTES
Commencement: 1 July 1995.

8   Supplementary provisions

(1)   The operation of any covenant implied in an instrument by virtue of this Part may be limited or extended by a term of that instrument.

(2)   Sections 81 and 83 of the Law of Property Act 1925 (effect of covenant with two or more jointly; construction of implied covenants) apply to a covenant implied by virtue of this Part as they apply to a covenant implied by virtue of that Act.

(3)   Where in an instrument effecting or purporting to effect a disposition of property a person is expressed to direct the disposition, this Part applies to him as if he were the person making the disposition.

(4)   This Part has effect—
  (a)   where "gyda gwarant teitl llawn" is used instead of "with full title guarantee", and
  (b)   where "gyda gwarant teitl cyfyngedig" is used instead of "with limited title guarantee",

as it has effect where the English words are used.

[746]

NOTES
Commencement: 1 July 1995.

9   Modifications of statutory forms

(1)   Where a form set out in an enactment, or in an instrument made under an enactment, includes words which (in an appropriate case) would have resulted in the implication of a covenant by virtue of section 76 of the Law of Property Act 1925, the form shall be taken to authorise instead the use of the words "with full title guarantee" or "with limited title guarantee" or their Welsh equivalent given in section 8(4).

(2)   This applies in particular to the forms set out in Schedule 1 to the Settled Land Act 1925 and Schedules 4 and 5 to the Law of Property Act 1925.

[747]

NOTES
Commencement: 1 July 1995.

Transitional provisions

10   General saving for covenants in old form

(1) Except as provided by section 11 below (cases in which covenants in old form implied on disposition after commencement), . . . as regards dispositions of property made after the commencement of this Part.

(2)   The repeal of those provisions by this Act accordingly does not affect the enforcement of a covenant implied by virtue of either of them on a disposition before the commencement of this Part.

[748]

NOTES

Commencement: 1 July 1995.

Sub-s (1): words omitted repeal the Law of Property Act 1925, s 76, and the Land Registration Act 1925, s 24(1)(a).

11   Covenants in old form implied in certain cases

(1)   Section 76 of the Law of Property Act 1925 applies in relation to a disposition of property made after the commencement of this Part in pursuance of a contract entered into before commencement where—

- (a)   the contract contains a term providing for a disposition to which that section would have applied if the disposition had been made before commencement, and
- (b)   the existence of the contract and of that term is apparent on the face of the instrument effecting the disposition,

unless there has been an intervening disposition of the property expressed, in accordance with this Part, to be made with full title guarantee.

(2)   Section 24(1)(a) of the Land Registration Act 1925 applies in relation to a disposition of a leasehold interest in land made after the commencement of this Part in pursuance of a contract entered into before commencement where—

- (a)   the covenant specified in that provision would have been implied on the disposition if it had been made before commencement, and
- (b)   the existence of the contract is apparent on the face of the instrument effecting the disposition,

unless there has been an intervening disposition of the leasehold interest expressed, in accordance with this Part, to be made with full title guarantee.

(3)   In subsections (1) and (2) an "intervening disposition" means a disposition after the commencement of this Part to, or to a predecessor in title of, the person by whom the disposition in question is made.

(4)   Where in order for subsection (1) or (2) to apply it is necessary for certain matters to be apparent on the face of the instrument effecting the disposition, the contract shall be deemed to contain an implied term that they should so appear.

[749]

NOTES

Commencement: 1 July 1995.

12   Covenants in new form to be implied in other cases

(1)   This section applies to a contract for the disposition of property entered into before the commencement of this Part where the disposition is made after

commencement and section 11 (cases in which covenants in old form to be implied) does not apply because there has been an intervening disposition expressed, in accordance with this Part, to be with full title guarantee.

(2)   A contract which contains a term that the person making the disposition shall do so as beneficial owner shall be construed as requiring that person to do so by an instrument expressed to be made with full title guarantee.

(3)   A contract which contains a term that the person making the disposition shall do so—
    (a)   as settlor, or
    (b)   as trustee or mortgagee or personal representative,

shall be construed as requiring that person to do so by an instrument expressed to be made with limited title guarantee.

(4)   A contract for the disposition of a leasehold interest in land entered into at a date when the title to the leasehold interest was registered shall be construed as requiring the person making the disposition for which it provides to do so by an instrument expressed to be made with full title guarantee.

(5)   Where this section applies and the contract provides that any of the covenants to be implied by virtue of section 76 of the Law of Property Act 1925 or section 24(1)(a) of the Land Registration Act 1925 shall be implied in a modified form, the contract shall be construed as requiring a corresponding modification of the covenants implied by virtue of this Part.

[750]

NOTES
Commencement: 1 July 1995.

13   Application of transitional provisions in relation to options

For the purposes of sections 11 and 12 (transitional provisions, implication of covenants in old form in certain cases and new form in others) as they apply in relation to a disposition of property in accordance with an option granted before the commencement of this Part and exercised after commencement, the contract for the disposition shall be deemed to have been entered into on the grant of the option.

[751]

NOTES
Commencement: 1 July 1995.

PART II
MATTERS ARISING IN CONNECTION WITH DEATH

14   Vesting of estate in case of intestacy or lack of executors

(1)   . . .

(2)   Any real or personal estate of a person dying before the commencement of this section shall, if it is property to which this subsection applies, vest in the Public Trustee on the commencement of this section.

(3)   Subsection (2) above applies to any property—
    (a)   if it was vested in the Probate Judge under section 9 of the Administration of Estates Act 1925 immediately before the commencement of this section, or

(b) if it was not so vested but as at commencement there has been no grant of representation in respect of it and there is no executor with power to obtain such a grant.

(4) Any property vesting in the Public Trustee by virtue of subsection (2) above shall—

(a) if the deceased died intestate, be treated as vesting in the Public Trustee under section 9(1) of the Administration of Estates Act 1925 (as substituted by subsection (1) above); and

(b) otherwise be treated as vesting in the Public Trustee under section 9(2) of that Act (as so substituted).

(5) Anything done by or in relation to the Probate Judge with respect to property vested in him as mentioned in subsection (3)(a) above shall be treated as having been done by or in relation to the Public Trustee.

(6) So far as may be necessary in consequence of the transfer to the Public Trustee of the functions of the Probate Judge under section 9 of the Administration of Estates Act 1925, any reference in an enactment or instrument to the Probate Judge shall be construed as a reference to the Public Trustee.

[752]

NOTES

Commencement: 1 July 1995.

Sub-s (1): substitutes the Administration of Estates Act 1925, s 9.

15   Registration of land charges after death

(1)–(4)   . . .

(5) The amendments made by this section do not apply where the application for registration was made before the commencement of this section, but without prejudice to a person's right to make a new application after commencement.

[753]

NOTES

Commencement: 1 July 1995.

Sub-ss (1)–(4): add the Land Charges Act 1972, ss 3(1A), 5(4A), 6(2A).

16   Concurrence of personal representatives in dealings with interests in land

(1)   . . .

(2) Section 2(2) of the Administration of Estates Act 1925 as amended by subsection (1) above (concurrence of all personal representatives required for conveyance of real estate or contract for such conveyance) applies in relation to an interest under a trust for sale of land as in relation to real estate.

(3) The amendments made by subsection (1) apply to contracts made after the commencement of this section; and subsection (2) applies to contracts made after the commencement of this section and to conveyances so made otherwise than in pursuance of a contract made before commencement.

[754]

NOTES

Commencement: 1 July 1995.

Sub-s (1): amends the Administration of Estates Act 1925, s 2(2).

17 Notices affecting land: absence of knowledge of intended recipient's death

(1) Service of a notice affecting land which would be effective but for the death of the intended recipient is effective despite his death if the person serving the notice has no reason to believe that he has died.

(2) Where the person serving a notice affecting land has no reason to believe that the intended recipient has died, the proper address for the purposes of section 7 of the Interpretation Act 1978 (service of documents by post) shall be what would be the proper address apart from his death.

(3) The above provisions do not apply to a notice authorised or required to be served for the purposes of proceedings before—

    (a) any court,

    (b) any tribunal specified in Schedule 1 to the Tribunals and Inquiries Act 1992 (tribunals within general supervision of Council on Tribunals), or

    (c) the Chief Land Registrar or any district registrar or assistant district registrar;

but this is without prejudice to the power to make provision in relation to such proceedings by rules of court, procedural rules within the meaning of section 8 of the Tribunals and Inquiries Act 1992 or rules under section 144 of the Land Registration Act 1925.

[755]

NOTES

Commencement: 1 July 1995.

18 Notices affecting land: service on personal representatives before filing of grant

(1) A notice affecting land which would have been authorised or required to be served on a person but for his death shall be sufficiently served before a grant of representation has been filed if—

    (a) it is addressed to "The Personal Representatives of" the deceased (naming him) and left at or sent by post to his last known place of residence or business in the United Kingdom, and

    (b) a copy of it, similarly addressed, is served on the Public Trustee.

(2) The reference in subsection (1) to the filing of a grant of representation is to the filing at the Principal Registry of the Family Division of the High Court of a copy of a grant of representation in respect of the deceased's estate or, as the case may be, the part of his estate which includes the land in question.

(3) The method of service provided for by this section is not available where provision is made—

    (a) by or under any enactment, or

    (b) by an agreement in writing,

requiring a different method of service, or expressly prohibiting the method of service provided for by this section, in the circumstances.

[756]

NOTES

Commencement: 1 July 1995.

19   Functions of Public Trustee in relation to notices, etc

(1)   The Public Trustee may give directions as to the office or offices at which documents may be served on him—

   (a)   by virtue of section 9 of the Administration of Estates Act 1925 (as substituted by section 14(1) above), or

   (b)   in pursuance of section 18(1)(b) above (service on Public Trustee of copy of certain notices affecting land);

and he shall publish such directions in such manner as he considers appropriate.

(2)   The Lord Chancellor may by regulations make provision with respect to the functions of the Public Trustee in relation to such documents; and the regulations may make different provision in relation to different descriptions of document or different circumstances.

(3)   The regulations may, in particular, make provision requiring the Public Trustee—

   (a)   to keep such documents for a specified period and thereafter to keep a copy or record of their contents in such form as may be specified;

   (b)   to keep such documents, copies and records available for inspection at such reasonable hours as may be specified; and

   (c)   to supply copies to any person on request.

In this subsection "specified" means specified by or under the regulations.

(4)   Regulations under this section shall be made by statutory instrument which shall be subject to annulment in pursuance of a resolution of either House of Parliament.

(5)   The following provisions of the Public Trustee Act 1906, namely—

   (a)   section 8(5) (payment of expenses out of money provided by Parliament), and

   (b)   section 9(1), (3) and (4) (provisions as to fees),

apply in relation to the functions of the Public Trustee in relation to documents to which this section applies as in relation to his functions under that Act.

[757]

NOTES

Commencement: 1 July 1995.

PART III
GENERAL PROVISIONS

20   Crown application

This Act binds the Crown.

[758]

NOTES

Commencement: 1 July 1995.

21   Consequential amendments and repeals

(1)   The enactments specified in Schedule 1 are amended in accordance with that Schedule, the amendments being consequential on the provisions of this Act.

(2)   The enactments specified in Schedule 2 are repealed to the extent specified.

(3)   In the case of section 76 of the Law of Property Act 1925 and section 24(1)(a) of the Land Registration Act 1925, those provisions are repealed in accordance with section 10(1) above (general saving for covenants in old form).

(4)   The amendments consequential on Part I of this Act (namely those in paragraphs 1, 2, 3, 5, 7, 9 and 12 of Schedule 1) shall not have effect in relation to any disposition of property to which, by virtue of section 10(1) or 11 above (transitional provisions), section 76 of the Law of Property Act 1925 or section 24(1)(a) of the Land Registration Act 1925 continues to apply.

[759]

NOTES
Commencement: 15 February 1995 (sub-s (1) certain purposes); 1 July 1995 (sub-s (1) remaining purposes, sub-ss (2)–(4)).

22   Extent

(1)   The provisions of this Act extend to England and Wales.

(2)   In addition—
    (a)   the provisions of Schedules 1 and 2 (consequential amendments and repeals) extend to Scotland so far as they relate to enactments which so extend; and
    (b)   the provisions of Schedule 1 extend to Northern Ireland so far as they relate to enactments which so extend.

[760]

NOTES
Commencement: 1 July 1995.

23   Commencement

(1)   The provisions of this Act come into force on such day as the Lord Chancellor may appoint by order made by statutory instrument.

(2)   Different days may be appointed for different provisions and for different purposes.

24   Short title

This Act may be cited as the Law of Property (Miscellaneous Provisions) Act 1994.

[761]

NOTES
Commencement: 1 July 1995.

INDEX

References are to paragraph number